ESSAYS
IN CLASSICAL AND MODERN
HINDU LAW

ESSAYS IN CLASSICAL AND MODERN HINDU LAW

BY

J. DUNCAN M. DERRETT

D.C.L. (Oxon.), LL.D., Ph.D. (Lond.) of Gray's Inn, Barrister;
Professor of Oriental Laws in the University of London

VOLUME ONE

DHARMAŚĀSTRA AND RELATED IDEAS

TUTA SUB AEGIDE PALLAS · EJB ·

LEIDEN
E. J. BRILL
1976

By the Same Author

The Hoysaḷas (Oxford University Press)
Hindu Law Past and Present (A. Mukherjee, Calcutta)
Introduction to Modern Hindu Law (Oxford University Press)
Religion, Law and the State in India (Faber & Faber, London)
Introduction to Legal Systems (edited) (Sweet & Maxwell, London)
Critique of Modern Hindu Law (Tripathi, Bombay)
Dharmaśāstra and Juridical Literature (Wiesbaden, Harrassowitz)
Bhāruci's Commentary on the Manusmṛti (Wiesbaden, Steiner)

also
Law in the New Testament (Darton, Longman & Todd, London)
Jesus's Audience (Darton, Longman & Todd)

and (translation)
R. Lingat, Classical Law of India (University of California Press)

ISBN 90 04 04475 2

PRINTED IN BELGIUM

TABLE OF CONTENTS
(with particulars of original locations)

PREFACE

Hindu law governs about one-sixth of the human race. The subjects in respect of which it is applied, and the territories in which it obtains as part of the *lex terrae*, are explained by Dr T. K. K. Iyer and myself in the second volume of the *International Encyclopedia of Comparative Law* (Hamburg). The scope of the subject as a spectrum of academic topics is revealed in the present series of four volumes of previously-published articles, chosen from a large field.

It was suggested by a colleague a few years back that at least a list of the two hundred or so articles ought to be available. I am not sure whether a research assistant can be found to devote the necessary time, or, if one were available, whether his efforts would be rewarding. It is more to the point to make available, in order to encourage others to take up a subject which has long been taught as a whole only in London, specimens of a single scholar's efforts over the important period 1950-1975. That quarter of a century saw, first, the total collapse of the subject as a matter of practical concern outside South Asia, South-East Asia and East Africa; until, with the massive immigrations of Hindus and Sikhs into Britain, the inwardnesses of 'Hindu law' once again attracted attention. By 1975 the reformed marriage law, which was enacted in India in 1955, was ripe for further and very substantial amendment. About the same time an adoption law for all India (a novelty) came on to the legislative anvil. The obvious shrinking of the world in terms of travel (the effect of American spaceflights is not to be underestimated), and in terms of humanitarian concern for the 'third world', in their turn stimulated a much more broadminded and adventurous attitude towards jurisprudence and legal science, which had for too long been dominated by western European experience and ideas. In the early years of this decade the Fritz Thyssen Stiftung promoted a scheme of research into the *Rechtsideen der Welt*, in which Hindu law could play its part. This hope had recently been strongly stimulated by Robert Lingat's *Classical Law of India*, now available in English as well as its original French. In Indology, too, Law came, rather late in the day, to play its part. My *Dharmaśāstra and Juridical Literature* (1973) forms a section in Jan Gonda's *History of Indian Literature* (Wiesbaden); my *History of Indian Law* finds a place in his *Indien*,

Part II of the *Handbuch der Orientalistik* edited by B. Spuler (Leiden, Brill, 1973). Bibliographies by Ludo Rocher and myself figure in the massive *Bibliographical Introduction to Legal History and Ethnology* being edited by J. Gilissen. The appearance of Ludwik Sternbach's *Bibliography on dharma and artha in Ancient and Mediaeval India* (Wiesbaden, 1973) proves the richness already at the command of those who wish to explore any but the purely ritual aspects of Hindu law and administration as they were before European rule commenced on a significant scale.

Meanwhile movements in India had repeatedly put into debate the possible roles of the ancient, traditional legal system and its leading ideas. Contributions on this subject continued to flow in legal periodicals no less than in periodicals of a more general character (see, e.g., Justice K. B. Panda's article on Hindu Judicial Administration in *Hindutva* 5/9, 1974, and subsequent issues). And the problems, as well as the benefits, bequeathed by the departing British rulers, continued to ferment. Of the dilemmas of India in the realm of law-reform I shall speak in my introduction to the last volume of this present series. Suffice it for the present that the last quarter-century has been one of constant movement, and of a renaissance of academic concern for what had been, for too long, dichotomised between Sanskritists without law, and lawyers without Sanskrit.

This brings me to an anecdote. In the early 1950's I attended an orientalists' congress at, I think, Munich. A respected Sanskrit scholar from East Germany, whose publications subsequently earned my abiding admiration, came up to me without warning and said, 'Which did you study first, Sanskrit or law?' I replied (for I knew that by 'study' he meant study as a University student, taught by University teachers), 'I studied neither, so that the question of priority does not arise!' He at once turned away in disgust, and neither he nor his have ever been in touch with me since.

The articles in these four volumes are therefore the work of a virtually selftaught man, animated by a passionate love of India. Something over a dozen of the more suitable of my *remaining* articles have already been presented in revised form, with supplementation, in my *Religion, Law and the State in India* (London, Faber, 1968). This present series is intended to give a sample of those to which I constantly made reference in that volume and elsewhere; and it should cure the embarrassment of scholars (whether orientalists, anthropologists, or lawyers) who, if domiciled in Europe, could not get access to journals printed in India, or, if domiciled in India, could not see periodicals or *Festschriften* which never circulate in the subcontinent.

Such republications cause automatic difficulties. Depending on the country of first publication and the journal, styles of citation, and even transliteration, differ. I must ask the reader to bear with me for not correcting *āchāra* to *ācāra*, nor *deshas* to *deṣa-s*. Such anomalies will not trouble the learned and should not preoccupy the tiro. He will not come to me, after all, for lessons in orthography. Further, the hand-set printing of India can often be charming, but it took much ingenuity on my part to mitigate the discomfort of the many misprints, and other anomalies : it is not likely that I have coped with all of them.

I do not seek to emulate the conventional *Gesammelte Aufsätze*. This often consists of past articles reprinted meticulously, with the original page-commencements indicated pedantically, the items collected, arranged and proof-read by the great man's many assistants, *without up-dating and (usually) without index*. As I do not share the facilities of those princes, 'all of [them] sons of the Most High' (Ps. 82.6), so it is the more incumbent on me both to attempt to deprecate the corrosion of time and to show where, amongst all this stuff, some items of interest ought to be found.

An author is not the best person to describe, still less to appraise his own work. Yet I think I may be allowed to say that I hate descriptive writing (one may, optimistically, leave it to the more laborious, the more confident, and the less ingenious), and I eschew repetition of what has been done (to my knowledge) by others. These articles were, in their day, each an adventure in ideas, each an act of defiance in the face of our monumental ignorance of one of the world's great intellectual systems.

The divisions between the volumes are not perfect. In bulk the second is the largest. India's shortage of paper and of patience explains the extreme brevity of many of the contributions in the fourth. But the collective picture all four paint is, I trust, faithful to the practical as well as to the academic scene.

J.D.M.D.

Acknowledgement: The source of each article is indicated in the Table of Contents. I am grateful to the editors and/or publishers for permission to reprint these items.

J.D.M.D.

ABBREVIATIONS

A. & N.	Assam and Nagaland
A.B.O.R.I.	Annals of the Bhandarkar Oriental Research Institute
AHL	Anglo-Hindu Law
A.I.R. or All Ind. Rep.	All India Reporter
A.O.R.	Annals of Oriental Research
A.R.E.	Annual Report of Epigraphy
A.R.I.E.	Annual Report of Indian Epigraphy
A.R.S.I.E.	Annual Report of South Indian Epigraphy
A.W.N.	Allahabad Weekly Notes
Adyar Lib. Bull.	Adyar Library Bulletin
All E.R.	All England Reports
All.	Allahabad
An.P. or A.P.	Andhra Pradesh
An.W.R.	Andhra Weekly Reporter
As.Res.	*Asiatic Researches*
Ass.	Assam
B.H.C.R.	Bombay High Court Reports
B.K.	Inscriptions gathered from the Bombay Karnatak (now in Mysore State) and published as appendices to the A.R.S.I.E. and A.R.I.E.
B.K. Ins.	Bombay Karnatak Inscriptions
B.S.O.A.S.	Bulletin of the School of Oriental and African Studies
Beng. L.R. or B.L.R.	Bengal Law Reports
Bhār.	Bhāruci
Bibl. Ind.	Bibliotheca Indica series
Bom.	Bombay
Bom. L.R.	Bombay Law Reporter
Bṛh.	Bṛhaspati
C.S.S.H.	Comparative Studies in Society and History
C.W.N.	Calcutta Weekly Notes
Cal.	Calcutta
Comm.	commentary
Dh.k.	L.S. Joshi's *Dharmakośa*
disc.	discussed by
E.C.	Epigraphia Carnatica
E.I.	Epigraphia Indica
F.B.	Full Bench (normally of three judges)
For. Not.	K. A. N. Sastri, Foreign Notices of S. India.
Gaut.	Gautama
HAMA	Hindu Adoptions and Maintenance Act
H.D.	History of Dharmaśāstra
H.L.	Hindu Law
HMA	Hindu Marriage Act
HMGA	Hindu Minority and Guardianship Act
H.P.	Himachal Pradesh
HSA	Hindu Succession Act
Hyd. Arch. Ser.	Hyderabad Archaeological Series
I.A.	Law Reports, Indian Appeals series

I.C.L.Q.	International and Comparative Law Quarterly
I.H.Q.	Indian Historical Quarterly
I.-I.J.	Indo-Iranian J.
I.M.H.L.	Introduction to Modern Hindu Law
I.O.	India Office
I.R.	Indian Reports (a Madras Law Journal reprint)
I.Y.B.I.A.	India Year-book of International Affairs
J.	Journal section
J. & K.	Jammu and Kashmir
J.A.	Journal asiatique (Paris)
J.A.O.S.	Journal of the American Oriental Society
J.A.S.B.	Journal of the Asiatic Society of Bengal
J.B.O.R.S.	Journal of the Bihar and Orissa Research Society
J.Bih.Res.Soc.	Journal of the Bihar Research Society
J.E.S.H.O.	Journal of the Economic and Social History of the Orient
J.I.L.I.	Journal of the Indian Law Institute
J.Ind.Hist.	Journal of Indian History
J.O.R.	Journal of Oriental Research
J.R.A.S.	Journal of the Royal Asiatic Society
Jur. Rev.	Juridical Review
Kar.	Karachi
K.I.	Karnatak Inscriptions
K.K.T.	Lakṣmīdhara's *Kṛtyakalpataru*
K.L.T.	Kerala Law Times
Kāty.	Kātyāyana
Kauṭ.	Kauṭilya
Ker.	Kerala
L.Q.R.	Law Quarterly Review
Luck.	Lucknow.
M.	Manu
M.A.R.	Mysore Archaeological Report
M.B.	Madhya Bharat
M.H.C.R.	Madras High Court Reports
MHL	Modern Hindu Law
M.I.A.	Moore's Indian Appeals
M.L.J.	Madras Law Journal
M.P.	Madhya Pradesh
M.W.N.	Madras Weekly Notes
Mad.	Madras
Madras G.O.Mss.Lib.	Madras Government Oriental Manuscripts Library
Mask.	Maskarī
Medh.	Medhātithi
Mit.	Mitāksharā
Mys.	Mysore
N.I.A.	New Indian Antiquary
N.U.C.	Notes of Unreported Cases
N.W.P.	North Western Provinces
Nag.	Nagpur
Nag. L.R.	Nagpur Law Reports
Nār.	Nārada
Norton	Norton's Leading Cases
O.H.	Our Heritage
Or.	Orissa

P.C.	Privy Council
P.L.D.	All Pakistan Legal Decisions
P.R.	Punjab Record
Pat.	Patna
Punj.	Punjab.
RabelsZ.	Rabels Zeitschrift, formerly Zeitschrift für ausländisches und internationales Privatrecht
ref.	referred to in
rev.	reviewed by
s.	see
S.B.	Special Bench (for matrimonial causes or for appeals before fuller benches)
Ś.B. or Śat.brā.	Śatapatha-brāhmaṇa
S.B.E.	Sacred Books of the East
S.C.	Supreme Court or Smṛti-candrikā
S.C.J.	Supreme Court Journal
S.C.R.	Supreme Court Reports
S.C.W.R.	Supreme Court Weekly Reporter
S.D.A.	Sadr Diwani Adalat (available in the original edition or the Indian Decisions (O.S.) *Select Reports* reprint)
S.I.I.	South Indian Inscriptions
Śab. bhā.	Śabara's *bhāṣya* on the Mīmāṃsā-sūtras
Sel. Rep.	Select Reports
S.V.	Sarasvatī-vilāsa
Suth.W.R.	Sutherland's Weekly Reporter
T.C.	Travancore-Cochin
T.L.L.	Tagore Law Lectures
Tit.	title
trans.	translated by
Trav.L.R.	Travancore Law Reports
v.	verse
Vas.	Vasiṣṭha
Vya.k.	Vyavahāra-kāṇḍa
Vya.may.	Vyavahāra-mayūkha
Vya.nir.	Varadarāja's *Vyavahāra-nirṇaya*
W.R. *see* Suth.W.R.	
W.Z.K.O.	Wiener Zeitschrift für die Kunde Süd- und Ostasiens
Yājñ.	Yājñavalkya
Z.D.M.G.	Zeitschrift der deutschen morgenländischen Gesellschaft
Z.V.R. or Z.f.vergl.Rechtsw.	Zeitschrift für vergleichende Rechtswissenschaft

* Asterisks in the margin refer to additions and corrections included at the end of the essay.

HINDU EMPIRES

Summary

In respect of Hindu empires, as equally of their successors, the Muslim empires in India and the British empire in India, it is desirable to summarise answers to the main questions. (1) How did an empire rise? By conquest and by voluntary or quasi-voluntary submissions to a would-be conqueror or leader. (2) How did it develop? By the same means; by the operation of rapacity, cupidity, and fear. (3) How and why did it fall? By failure of personalities, by foreign invasions, or by natural causes such as tend to equalise power between the centre and the constituent parts. (4) It will be noted that in all three aspects the same psychological factors played a decisive role. This is important, because the invading Muslims and the invading and even transient British betrayed, in due course, symptoms of the same complaints which affected native Hindu rulers, and the British (for all their excellent organisation) succumbed, in reality, as much through internal failures as through positive pressure within and negative failure of resources outside India.

Definition

The definition of 'empire' presents no problem. A king is *rāja*, an emperor *rājādhirāja*, or *mahārājādhirāja*, 'overlord of kings', 'overlord of great kings'. There is no special word in Sanskrit for 'empire'. The nearest is *sāmrājya*, which means universal or total sovereignty, the state appertaining to a *samrāj* (nom. *samrāṭ*), who is the overlord of at least one king. A king (*rāja*) is one who exercises rule, a ruler. The definition should not be complicated by reference to the partly mystical, certainly poetical, concept of *chakravartī*. The *chakravartī* is one who exercises imperial rule extending in a circle (*chakra*) towards all quarters. All actual emperors wished to be, and, if they were not, wished to be thought to be or to be called, *chakravartī*. All wanted to be lords, 'husbands', of the Earth. The actual condition of the *samrāṭ* (which is an objective term) and the theoretical status of *chakravartī* were connected in point of psychology. The following will deal with both topics under the heading of 'empire'. Little could be gained by the repetition of the abundance of material on the actual history of any of the many small and numerous large empires; and this paper will concentrate on the essence of the practical, rather than the poetic concept of empire.

Introduction

The subject of 'empires' is of great interest for Indian historiography. What is known and what is not known, and how both are written about are necessarily essential aspects of history. Why and how the Hindu kingdoms and empires fell to Muslim invaders and conquerors; why, even earlier, Alexander was able to build a short-lived empire in the North-West, and the Indo-Greeks, Śakas and Prathians after him; why, lastly the French were nearly able to build an empire, and Portuguese and the Dutch were able in different measures to acquire territory at the expense of the native powers, and lastly the British were able gradually but surely to obtain dominion or paramountcy over the indigenous rulers: these questions have agitated the minds of Indian historians, and coloured their approach towards, or failure to approach, the clue to these facts. The same clue explains the rise, duration, and fall of Hindu empires. But it is a clue of a character for which the Indian historians themselves are at present little prepared. The Indian-born historian of his own country is predisposed, by training, habit, and the conventions of a recently-established independence, to see his ancestors is a pious light. They had the virtues and merits which he has (so he supposes), and would not be guilty of behaviour such as would either justify foreign rule or provoke the unmeritorious behaviour which he often rightly castigates (by foreign standards) in the former imperial power. Anything which tends to describe them in terms which would not be equally applicable to western people (in particular the British) is distasteful to him. To treat his ancestors (however remote) as objects of objective sociological study seems to him irreverent and unpatriotic. Sociology and history are not yet linked in India (if we may except the as yet slender attempts of Dhirendra Narain [1]) just as sociology and law have still to join hands. Thus the *real* reasons why empires rose and fell are not attended to, and the copious facts (or apparent facts) of social life, which determined the behaviour of the people, are noted in a dry fashion, seldom tending towards an explanation beyond depiction.

A recent thorough study of historiography in India [2] reveals no awareness of the psychological factors which lie at the bottom of this story. Yet the continuity and identity of those factors from before the Mauryan empire until the consolidation of British rule is astonishing. The purpose of this contribution is to simplify the picture so that the factors may easily be grasped.

Equally astonishing is the fact that the causes of the fall of Hindu empires are not in doubt. The details of the facts in some ancient and mediaeval instances may not be available, but the

[1] *Hindu Character (a Few Glimpses)*, Bombay (University of Bombay Sociological Ser., N°. 8), 1957.

[2] C.H. Philips, ed., *Historians of India, Pakistan and Ceylon*, London (Oxford University Press), 1962.

pattern is clear. Most Indian phenomena are complicated and involved. Generalisations on Indian matters are more insecure than in any comparable field. Yet here we have not only virtual unanimity between scholars as to the broad outlines of the pattern, but the nature, size and character of our problem are either agreed among the savants or are easily capable of agreement. This is odd : but if, as the present writer supposes, the factors are psychological, and due to geography, human and environmental, it could hardly be otherwise.

The historical map of India is depressing to the newcomer. The swarm of names, the constant series of wars and revolutions and conquests and defeats, the apparent lack of consequence between the political changes and the social and political conditions of the inhabitants, and the impression of hopeless confusion thus created, makes the newcomer despondent of obtaining any useful information from the relations of historians. In this paper a minimum use of proper names and dates can safely be made, since from the items in the bibliography the serious student can readily obtain access to the abundant, perhaps excessive, detailed information which the more famous and competent Indian historians have lavishly supplied in the epigraphical journals and the advanced histories.

The Rise of Empires

We must approach this question from two standpoints, the practical, and the theoretical. The reader will already be aware [3] that a vast theoretical literature exists on the subject of kingship and empire. The explanation for the bellicosity of the literature is not readily accepted by all contemporary Indian thinkers [4], but

---

[3] 'The maintenance of peace in the Hindu world : practice and theory', *Recueils de la Société Jean Bodin*, XIV (La Paix), 143 ff. This was published in a nearly identical form in *Indian Year Book of International Affairs*, 1958.

[4] M. Kulasrestha, ed., *Tagore Centenary Volume*, Hoshiapur (1961), p. 257-262;

this writer retains his original conception, *viz.* that public security (and the word *security* must be emphasised) required a bellicose king and the positive rather than a negative attitude towards empire building. The practical standpoint of our study relates to the geographical, climatic and population factors of an objective character.

To commence with the practical aspect: several political units, whether these are oligarchical polities of the ancient type known to India in the Buddhist era or kingdoms of the classical type, required mutual protection and mutual support. The larger units of society were in the plains, since those in the hills and forests were naturally scattered and incohesive. Society in the great northern plains required protection for purposes of agriculture, and was exceptionally exposed to attack due to the level nature of the ground and the scarcity of natural obstacles to military advance. In such areas the only natural boundaries were the edges of the forests and the rivers themselves. The latter were easily crossed at most seasons of the year. The former were not true frontiers, since they could be crossed and recrossed at pleasure by the wild forest and mountain tribes. At the edges of cultivation and civilisation protection of the settlements was a full-time task for someone: and nearly always beyond the means of the cultivators themselves. Hence the need for subjection to an imperial power which could levy taxes for protection over a wide area, thus spreading the burden, and with the proceeds employ standing forces to police the frontiers. Boundaries were vague on the great plains, and the urge to unite with neighbouring settlements and so to extend the frontiers, pushing the area of protection and intermittent conflict further and further from wealthy settlements, was natural and constant. An empire offered to minimise wasteful expenditure of men and materials and the larger it was the more efficient it was for the purposes of keeping

T.K. Tope in M.J. Sethna, ed., *Contributions to Synthetic Jurisprudence* (Bombay, 1962), p. 84-98. See also M. Anantanarayanan, 'Hindu law', in A. Larson and C. Wilfred Jenks, edd., *Sovereignty within the Law* (New York/London, 1965), p. 184-209.

internal peace and minimising risks of invasion. Wherever risks were large or unusual the centrally organised forces would be available: but the tendency in fact to let local rulers mind their own problems seems never to have been disputed. Self-sufficiency within the empire to which taxes were paid seems to have been the more common situation — a fact hostile to the stability of empires.

If one can shepherd men as one shepherds flocks, men too can be exploited. The soldiers who can police frontiers are capable of adquiring for the emperor new subjects who have not so far desired his protection. Weaker peoples, foreign to the basic populations whose ruler is now predatory, are naturally open to be exploited. In both these ways the first well-known great empire of India, the Mauryan, seems to have started [5]. A political and even cultural unity extending over the greater part of the sub-continent and into modern Afghanistan offered rewards and a standard of civilization which subsequent ages were hardly able to rival. At one stage the emperor Aśoka caused an adjoining people (of Kalinga), who did not require to be subject to him, to be subdued with enormous loss of life (itself not unique in Indian experience). We are told that this was a turning point of his religious life and his imperial policies. But, whatever may and must be said about Aśoka's ideals and policies [6], the general pattern of Indian imperialism, namely to subdue those able to be subdued, is only temporarily broken by Mauryan (Aśokan) pacifism and benevolence.

Practically, too, empires serve the ambitions of the administrator 'type' of personality. Irrespective of the caste system which deprecated administration as a role for the Brahmin caste, numerous Brahmins, by reason of their intellectual ability and inherited prestige took to government, and even generalship was not abhorred by that traditionally pacific people. The point about *ambition* also needs to be empasised, for the optimism and persistence of the

---

[5] R.D. Mookerji, 'Rise of Magadhan imperialism', *The Age of Imperial Unity* (Bombay, 1951), ch. 2; the Mauryan epoch was at its height from c. 273 B.C. to c. 187 B.C.

imperial careerist is a constant feature of the Indian scene, and the reasons for this must be explored.

The ideological factor must not be ignored. Empire would be extended not merely by conquest but also by belief that the imperial family intended to facilitate or foster a particular ideological approach to life, private and public. The Mauryan connection with Buddhism, and the attitude of later emperors to religious questions, cannot be shown not to have had a role to play in the willingness of people to subject themselves to this rule, or to remain subject to it against fissiparous tendencies. A point is sometimes made that dharma ('righteousness') has been violated by a ruler, and therefore a usuper is justified in acquiring the loyalties forfeited by the culprit [7]. Rulers whose families have disobeyed the canons of right behaviour are insecure, and, at any rate in South India, many changes in government can be traced to such movements [8]. The king, and more certainly, the emperor must always set a good example : and it is astonishing how often the burdens of office naturally distract him from that duty. Kings in India seem seldom to have learnt by experience (due to the low development of historical scholarship in India?), another curious fact which our 'clue' will help to explain.

Theoretically the ideal Hindu king was a potential emperor, as he was a potential conqueror [9]. Empire, rather than mere king-

---

[6] P.H.L. Eggermont and J. Hoftijzer, *The Moral Edicts of King Asoka* (texts only), Leiden (Brill), 1962. R. Thapar, *Asoka and the Decline of the Mauryas*, London (O.U.P.), 1961. N.A. Nikam and R. Mc Keon, *The Edicts of Asoka*, Chicago (Chicago Univ. Press), 1959, also Chicago (Pheonix), 1966; D.C. Sircar, *Inscriptions of Asoka*, Delhi (Ministry of Information), 1957. F. Kern, *Asoka : Kaiser und Missionar*, Bern (Francke), 1956. G. Srinivasa Murti, A.N. Krishna Aiyangar, and K.V. Rangaswami Aiyangar, ed., *Edicts of Asoka, Priyadarśin*, Adyar (Library), 1951.

[7] For example, propaganda put out by a usurping member of the Rāṣṭrakūṭa dynasty against a close relation who was really entitled to the throne.

[8] Strikingly in Vijayanagar. For instance the usurpation of Sāluva Narasiṃha. K.A. Nilakanta Sastri, *History of South India*, 2nd. edn., p. 263.

[9] See citation from the same work below.

ship gave the kingly caste its natural scope and goal. Learning was in the hands of Brahmins. Brahmin supreme rulers were rare. They would become virtually Kshatriyas thereby, thus descending in the hierarchical caste order, by assuming governmental responsibility. Brahmins, the true custodians of religion, political science, and literature generally, were constantly conscious of their dependence upon the ruler, and upon him and his deputies for gifts and other endowments. Brahmins preached conquest, and, as a prophylatic against being conquered, readiness for war. They themselves would not fight, but they would profit enormously from victory and conquest, since the successful fighter's first duties included the endowment or re-endowment of priests, temples, and educational and other charitable establishments. This does not mean that conquest was the only method of empire-building. Peoples too weak to resist were called upon to submit, or their security was subverted by other means. If a ruler was able to become an emperor by subverting neighbouring peoples without losing his soldiers so much the better [10]. Other means of expansion were acceptable, provided they were efficient.

Practice and theory established the notion that empires were better than kingdoms, and nobody doubted but that a non-expansionist ruler was a weak one, who was about to forfeit his and his family's title to rule.

The Development of Empires

India, for all its very long history, has seen very few long-lasting or extensive empires. The truly great empires were those of the Mauryas, the Kushāṇas, the Sātavāhanas, the Guptas, the Vākāṭakas; the greater amongst the lesser empires were those of

[10] Another way of putting what Indra says at Kulasrestha (cited above): every means was tried before war was resorted to, which even the most absolute pacifist would commend!

the Pratihāras and Pālas in the north and east, the Rāṣṭrakūṭas followed by the Chālukyas in the Deccan, and the Chōḷas and Pāṇḍyas in the South. Apart from these the empire of Harṣa in the north is often referred to as a leading empire. For greatness of extent, duration of rule and general efficiency the Mauryan was equalled only by the Gupta, but neither of these seems really to have ruled in the Deccan and South, irrespective of a nominal acceptance of their sovereignty by local chiefs. On the other hand we must not forget the Vijayanagar empire which, as the last Hindu empire, ruled for at least three centuries in the Deccan and South, and for long resisted the threat of Muslim power and ideology more or less continuously pressing from the North.

An empire could not develop unless a king acquired rule over other kings. It was a feature of Indian imperialism that the conqueed rulers were deprived of their kingdoms, and then *reinstated* as 'feudatories'. This process was apperently mild and benevolent and likely to avoid desparate jealousies at the edges of the empire, but it operated to the empire's disadvantage. Medhātithi, the famous 10th century commentator on the *Manu-smṛti* says (on M.VII. 202, see Jha's trans., III, 2, p. 407) that the conqueror should discover the inhabitants' preferences and should make a treaty with a member of the original dynasty in such terms as these: 'You must give me an equal share in your treasury, etc., and you must take an equal share in my fortune and misfortune (or 'sin'); in activity or inactivity, at the proper time, you must personally adhere to me, both with your forces and your treasury'. In this way the emperor obtained a willing, and *pro tempore* grateful subordinate and ally, both against foreign agression and against internal disorder. But since the treaty did not bind those who did not enter into it, and since princes readily combined against their sovereign or his successor, the vassal prince was a potential source of weakness. During the decay of the Western Chālukya empire and during the short-lived empire of the usurping successor state which attempted to prolong its life, the Hoysaḷa king, who was aiming from the dry south to build up an empire which should include the moister and thus more fertile parts of the southern and western edges of the Chālukya territories, conquered and forced into such a position as Medhātithi describes several important *rājas*. They duly kept loyalty to the Hoysaḷa, and recited his titles before their own on their inscriptions, until the sphere of influence from the north became too strong, and the preoccupations of the Hoysaḷa elsewhere became too many, whereupon they omitted the overlord's titles, sought independence, and eventually joined another empire on (we hope) more advantageous terms. Generally we hear of vassal kings attending the durbar of their emperor, and poetically they are depicted as waiting upon the emperor like servants. But evidence suggests, certainly in South India, where our materials are more abundant, that the subject kings accepted titles from their conquerors and went back to their homes to rule as before, but subject to pay tribute to the emperor and to assist him with men and materials in his wars. Occasionally imperial status was granted to an individual person because of his personal qualities in order to terminate a period of anarchy [11].

The development of the empire by way of conquest would be balanced by developments in point of security by way of alliances. Kings that could not be conquered were placated by alliances. The loyalty of conquered kings and rulers was obtained by their compulsorily giving daughters in marriage to the conqueror. An instance of a son being given as a hostage is met with here and there, when the Muslims were the victors : it is not impossible that sons were

[11] The case of Gopāla (c. A.D. 750-770) in Bengal is the best known, but another may be taken from Pallava history. See R.C. Majumdar and A.D. Pusalker, *The Age of Imperial Kanauj*, Bombay (1955), p. 44. Ibid., p. 52, the responsibility was unworthily held by successors. Vigrahapāla abdicated and retired to an ascetic life. His son and successor Nārāyaṇapāla ruled for more than half a century, but he was also of a pacific and religious disposition. During the reigns of these two unmartial kings the Pāla empire fell to pieces. Some time after A.D. 860 the far-off Rāṣṭrakūṭas (coming from the poor Deccan) defeated the Pāla rulers.

given as hostages even in warfare between Hindu rulers [12]. The loyalty of allies could not be secured by a hostage, and was regarded theoretically as a somewhat insecure advantage. Nevertheless the alliance enabled the emperor to turn greater attention to areas where the forces of the empire could be profitably employed at greater risk.

The success of the adventures depended on the efficiency of the machinery of government. If the objects of the empire were negative, namely to protect the territory from invasions, it would be sufficient to secure the loyalty of the rulers of the border districts or other sensitive areas. If the objects were positive and aggressive, military leaders and officials competent in the art of internal security were both needed, and their employment and encouragement were amongst the emperors' chiefs concerns. The recruitment and payment of these people was thus a key factor. In the Mauryan empire and in subsequent Muslim empires at their height care was taken to employ officials for wages, thereby attaching them to the centre. Later it was found impossible to achieve this, for reasons which will be outlined below, and grants of territory were made to the ministers and generals: and it is generally agreed that this was a contributory factor to the decay of empires almost as soon as they were consolidated [13].

An empire would grow with success, as more and more areas felt that the cost of submission to it would be outweighed by the strength of its protection or the likelihood of participation in booty or other gains. It is noticeable while studying the history of the Deccan, which is a dry, hard area, how often the imperial families are those best suited to lead the inhabitants out of the Deccan and down into

12 Kampili was founded by returning hostages from Delhi. Ballāḷa III Hoysaḷa gave his son as a hostage to the same court.

13 For great detail in connexion with grants of land by way of remuneration, and the weakening effect this had upon the thrones from which the grants came, see R.S. Sharma, *Indian Feudalism : c. 300-1200*, Calcutta (University of Calcutta), 1965.

the favourable, rich areas, whether along the West Coast where the ports were and rich trade flowed from the Arabian Sea into the Peninsula, or into the rice-growing regions of the great river deltas and the well-irrigated valleys [14]. People wanted to be ruled by a leader who could give shares in wealth stripped from foreigners, as well as security within the borders. An empire could as easily collapse if the reigning family ceased to provide these advantages, or if its efficiency was impaired by causes we shall presently review.

The situation in times of success is best illustrated by an extract from the celebrated and impartial historian, R.C. Majumdar, discussing the empire of the Guptas [15] at its height:

'The inscription of Parṇadatta is a beautiful composition and holds out before us the picture of a strong united empire under the vigorous administration of a benevolent and popular ruler. The Gupta empire, which now stretched literally from the Bay of Bengal to the Arabian Sea, was the undisputed possession of one master whose commands were implicitly obeyed by the governors, appointed by him, from one end to the other of this vast region. The foundations of the empire were strong enough to survive great internal shocks, and even the redoubtable Hūṇas failed to break through its defences. For nearly a century the empire had stood as a symbol of the unity, integrity and independence of Āryāvarta. The poet who referred (in A.D. 460) to the tranquil reign of Skanda-gupta, the lord of a hundred kings, did not probably exaggerate the condition of things. We have every reason to believe that peace and prosperity prevailed over the vast empire, and the new era of cultural progress continued its course unchecked under the protective wing of the unparalleled material power and splendour of the age. When Skanda-gupta died about A.D. 467, he had the supreme satis-

---

[14] The principles are illustrated in J.D.M. Derrett, *The Hoysaḷas*, Madras (Oxford University Press), 1957.

[15] *The Classical Age*, Bombay (Bharatiya Vidya Bhavan), 1954, p. 28.

faction of leaving intact a mighty empire built up by his great predecessors'.

An attack from abroad stengthened the hand of one who wished for empire. The Śakas as enemies of the Hindu rulers of the North and Central Indian plains; the Hūṇas as invaders of the Punjab and Ganges Valley; the Muslims of Dehli and later of the Bahmani Sultanate and its successors as invaders and potential invaders of the Deccan and the South : all these acted as incipient empire-builders for the most worthy Hindu monarch amongst those whom they threatened. Yet it was exactly such circumstances as would be favourable to the consolidation of a sound empire that actually precipitated the break-up of an unsound one. For the boldness of the invader was whetted by the prosperity of the land chosen to be invaded, and by the dissensions within between those who wished for larger shares in its profits. On the other hand, if the pressure on the frontiers relaxed, so that the emperor could go forward and add to his territories, his movement was dictated not only by a spirit of grandeur, by desire for revenge, or by mere rapacity, but also by the vacuum — the vacuum of a relatively weak political power, into which a stronger is inevitably sucked. Hindu students of politics were emphatically aware of this.

The physical growth of an empire was the erection of a pyramid. The village depended on the personality and competence of the headman or joint headmen. The group of villages depended upon group arrangements for defence. The district depended upon the leaders of the district, the people most to be relied upon to resolve disputes and to represent the district in contact with any higher power. Prestige was the key quality, and its foundations were purely practical. Wealth, freedom from suspicion of corruptibility, strength of purpose, and power instinctively to represent the people and to protect them; the ability, in short, to call upon them for their services without fear of a refusal, and to reward and punish in such a manner as to retain universal regard : these were the natural ingredients of prestige. This delicate ability is more often than not hereditary, especially when combined with the knowledge of minute local matters which is essential before such qualities can be employed. Any kingdom consisted of districts which chose or accepted or endured a particular family as its leader in peace and war, its supreme judge (so long as it was independent) and its organiser for purposes of growth, spiritual and temporal alike, and for purposes of defence. The instinct to form a pyramid was a perpetual characteristic. But the problem remained that, when many districts joined, jealousies and insecurity developed between the heads of districts of various powers and values. It was part of the price which had to be paid. The ruler of a small area would wish to form a connection with one greater than his overlord, in order to balance the pressures which his immediate equals would otherwise place upon him. Absolute equality was rare, and a search for this almost impossible goal led to discontent amongst those whose contented loyalty was essential to the empire's reality. When a kingdom absorbed another or others, the loyalties of the lower courses of the pyramid could as easily be available to one family as to another of the upper courses, so that the firmness of attachment between family and village, and between village and district which was based on race, language, geography and economic interdependence was not reproduced in an equal firmness of attachment to the leaders whose duties were less well defined, and must fluctuate with opportunity and means.

The metaphor of the pyramid requires emphasis, since it is not to be assumed that the independent rulers who were compelled or preferred to form an integral part of an empire felt that they were thereby lowered in prestige : on the contrary, the acquisition of a superior who proved worthy of their attachment was a proof of their own eminence, and the function of each course in the pyramid was related to the others. The obligations of the supreme overlord, his subject kings and ministers, downwards towards the inhabitants of town and countryside were, in a general way, reciprocal.

The juridical theory accepted this, though we cannot be sure exactly what practical conclusions to draw from it. The *samrāṭ* took tribute (*kara*) from the subordinate ruler (*sakara*); to some he gave jurisdiction to keep order and to execute sentence on criminals. In practice it must have been a common thing to find a trustworthy *rāja* invested with such jurisdiction. In other cases he may well have reserved jurisdiction to himself, thereby attempting to clip the wings of any incipient revolt by constant knowledge of misbehavior of all kinds within the subject kingdom. The fourteenth-century jurist Chaṇḍeśvara, in his *Rājanīti-ratnākara*, explains these two kinds of *sakaras*, Where the *sakara rāja* arbitrarily hears a case though he has not been invested with jurisdiction, if it is a criminal case in which the *rāja* has levied a fine the *rāja* himself is fined by the *samrāṭ* an amount equal to the original fine, so that the imperial treasury obtains its due; if it is a civil case the *rāja* should be summoned, or the occasion of his ceremonial visit should be awaited, and his offer of a present should not be accepted and he himself should be kept waiting for a few days, to show the emperor's displeasure. But the decree, though given without jurisdiction, should not be rescinded or annulled, because the *rāja* is after all king in his own territory and his prestige should not be lowered in the eyes of his subjects (an event which would cost the emperor ultimately much more severe loss).

The Fall of Empires

The desire to be an emperor was too widely shared. It was shared by competing subordinate families under a weak or weakened emperor. It was shared equally by members of an imperial family. For the law of succession did not choose or determine that the heir should be prestige-worthy; still less did it choose the prestige-worthy amongst possible heirs. Along with the desire to be emperor ran the opposing desire not to be subordinate if no need arose for protection: there seemed to be no point in paying taxes and yielding jurisdiction to a superior if one had more efficacious, or sufficient, means to resist attacks or subversion.

The acquisition of wealth led to prestige, since one could award favours and buy loyalties and respect if one was rich, not least by lavish gifts for religion and charity. Kingship was a way of accumulating wealth, likewise the right to be a minister or governor, or to act as some other channel for the in-bringing of taxes. The desire for prestige led automatically to a desire for wealth. Prestige, however, was on the whole the dominant motive, as it still is. The search for prestige within Hindu society was so strong that factors of a more objective kind were frequently ignored as unimportant. In Northern India, in the Deccan, and in Vijayanagar and in the face of the European powers, the Hindu rulers characterisically feuded amongst themselves while the common enemy was at the gate. They would repeatedly seek the help of the common enemy in order to get the better of a rival, perhaps a relation who was a rival. It was the order of priorities which constantly proved to be the weak link in the system of empire-seeking and empire-building in ancient and mediaeval India.

Just as we have abundant evidence that the emergence of a particular personality, such as Harṣa or Kṛṣṇadeva-rāja (the greatest empire-builder amongst the Vijayanagar rulers), made for the growth of an empire, so we can be sure that the accession of a weak personality led rapidly to the empire's decline. Empire therefore hinged heavily upon the personality of the emperor, or, to be more accurate for the periods and areas about which we have abundant evidence, upon the security and self-discipline of the imperial family (which could replace a weak successor by a strong one without necessarily dislodging the family's own advantages or incurring factions within the family).

The brilliance of the Mauryan empire, which may have owed something to Hellenic and Achaemenian influence, was such that the rapid decline of the dynasty and the lapse of Northern India into the chaos which seems to have been its resting condition needed explanation. At the other end of the time-scale, the extremely well-organized and highly diversified and prosperous empire of Vijayanagar had a long experience of maintaining internal balance and could have withstood, and indeed did withstand many invasions and small-scale attacks from the Muslims in the north. Why did it collapse and go into fragments all of a sudden, with the looting and destruction of the capital city? The cause of the fall of the Mauryas is a matter of speculation. In the case of Vijayanagar we know the causes. It is reasonable to suppose that they had something, or more than something, in common.

It is argued that Aśoka weakened the empire by his pacifist policies [16], and by his inordinate partiality towards Buddhism, i.e. by angering adherents of the Brahminical religion by withholding proportionate patronage from them. R.D. Mookerji comments that the size of the empire was remarkable, and that it is more difficult to account for its longevity than its decline — and this point of view may be correct. He would say that generally the causes of the decline were (1) a spirit of local autonomy due perhaps to prosperity and jealousy of interference inspired by officials of a different nationality; (2) the difficulties of communicating with distant provinces, especially if they had no desire to be communicated with; (3) oppressive rule, unduly bureaucratic methods, harsh rule of the subjects by governors who, if successful, could use their strength against the centre, and if unsuccessful merely provoked rebellions against both themselves and the power on whose behalf they acted (4); palace intrigues and treachery amongst officials; and finally (5) foreign invasions provoked by instability within. This is borne out by the fact that Taxila, a town far removed from the centre, repeatedly revolted. It was rich, far off, culturally specialised and continually in touch with foreign neighbours of the state. The immediate cause of the decline of the Mauryas and the accession of Puṣyamitra seems to have been the invasion of the Bactrian Greeks, which called for radical reforms within the empire.

Speaking of the downfall of the great Gupta empire, R.C. Majumdar says [17],

---

[16] Buddha PRAKASH, *Studies in Indian History and Civilisation*, Agra (Shiv Lal Agarwala), 1962, p. 207.

[17] *The Classical Age*, p. 44.

'... the end of the Gupta empire offers a striking analogy to that of the Mughal empire. The decline and downfall of both were brought about mainly by internal dissensions in the royal family and the rebellions of feudal chiefs and provincial satraps, though foreign invasion was an important contributory factor. There is a general belief among historians that the Hūṇa invasion was the principal cause of the downfall of the Gupta empire... So far as the evidence goes, the death-blow to the Gupta empire was dealt not by the Hūṇas but by ambitious chiefs like Yaśoddharman... The rift caused by Yaśoddharman... gradually widened till the mighty imperial structure was engulfed in the chasm'.

C.V. Vaidya deals with the downfall of Hindu India before the threat of Muslim incursions in Northern India [18]. His view is that the prime cause of failure to ward off Muslim imperialism was internecine fighting. One who conquered gained no increase in resources or dominion, a fact perhaps truer in general of the North than of Central India or the South. Due to the caste system there was no natural social cohesion which gave Hindus more in common with each other than with a powerful foreigner anxious to divide and rule. Likewise no sentiment of nationality existed between areas speaking different dialects and even different languages. Lastly there existed a superstitious trend inducing the belief that ultimately *mlecchas* (non-Hindus) must win in the political sphere — an aspect of fatalism which truly reflects the debilitating effects not only of the Indian climate but especially of Indian traditional social conditions.

The great historian K.A. Nilakanta Sastri speaks of the political condition of South India at a somewhat earlier period in these terms [19]:

'...the duty of protecting society was cast by theory on a special

[18] *Downfall of Hindu India* (c. *1000 A.D.-1200 A.D.*), Poona (1926), p. 361-370. See also B.P. Sinha, *The Decline of the Kingdom of Magadha* (c. *455-1000 A.D.*), Bankipore/Patna, 1954.

[19] *History of South India*, 2nd edn., Madras (1958), p. 157-8.

class, the Kshatriyas, and by a natural and easy transition anyone who felt equal to the task of undertaking the rule of a particular area and did not hesitate to do so was more or less readily accepted as the ruler. Each successful adventurer became a king and gained respectability by maintaining a liberal court, patronizing learning and the arts, and causing *praśastis* (praises) to be composed in honour of himself and his family. Moreover, aggrandizement was the recognised duty of the ruler; he had to be a *vijigīshu* (one who wishes to conquer) and the general acceptance of this ideal led to frequent wars and skirmishes resulting in changes in the relative precedence of the different powers involved'.

Just as the empire flourished in the hands of a strong and determined ruler, so he built up for himself and his family an institution carrying within itself the seeds of rapid decay. His trusted officials were paid largely out of the revenues of areas of land, on which they or their families and dependants resided, controlling the multitudes of semi-servile agriculturists. The revenue-payers were loyal to them rather than to the emperor. If these chiefs, whether appointed by the ruler, or hereditarily ruling areas which had submitted to the empire, supplied arms, men, and money the empire could flourish. But the very strength of the empire induced individuals who were ambitious for promotion to intrigue against the ruler in favour either of one of themselves or of a member of the imperial family of whom they approved. Only if the imperial family was extremely well united in every way was it collectively proof against these intrigues. The intrigues themselves has peculiar chances of success because of the unsteadiness which, in spite of all the talk of loyalty, affected the Indian temperament of ancient times very severely. Courts were repeatedly the asylums of ambitious and embittered scions of neighbouring royal houses, waiting for their chance to return, or to be put upon the throne, no matter what price their country might have to pay for this dubious privilege.

Having achieved, by birth, choice, or conquest, or even a usurpation, the imperial position, the successful ruler would not always do as the textbooks required of him, namely divide his time properly between the various departments of imperial administration and organization. On the contrary he might relapse into the hieratic and superstitious aspects of the role which he had acquired. Again and again we hear of rulers who slid into debauchery, preoccupied with women and liquor and foolish habits of conspicuous consumption [20], and who are thus not merely sitting targets for rivals, likely to retain power only by such capricious cruelty as will serve to create sympathy for their enemies, but also wielders of power and enjoyers of wealth which almost any competent person might envy and seek to take from them. They could as easily become addicted to religion — the *Nītivākyāmṛta* of *Soma-deva* quaintly says that kingship is not for the purpose of assuming the trappings of a religious mendicant or ascetic — with the same results.

We have already noticed the highly personal aspect of empire, and it would be impossible unduly to emphasise this. The Indian legends about rulers, both those which appear in official documents and others, abound with tales which suggest that governmental policy was directed by personal considerations, such as avenging an insult, rather than objective attention to public welfare; this the Indian public readily believed, and they could not have believed this if it were not accepted that kingship, and, still more, empire, rested upon the personalities' capacities and preferences.

In illustration of all these points we may take the last days of the Vijayanagar empire. The usurper Rāma Raya was an able administrator and a man of vigour into old age. But to achieve and keep his position he must be suspicious or all possible rivals and he acted as many in mediaeval Europe did in such cases. He destroyed many of the ancient nobility and raised his own family to the highest ranks. He also thought to keep loyal servants by employing Muslims, and, what is worse, employing them in his army and in his privy councils. The Muslim states of the Deccan which had, Hindu

[20] *Ibid.*, 243, 262, 263. The story of Vijayanagar proceeds with frequent assassinations, intrigues and civil wars, while the Muslim rulers to the North were perpetually ready to attack.

fashion, split off from the now long defunct Bahmani kingdom, especially the Sultanates of Ahmadnagar, Bijapur and Golconda were mutually jealous and predatory upon the borders of Vijayanagar and upon each other. Rāma Raya played each one of these three off against the others. While he kept them in suspense they so kept him. His capital was far too near the frontier, and was in reality the hub of Hindu resistance to the predatory, oppresive, mercenary and brutal forces which the Muslim states kept alert on the Hindus' doorstep. Meanwhile energy was distracted from the far South. There revolts occurred on the part of rulers who felt Vijayanagar to be too far off to be a danger to them. St. Francis Xavier and the Portuguese fomented rebellion and aimed to detach areas of territory (true, of no great size) from their alliance to the emperor. China Timma, a cousin of Rāma Raya, led a punitive expedition to the South where his cruelties were the less effective for their momentary severity. The Sultan of Bijapur, the weakest of the three Sultans, sought Rāma's friendship. There was the farce of his being adopted by the Hindu emperor as his son. To keep the balance Rāma did what other Hindu kings had attempted before, with equal failure: to mediate between the Sultans. The Peace of the Four Kings lasted from 1557 to 1560. Hereupon the Muslims learnt from experience. Dynastic marriages cemented political alliances between Ahmadnagar and Bijapur. All the Muslim rulers combined against Rāma Raya. The attack was launched on a vast scale in 1564. At the beginning of 1565 the battle was joined at Rakshasi-Tangadi or Talikota. Rāma's well prepared forces would have won but for the desertion to the enemy of two Muslim commanders in Rāma's pay. The defeat which followed was strategic as well as tactical. The city of Vijayanagar was looted and reduced to the ruins which have survived to this day. The desolation of the city was the desolation of the empire. Rāma was beheaded, the troops fled, the empire collapsed, and no attempts to recreate it found any success. The Muslims would divide the South of India between them, and the valuable parts were taken, only the geographically and economically less attractive were left to Hindu rulers.

Vijayanagar as a nominal empire came to an end between 1652 and 1675, but the organisation and spirit of common subordination to a single ruler died in 1565. There was no South Indian empire, Hindu or Muslim, except in name, until the British came and put an end to internecine strife which had become worse and more destructive and embittered as time went on.

The relatively short lives of the greater empires, and the lack of continuity and stability amongst the lesser empires, are equally to be explained by the pyramidal structure of political dependence and the peculiar character of that dependence to which we must now, in conclusion, turn.

Conclusion

We have already seen how a potential weakness of the Indian kingdom lay in the method of paying officials by giving them grants of revenue from the land, or, what amounted to much the same thing in practice, the land itself. This system must have arisen out of the impossibility of satisfactorily paying them otherwise. That this lasted over an immense area of territory and for a very long period of time can be explained by psychological factors. These are quite clearly to be observed today, and thus present no problem. Those who have any kind of official position believe that they do others a favour for doing what in the rest of the world is regarded as a duty. This is because of the ancient hieratic and superstitious concept of rule and the ruler's position. The ruler also has his duty, but his role and function is of enjoyment. The ruler's duty to protect the subjects cannot be visualised as a duty towards any particular subject in any particular situation. All subjects adopt a toadying attitude towards officials. Toadyism (*flagornerie*) and sycophancy run throughout the system. If money is to be paid out this may not be completed unless pressure is placed on the payer, or he is induced to concede payment as a favour — for which some reciprocity is naturally required. Officials whose incomes depended on the payment by individuals whom they could not personally squeeze would be insecure and dependent upon those officials, and this would reverse the order of precedence. Thus the characteristic Indian situation was of a pyramid of dependence, the topmost individual depending upon all his immediate subjects for his income, but with all of them dependent upon him for their own progress, security, and general welfare. The king in turn depended on the rulers for his income and troops, and they depended on him for the security and prosperity of the empire.

The insecurity of the Indian mind is, and obviously was, its predominant feature. Life in the joint family deprived every individual of a trust or belief in the stability of any person. Hence the great interest in otherworldly values, in 'merit', and in escape from the apparently endless flux of existence, between this life which might be endlessly repeated and other forms of existence which were none the less strongly feared for their being unknown. *Moksha* ('release') was (and indeed is) a constituent part of *dharma* ('righteousness'). The natural search for security went on ceaselessly. Prestige belonged to one who could pretend or offer to give security (*abhaya*) to his dependants, i.e. those who pretended or needed to expect security from him. Prestige-bearing persons themselves needed security from those who offered it to them, i.e. the upper courses of the pyramid of power. Loyalty was thus to a hypothesis, namely to those people only who actually offer security, not to an individual or a family. Long experience shows that certain families and certain hnman types are more likely to be worthy of confidence under imaginable conditions, and to these dependence automatically attaches itself by a kind of natural agglutination. In this way individuals are built up into kingly figures, intrigues are fomented, rebellions are organised, and dynasties are ousted by usurpers. Insecurity thus made empires, and broke them. We could reconstruct the chain in this way:

(1) Empire leads to security and wealth.

(2) Wealth attracts invasions and intrigues which in turn tend to perfect the organisation and bind the elements of the state together.

(3) Any weakness, whether in point of resources or in point of jealousies or intrigues, attracted invasions. Thus in the Deccan and South India it was axiomatic that if your neighbour's army was occupied on the western border you should attack him in the east, and so on.

(4) The vaster the organization the more responsibility would be given to officials and relatives, preferably the latter. But the mild methods of government left subordinates a very great freedom, certainly sufficient freedom to attempt to build little empires for themselves within the greater empire.

(5) If the organization became top-heavy, and communication between higher and lower elements was poor, the government could only be weak, except when employing capricious and intermittent punishments for an inefficiently chosen selection of culprits. Indian adminstration lay perpetually open to petty corruptions. This gave an opening for discontent.

(6) Competition between relatives expecting to succeed to the throne would bring in certain subordinates or even foreigners as 'mediators', i.e. the state would suffer due to promises or obligations either to subordinate elements, whose subsequent rise would be resented by their former equals, or the integrity of the state itself would be threatened by the interference of neighbouring states, who could not but gain from their help.

(7) Internecine feuding between relatives, between comparable but independent powers, between the feudatories of a single weak emperor, and generally throughout Hindu society rendered an empire weak in the face of any common threat. The only sanction seems to have been force; while society as a whole attempted to live in indifference to the ineptitudes of kings and emperors, an indifference which in fact it could hardly afford.

(8) From top to bottom of the chain runs the thread of personal dependence and the search for prestige. Support could not be obtained except upon terms. What would now be called dishonest dealing in terms of revenue collection or any kind of undertaking was so common that nothing but transient self-interest held people together

beyond the level of the family, and even families broke up under the strain of the temptations of empire. The state was in constant flux which only a few highly talented individuals were able to keep in relative check [21].

Insecurity is thus the mother of empires in India and also their end. The insecurity is both of a climatic and geographical nature and psychological. The first reinforces the second. The teachings of Indian scholars showed abundant awareness of this and did all that teachings could do to overcome the effects. But apart from efficient government, apt to advance into the vacuum of which we have spoken and able to defend against adversaries, there was no offer of relief except escape into fantasy by abandoning the world — which even kings might do! In practice the determination to be a receptacle of prestige and to merit it in the eyes of the pyramid of dependants was the undoing of kingdoms and of empires; of the first because kings would fight to the last over trifling questions of honour; of the second because competitors for empire were obliged to try their luck, and to gamble with their lives and those even of their toadies, come what might. In this way features of perennial Indian psychology explain the main lines of Indian history up to and beyond the commencement of the British period.

Appendix I: Muslim empires.

After invasions from the west from A.D. 711 onwards during which wealthy cities were looted, temples destroyed, and other transient

---

21 It is of interest that the researches of R.E. Frykenberg, *Guntur District 1788-1848. A History of Local influence on Central Authority in South India*, Madras (Oxford University Press), 1965, conducted upon principles of historical sociology, reveal old Indian methods at work even during the early British period. The present writer's contention that the methods run through all periods is easily sustained from R.C. Majumdar's emphasis on instances of discontent with British rule throughout the British period (see bibliography below).

benefits were obtained from India without corresponding advantages for her, Muslim rulers established themselves at Delhi and a Sultanate of Delhi grew up. In succession a large part of Northern India was ruled by the so called Slave Kings (Turks), the Khaljis (1296-1316), the Tughlaks (to 1351), and, after the invasions of Timur (1398) and others, the Sayyids (1414-1451). After the Lodi dynasty (1451-1526) independent Sultanates took the place of the unwieldy empire nominally ruled from Delhi. The Bahmani kingdom, followed by a fragmentary successor state consisting of five independent Sultanates of the Deccan was one of the nominal successors to this Dehli empire. The Mughal empire was founded by a Turk called Babur, whose personal energy and enterprise carved out this estate for himself and his family. Amongst the more famous Mughal emperors were Akbar (1556-1605), who ruled the greater part of Northern, Central and Eastern India, Jahangir (1605-1627) during whose reign the Mughal empire reached its zenith, and Aurangzeb (1658-1707) during whose lifetime an attempt to make the Mughal empire pan-Indian nearly succeeded, prosperity increased considerably, yet decay rapidly developed and the empire began to fall apart. It was from the decayed limbs of this empire that the European powers began to build their own little nuclei of empires, of which only the British succeeded.

The basis of Muslim rule initially was simply rapine. Hindus did not effectively resist Muslim rulers not chiefly because of the terrain or the better quality of the Turkish and other foreign troops, but because of their psychological inability to combine and organise themselves. The case of Shivājī, whose organisation enabled a Hindu state to be carved from the western Deccan under the eyes of the Mughal emperor, is unique and illustrates the weakness and handicaps of the rest of the sub-continent. The Hindu desire to take advantage of a strong ruler to protect himself against his competitors and if possible to obtain some advantage over his Hindu rivals, gave the Muslims, for all their atrocious treatment of Indians, a free ticket into power. The collapse of various Muslim empires, including that of Aurangzeb, was due to the size of the prizes that easily fell to rebels, to the tendency of Muslim families to feud, and to the inordinate centralisation of business which fear of delegating and fear of trusting anyone subject to any temptation must necessarily bring with it. Far too much weight lay upon personalities; what would be virtues in one might be vices in another, and the ease with which treachery and murder could lead to wealth and power, and the total absence of moral indignation as a restraining factor, helped to build empires which carried their own seeds of collapse.

Appendix II : The British Empire

The story of the British empire in India has been told from many angles and its fascination leads us to expect even more attem pts to explain what happened. The Indian historian of today, forgetting that his ancestors did not resemble him in all respects, and forgetting that the standards which he now takes for granted was actually imported into India by the British, professes disgust at the way in which the British empire in India was built, and contempt for the apparent hypocrisy with which the various episodes were adorned by the British actors in the dramas themselves.

In 1765 the East India Company found itself able to rule, as nominal minister of the Mughal emperor, the rich provinces of Bengal, Bihar and Orissa. By the time of the Mutiny (1857) the emperor, who had lost all power except in his palace, was a mere pensioner of the Company, and indeed he was tried and exiled for his part in the Mutiny, and his banishment put an end to the Mughal empire in name as well as in fact. During that period of something less than a century that vast sub-continent had been brought under British rule or at least decisive influence. The methods adopted in each case varied, but the result was the same. Briefly, the parts of India ruled by grant from the emperor were the nucleus which paid for the adventures elsewhere; other portions were acquired by a variety of devices, the first of which was annexation, then subsidiary alliances which more or less drove the native ally into surrendering territory to pay for expensive troops which he fancied he needed to protect him against his neighbours, then conquest in war, then acquisition by lapse when the native rulers died without legitimate (and acceptable) issue. In the end more than a half of India was directly ruled by the British and the remainder, the so-called Native States, remained under the nominal control of the native hereditary ruler, whilst a British Resident interfered constantly with their affairs, not merely external but even internal. The doctrine of the Paramountcy of the British Crown, which acquired India by Parliamentary enactment after the Mutiny, enabled autocratic interference with the States to occur as a matter of course.

The speed and vigour of the annexations and other acquisitions were justified at the time (against suspicious reactions from Britain herself) by referring to the fact that the natives required peace and prosperity, which constant wars and rebellions had made impossible for several centuries (which was true so far as it went), and by trumped-up excuses consisting in accusations against the rulers whose territory was coveted. Attempts on the part of Tipu Sultan to get into touch with foreign powers, e.g. the French, were a sufficient excuse to support a war in which the state of Mysore was simply taken over, though, in true Indian fashion, it was handed back to a native ruler, if with a British garrison in the heart of his dominions (which was an improvement on traditional Indian methods). Until Independence in 1947 many Indians regarded British rule as valid and tolerable. The advantages outweighed the disadvantages. But the British taught (in their strange way) liberty and equality to people with whom they then admitted no equality and to whom they yielded freedom only in domestic and local affairs such as would offer no competition with British interests. India was certainly exploited, and the efforts expended to develop her economically and otherwise tended to coincide with the imperial power's overall projects rather than with the needs (as contrasted with the very modest demands) of the Indian people.

To sum up the character of the empire and the causes of its fall in a few words is bound to be unfair to the multitude of persons and episodes on which abundant information is available. But it would be on the whole true to say that Britain taught India to be tired not merely of the British, but of the Indian characteristics which enabled the British (as previously the Muslims) to acquire power, and to keep it. The decay of the British Empire at large coincided with the powerful demand for Independence in India, a demand supported by a new moral sense in Britain, an impatience in other countries to whom Britain was obliged (notably the United States, whose own motives are now emerging more clearly), and the greater unity within India which only acute common disgust with their subject position could forge amongst otherwise inharmonious subjects. This disgust the British could easily have obviated had they not been taught by Indians of the previous century to behave as if their prestige-rating put them in another bracket of humanity : so long as Indian toadyism and sycophancy required that someone should play this role the bad behaviour, casuistry, hypocrisy, and selfishness of a significant and influential proportion of the ruling race was indirectly justified [22]. But a marked contribution to the independence movement was made by the repeated discovery of life in England by Indian students and others, to whom the true nature of the toadyism-racial-superiority syndrome was painfully revealed.

---

[22] Yet note how Majumdar, a violent critic of the British period, sees it only as another phase of a long story (rightly). *British Paramountcy*, pt.1 (1963), p. 12,17 : 'India presented the spectacle of gardens full of ripe mangoes without any strong watchmen to protect them from intruders, and the Governor-Generals were overcome by the irresistible temptation to swallow them'; 'The British empire in India rose and fell very much like all empires in ancient, mediæval and modern ages, and if the method pursued can hardly claim any special virtue, it does not call for any special condemnation'. The behaviour of Governor-General Ellenborough towards the Hindu prince Sindhia was like that of the wolf towards the lamb in Aesop's fable : but no one contends that pre-British rulers treated their weaker contemporaries any better.

Thus the award of honours from the Vice-regal throne at New Delhi by the representative of the imperial power could not offer any equivalent for the services which Indians gave merely by their acquiescence in a subjection they themselves had ceased to require. When it was known that peace and security of the state could be left in Indian hands, and when it was obvious that a sufficient number of Indian officials could manage the machine the British imperialists had forged, the obstacles to freedom were removed. The Indian successors to the Indian (as contrasted with the Pakistani) portion of the former British Indian Empire are now coping with traditional Indian psychological characteristics: but they are obviously better fitted to cope with them constructively than even the British were, and a happy outcome is to be expected.

On Jan. 1st, 1877 Queen Victoria was proclaimed Empress of India, and all her successors carried this title until 1947. The Royal Titles Act, 1876 (39 & 40 Vict., c. 10) which authorised the Queen to assume this title was passed despite opposition in both Houses of Parliament [23]. The British people were sceptical of the utility of this move. Did it make India into an empire that she had not been before? Did the title *Kaisar-i-Hind* help to endear the Indian peoples to their foreign sovereign? The Durbar held by King George V in Delhi may or may not have been a pleasant pageant, but did the concept do anything to foster reconcilation between the races? We know now that it did not. What was wanted was not Indian-type prestige-pyramid-building but a correspondence between the best British plans for India and the best notions of the British 'mission' in Asia, such as these were, with the actual facts of Indian political, military, and economic partnership with the other countries of the then Empire. Queen Victoria's title did not achieve anything. K.A.N. Sastri quotes Jadunath Sarkar, commenting upon the dismal end of all Aurangzeb's austere campaignings, that the

[23] Lytton Strachey's biography of Queen Victoria, ch. 8, iii. W.F. Moneypenny and G.E. Buckle's standard biography of B. Disraeli, vol. 5, 456-468.

failure of his reign 'lay deeper than his personal character. Though it is not true that he alone caused the fall of the Mughal empire, yet he did nothing to avert it; but rather quickened the destructive forces already in operation in the land; he never realized that there cannot be a great empire without a great people'. The sly comment from an expert on the Mughal period could as well be applied to the British period: had the British made a 'great people' out of themselves and their subjects their empire would have endured.

BIBLIOGRAPHY

It is not necessary to repeat here what was made available in the volumes devoted to 'Peace', to 'Monocracy', and to 'Rulers and Ruled'. [But see also W. RUBEN and K. FISCHER, *Der Maurya- und der Mogul-Staat* (D.A.W., Berlin, K.S.L.K., SB, 1965, N°. 5), Berlin (1965).] The scope of historical writing is vast, and the student of Empires will waste much of his time. It is necessary only to advise him to read introductory books which summarise what is known of the main features of the subject and which, in most cases, provide their own bibliographies. The series known as the *History and Culture of the Indian People*, published by the Bharatiya Vidya Bhavan (Bombay), is of great value for our purpose. Vol. 2 (1951), *The Age of Imperial Unity*, deals with Magadhan imperialism and especially with the Mauryas. An earlier period is covered by Vishuddhanand PATHAK, *History of Kosala upto the Rise of the Mauryas*, Delhi, etc., 1963. Of great value for the rapid reader is K.A. Nilakanta SASTRI, ed., *A Comprehensive History of India, II, Mauryas and Satavahanas*, Calcutta (Orient Longmans), 1957. Vol. 3 of the *History and Culture of the Indian People, The Classical Age* (1954) covers the Guptas and Harṣa. R.C. Majumdar and A.D. Pusalker again collaborated in Vol. 5 (1957), which deals only with the minor dynasties including the Southern dynasties. That topic is much more fully and even luxurioulsy handled in the two-volume work edited by G. YAZDANI, *Early History of the Deccan* (London, Oxford University Press, 1960): there the great empires are handled in the first and the independent sovereigns in the second volume. Meanwhole in Vol. 4 of the *H.C.I.P.* Majumdar and Pusalker deal with the Pratihāras, Pālas, and Rāṣṭrakūṭas (*The Age of Imperial Kanauj*). All these works have extensive bibliographies. On Vijayanagar no comprehensive work is up to date. K.A. Nilakanta SASTRI's *History of South India from Prehistoric Times to the Fall of Vijayanagar*, 3rd edn. (Madras, Oxford University Press, 1966) gives all that a student of imperialism in Hindu India will require relative to the Sātavāhanas, the conflicts of the 'three emperors' (Chālukya, Rāṣṭrakūṭa, Pallava), the balance of the 'two empires' (Chālukya and Cōḷa), the emergence of Vijayanagar and its series of dynasties. Amongst the works which may be consulted for picturesque and lively details of Vijayanagar politics and vicissitudes are R. SEWELL, *A Forgotten Empire* (1900), N. VENKATARAMANAYYA, *Vijayanagara, Origin of the City and the Empire* (1933), the *Vijayanagar Sexcentenary Commemoration Volume* (1936), and K.A. Nilakanta SASTRI and N. VENKATARAMANAYYA, *Further Sources of Vijayanagara History* (Madras, 1946).

The interminable vicissitudes of the Muslim rulers are conveniently summarised, in a work which may appeal to many readers pressed for time : R.C. MAJUMDAR H.C. RAYCHAUDHURI, and KALIKINKAR DATTA, *An Advanced History of India* (London, 1946) which gives a compressed, and fair, view of the British period then about to close. The last one-man effort at disgesting the history of India up to the end of the last important Muslim emperor's reign, namely K.A. Nilakanta SASTRI, *History of India*, 2 vols., Madras (S. Viswanathan), 1950 attempts to paint the picture from the standpoint of the love of freedom. Ishwari PRASAD, *History of Mediaeval India (from A.D.* 647 *to the Mughal conquest*), Allahabad, 1928 — also available in CAVAIGNAC'S *Histoire du Monde* under the title *L'Inde du vii*[e] *au xvi*[e] *siècle*, Paris (E. de Boccard), 1930 — and S.M. EDWARDS and H.L.O. GARRETT, *Mughal Rule in India* (Oxford, 1930) are still consulted. For the British period the *Cambridge History of India*, the last two volumes, are still good on the mechanics of imperialism as seen through British eyes (mostly by uncritical British eyes); but the last volume to appear in the *H.C.I.P.* series, ed. again by R.C. MAJUMDAR and largely written by him, *British Paramountcy and Indian Renaissance*, in two parts (Bombay, 1963-5) is an essential compendium with helpful bibliographies. The pendulum swung perhaps a little too far towards a sentimental view of Indian sufferings, and the effects upon British residents of the Indian sociological as well as political climate in the late eighteenth and early nineteenth century is minimised : however this is the work with which to approach the subject. On paramountcy the standard work is W. LEE-WARNER'S *Native States of India*, London (1910) and *Protected Princes of India*, London (1894). A recent view from the British side may be of value : works in appreciation of the actual rulers of India during the British period include Philip MASON'S *Men who Ruled India*, 2 vols., London (Cape) 1953-4, while one may see D.K. FIELDHOUSE, *The Colonial Empires*, London (Weidenfeld and Nicolson), 1966 for a comparative survey from the eighteenth century.

Postscript : R.K. MOOKERJI, *Harsha* (Delhi, 1965); R.V. NADKARNI, *The Rise and Fall of the Maratha Empire* (Bombay, 1966); R.P. TRIPATHI, *Rise and Fall of the Mughal Empire* (Allahabad, 1965); W. IRVINE, *Later Mughals* (Calcutta/London, n.d.); S.N. PRASAD, *Paramountcy under Dalhousie* (Delhi, 1964); K.L. PANJABI, ed., *The Civil Servant in India* (Bombay, 1966); M. GILBERT, *Servant of India* (London, 1966); V.B. KULKARNI, *British Statesmen in India* (Bombay, 1961); and C. SCHRENCK-NOTZING, *Hundert Jahre Indien. Die politische Entwicklung von 1857-1960* (1961) should be added. A.T. EMBREE and F. WILHELM, *Indien* (Fischer Weltgeschichte 17) (Frankfurt, 1967) is a most useful compendium.

BHŪ-BHARAṆA, BHŪ-PĀLANA, BHŪ-BHOJANA: AN INDIAN CONUNDRUM *

THE attributes of the Indian king have long been familiar, but taken together they have an inexplicable feature—their apparent incompatibility. An explanation for one, *bhū-bhojana*, is hinted at by J. J. Meyer's *Trilogie altindischer Mächte und Feste der Vegetation* (Zürich and Leipzig, 1937), and the setting in which the subject is to be reviewed has been entirely recast by the lengthy and exhaustive article by J. Gonda, entitled 'Ancient Indian kingship from the religious point of view' (*Numen*, III–IV, 1956–7). It is much to be hoped that these works will not escape the notice of historians of India, and it is assumed in this paper that Professor Gonda's article is accessible to the reader.

The question posed here is, in itself, narrow. Why was the king supposed to be the Earth's lover or husband, and what is the significance of the metaphor? In the *brāhmaṇas* we know that the Earth is called the wife of Agni and of the *devas*,[1] but why is this relationship posited of the king? The mythological marriage to Pṛthu we take for granted, but he was not her last 'husband'. This is not merely poetical imagery, nor, as we shall see, does the Earth stand, metonymically, for her inhabitants. The constant repetition of such an image implies a meeting of a fundamental concept, or psychological position, with an expression which can release it; repetition deprives it of charm, but not of validity. In the *Aitareya-brāhmaṇa* there appears an obscure text[2] in which one individual says to another, 'I am sky, thou art Earth'; it is usually assumed that the speaker is the king and the person addressed is the *purohita*, the context being the 'coronation'-ceremony. A. K. Coomaraswamy attempted to show, in *Spiritual authority and temporal power in the Indian theory of government*,[3] that the roles were reversed and that the king accepted a feminine role as Earth. For reasons which appear below the argument may not now convince, but it does not seem that, apart from Coomaraswamy's pioneering venture, the problem has been probed critically in modern times. It may be that the true meaning of the *Aitareya-brāhmaṇa* text will emerge from a better acquaintance with the king's normal attributes.

Gonda amply proves the 'sacred' character of the Indian king (though he naturally hesitates to draw political conclusions from this 'sacredness')

[1] Haṃsarāja, *Vedic Koṣa*, I, Lahore, 1926, 298 ff., esp. citations from *Gopatha-br.* and *Śatapatha-br.* (cited below as *ŚB*).

[2] VIII, 27: discussed K. V. Rangaswami Aiyangar, *Kṛtyakalpataru of Bhaṭṭa Lakṣmīdhara. XI. Rājadharmakāṇḍa*, Baroda, 1943, introd., 59.

[3] Am. Or. Ser. No. 22, New Haven, 1942: reviewed in *BSOAS*, XI, 2, 1944, 438–9. Our problem is not dealt with in objective treatments of royalty, e.g. Narendranatha Law, *Ancient Indian polity*, ch. viii; V. R. Ramachandra Dikshitar, *Hindu administrative institutions*, ch. ii; P. V. Kane, *History of dharmaśāstra* (cited below).

and finds Indo-European kingship, ' in important respects ', a sacred institution; but no other branch of this family of peoples has, so far as we know, seen the king as ' husband of the Earth '. For the ceremony performed by the Doge resembles, if anything, the Hindu's annual worship of the implements of his craft or trade, and Elizabeth I was ' wedded ' to her people much as one is ' wedded ' to principles, and the like. Indian worshippers, particularly Vaiṣṇavas, believe God to be related to the individual (even where the latter is masculine) as lover and beloved (*nāyaka-nāyakī-bhāva*) and the imagery used to describe the relation approaches, as elsewhere further West, the sexual.[1] But it is very doubtful whether this throws any light on our problem.

As for the Earth herself: she is the great Mother, the supporter of all living creatures.[2] Poets compare her with the mythical Wishing-cow, or indeed with any cow.[3] As a cow she was, says the *Vāyu-purāṇa*,[4] repeatedly milked by Brahmā and others, and once Indra (to whom we shall return) acted as her calf to assist the operation.[5] The cow is a well-recognized mother-figure in modern as well as ancient Hindu thought. The Earth pours forth streams,[6] like a cow milk.

nivartya rājā dayitāṃ dayālus tāṃ saurabheyīṃ surabhir yaśobhiḥ |
payodharī-bhūta-catuḥ-samudrāṃ jugopa go-rūpa-dharām ivorvīm || [7]

She bears fire, jewels, minerals, and so on, in her womb.[8]

kintu vadhvāṃ tavaitasyām adṛṣṭa-sadṛśa-prajam |
na mām avati sa-dvīpā ratnasūr api medinī || [9]

She is penetrated by snakes, and *bhūjaṅga* appropriately means a snake or a gallant: small wonder that the Nāgas were reputed to be very handsome!

[1] On the Tamil Āḷvārs see Surendranath Dasgupta, *History of Indian philosophy*, III, Cambridge, 1940, 70; on the Gauḍīya Vaiṣṇavas see Rūpa-kavirāja (attrib.), *Sārasaṅgraha*, ed. K. Goswami Sastri, Calcutta, 1949, with an introd. by Professor Satkari Mookerjee, which might facilitate the researches of Dr. Morris Carstairs (see p. 116, n. 6, below). The sexual image is used to describe even the relationship between the (masculine) *puruṣa* and the (feminine) *prakṛti* in the Sāṃkhya philosophy. There is mutual dependence there also (cf. the *paṅgvandha* simile). The *puruṣa* through the aid of *prakṛti* attains *mukti*, and *prakṛti* ceases to function ' just as an unchaste woman who has been found out by her husband-maintainor does not resort to her (or ? a) husband again, or like a dancing girl, who has played her part and departs '. Mādhavācārya, *Sarva-darśana-saṅgraha* (Bibl. Ind.), Calcutta, 1858, 153, where a *śloka* is cited. A comprehensive study of the scope of sexual images in Indian thought would be rewarding.

[2] *ṚV*, VII, 101, 3 with Sāyaṇa; *VS*, x, 23; *TS*, III, 3, 2, 2; *ŚB*, v, 4, 3, 20; *TB*, II, 2, 4, 6, 8. M. Bloomfield, *Vedic concordance*, Cambridge (Mass.), 1906, 602 ff.; Haṃsarāja, cit. sup.; text cited below, p. 119. Kalhaṇa, *Rājataraṅgiṇī*, III, 86, 108. Meyer, op. cit., I, 207, 213; II, 38, 64 (as Mother); as Fertility-goddess *passim*.

[3] *ŚB*, II, 2, 1, 21; XII, 9, 2, 11. See synonyms for ' Earth ' in *Amarakośa*, II, 1, 2 ff., also Halāyudha, *Abhidhāna-ratnamālā*, II, 1.

[4] LXIII, 12–19. J. Gonda, ' Ancient Indian kingship . . .', *Numen*, III–IV, 1956–7 (cited below as Gonda, III or IV), at IV, 151. I owe the reference to this invaluable article to Dr. L. J. Rocher, and a copy to the kindness of Professor Gonda.

[5] *Bhāgavata-purāṇa*, 1916, IV, 18.

[6] *Rājat.*, IV, 300.

[7] Kālidāsa, *Raghuvaṃśa*, II, 3.

[8] After all, she is *vasudhā*, etc. *ŚB*, XIV, 9, 4, 21; *Rājat.*, III, 300, *et alibi*.

[9] *Ragh.*, I, 65.

She is the Queen of the snakes.[1] Moreover she is fertilized by rain. The union of Heaven and Earth, the intercourse between Parjanya (Rain) and Pṛthivī, begets plants and is the sole (intermediate) cause of living creatures.[2] The importance of rain-water cannot be overestimated; it is even said that all society and decency depend on rain.[3] If Heaven is our father, Rain is also our father.[4]

The king performs *bhū-bharaṇa*. *Bharaṇa* from very early times meant (i) carrying, and hence (ii) maintaining. How can the king be said to maintain the Earth? The Earth is visualized as the king's dependant. This is odd, since he manifestly depends upon her. A mother is a maintainee if she is widowed or her husband has deserted her. The Earth is never compared to so inauspicious a person as a widow, for, even when she is deprived of her lord by his death in battle the furthest the poet will go in this direction is to admit that the *kingdom*, and of course the queens of the deceased, have been made widows. However, the king participated in, or provided for, sacrifices which were intended to secure rainfall,[5] and one of his chief duties was to protect Brahmans whose daily offerings, ascended into the heavens and received (in a non-technical sense) by the *devas* headed by Indra, the rain-cloud-splitter, gave rise to rainfall in return.

> *dudoha gāṃ sa yajñāya sasyāya Maghavā divam* |
> *saṃpad-vinimayenobhau dadhatur bhuvana-dvayam* || [6]
> *havir āvarjitaṃ hotas tvayā vidhivad agniṣu* |
> *vṛṣṭir bhavati sasyānām avagraha-viśoṣiṇām* || [7]

For this there is very ancient authority. *Ṛgveda*, I, 121, 2–5 bring together the cow, the 'parents' (who, according to Sāyaṇa, are Heaven and Earth), the oblation they provide, Indra, and rain, in the very plainest conjunction. Thence, no doubt, ultimately we have

> *agnau prāstāhutiḥ saṃyag ādityam upatiṣṭhate* |
> *ādityāj jāyate vṛṣṭir vṛṣṭer annaṃ tataḥ prajāḥ* || [8]

Prajāḥ, like the word 'creatures' in English, means both *subjects* and 'dependants'. The Indian king's duties included the performance of the *Indra-vratam* to secure regular rain [9]; the liberation of cows (reminiscent of

[1] Meyer, III, 231, n. 3.

[2] *AV*, XII, 1, 12. On *dyāvāpṛthivī* see below, p. 123, and *AB*, IV, 27, 5; *AA*, III, 1, 2; *ŚB*, I, 8, 3, 12.

[3] *ŚB*, XI, 1, 6, 24. Kane, op. cit., III, Poona, 1946, 21.

[4] Yāska, *Nirukta*, X, 10; cf. Gonda, III, 136.

[5] R. Aiyangar, op. cit., 82; W. Rau, *Staat und Gesellschaft im alten Indien* . . ., Wiesbaden, 1957, 90–2, para. 59. N. Law, op. cit., ch. viii, 112 ff., and ch. ix (on *rājasūya*, *aśvamedha*, etc.) touches the fringes of our problem, but from what Gonda says (III, 41–6; IV, 162) it is plain that *abhiṣeka*, 'coronation', anointing, and the king's duty to make rain are very intimately connected. Note that fertility-symbols and water must be looked at by a king commencing a *yātrā*: evidently a mass of ritual data needs to be examined in a fresh light.

[6] *Ragh.*, I, 26. [7] ibid., I, 62. [8] Manu, III, 76. [9] *Matsya-purāṇa*, CCXXVI, 10.

Indra's exploit) in the month of Kārtika was believed to give relief from excessive or inadequate rain; and the erecting of the *Indra-dhvaja*, or 'Indra's flagstaff',[1] as a simultaneous assertion of sovereignty and method of assuring rainfall, brings to mind parallels, to which we shall return. The righteous king secures regular rain by good government as well as by his sacrifices.[2] Indirectly, therefore, the king maintains the Earth; but this was not enough for poets. Both in pure *kāvya* and in poetical inscriptions the king is repeatedly shown actually carrying the Earth. The Earth is taken up on his arm, is cradled there, is hoisted upon his shoulder, and there carried as if by an Atlas.[3]

santānārthāya vidhaye sva-bhujād avatāritā |
tena dhur jagato gurvī saciveṣu nicikṣipe || [4]
puraṃdara-śrīḥ puram utpatākaṃ praviśya paurair abhinandyamānaḥ |
bhuje bhujaṅgendra-samāna-sāre bhūyaḥ sa bhūmer dhuram āsasañja || [5]

Only Śeṣa, the primeval snake, shares this role with the king, though, as we have seen, he shares with him another. In Kannaḍa the Sanskrit *bhū-bhuk* 'earth-enjoyer' forms the *tadbhava* equivalent *bhū-bhujaṃ* (mod. Kan. *bhū-bhujanu*), and thus *bhū-bhuja* may be used, by way of a pun,[6] to refer to the king in both roles at once.

The second role requires little elaboration and no citation. *Bhū-pālana*, 'protection' of the Earth, has been the king's duty since Kauṭilya's time at the latest.[7] Protection implies services which distinctly recall the duties of a

[1] R. Aiyangar, op. cit., 78, and refs. there given; Kane, op. cit., II, 825–6 (note the pole may be made of bamboo or *sugar-cane*); Meyer, see below, p. 120, n. 6; Gonda, III, 64; IV, 27. Investigation is required of Indra, his *pārijāta* tree (a tree which showers 'wishes'), and the latter's 'sister' Lakṣmī. See Meyer, II, 85–9, and, on unexpected functions of Lakṣmī-Śrī, Gonda, III, 131; IV, 35.

[2] Vālmīki, *Rāmāyaṇa*, I, 9, 7–8 (eds. Bombay, 1905; Banaras, 1956; cf. Gorresio, 1843, I, 8, 11–12); VI, 131, 99 (Bombay, 1905) or VI, 128, 102 (Bombay, 1919), 110, 8 (Lahore, 1944), 131, 103 (Banaras, 1956); cf. Gorresio, 1850, VI, 113, 6; *MBh.*, XII, 139, 9; and other refs. in R. Aiyangar, *Ancient Indian polity. Second ed.*, Madras, 1935, 108. Tiruvaḷḷuva-nāyaṉār, *Tirukkuṟaḷ*, Thirunelveli and Madras, 1949, 559, p. 213: *muṟai-kōḍi maṉṉavaṉ ceyyi=nuṟai-kōḍi=* | *yollādu vāṉam peyal.* Compare the references given in the footnote, same page. Meyer, II, 255 ff.; III, 268. Gonda, IV, 162–3.

[3] In *Rājat.* alone instances occur at I, 64, 101, 346; III, 58, 98, 529 (where Śeṣa is referred to); IV, 119, 481–2; *et alibi.* That the idea was very popular is shown by the story given in Merutuṅga, *Prabandha-cintāmaṇi*, ed. Jinavijaya-muni, 70–1, trans. Tawney, 106, where a buffoon leans on the king's shoulder and then expresses surprise at his remonstrance. In Kannaḍa inscriptions the idea is a commonplace: see, e.g., *Epigraphia Carnatica*, V, Hassan 53: *Hima-Setuvindoḷagāda bhūmiyaṃ bhuja-baḷāvaṣṭambhadiṃ tāḷdi* . . ., whereas in ibid., 65 we find *ivan ī tōḷ-gambadoḷ puttaḷigevol avanī-dēvi tān vippaḷ enduṃ* . . . . Note the significant picture in the Daulatabad Plates of Jayasiṃha II (A.D. 1017), *Hyderabad Archaeological Series*, II, p. 7, where the Earth is lifted on high *as if a bracelet*, i.e. the *daṇḍa* or *liṅgaṃ* of the arm (see below, p. 122, n. 4) penetrates the *yoni* of the Earth.

[4] *Ragh.*, I, 34.

[5] ibid., II, 74.

[6] By analogy with *śaṅkha-pāṇi* or *śastra-hasta.* An instance of the idea is seen at *Ep. Carn.*, V, Arsikere 79 (lines 30–1), where *śākhe* = 'arm'; and there are less obvious examples at lines 23–5 and 33 of ibid., Belur 58. Professor K. A. Nilakanta Sastri seems to have missed this in a remark at *JIH*, XXXV, 2, 1957, 282–3.

[7] *Arthaśāstra*, I, i.

cowherd, and it is for this reason that King Dilīpa's task in reference to the cow Nandinī was so appropriately invented.

Finally the king enjoys the Earth, much as Indra enjoys Heaven.[1] The significance of the root *bhuj* is wide (cf. Agni's titles *havir-bhuk,* etc.), but in this context the word is precise. *Bhū-bhuk, mahī-bhuk, jagatī-bhuk,* and the other commonplace titles refer to physical enjoyments, with a distinct implication of that particular type which is thought of in India as the highest type of 'enjoyment'. *Bhogin* 'enjoyer' is glossed by Śāśvata as *rāja.*[2] Indian speakers of English refer to the 'enjoyment' of women in a precise sense. The king is called *bhū-vallabha,* the Earth's beloved, and when he is called *-deśa-varādhipa* we can be sure that the country is visualized as choosing him as if in
* *svayaṃvara.* Stories relate the Earth declaring herself the wife of a particular king.[3] The king's relationship to her is thought of as sexual. Of this there are many illustrations,[4] some delicate and some gross :

priyam anucitaṃ kṣmā-paṇya-strī-kṣaṇa-prabhur īśvaro
ramayati yato dhik tān bhṛtyān sva-vṛtti-sukhārthinaḥ || [5]

The same author refers to Kālidāsa's picture of the king, possessed of produce in the way of jewels from the Earth but devoid of male issue, in an apt verse :

sa mahīṃ rāja-kanyāṃ ca prāptavān ekataḥ kulāt |
ratnānāṃ ca sutānāṃ ca rājābhūd bhājanaṃ śanaiḥ || [6]

When the king conquers a region he may be said to have snatched at its breasts, the mountains.[7] When he takes a city it is described, honorifically, as a rape.[8] There is a point at which two roles coalesce. *Bhāryā* 'wife', is *the* maintainee, the dependant *par excellence.*[9] *Pati* and *bhartṛ,* 'husband', imply 'protector' and 'maintainor'. The Earth, sitting comfortably on the king's knee,[10] is both his maintainee and his 'enjoyed one'. She is not the only one in that position.

[1] See below, p. 118, n. 9, and *ṚV,* I, 33, 9, where the root *bhuj* appears.

[2] *Anekārtha-samuccaya,* Poona, 1929, 105, p. 10.

[3] *Kathā-sarit-sāgara,* trans. Tawney, *Ocean of story,* IV, 175–6 ; VI, 194.

[4] *Ragh.,* VIII, 3, 7 (which is the plainest of all) ; XIX, 3 ; *Rājat.,* I, 72, 273, 287, 309 ; II, 8, 9, 63 III, 96, 470 ; IV, 2, 44, 282 ; *et alibi,* notably IV, 398, which runs : *saptābdān vasudhāṃ bhuktvā so 'ti-saṃbhoga-janmanāṃ* | *jagāma saṃkṣayaṃ kṣmābhṛt kṣaya-rogeṇa kilbiṣī* || In a beautiful and apt passage in *Ep. Carn.,* XII, Nanj. 269, pp. 225–6 (A.D. 904) we are told that (while acting as his elder brother's viceroy) Vijayāditya treated the Earth with the chaste respect due to a sister-in-law.

[5] *Rājat.,* IV, 32.

[6] ibid., IV, 2.

[7] *Ep. Carn.,* VI, Kadur 21, dated Cāl. Vik. 13 = A.D. 1089.

[8] The well-known *janapada* Kuntala (in Skt. = 'tresses') offered poets an obvious pun : e.g. in *Epigraphia Indica,* XX, p. 115 (A.D. 1167) we are told that by force of arms Bijjaṇa seized the hair of the lady, the land of Kuntala (sc. as a prelude to rape). He was in fact a usurper. *South Indian inscr.,* III, no. 205, p. 395, v. 5 : the Cōḷa king seized the city of Tanjore, capital of a great kingdom, as if she had been his own wife.

[9] Rau, op. cit., 35–7, para. 26.

[10] See Bāṇa-bhaṭṭa, *Harṣacarita,* VI, 13 : *utsaṅge bhuvā* . . . .

He is *śrī-pṛthvī-vallabha*,[1] and he must be wedded to both Earth and Fortune if he is to remain king. Lakṣmī appears in various guises, such as *rājya-śrī*, *vīrya-śrī*, and *jaya-śrī*, and is notoriously fickle.[2] The name Śrī-vallabha is an apt one for a prince.[3] She is the king's darling (for the time being), and he has all the women-folk he needs if both Pṛthivī and Lakṣmī are faithful to him.

kalatravantam ātmānam avarodhe mahaty api |
tayā mene manasvinyā Lakṣmyā ca vasudhādhipaḥ || [4]
urasy aparyāpta-niveśa-bhāgā prauḍhī-bhaviṣyantam udīkṣamāṇā |
sañjāta-lajjeva tam ātapatra-cchāyā-cchalenopajugūha Lakṣmīḥ || [5]

But just as Lakṣmī may be unfaithful, Pṛthivī is not less capable of being divorced and remarried, and the Earth is enjoyed by many kings,[6] as the adage goes, from Sagara in succession. So he 'enjoys' the mother of all creatures: yet we shall not proceed far if we assume that he suffered, professionally, from an Oedipus complex.

The mystery surrounding the epithet, 'enjoyer', is heightened by its total absence from *dharmaśāstra* literature. By way of *stuti* those texts tell us that the king is made up of the 'heavy' particles of many deities and deserves obedience, etc.,[7] and by way of *ādeśa* the king is warned of the effects of anarchy, the extent of his responsibilities, and the need to control his natural proclivities.[8] In the *Arthaśāstra* the notion that a kingdom is to be enjoyed is asserted at an early stage,[9] but the image of the king's conjugal relationship with the Earth is not found. The Earth is *artha*; the king is *arthapati*; but the king's exploitation of the Earth is regarded as a duty requiring no such justification as this.

[1] R. C. Majumdar, H. C. Raychaudhuri, and Kalikinkar Datta, *Advanced history of India*, London, 1946, 191–2, comment that this makes him equal to Viṣṇu. Compare *nāviṣṇuḥ pṛthvīpatiḥ*. Vīra-Rājēndra Cōḷa is called *Śrī-medinī-vallabha* in *Epigraphia Indica*, XXV, p. 265. A title of the Rāṣṭrakūṭas, *inter alios*, and after them of the Western Cālukyas and later the Hoysaḷas: e.g. *Ep. Carn.*, V, Hassan 114 of A.D. 1139. *Vallabha* came with time to mean 'emperor' in the Deccan.

[2] *Ragh.*, XVII, 46. But she observed a vow of chastity in the house of King Raṇaraṅga-Bhīma: *Ep. Ind.*, XI, p. 218, ll. 40–2. As a wife she appears in the Junagadh inscription of Skanda Gupta, *Corpus ins. Ind.*, III, p. 59, v. 5 of c. A.D. 455.

[3] *South Indian inscr.*, III, p. 451, provides one of many examples.

[4] *Ragh.*, I, 32. *South Indian inscr.*, III, no. 69, p. 147, lines 4–5: Kulōttuṅga I put an end to the commonness of the Lakṣmī of the South and the loneliness of the goddess of the Kāvērī country. Here *podumai* = commonness (not 'ownerlessness'), cf. *podu-stiri*, 'prostitute'.

[5] ibid., XVIII, 47. Note also *Rājat.*, III, 126; IV, 373, 467, 589–90. For the text *Śrīś ca te Lakṣmīś ca patnyau* see Mitra-miśra, cit. inf., 18–19. Also *Ep. Carn.*, V, Hassan 65: *kula-vadhu vijaya-śrī*; and in both ibid., Belur 58 and 71 (of the year A.D. 1117) we find: *piṅgade tōḷol korvvi malaṅgire jaya-lakṣmi lakṣmi varddhise suttaṃ*.

[6] Bāṇa, op. cit., IV, 27. *

[7] Lakṣmīdhara, *Rājadharmakāṇḍa*, 1–8; Mitra-miśra, *Vīramitrodaya*, *Rājanītiprakāśa*, Banaras, 1916, 15–31. It is noted that in several texts it is Indra that is first mentioned as supplying parts of the king, and see Nārada, XVII, 27. Gonda, III, 65.

[8] Lakṣmīdhara, ubi cit., 18–21, 142–8; Mitra-miśra, ubi cit., 116–21. Manu, I, 89, is faintly comical in view of the traditional *rāja-vyasanas*: the king's divinely appointed duties are (i) protection of the people, and (ii) non-surrender to appetites.

[9] I, 18 (Trivandrum ed., 92).

It might be suggested that the *smṛtis*, despite their occasional poetical turn, are practical works, not in need of poetical images; while, on the other hand, moral responsibilities are incompatible with the freedom of behaviour suggested to an Indian by this notion.[1] But this is not true. The special relationship, so far from being foreign to the *śāstra*, is required to explain legal facts; and figures of this kind are intimately connected with very practical concepts. So long as the king treats his 'wife' in a husbandly fashion he is acting distinctly in accordance with *dharma*. The king's legal rights were *bhogas* ('enjoyments'), and when these were passed on to tenants by grant the latter estimated the value of their tenure in terms of the number of *bhogas* it involved.[2] In Indian law *bhogas* were easily severed, and, for example, land could be sold without the right to use a well in it, and trees could be sold, leased, or mortgaged, without affecting the ownership of the soil. With two exceptions the king was 'lord of all'.[3] MM Dr. P. V. Kane has discovered in an unpublished work a *śloka* of unknown authorship but unquestionable accuracy. The point it makes is elaborately worked out in *dharmaśāstra* and *arthaśāstra* texts.

dhanānām īśvaro rājā Brahmaṇā parikalpitaḥ |
bhū-gatānāṃ viśeṣeṇa, bhartā 'sau vibudhādhipaḥ || [4]

He translates up to the comma as follows: 'Brahmā arranged that the king was (to be) the owner of all wealth and specially (wealth) that is inside the earth'. He does not proceed, but one may point out that quite literally, the remaining quarter-*śloka* says, 'the *bhartṛ* ('husband', 'maintainor', 'master', 'lord') is he, ⟨*videlicet*⟩ the "overlord of the gods" (i.e. Indra)'. Thus the labour of the *prajāḥ* was his to tax, whether by forced labour or otherwise. A full list of his actual exactions from them would be lengthy and unnecessary.[5] Sufficient attention, however, has not been given to the right to fruit, vegetables,

[1] Kane, op. cit., III, 27, notes the relative scarcity of matter in the *śāstra* dealing with privileges as opposed to responsibilities.

[2] Grants reserving certain rights, particularly in cases of disobedience, laid down in the grants themselves, are well authenticated. The nearest to an 'out-and-out' grant was that of *aṣṭa-bhoga-tejas-svāmya*, in other words *nidhi*, *nikṣepa*, *pāṣāṇa*, *siddha*, *sādhya*, *jala*, *akṣiṇi*, and *āgāmi*, on which see the verse cited by F. W. Ellis in his letter to the Madras Govt. dated 2 August 1814 (?), pub. C. P. Brown, *Three treatises on Mirasi right* . . ., Madras, 1852, at p. 17, n. 49; also A. K. Majumdar, *The Chaulukyas*, Bombay, 1956, 248; and cf. A. Master, 'Some Marathi inscriptions, A.D. 1060–1300', *BSOAS*, XX, 1957, 428–9. Majumdar, cit. sup., is most useful on the king's rights, and one may usefully consult S. K. Maity, *Economic life of northern India* . . ., Calcutta, 1957. In revenue terminology *bhoga* means, apparently, the right to maintenance from the inhabitants when in their vicinity, as contrasted with *bhāga*, the regular share in the crops by way of land-revenue.

[3] See below, p. 116.

[4] *Paraśurāmapratāpa* (on which see Kane, op. cit., I, 578) cited from 'f. 27a' (prob. Deccan Coll. MS), ibid., III, 196, n. 252a.

[5] Details of these rights are to be found in T. V. Mahalingam, *South Indian polity*, Madras, 1955; Maity, cit. sup.; and Derrett, *The Hoysaḷas*, O.U.P., 1957. See also Book II of the *Arthaśāstra* and ibid., Bk. V, ch. ii. It is well known that the king was entitled to order householders to contribute to the maintenance of dancing-girls; for his right to compel rich persons to be generous see Medhātithi on Manu, IX, 333.

grain, fodder, lodging, conveyance, and the like, which he and his court enjoyed when on campaign or progress. The political and social effects of this right, and of the illegal exactions of the royal purveyors by virtue of their ill-defined authority, were enormous: it typified the king's position admirably and, incidentally, was inherited by the East India Company.[1] No less significant is the fact that jurists saw the king exercising his rights over the soil and its produce when he confiscated a delinquent's property (a common punishment), and when he seized it or auctioned it in execution of a decretal debt or for default in payment of revenue.[2]

Perhaps it is in this way that we may explain a curious, if notorious, fact of Indian history. A king's sovereignty extended to his boundaries; dissatisfied subjects merely decamped to his neighbour, who at once became their ruler. This right to change one's allegiance was never questioned or hampered; the simplest way to rid oneself of loyalty to a ruler was to change the soil under one's feet: a position which no modern and few western medieval States could tolerate.

The king's ultimate lordship of the soil would not still be open to debate, if some Indian historians, misled by publicists early in this century, had not assumed that ownership in India was like ownership in England, and that there was something unsatisfactory about concurrent, though distinct, rights of ownership in land between the ruler and the ruled.[3] In medieval times the monarch seemed incredibly forbearing if he paid for a plot of land he required for his own purposes.[4] In order to 'satisfy' the subjects a king observed certain conventions—yet the former were always complaining that in practice the king's agents interpreted them too far in their master's favour. But his inherent superiority in the allocation of 'enjoyments' was a source of pride, and not resentment. It was only when foreigners were found utilizing the very large benefits of this situation to their own advantage, that Indians awoke to the undoubted peculiarity of their *rāja's* position, and, if they were educated in Western ideas, rejected it.

[1] Many land-grants provide that the demesne shall not be entered by *cāṭas* or *bhaṭas* (who would levy contributions on the pretext that the court required them). On the abuse called *begārī*, see Bengal Regs. XI of 1806 and III of 1820; T. K. Banerjee, *Administration of criminal justice* . . . [thesis], London, 1955, 135 ff.

[2] Jagannātha-tarkapañcānana, *Vivāda-bhaṅgārṇava*, I.O. MS Skt. 1770 = Egg. 1534, f. 5 = Colebrooke's *Digest*, Madras, 1864, I, 306-7. Kātyāyana (Kane's text), v. 16, and editor's comments thereon, p. 121, n., also Kane, III, 189, n. 243. The king's right to taxes was sometimes attributed to the tax-payer's own motives (e.g. Aparārka on Yājñ, I, 366, cited Kane, III, 38–9), but this does not diminish the king's rights in respect of the soil.

[3] A. L. Basham, *The wonder that was India*, London, 1954, 109 ff.; Derrett, 233 ff.; Maity, 15–23; Gonda, IV, 128, n. 656. The less satisfactory view continues to be stated by epigraphists, such as MM V. V. Mirashi, and historians, e.g. Professor Nilakanta Sastri, ubi cit. sup. Śabara on Jaimini, VI, 7, 3, is widely misunderstood. The king who serves the Earth by 'upholding' and being valorous has no exclusive ownership over the Earth that can be given to priests, but only the rights not already assigned to the subjects. These could be, and often were, alienated in religious donations—and sometimes bought back again!

[4] *Rājat.*, IV, 55 ff.

Most remarkable among the exceptions were the immunities of Brahmans, personally and in respect of their property—immunities which were on the whole carefully observed.[1] Soma, they protested at the coronation (or rather the 'sprinkling ceremony'), was their king.[2] The *śāstra* makes no effort to conceal the king's debt to the Brahman community [3] and his duty to facilitate their work. It is easy to understand that property nominally belonging to the *devas* was immune from the king's lordship, so long, that is to say, as necessity or temptation was not too strong for his piety.

It may be urged that the *śāstra* at length saw the king's *bhogas* as a repayment for his services in *prajā-pālana*. It is boldly asserted (e.g. in Nārada, XVII, 47) that revenue is the king's wages.[4] But this argument is unrealistic. No one imagines that he 'enjoys' his human dependants in right of wage, as it were, for maintaining them: it is quite the other way about. We need not investigate here the quite relevant Indian notion that while the *bhṛtya* must be supported by his master, the *bhartṛ*, at the same time the *bhṛtya* himself supports the *bhartṛ* [5]: this reciprocity at first seems a paradox, but, like many such, expresses a nexus of psychological attitudes implicit in a stable relationship. We must accept that, just as *bhṛti* means *wages*, so, notwithstanding this important notion, the *bhartṛ* maintains wholly or in part in lieu of wages, as every widower who marries his housekeeper will readily affirm. Moreover the notion that the ruler is the servant of the people, agreeable in times of revolution and the like, does not accord with Hindu traditional sentiment. He shows his qualities by lending a ready ear to their grievances, and so on, but he is emphatically if not always their leader, at any rate the *prajā-svāmi*, their lord. Even to those not actually employed in the royal household he is *anna-dātṛ*, the 'giver of food'.[6] Without him the stronger would roast the weaker, like fish on a spit: no exaggeration, as everyone knows. Perhaps the reference to the king's relationship to the Earth cannot be found in the *śāstra* because the jurists wanted to minimize a feature with which the public were all too familiar, and which tended to impede their inculcation of the *śāstra's* chief lesson, namely that, 'divinity' or not, the king must *not* consider himself a superhuman being and must concentrate on his duty and not upon the delights which his position may afford. Gonda rightly points out the distinction between

[1] R. Aiyangar, introd. to *Rājadharmakāṇḍa*, 54 ff. Kane, III, 190, 228, 384, 762, 942. A fundamental text commences *na viṣam viṣam*, ibid., p. 1273, No. 11. On Bhats and Charans in western India in the eighteenth century see J. Tod, *Annals and antiquities* . . ., II, 500; J. Forbes, *Oriental memoirs*, 1834, I, 377–80. Chintaman Rao, negotiating with Elphinstone in 1819, demanded that Brahmans should be exempt from *begārī*: K. Ballhatchet, *Social policy and social change* . . ., London, 1957, 68.

[2] Rau, 65, para. 43; Gonda, III, 135. *MBh.*, XII, 47, 24; *Vas.*, I, 42–3.

[3] Kane, II, 36 ff.; Dikshitar, *Hindu administrative institutions*, 114 ff.

[4] Dikshitar, op. cit., 166 ff.; Kane, III, 187; R. Aiyangar, *Rājadharma*, Adyar, 1941, 35, 107; *MBh.*, XII, 57, 11.

[5] e.g. Rāmānuja, *Vedārthasaṅgraha*, ed. van Beutenen, Poona, 1957, trans., 275.

[6] Nār., XVII, 25; E. M. Carstairs, *The twice-born*, London, 1957, 21.

the divine kingship and the all-too-human individual who represents it, and the anomalies to which this distinction gave rise.

Another suggestion is made, that in the phrases cited the word *bhū* really stands for *prajāḥ*.[1] He maintains the public, fostering the good and rooting out the 'thorns'; he protects not more by warding off attacks than by increasing his material resources; and where there were no inhabitants there was, it is alleged with doubtful authority, no kingdom. But this will not serve. For *prajā-bhojana* is a revolting concept. The king, given normal conditions, is no parasite; rather it is upon him that all the *prajāḥ* depend. If they contribute to his maintenance by their labour, his own contributions serve, in precisely the same way, to support the Brahman community. Even in emergencies, when he may take the goods of wealthy merchants,[2] he is not acting parasitically, for his authority to do this is not challenged. It is only if they stop 'feeding' him, or fail in their duty, or he is overcome with greed, that the relationship breaks down, and he 'preys upon' them.[3] This is distinctly a morbid, and not a normal characteristic. Nor is this a case where reciprocity applies, for one does not hear of *bhṛtya-bhojana*, where, if anywhere, such an expression might have been expected. All the difficulty lies in the word *bhojana*, which calls to mind the harem, who certainly do not support their master, except in very peculiar circumstances. It is true that the *rāja*, the *rāja's* friend, and the dacoit, are the conventional hazards that beset peaceful citizens,[4] but this is not evidence of *prajā-bhojana*—for who has heard a thief described as 'enjoyer of the robbed'?

Perhaps it is Indra who provides the explanation. He and his ancient colleague or substitute, Parjanya, give or withhold rain, and similarly, and perhaps accordingly, all wealth.[5] Like a real king Indra divides the spoil between his dependants, and in return for offerings is believed to be morally bound to provide cattle.[6] In the *Ṛgveda* he is plainly the embodiment of brilliant power, loosing the bound, opening up the riches of enemies to his followers,

[1] *Śrīmūla*, on *Arthaśāstra*, I, i; Manu, IX, 311 and commentaries.

[2] *Arthaśāstra*, IV, 3; V, 2: Kane, III, 188, n. 240.

[3] In *AB*, VIII, 12, 5 (cf. 17, 5) he is called *viśām attā* 'eater of the folk'; Gonda, IV, 35. From the context this may mean 'devourer' in the sense of 'destroyer'; cf. *MBh.*, XII, 47, 37–8. For 'preying upon' see *Arthaś.*, II, 1; Kane, III, 184 ff. In another sense the food-producing classes are 'eaten' by those who protect them by arms or *mantras*, and the latter even 'eat' the king: *TS*, VII, 1, 1, 4–6; *PB*, VI, 1, 6–11 (U. N. Ghoshal, *History of Hindu public life*, I, Calcutta, 1945, 51–2); also *ŚB*, V, 4, 2, 3. A thorough study of the problem will take into account texts such as Nārada, XVII, 22, where the subject is compared with the king's wife; and *Ragh.*, VIII, 8, where the good king acts impartially to each subject, just as the ocean behaves to hundreds of rivers. The ocean is, of course, the *husband* of the rivers: *sarit-pati*—cf. Kālidāsa, *Mālavikā.*, V, 19.

[4] A commonplace in *dharmaśāstra*. In Meyer, II, 128–9, a hint is not followed up.

[5] Sāyaṇa on *ṚV*, I, 52, 14. Indra resorted to for fertility ('offspring'), victory, and wealth: ibid., I, 8, 6 and *passim* particularly in the first *maṇḍala*.

[6] Another commonplace. See e.g. *ṚV*, I, 33; IV, 34 and 35; cf. *AV*, III, 4, 2. The sexual aspects of Indra: Meyer, III. A critical, but non-sexual study: E. Benveniste and L. Renou, *Vṛtra et Vṛθragna: étude de mythologie indo-iranienne*, Paris, 1934.

and stimulating the warrior and raider. The notions of violent robbery and impregnation seem to be linked.[1] Was he called the king of the *devas* because he shared these attributes with the earthly chief, to whom he is constantly and tediously likened ?[2] A prayer in the *Atharva-veda* seeks to make the ' sprinkled ' king like Indra, in order that the people may have rain[3]; the warrior king in history sought ' Indra-hood ' in this very life.[4] The very word *kṣatriya*, says Śabara-svāmi, calls to mind Indra.[5] If Indra is not precisely wedded to Pṛthivī, Parjanya certainly is,[6] and there is a complete parallel.[7] Earth is the mother, Parjanya (we have seen) is the father, and Parjanya is therefore (like Indra) our ruler.[8] Sudakṣiṇā, hoping that her expected son will enjoy the Earth as Indra enjoys Heaven, takes to eating soil . . .

divaṃ Marutvān iva bhokṣyate bhuvaṃ dig-anta-viśrānta-ratho hi tat-sutaḥ |
ato 'bhilāṣe prathamaṃ tathāvidhe mano babandhānya-rasān vilaṅghya sā || [9]

Since they are of a kind, the king and Indra are on visiting terms.[10] Like Indra, the king is a ' rainer '.[11] Gonda, who notes the parallelism, points to the mystical possession of *ojas* (' creative vital energy ') as a kingly quality.[12] Similar expressions deserve scrutiny. *Retas* ' rain-water ' also means ' semen ',[13] and it is with *retas* that Parjanya *satisfies* the Earth.[14] Modern Indian speech employs ' water ' as a euphemism for several fluids, and the *Bhāgavata-purāṇa* in an odd story about Indra sees a large range of fluids with distinct fertility-connotations as

[1] Ruler : *ṚV*, VIII, 37, 3. Bull, lord, ' rainer ', protector, ' showerer ' : *ṚV*, I, 7, 8 ; 9, 4 ; 10, 10 ; 32. Even in countries where rainfall can be a nuisance ' showering blessings ' is an accepted metaphor—and, since we have mentioned a Western usage, are not the uses to which the English word *husband* is put significant in our context ?

[2] He is *bhū-śakra* (' the Earth's Indra ' ?): Śrī-Harṣa cited *Sūkti-muktāvalī*, Baroda, 1938, 338, No. 25. *MBh.*, XII, 67, 4 ; *Arthaś.*, I, 13. The king's mother is Indra's mother : *AV*, VI, 38 ; his bow Indra's weapon : Gonda, III, 131. *Rājat.*, I, 99, 100, 174 ; II, 63 ; III, 329, 475 ; IV, 108, 164, 194, 217, 372 ; and so forth. Indra survived in *abhiṣeka* ceremonies and the rituals for increasing sovereignty ; and also in the South Indian *poṅgal* festival, upon which see Meyer, III, 118 ff. Gonda takes the identification as established : III, 63–4, 134, 138 ; IV, 51. What is the relationship of Indra to Gautama Buddha ? The concept of Indra held by Buddhist writers is sketched ibid., III, 144.

[3] VI, 54, cited V. R. Ramachandra Dikshitar, *War in ancient India. Second ed.*, Madras, etc., 1948, at p. 36.

[4] *Aindrapadam. MBh.*, XII, 78, 34, promises him *Indra-salokatā* after his death, but that is not enough. The ' state of Indra ' is the conventional boon with which *sannyāsis* are tempted. The whole point, so far as it relates to kings, is well elaborated by Dikshitar, *War*, 31 and ff.

[5] On Jaimini, I, 4, 13.

[6] *AV*, XII, 1, 42.

[7] See p. 110, n. 2, above and p. 119, n. 4, below, also *MBh.*, XII, 92, 1.

[8] *ṚV.*, VII, 101, 2.

[9] *Ragh.*, III, 4.

[10] ibid., I, 75 ; *Rājat.*, IV, 222–40. Indra also gives lessons in statecraft : *MBh.*, XII, 140, 17.

[11] R. Aiyangar, introd. to *Rājadharmakāṇḍa*, 17. The most explicit text is Manu, IX, 304.

[12] III, 64, 134.

[13] See Meyer, op. cit., III, 150.

[14] *ṚV.*, V, 83, 4–5, with Sāyaṇa thereon, is extraordinarily suggestive, since the word *avati* aptly implies sexual satisfaction (cf. *Ragh.*, I, 65, cit. sup.). On *retas* and Parjanya as an impregnator see also *ṚV.*, V, 83, 1 ; VII, 101, 6 ; and 103, 2.

mystical representatives of rain-water.[1] The root *vṛṣ* 'to rain' has a most ancient duality of meaning: it suggests the pouring or scattering of generative fluid. *Vṛṣa* implies any male animal, and the mightiest of its kind. The *Atharva-veda* prays for sovereignty even over Indra, over Heaven, and over the Earth, for the chief, in these suggestive words[2]:

vṛṣendrasya vṛṣā divo vṛṣā pṛthivyā ayam |
vṛṣā viśvasya bhūtasya tvam ekavṛṣo bhava ||

Vṛṣabha, with which the *Ṛgveda* compares Parjanya and Indra,[3] came to be a bull, but how did *mahiṣī* come to mean 'chief queen' when its principal meaning is 'she-buffalo'? Wilhelm Rau recently pointed out the curious * connexion here between the Queen, a cow, the Mother, and the Earth.[4] The king is a bull amongst men; the idea of a king growing past potency in office is distasteful to traditional Hindu notions, and the large (but curiously often unfruitful) harem was always an ostensible sign of the king's possession of the necessary qualification. Two classes of humans should not die a natural death: they should be buried alive or drowned, starve themselves to death, or, in the case of the first only, die in battle or of wounds received in battle. These are the king, and the *sannyāsi*.[5] It has been observed that they are the only persons to possess *tejas*,[6] that characteristic Indian attribute of males, and they are the only persons marked out for their possession—though in different contexts and for different purposes—of abundant semen.

pṛthivī sarva-bhūtānāṃ janitrī tad-vidhāḥ striyaḥ |
pumān prajā-patis tatra śukraṃ tejo-mayaṃ viduḥ || [7]

And what is the *yaśas* of the king, the clear white fluid fit to be drunk, particularly by dependants or those humiliated? Drinking fame is a notable Indian metaphor.

[1] vi, 7, 2–40; 8, 42; 9, 4–11.

[2] Cited in Dikshitar, *War*, 37, n. 63a; Gonda, iv, 28. *

[3] See p. 118, n. 1, above, and compare the warrior's hymn to the virile *vṛṣan* Indra in *AV*, xix, 13.

[4] op. cit., 106, para. 71, ref. *ŚB*, v, 3, 1, 4. The learned author assembles further references suggesting that the *uttaravedi*, the lioness, and the female buffalo are supernaturally related. Indra's and Parjanya's relationship with Pṛthivī, and Indra's other sexual exploits, were taken for granted in medieval times; Sāyaṇa tells us that 'for fun' Indra had intercourse with a mare and begot a cow: comm. on *ṚV*, i, 121, 2.

[5] King: refs. in Dikshitar, *War*, 19, 387–91; R. Aiyangar, op. cit., introd., 75, n. 1; Kane, op. cit., iii, 57–8; iv, 605; *sannyāsi*: Kane, ii, ch. xxviii. See Medhātithi on Manu, vii, 89. History abounds with examples of *sannyāsis* or would-be *sannyāsis* who have committed suicide by fire or water, and burial alive, as a literal interpretation of the requirement of death by *samādhi* (with which compare the Jainas' *sallekhanā*), takes place even to-day. Note that only babies and *sannyāsis* are entitled to burial as distinct from cremation. Moreover there is a reciprocity between *rājas* and *sannyāsis* of a most unexpected kind. They appear to be at opposite poles of existence: but the royal *ṛṣi* (Gonda, iii, 45) and the *rāja* whose *rājyam* is his *āśrama* or *tapas*, are commonplaces, whence *Ragh.*, i, 58, is beautifully apt. See also *Śākunt.*, ii, 14. Both *rāja* and *sannyāsi* in the form of *ṛṣi* are, of course, perfect father-figures.

[6] Gonda, iii, 71; iv, 133. The last reference links *tejas* and *vīrya*, mystical efficiency and sexual potency. Professor Gonda sees in the Aśvamedha sacrifice (iv, 134–5) a ritual primarily intended to increase the king's potency (and thence his qualification to rule widely).

[7] *MBh.*, xii, 183, 15: for the printed *śukram* many manuscripts read *śuklam*.

sa nandinī-stanyam aninditātmā sad-vatsalo vatsa-hutāvaśeṣam |
papau Vasiṣṭhena kṛtābhyanujñaḥ śubhraṃ yaśo mūrtam ivātitṛṣṇaḥ || [1]
bhūpeṣu kūpeṣv iva rikta-bhāvaṃ kṛtvā prapāpālikayaiva yasya |
vīra-śriyā kīrti-sudhā-rasasya diśāṃ mukhāni praṇayī-kṛtāni || [2]

A prolongation of Morris Carstairs' brilliant discoveries in the psychological connotations of white fluids, white foods, and related matters, may throw light on this question.[3]

Apparently, quite apart from considerations of 'sacredness', the Indian king was first and foremost a *male*. Royal titles, like Dhārāvarṣa, Akālavarṣa, Amoghavarṣa, and so on, combine the 'raining' and masculine attributes. At the 'coronation' fluids, viscous and clear, play varied and essential parts.[4] Just as *abhiṣecana* with water over the head is essential for the king's authority, so the *dharmaśāstra* recommends that he be *abhiṣikta* annually and on special occasions. We wonder what is behind the symbolism of the *vasordhārā*, which as Rangaswami Aiyangar pointed out [5] may be performed to destroy enemies, at anniversaries of *abhiṣekas*, or the births of princes, etc., and mimetically promises the 'shower' of wealth and other blessings which the *devas* give in return—a 'shower' which pours over the head of the sacrifier, i.e. the king himself. For the rite consists in a very slow trickling of ghee into a consecrated fire kindled at the bottom of a pit in the middle of a dwelling. The learned commentator, quoting Kālidāsa, points out that here showering, sprinkling, blessings, martial potency, and reciprocity between Heaven and Earth are all inextricably associated: and doubtless we might go further. Why does the king have to erect the 'flagstaff of Indra', on which there seems to be a large literature, and which is, as Meyer has abundantly proved,[6] as much a phallic symbol as any of the poles, *liṅgams*, obelisks, *vīragals*, or other tall stones, whether actually worshipped or not? For the sake of rain and 'to become lord of the world' he erects what Gonda identifies as a maypole. For fertility

[1] *Ragh.*, II, 69. *Sūktim.*, 339—a verse calling *yaśas* by the suggestive word *śukla*. *Vājapeya* = 'drink of vigour', on which see refs. in Gonda, IV, 37; ibid., 38, 134–5, for the meanings of *vāja*. It is not precisely *retas*, but it is evidently the condition of having ample *retas* pent up. Carstairs enlarges on secret rites involving incest, etc., and no doubt holiness and horror are often related. The relation between sexuality and holiness seems to maintain similar features throughout the Indo-European world, but as Professor Gonda emphasizes, India provides quite special developments of the common heritage.

[2] Bilhaṇa, *Vikramāṅkadeva-carita*, Banaras, 1945, I, 89. The pure *yaśas* of one king was so abundant that it had to be stored in a reservoir (like the seed of Prajāpati that formed the lake Mānasa): *Ep. Ind.*, VII, p. 43; cf. Heesterman, cit. inf., 190. Somadeva's *Yaśastilaka* bears an intriguing and doubtless apt title. *South Indian inscr.*, III, p. 398, v. 92: the son of Rājarāja seized the pure pearls which had become *seeds*, as it were, of the pure fame (in the plural) of the Pāṇḍya king.

[3] op. cit., 83 ff., 166. Meyer, index, 'Honig', 'Milch'. The king's couch at the 'coronation' may be made of wood yielding a milk-white sap.

[4] N. Law, ubi cit.; Kane, III, 72 ff.; Gonda, III, 43; IV, 33 ff., 46 ff.

[5] Introd. to *Rājadharmakāṇḍa*, 80–1. Meyer seems to have omitted to mention this.

[6] III, 7 ff.; 192. It is Indra himself, III, 13, 24, 40, 41, 98. On stones see ibid., I, 57.

southern Indians to this day pour ghee on the tall stones erected to commemorate the deaths of heroes in battle, and such stones are erected elsewhere to assert prestige, and to secure good crops. Planting columns was a sign of virility and a sop to vanity as much in India as in the West [1]: one planted a Kadamba tree in one's own soil [2] and a 'column of victory' in one's neighbour's.

Perhaps the king was the lover of the Earth because of the physical prowess constantly attributed to him *ex officio*. It enabled him to capture her as the *kṣatriyas* were supposed to capture their brides. Perhaps he felt towards her that peculiar complex of animal power, jealous subjection, dutiful protection, and fearful worship which has been observed between husband and wife in orthodox Hindu societies, where marriage still takes place in childhood and precedes love. Is the phrase *bhū-bhojana* an admission that the king's possession of the Earth was not different in kind from an ordinary citizen's possession of his wife? If so we are a long way towards understanding the attitude of the subject towards his king as a second father, an attitude which alone made possible the deviations on the part of kings from what was admitted on every side to be their duty.[3] Perhaps the whole notion grew from the primitive observation that extraverted zeal and physical prowess, the absolute requirements of a successful brigand or champion, were in some way associated with *vīrya*, a characteristic inseparable from possession of abundant semen.[4] Similarly, though perhaps by coincidence, the power that enabled a chief to possess the Earth, whether personally or through his dependants and associates, was thought of as a fertilizing power, for the acts of cultivation (at least in one part of India, these were acts that could not prosper without the *kṣatriya's* inauguration) [5] must have been seen as distinctly masculine, ever since the story of Sītā started on its long journey, if not before—and hence perhaps the connexion between the king and Indra. That the king himself undertook to produce rain by keeping up brahmanical offerings and attending to the requirements of *dharma* may have been a secondary development.

If *bhū-pālana* and *bhū-bhojana* have happily coalesced, what remains to be said of *bhū-bharaṇa*? If the enjoyed one is kept happy one aspect of *bharaṇa* is accounted for, but what of the other? Is the physical carrying another secondary development, made at the time when the king discovered that rule

[1] Alexander probably did *not* bring the custom to India. The custom of erecting monoliths is still alive in England. A gigantic partly-hewn pillar is to be seen on the village green in Westwell, Oxon., erected after the first World War to commemorate two soldiers. It is a splendid *vīragal*.

[2] Evidence from South India. On trees as fertility symbols, lordly and phallic: Meyer, I, 214 ff.; III, 190–5.

[3] On attitudes to fathers: Carstairs, 67–9, 159–67. Texts emphasizing the father-like status of the king: Kane, III, 62–3.

[4] On *vīrya*; Gonda, IV, 133, 158. After this paper was written the writer discovered with pleasure that Professor Gonda had found, in *TB*, III, 9, 7, 4, and *ŚB*, XIII, 2, 9, 6, identifications of the *rāṣṭra* (which he translates 'royal sway') with the *membrum virile*.

[5] *Vāpya-maṅgala* ceremony, cited by Dev Raj, *L'esclavage dans l'Inde ancienne*, Pondichéry, 1957, 53. Heesterman's guess, op. cit. inf. 166, seems appropriate.

was a burden ? A wife is *bhāryā* because she was originally carried along, and thence her master's responsibility. The Earth could hardly have become a burden because she was a wife, but rather because protecting her became burdensome. *Prajāḥ* are not in any case a burden, any more than they are enjoyed ; dependency alone must have ceased to imply a burden long before the king's responsibility appeared as such. But if we assert that the image of the king with the Earth upon his shoulder is a derivative notion we are not rising above conjecture, since the Ṛgvedic *sūkta* we have already consulted (I, 121, 2–3) explicitly tells us that Indra *holds up* the Heavens for the good of creatures, while in the *Atharvaveda* we find the prayer,[1] 'may you stand firm in the world like Indra and may you uphold the kingdom!'. There are evidently depths to this problem which can hardly be plumbed with assurance, though we may attempt to apprehend them. There remains a fact, however, which it may be presumptuous to claim as a clue, but seems worth citing. The word used in the *sūkta* for 'holding up' is derived from the root *stambh* 'to prop up'. Now *stambha* is a pillar. We are told repeatedly that a king supports the world on his arm, which is 'like a pillar',[2] very much as Krishna holds up the mountain. * The arm-pillar is of course a phallic symbol. Hindus believe the three worlds to be supported upon a pillar. The pillar on the round flat ground (the flatness has its significance, and the roundness no less)[3] at once calls to mind Mahādeva, the predominant fertility deity.[4] But we have also the reverse, the pillar, apart from other characteristics which do not seem relevant here, holding up the three worlds in the form of a (? flat) inhabited place. A commonplace stanza says this is Śiva, the Phallus.

namas tuṅga-śiraś-cumbi-candra-cāmara-cārave |
trailokya-nagarārambha-mūla-stambhāya Śaṃbhave || [5]

If Indra propped up the Heavens, perhaps because by splitting the clouds he

[1] VI, 87, 1–2.

[2] Kannaḍa examples cited p. 111, n. 3, above.

[3] Gonda, IV, 53 ff., on the Earth's *broadness*, and Heaven's. On the circularity of the king's Earth, ibid., 144 ff. The king should be in the centre of his *maṇḍala* or *cakra* (ibid., 148), just, we note, as the *liṅgam* of Mahādeva shows the upright portion in the centre of the *yoni* portion.

[4] In Śiva-Mahādeva the *yoni* is underneath, the *liṅgam* above. But the image we have here is reversed, as well it may be since the arm, which is the phallic symbol (see the instance cited above, p. 111, n. 3), must of necessity be visualized *surmounted* by that which it is supporting and penetrating. The arm with the clenched fist is often used suggestively in India. The king's arm appears as phallic, doubtless as a symbol of Indra, and as a deity, it seems, in the otherwise inexplicable passage in the Kaluchumbarru grant of Vijayāditya Amma II, the Eastern Cāḷukya of the tenth century (*Ep. Ind.*, VII, p. 186). He is described as *sākṣād Vallabha-nṛpa-samabhyarcita-bhujaḥ* 'whose arm was personally (or 'publicly') worshipped by king Vallabha (i.e. the Rāṣṭrakūṭa emperor, so termed disrespectfully)'. *samabhyarcita* is a very strong word, suggesting worship of the *liṅgam* of Śiva, and *bhuja* means nothing but 'arm'.

[5] See p. 123, n. 3. This verse commences about seven out of every ten inscriptions (mostly engraved on tall monoliths) now standing in the villages or fields of Karṇāṭaka. The white *cāmara*, white umbrellas, and the *victorious* white pennant, all related to the king and to poles, deserve study along the lines suggested here.

reinstated daylight (he is elsewhere said to have placed the sun in the sky),[1] we are told also that he kept Heaven separate from Earth. But in the same *sūkta* (I, 62, 7), Indra not merely keeps them apart, but also upholds them. The *dyāvāpṛthivī*, who appear with Indra in several contexts, sometimes supporting him and sometimes supported by him,[2] are actually held by him, and the commentator Sāyaṇa goes out of his way to point out that this may well place Indra in a (characteristic) masculine role, and Heaven and Earth in feminine roles, while the holding may be a maintaining or nourishing.

dvitā vi vavre sanajā sanīḷe ayāsyaḥ stavamānebhir arkaiḥ |
bhago na mene parame vyomann adhārayad rodasī sudaṃsāḥ ||

(Sāyaṇa :) . . . *rodasī* dyāvāpṛthivyau *adhārayat* apoṣayat. yadvā. *menā* iti strī-nāma. tathā ca Yāskaḥ : menā gnā iti strīṇāṃ menā mānayanty enāḥ (Nir. III, 21) iti. strī-rūpam āpanne rodasī Indro 'puṣyad ity arthaḥ.

Thus Indra, the personification of the masculine, the prototype of the column of victory, bears up, supports, maintains and protects—or was thought to do so by the very people who attributed the same characteristics to their kings. Masculinity, it seems, may be the key to all this. The *yoni* that is the Earth requires, it seems, the *liṅgam* that is the King.[3] Should this ultimately be proved, its effects upon our understanding of Indian social and political history cannot be small, and one of the origins, if not the chief origin, of the ' divinity ' of Indo-European kingship may have been discovered.

[1] Gonda, IV, 141, 143–4, emphasizes how Indra's expansion is so great that he *fills* Earth and Heaven and the space between, or rather that in extent he surpasses them. Extension, swelling so as fully to occupy : this attribute of both Indra and the king is carefully expounded by Professor Gonda. J. C. Heesterman, *The ancient Indian royal consecration*, The Hague, 1957, 191, n. 58, points out that the *indriya* force rises upwards through the three worlds and that it is only by rising to the third world that Indra can master it. His work refers to what he calls *indriya- vīrya-* frequently, pointing out its importance in the *rājasūya*.

[2] In particular note *ṚV.*, III, 30, 5 : *ime cid Indra rodasī apāre yat saṃgṛbhṇā Maghavan kāśir it te*, which Śabara (on Jaimini, IX, 1, 6 and 9) hastens to explain away, because though Indra grips them in a ' fistful ' (*kāśiḥ* = *muṣṭiḥ*, which, N.B., is suspected to mean *penis* in one citation in Monier-Williams), the jurist is reluctant to ascribe either possession or ownership to a *devatā*.

[3] Nothing depicts the king's nature as phallus-pillar-Indra more clearly than the *axis mundi* pose of the king, about to be ' sprinkled ', standing erect on his throne (the navel of the Earth), with both arms reaching to the sky : *MS*, 4, 4, 3 : 53.16 referred to and expounded brilliantly by Heesterman, op. cit., 101 and n. 51.

ADDITIONAL ANNOTATIONS

Tit. Cited E. S. Drower, *Theol. Lit. Zeit.* 1961, pt. 3, 174f. On the subject see J. W. Spellman, *Political Theory of Ancient India* (Oxford, 1964), 208-9. Useful material appears at J. Gonda, 'Ascetics and courtesans', *Adyar Lib. Bull.* 25 (Jub. Vol.), 1961, 78ff. (on sacrifices and sex).

p. [33], l. 15. Medh. on M. IX. 44 is clear on this. R. M. Huntington, 'Legend of Pṛithu', *Purāṇa* 2 (1960), 188ff. On this subject a publication of Dr W.D. O'Flaherty is awaited.

p. [37]. Bṛhaddharma-purāṇa III. 4, 33-4 compares a land without a king to a woman without a husband (U. Ghoshal, *Hist. Ind. Pol. Ideas*, Oxford, 1959, 441). 'Shame on avarice! That land is like a widow, the sovereign of which is despised' : Tipura Copper Plate (A.D. 1219), *v.* 8 : Colebrooke at *Essays* (London, 1873), II, 216-220 (= *As. Res.* IX, 1807, 398ff.).

p. [38], n. 6. Medh. on M. IX. 44.

p. [39], n. 2. For *vv.* explaining these items : Manu and Bṛh. quoted in the *Vya.nir.*, 342, trans. L. Renou, *I.-I.J.* 6/2 (1962), 95. Also my art. on Property (*Z.V.R.* 64, 1962, below, Vol. 2), at p. 93.

p. [40], n. 1. Now T. K. Banerjee, *Background to Indian Criminal Law* (Orient Longmans, 1963).

p. [40], n. 3. Satisfactory attempts to understand the rights of the king over the soil are to be seen at L. Gopal, 'Ownership of agricultural land in ancient India', *J.E.S.H.O.* 4/3 (1961), 240-63 ; D. N. Jha, *Revenue System in Post-Maurya and Gupta Times* (Calcutta, 1967), chh. 2, 9.

p. [44], l. 10. S. Ṛgveda III. 46, 2 quoted and trans. by B. Schlerath in his important *Das Königtum im Rig- und Atharvaveda* (Wiesbaden, 1960), 58. Note also ibid., 50, quotation of Śat.brā. XIII.2.9,6 : viḍ vai gabho rāṣṭram pasas, 'The vagina is the people, the penis is the kingdom/government'.

p. [44], n. 2. Schlerath (supra), 68.

p. [47], l. 18. Kṣemendra, *Aucitya-vicāra-carcā* v. 12, trans., Suryakanta, *Kṣemendra St.* (Poona, 1954), 122.

RULERS AND RULED IN INDIA

The subject of this study interested Indian scholars and publicists from at least as early as the middle of last century. The question whether Indians were fit to rule themselves, or at any rate to have responsibility for decisions affecting important national issues agitated all western-educated classes, whose preoccupation with a defence of India's claims to 'freedom' affected in turn vast numbers of their compatriots whose contact with the West was limited or at second hand. There is therefore a vast literature bearing directly or indirectly upon the question whether, in pre-British periods, Indians had been subject to a benevolent despotism, and if not, upon what basis they had been governed : and the desire to show that Indians were hereditarily not unfit to control their own political lives took so large a control of the research, and what passed for research, that the majority of the works produced, in particular since the beginning of this century, must be read with great caution. Professor R.S. Sharma has, in a recent paper [1], very properly pointed out the tendentious and biassed approaches of Indian scholars, and the lack of objectivity in their writing, and it is refreshing to find from a broad-minded patriot so frank, as well as truthful, an exposure of the limitations of our

[1] « Historiography of the ancient Indian social order » in C.H. Philips, ed., *Historians of India, Pakistan and Ceylon*, London 1961, at pp. 102 ff.

recent secondary literature. There are other limitations besides those imposed by the ardent desire for 'freedom'. Indian writers in particular Kasi Prasad Jayaswal have tended to read books on political theory in the West, and then searched in Indian material for ideas and features which could be set out in language originally suited to the western discussions, but which are by no means truly representative of Indian situations. The spirit that 'we have everything which you have, only better' is so pervasive that few works in English or French by Indian authors are devoid of that peculiar mixture of emulation and self-justification which taints most works of the pre-Independence period [2]. One has to remember that promotion in that ill-remunerated sphere, university teaching, was to be obtained for publications which were loyal to India, her past and her aspirations, provided they were written in a style and from a viewpoint capable of being labeled 'scholarly' by western (principally English) critics.

The literature in European languages about Indian political thought and history is subject to a further weakness, which gave the tendencies adverted to above the fullest possible scope. In order to determine what were in, say, 1919, the political capabilities of Indians, that is to say Muslims, Hindus, Christians, Parsis, Jews, outcaste-untouchables, primitive peoples, Buddhist or quasi-Buddhist peoples of the remote sub-Himalayan tracts, and others, no one suggested that reference should be made to their own actual behaviour and record. The relatively recent experience of local self-government revealed faction, friction, limited capacity for cooperation. The divergencies between the castes and religious and ethnic groups seemed to suggest, upon their very face, the unlike-

[2] An exception is Ramaprasad Dasgupta's posthumous work, *A Study in Hindu and European Political System*, Calcutta, 1959. His approach is to say, « Absolute government was a requisite in Europe, and only by an accident gave way to parliamentary government : in India how could anything as good have developed? » But in his use of the comparative technique to fill gaps in our documents he is not so far from his opponent, Jayaswal. His approach follows out a hint of P.V. Kane, *History of Dharmaśāstra*, III, Poona, 1946, p. 94.

lihood of democratic government as known in other countries in the British Empire. In the realms where Hindus had always been self-governing, namely caste-regulation in matters of social etiquette and religion, it was notorious that impartiality and responsible administration were hard to find. Indians themselves, when approached in these connexions, all agreed that, whatever the shortcomings of the British and other foreign rulers, they were at least fair and impartial, and this was a consideration of enormous importance. The fairness of the open mind, even if it was an ill-instructed mind, had its decided charms. The material for the study of Indian self-government, where it existed, was not encouraging and hardly adapted to an idealistic purpose [3]. Hence the appeal was invariably to the 'golden age', before the British period commenced, before the Muslims intruded into India, to the period represented by the Sanskrit *nīti-śāstra*, 'science of government', the *artha-śāstra*, 'science of ways and means', and the *dharma-śāstra*, queen of sciences, the science of righteousness, within which was contained what we call 'law'. But did these voluminous literatures really represent what *happened* in the, somewhat vaguely defined, centuries or ages prior to the British period? How far could one rely upon statements to be found there for any proposition as to *fact*? Naturally writers assumed that any written propositions supporting their theses were actually fact, whereas a more objective appraisal of the sources induces more caution.

It is not the purpose of this paper to exceed the bounds of our Society's investigation, which is not into the full nature of kingship, or the various theories of government, but simply into the participation of the public in the process of government. As we approach,

[3] A work which throws a lot of light on the outlook and literature on the pre-First World War period, when independence was about to be sought with increasing violence and desperation, is J. MATTHAI's excellent and informative *Village Government in British India*, London, 1915. This work, despite its title, gives ample and often valuable information on village self-government prior to the British period. His chapters handle education (2), poor relief (3), sanitation (4), public works (5), watch and ward (6), and the administration of justice (7).

in the prearranged order, the questions here investigated in parallel schemes for each country and civilisation, we should attempt to compare the statements in the technical literature with the evidence, so far as it survives, for actual behaviour in India. It will be evident that, day-dreams aside, the claims of India to be, traditionally and actually, a member of a group of democratically-governed nations is very tenuous, and that, though India's democratic form of government is likely to continue (by contrast with the experience of Pakistan, Burma, etc.), democracy as known in India must be accepted as different in nature from that experienced elsewhere in the Commonwealth, with the possible exception of its most recent recruits in Africa and South East Asia. The recent studies of politics in India reveal an awareness that this must be so [4] : it is to be regretted that, by and large, too few of the many students of Indian affairs are equipped with first-hand knowledge of the 'old' India, and they are therefore handicapped when it comes to the question how much of the present-day scene is traditional, and quite what an ancient historian would expect [5]. It is further to be borne in mind that writers who are backing the 'new' India, as against the heavy competition of the 'old' India as it survives and pervades Indian life, are bound to pretend an ignorance they may not have [6], in order to lend strength to the now struggling impression that the 'new' India, the cosmopolitan, Commonwealth India, must prevail, and that the future is on its side — whereas in reality the survival of the 'new' India in any but superficial senses is by no means to be counted upon : though

4 See the studies by C. VON FÜRER-HAIMENDORF, F.G. BAILEY, A.C. MAYER, and W.H. MORRIS-JONES in C.H. PHILIPS, ed., *Politics and Society in India*, 1963.

5 An exception is J.C. HEESTERMAN, whose « Tradition in Modern India », *Bijdragen tot de Taal-, Land- en Volkenkunde*, 119, 1963, pp. 237 ff., reveals a realisation of the oneness of Indian experience.

6 A recent monumental study in the 'new India' interest is D.E. SMITH, *India as a Secular State*, Princeton, 1963, where the conflict between the constitution's nominal protection of the right to freedom of religion and the actual working out of religious problems is graphically demonstrated.

those who are loyal to it and believe in it must not breathe a word of their doubts.

I

The earliest period of historical India is the Vedic period. The polity of that period can be made out with some difficulty, since the Vedic literature hints at it only in passing [7]. Assemblies of a popular character existed, in which it appears both men and women participated, and there is no reason to doubt but that the government of the tribe at all levels was popular, the chiefs being appointed by, and exercising their functions under the authority of, the popular assembly [8]. It seems also clear that for some purposes an assembly of warriors, and for others a joint assembly of warriors and elders, would exercise government. When, long afterwards, settlements in agricultural areas were numerous and established, a form of government retaining the popular principle was in existence. The age of the Buddha (c. 500 B.C.) knew republics as well as kingdoms, and these republics had a form of government which was aristocratic from the point of view of the entire population of the area, but democratic from the point of view of the governing class. The method of governing the Buddhist *saṅgha*, which was taken from contemporary governmental techniques, reveals a tradition of democratic forms, of participation by the public in the making of decisions by the rulers, indeed, it approaches elemental democracy [9]. But already by the age of the Buddha

[7] DASGUPTA, Bk. 2, ch. 1; R.S. SHARMA, *Aspects*, 1959, ch. 5, ch. 6.

[8] SHARMA, ubi cit., ch. 4, explores the contractual theory of the origin of the State. Such theories go back perhaps to the Vedic or early post-Vedic period.

[9] ALTEKAR, *State and Government*, 1962, ch. 6 deals with the republican government of Buddhist times; GHOSHAL, *History*, 1959, ch. 4 deals with the political theories of the Buddhist literature. JAGDISH PRASAD SHARMA, *Republican and quasi-republican Institutions in Ancient India, with Special Reference to the times of the Buddha*, Thesis, Ph. D., London (unpublished), 1962, gives a thorough examination to the polity of the Licchavis. But was there a democratic spirit : N. WAGLE, *Society at the time of the Buddha*, 1966 ? *

popular participation in government had declined with the extension of the public in vast areas, the elaboration of a complicated inter-relation of time-consuming occupations, and the experience (evidently over centuries) that kingly rule was successful and necessary. When Alexander the Great invaded India both forms of government existed, republican, whether aristocratic or oligarchic, and monarchical [10]. The greater efficiency of monarchical institutions seems even by that period to have been recognised, and it is not surprising that the ensuing period of the Mauryan emperors saw the beginnings, if not the finished product, of the school of *artha-śāstra*, of which the vast and complex text-book of Kauṭilya is the best-known example, in which monarchy is taken for granted as the only typically Indian form of government.

The ruling classes — and Indian populations were already divided according to occupation and function by Alexander's time — had already resigned priestly, and perhaps most of the academic, functions to the caste of Brahmans (originally 'medicine-men', specialists in sacrificial formulas, and not confined to a hereditary caste) who from then onwards monopolised writing, if not discussion, on the sciences mentioned above. Their long contest with the Buddhists, who for at least a thousand years after the death of the Buddha asserted the right of all classes to education and to intellectual participation in public affairs, ended eventually in the absorption of Buddhism as a living religion once again into Hinduism, and the extinction of specifically Buddhist learning in the fields that concern us. Similarly, other heterodox sects cutting across caste divisions, such as the Jainas, made their own contributions until the middle ages, and then fade from the scene.

At the time of the Mauryas it is evident that a class of administrator was developing. We are not entitled to assume that administration was a hereditary occupation so early as the third

10 DASGUPTA, pp 212 ff. MEGASTHENES is confirmed to a large extent by references in the Kauṭilīya Arthaśāstra. See *Der kleine Pauly*, 3, 'Megasthenes'.

century B.C., but from the recommendation that officers should be chosen from families which had already served the king in administrative posts, a recommendation which is found throughout the literature, it is plausible to conjecture that with imperial, highly concentrated and somewhat centralised government came the discovery that as there were no academies in which the practice (as opposed to the theory) of government could be taught, and as there is no apprenticeship so good as apprenticeship at home, hereditary acquaintance with the nature of responsibilities might very well lead to hereditary aptitudes. This theory is amply borne out by our experience with Brahmans, whose hereditary aptitudes were, to the dismay of their non-Brahman compatriots, soon put to use in very un-Brahmanical contexts during the British period. Groups, even as early as the Maurya period, must have emerged with a special interest in and capacity for administration. But the mass of the public was not concerned with major matters of policy. Details of administration beyond the village-polity or family level were never, so far as we know, the concern of popular gatherings [11].

Mediaeval India, though not so highly organised, continued in the same theoretical tradition. In practice organisation was less thorough, empires were smaller and more fragile, and stability generally less certain. The public, the 'ruled', showed more or less indifference to a change of rulers. Our inscriptional evidence, which from the fourth century A.D. onwards provides an increasingly comprehensive check upon the theoretical literature, supports the prevailing doctrine, namely that the task of the king was to rule, and that this task was not to be shared with others. Nostalgic

[11] This is not to underrate the extent of village self-administration, on which see MATTHAI, cited above. How far the *gaṇas*, the supposed incipient republics, SARMA, *Aspects*, ch. 6, wielded sway over more than a tribe at a time is very doubtful. K.A. NILAKANTA SASTRI, *Studies*, p. 98 : " ... to cast a doubt on the democratic nature of ancient Indian society and government is no longer a mortal sin against patriotism ".

references to non-monarchical organisations appear, suggesting that these were more than memories. Possibly aristocratic or even popular societies survived during this period, but we hear very little of them. Certainly the hill and forest tribes, which had their chiefs, must have been in practice democratic, the chiefs acting as the public's servants (as with our reconstruction of the Vedic age), for the same is found to this day amongst the Scheduled Tribes. But classical Hindu literature does not take account of the *antyajas*, the fringe populations. The literature speaks of the king, a theory so well embedded that the word *rāja* is not displaced by that for emperor, except in specific contexts, and with the arrival of the East India Company the Governor-General and Council were referred to by Hindu scholars as *rāja*, as they were the *de facto* 'king' of their Indian subjects.

The theory of monarchical rule implicitly eliminates popular participation. The *prajāh*, the 'subjects', are related to the king in a number of ways, each of which excludes parity between them. The *rāja* looks after the spiritual needs of the kingdom by exercising his special priestly functions, without which fertility and security will be endangered [12]. The relationship between the earth which the subjects cultivate and the *rāja* is depicted as a mystical relationship symbolised by human marriage. The subjects must obey, and must feed their *rāja*. Certain classes, particularly Vaiśyas, exist primarily to perform this function of feeding, their wealth being available for the replenishing of the royal treasury. There was a kind of natural bargain between the ruler and his subjects,

[12] This aspect of kingship cannot be overemphasised, since the religious functions of the king were, in the public mind, every bit as important as his duties to 'satisfy' the people and protect them from revolution and invasion. See J. GONDA, *Ancient Indian Kingship from the Religious Point of View*, reprint from *Numen*, III and IV, 1956-7; B. SCHLERATH, *Das Königtum im Rig- und Atharvaveda*, Wiesbaden, 1960; J.C. HEESTERMAN, *The Ancient Indian Royal Consecration*, The Hague 1957; J.D.M. DERRETT, « Bhū-bharaṇa, bhū-pālana, bhū-bhojana : an Indian conundrum », *B.S.O.A.S.* 22, 1959, pp. 108 ff.; J.W. SPELLMAN, « Symbolic significance of the number twelve in Ancient India », *J. As. St.*, 22, 1962, pp. 79 ff.

subject to the omniopotent rule of *dharma* ('righteousness'), and it was not an equal bargain. The ruler must, it is alleged, satisfy the subjects. He pleases them by providing them with safety from external attack, and by 'removing thorns', i.e. purging the kingdom of thieves, vagabonds, and the like, and principally by keeping the reign of *dharma* intact. This in principle meant the effectuating of an extremely complex balance of forces, preventing the development of new castes or classes by irregular intermarriages, preventing the increase in non-traditional occupations by the various castes, preventing all deviations from the established order of life, and so not allowing one group to progress at the expense of others. This extremely intricate task, well beyond the powers of even the most competent modern administration, but not altogether outside the aims of a modern Indian government, was indeed the imposition upon society through the *rāja* of a concept of a theoretical character emanating undoubtedly from society itself, fragmented and competitive as it was. But it was the negation of popular participation in government. The *rāja* was needed precisely because the public could never directly attend to the task of repression and balance, often as we find the subjects of relatively weak rulers attempting to do this.

While the groups which made up the public could bring pressure to bear upon the *rāja*, his sacral functions and transcendant duty towards *dharma* enabled him to keep his distance from all of them — a fact facilitating his task of maintaining the established order. Every element of self-government was within the framework of monarchy, and for even village headmen were appointed by the king, and the notion that a group could determine its own future without reference to the *rāja* was foreign to the Hindu outlook. There may have been legally or *de facto* 'self-governing' bodies, particularly where central government was wanting : but there was no government by the 'public' as such. What participation there was was extremely indirect, and only conclusive on the very rare occasions of a rebellion, when one *rāja* was substituted for another. There are no examples of monarchy being overturned and replaced by an aristocracy or oligarchy, or democracy, or indeed by any Indian variant or version of these non-monarchical forms. Republics were, as we have seen, virtually dead before our literature commences.

The notion that India was a land of oriental despotism is easily traced, when we see the facts being analysed and described by the earliest European visitors. These were unaware of the functions of courtiers, and of the pressures exerted by sections of the public; they were dazzled by the poverty of the mass of the people supporting a vast conspicuous expenditure on the part of the *rāja*. In fact the checks and balances of Indian political life kept most *rājas* within reasonable bounds most of the time, and the doctrine that *dharma* was the king whom the *rāja* himself must obey was asserted without shame or fear throughout the historical period. The king has power to do what he wills, but whether he should will it, and what will befall him if he attempts to act contrary to the public's concept of *dharma* are questions that will be ventilated, and decided upon before the apparently boundless powers are used. Indeed the *rāja* is expected to act, whether or not he has ascertained the possible reactions of the public or any section of it : but then it is assumed at the commencement that he has been thoroughly indoctrinated as to his rôle as the spiritual and secular 'father' of his people, and when he is in doubt he has specialist advisers who can tell him what *dharma* requires, a criterion above that of the public's convenience.

European rule led eventually to representative and finally responsible government. The public still retained the idea of *sirkar* ('Government') as a personality, as a kind of *rāja*, even though its decisions might be those of an instable and partial group, whom party-politics had thrown to the top. The public, through its elected representatives, has acquired an indirect voice in national as well as local concerns. This development was the more ardently desired because the fruits of power were visualised as the natural privileges of those whom the *rāja* trusted, and who, for the time being, were able to utilise the immense authority which the royal service conveyed. It would be false to suggest that now the *prajāh* have become *rāja*. The true position is that the subjects (now the 'lower classes', 'lower orders', 'peasantry' and so on) as distinct from the classes having access to power, are ruled by a more complex *rāja*, not more unpredictable that the traditional *rājas*, who disappeared in 1950, but more inexorable, more pervasive, more demanding, and more burdensome. The quarrels between those who have acquired access to power are concerned in reality with the competition between them, which is nothing new, but they are all agreed that the 'lower orders' exist to be milked, just as the *rāja* was taught that the subjects, and their sources of production, existed as the natural 'food' for their ruler. Majority rule now enables the voters to obtain directly and indirectly attention to public complaints of a kind not formerly likely to obtain a hearing; but in the process devastating legislation is passed in furtherance of vast and, some think, visionary schemes, in which the aims and objections of the inert multitude obtain no recognition. The ruthless, planned, motion forward of modern governors in India is in striking contrast to the timid and unprogressive attitude of previous rulers, to whom the comfort and stability of the majority was more of an aim than the remoter prospect of their systematic 'uplift' and improvement. As with everything else Indian, the past casts a shadow over the present, and where the public attempt to participate it is always subject to the reservation that what the *Sirkar* ultimately decides is important must be respected, and this strengthens the hands of those who have sectional, regional, or purely selfish aims to prosecute.

II

Direct government by the public can be posited for the Vedic period. Amongst the republics in northern India assemblies of the entire governing body were known. But sections of the population probably had no direct representation there. Government by assembly direct is otherwise unknown in India.

Representative government as such was introduced by the British, first at the local government, and finally at the provincial and central level, in very gradual stages [13]. Modern India has adopted adult suffrage and representative government at all levels [14].

Representation of the public during mediaeval times is, however, very widely evidenced. But we must not misunderstand the nature of that representation, or its motives. From our texts themselves we obtain information about regional entities (we can hardly call them 'corporations') which could voice local opinion, and which enjoyed some identity, notwithstanding the conflicting interests and diverse origins and ways of life of the groups that made up the population. The phrase *paura-janapada*, 'citizens of the cities and population of the rural areas', and even the word *janapada* itself, which conveys the notion of a district, show that the public, in some vague sense, were a force to contend with, and not a mass upon which a tyrant might play as upon some orchestra. From our inscriptions, as well as from the legal texts, we learn of the common activity of villages, paying revenue, entering into contractual relations with neighbouring villages, joining with other villages of the district to achieve some common object, settling disputes or taking steps to have disputes settled. Not only villages, and even hamlets, are spoken of as acting in these and other ways. The neighbourhood, the sub-division, the district, the country, and rarely (and in poetic terms) the nation are all spoken of as acting, deciding, achieving something, or suffering something [15]. In all

---

[13] A.B. KEITH, *Constitutional History of India*, Oxford, 1935; A. GLEDHILL, *The British Commonwealth... India*², London, 1964. A valuable detailed study is V. VENKATA RAO, *A Hundred Years of Local Self-government and Administration in the Andhra and Madras States* 1850-1950, Bombay, 1960. R.N. Spann, ed., *Constitutionalism in Asia*, London, 1964.

[14] G. AUSTIN, *The Indian Constitution : Cornerstone of a Nation*, Oxford, 1966; M.V. PYLEE, *Constitutional Government in India*², Bombay, 1965; D.D. BASU, *Commentary on the Constitution of India*⁴⁻⁵, 5 vols., Calcutta, 1964-5.

[15] Inscriptional evidence of this phenomenon is handled in the present writer's *Religion, Law and the State in India*, London, 1968, ch. 7.

these contexts, even the poetic and imaginary ones, *representation* is unquestionably envisaged.

Within the village the families were represented by their heads, castes and sub-castes by their natural leaders. A village council, consisting of a group of natural leaders, would speak through a small group, or natural head. Many such heads would meet, but our evidence suggests that they went to the meeting with others who, without diminishing their representative faculty, supported them and assisted them in their rôle. Such a meeting spoke in the name of the unit, whether it was the district, in some matter affecting a locality, or a major caste, in some question relating to caste discipline, morality, or way of life. Evidence of cooperation of many such units, such cross-categories of the population, is ample for the South of India, and we have no reason to doubt its existence in the North likewise.

The intimate blend of religion, caste, land-tenure, revenue, politics, and foreign policy in India made it impossible for any governmental action to take place without attention to the web of pressures and interests that any Indian population must create [16]. No king could function without knowing what degree of cooperation could be obtained from the bodies, categories, cross-categories affected by his plans. To take an example : suppose a rich merchant wanted to leave a memorial to his own wealth (i.e. success) and piety, and favoured the construction of a dam across a valley for the irrigation of his native territory. To flood part of a valley would require considerable administrative activity. To obtain the labour and materials for the dam would likewise mean some dis-

[16] A typically Indian nexus was that between Hindu villages, acting through their headman and *panchayat*, and the chiefs of criminal tribes settled nearby. The chiefs sometimes even resided, or kept their deputies in the villages. It was a system of blackmail whereby the village employed these chiefs to prevent raids on the cattle, housebreaking, and the like. If property was stolen the chiefs had to pay its value (which they no doubt recovered from their 'subjects' afterwards). This system was far more efficient than the governmental police, and often existed alongside the police. See Matthai, ch. 6.

turbance of existing arrangements. It was not merely a question of laying out money. Much goodwill would be needed, and many jealousies must be overcome. The merchant could get his village on his side, and the villages which would be benefitted by the proposed irrigation scheme; but there would be some likelihood that the revenue demand for that villages would be increased, and that possibility would have to be investigated. The inhabitants of the valley above the proposed dam would have to be resettled, and this would involve quarrels with the inhabitants in surrounding areas. The delicate balance between families and even sub-castes would be disturbed, and a great many consents would have to be purchased. Even gods, whose temples would be submerged, would have to be pacified with suitable alternatives. All this would be the task of the king, delegated to his civil representative (who might also be the military governor) in the area. If more than one area were affected two such governors would have to cooperate. At various stages public meetings would be held in which the proposal would be discussed, and a decision made (if possible). The scheme could not succeed unless all the strands of the web were as tight as before the disruption was mooted.

In the interminable consultation and bargaining all groups which were at all concerned would have their say. Even the untouchable castes, whose leaders could hardly form a common committee with the leaders of the 'clean' castes, would be able to exert pressure; since the withdrawal of their labour would make life intolerable for all, particularly the Brahmans, whose prestige was highest [17] and whose access to power was always shorter, if not always more decisive that that of lower castes.

Nowhere was participation by the public completely absent. Even when the king decided to lead or send an army into his neighbour's territory the success of the expedition depended in

[17] One bears in mind that brahmanical ideologies triumphed eventually, but that during the times portrayed by the Buddhist *jātaka* tales and at other periods, for example in mediaeval Tamil-nāḍ, as nowadays in Ceylon, the ruling classes (*kshatriyas* by *varṇa*) were socially superior to the Brahmans.

some measure upon the inhabitants' willingness to find food, fuel, and fodder for the army, and if they heartily disapproved of the scheme they could frustrate his plans, and their cooperation was by no means to be taken for granted, notwithstanding the sacral aspect of kingship and the glorification of war — the question of revenue was the ultimate test of loyalty, and we know that every trick in the king's power was tried before a frank raising of the rate of land-revenue was resorted to [18]. Though the public did not decide upon the size of the revenue demand from an area (this was determined by the kings' ministers) their resistance to demands and insistence upon custom as the arbiter in such matters was a force with which those ministers were perpetually wrestling.

III

We may now approach some of the terms for a meeting of leaders to determine something. The word *sabhā* is ancient, ubiquitous, and of various implications [19]. The *sabhā* (which survives in the words Rajya-sabhā and Lok-sabhā for the two houses of the Indian Parliament since 1950) was a deliberative body. Only since the British period have such bodies had a definite constitution. In earlier times *sabhā* existed for recurrent purposes, or *ad hoc*. In the texts we are told that the king must have a *sabhā* to advise him. With the king or his deputy added to it the *sabhā* became both advisory and, indirectly, executive. This is particularly to be noted in juridical matters, though the rule that the ruler must have a 'court' in such connexions seems not to have been obeyed in all parts of the country at all times. In pre-British times a *sabhā* was properly constituted if it contained properly qualified people, whose views were likely to be objective [20], and did not exclude

[18] See J.D.M. Derrett, *The Hoysalas*, Madras, 1957, ch. 7.

[19] See Sharma, *Aspects*, index, s.v.; Kane, op. cit., pp. 92 ff. Also n. 20 below.

[20] The subject of ministers (*amātya, saciva, mantri*) is different, but the recommendations of the *śāstras* as to the qualifications of ministers and members of a *sabhā* had similarities. For the *sabhyas* who acted as assessors in judicial work and their qualifications see Kane, op. cit., 272-3.

personalities whose consent to the ultimate decision would have been desired by a substantial group in order to give it validity in their eyes. The *sabhā* thus had a 'natural' membership, based ultimately upon the acceptance and respect of the public, or the parts of the public that would be affected by the decision.

The *pariṣad* was an expert committee. The origin of the word is obscure. Perhaps it implies a committee sitting around their chief [21]. It is found in various contexts, e.g. a *pariṣad* of Brahmans to advise authoritatively on law, or of ministers or officials to advise the king. Other names for committees or public gatherings are found [22]. In all cases we suppose that consultation, and decision are implied, but where the body concerned is advisory it was naturally left to the official who was being advised to make up his mind. The leaders' judgment was respected, and was binding upon those whom they represented, but there is no trace whatever of a rule that the king, or any of his deputies or ministers should be bound by the advice of any committee or public meeting.

Many consultative bodies were of great age and required no authorisation from the ruler in order to be convened. In mediaeval times we find traces of a notion that a representative of the ruler should summon a meeting, or be present at a meeting in order to lend some prestige to the proceedings and, if possible, weight and decisiveness to the decision, if any, to be arrived at. District, professional, or caste meetings could be held at the summons of the leaders or headmen of the caste and without royal command.

We often hear of the 'district', which was in a sense permanent, but permanent bodies as such did not exist. Members of a *sabhā* were called *sabhāsad(s)*; the term does not imply permanent, or any other long membership, since the qualifications could be lost, often unpredictably, as by an indiscreet proposal, and confidence

[21] SHARMA, op. cit., 191, K.V.R. AIYANGAR, *Rājadharma*, pp. 99-100. A specialised use of the term is discussed at length in KANE, op. cit., vol. 2, pt. 2, 966-72.

[22] *Samiti, vidatha* : attempts to lay down their functions and composition have failed. SHARMA at *J.R.A.S.* 1965, pp. 43-56 attributes *religious* functions to the latter. *Pūga* may have been the village assembly.

could be withdrawn from below, or a better-equipped rival could oust the former representative. In modern India by contrast the members of the central and state legislatures have tenures limited by the constitution. The traditionally-minded assumed that membership should be for life, unless the representative disqualified himself by indiscretions; but equally strange to them is the principle of election.

Designation of members of consultative and executive bodies was by birth only in the early republics of which we have spoken, and to the extent that membership of a caste was by birth. In later times, that is to say in the typical Hindu polity, age, character, prestige selected the 'natural' leader. No voting to elect a member took place until the introduction of this notion by the British. The ancient arrangement still survives in caste-councils and *panchayats*, which by no means always coincide with the new statutory, elected *grām-panchayats* and *nyāya-panchayats* that function in the same areas [23]. The traditional *panchayats* still function in matrimonial matters, attempting to reconcile spouses who are estranged, and ultimately, if necessary, granting them divorces. The hostility with which such divorces, and the traditional procedure by which they are granted, are viewed by the established courts (which are necessarily largely Anglo-Indian in tone and outlook) as evidence of the clash between the 'old' India and the 'new' which finds expression even in this field [24]. Like the ancient *pariṣad* the modern

[23] The constitution of modern *panchayats* and their varied functions are dealt with in a comprehensive article by H. Tinker, « The Village in the Framework of Development,» in Braibanti and Spengler, ed., *Administration*, 1963, at p. 94 ff. The *nyāya*, or judicial *panchayat*, is a controversial institution. See *Law Commission of India*, 14th Report (Judicial Administration), 1958, vol. 2, ch. 43, pp. 874-925; *Report of the Study Team on Nyaya Panchayats*, April, 1962, Govt. of India, Ministry of Law; also R.S. Robins, « India : Judicial panchayats in Uttar Pradesh », *Am. J. Comp. L.*, 11, 1962, pp. 239-46. A useful work is S.V. Samant, *Village Panchayats*, Bombay, 1957, ch. 2 of which deals with village *panchayats* in ancient India and in the middle ages. *

[24] The tone is evidenced in *Kishenlal* v. *Mst. Prabhu* All India Reporter, 1963, Rajasthan section, p. 95.

traditional *panchayat* may well amount only to one 'expert' in whom the public should, for the limited purpose in hand, repose confidence.

IV

Assemblies and committees in mediaeval, and to a limited extent likewise in modern India, met and meet to consult; not as a means of validating pre-conceived policies and schemes. The power of decision, as we have seen, rested with the ruler in those contexts where the meeting met to advise the ruler. But on the other hand the *sabhā* might well meet, as otherwise individual ministers might approach the ruler independently, in order to discuss a project initiated entirely by the *janapada*, or by a caste, or by some individual such as the merchant in our illustration. Where the project came before a ruler already furnished with the consents of the relevant prestigious or powerful groups it would be a relatively simple matter to obtain the ruler's *fiat*. The duty of the ruler to satisfy the public enabled them to rely upon his favourable reception of a petition for royal assent to a properly investigated scheme. The decision of a traditional assembly, especially if it purported to declare custom, or to re-establish or reform custom, could be sure of royal approval, which would sometimes be necessary to coerce dissidents, especially if the latter were intending to leave the caste and or the locality in any event.

The British period introduced a novelty. The ruler, i.e. first the East India company and later the Crown, allowed, without authorising, the decisions of traditional assemblies, such a caste-*panchayat*, provided that these were consistent with natural justice (a requirement related only to judicial activity). The theory that the decision was that of the ruler advised by the *panchayat* seems to have survived. It is most unfortunate that we have no evidence of a decision of a *sabhā* or *pariṣad* being taken to a ruler for his cancellation [25]. But the practice of having, if possible, a representative of the ruler present at the debates shows a fear that a decision might be upset ultimately by the ruler. The fact that in the early days of the East India Company's rule decisions by caste-tribunals. including those relating to nominations for headship of religious institutions, were eagerly sought be to set aside, whether by cancellation or appeal judicially, supports the view that the ruler's ultimate responsibility for the spiritual and secular welfare of the subjects was sufficient authority for his setting aside (if he dared) a decision of a popular or other traditional assembly. But our evidence for medieval times does not amount to this. On the contrary, what we find is that solemn decisions of high-powered and numerous tribunals representative of many points of view and many conflicting interests were reopened by further complaints and further investigations, until ultimately the antagonists, worn out by the conflict, accepted some practical and 'just' solution [26].

Redressing of grievances was a favourite topic for debate. The duty to abate a grievance was that of the ruler, and apparently that of the ruler alone.

Public control over the ruler or his deputy was exercised indirectly by dilatoriness in paying taxes, refusal of cooperation, threats of revolution. No doubt great tact was used in all such * crises. Appeals were made to the higher order of things, trans-

[25] We have evidence of a regular court's refusing to allow a *panchayat* to annul a marriage. Instances are not rare where action in a caste *panchayat* has led to, or has been followed by, litigation in a regular court, and there is one instance where the custom upon which a *panchayat* purported to settle a dispute was held void as contrary to public policy : *Keshav Hargovan* v. *Bai Gandi*, Indian Law Reports, 1915, Bombay series, vol. 39, p. 538. Nowadays the courts refuse to handle caste custom, and where a divorce may be obtained according to such custom the regular court will not have any part in the proceedings : *Mt. Savitri Devi* A.I.R., 1958, Himachal Pradesh section, p. 15.

[26] For mediaeval instances see *Annual Reports of Epigraphy* (Madras) for 1922, stone inscription no. 416 of 1921; ibid. for 1913, no. 195 of 1912. And see also the sanctions of the *rājaguru* (royal spiritual teacher) and the *samaya* ('assembly') mentioned in *Mysore Archaelogical Report* for 1910-11, para. 105.

cendental obligations, moral law, to *dharma*. This is the reason for all the vague and highflying exhortations in the *dharma-śāstra* in its *rāja-dharma-kāṇḍa* [27]. A ruler whose schemes dismayed many could be frustrated by having his audience-chambers besieged by daily visits from caste-leaders or their spokesmen and representatives of merchant and other powerful classes, patiently waiting for grievances to be redressed!

We are in a position to see public participation in government from two points of view. In the background, ever-present, is the half-detached, half-jealous concern of the people that the ruler shall perform his traditional functions. Their views are voiced by 'natural' representatives. In the foreground the public participates in two obvious ways : (i) by supplying a caste or cadre of skilled administrators competent to look after, primarily, finance and the 'peace' of the population; (ii) by providing assessors or even judges, and expert committees of jurists to deal with legal business. At periods with a lack of a sufficient number of people with a belief in or skill in the relevant *śāstras*, and the will to apply their knowledge, together with, perhaps, a state of affairs in which appeal to traditional learning was ineffective to settle disputes, deputies of the ruler acted as adjudicators. There is little ground for expecting a third contribution from the public, namely by way of the army (which was also the force to maintain order in other than minor village disturbances). Most soldiers were, in mediaeval times, persons of low caste, criminals, slaves [28], or part-time soldiers who were also agriculturalists.

But in contrast to this situation, sometimes wrongly described as possessing the features of permanent institutions and 'local

[27] See A.K. Sen, *Studies*, 1926, pp. 65 ff.; Kane, *H.D.*, III, pp. 56 ff., is particularly rich, compiled with the author's usual balance, discrimination and compression.

[28] The legal status of slaves in India until the early decades of the British period is not without its obscurities : the subject is handled, with complete bibliography in Yvonne Bongert's « Réflexions sur le problème de l'esclavage dans l'Inde ancienne », *B. l'Ecole Francaise d'Extrême-Orient*, 51, 1963, pp. 143-194.

self-government' upon western lines, there is evidence of a modification which deserves very close examination. It remains to be determined whether what we find in this evidence is an exception to the general rule, or merely a particular instance of the spirit and practice of mediaeval India which would be more generalised if the conditions had been more general. In South India there existed numerous *agrahāras*, namely colonies or settlements of Brahmans, living upon lands donated to them for the maintenance of their various *śāstras*. The holdings of land were approximately equal, but the lands were naturally not tilled by the Brahmans themselves but by their dependants, families of lower castes who were specialists in agriculture. The internal government of these *agrahāras* was established in the charters granted at the time of their foundations. According to these the committee of government was actually elected, and there were rules preventing the re-election of persons who had held a seat on the committee after a certain length of time. Rules of procedure were laid down to ensure a democratic control of the affairs of the colony, but of course the electing of the members, and the right to be a member, were confined to the share-holders themselves. The rules and constitution of such *agrahāras* have aroused a merited interest [29]. But they are to be seen as elaborate schemes intended to secure the peaceful management of what was virtually a club in respect of its domestic affairs. The district as a whole, and the kingdom, were certainly not run upon any such lines. It was an exception which proved a rule.

No legislative power lay with any assembly without the actual or nominal consent and 'enactment' of the ruler. But here it is very difficult to generalise. There *is* evidence of villages, and even subdivisions, making ordinances which shall be binding upon inhabitants; likewise castes and communities in full assembly make

[29] Uttaramērūr. Dealt with exhaustively by K.A. Nilakanta Sastri, *Studies in Cōla History and Administration*, Madras, 1932, especially ch. 3-6; and handled at Altekar, *State and Government*, pp. 230-4; Matthai, pp 25-9. *

regulations to be binding thenceforward upon their members — in both cases without overt reference to the ruler or his deputy [30]. It would appear that in matters of custom which did *not* affect the revenue, and where outsiders could not be affected, the powers of excommunication possessed by the local assemblies were sufficient to enable legislation to be effective, and constitutionally allowable, even without the ruler's participation. It was otherwise where the ruler was the patron of the region, where local committees were weak, or where it was necessary to coerce persons outside the reach of bodies which could exert force only by way of excommunication. We have to remember that, in general, force of a coercive character such as mutilations and imprisonment were beyond the powers of any but the ruler and his deputies. The king's own powers of legislation were confined to his traditional fields of secular regulation. He could not interfere with ritual or moral ordinances, though he could certainly, by regulation, take away one of the alternatives which the religious law might allow, or require some conditions to be observed, provided that this could be supported from the *dharma-śāstra.*

The villages themselves, basing their activity upon the sanction of custom, exercised considerable executive powers, particularly in the way of apportioning the revenue, and in policing their districts.

---

30 On law-making and rule-making in ancient India there are divergent views. The majority believe that no legislative power existed. This is not accepted by A.K. SEN, who has (rightly) no hesitation in speaking of 'positive law'. See J.D. M. DERRETT « Law and custom in ancient India : Sources and authority », *Rev. Int. Dr. Ant.*, 3rd. ser., 9, 1962, pp. 11-32. One may note in addition to primary and secondary references there given that in Yājñ. II, 166 (with the commentary *Mitākṣarā* by Vijñāneśvara) we learn of the king (!) or the village settling the extent of pastures. This is by-law, but none the less law. ALTEKAR joins issue with JAYASWAL as to whether *déśa-samaya* (lit. 'country-agreement' --- in Arth. III. ch. 10) or *grāma-samaya* (lit. 'village-agreement') mean law or resolutions by village or district 'legislative' bodies (*State and Government*, p. 149-150). In ALTEKAR's view the words mean agreements between individuals and their village or district corporate bodies. This may not be impossible, but JAYASWAL's interpretation accords better with the present writer's reading of the obscure sources. See *J.A.O.S.* 84, 1964, pp. 392-5.

Control of the police, exercise of petty criminal jurisdiction, and supervision of the market were in the hands of officials appointed by the village elders. In times of poor central organisation we find judicial powers exercised by very large courts, whose members represented wide areas of territory and perhaps the main castes in the region. The larger the court, the greater chance that the decision would be respected by the parties [31].

Historical instances of ministers supplanting their masters and becoming *de facto* and even *de jure* kings themselves are not rare. Political theory in mediaeval South India contemplated constitutions in which the kings delegated large responsibility to their ministers and virtually ruled along with them [31a].

Modern India allows participation of the public indirectly through local committees known as *panchayats* (referred to above) whose scope of activities is naturally narrow [32], and through the state and central legislatures, to which ultimately the municipal and government authorities are responsible. Public participation in justice exists by way of the caste-*panchayats* referred to above and in the jury-system for criminal trials in certain courts : both of these fields for participation are so narrow that they may virtually be ignored. The civil service, as trained specialists, handle the day-to-day business of government, subject to the interference of politicians who want favours for their supporters.

V

The method of deliberation, both in ancient times and today, appears to have been with the seniormost speaking first. The young,

---

[31] That appears to be the explanation of the very large courts evidenced in V.T. Gune's *Judicial System of the Marathas*, Poona, 1953.

[31a] It is to be regretted that historical evidence of this is wanting (there is evidence of subinfeudation leading to weakness at the centre, but that is different). For the theory of the three kinds of constitution see Someśvara, *Abhilashitārthachintāmaṇi* (*Mānasollāsa*), II, 8, Mysore, 1926, pp. 110-111.

[32] The avowed policy of the present constitution, and its implementation, is more and more decentralisation. See article of Tinker referred to above.

no matter how qualified, are supposed to remain silent in the presence of elders, unless invited to contribute. The concept of an individual putting his own view-point is un-Indian. There are two reasons for this. Firstly speech, especially public speech, is not a method of frank and uninhibited self-expression. One must observe one's relationships in all contexts, particularly in public; and the relationship which is for the moment uppermost may remove completely a consciousness of a private and individual view-point. Secondly individuals whose own interests conflicted with those of the group to which they belonged must always have been rare. An individual without a group would in any case never obtain a hearing in, or membership of, a *sabhā* of any kind. The principles governing debate in any worldly *sabhā* would apply equally to meetings of unwordly people, *sanyāsīs* who had nominally abandoned the world and its etiquette; and deference and disinclination to obtrude a selfish or individual viewpoint would be as much required of a *sanyāsī* as of a householder.

In the Vedic period decision *may* have taken place by majority. Traces of majority decision exist in Buddhist texts, based, as we suppose, upon the secular practice of the aristocratic societies. Acclamation and even voting with voting tickets are referred to. With the disappearance of institutions (save for the *agrahāras* referred to above) in which members were theoretically equal, decision by majority disappeared. All decisions in India were, until the advent of European-type institutions, unanimous. Until unanimity was achieved decision was postponed [33]. If it became imperative to take a decision, schism was risked. Hence voting, and counting of heads are quite uncharacteristic of India, and modern

[33] There was no majority vote in historical times. The present writer is preparing a treatment of the majority principle in India, of which traces remain from extremely early times, only to disappear gradually, even in regard to the composition and size of judicial tribunals. See Speech of SIR HERBERT RISLEY in the Bengal Legislative Council, July 23, 1892, quoted by MATTHAI, p. 31; and when DASGUPTA speaks of elective monarchy at his p. 178 ff., it is made clear that he does not envisage majority decision as such even in the very remote times under discussion.

India had has difficulty in assimilating this innovation. The tendency seems to be to elect the man whom one would, on traditional grounds, wish to have as one's representative; the notion that the candidate who has failed to win the election does *not* represent anybody is also an uncongenial notion. Appeals to the electorate for votes are a novel feature of the Indian scene, they frequently take the form of attempting to associate the candidate with some principle (cutting across caste where possible and utilising caste-alignments where not) which the voter is expected to approve of, whoever the candidate might be. This is an uneasy combination of Indian and western approaches to selection of a representative. To test the theory that counting of heads is anathema to traditional India one might observe how decisions are made in so westernised an organisation as a trade-union meeting. The present writer would be very surprised to learn that decisions are made by a show of hands. If this ever occurs the union is indeed far from the 'old' India.

VI

By associating the ruler or his deputy with the committee or assembly an attempt was made, where possible, to unite the prestige of government with the prestige of social opinion. Only in highly technical fields, such as Brahmanical ritual and secrets of artisan and other guilds, would the ruler be excluded. The organs of power and the organs of public expression were thus normally interdependent if they had any force at all. Public resistance to un-traditional acts on the part of the ruler could amount to prohibition. By evading participation in the schemes of A the general public could convey prestige away from A and towards B. No one was compelled to take part in anything unless he would transgress caste usage by idleness. The result must have been the same self-contained character of the habitual 'participators' that we find in modern, non-bureaucratic countries.

Since leaders were natural and not elective they were not responsible to the public whom they represented. This historical background explains a feature of modern Indian politics. Members of the legislatures, even members of cabinets, are likely to be re-elected even if their policies are disapproved of by the majority of the legislature in question and all the organs of public opinion.

VII

The movement towards a government responsible to the 'man in the street' requires the development of two non-traditional entities. Firstly the concept of the 'man in the street', the citizen as such detached from the pervasive mutual bargaining, the casteism and regionalism of which modern politicians constantly complain; and secondly a concept of a representative's dependence upon his constitituents. At present the individual Indian, especially in the vast rural areas, is lacking in personality and sees himself, and is seen by politicians, as merely a member of a group, or rather of many concentric groups, the interests of which, in sum, can be predicted. Corruption, the oiling of the wheels of administration, favouritism, and all the inequalities of which people complain, happen because the only interests which strike the politician as real are those of his immediate supporters and those of the vast, scarcely comprehensible unit, the state or region from which he is sent to Parliament or the Legislative Assembly. Personal participation in government is therefore that of the politician and of those to whose pressures he must submit. He is not dependant upon all the constituents, for if he still carries with them an inherited prestige or a prestige acquired by any of the traditional methods, he can be re-elected whatever his policies, or even if he has no policies. Responsible government, which is not merely a question of governing so as not to lose the confidence of the legislative body, cannot occur without a much tighter link between the constituent and the politician than subsists at present. At present, while the Indian government is still the bearer of the prestige of the pre-

Independence *Sirkar*, the members of Parliament and M.L.A.'s are petty *rājas*, a rôle for which many of them are hardly equipped. But the people get a governemnt which they deserve, and the average Indian does not see, as yet, a perceptible shortening of the distance between the *Sirkar* and himself; and it will be long before he can view himself as a distinct entity in this process of communication.

It is conceivable that a more genuine trend will appear. Instead of the dramatic choices at the polls and the secret influences exerted on M.P.'s and M.L.A.'s, ideals may be achieved through compromises and delays. The *Sirkar* of today is much too precipitate and active for the liking of the traditionally minded. There is too much government. Public money, in too large quantities, flows too fast and in too many directions. Upon the theory of the consent of the people, schemes are inaugurated in great numbers, to which no recognisable people can be assumed to have consented. The fact that a government remains in office is taken largely as carte blanche, and the credit for achieving Independence enabled the Congress Party to remain in power without effective opposition. The traditional deference goes to untraditional lengths for untraditional ends. The best illustration is the draconic alteration of the personal laws of the Hindus, an example of what appears to be a tyrannical reform of society, in the best humanitarian and 'civilising' interests of the nation [34]. There the lack of an intimate connexion between the public and the legislature enabled a very radical, and in places a rather poorly-drafted, code to be enacted, irrespective of the question whether it would be known to or understood, let alone obeyed, by the multitude of Hindus. Perhaps a new method of democratic government will evolve rather than the present adaptation of democratic forms to ends which are not noticeably democratic as that word is understood in democratic

[34] J.D.M. Derrett, « The codification of personal law in India : Hindu law », *Ind. Y. Book of Int. Aff.*, 1956; the same, «Statutory amendments of the personal law of Hindus since Indian Independence», *Rapp. Gén. Ve. Cong. Int. Dr. Comparé*, 1958, Bruxelles, 1960, pp. 101-24.

countries. Yet it must be admitted of the present set-up in India that it is no tyranny as that word is understood in the West. Elements which are at odds with the government are free to exist, if not always to express themselves, and dissidence is as free as it was before Independence, or indeed before the British period[35]. Prestige-worthy elements in the population obtain a hearing in the highest quarters, and that is roughly what could be hoped of traditional Indian governmental machinery, at its best, at any time prior to, and even sometimes during, the Muslim period.

* * *

BIBLIOGRAPHY

The work of U.N. Ghoshal, though — as are most of the works by single authors — flat and pedestrian, is the most complete and reliable. An instinct to check theory by evidence of fact is curiously missing in all quarters, but an ability to utilise factual material is well evidenced in A.S. Altekar's book, for he was a political historian and epigraphist as well as a historian of Indian thought. That by B.A. Saletore has the scope of a comprehensive work, but the author has a reputation for more industry than accuracy or judgment.

Radhakumud Mookerji, *Local Governmment in Ancient India*, 2nd. edn., Oxford 1920, repr. 1958.
N.N. Law, *Aspects of Ancient Indian Polity*, Oxford, 1921.
R.C. Majumdar, *Corporate Life in Ancient India*, 2nd. edn., Calcutta, 1922.
A. Hillebrandt, *Altindische Politik*, Jena, 1923.
K.P. Jayaswal, *Hindu Polity*, Calcutta, 1924.
Ajit K. Sen, *Studies in Hindu Political Thought*, Calcutta, 1926.
N.C. Bandyopadhyaya, *Development of Hindu Polity and Political Theories*, Calcutta, 1927.
Beni Prasad, *The State in Ancient India*, Allahabad, 1928.
D.R. Bhandarkar, *Some Aspects of Ancient Indian Polity*, Benares, 1929.

[35] This must be stated subject to the government's exercise of its constitutional powers of Preventive Detention, and to the conditions which obtain in a State of Emergency. See also the Unlawful Activities (Prevention) Act, 1967.

V.R.R. Dikshitar, *Hindu Administrative Institutions*, Madras, 1929.
V.R.R. Dikshitar, *Mauryan Polity*, Madras, 1932.
K.V. Rangaswami Aiyangar, *Aspects of Ancient Indian Economic Thought*, Benares, 1934.
K.V. Rangaswami Aiyangar, *Rājadharma*, Adyar, 1941.
K.A. Nilakanta Sastri, *Studies in Cōḷa History and Administration*, Madras, 1932.
A.S. Altekar, *State and Government in Ancient India*, 1949, 4th edn., Delhi, etc., 1962.
K.V. Rangaswami Aiyangar, *Aspects of the Social and Political System of Manusmṛti*, Lucknow, 1949.
T.V. Mahalingam, *South Indian Polity*, Madras, 1955.
W.H. Morris-Jones, *Parliament in India*, London, 1957.
Myron Weiner, *Party Politics in India*, 1957.
U.N. Ghoshal, *History of Indian Political Ideas*, Bombay, Oxford U.P., 1959.
R.S. Sharma, *Śūdras in Ancient India*, Delhi, 1958.
R.S. Sharma, *Aspects of Political Ideas and Institutions in Ancient India*, Delhi, 1959.
C.H. Philips, ed., *Politics and Society in India*, London, 1963.
B.A. Saletore, *Ancient Indian Political Thought and Institutions*, London, 1963.
J.W. Spellman, *Political Theory of Ancient India*, Oxford, 1964.
C. Drekmeier, *Kingship and Community in Early India*, Stanford, 1962.
R. Braibanti and J.J. Spengler, ed., *Administration and Economic Development in India*, Durham, N.C./Cambridge, 1963.
R.H. Retzlaff, *Village Government in India*, New York, 1962.
D.E. Smith, ed., *South Asian Politics and Religion*, Princeton, 1966.
G.S. Sharma, ed., *Secularism : its Implications for Law and Life in India*, Bombay, 1966.
M.P. Jain, *Outlines of Indian Legal History*, 2d edn., Bombay, 1966.
H.R. Tinker, *The Foundations of Local Self-government in India, Pakistan and Burma*, London, 1954.
H.R. Tinker, *South Asia, a short History*, London, 1966.
G.S. Dikshit, *Local Self-Government in Mediaeval Karṇātaka*, Dharwar, 1964.
D. Rothermund, *Die politische Willensbildung in Indien 1900-1960*, Wiesbaden, 1965.
R.P. Kangle, *The Kauṭilīya Arthaśāstra. Part III. A Study*, Bombay, 1965.
M. Hidayatullah, *Democracy in India and the Judicial Process*, London, 1966.
Myron Weiner : *Party Building in a New Nation. The Indian National Congress*, Chicago, 1968.

ADDITIONAL ANNOTATIONS

p. [54], n. 9. J.P. Sharma, *Republics in Ancient India c. 1500 B.C. - 500 B.C.* (Leiden, 1968), rev. T. Burrow, *B.S.O.A.S.* 34/2 (1971), 416-17. Shobha Mukerji, *The Republican Trends in Ancient India* (Delhi, 1969), rev. W.D. O'Flaherty, *B.S.O.A.S.* 34/1 (1971), 208.

p. [66], n. 23. *Processual Justice to the People. Report of the Expert Committee on Legal Aid (May 1973)* (Delhi, Govt. of India, 1974), 39-40, 137-45.

p. [68], l. 22. W. Ruben, 'Fighting against despots in the Old Indian literature', *A.B.O.R.I.*, 48-9 (1968), 111-18.

p. [70], n. 29. F. Gros, 'Uttaramerur revisited', *Prof. K.A.N. Sastri Fel. Vol.* (Madras, 1971), 191-4. F. Gros and R. Nagaswamy, *Uttaramerur, Légendes, Histoire, Monuments* (Pondichery, 1970).

VYAVAHĀRA: LIGHT ON A VANISHED CONTROVERSY FROM AN UNPUBLISHED FRAGMENT *

No one interested in the Classical Hindu Law could read Dr. S. K. Belvalkar's *Critical Note to Śāntiparva, Adhyāya* 121, *śl.* 14 and ff.,[1] without experiencing a great curiosity. The important account given by Bhīṣma of the nature and purpose of *Daṇḍa* (Punishment) incidentally produces an Indian counterpart to the Roman *jus naturale*, the full implications of which deserve investigation elsewhere. Amongst the details we find a description of *Daṇḍa* as follows :—

nīlōtpala-dala-śyāmaś=caturdaṃṣṭraś=caturbhujaḥ
aṣṭapān=naikanayanaś=śaṅkukarṇōrdhvarōmavān
jaṭī dvi-jihvas tāmrāsyō mṛga-rāja-tanucchadaḥ
ētad-rūpaṃ bibharty=ugraṃ Daṇḍō nityaṃ durāvaraḥ.

Because it is awe-inspiring, yet systematic, its qualities capable of classification, Bhīṣma finds it convenient to personify *Daṇḍa*, which he later exalts as a divinely instituted means whereby Kings may preserve their position and thereby the ' everlasting order ' which human life, amongst other kinds of existence, was supposed to exemplify. The metaphor is not expounded, and we are forced to turn for an explanation to the commentaries, of which Dr. Belvalkar gives a brief account. From the end of his summary it appears that whereas Arjunamiśra in his *Bhāratārtha-dīpikā* and Nīlakaṇṭha in his *Bhārata-bhāva-dīpa* pretty generally agree as to the meaning of the passage, Vimalabōdha in his *Durghaṭārthaprakāśini* quotes a ' somewhat different interpretation ' by Bhōja-dēva as given in his *Vyavahāra-mañjarī.* This * reference is of the greatest importance as, though it has been known for a long time that the polymath Bhōja, King of Dhārā, was devoted to the study of the Dharmaśāstra among other *śāstras*, and made numerous original contributions to it,[2] the name of his chief legal work was not known until this discovery from Vimalabōdha. Moreover, whereas a close consideration of this riddle-like text * is not out of place in a commentary on the *Mahābhārata* itself, it is curious that a practical mind such as Bhōja's should have found it worth while to expend time and energy on what seems a laudatory fantasy. Bhōja, who preceded Vijñānēśvara by not more than half a century (he lived between A.D. 1000 and 1055), can hardly have taken pains to interpret this passage, which not only Vijñānēśvara but his illustrious predecessors Asahāya, Medhātithi, Bhavaswāmi and Viśvarūpa, and all his successors, with one exception, ignore, unless he had some special object in view.

The present writer has not inspected the text of Vimalabōdha's work,[3] but a copy of a fragment of a work on judicial administration, *Vyavahāra-vidhāna*,

[1] Fasciscule 19 of the B.O.R.I. edition, published 1950. *
[2] Kane, *History of Dharmaśāstra*, vol. i, pp. 275–9, also *J.B.B.R.A.S.*, 1925, pp. 223–4.
[3] It is MS. no. 84 of 1869–1870 in the Bombay Government Collection at the B.O.R.I., Poona.

recently obtained from the Sarasvati Mahal Library at Tanjore [1] shows that its anonymous author found it necessary to copy, or virtually to copy, Vimalabodha's treatment of the point, and from the fragment it is possible to reconstruct Bhōja's attitude to this curious passage. In the first place Bhōja cut down the quotation from the *Śāntiparva* to one and a half *ślōkas*, so that the half-*ślōka* which applies the description to *Daṇḍa* is omitted, leaving it open to him to apply the words to *Vyavahāra*. This is not so unwarranted as it might seem, for Bhīṣma's speech makes it clear that *Vyavahāra*, in the wide sense of ' order ' or ' world-plan ',[2] comes down to earth, as it were, so as to coalesce at one point with *Daṇḍa*. This occurs when a case comes up before the King and it becomes possible that a penalty must be awarded against one of the parties, the decision depending not upon the self-evident text of the *Vēda* or of the *smṛti* as a *Vēda*-inspired authority, but upon the interpretative faculty of the ruler. This class of *Daṇḍa* he calls *bhartṛ-pratyaya-lakṣaṇa*. This expression Dr. Belvalkar would translate, ' characterized by its dependence upon evidence produced by the parties', giving *bhartṛ* the meaning ' litigant '. It seems, rather, that the author of that portion of the *Mahābhārata* viewed the King in his Court as dispensing a justice which, though depending upon the ultimate, superior *Vyavahāra*, in practice amounted to a personal responsibility, in which the parties must have confidence if *Daṇḍa* in its civil and criminal contexts was to have its proper effect. Thus both *Daṇḍa* and *Vyavahāra* could be, as Bhīṣma says in *ślōkas* 48, 50, and 56, *bhartṛ-pratyaya-lakṣaṇa*, and to that extent the two amounted to the same thing. But could this conception affect the actual administration of justice ? Bhōja-dēva evidently thought that it could, and he was followed in this notion not only by Vimalabōdha, who may not have been a lawyer, but also by the author of the *Vyavahāra-vidhāna* who sought to satisfy an 18th-century ruler of Tanjore, a member of a family that took its judicial responsibilities very seriously.[3] A glance at the parallel interpretations of the *sārdha-ślōka* will make the reason apparent.

> ' *Dark like the petal of a blue lotus* ' (?)—Arjunamiśra and T (the Tanjore MS.) : black and white because of the manifestation of truth and falsehood on the part of the plaintiff and defendant ; Bhōja : *Vyavahāra* is a contradiction between the plaintiff and defendant who are both manifesting truth and falsehood, and he (i.e. *Vyavahāra*) is a person partaking of both

[1] Where it is MS. no. 670B/19001D.

[2] To Kane's account of the meaning of *Vyavahāra* (op. cit., vol. iii, pp. 245–8) one must add a note to the effect that the *Kauṭilīya* uses the word in III i (Triv. ed. ii, pp. 1 and ff.) in the sense of contract capable of legal effect. In the established context of ' lawsuit ' the best discussion of the real meaning of the word is found in the *Vīramitrōdaya* at the commencement of the *Vyavahāra-prakāśa*. From Kane's summary alone it is evident that the problem raised by this *Śāntiparva* text was relegated to the background before those controversies started. Whether *vyavahāra* was a matter of ventilation of grievances, or the actual adjudication, or the process of trial could be discussed only among those who were certain that it was a phenomenon independent of theological and teleological associations.

[3] T bears the name of its owner, Tuljā-jī. Śarabho-jī (Serfoji) was particularly zealous in this subject.

characters on account of his comprehending the *dharmas* of both of them. The expression '*nīlōtpala-dala-śyāmaḥ*' signifies properly one whose character is part black and part white (like the Ganges and Jumna at Prayāga), because (here) both parties manifest truth and falsehood.

'*Of four tusks*'—Nīlakaṇṭha : the modes of punishment (rebuke, fine, mutilation, putting to death). T : the four knowers of the *Vēda* and *Dharma*, for they are the means by which lawlessness is put down : reference to Yājñavalkya i, 9. Bhōja : no comment.

'*Of four arms*'—Arjunamiśra and T : he enjoys and protects the four castes and four *āśramas*, because without *Vyavahāra* the result would be chaos. Nīlakaṇṭha : four arms with which to take four kinds of revenue (this clearly applies only to *Daṇḍa*). Bhōja : (probably, as what follows * must be transposed from after *ubhayor nayanāni yasmin* to before *tathobhayoś=catvāraḥ pādāḥ*) because of the four syllables in *vya-va-hā-ra* : reference to the text [1] *caturakṣare tu nivṛtta.*

'*Of eight feet*'—(Here we might have expected either a reproduction of Nārada i, 10, on the bases of Law, or a reference to the *vyavahāra-padas*, or subdivisions of litigation.) T's point of view does not square with that referred to by Dr. Belvalkar nor with that of Nīlakaṇṭha : the eight feet consist of the four defences (equivalent to the English denial, admission, confession and avoidance and *res judicata*), where Nīlakaṇṭha suggests the eight possible elements of a lawsuit, *plus* the two methods of investigation, human and divine, and the decision—here one *pāda* seems to be omitted. Bhōja : the four feet of the parties themselves (!) *plus* the group of four consisting of plaint,[2] reply and settlement of burden of proof (which * generally involves the decision itself with it).

'*Of many eyes*'—Arjunamiśra, Vimalabōdha, and T : means of proof (capable of leading to a decision) consisting of documents, witnesses, and possession.[3] Nīlakaṇṭha : the eyes consist of the King, his ministers and priests, and the Court. Bhōja : the many eyes of the parties.

'*Of pointed ears*'—Arjunamiśra : the ears are anger and greed. T : the two *firm* ears signify the *dharmaśāstra* and the *arthaśāstra* which must be used to guide the *Vyavahāra* along : reference to Nārada i, 31/38. Bhōja : he has spear-like ears consisting of obstinate anger and greed (on the part of the parties, scil.).

'*Of hair standing on end*'—T : *ūrdhvāni sthirī-bhūtāni lōmāni sthūla-bhūta-puruṣāśraya-rūpāni nyāya-śarīra-bahir-bhūtāni yasya tadvān*, which presumably (but by no means certainly) means that the hairs standing stiff on the body of *Vyavahāra* represent hairs such as one would associate with

[1] As yet unidentified.

[2] Reading *bhāṣottara* for T's *bhāvottara*.

[3] The reference given for this is said to be ' in *dharmaśāstra* and *arthaśāstra* ' and corresponds to Yājñ. ii, 22, as quoted by the Smṛtisāra on p. 15, similar to Kāty. as quoted by the *Vyavahāra-cintāmaṇi* on p. 33. See *Dharmakośa, Vyavahāra-kāṇḍa*, vol. i, pt. i, pp. 213 and 227.

a materialized human being emerging from a body which represents *nyāya*, or judicial activity. Bhōja : his hair stands on end because of the anger of the parties.

'*Of matted top-knot*'—Nīlakaṇṭha : having a multitude of involved uncertainties (in the trial) ; T says, *nānā ūhakādijaṭā-yuktaḥ*, 'having a top-knot consisting of various analogies, or deductions'. Bhōja says laconically, '*jaṭī* : *dṛḍhamūla*', i.e. the word means root, not top-knot, as it usually does, as *Vyavahāra* is an obstinate, tough affair, almost impossible to eradicate once it has been commenced.

'*Of two tongues*'—T says that the two tongues belong to the plaintiff and defendant *jaya-parājaya-phalāsvādike*, 'savouring the fruits consisting of victory and defeat'. Bhōja does not comment and he apparently follows the obvious view that the two tongues represent the two parties at the Bar.

'*Of brazen visage*'—Arjunamiśra takes this to be the material of which the face is composed, representing the wager in coins [1] which the litigants were at times compelled to put down before the trial commenced, that of the loser being forfeited to the Crown. T follows this. Bhōja : the eyes of the two parties are reddened in colour through anger.

Finally, *mṛga-rāja-tanucchadaḥ*—Arjunamiśra : wrapped in a tiger-skin ; Nīlakaṇṭha : wrapped in deer-hide ; T : having a tiger-skin as a covering, that is to say, being of variegated appearance, such as the foregoing suggests. Bhōja : *upaveśanārtham . . . vyāghrasya . . . carma-puṭaṃ yasmin sa tathā*, 'having a fold, or pouch, of tiger-skin to sit on', in support of which inter-
* pretation he quotes a hitherto unknown *ślōka* from the Bṛhan-Nāradīya [*sic*], of which the meaning is that a litigant who hopes to win a lawsuit should provide himself with a tiger-skin to sit on, should concentrate on Viṣṇu, should have a piece of gold in his hand (as a talisman, presumably, not as
* a bribe for the judge or a sign of willingness to pay damages), and a smile on his face (to indicate absence of malice).[2] This strange advice is not quoted in the principal digests (the publication of Lakṣmīdhara on
* *Vyavahāra* is awaited) and is interesting as tending to prove that there was a *Bṛhan-Nārada-smṛti*, which has long been doubted.[3]

What is the conclusion to be drawn from Bhōja's interpretation and his attribution of it to *Vyavahāra* rather than *Daṇḍa* ? Briefly, it would appear to be this : the other party followed the author of the *Śāntiparva* in considering *Vyavahāra* as a means of achieving the King's mission and in particular of inflicting punishment both retributive and deterrent ; the parties came to Court not so much to have their disputes settled as to provide the King with an opportunity to punish the unrighteous. Bhōja would have none of this. That

[1] *paṇa.*

[2] *vyāghra-carmaṇi saṃviṣṭaś=cintayan garuḍa-dhvajam*
suvarṇa-pāṇiḥ sumukhaḥ vyavahāre jayaṃ labhed.

[3] See Kane, op. cit., vol. i, pp. 204, 206. Also Jolly, Introduction to translation of *Nārada-smṛti* (1876), p. xii, note.

that view of the nature and function of *Vyavahāra* was ancient and persistent is proved by the fact that the defeated litigant was always fined; by the fact that of the King's duties, *duṣṭa-nigraha-śiṣṭa-pratipālana*, repression conventionally comes first; by the statement in the *Mitākṣarā* (on Yājñ. i, 360) that the King should attend to judicial business *duṣṭāduṣṭa-parijñānārtham*, where the choice of words is significant; and by the survival in the *Sarasvati-vilāsa* (*c*. 1520) of the view that one of the principal ends of *Vyavahāra* is repression of the wicked: *duṣṭa-parijñānaṃ vyavahāra-darśanamantareṇa na siddhyati.*[1] It is essentially a tendentious view, inseparable from a particular philosophical approach to Society. Its effect on legal practice could be pernicious. In a fair number of disputes both parties are more or less in the wrong, and the application of the science of jurisprudence according to the prevailing system of the country and period merely obliges the complainant to formulate his complaint and detects whether he is or is not entitled to a particular remedy, and though the position is complicated in modern times by the existence of pleas of the Crown, which were impossible in ancient India,[2] it was never practicable, whether in India or elsewhere, to view litigation as an organ of State policy. A judicial organization which saw litigants as prospective criminals, and litigation as a source of income for the Crown, suffered from an initial bias that must have been fatal to justice. None of the digest-writers views *Vyavahāra* in the same light as the author of the *Śāntiparva*, and it seems that we may owe this as much to the effort of Bhōja-dēva as to the effect of practical experience. The text could not be perpetually ignored, for the theory of *ēka-vākyatā* did not permit of inconsistency even on the part of the epics with the *smṛti*. Hence Bhōja explains that while the others personify *Vyavahāra* as an organ of the State, as it were a tool of the King, not connected by nature with the actual origins of litigation and standing apart from the parties, he himself saw it as the duel itself personified. *Vyavahāra* to him was the essence of all legal battles, made up of the passions of the all-too-human adversaries, sprinkled with the dust of the forum itself. Accordingly it was not only a mere everyday phenomenon, but also one capable of rationalization and progressive analysis.

The author of T concludes his summary with the words:—

ayaṃ pakṣo bahubhir Dhārēśvarādibhir nibandhibhiḥ anumata iti yatheṣṭaṃ vyavahartavyam.

This was no 'academic' matter. If his royal patron cared to follow the view which had the approval of many digest-writers commencing with the King of Dhārā, it was open to him to arrange his judicial administration accordingly. Most modern lawyers will agree with Bhōja.

[1] Mysore edition, p. 16.
[2] See Manu viii, 43.

ADDITIONAL ANNOTATIONS

p. [80], tit. Ref. J.O.R. 33 (1954), 94-127.

p. [80], l. 21. P. K. Gode, *Studies in Indian Literary History* I (1953), 212-14 (previously at *Mīmāṃsā-prakāśa* (Poona), I, 10-11) reproduces Vimalabodha on this (f. 63b): evaṃ nānārūpe vyavahāra-puruṣa iti ayaṃ ca sārdha-śloko Bhojarājena Vyavahāra-mañjaryām anyathā vyākhyātaḥ. ubhayoḥ satyānṛta-pravṛttayor vādi-prativādinor viruddho vyavahāraḥ. sa cobhaya-dharma-grāhitatvāt. ubhayātmā puruṣaḥ ko 'pi nīlotpala-dalaśyāmaḥ śitāśitātmā satyānṛta-pravṛttatvāt. ubhayoś catrasro daṃṣṭrā yasmin sa tathā. evam ubhayoś catvāraḥ pādāḥ. bhāṣottara-kriyā-pratyākalita-pāda-catuṣṭaya-sahitā aṣṭau pādāḥ yasmin sa tathā. naikāni bahūni ubhayor nayanāni yasmin sa tathā. caturakṣaratvāt vyavahārasya.

p. [80], l. 26. According to Gode (supra) Vimalabodha lived after 1150 (see *St. Ind. Lit. Hist.* I, p. 319).

p. [80], n. 1. The passage was much used in the pseudo-historical study of T. J. Kedar, 'Lecture on some aspects of early Hindu law', All Ind. Rep. 1941 Journal 14-19.

p. [82], l. 12. Cf. Vimalabodha's account (sup.).

p. [82], l. 25. Since Vimalabodha gives *kriyā* (missing in T) our text must be corrected.

p. [83], l. 24. This must be the *Bṛhan-nāradīya-purāṇa* cited in legal contexts (e.g. Dave's edn. of part of the *Pṛthvīcandrodaya*, 55 Bom.L.R., J., 31, and Kane, H.D., III, 656, n. 1242) but the *v.* is as yet untraced.

p. [83], l. 28. S. *Taitt. brā.* II,ii,4.6 disc. *Śab. bhā.* II.iv,8.20-24. The enemy becomes pale. A litigant, in a case where neither human oral or documentary nor 'divine' evidence supplies a solution, nor even inference, may be called upon to take a decisory oath. According to Nār. IV.248, Viṣṇu IX.5-10, and Somadevasūri's *Nītivākyāmṛta*, pp. 305-7 (see A. Thakur, *Hindu Law of Evidence*, Calcutta, 1933), 145-6) various *varṇa-s* may swear with gold in hand.

p. [83], l. 31. K. V. Rangaswami Aiyangar's index to Lakṣmīdhara's *Kṛtyakalpataru, Vyavahāra-kāṇḍa* (1958) does not indicate this *v.* On the B.n. see n. above.

Two Inscriptions Concerning the Status of Kammalas and the Application of Dharmasastra

The most recent writers on the *dharmaśāstra*, R. Lingat and W. Ruben,[1] are unable to say what exactly was the role in practice of the *dharmaśāstra* texts in disputes of sufficient importance to call for their scientific application. The *śāstra* tells us how its texts should be inquired into and utilised, but that is a different matter. There are very few interesting and illuminating instances of the texts being relied upon in literature, including legal literature, and the absence of reported cases is a notorious stumbling-block for the student. The Anglo-Hindu law went upon the assumption that the Sanskrit texts were sources of law, to be applied to any litigant who could not plead and prove a custom to the contrary.[2] The pre-British situation has been misjudged by some, who believed that written sources of law were never consulted by judges, and that the practical role of the jurist had disappeared under Muslim rule. Now we do have an example of a *literary* account of the settlement of a caste dispute in the fifteenth century, in which a mass of Hindu literature, including *smṛtis* and digests, was consulted, and this gives a fairly clear impression of how a long-standing dispute of a social character was solved.[3] Hindu culture as a whole was laid under contribution, not the *smṛti* alone. But no actual examples, no ancient *vyavasthās*, have come to light in which the sources were cited, quoted, and applied by official experts, with jurisdiction to settle the question at issue.

---

1. R. Lingat, Les Sources du Droit dans le Système traditionnel de l'Inde, Paris and The Hague, 1967 (an English version of this will appear from the University of California Press under the title "The Classical Law of India"). W. Ruben, Die gesellschaftliche Entwicklung im alten Indien. II. Die Entwicklung von Staat und Recht, Berlin, 1968.

2. J. D. M. Derrett, Religion, Law and the State in India, London, 1968, 292-3. 305.

3. Vaiśya-vaṁśa-sudhākara: V. Raghavan in A Volume presented to Sir Denison Ross, Bombay, 1939, 234-40. P. V. Kane, History of Dharmaśāstra, III (Poona, 1946, 252 n. The affair took place c. 1422-1466.

The next best thing has now turned up *a propos* of the status of the Rathakāras of South India. These were equated with Kammālas, of whom it is known that some are untouchables (in traditional terms) and some craftsmen of relatively high status. It has been known for a long time that Rathakāras challenged Brahmins. Well they might at a period, as for example from the tenth century onwards, when there was a boom in temple building and all that went with it. Architects and masons must have been in great demand and they could command substantial incomes. As to the claims of inferior Kammālas to belong to the Rathakāras, with the possible right to share the hereditary monopolistic practice of arts and crafts connected with temple and other construction, doubts seem to have cropped up fairly frequently in South India.[1] As this was a matter of *varṇāśrama-dharma* the arbiters were Brahmins. Their decision was expected to be objective, though they might prevent their own youth from intruding upon any aspect of the monopolies; and their own fees would be affected by excluding from non-Śūdra and *pratiloma* castes any groups which might otherwise have called for their services as *purohitas*.

It is a matter of great satisfaction to be able to consult two of the three Tamil and Sanskrit inscriptions which deal with claims on the part of certain Rathakāras, settling the rights and duties of that caste. A.R. No. 558 of 1904 has been published as S.I.I. xvii (1964), No. 603. A.R. No. 479 of 1908 was most kindly copied and sent to me by Dr. G. S. Gai, Chief Epigraphist, Archaeological Survey of India. There is also A.R. No. 189 of 1925, of which he sent me a copy: it is, however, broken off short.

The great advantage of these inscriptions is that they provide certain answers to questions we had been asking. Firstly, the referees were Brahmins exclusively. Next they took personal responsibility for their prescriptions of law, that is to say, they identified themselves as holding the opinions they stated for the reasons they stated. Next, they cited their sources and even quoted them. The fact that incompetent copying by the (non-Brahmin) scribe(s) had the effect of losing or mutilating some of the Sanskrit texts (which the scribes probably did not understand) does not diminish the interest of the citations. Many of them have not survived in *dharmaṣāstra* works now in print. Of the standard commentators the only one recognisable is Maskari, whose date had been

1. K. A. Nilakanta Sastri, Colas, 1st edn. I/2, Madras, 1937, 658, 739, also 603. Colas 2nd edn., 549. Derrett, Religion, Law and the State, cited above, 175.

doubted.[1] One inscription cites Kauṭilya (in a Tamilised form as Gauṭilya), but unfortunately the quotation which must have followed has dropped out, probably through the scribe's incompetence. The date of No. 603 is vague, 'the twelfth century': that of No. 479 is apparently A.D. 1118; that of No. 189 seems to be in the region of 1166. At this period the *Mitakṣara* is not cited, nor the much earlier Medhātithi, nor Viśvarūpa's *Balakrīḍa*. The well-known *smṛtikara* Yājñavalkya is quoted both in the form we know, and in another form. In so far as the quotation agrees with our text it is the form known from the *Mitakṣara* and Aparārka, nor the *Balakrīḍa*. An apparently unknown commentary on Gautama is quoted.

The proportion of anonymous texts quoted is high, including amongst them one which is cited prominently. The referees had no compunction in quoting a text with its attribution and immediately following it with an anonymous text. Yet in spite of the loss of some texts, the slight changes in texts we still possess, and the amalgamation of texts having attributions with anonymous texts, the style and quality of the śāstric material is not markedly different from that what we find in medieval commentaries known to us from their manuscript traditions and printed (more or less critically) in our own day.

No. 603 will be studied in detail here, because of its very extensive use ot architectural material, quoted *in extenso*. It is hoped that the eventual editor of No. 479 may be assisted by further information and references which readers of this article may contribute hereafter towards a better appreciation of No. 603.

Since the texts are quoted and relied upon there can be no doubt but that, save for the errors of the scribe and/or copyists, they were taken for genuine and reliable in their day, and the extent of verbal agreement between No. 479 and No. 603 confirms this.

1. P. V. Kane, History of Dharmaśāstra, I, (Poona, 1930) deals with Haradatta at sec. 86. He assigns him a date c. 1200. At p. 19 he says of Maskari that his commentary "is also a learned one, but may probably be latter than Haradatta, since the interpretations which he quotes as given by others are found to be those of Haradatta". In fact Maskari is cited Vaguely by Lakṣmīdhara, Kṛtyakalpataru, Mokṣakāṇḍa, p. 49, which shows that he existed well before the end of the eleventh century.

The śāstric position:

The śastric position was considered briefly by Bālaṃbhaṭṭa in the last quarter of the nineteenth century[1]. It would be an error to read back into the twelfth century (with which we are concerned) the ideas of the nineteenth. But the materials which Bālaṃbhaṭṭa uses were presumably available much earlier, if not in the same form. Thus while we survey the material we are justified in bearing in mind the continuity from the earliest commentaries which we possess to the latest, and then only can we see the validity of our referees' decisions in its true perspective. They did not cite all the information available to them, and Bālaṃbhaṭṭa and other jurists do not cite all the information available to our referees, naturally. But if we pool the information we have we shall be able to size up what was done, and to appreciate the function of the referees, which is what gives the inscriptions their interest.

The materials themselves have a tedious air, and the confused topic of the mixed castes is one which perplexes and annoys the reader. It is almost impossible to make the topic exciting or even pleasurable. An air of artificiality hangs over it. But our inscriptions prove that the public were deeply interested in at least one aspect of the problem, and this we must pursue as best we may. We must first refer to texts establishing a high status for Rathakāras (and thus of those Kammālas who could claim to be Rathakāras), and then turn to those which attributed a low status to them. Those who had a high status were, in part, rivals of Brahmins, and were entitled to noble and intellectual functions. Those with a low status were confined to menial tasks.

Rathakāras of high caste:

A good starting-point would be Yājñavalkya I. 95. 'From a Māhiṣya male upon a Karaṇī is produced a Rathakāra. Bad and good (respectively) are to be considered the progeny born of the Pratilōma and Anuloma' The meaning of this is sufficiently indicated in the commentaries of Viśvarūpa (which was probably available to our referees),[2] of Vijñāneśvara (which may not have been),[3]

1. For Bālaṁbhaṭṭa see Kane, op. cit., I, sec. 111. B.'s very extensive gloss on Yājñ. I. 94 is paraphrased by S'riśa Chandra Vidyārṇava in his translation of the Yājñavalkya.smṛti with the Mitākṣarā published in Allahabad, 1918, pp. 193-200. *

2. The Bālakrīḍā on the Yājñavalkya-smṛti was published by T. Gaṇapati S'āstri from Trivandrum in 1922. See I. 94, p. 901.

3. The Nirṇayasāgara Press edition has been frequently reprinted. The edition by S. S. Setlur from Madras, 1912, is also valuable. In my view the Mitākṣarā belongs

of Aparārka (which may not have been).[1] and of Mitra Miśra (which certainly was not).[2] According to an earlier verse (see *v.* 92) the scheme is clear. A Māhiṣya is the son of a Kṣatriya by a Vaiśya wife. He is therefore an *anulomaja*, born in the natural order of *varṇas*, and of parents only one degree removed, and by a valid marriage. He has thus three claims to respectability. He is a twice-born, though of a mixed caste, and he is entitled to the sacred thread and to Vedic education—at least in theory. He is not a S'ūdra, still less an outcaste. A Karaṇa, somewhat similarly, is the son of a Vaiśya by a S'ūdra wife. He too is an *anulomaja*. His right to the sacred thread subsists, though he is at the extreme edge of the *anuloma* mixed castes. Now where a Māhiṣya male marries a Karaṇa female the offspring must, logically, be twice-born, entitled to the *upanayana* ceremony and the sacred thread. This is what Yājña-valkya says, and he proceeds to comment upon the whole series of verses by saying that progeny born of *pratilomas* and *anulomas* are respectively 'bad' and 'good'. Status and worth depend on the answer to the question whether the parents of the person in question were united in the *anuloma* or the *pratiloma* order, and whether the parents were themselves the fruit of such unions. Now this is a general proposition, and so far as the Rathakāras are concerned it is evident that they are, according to Yājñavalkya, *anulomajas*, born in *anuloma* unions between *anulomajas*. But a hasty reading of the verse might suggest that the second line applies to and controls the first, namely that there are Rathakāras born in the *pratiloma* manner, in other words Rathakāras other than those specified in the first line of the verse.

Manu and Nārada, though they deal in general with the problem of mixed *varṇas*, do not specify the Rathakāra. The Mitākṣarā[3] and other sources[4] quote

---

to c. 1125, It would not have been a celebrated work in the Tamil country until the century was out.

1. Aparārka's commentary on the Yājñavalkya-smṛti was roughly contemporary with the Mitākṣarā, but belonged to the Koṅkaṇ, whereas the Mitākṣarā belonged to the central Deccan. The edition of Aparārka is by the Ananāśrama Skt. Ser. pandits under the name of H. N. Apte, Poona, 1903.

2. The Vīramitrodaya belongs to the seventeenth century.

3. I.95. For the position in the Kṛtyakalpataru, Vyavahārakāṇḍa, where the editor may have misunderstood the inference to be drawn from the manuscripts, see K. V. Rangaswami Aiyangar, ed., Lakṣmidhara, Kṛtyakalpataru, XII, Baroda, 1953, p. 823. For S'aṅkha's text see also Mitra Miśra, Vīramitrodaya (digest), Benares 1906, Saṁskāraprakāśa, 399.

4. It is doubtful whether Aparārka quotes the whole of the passage (on Yājñ. 1. 95ab).

Śaṅkha as saying, 'From the Kṣatriya and Vaiśya anuloma progeny a son begotten on lower orders is a Rathakāra. He is entitled to rituals for the kindling of the fire, giving alms, and the *upanayana* ceremony. His livelihood is by studying the science of horses[1], foundation or consecration (*pratiṣṭhā*), the business of chariots, carpentry, and building in general (*vāstu*).' This, perhaps, is the key text on our Rathakāras, and a full commentary on it is provided by Mitra Miśra (seventeenth century) in his digest.[2] At that time it was suggested that the Pūrva Mīmāṃsā position on Rathakāras[3] conflicted with Śaṅkha's text, since the latter suggested that *anuloma* mixed castes had the right to *upanayana*, whereas Jaimini spoke of an exceptional right of *ādhāna* (fire-laying) conferred on castes which had *no* right to the *upanayana*. The solution adopted by Mitra Miśra was that Rathakāras alone amongst the mixed castes normally disqualified from *upanayana* (e,g. Ṛbhu, Sudhanvan), were allowed to perform the Vedic *ādhāna*.

After Śaṅkha appear a series of lines which form two *ślokas*. Since there appears to have been no caesura in the second line of the first *śloka* it is not surprising, perhaps that it is defectively copied in both No. 603 and No. 479 of 1908. I have not been able to track it down to a printed source. Its function is to reassure the sceptics that Rathakāras and other *anulomas* who are entitled to the sacred thread that the latter does not imply that they enjo y characteristic Brahminical privileges or ritual duties.

anulomyopaneyānāṃ na sandhyāyām upāsanam
na samit-sannidhānāgnihotraṃ naupāsanaṃ tathā.
na ca pañcamahāyajñā vedādhyayanas tathā
mantreṇa rahitā teṣām upanītir api śmṛtā.

Assuming that my reconstruction of the second line of the first *śloka* is correct, that is hardly more than a poor versification of a prose passage which is actually given as an anonymous *smṛti* in the authentic commentary of Maskari on *Gautama-dharma-sūtra* (IV. 22), on which see below.

The text of Yājñavalkya, the general theory of *anuloma* mixed castes, and the text of Śaṅkha, point to a qualified Vedic initiation, as Bālaṃbhaṭṭa, relying

1. Our inscriptions read *aśva-ratha-*. The printed texts read *aśva-pratiṣṭhā-*.
2. p. 399.
3. Jaimini VI. 1, 44-50. P. V. Kane, History of Dharmaśāstra, I, 45.

*

on the authority of Karkācārya,[1] explains (in a passage to be cited again below). Brahmins, indeed, had the initiation of *upanayana* and thereafter were entitled to the six *karmas* of *yajana, yājana, dāna, pratigraha, adhyayana,* and *adhyāpana*. Whatever the factual situation might have been (did no Rathakāras ever teach the *sūtras,* and *smṛtis* and other scriptures, including Vedic *mantras,* relating to architecture in all its phases ?), the Rathakāras were entitled to the thread ceremony. Vedic material confirms this.[2] They might therefore study, but not teach, perform sacrificial rites (connected with practical architecture), and make offerings (but not receive them with spiritual effect for the donor). That they were in some sense in a limited ritual competition with Brahmins is thus evident. If a Rathakāra could be an *ācārya* in the sense in which that term is used in architectural scriptures, this would no doubt be convenient, but it would trench upon the Brahmins' privileges at many points. In A. R. No. 189 of 1925 two leading Kammālas appear with the names Rājanārāyaṇa ācārya and Mūlabharuṣai ācārya.

The complications of the śāstric texts on the mixed castes are notorious. Various castes have different names. There is the additional complication which arises when the intercourse which produced the child was illicit. To be born in the inverse order of castes was to be a *pratilomaja,* but that was not all. Worse *pratilomajas* were those whose fathers were in the lowest rank and whose mothers were in the highest, but the lowest even of these were born of an illicit intercourse. Practical questions, such as how the parentage was known and how and even whether castes were formed in this manner can be left out of account, since they could hardly have been ventilated before our referees in this case. The discussion turned on the śāstric position; were Rathakāras *twice-born* with the exclusive right to undertake those valuable and expanding craft activities ?

The relevant text of Baudhāyana[3] is a śāstric authority which our referees will have known, though they neither cite it nor quote it. It says that the Rathakāra is born to a Vaiśya male from a Śūdra woman—a proposition quite different from that laid down by Yājñavalkya. But he is

1. Very little is known of this author. Kane places him before 1100 (*HD*, I, 684), a commentator on *gṛhya-sūtras*. The passage is to be found in Bālaṁbhaṭṭa, ed Gharpure, Bombay, 1914, p. 293.

2. Kane, *HD*, II/1, 43, 45, 57, 94.

3. I, 9, 6. Ed. A. Chinnaswāmi Śāstri, Benares, 1934, p. 87. See also I, 3, 9.

still an *anulomaja*. The commentary of Govindasvāmī, which is of great but unknown age, explains that the Rathakāra born to a Vaiśya male from a Śūdra woman has the right to lay Vedic fires according to the Vedic passage *varṣāsu rathakāraḥ*.[1] His parentage has a Śūdra element, which we should have thought fatal. Saṅkha, quoted by Nanda-paṇḍita on Viṣṇu XVI. 2, says *vaiśyena śūdrāyām śūdra eva*, and similarly Devala as quoted in the *Kalpataru* says *vaiśyāc chūdrasya kanyāyām śūdra eva prajāyate*. But because of the Vedic passage the right to perform *ādhāna* is there. A right to initiation is therefore to be contemplated. Govindasvāmī does not say that the Rathakāra is a twice-born, perhaps prudently. Our inscription at S.I.I. xvii No. 603 does not mention Baudhāyana: perhaps the other texts were more gratifying to Rathakāras, about whom some pleasant things are said in quotations to which we shall come presently. But it is proper to note here that Śūlapāṇi (fourteenth to fifteenth centuries) in his comments on Yājñ. I. 95 clearly says that the Rathakāra referred to by Baudhāyana (I. 9.5) is another caste having the same name as that figuring in Yājñavalkya's text. This would seem to be good traditional interpretation (*go-śabdavad anekārthatā*) which would leave it in doubt whether this new class of Rathakāra had the privilege of *ādhāna*.

Our referees however cite and quote[2] as a text of Yāñavalkya a passage which the Brahmins of No. 603 claim to find in an unknown commentary on Gautama: [3]

māhiṣyena karaṇyām tu rathakāraḥ prajāyate
nāsyopanayanam nejyā nādhānam ca niṣidhyate.

This is curious. The first line is Yājñ. I. 95ab. The second has not been traced, and has a suspicious air. It means, evidently, that neither the thread ceremony, nor sacrificial acts, nor the laying of the (Vedic) fires are prohibited to him. And this suspect line, conflicting in spirit (if not in the letter) with the anonymous passage *anulomyopaneyānām* which I have reproduced above, has been substituted silently for that possibly embarrassing line we have already studied, in which the 'badness' or 'goodness' of mixed castes is mentioned. It is not

1. Tai. Br. I, 1, 4. See also Baud. gṛhya-sūtra II, 5, 6.
2. No. 603, para 1; No. 479, para 2.
3. No. 603, para I2. The vivaraṇa (could it have been by Bhāruci?) is not known to Kane (on Gautama in *HD*, I).

as if Yājñavalkya's *śloka* was not known as we know it from the *Mitākṣarā*, Aparārka, or independent manuscript tradition: for that *śloka* does appear in No. 479, though not under Yājñavalkya's name!

Next we are given an anonymous text upon which both the referees in No. 603 and in No. 479 rely.[1]

vaiśyataḥ śūdra-kanyāyāṃ saṃjātaḥ karaṇas striyām
asmād ambaṣṭhato jāto rathakāra iti smṛtaḥ.

The statement that a Karaṇa is born of a Vaiśya male to a S'ūdra female, who is not necessarily his wife, agrees with other known authorities, e.g. Gautama, Baudhāyana, Yājñavalkya. If we take the word *asmād* in the somewhat unexpected sense of 'hence', 'from that quarter' (instead of 'from him') we obtain the sense which the referees must certainly have had in mind, namely that the Rathakāra is born to a Karaṇa *female* by an Ambaṣṭha male. Otherwise we should have been forced to find the Rathakāra a *pratiloma* caste, for Ambaṣṭhas are certainly ritually superior to Karaṇas.

Next we turn to the text of Maskari which is correctly quoted in both No. 603 and No. 479.[2] The purpose of the quotation is to authenticate another anonymous *smṛti* which Maskari reads and therefore certifies as authoritative. What a pity the same was not done for the text *vaiśyataḥ śūdra-kanyāyām*! Obviously it was of unquestioned authenticity. Maskari's apocryphal *smṛti* reads:

anulomānām upanayanam eva na vedādhyayanaṃ na
pañca-mahāyajñaṃ naupāsanaṃ nāgnihotraṃ na samit-kāryaṃ na
sandhyopāsanam upanayanam api tūṣṇīm eva.[3]

It is a rather poor versification of this which we have already seen as an appendix to the text of S'aṅkha above. It is further evidence of our referees' care to quote each and every text they felt to be relevant even when repetition would result. *Anulomas* may not, after their *upanayana* (performed in silence), study the Veda, perform the five 'great' sacrifices of the householder or make oblations

1. No. 603, para 12; No. 479, para 2.

2. No. 603, para 2, No. 479, para 3-4. Barring insignificant deviations they agree with Maskari on Gautama IV. 22, p. 82 of the Mysore edition.

3. Both inscriptions read *pañca-mahā-yajña*, which should be added to the apparatus when a critical edition is contemplated. On the Rathakāras' *upanayana* see also Baud. gṛhya-sūtra II. 8 (Kane, *HD*, II/1, 299.)

in the Aupāsana fire, or perform the *agnihotra*, preparation of fuel, or the twilight worship. In other words a form of distinction, in ritual terms, between the *anulomas* (which our referees understood to include some at least of the Rathakāras) and the twice-born, and in particular Brahmins, was set out. Thus, in a respectable view, adopted by our referees, some *anuloma* castes were entitled to *upanayana* (and the sacred thread) but that did not constitute a challenge of any substantial moment to the Brahmins in ritual terms. We are already half-way to observing that if Rathakāras, or some of them, are acknowledged *anuloma* status this does not amount to serious rivalry, at least in ritual terms, to the Brahmins. The citation from Maskari is followed in S.I.I. xvii No. 603 by a passage from a work on architecture called *Viśva-karmīya*, which may yet be traced and verified. It includes the following undamaged lines:

ambaṣṭhena karaṇyāṃ tu rathakāraḥ prajāyate...
anulomeṣu sarveṣu tūṣṇīm upanayaḥ kriyā
savarṇāmbaṣṭhayor eva sāpi tatra vidhīyate
rathakārādi-jātīnām upanītir amantrakam[1]
na yajño nāpi sandhyādi kiṃcānyad yat tu[2] *vaidikam*
ādhāna-mātraṃ kurvīta rathakāras tu viśvakṛt.

The Rathakāra is the son of an Ambaṣṭha by a Karaṇa woman, which agrees with the anonymous text *vaiśyataḥ śūdra-kanyāyām* as we have tentatively construed it. Next we learn, from a sympathetic source, that the Rathakāra who is an *anulomaja* has his thread ceremony in silence. Two high-grade *anuloma* castes, Savarṇa and Ambaṣṭha, are in the same position. If I have understood the line correctly, no sacrifice, no twilight prayers, nor any other Vedic ceremony is permitted, except that the Rathakāra architect or craftsman, called *viśvakṛt* in reminiscence of their patron deity Viśvakarma, may simply perform *ādhāna*, the laying of Vedic fires, though in the context of architectural lore it may well have other meanings relative to the foundation and/or consecration of buildings.

Rathakāras of low caste

The śāstric position we have seen was not a simple or uniform one. Two kinds of Rathakāras amongst the *anuloma* castes have been observed

1. *amantram* in the ins.
2. *yaṃ tu* in the ins.

or alternatively two distinct traditions about the origins of the Rathakāras. But there is agreement that they are concerned with chariots, wagons, carpentary, metal work, architecture, house-building, and related crafts. But there were artisans called Rathakāras, like our Kammālas, who were of low social rank, as is evident from texts of no less authoritative status.

Perhaps we do well to start with the equivocal opinion of Jaimini himself.[1] I am not saying that Jaimini said Rathakāras were *pratilomajas*. But he did say that they were identical with the Sudhanvan and Ācarya born of a *vrātya* Vaiśya. *Upanayana* would consequently be in abeyance. This would fit a social position, in which some Rathakāras claimed that if sufficient ritual pains were taken the practice of *upanayana* could be restarted; it would even protect from Brahmin fury some groups of Rathakāras who assumed the sacred thread but whose right to *upanayana* was doubtful.

Meanwhile so important and ancient a śāstric commentator as Viśvarūpa says (on Yājñ. I. 10) that Rathakāras are not among the higher castes. They are not, in his view, entitled to *upanayana*. The *smṛti* which says that they are (obviously Śaṅkha or Vasiṣṭha, both originally quoted by Lakṣmīdhara in the *Kalpataru*) is based on an error, he says, due to their having the (Vedic) right to perform *ādhāna*, a right, he implies, which could exist without *upanayana*. Here is a South Indian explaining, in effect, that architectural requirements and the social developments to which these led did not necessarily make the Rathakāras twice-born. This fits with the background to our own inscriptions. Viśvarūpa's own teacher took the view that this was *not* a case where the right to *upanayana* might be held to exist, optionally. They simply had no right to it at all. Viśvarūpa goes on to explain (on Yājñ. I. 94) that *in former ages* there were *anuloma* castes which had the privilege of *ādhāna* because of their status, whereas the *pratiloma* castes were of low status (and consequently had not that privilege). We have seen already that one might be a *pratilomaja* though one's parents and one's grandparents indefinitely were born in twice-born castes, e.g. the child of a Vaiśya male by a Brahmin female.

At this point it is convenient to take up the view of that very late jurist, Bālambhaṭṭa, who, somehow, seems to have been aware of our very problem.[2] Knowing, as he does, that Śaṅkha asserts the right to *upanayana*

1. See above, n. 15.
2. See above, n. 16.

and citing the text of Vasiṣṭha which says the same *as the view of some jurists* (a text which does not belong to the printed editions of Vasiṣṭha, but which pre-existed the *Kalpataru* and was therefore anterior to our inscriptions), he comes to the conclusion that the Rathakāra, though like a Sūdra, is entitled to the *upanayana*. This he does by asserting the validity of the literal texts of those antiquated *sūtras* as against a peculiar anonymous text, which we are bound to note here. It reads:

naivopanayanaṃ tasya śūdra - dharmād bahiḥ kvacit
vartanaṃ śilpa - vṛttyā 'tra loke śilpasya śāstra - vit.

This miserable little text evidently refers to craftsmen, and we can take Bālaṃbhaṭṭa's word for it, that it referred to Rathakāras. It may well come from an architectural work, which he does not specify. It denied the caste's right to *upanayana* and assigned it to the *dharma* of a *śūdra* (if I understand it rightly), although it was entitled to knowledge of the *śāstra* relating to sculpture and the like, by which it obtained its livelihood. Since this wretched text survived until almost the beginning of the nineteenth century we can be sure that antagonism to the wearing of the sacred thread by people calling themselves Rathakāras and practising the plastic arts and crafts was widespread and deeprooted.

The *Vaikhānasa-dharma-sūtra*, otherwise known as *Vaikhānasa-dharma-praśna*, most unfortunately gives an ancient list of *varṇas* and mixed castes contradicting the orthodox *smṛtī* material. Vaikhānasa sources were not 'bogus', and like the Pañcarātra material which was in a way competitive with them, could claim to be almost as respectable in South India as Manu himself.[1] The Vaikhānasa *sūtras* say that the first *pratilomas* is the Sūta, born to a Kṣatriya from a Brahmin wife. He is initiated without *mantras* and is unworthy of twice-born *dharmas*. This is more or less what would be expected of *pratilomajas*. To continue: his duties are relating matters of *dharma* (as a reciter?) and preparing the food of the king (or Kṣatriyas?). But if the child is born to parents of those same castes but by adultery the child's caste is Rathakāra. He is not entitled to *mantras*, he is unworthy of twice-born status, his functions are those of S'ūdras. He lives by feeding and training horses, and similar tasks, a life (in

1. On the Vaikhānasa doctrines and literature see J. Gonda. 'Religious thought and practice in Vaikhānasa Viṣṇuism', to be published in the collection of seminar papers on the Religions of India, Pakistan, Ceylon and Nepal, S.O.A.S., London (1970-1). No information about Rathakāras is to be obtained from the ancient Vaikhānasāgama of Marīci, published by K. Sāmbaśiva S'āstri, Trivandrum, 1935.

short) of a menial servant.[1] The *Kaśyapa-jñāna-kāṇḍa,* another Vaikhānasa text, places Sūta and Rathakāra together as jointly chief of the *pratilomas.*[2] The ancient sage Paiṭhīnasi, if the text attributed to him is genuine, implied, if he did not actually say, much the same. [3]

Uśanas, which may be called an older 'bogus' *smṛti,* having perhaps no relation to the work of Uśanas cited by ancient jurists like Lakṣmīdhara, contains two verses on the rare subject of Rathakāras.[4] In the view of the author the Rathakāra is born in a *pratiloma* union. So far this agrees with the Vaikhānasa text. The Rathakāra's father is a Kṣatriya, his mother a Brahmin, and the union itself 'by stealth'. His livelihood is that of a Śūdra, and twice-born rank is forbidden to him (hence no *upanayana*!). His way of life is that a Śūdra, and he must not perform the *dharma* of the Kṣatriya. What we might call *ad hoc* the Vaikhānasa position is here badly versified. The text of Uśanas quoted in the *Kalpataru*[5] merely says that the Rathakāra is the first of all the mixed castes, apparently senior to the Ambaṣṭha, which implies, on the contrary that Rathakāras are *anulomas*. Our inscription No. 603 quotes neither Vaikhānasa text nor Uśanas; but we cannot be sure that such material was not cited to our referees during their investigation.

The notion that Rathakāras were *pratilomajas,* even though born of *anuloma* castes by cross-caste union, can be found elsewhere. The *Smṛtyartha-sāra* of Śrīdhara-bhaṭṭa, who seems to have been a southerner, is of particular interest. It must have been composed 1150 — 1200 and is thus contemporary with our enquiries.[6] The view is stated [7] that a Māhiṣya is born to a Vaiśya woman from a Kṣatriya, and a Karṇa is born from a Vaiśya to a Śūdra woman, and both are (naturally) *anulomas,* twice-born, entitled to the *saṃskāras.* Later, dealing with *pratilomas,* the author states that a Vaiśya woman bears

1. Caland's Vaikhānasa-smārta-sūtra, X. 13 (text, 1927, p. 143; trans. 1929, 227). Also Vaikhānasa-dharma-praśna, ed. T. Gaṇapati Śāstrī, Trivandrum, 1913, pp. 47-49.
2. Ed. R. B. Parthasārathi Bhaṭṭācārya, Tirupati, 1948, ch. 91. T. Goudriaan, Kāśyapa's Book of Wisdom, The Hague, 1965.
3. Lakṣmīdhara, Kṛtyakalpataru, Vyavahārakāṇḍa, p. 818.
4. Uśanas 5-6 (ed. Jīvānanda, Dharmaśāstra saṅgraha, 1876, I, p. 497). Cf. Uśanas at Kṛtyakalpataru, Vy. K., p. 814.
5. See last note.
6. Kane, *HD*, I, sec. 81.
7. Ed. R. S. Vaidya, Ānandāśrama Skt. Ser. 70 (1912), p. 13.

an Āyogava to a Sūdra male (and this is evidently an example of *pratiloma* birth). Immediately afterwards he says that the Rathakāra is born of a Karaṇa woman by a Māhiṣya male (using exactly the words of Yājñavalkya I. 95ab), and immediately afterwards says that 'all these are *pratilomas*, excluded from the *dharma* of the twice-born.' I, for one, find it difficult to see how the offspring of a Māhiṣya by a Karaṇa woman can be *pratiloma*: for the Māhiṣya, who has a Kṣatriya father, is surely superior to a Karaṇa, whose father is a Vaiśya—it would be a *pratiloma* union if a Karaṇa male had intercourse with a Māhiṣya female. The view which Śrīdhara-bhaṭṭa took could conceivably make sense if we assume that a different Rathakāra from our *anuloma* Rathakāra had somehow been intruded into the picture without warning—perhaps a defect in the text as transmitted. But a certain ambiguity existed in the position, as is emphasised by the curious comment of the 'bogus' *smṛti*, Vṛddha-Hārīta which, rewriting Yājñavalkya, as it were says,[1] after explaining the Māhiṣya and the Karaṇa as above, that the Rathakāra is born to a Māhiṣya male from a Karaṇa female, and immediately afterwards that the *anulomas*' and *pratilomas*' offspring may be known as 'bad' lineages (the text looks like a misreading or deliberate perversion of Yājñavalkya I. 95cd). In other words the Rathakāra is there placed at the end of examples of mixture of caste between two *anuloma* mixed castes. How this could be construed into making him into a *pratilomaja* is a puzzle to me, but it appears to have happened. It is barely satisfactory to suggest that he was a borderline case: it is more plausible to say that two elements in society claimed Rathakāra backgrounds, and that the śāstric material did not conclusively distinguish between them.

That the Pañcarātras regarded Rathakāras as Śūdras or at any rāte not as twice-born, and that too in an architectural context, is indicated in an important architectural text of uncertain age. The *Pāñcarātra-prāsāda-prasādhanam* (a part of the *Padma-saṃhitā*), I. 21 reads;

> *bhū-parīkṣādikaṁ sarvaṃ Rathakāreṇa vai saha*
> *ācāryaḥ pāñcarātrajñaḥ kuryāt abhyudita-kramāt.*

And I. 40:

> *vāstu-vidyāsu kṛtinā kriyāsu nipuṇena ca*
> *Rathakāreṇa sahitaḥ kuśalaḥ pāñcarātravit*

---

1. VII, 149 ff. 152, 155.

The Rathakāra is here obviously the artisan.[1] very much inferior to the *acarya* who, more and more, came to be thought of as a Brahmin expert in the lore of architecture. At the same time elements of Pāñcarātra literature connect Rathakāra as a caste name with *takṣaka*, literally the carpenter.[2]

We come to the final textual authority. Bālaṃbhaṭṭa frequently quotes the *Sūta-saṃhitā* in this context.[3] But he does not quote it fully, naturally enough, his work being dangerously extensive as it is. This S'aivite work agrees[4] so far with the Vaiṣṇavite works we have been consulting in that it shows that the Rathakāra is born by stealth to a Brahmin woman from a Kṣatriya male—evidently he is a *pratilomaja*. Apart from this there is a caste bearing (it would seem) the names or designations Takṣā (carpenter), Rathakāra, Śilpī (craftsman), Vardhakī (carpenter), Lohakāra (smith), and Karmāra (mechanic). The *Sūta-saṃhitā* continues that the son of a Brahmin girl by an Ugra has the livelihood of a carpenter. Both these pieces of information belong to *pratiloma* unions and their progeny.

Architectural material on this subject

We have already seen that Vaikhānasa and Pāñcarātra architectural texts deal with the status and duties of Rathakāras. There was also the *Viśvakarmīya*, an unverified text favourable to Rathakāras' twice-born status, which our referees quoted. Would further search in architectural materials throw light on the subject ? Architectural literature as it now survives is only partly available in print. It is going through a second phase of public interest amongst Indologists,[5] but the whole range of available works is far from well

1. See the interesting and valuable note by H. Daniel Smith, Pāñcarātra-prasāda-prasādhanam. Chapters 1-10 of the 'kriyāpāda', Pādmasaṃhitā, Madras: 1963' p. 8, n. 26.

2. Note how in No. 189 of 1925 (the sadly truncated inscription apparently originally connected with our topic) the Rathakāra leaders bear the word *taccan* in their titles. I do not know if the *Sanatkumāra-Saṃhitā* of the Pañcarātrāgama (Adyar 1969) throws any further light, as it is not available to me.

3. E.g. at p. 214.

4. Ed.S. Rāmachandra Śāstrī and K. Kuppuswāmy Śāstrī, Madras, 1913, ch. 12 (see verses 18, 19, 29, 30).

5. The first phase was initiated by P. K. Acharya in his series of works on the Mānasāra. Amongst comparatively recent works are N. V. Mallaya's Studies in Sanskrit Texts on Temple Architecture, Annamalai 1949 and D. N. Shukla's Vāstu-s'āstra, vol. I. Lucknow 1961 (?).

known, even though the community of *sthapatis* (traditional sculptors and architects) is being kept alive and recruits apprentices, especially in South India (e.g. at Mamallapuram). The efforts of specialist editors, e.g. at Tanjore, are bringing more and more ancient works to light. These do not, so far as I could discover, deal specifically with Rathakāras. Some incidental references, were fortunately noted, by H. Daniel Smith (as we have seen above).

For the *argument* of this article it is not necessary to spend too much time on our referees' long quotations from architectural and other works as yet unidentified. But there is a sufficient reason to quote what is still capable of use, first because the referees thought that since a *sthapati*, an inferior craftsman, must be learned in Vedic and other orthodox religious lore he must be entitled to *upanayana* and to be called *ācārya* (their motive for such extensive citations); and secondly because unless the texts are readily available the task of verifying them and identifying which works were in notorious authoritative use in the twelfth century would be harder. I thus proceed to copy out the passages concerned, with the minimum of comment, contenting myself with the warning that in this class of literature bad Sanskrit does not mean, necessarily, an incompetent transmission of the text, and the conclusion that such passages do prove the superior caste status of Rathakāras if Rathakāras, in pursuing the livelihood set out for them in S'aṅkha's text (which our referees rely upon), act as *sthapatis* and immerse themselves in *vāstu-śāstra*, which is Architecture in its widest sense.

Viśvakarmīye[1] :

After the verses quoted above, they set out the following:

vāstu-śilpaka vidyābhyāṃ vartayed eṣa nityaśaḥ
devatā-pratimāṃ cāpi kuryāc citraṃ tathaiva ca.
yāntrānām[2] *api patrāṇi prati pūrvaṃ prakalpayet*
suvarṇābharaṇānāṃ ca kañcavyaya striyā.
devatādi-tanūnāṃ ca karaṇaṃ śilpa-jivitā
sauvarṇa-vastu-nirmāṇaṃ svarṇakāra itīṣyate.

1. See above. The work has not been identified. Not the Vis'vakarma Vāstuśāstram in the Tanjore S. M. Ser no. 85, 1958. Perhaps this is the Vis'vakarmas'ilpam, No. 15447 in the Tanjore Skt. Catalogue.

2 *yañcānām* in the ins.

ayas-karmaṇy ayaskāras takṣā takṣaka-karmaṇi
tanūnām karaṇam tvaṣṭā sa eva rathakṛt *bhavet.*
prāsādam devatādinām sthāpanāt sthapatiḥ smṛtaḥ
sthapatir viśvakṛt takṣā tvaṣṭā ca rathakārakaḥ
kāṣṭhiko vardhakiś ceti śilpi-paryāya-vācakaḥ.

Āgamam...ditta vacanam is now quoted, but both verses are badly damaged and it is not possible to make much of them, but I suspect that their point was similar to that of the citation first taken from the *Pādma-saṃhitā* above.

Bhīma-Saṃhitāyām :

sulekhas suguṇaś śilpa-śāstra jñaḥ karma-yogyakaḥ
mānādi-rasa-māna-jñaś śalyoddhāra-viśāradaḥ.
vāstu-vidyā-kṛtābhyāsaś śilā-doṣa-parīkṣakaḥ
sarva-lakṣaṇa-saṁyuktaḥ sthapatis sa udāhṛtaḥ.

Kāraṇe (*i.e. Kāraṇāgame*)[1] :

sulekhas suguṇo dhīmān śāstra-jñaḥ karma-yogyakaḥ
vastū-vidyā-kṛtābhyāsaś śalyoddhāra-viśāradaḥ.

Yogaje (*i e. Yogajāgame*) :

sthapatir vāstu-tantra-jñas sarva-śāstra-viśāradaḥ
mahā-deśa-sthas[2] *saṁkīrṇotpanna-janmā kulādhamaḥ*[3]
sthāpako deva-devas syād yajamāno Janārdanaḥ
vidhātā sthapatis sākṣād etair dharma-sthitis tribhiḥ

* 1. These S'aiva *āgamas* have long been known as architectural works, but were hardly used by Āchārya though he lists them. This verse is not in the Uttara-Kāraṇāgama which is all of the name I have seen in published form.

2. —*stha* in the ins.

3. The ins. is read *janmā (ku) lā (dhamaḥ)*. This does not look satisfactory, but all restoration is hampered by the well-known eccentricity of the style of Sanskrit architectural works, the despair of the grammarian and prosodist.

Suprabhede (i.e. *Suprabhedāgame*) :[1]

ācāryam uktavāṁś caiva pūrvoktān sampragṛhya ca
ta syānveṣayet tadvat śilpinaṃ sukulotbhavam.
sthapatis sūtra-grāhī ca vardhakis takṣakas tathā
tanū-karaṇa . . . . .

sthapatis sūtra-grāhibhyāṃ prāsāda-pratimāṃs tathā
akṣi-mokṣādikam sarvaṃ kārayet takṣakottamaḥ.
sthapatiś śāstra-karma-jñaḥ kṛta-karmābhijātavān
īdṛśaṃ śilpinaṃ gṛhya prārabhet sarva-karmakam.

From the *Prapañcottara Vidyā-sūtra* they quote a verse agreeing exactly with the quotation from the *Kāraṇāgama*, which they have already cited above.

Lakṣaṇa-pramāṇe :

sarva-lakṣaṇa-sampanno nīrogaḥ kopa-varjitaḥ
upāya-jñas suśīla-jñaḥ kṛta-hasto vicakṣaṇaḥ.

Prapañca-tantre Lakṣaṇa-pramāṇe :

prasiddha-deśa-saṃkīrṇa-jātijo 'bhīṣṭa-kāraṇaḥ[2]
vāstu-vidyā-vidhāna-jñas tūnāpoha-samanvitaḥ.
nimitta[3]*-śakuna-jyoti-jñāne samyak prabodhakaḥ.*[4]
veda-vid dharma-vid dhīmān ācāryaḥ[5] *prokṣitas sudhīḥ*
prāsāda-liṅga-kāryeṣu mānasa[6]*-kāya-karmabhiḥ.*
Brahmaiva[7] *sthapatis sākṣāt yajamānas tu Keśavaḥ*
gurus sarvasya kāryasya Mahādevas sakāraṇam.

1. I could not find these verses in the published Suprabhedāgama.
2. The syllables *kāra* are illegible in the ins.
3. *nimittaś* in the ins.
4. *dhakaḥ* is conjectural.
5. Or *ācārya* ?
6. *mānosura* in the inscription.
7. The ins. is read '...*brahaiva*'.

Śrī Pāñcarātre Kāpiṃjale[1] :

> *bhuvaṃ khātvā śilāṃ paśyed ācāryaś śilpibhis saha*
> *śilpinaṃ pūjayet kāle dhana-dhānya-gajādibhiḥ.*

There follows what appears to be a one-line quotation from the *Parama-puruṣa-saṃhitā*,[2] but it was not to be identified because the fragment is too badly damaged. There follows—

Śrī Vaikhānasa–Mahāstave:

> *śilpa–śāstrokta-vidhinā śilpinas samyag ācaret*
> *sthāpayitvaivaṃ sahitas*[3] *śilpibhis śāstra-kovidaiḥ.*

Āgastya–vāstu–śāstre[4] :

> *svatantra-paratantra-jñaḥ kṛta–kṛtyas sumānasaḥ*
> *dharma–jñas satya-sampannas sarvendriya-jitendriyaḥ.*
> *itihāsa-purāṇa-jñaḥ smṛtivit vāstuvit sudhīḥ*
> *atandrī śuddha-bhaktiś*[5] *ca*[6] *alubdhaś cāmalātmakaḥ.*
> *nimittānāṃ krama jñaś ca citra-karma-viśāradaḥ*
> *sarvāvayava-niṣpanne vimāne cottarāyaṇe*
> *praśasta-pakṣa--nakṣatre yajamāno Janārdanaḥ*
> . . . . *sthapatiś*[7] *ca mahātmanaḥ*
> . . . *śarīrāṃgaṃ pāce* (?) *bhautika-saṃjñitam*
> *vimānaṃ vidhinā samyak jala-samprokṣaṇaṃ caret.*

---

1. The Kapiñjala-saṁhitā was published, according to H. D. Smith, in 1896.
2. Ed. P. Sitārāmāchārya, according to Smith.
3. This word is omitted in error in the ins.
4. * Of the many architectural texts attributed to Agastya, including an Agastya-pañcarātra, none seems to have been published?
5. In the ins. this is read as '*ata...dha–bhaktas*'. For these qualifications, which became standardised, see S'rī Kumāra, S'ilparatna, ed. T. Gaṇapati S'āstrī, Trivandrum 1922, I. 34-38.
6. A want of *sandhi* is consistent with the style of such works.
7. The ins. provides only...*patis*.

Vastu-vidyāyām[1] :

Viśvakarmā cācāryo gurutvāt viśva-karmaṇām
sthapatiḥ sthāpanaṃ kurvan iti śilpīr vidhīyate.[2]
sthapatis satya-śāstra-karma-vicakṣaṇaḥ.
kṛta-kṛtyaḥ kulīnaś ca[3] *ahīnādhika-lakṣanaḥ.*
dhārmikaḥ satyavādī ca gaṇita-jñaḥ purāṇa-vit
citravit sarva-deśa-jñas sunāma yamanāmayaḥ (?)
dṛḍha-yonisū ... ... yonalasobhayaḥ (?)
alubdho 'śanado 'dīno 'pramādī ca jitendriyaḥ
sapta-vyasana-jid dhīmān ūhāpoha-vicakṣaṇaḥ

Sarasvatīye[4] :

Viśvakarmā ṛṣer nāmnā gurutvāt viśva-karmaṇaḥ
sthapatiḥ sthāpanaṃ kurvan iti śilpir vidhīyate.
tattva-jñaḥ sthapatis sarva-śastrānāṃ ca viśeṣataḥ
dhārmikas satya-vādī ca kṛta-kṛtyaḥ kulodbhavaḥ

Finally two verses are quoted from the *Gautamīya-vivaraṇe*, an unknown commentary on Gautama, perhaps the *dharma-sūtra* or even, equally probably, a *purāṇa* or architectural *saṃhitā*, now lost, attributed to that sage. It is comical that it starts with a borrowing from Yājñavalkya (I. 95ab).

māhiṣyeṇa karaṇyāṃ tu rathakāraḥ *prajāyate*
nāsyopanayanaṃ nejyā nādhānaṃ ca niṣidhyate.
sūtrasya vājino vāstu-śilpayos syandanasya ca
vidyayātītayā[5] *svasya śarīraṃ vartayed ayam.*

---

1. This is an older work than the published Vāstu-vidyā (ed. T. Gaṇapati S'āstri, 1913), which is well worthy (however) of comparison with this passage (I. 12-15). K. C. Chatterji's trans. at Calcutta Oriental Journal, 1934, is better than P. K. Acharya's (Encyclopaedia of Hindu Architecture, Mānasāra Ser., vol. 7, Oxford 1946: a work in which, unfortunately Rathakāra does not appear).
2. The ins. reads only *iti s'ilpī...*
3. See note 60 above.
4. Not in the Sārasvatīya Citrakarmas'āstra, ed. K. S. Subrahmanya S'āstri, Tanjore-1960.
5. No. 603, para. 12 reads *vidyayā (sya*) dhika (ḥ*) svasya.* No. 479 at para. 2 seem to read *vidyayādhītayā svasya.*

All these texts establish the respectability, responsibility, and caste-duties of the Rathakāra in his quality as *sthapati*, architect.

The referees' decision.

We are now in a position to see what the Brahmins decided and how they did it. The question put to them S.I.I. XVII No. 603, which is recited at the outset, was what was the *vṛtti*, or approved livelihood, for a Kammāla who was a Rathakāra. The answer, as I have said, is broken accidentally by what appear to be faults in copying (haplography) and damage to the stone, but the structure is clear enough. The referees apply their minds to the *smṛtis* which explain that livelihood, and say that the (anonymous) text *vaiśyataḥ śūdra-kanyāyām* (above) governs him because he has been identified as an *anuloma* in the text (of Śaṅkha, above) *kṣatriya-vaiśyānulomāntarajotpanno*, in view of the text of Gautama, the text of Nārada, the text of Maskara (*sic*), the text of Yājñavalkya, a text from a *vṛtti* on ...lla (?), and the text of the *Brāhma-purāṇa*. I may be permitted to comment that this is an extremely neat way of reconciling those verses, though we do not in fact have in front of us *all* the material which they were using and they for their part do not explain (how could they have done ?) their failure to use material available to us.

They then begin at once to set out the texts, which I need not repeat. Yājñavalkya I. 95 appears in the strange guise noted above. Then comes the *Gautamīya-vivaraṇa* passage which will recur towards the end of our inscription as it stands now. Then Śaṅkha's text. Then the *smṛti* read by 'Maskara' in his *Gautamīya-vivaraṇa* apparently *not* the commentary utilised twice as above. Next comes the long quotation from the *Viśvakarmīya*. Then comes the statement that to this same effect is the information about the origins and livelihood of the man (caste) concerned contained in 'the Pañcarātrasaṃhitās, the Vaikhānasa books, the Viśvakarmīya, Āgastya[1] and related *śāstras*'. His duty is this: he must practise the arts of the *vāstu* (architecture) of villages, etc., the *vāstu* of temples, etc., sculpting images, the making of the weapons of the Fire-weaponed one, etc., ceremonies such as the Brahma-sṛṣṭi (a ceremonial at the foundation of temples ?). That being so the undersigned order that the fact

1. I have mentioned at n. 4 of p. 50 the existence of architectural works attributed to Agastya the sum total of which may be discovered readily from the New Catalogus Catalogorum. The inscription takes this way of indicating that all literature on the sbuject had been scrutinised, both Vaiṣnava and Śaiva.

that he will perform all this, he, the Kammāla who is an *anuloma* Rathakāra belonging to this place,[1] is to be engraved on stone and on a copper plate. Then follow the eleven surviving signatures.

What then follows commences with fragments of a Tamil translation of some statement in Sanskrit, or conceivably a statement originally in mixed Sanskrit and Tamil, in which the caste position of the Rathakāra is related to the Kṣatriya and Vaiśya castes *and* to the S'ūdra caste (relating, it would appear, to the ingenious reconcilation mentioned above, but too damaged to provide a positive conclusion) and there follows a citation from what is apparently '*Āgamam......ditta-vacanam*'. Thereafter follow immediately quotations, set out above, from the *Bhīma-saṃhita, Kāraṇa, Yogaja, Suprabheda, Prapañcottara-vidyā-sūtra, Lakṣaṇa-pramāṇa, Prapañca-tantra Lakṣaṇa-pramāṇa, Śrī Pañcarātra Kāpiṃjala, Parama-puruṣa-saṃhitā, S'rī Vaikhānasamahāstava, Āgastya-vāstu-śāstra, Vāstu-vidyā, Sārasvatīya.* Next come what appear to be three signatures (two referees having the same personal name),[2] since, evidently, the authenticity of the material quoted could be vouched for by specialists other than those who put their names to a proposition of *dharmaśāstra.*

The inscription abruptly starts again with *svasti śrī.* The text *vaiśyataḥ śūdra-kanyāyām* is repeated, and translated into Tamil, the Tamil equivalent of S'ūdra being Veḷḷāḷa (which as everyone knows is a respectable caste in Tamilnāḍ). The equivalent of Rathakāra is *taccan,* i.e. 'carpenter', equally 'mason'. Then the *Gautamīya-vivaraṇa* is set out again, followed by a literal Tamil translation (*vṛtti - toḻil*), in which it appears that *ilakkaṇam* (presumably the five components of grammar) was thought to be one of the necessary arts (rather than work with horses ?). Yājñavalkya is invoked for this proposition, too, and the words *atra Śaṃkha-vacanam* introduce the text of Śaṅkha again, but this time it is not given in full, stopping with the word 'Rathakāra' followed by a Tamil translation, saying merely that Kammālas who are these (Rathakāras) are '*anulomas*'. The inscription goes on to allege that he (who?) says that menial tasks (*iḻitoḻil*) must be done in the castes which are *pratiḻomas.*

1. No. 603 at para - 4. *ivvariṣṭomāpattiyaiyuḍaiya rathakārānulomanāgiya karmmārane ivaiayellāñ ceyavānenṛu kallilum cempilum veṭṭikkoḷka venṛu connom.*

2. Note that the Brahmin specialists in architectural texts *seem* much fewer than those who deal with and certify the *dharmas'āstra* position. Here the referees are Narāyaṇa.bhaṭṭa Somayāji, S'rī Raṅganātha-bhaṭṭa-Vājapeyi (the name is given as *-vājape (ya*) yāji*, and S'rī-Raṅganātha-bhaṭṭa. But it will be noticed that the section appears to be incomplete, and there *might* have been other names.

The Rathakāras themselves take up the tale, saying that 'we' have acted accordingly because it is stated in the texts of *smṛti* that menial tasks must be done by...(and the inscription is damaged here). The text of S'aṅkha is commenced again, but has a slightly different ending,[1] which may or may not be an error, for the Tamil translation which follows is broken off as the inscription abruptly ceases.

The information suffices to show that the referees expounded, and obtained the Rathakāra's, alias Kammāla's, agreement to a solution as simple as it was intelligent. If any Rathakāras were doing menial tasks these were * *pratiloma* Rathakāras, who had no right to participate in architecture; while those who could claim to be *anulomas* would be entitled to the architectural activities prescribed in the texts. Under the caste system as then in operation no Rathakāra could move from one category to the other: and so the solution would be permanent.

A.R. No. 479 of 1908

The Brahmins of Rājāśraya-caturvedimaṅgalam dealt with the problem more shortly, though there was a close similarity of treatment. They purported, both at the commencement and the end of the inscription, merely to give the purport of the *śāstra* on the subject (*śāstrārtham*) with regard to a subdivision of a caste (*jāti-vibhāgam* (sic)).

They started with the text *vaiśyataḥ śūdra-kanyāyām*, here too anonymous. They proceeded to quote Yājñavalkya I. 95ab followed by the curious unknown second line which we saw in No. 603, followed by an *iti*, continuing with *sutrasya vājino*, etc., which we have supposed (from No. 603) to have been taken from a *Gautamīya-vivaraṇa*. Then what would appear to be Śaṅkha's text[2] *kṣatriya-vaiśyānulomānantaraj otpanno*, followed by the two *ślokas*, commencing with *anulomyupaneyānām*, the provenance of which is unclear. Next comes the same quotation of 'another *smṛti* from Maskari (this time properly spelt) described as the 'author of a (or the) *Gautamīya-vivaraṇa*.' After an *iti* there follows a half-*śloka* commencing *māhiṣya iti nāmnā* but in

1. *tasyās'varathasūtras'ilpavāstuvidyā dhanurvvidyānvitās'ceti*. It is the reference to *dhanurvvidyā* which is novel. Such discrepancies would not trouble scholars of a civilisation which regarded all traditional texts as equally valid in the form they were received in by the learned. 2. See p. 37 (top).

so bad a shape that it is not clear what it means. Next Yājñavalkya is cited for a rather poor reproduction of Yājñ. I. 92—complete this time. After an *iti* appears another half-*śloka*, also in bad condition commencing *savarṇa*, and ending *ākarṇyate janaiḥ*, which is not attributed to any particular author and I have found impossible to trace. Then follows *atra Kauṭilya-vacanam* As mentioned above, this must indicate that the author of the original text of the inscription believed he was about to cite Kauṭilya. The appropriate text is III. 7.35, but it is difficult to see how it could have been left out by haplography: *karmaṇā vaiśyo Rathakāraḥ*. However, it would have fitted well enough had it actually been copied out. Later we shall see that another author is merely cited, and not quoted. What does follow the citation of Kauṭilya is Yājñavalkya I. 95abc, followed by an unintelligible half-*śloka* (apparently) in which the word Rathakāra appears. Next comes the phrase *tathā hi Bodhāyana-vacanam*. But the words of Baudhāyana on the subject (see above) are not quoted.

There follows a long Tamil and Sanskrit sentence in which the Brahmins state that the *anuloma* Rathakāra is born of a Māhiṣya male to a Karaṇa female, the Māhiṣya himself being the offspring of a Kṣatriya male by a Vaiśya female and the Karaṇa female being the offspring of a Vaiśya male by a Śūdra female as is unexceptionable (following Yājñavalkya in preference to other sources). This Rathakāra's ways of earning a livelihood are stated as comprising *vāstuśāstra*, chariots, carts and the like; sculpture and engineering: the making of what is called *brahmayāgādi*-(?) which calls for some investigation, if it is correctly transcribed; the making of sacrificial implements, statues, palaces, halls, gopuras; certain other tasks which are not clear; then the production of crowns, bracelets, threads and thrones for the royal palace, and above all, the painting of idols or images.

ADDITIONAL ANNOTATIONS

p. [87], l. 2. Kammāḷa comes from Karmāra (smith) and is therefore a Sanskritic term: T. Burrow, *Adyar Lib. Bull.* 25 (1961), 69ff.

p. [87], l. 7-8. This would be supported easily from inscriptional references. Craftsmen often gave themselves high-sounding titles: E.C. IV Gu. 20 (a sculptor called, inter alia, *bhaṭṭācārī*, which is a distinctively brahminical title); E.C. IV Kp 68 (A.D. 1116): a craftsman like Viśvakarmā; ibid., V Cn 265 (A.D. 1206) ditto; S.I.I. XI/2, no. 127 a *kammāra* (s. supr.) ditto. At E.C. X Kl 106d (c. A.D. 1071) we see a brahmin Mārasiṅga-bhaṭṭa receiving 60 *kalam* of paddy p.a. for conducting the worship in the temple, while the mason (who no doubt had other duties also elsewhere) gets 30 *kalam*; the temple accountant gets as much; other temple servants half as much.

p. [89], n. 1. The *Jāti-mālā*, an extract from the *Rudra-yāmala-tantra* gives abundant detail on mixed castes. See H. T. Colebrooke, *Essays* II (London, 1873), 157-70 (= *As. Res.* V, 1798, 53-67). For a guess as to the origin of two divisions of Rathakāras see Shivaji Singh, *Evolution of the Smṛti Law* (Varanasi, 1972), 171.

p. [91], n. 3. S. G. Jha, *Pūrva-mīmāṃsā in its Sources* (Benares, 1942), 314; also Kane, *H.D.* V, 1290-1, dealing with Jaim. VI.I.44-50. He quotes the *Smṛtikaustubha* (p. 168) as using the Rathakāra to illustrate a limited right to use Vedic *mantra-s*.

p. [97], n. 1. Add: Kane, *H.D.* I^2 (1968), 260, contradicts Caland and dates the *Vaikhānasa-dharma-sūtra c.* A.D. 300-400.

p. [102], n. 1. The relation of the work to the *Kiraṇāgama* (see H. Brunner, *J.A.* 253, 1965, 309-28) is not clear.

p. [104], n. 4. On the *Agastya-saṃhitā* see H. Daniel Smith at *Adyar Lib. Bull.* 27 (1963), 1-17 (identified as a Pāñcarātrāgama text).

p. [108], l. 10. The *Samūrtārcanādhikaraṇam (Atri-saṃhitā)* (Tirupati, 1943), a Vaikhānasa work, says (I.42-4) that *anuloma* Śūdras may be *yajamāna-s*, but not *sūtādi-pratiloma*.

MODES OF SANNYĀSĪS AND THE REFORM OF A SOUTH INDIAN MAṬHA CARRIED OUT IN 1584 *

Inscriptions help to show how the *dharmaśāstra* was actually administered. Inscriptions from the Tamil country (see R. Lingat, *The Classical Law of India*, University of California Press, 1973, pp. 273-4) reveal how *dharmaśāstra* texts were cited and quoted in a caste-problem, along with references to Kauṭilya (*sic*) and works in the field of architecture. Here we consider the implications of an inscription which tries to persuade the reader that the conversion of a *maṭha* which had been governed by a celibate into one to be ruled by a married mahant was not repugnant to Hinduism. The quotation of śāstric sources in association with purāṇic and sectarian works, proves that the *śāstra* was resorted to (in association with other culturally relevant materials) even at a time when (it was supposed) it could not have been widely known. These people were Pāśupatas.

There are some features of the ancient Hindu law which are still alive today, in spite of the contention (heard from time to time) that the *dharmaśāstra* is dead and no one need trouble himself to learn about it. Miniskirts are to be seen even in Poona, and the ancient *munis* must fry their own fish. Below I attempt a study of a fascinating inscription from Tamil Nad; but before anyone writes it off as irrelevant to the modern world I must draw attention to very recent case-law in which these topics figured.

Religious endowments are a magnet for money. Widows still make gifts out of their husbands' estates, provided, that is to say, the deceased husbands have not bequeathed a great deal of them in that direction already. *Maṭhas* (in Anglo-Hindu language maths, or even 'mutts') are a well-known variety of 'religious endowment'. Two questions have come to the fore. Can Śūdras be heads of *maṭhas*? And can married men, family men, occupy places much more naturally reserved for celibate teachers, founders or leaders of a school of Hinduism, dedicated to religion and divorced from the world and its pleasures? The *śāstra*, as understood in Anglo-Hindu law, conceives only of a celibate and a renunciate as a *sannyāsī*, and only a *sannyāsī* as the head of a *maṭha*. When it is a question of the right to act as mahant (= *maṭhādhikārī*), or to succeed to one deceased, litigants are heard to contend that the deceased was no real *sannyāsī*, and that, unless a custom to the contrary could be proved, the law to be applied must be that of Hindu males who are not *sannyāsis*. Recent decisions have repelled these contentions in the individual sets of facts.[1] It seems to be the case that, even where a custom cannot be proved contrary to the book-law, Śūdras can be *sannyāsis* (though not of the Vedic, i.e., *śrauta* or *smārta*, type), and that too whether or not they have actually abandoned the world, whether by any particular ceremony or not, and even where they are married; the community must accept them as mahants, whatever the book-law may say on the subject. Such decisions have the merit of flexibility and realism, and the rigidity of the Anglo-Hindu law is properly modified by them.

On the other hand the case-law reveals only too clearly the evils of *gṛhastha* (i.e., householder) mahants, when the squabbles between the surviving members of Vaiṣṇava Mahāprabhūs' families waste their estates, private and trust-endowed alike.[2] But when the requirements of the modern world and ancient tradition conflict the court listens attentively to the ancient *śāstras*, and their exponents.[2a]

---

[1] *Lalnarayan Prasad* v. *Amereshwari* A.I.R. (= All India Reporter) 1972 Pat. 242 (a Śūdra bairagi's estate). *Krishna Singh* v. *Mathura Ahir* A.I.R. 1972 All. 273.

[2] *Goswami* v. *Shah* A.I.R. 1970 S.C. 2025.

[2a] *E.R.J. Swami* v. *State of Tamil Nad* A.I.R. 1972 S.C. 1586 is a wonderful example of the Indian Supreme Court's ability to balance the modern ideas of the Con-

The inscription is No. 135, from Jambukēśvaram, dated Śaka 1506 = A.D. 1584, at the beginning of the reign of Veṅkaṭa I, reported by C. R. Krishnamacharlu in 1940 in his *Annual Report on South Indian Epigraphy* for 1936-7 at §. 79, the inscription being transcribed in roman characters at pp. 92–3. The editorial note reads as follows:

> "It is couched in a high-flown *maṇipravāḷa* style and appears to be an apologia for the selection of a married person (gṛhastha) to the pontificate of the Pāśupata-maṭha at Tiruvāṉaikkā, which had till then been probably in the keeping of a celibate only. The quaint style of the record bristles with bombastic quotations from several works in seeming support of this transition, and affords interesting reading."

The reasons for the change are paraphrased in English, and the whole was taken more or less word for word by T. V. Mahalingam in his article at *Journal of Oriental Research* (Madras) Vol. 25 (1957), pp. 78–9. I found the thing very interesting. The inscription is unique, but it supplements what we know from other references to the *dharmaśāstra* and related materials in a few other inscriptions. A reference to the *Mahābhārata* and "principles followed by kings" appears with reference to relief from taxation in an eleventh-century inscription.[3] A galaxy of *dharmaśāstra* citations, with the Brahmins' deductions from them, appear in twelfth-century inscriptions[4] concerning the status and privileges of Rathakāras. What we have here, however, is what is virtually a public decision made in the name of a deity, with the consent of interested Brahmins, but with the intended effect of a legal settlement of a pecuniary, and not merely social bearing, like a scheme framed and decreed in the Chancery division in England or by the High Court in India. I felt that the editor's sceptical tone was a little harsh, and perhaps prejudiced. I entered into a brief correspondence about the record with D. C. Sircar (then at Ootacamund) in early 1959. It is only now that I have an opportunity of improving upon my reference to the inscription in my *Religion, Law and the State in India*.[5]

Neither the editor nor Mahalingam attempted to assess the meaning or value of the event described in the inscription, and, as so often, many technical terms were left untranslated and unexplained. I cannot hope to improve upon their handling in all respects, since time and effort, though deserved by this inscription, are bound to be limited by other competing concerns. But we shall, I hope, have a better chance of estimating how such matters were handled, and why.

The Pāśupata sect was evidently an ancient Śaivite sect long established in South India, and particularly strong in the Tamil country. The sect's religion and religious practices were not of a type which is nowadays considered very edifying; the preoccupation with externals and observances, the endless concern with vows and austerities and marvellous aberrations from normal living in a parade of holiness—all these features make the behaviour, let alone the doctrines, of this ancient religion less than attractive even to the simpler villager of today.[6] Other forms of Śaivism, with greater emphasis upon morality and devotion to the deity to be expressed in terms of personal conversion and reform, have become more popular. But at the times with which we are concerned Pāśupatas were powerful and significant. I think it will be admitted that it is a feature of the Indian scene that competing religions are less competing faiths than competing social assertions. The group identifies itself with a particular religion or sect, endows it, and seeks to

stitution with the traditional notions of the *āgamas* according to which a great temple is run by its priests.

In *Kalyan Dass* v. *State* A.I.R. 1973 Mad. 264 a problem concerning temple-entry was solved with the aid of consultation of Śaiva and Vaiṣṇava āgamas.

[3] 358 of 1927. A.R.S.I.E. 1926–7, p. 101.

[4] 558 of 1904. S.I.I., vol. xvii (Madras/Delhi, 1964), No. 603. See App. to R. Lingat, *The Classical Law of India* (Berkeley, 1973). Also J. D. M. Derrett, 'Two inscriptions concerning the status of Kammālas,' *K. A. Nilakanta Sastri Fel. Vol.* (Madras, 1971), pp. 32–55.

[5] London, 1968, p. 168 n. 1. I then inclined to the view expressed by the *original* editor (List of the Inscriptions copied in the year 1936–7, p. 22, 'remarks') that Ādi-Caṇḍeśvara was the deity himself.

[6] For the sect see R. G. Bhandarkar, *Vaishnavism, Śaivism*, p. 112; T. V. Mahalingam, "The Pāśupatas in South India," *Journal of Indian History* 27 (1949), 43ff. at 52–3; also H. M. Sadasivaiah, *A Comparative Study of Two Virasaiva Monasteries. A Study in Sociology of Religion* (Mysore, 1967), 6ff.; M. Rajamanikkam, "The Tamil Saiva Mathas under the Coḷas (A.H. 900–1300)", in *Essays in Philosophy*, ed., C. T. K. Chari (T. M. P. Mahadevan Vol.) (Madras, 1962), 217–225. Also T. V. Mahalingan, *Administration and Social Life under Vijayanagar* (Madras, 1940), 333–338. *

enhance its own prestige relative to its competitors through and by means of its religious activities. In this way sects rise and fall, and allegiance waxes and wanes, sometimes without any rational explanation. In these days of anti-caste agitation it is odd that caste-sentiments should figure in this development. But field studies in different parts of India show that they do, and perhaps they always have done.

The law relating to maths is a well-known, but not an edifying, chapter of the Hindu law applied by the Indian courts.[7] In a recent case the learned judge expatiated on the unseemliness of the dispute between two would-be mahants.[8] Cases in which math properties are wasted in squabbles over the appointment of the next mahant are many, and litigation up to the Supreme Court about rights in and to math properties is frequent.[9] There is no doubt but that maths of all denominations and sects attract money and accumulate wealth, and some even take to money-lending as their primary pursuit.[10] It is odd that the more the mahant seeks to live an unworldly life the more gifts are showered upon him and his math. The genuineness of the mahant is thus an essential question about him, and Indians, with their characteristic mixture of optimism and cynicism, equate *sannyāsis* who are mahants with bogus spiritual teachers of the kinds which Kauṭilya urges the king to enlist in his secret service: the holy and the fraudulent are somehow symbiotic, and no one minds. Until, that is to say, some particularly appalling scandal break out, whereupon the "king" must take action, and the endowment is "visited" and "reformed," much after the style of the Hindu Religious Endowments Commission, which was a sort of royal visitation.[11]

When we study this inscription we wonder whether the reform, by which the incumbent mahant was "ordered" to become a grhastha, whereas he had previously been (we are bound to assume) unmarried (whether or not he was celibate), was a reform intended to deal with a situation in which the math had fallen into decay due to a succession of unchaste and disreputable *sannyāsī* mahants[12] (a reform which would occur to the mind of a student of the Reformation in western Europe), or whether it was something else. My reading of the inscription leads me to think it was something else, conceivably like this. The math was flourishing, though physically, it seems, a small affair, in association with the temple, placed strategically in the rich Kaveri valley. The Pāśupatas were no longer in opposition as they once were, as Tamil radicals, to the Brahminical faiths which had dominated the scene and obtained ascendancy; they no longer took the place of the ancient opponents of Brahminism in the South, namely Jainism and Buddhism, which had vanished. Other sects of Śaivism would maintain their religious hold upon those who were doubtful of the value of the Brahminical *varṇāśrama-dharma*, always a suspect import into the extreme South: devotion to a personal deity would absorb the religious energies of Śaivites and Vaiṣṇavas and undermine the spread of Brahminical doctrines of observances, of sacraments, and of an eternal *varṇa* hierarchy. Yet the unification of the culture demanded a synthesis of these apparently conflicting trends and desires. Those whose religion was utter devotion to Śiva wanted still to be part and parcel of the caste system, and there was no caste theory other than that expressed by Brahmins in the *varṇāśrama-dharma*. An antinomian and defiant archaic Dravidian religion became at some points compatible with normative Hinduism, as the religious teachers, absorbing the Brahminical learning, offered to the generality of the public everything that the Brahmins had to offer. Thus castes higher

[7] N. R. Raghavachariar, *Hindu Law, Principles and Precedents*, 5th edn. (Madras, 1965), ch. 15. Derrett, "The reform of Hindu religious endowments," ch. 14 in D. E. Smith, ed., *South Asian Politics and Religion* (Princeton, 1966). P. V. Kane, *History of Dharmaśāstra* II, pt. 2 (Poona, 1941), p. 906ff., 948ff. Signs of bias are present in the last-mentioned study (though the statements are supported by facts), which will be corrected by H. M. Sadasivaiah's excellent work (cited above).

[8] *Swamy Premananda* v. *Swamy Yogananda* 1965 Kerala law Times, p. 824.

[9] *Biram Prakash* v. *Narendra Dass* A.I.R. 1966 S.C. 1011 and *Dhyan Singh* v. *Chandradip Singh* (1969) 1 S.C.W. R. 242 illustrate the position. See Kane, *op. cit.*, 949.

[10] *Gurcharan Prasad* v. *P. Krishnanand Giri* A.I.R. 1968 S.C. 1032.

[11] Discussed in my chapter cited at n. 7 above. On the mahants' property rights, much debated in the *Report* of that Commission, see H. M. Jain, *Right of Property* (1968), pp. 69–70, pp. 307–8.

[12] As seems to have happened with a twelfth-century *guhai* (A.R.E. 1913, pt. 2, § 42). In S.I.I. IX (1), No. 102 (A.D. 1046), however, the *mahājanas* are instructed to drive away any *gṛhastha* appointed (Bellary Dist.).

in the scale than the humble agriculturalist gave their adherence to Śaivite sects such as the Pāśupatas, and the result was (as I think) that the Pāśupata doctrine had to become "respectable." In order to teach *varṇāśrama-dharma*, no doubt with many modifications to meet the requirements of local prejudices, the teachers, the maṭhādhipatis, had to be orthodox themselves, and had to take on Brahminical observances as well as the vows of the Pāśupatas. The problem was whether the two types of observance were compatible. It is notorious that in *purāṇas* and *tantras*, persistent and successful efforts were made to integrate popular notions and notions essentially competitive with Brahminism, into the orthodox normative system. And Brahmins themselves taught doctrines and practices which had no Vedic authority, but relied for their authority upon *sadācāra*—the fact that learned Vaidik Brahmins believed in and practised them.

In this case what I believe happened was that a fashion was started of appointing to the headship of maths married men who would found dynasties of holiness, performing the rituals open to householders, carrying out the duties appropriate to that *āśrama*, whilst serving as teachers and spiritual preceptors of Pāśupatas of all castes. The *dharmaśāstra* itself was not clear on the point whether a true *sannyāsī* could perform all the functions mentioned. How could a *sannyāsī* be the effective (as opposed to nominal) head of a religious institution? It is established in Hindu law that the essential of a math is that religious instruction is given there to students.[13] If it is still the case it was even more so in earlier ages. And regular institutional instruction implies an endowment, and a business head. A householder head would make much better sense, and it is clear that in the next century Jambukēśvaram knew families of Śaivite spiritual gurus, as their surviving inscriptions testify. The math would also be a *guru-kula* in the traditional sense. But the fascination for the life of the perpetual *brahmacārī*, the awe attached to the (supposedly) perpetual celibate, went a long way towards securing the public's regard, towards certifying the holiness of the establishment, and thus bringing in funds. To convert an existing post as head of a math, and, at the same time, shebait of the temple with which it was immediately associated, into a different kind of post, the holder of which would enjoy householder status and comfort whilst retaining the privileges and the profits, was something that could be achieved only by the concerted action of the sect, represented by their most prestige-worthy members, upon grounds which must be transparently lawful and righteous at the same time, with the consent and approval of the ruler, whose support would be needed to restrain counter-reform movements which would otherwise put forward an anti-mahant (this time a confirmed and conforming *sannyāsī*) as their protagonist.

The *dharmaśāstra* absorbed and regularised the concept of the perpetual celibate, the *naiṣṭika-brahmacārī*, but he remained attached to his teacher. The idea of a sannyāsī heading a wealthy establishment, even an expert in agriculture and money-lending as we know them today, did not fit with *śāstric* notions. There was never complete certainty whether a man might pass from *brahmacarya* to *sannyāsa* without going through the intermediate *āśramas*.[14] However it was open to argue that the true teaching of the *śāstra* was that even twice-born should pass through the householder stage, and there were reasons to believe that a Brahmin must perform the *karmas* laid down by the *śāstra* if he was not to lose esteem as a member of his *varṇa*. Naturally the Brahmin head of a wealthy and influential math could not afford to risk diminution or loss of prestige: once, at any rate, it had been accepted that orthodox Brahmins were natural, or possible, heads of Pāśupata maths.

This, then, is what this inscription may mean. Of the two alternatives, celibacy, and householder status, both could be supported on śāstric and traditional grounds somehow. The legal texts, and the religious texts of the Śaivites were called upon to authorise the latter position, and the decision was framed as an order directed to the mahant from the god Śiva, pronounced by his

---

13 *Administrator of Shringeri Math* v. *Charity Commissioner, Bombay* A.I.R. 1967 Bom. 194, A.I.R. 1969 S.C. 566, 71 Bom. L. R. 678 (SC).

14 Kane, *op. cit.*, II, pt. 1 (1941), pp. 418–426. Baudhāyana I.2.3,5 (the Veda says the fires are to be kindled while the hair is still black, and this limits the scope for prolonged *brahmacarya*). The text of the *Jābālopaniṣad* (§. 4) discussed by Kane at p. 421 (also II, pt. 2, 930) authorises both procedures, i.e., passing through *or* bypassing the *gṛhastha āśrama*. The question was never resolved: there remain the two alternatives. *Viṣṇupurāṇa* III. 10,13–15 quoted by Lakṣmīdhara, *Kṛtyakalpataru*, Brahmacāri-kāṇḍa, 268–9.

hereditary representative (see below), the shebait (it seems) of the principal temple in association with which the mahant's rights had been created, a gentleman, no doubt, of considerable prestige in the state government as well as that of religious affairs. The authors of this *vyavasthā* knew very well that their decision would be contradicted. It obviously was capable of contradiction. Householder mahants apparently existed in the Tamil country but history shows that the concept died out, and it is taken for granted there nowadays that mahants are sannyāsīs. But the authors of this document went about their work in such a way as to suggest that it was clear to them that government, the State, would not interfere to reverse the decision, but would, on the contrary, uphold it as an authentic legal alternative against all possible dissidents. The curses pronounced upon any individuals who interfere with the arrangement show that the Brahmins of the locality and the spiritual leaders of the sect had made up their minds in favour of the orthodox complexion which the sect's doctrines were to take on from thence forward, and it was assumed that the resulting gain in prestige to the math and its adherents could operate only in favour of the society, the culture, and the *śāstric* norm.

The inscription opens with the statement that it is the *tirumugam* or sacred order addressed to Candraśekhara-guru by one Ādi-Caṇḍeśvara-devar, who describes himself as *mūla-bhṛtya* of the (god) Tribhuvana-pati in the temple described. I suggest that he was named after the Ādi-Caṇḍeśvara-deva (Śiva) who was the deity of Tiruvarur, Nagapattinam taluk, Tanjore district,[15] rather than the deity of the same name at Sivapuri, Tiruppattur taluk, Ramanathapuram district.[16] I regard it as highly likely that he was born in Tiruvarur, perhaps the first son of his parents. He seems to have become the manager of the whole temple complex, responsible to government ultimately for the good conduct of the entire religious trust in which the math in question was physically situated. I wish we knew more about him. The verse at the end of the inscription suggests that he, as a patron-devotee of Candraśekhara-guru, was an official as well as an endowment trustee (*dharmakartā*). The voluminous works of T. V. Mahalingam and B. A. Saletore about Vijayanagara throw no more light on the man, and it may be that he was politically quite obscure.

The operative part of the "order" falls into two parts: (1) Candraśekara, in his quality as "our" (i.e., Śiva's) *tambirāṉār*, i.e., *maṭhādhipati*, shall continue to perform and enjoy the rights and obligations of worship of the deity, service of the idol, superintendence of the temple, drawing up[17] of accounts, the right to mark devotees with the seal (*muddirai*),[18] independence of management, and the Pāśupata-vow from teacher to pupil in succession; (ii) he shall do this as a householder, performing the Pāśupata rites and the *karmas* of sacrifices (e.g., *pañca-mahā-yajña*, presumably), worshipping, etc., for the god Jembunāthar Akhilāṇḍa-Īśvara, but with succession from father to son, on the basis of this order, as long as moon and sun endure, and upon that footing succession shall be to the son who is eldest in age *and* learning and he must maintain his brothers and protect the endowment.

The most interesting part of the document is the list of quotations supporting the revolutionary reform which this involved. It need hardly be emphasised that to convert a (śāstric) *sannyāsī* math into a *gṛhastha* math on this basis would not merely subsidise the mahant's enjoyment as a householder (he might have a succession of wives, since the presence of a valuable endowment would attract an unceasing flow of offers of girls in marriage), but also burden the math, and therefore its devotees, with generations of collaterals of the reigning mahant, who would be kept in idleness at the expense of the endowment (unlike the families of *gurus* who partition their disciples and all perform religious functions on tour).[19] A move from the one kind of math to the other would thus be an example of conspicuous consumption, in itself tending to raise the prestige of the math. I now reproduce the citations which supported the decision.

dirgha-kāla-brahmacaryaṃ dhāraṇaṃ ca kamaṇḍaloḥ|
narāśvamedhau madyaṃ ca Kalau varjyā dvijātibhiḥ ||
"Lengthy *brahmacarya*, the carrying of the water-pot, sacrifices of human-beings and horses, and spirituous

[15] S.I.I. vol. XVII (1964), Nos. 578, 586, 590, 598, 604, 605, 607, 608, 609.

[16] S.I.I. vol. XIV (1962), Nos. 218 and 253.

[17] And auditing?

[18] The practice seems to have been common to Śaivites and Vaiṣṇavites. Or does *Muddirai* (*mudrā*, a seal) imply legal personality (as a corporator sole)?

[19] *Tiruvenkatachariar* v. *Andalamma* 1969 1 Andhra W. R. 142 (FB) = A.I.R. 1969 An. P. 303 (FB) (on *śiṣya-saṃcāram*).

liquor are to be avoided by twice-born in the Kali Age."

This is cited as from the *Parāśara-Mādhavīya*, the then leading legal digest of the Tamil country, where it is indeed to be found without difficulty.[20] Its ultimate source is typically vague. Lakṣmīdhara attributes it to the *Brahma-purāṇa*, as does Aparārka.[21] The *Smṛticandrikā*, another lawbook of importance in the Tamil-nāḍ, perhaps now regarded more highly than Mādhava's work, attributes it to the *Āditya-purāṇa*,[22] but alas the *Nirṇaya-sindhu* attributes it to the *Ādi-purāṇa*.[23] It may once have existed in all three.[24] From the text our inscription gratuitously concludes that lengthy celibacy is *niṣiddham* ("forbidden")!

yo vidvān brahmacārī gṛhastho yatir vā |

This is attributed to the minor *upaniṣad* called *Kālāgni-rudropaniṣad*, which is evidently a holy book of the Pāśupata sect. It is indeed to be found there at para. 9, which however reads, in the most careful edition,[25]

tripuṇḍra-vidhiṃ bhasmanā karoti | yo vidvān brahmacārī gṛhastho vāna-prastho yatir vā samasta-mahāpātakopapātakebhyaḥ pūto bhavati | sa sarveṣu tīrtheṣu snāto bhavati . . . '. . . he who performs the marking called *tripuṇḍra* with the (holy) ash, being learned, whether he be *brahmacārī*, householder, forest-recluse, or renunciate, becomes cleansed from all the greater and lesser sins, becomes as if he had bathed in all the *tīrthas* (and so on, eventually becoming united with Śiva, without fear of rebirth—so says the blessed Kālāgnirudra).'

Now the inscription's text shows that our copyist did not copy correctly, as the word *vānaprastho* was omitted through that common copyists's error, haplography.

vratam Pāśupataṃ śuddhaṃ dvādaśābdādi-lakṣitam |
mat-bhakte tat pradātavyaṃ māheśvara-parāyaṇe ||
gṛhasthebhyo viśeṣeṇa yatīnāṃ tv agni-varjjitam |
aupanāyanike vanhau śrotriya-brahmacāriṇām |
vāyavye 'tha Pāśupataṃ sākṣāt vrataṃ dvādaśa-māsikam ||

The next text is attributed to the *Sanatkumāra-saṃhitā*:

'The pure Pāśupata vow, which lasts twelve years, should be committed to the devotee who is devoted to the servants (ministrants) of Maheśvara (Śiva): especially to householders; but without fire in the case of renunciates; in the fire of the Vedic initiation in the case of *brahmacāris* who are *śrotriyas* (faithful to Vedic *karmas*). Where the windy humour is disturbed (i.e., in ill health?) the Pāśupata vow lasts actually for twelve months only.'

This text plainly claims that even the most orthodox Brahmins can be initiated into the Pāśupata sect, and householders are indeed preferred.

It is difficult to track down and verify the text because the name *Sanatkumāra-saṃhitā* is given to four works, (i) the *purāṇa* of that name published in the *Purāṇa-saṃhitā* in the Chowkhamba Sanskrit Series,[26] in which the text does *not* appear; (ii) a portion of the *Skanda-purāṇa*, which seems a most likely choice;[27] (iii) a portion of the *Brahmāṇḍa-purāṇa*;[28] and (iv) a portion of the *Rudra-yāmala*, which was cited in *dharmaśāstra*[29] works and even in a *rājanīti* work.[30] Perhaps it will be tracked down one day. *

dvādaśābdam athābdaṃ vā tad-arddhaṃ vā tad-arddhakam |
prakuryyād dvādaśāhaṃ vā saṅkalpyaitacchirovratam ||

[20] *Pa. Mā.* I. 1, ed. Chandrakanta Tarkalankara (Calcutta, 1889), on *śloka* 34 (p. 123). Between the two lines he reads *gotrān mātṛ-sapiṇḍāt tu vivāho go-vadhas tathā* (readings are disputed: and did some Southerners object to that line?). Kane, *op. cit.*, III, 928 n. 1799. B. Bhattacharya, *The 'Kalivarjyas'* (Calcutta, 1943), 2 (No. VI amongst the *kalivarjyas* discussed).

[21] Lakṣmīdhara, *op. cit.*, *Brahmacāri-kāṇḍa*, p. 264; Aparārka on the *Yājñavalkya-smṛti* (Anandasrama Skt. Ser.), p. 15.

[22] *S.C.* (Mysore edn.), I, p. 12.

[23] *N.S.*, p. 286.

[24] It is notorious that digest-writers took quotations from collections as well as from the original sources. But many *purāṇas* now in print do not correspond to *purāṇas* utilised in such works: hence verification is difficult.

[25] By G. A. Jacob, *Eleven Atharvaṇa Upanishads* (Bombay, 1891). 20. The readings of the editions of A. Mahadeva Sastri, *The Śaiva Upanishads* (Adyar, 1925), 43 and Haripada Chatterji (Calcutta, 1920–1), agree with each other in *sa* for *samasta*.

[26] Ed. Shri Krishna Priyacharya, Banaras, 1951.

[27] See Eggeling's Catalogue of Sanskrit Manuscripts at the India Office Library, Nos. 3737–8, p. 1413b.

[28] Keith, continuation of Eggeling (above), II, No. 6664, also 6211.

[29] Anantadeva, *Smṛtikaustubha*; Bhavadeva, *Śrāddhakalā*; Viśvakarman, *Dharmaviveka*; Dinakara, *Dinakaroddyota* (on *śrāddhas*). See R. C. Hazra at *Our Herit.* 1/1 (1953), 46ff. *

[30] Keith, *op. cit.*, II, No. 7934.

This proves that the Pāśupata vow can be accomplished in various periods (not involving perpetual celibacy),

'for twelve years or for a year, for half a year, or a quarter of it, he should perform the "Head (-shaving) Vow"[31]—or even with intention (devotion) for twelve days.'

The text is attributed to the *Saura-saṃhitā*, which is a part of the *Skanda-purāṇa*, and not available to me for verification.[32] These two last texts show that the vows can be performed by householders, and for short periods: our inscription goes on to assert that Upamanyu,[33] Dadhīci,[34] Agastya,[35] Rama and Kṛṣṇa were householders and performed the Pāśupata vow. The argument next moves to the positive requirement of performance of *karma*.

ṛṇam asmin sannayaty amṛtatvaṃ ca gacchati |
pitā putrasya jātasya paśyec cej jīvato mukham ||
nāputrasya loko 'sti . . .

'When a father sees the face of a living son he casts his debt onto him and acquires immortality. There is no world for the sonless man . . .'

This is stated to have come, along with the passage which immediately follows, from a *Ṛg-brāhmaṇa*, which is true enough since it is *Ait. Brā.* XXXIII. 1, quoted by Viṣṇu XV. 45 and Vasiṣṭha XVII. 1, and thus very well known.[36]

yajuṣā (?) *jāyamāno vai brāhmaṇa-sthitau |*
ṛṇāni triṇyapākṛtya mano mokṣe niveśayet ||

The first word appears to be corrupt.

'Even by being born in the status of a Brahmin he should fix his mind on release having paid the three debts.'

This is a versified paraphrase of *Tai. Saṃ.* VI.3.10.5, which is in fact quoted in the original in the *Parāśara-Mādhavīya*.[37] It is a commonplace that the Brahmin is born with three debts, which three he cannot work off unless he marries and begets a legitimate son. True enough the view that an unmarried man can work off the debts to his parents by performing the *agnihotra* is set out (as an example of the consolatory provisions of the *śāstra*) in *Ait. Brā.* VII.2.8-9 (9-10).[38]. But that is rather a different matter. The theory of the three debts, once accepted, is fatal to perpetual celibacy on the part of those qualified for marriage. Our inscription urges that the three debts must be paid, from which it follows that sacrifices must be performed, whence it follows, in turn, that marriage is requisite . . .

jāyām avāpya daśame 'hany agnīn ādadhīta |
jātaputro 'gnīn ādadhīta |
uparāge kurukṣetre meṣa-kṛṣṇājinādikaṃ caṇḍālāt pratigṛhyāpi yajed avaśyakair makhaiḥ |

The first of these ("Having acquired a wife he should lay the fires on the tenth day") I have been unable to locate, though the inscription would attribute it to the Veda and *smṛti*. The second ("When a son is born he should lay the fires") is a commonplace Vedic citation which no one can locate in a Vedic passage now extant.[39] The third too I cannot trace: "In the dark, at Kurukṣetra, even if one has to accept a sheep or black antelope's skin, etc., from a *Caṇḍāla*, he should sacrifice with the essential sacrifices." The word *makha* interests us momentarily since the little dynasty of Śaivite gurus at Jambukesvaram in the seventeenth century were called *makhī* (e.g., Sadāśiva-makhī), indicating that a Śaivite pontiff at this very place was a married man performing Vedic sacrifices. The texts cited tend to show that sacrifices are obligatory and that marriage is needed in order to perform them. That a man is completed by his wife, in all respects and with special references to sacrifices, is a commonplace of the Vedic tradition (*Śat. Brā.* V.2.1, 10).

The inscription goes on to assert that he who fails to perform the necessary sacrifices is a sinner, the implication being that he is fit to be outcasted: and this would apply also to Brahmins who were

---

[31] *Muṇḍakopaniṣad* III.2.10

[32] Eggeling, *op. cit.*, II, Nos. 3693, 3737–8, p. 1414a.

[33] A *śrutarṣi*, and *madhyamādhvaryu*. For these sages see V. R. Ramachandra Dikshitar, *Purāṇa Index* (Madras 1951–5). Information from Śaivite purāṇic material is also to be wished for here.

[34] *Ibid.* Dadhīci gave up his life in service (I). But there is also a Dadhīci (II) who was the son of Cyavana Bhārgava, a married man, a sage by *garbha* (?) and a *mantrakṛt*.

[35] This is probably the Agastya (III) in V.R.R. Dikshitar's list. His wife was Lopāmudrā.

[36] Lakṣmīdhara, *op. cit.*, Gṛhastha-kāṇḍa, 431. Kane, *op. cit.*, II, 560 n. 1302.

[37] III (Bombay, 1911), 263.

[38] *tasmād apatnīko 'py agnihotram āharet.*

[39] Kane, *op. cit.*, II, 350 (referring to Śabara on Jaimini's *Mīmāṃsā-sūtra* I. 3.3).

members of the Pāśupata sect, as they did not cease to be Brahmins by belonging to it.

yasya Vedaś ca vedī ca vicchidyete tripuruṣam |
sa vai durbrāhmaṇo nāma sarva-karma-bahiṣkṛtaḥ ||
'He whose Veda and sacrificial altar are cut off for three generations is called an Evil Brahmin, cast out from all rituals.'

I do not doubt but that this can be identified and verified, because the pandits of the Adyar Library report it as located in their manuscript copy of the *Jābāla-smṛti*, a work of comparative rarity. They sought for it because it is quoted as from Jābāla at p. 626 of the (Adyar) edition of the commentary of Nanda-paṇḍita (who lived not so very long after our inscription) on the *Viṣṇu-smṛti* (LIV. 13). It is interesting to see such rare and marginal *smṛti* works relied upon for such an important purpose. But we must admit that the principle enunciated is an obvious one. The next work to be cited defeats me.

śruti-smṛti-mamaivājñā yas tām ullaṅghya varttate |
ājñā-cchedī mama drohī mat-buddhi-pratiloma-kṛt ||
"He who lives in defiance of the Veda, *smṛti* and my order is disobedient, a traitor to me, acting contrary to my wisdom."

No doubt this comes from a Śaivite purāṇic work. Its tendency is plainly to show that Śaivism is fully consistent with Veda and with *smṛti*, and that devotees of Śiva must conform to *varṇāśrama-dharma*, which is what the authors of our inscription must have wanted. This is the last of the authorities quoted. There follows the effect of the allegations, and the whole is wound up with an elegant Sanskrit verse to which we shall come immediately,[40] a very free Tamil paraphrase of it, a curse in Tamil only, to the effect that one who breaks this "order" will be guilty of killing a cow in milk and his two parents on the banks of the Ganges.

Then comes an interesting list of persons who are to be bound by the decision, including Brahmins bearing the title *paṇḍita*, Nambi, *bhaṭṭa*, and the accountants or treasurers of the temple and of the assembly, and then the whole is wound up with a Sanskrit verse in praise of the guru, Candraśekhara, himself.

Here is the longer verse referred to above. After a *śloka* we have two couplets in the Śārdūlavikrīḍita metre and one in Upendravajrā.

evaṃ Śiva-preraṇayā dattaṃ Caṇḍena śāsanam |
tad idaṃ śāsanaṃ pālyaṃ sarvadā sarva-mānavaiḥ ||
Caṇḍeśasya śaśāṅka-śekhara-camū-dhaureyatām eyuṣo |
Lakṣmikānta-Viriñca-mukhya-viduṣo[41] *mauḷi-sthitājñā-juṣaḥ |*
ājñāṃ prājñatamāṃ nikāmam avatu kṣoṇī-dhendras sadā- |
treyas santati-kāriṇīm abhimatāṃ Candrārddha-cūḍā-maṇeḥ ||
avaśyam ājñā paripālanīyā Śivasya devair upalālanīyā |
vilikhyatāṃ Dakṣa-purassarāṇāṃ pramādyatāṃ paśyata pūr-vipākam ||

"Thus a decree was given at the command of Śiva by Caṇḍa:[42] that very decree must always be protected by all men. May the Ātreya king ever fully protect the order, most wise, productive of issue,[43] approved by him whose crest-jewel is the crescent moon,[44] made by Caṇḍeśa, who has become the commander-in-chief of the army of him whose crest is topped by the moon,[45] who is a leading devotee of Viṣṇu and Brahmā,[46] who delights in the order which he has placed on his head. Necessarily the order of Śiva must be observed, delightfully regarded by the *devas*. Let it be inscribed! Consider the disaster that befell the city of the incautious Dakṣa and those like him!"[47]

The final, neat lines are these:

ubhayor iyam eva bhidā vaśinor iha jagati Candraśekharayoḥ |
makuṭa-gata-rāja-pādaḥ kaścana pāda-gata-rāja-makuṭo 'nyaḥ ||
"Between the two Candraśekharas who are alike lords on this earth there is only this difference: one has a King (i.e. Soma, the moon) on his diadem, the other has a king's crown at his feet."

[40] I am obliged to Prof. J. C. Wright for help with this corruptly copied verse, and to Mr. T. K. K. Iyer for a re-reading of the Tamil portions of this extraordinary inscription and an explanation of certain terms.

[41] The text corruptly reads *mukhyaṃ viṣan*. *

[42] Or 'vehemently'. Caṇḍa is, also, a name of Śiva.

[43] Auspicious for those who protect it, productive of a succession for the math and the sect, and productive of issue for Candraśekhara-guru himself! But I have seen no Jambukêśvaram inscription about his descendants.

[44] Śiva or Candraśekhara (the beneficiary) himself.

[45] Caṇḍeśvara is the leading trustee of the Pāśupata sect in the vicinity, viewed as Śiva's *gaṇa*. He might even have been a military governor of the district as well.

[46] *Viduṣo* is my guess. Moreover, Caṇḍeśvara admits the *trimūrti* as a whole.

[47] Dakṣa was decapitated because he did not invite Śiva to his sacrifice, the point here being that Śiva caused destruction or harm even to the *devas* and sages because of his interest in sacrifices!

ADDITIONAL ANNOTATIONS

Tit. Basically the same article appeared under the title 'An inscription dated 1584 concerning reform of a Maṭha', in S. Ritti, B. R. Gopal, edd., *Studies in Indian History and Culture: Volume presented to P. B. Desai* (Karnatak University, Dharwar, 1971), 91-104.

p. [112], n. 6. B. G. L. Swamy, 'The four Śaivite Samayācāryas of the Tamil country in epigraphy', *J.Ind.H.* 50/1 (1972), 95-128, at pp. 113ff. S. Chattopadhyaya, *Evolution of Hindu Sects* (New Delhi, 1970); D. N. Lorenzen, *Kāpālikas and Kālāmukhas. Two Lost Śaivite Sects* (Delhi, 1973); R. N. Nandi, *Religious Institutions and Cults in the Deccan (A.D. 600-1000)* (Delhi, 1973); B. Hanumantha Rao, *Religion in Andhra (A Survey of Religious Developments in Andhra from Early Times up to A.D. 1325)* (Guntur, 1973). There is also the more superficial K. A. Nilakanta Sastri, *Development of Religion in South India* (Orient Longmans, 1963).

p. [116], col. ii, l. 36-7. In fact there are two more *Sanatkumāra-saṃhitā-s*! The most obviously relevant one is the earliest of the extant *saṃhitā-s* of the Śiva-purāṇa, thoroughly considered by R. C. Hazra, 'The problems relating to the Śiva-purāṇa', *O.H.* 1/1 (1953), 46ff., at 46, 51-2, 59-61, 66-8. This is a pro-Vedic, anti-*āgama* Pāśupata work. Not later than A.D. 900, because quoted by Govindānanda in his *Dāna-kaumudī*, and by Vallālasena in his *Dāna-sāgara*; nor much earlier than A.D. 750 because it incorporates ch. 54 of the *Vāyu-purāṇa*. Originally a Bengali work. Further, there is a *Sanatkumāra-saṃhitā* belonging to the Pañcarātra sect of Vaiṣṇavas: V. Varadachari, 'The Sanatkumāra Saṃhitā', *Adyar Lib. Bull.* 35 (1971), 227-57. The latter can have no connection with our subject.

p. [116], n. 29. The *Sanatkumāra-saṃhitā* (Calcutta, 1314/1907), disc. by Hazra (supra), does not contain our *vv*.

p. [118], n. 41. By a double entendre *mukhya* may signify also Śiva.

A Newly-discovered Contact between Arthaśāstra and Dharmaśastra: the Role of Bhāruci

When the late Professor T. R. CHINTĀMAṆI introduced to the world[1] the work of Ṛju-vimala, *alias* Bhāruci , the long-lost ancient commentator upon the Manu-smṛti, he made it possible to do far more than he himself, with a cursory survey, was able to visualise. At the kind suggestion of Professor (then Dr.) V. RAGHAVAN the present writer acquired from the manuscript library at the University of Travancore, Trivandrum, a devanāgarī copy of the old, damaged, copy of Bhārucin's *Manuśāstra-vivaraṇa* (*alias* 'the Vivaraṇa'), written in the Malayālam script, and, after some delays, has been able to commence the task of transcribing and translating it.[1a] The copy commences with the last sections of Book VI. A perusal of Book VII was hardly commenced when it became obvious that Bhāruci was making considerable use of Kauṭilya's *Arthaśāstra*, though it was not clear whether he used any particular commentary thereupon, and though he did not refer to that work or to its author by name. Citations of the artha-śāstra, as such, in dharma-śāstra works are extremely rare. The two śāstras stand for different approaches to the problems of self-government and society, and we are familiar with the rule that in the case of conflict between them (which is envisaged as a matter of course) the dharma-śāstra must prevail.[2] The citation of the Arthaśāstra of Kauṭilya in Varadarāja's digest is indeed remarkable.[3]

However, it has been evident for long that the Manu-smṛti, which owes a great deal of its popularity and importance to its attempt to cover all aspects of religious and civil law and politics exhaustively and

[1] *Bhāruci, a new commentator on Manusmṛti*, Proceedings and Transactions of the Twelfth All-India Oriental Conference (1943—4), vol. 2, Benares, 1946, pp. 352—60. The connection between Medhātithi and Bhārucin is proposed at pp. 357ff.

[1a] The text with translation, introduction and notes, is to be published by the *Centre du sud-est asiatique*, University of Brussels.

[2] Yājñavalkya-smṛti, II. 21. The relationship between the śāstras is still a matter for debate. The view of K. V. RAṄGASWĀMĪ AIYAṄGĀR seems to the present writer to be correct. It is expressed *passim* in his works: see, e.g. *Rajadharma*, Adyar, 1941, 13, 82—3, 93—3, 132—4; *Indian Cameralism*, * Adyar, 1949, 46—52. See Bṛhaspati-smṛti, vyav. I, 113; KĀṆE (cit. inf.), III, 9–10, 868.

[3] *Vyavahāra-nirṇaya*, ed. K. V. R. AIYAṄGĀR and A. N. KṚISHṆA AIYAṄGĀR, Adyar, 1942, 284—5 (cf. Kauṭ. 3. 14, 29—31, KĀṄGLE's edn., p. 120).

(difficult though this was) consistently, in the course of that arduous task combined artha-śāstra material with the fundamentally dharma-śāstra character of the scheme. Book VII, which is devoted to rāja-dharma, a term which covers constitutional law, governmental policy, statecraft, and politics under the somewhat misleading expression 'duties of the king', would naturally require some attention to artha-śāstra. Manu in fact plainly shows this dependence by actually using terms[4] which are meaningless without reference to that science. The same tendency is evident also in the Mahābhārata, where also encyclopedism was (more luxuriantly) at work.[5] But the brevity of Manu demanded something of a commentary from the first, though more evidently in Book VII than in any other of the twelve books. One of the most striking features of Book VII is the author's simple adherence to artha-śāstra technique until nearly the end of his exposition, when, fearing that, if he added no *caveant lectores*, his overall scheme would be spoiled, he inserted passages palliating the picture of unethical opportunism he had already painted and subordinating his material to fundamental dharmic principles. But this is a feature which cannot be treated here.

Since Manu, and Yājñavalkya too, used arthaśāstra material, it is clear that commentators upon them would be justified in turning to arthaśāstra authorities for the elucidation and supplementation (where necessary) of their texts. In view of the dichotomy between the śāstras a certain self-consciousness would be expected, and we have seen how rare such references to the arthaśāstra are. However, it has been known since BÜHLER published his translation of Manu (1886) that commentators other than Medhātithi on VII. 156 used either the *Kāmandakīya Nīti-śāstra*, or a prose work from the same school.[5a] Much more significant are the quotations of Bṛhaspati's arthaśāstra work by Viśvarūpa in his * *Bālakrīḍā* on the *Yājñavalkya-smṛti* (I. 307, 323) and a citation by the same author of Viśālākṣa *ibid.* 328. These quotations have been available since 1922 and attention was pointedly drawn to them in 1924.[5b] The

[4] E.g. at VII. 154. The view that Manu relied on an arthaśāstra work anterior to Kauṭ. has much to recommend it. This is not the place to reexamine the evidence, but see R. P. KĀṄGLE, *Manu and Kautilya*, Indian Antiquary (New Ser.), I, 1 (advertised in 1963/4 but not yet come to hand).

[5] E.g. MBh. XII. 101, 44. The meaning of these types of array is to be found out from the arthaśāstra.

[5a] G. BÜHLER, *Laws of Manu*, S. B. E. vol. 25, Oxford, 1886, on M. VII. 155—6. J. JOLLY, "Arthaśāstra und Dharmaśāstra," ZDMG., lxvii, 1913, 49—96, at 96: "... in Wirklichkeit aber aus einem Prosawerk über Nīti, und zwar augenscheinlich aus K. A. 258 entnommen sind."

[5b] T. GAṆAPATI ŚĀSTRĪ, introd. to *Arthaśāstra of Kauṭalya...*, Pt. II (Triv. Skt. Ser. 80), Trivandrum, 1924, p. 7.

delicate balance between the śāstras could not be investigated without further references and identifications, which would allow us to see how much specialists in one school would permit themselves to utilise the other, and subject to what conventions. Strangely the known utilisations of the arthaśāstra by Medhātithi have not been studied, and this failure is unaccounted for.

The principal commentaries on the Manu-smṛti were published conveniently in two volumes by V. N. MAṆḌALIKA (MANDLIK).[6] The commentary of Kullūka, who belongs to the 13th century,[7] has been published frequently, and the text of Manu there given can be called the vulgate Manu. Kullūka makes extensive use of Medhātithi, but almost everywhere abridges or merely plagiarises him without acknowledgement. Where Medhātithi (hereafter referred to as Medh.) is most interesting, whether in his long and involved mīmāṃsā disquisitions, or in his illuminating and sometimes comical practical illustrations, Kullūka omits the material. What is most characteristic about Medh. could be obtained only from Medh. himself. No other commentator upon Manu so far published, excepting Govindarāja (c. 1050—1080) who plagiarises Medh., gives anything like the attention to his text that Medh. gave, and because of his vast size and complexity of explanation in some places Medh. himself became scarce. According to GAṄGĀNĀTHA JHĀ's explanation of what took place,[8] a northern Indian ruler was obliged to have a jīrṇoddhāra made in the course of the 14th century, as a result of which we have manuscripts, all more or less corrupt, descended from a restoration of the commentary from materials which were not only scarce but damaged. About the time when Kauṭ. was discovered and the results were causing their unprecedented excitement JHĀ was approaching, and undertaking, the gigantic task of revising the previous editions of Medh., publishing his translation, and finally (1932—9) publishing his revised text (which deviates from his translation). It never occurred to him to consult the *Arthaśāstra* for the purposes of settling his text. Admittedly that differed in many respects (which require explanation) from the then available Kauṭ. But since his researches into dharmaśāstra material were exhaustive, as evidenced by his two volumes of notes and explanations,

[6] *Mánava-Dharma Śástra (Institutes of Manu) with the commentaries of Medhátithi* . . ., 2 vols., Bombay, 1886. J. R. GHĀRPURE's edition (which is rare) closely followed it.

[7] P. V. KĀṆE, *History of Dharmaśāstra*, I, Poona, 1930, 359 ff. It was with the aid of this commentary that Sir William JONES learnt his Manu-smṛti.

[8] MM. GAṄGĀNĀTHA JHĀ. *Manu-Smṛti with the 'Manubhāṣya' of Medhātithi*, III, Calcutta, 1939, 'Editor's Apologia,' pp. i—ii.

it is remarkable that he did not think of turning to the then notorious and controversial Kauṭilya.

Jhā's translation of Book VII of the *Manu-bhāṣya* appeared in 1924. In 1923 in Lahore was published J. Jolly's edition of Kauṭilya (Vol. I), at p. 11 of the Introduction to which the reliance of Medhātithi upon the *Arthaśāstra* is noted. Since Jhā does not take up Jolly's identification of Medh.'s source (samāna-tantra, i.e. a treatise on a similar subject[8a]) as Kauṭ. (cf. pp. 401, 409 of Jhā's trans.), we can be confident that he did not see Jolly's book. The point was taken up by T. Ganapati Śāstrin also in 1924, with no further result.[8b] Jhā's text of Medh. published so many years later likewise shows no reaction to the discovery. Jolly had found that Medh. used Kauṭ. at VII, 61 and 81, where the * section (II) is referred to as *Adhyakṣapracāra*. He adds that Medh. uses Kauṭ. without acknowledgement at VII, 53, 54, and 104. The matter is not pursued further, nor does anyone inquire why Medh. used only these passages or in that form. Apparently independently of Jolly, Pāṇḍuraṅga V. Kāṇe in the first volume of his *History of Dharmaśāstra* (1930) notes Medh.'s dependence on Kauṭ. at VII, 54, 148, and 155.[9] A brief note by Kāṇe evoked no further response from Jhā than Jolly's note had done, and indeed provoked no further research from anyone, including Kāṇe himself. Another learned writer, K. V. Raṅgaswāmī Aiyaṅgār, whose contributions to the study of both arthaśāstra and dharmaśāstra are well known, seems to have ignored both the discovery and its implications. The recent author of the authoritative text of Kauṭ. and its translation,[10] R. P. Kāṅgle, whose additions to our knowledge of the *Arthaśāstra* are unique, apparently decided against utilising Medh. for his textual apparatus except at I. 12, 23—4 (p. 30 of the trans.). His reason may possibly have been that Medh.'s correspondence with Kauṭ. was not sufficiently precise, or was fleeting and insecure, in view of the doubts as to the reliability of the jīrṇoddhāra text to which we have referred, and that uncertainties in his apparatus should not be increased thereby.

The questions remained, did Medh. copy from Kauṭ., and if he did are his readings useful for determining the text of that very difficult and ill-evidenced work? To these questions a possible field of clarification has been opened up by the rediscovery of the *Vivaraṇa*, unknown alike to Jolly, Meyer, Jhā, T. Gaṇapati Śāstrin, Kāṇe, and Kāṅgle.

[8a] T. Gaṇapati Śāstrī, ubi cit. sup., at pp. 7—8.
[8b] Ibid., p. 8. [9] Op. cit., p. 270.
[10] *Kauṭilīya Arthaśāstra, Pt. II* (Univ. of Bombay Stud., Skt., Pkt. and Pali, No. 2), Bombay, 1963.

The result is very curious. The passages which Medh. takes without acknowledgement from Kauṭ. are not obtained from the *Arthaśāstra* direct, but from Bhāruci, who is quoting, with occasional adjustments, from Kauṭ. This signifies that Medh. did not know (since Bhār. does not refer to his own source by name) that he was reproducing the *Arthaśāstra*. The passages which Medh. himself refers to as a *samāna-tantra* (an obtrusively anonymous source) are not present in Bhār. Likewise the quotations of Medh. from the *Adhyakṣapracāra* are missing from Bhār. This leaves it open to be supposed that an anonymous work which was essentially an excerpt from the *Arthaśāstra*, and another section passing under the name *Adhyakṣapracāra* were available (with commentaries?) to Medh., but the passages quoted (evidently) from Kauṭ. indirectly from Bhār. were not otherwise available. The curiosity is deepened by the fact that these passages are taken from various places in the *Arthaśāstra* and not from one or more closely linked sections. However, the general tentative conclusion that Medh., who was supplied with many copies and versions of Manu, could not be furnished with a complete copy of the *Arthaśāstra* under the name of the Kauṭilīya seems inescapable.

Something even more unexpected emerges. Of no writer on Manu does Medh. make more constant and close use than Bhāruci, especially in Book VII. Yet Medh.'s knowledge of Bhār. himself seems to derive solely from one manuscript. This is after all not unlikely. But the evidence is all too compelling that that manuscript was defective. It seems that in places he could not read it. Some of the many deviations of Medh. from Bhār. can be explained most readily upon the footing that his Bhār. was here and there illegible or unintelligible.[11]

This is by no means an impossibility. Medh. wrote somewhere between about A.D. 825 and 900, according to the opinion of that expert and conservative dater of dharma-śāstra works, KĀṆE, an opinion which JHĀ accepts.[12] By that period regional scripts had diverged so widely as to make Sanskrit works unintelligible in a foreign deśa. If Bhār. was a Tamilian or Malayālī (which is not unlikely)[12a] his work would have had

[11] In our passage III below the content of the purohita's enticement seems to have been illegible. For āmiṣaṃ/viṣaṃ see p. 142 n. 24 inf. There are more than sufficient examples in our passages without adding others from elsewhere. Note *āsevanena/eva tena* (I); *kṛcchreṣu/kṛta-kṛtyeṣu; kupyati/(na) kṛṣyate; anusavanaṃ/anubhavanam; nṛttādiṣu/anṛtādiṣu* (all in I); *avāpt-ārthaḥ/prārthanā* (IV); *Kārūṣaṃ (? -śaṃ)/ku-puruṣa* (see p. 148 n. 56 inf.). Also from VI, *vargam/karm-; sattrinas/mantrinas* (bis); *'vaśyaṃ/vaṃśa; aṅga/saṅga*. Gross misreadings took place in the verses at the end of VI, and some misreading in the first śloka in II. [12] KĀṆE, ubi cit. sup., at p. 275.

[12a] His readings of Manu resemble in places those adopted by Mādhava in the Parāśara-mādhavīya, e.g. at VII. 49, 53, 54, 99, 134, 182, 185, 193, 194,

to be transcribed into a northern Indian script before Medh. could read it. Such a process always involves difficulties as soon as the subject-matter becomes difficult, the style laconic, technical, or poetical. In such contexts Bhār.'s manuscript was not faithfully reproduced and Medh. was obliged to reconstruct the sense as best he could.

Apart from these discrepancies he gives the sense and actual words of Bhār., except where two, or one of two, processes occur: firstly his own rethinking of the notions which Bhār. adopts, as a result of which changes, editing, amplification, illustration take place at sufficient length to show Medh.'s own mind at work; secondly the decay or obscurity of Medh.'s own text by the time of the jīrṇoddhāra has given rise to editorial activity on the part of the pandits—this is usually evident from a vapid and unconstructive tampering with what would otherwise be a valuable text. Jhā's interference with the text might have been supposed to be considerable from what he himself says,[13] but in fact a comparison with MANDLIK's edition reveals that his alterations were, if not few in number, at least not very drastic.

Medh.'s dissatisfaction with Bhār. stems from the different role which Manu was destined (to his mind) to play. Bhār. had had fewer alternative readings before him; fewer ideas; fewer academic or practical problems. Bhār. was nearer to the smṛti itself in point of time and language. Far fewer words needed to be explained, and fewer ślokas. Bhār. was old-fashioned, and antiquated. His rarity, which is evidenced by the paucity of citations from him in later works, and the presence of for the most part mere references to his opinions,[14] in itself suggests that his views were as good as superseded. A detailed comparison between Medh. and Bhār. would reveal the difference of their outlook, and their aims. We do not know the date of Bhāruci, but it can hardly have been later than A.D. 800, and the present writer would be content to believe that

200 (incompletely). [Mādhava may be citing 'Uśanas' from Bhār. on 154 at his Ācāra-k., 411, but Medh. is more likely as his source.] The correspondence with the P. M. is not however constant, as a glance through JHĀ's Notes, Pt. 1 (1924) on 'Discourse VII' will reveal. There are instances where Bhār. is agreed with in the (northern) Vīramitrodaya (e.g. VII. 40b), but Mitramiśra obtained his material from all quarters, and some of his readings have an affinity with the (distinctively southern) P. M., e.g. at VII. 49. Medhātithi sometimes follows Bhār.'s reading of Manu, but is not bound by him, e.g. in the order of verses at VII. 128/9. Where Bhār.'s text is the one cited in Aparārka, e.g. VII. 85, we have additional evidence of Bhār.'s version being southern. Evidence of his text standing apart from all the surviving traditions appears in, e.g., VII. 145. However, ecclectic habits surely did not commence after Bhāruci.

[13] Ubi cit. sup., at pp. iii—iv.

[14] See KĀṆE, ubi cit., 264—6.

it is nearer A.D. 700 than the c. 800—850 which KĀṆE cautiously places as Bhāruci's latest likely *floruit*.[15]

At present the questions suitable for discussion here are these:

1. Assuming that the text of Bhār. can be established with the aid of Medh. and Kauṭ. as we know them, or otherwise, can the text of Bhār. throw light on the text of Kauṭ. as available about A.D. 700—800 (which is very early in comparison with most of our evidence on that subject)?

2. Assuming, once again, that the text of Bhār. can be established, can it throw light on the pre-jīrṇoddhāra text of Medh. (which would be immensely valuable in view of the unique importance of that author)?

3. Can a comparison of the texts of Bhār. and Medh., so established, throw any light upon the methods of Medh., and in particular his utilisation of previous authors?

To all these questions this writer would be inclined to give a positive answer, for the following reasons:

1. Bhār. obviously used a version of Kauṭ. anterior to those known to some extent from records of surviving manuscript material of Kauṭilya himself.[16] His numerous deviations from Kauṭ. suit his purpose as a commentator on Manu; but one striking instance of a real distortion of Kauṭ. to suit the obviously different scheme of Manu (the rāja-vyasanas)[17] shows that he was master of his material. The fact that he does not bother to cite Kauṭ. by name shows that he expected the source to be recognised automatically. In numerous cases he merelly alludes to Kauṭ. or borrows his vocabulary without copying the passage verbatim,[18] and this too helps us to recognise where he is deliberately incorporating Kauṭ. as distinct from merely utilising him and his science.

2. It is a matter of great difficulty to see which of Medh.'s deviations from Bhār. are due to him and which to his restorers, especially since we can be sure that his copy of Bhār. was defective. But there are a few

[15] Ibid., 265.

[16] He agrees with Cn (a South Indian comm.) at 8. 3, 44 (see KĀṄGLE's trans. ad loc.); but he agrees with D at 1. 10, 7—8; 1. 11, 4, 14; and 1. 20, 15. He agrees with GM at 1. 11, 14. D is a ms. found at Patan in Gujarat, recently published by Muni Jinavijayaji. Bhār. differs as frequently from D as from the Grantha and the Malayālam mss.

[17] Passage I below, on M. VII. 52. We note that Bhār. cites views *denied* by K., but the evidence is too slight to enable us to suppose that Bhār. was copying from predecessors of K. On the contrary what evidence there is, especially the verses at the end of VI below, points to Bhār.'s having K. in front of him.

[18] Allusions to Kaut. appear at VII. 70 (cf. K. 2. 3, 7); 152 (cf. K. 1. 17, 34); 155 (cf. K. 6. 2, 19 (?), 21, 22); 160 (cf. K. 7. 1, 6, 20); 187 (cf. K. 10. 2).

instances where it seems highly likely that our printed Medh. does not represent what he could have written. The best test is whether, if Bhār. is likely to have been clear to him, Medh. could have written what he is represented as having written. The test applies to a couple of instances available below.[19] A general impression achieved from a preliminary reading of Medh. with Bhār. is that the reliability of the printed text is high, and that the damage due by the jīrṇoddhāra is slight.

3. Medh.'s independence from Bhār. and indeed from previous writers is proved by the overall comparison. He prefers to follow and where necessary improve upon Bhār. in places where the latter has rare information (e.g. from Kauṭ.). But his respect for Bhār., evidenced by direct allusions to him,[20] is proved in the majority of passages. It is legitimate to ask whether without previous scholars of the stature of Bhār. Medh. could have written his important treatise.

Better than any such general discussion is a detailed comparison of passages, some of which KĀṆE himself alluded to. The relationship between the three authors, and their respective capacities to be purged or improved as a result of this comparison, are at once evident. The present writer has not adopted a consistent style of romanisation, especially in respect of resolving sandhi, preferring to follow, for the most part, the texts as printed by JHĀ and KĀṄGLE. The resulting anomalies should not prove to be an embarrassment. In several cases the corrupt state of the *Vivaraṇa* manuscript is given, since it may be more helpful than the conjecture which will eventually take its place in the edition.

I

Kauṭ. 8, 3, 38: *kāmajastu mṛgayā dyūtaṃ striyaḥ pānam iti caturvargaḥ.*
Manu VII, 50: *pānam akṣāḥ striyaścaiva mṛgayā ca yathā-kramam*
etat kaṣṭataraṃ vidyāccatuṣkaṃ kāmaje gaṇe.

Bhār.	Medh.	Kauṭ.
pāna-dyūtayoḥ pānaṃ garīyaḥ. tatra hi saṃ-	*pāna-dyūtayoḥ pānaṃ garīyaḥ. tatra hi saṃ-*	*pāna-sampat saṃjñā- -nāśo 'nunmattasyon-*

[19] *rata* for *rahasya* in I below is doubtful; *grāmya-jana-parijayaśca* at the end of I might be Medh.'s reaction to *paracaya* misread as *parijaya*, but it looks like *jīrṇoddhāra* panditry. *paramarma/parama-dharma* at VI is a certain example because we know from Govindarāja *ad loc.* that Medh. read *paramarma* at that time.

[20] He is cited as Ṛju at M. VIII. 151 (cf. VIII. 150, Yajvan ought to be *
Ṛju ?); as Smṛti-vivaraṇa-kārāḥ at II. 25. The *Vivaraṇa* as such is cited at II. 6. KĀṆE's statement that Medh. does not cite Bhār. is thus literally (op. cit., 275) but not substantially correct.

jñā-pranāśaḥ.anunmattasyonmattatva(m apreta)sya pretatvaṃ śruta-prajñā-prahāṇaṃ mitra-hāniḥ sadbhir viyogaḥ asadbhiśca prayogaḥ. gītādiṣu cārtha-svapneṣu[23] *prasaṅgaḥ. rahasya-mantra-prakāśaṃ, mada-vegeneti pāna-doṣaḥ.*	*jñā-pranāśaḥ,anunmattasyonmattatvam, apretasya pretatvam kaupīna-prakāśanam,*[21] *śruta-prajñā-prahāṇam, mitra-hāniḥ, sadbhir viyogaḥ, asadbhiśca samprayogaḥ,gītādiṣvarthaghneṣu prasaṅgaḥ, rata-mantra-prakāśanaṃca, mānino 'pyupahāsyatā, gambhīra-prakṛter api yat-kiñcana-vāditā mada-vegeneti pāna-doṣāḥ.*	*mattatvam apretasya pretatvaṃ kaupīna-darśanaṃ śruta-prajñā-prāṇa*[22]*-vitta-mitra-hāniḥ sadbhir viyogo 'narthya-saṃyogas tantrī-gīta-naipuṇyeṣu cārtha-ghneṣu prasaṅga iti (61).*
dyute jitam evākṣa-viduṣā anakṣa-jñasyāpi pākṣikaḥ parājayaḥ.	*dyūte tu jitam evākṣa-viduṣā, anakṣa-jñasyāpi pākṣikaḥ parājayaḥ.*	*dyūte tu jitam evākṣa-viduṣā yathā Jayatsena-Duryodhanābhyām iti (41).*
dyūta-strī-vyasanayośca dyūtaṃ garīyaḥ. yena tadaiva jita-dravyaḥ tasyāpi bhavati, tathā tan-nimitto vairānubandhaḥ jayaḥ sādhāraṇaḥ kevalaḥ parājayaḥ anubhakta[25]*-nāśaḥ.*	*strī-dyūta-vyasanayor dyūta-vyasanaṃ garīyaḥ. yena tad eva jitaṃ dravyaṃtasyāpi viṣaṃ*[24] *bhavati. tathā ca tan-nimitto vairānubandho jayaḥ, sādhāraṇaḥ kevalaṃ parājayaḥ, bhukta-nāśaḥ.*	*tad eva vijita-dravyam āmiṣaṃ vairānubandhaśca. sato 'rthasya vipratipattir asataścārjanam apratibhukta-nāśo*
mūtra-purīṣa-vega-dhāraṇācca śarīra-tantra-śaithilyaṃ vyādhi-nidānam āsevanena kṣudrādibhiścapīḍātiśayena. mātaryapi ca mṛtāyāṃ dīvyatyeva kitavaḥ. kṛcchreṣu ca pṛcchyamānaḥ suhṛdbhir api kupyatīti dyūta-doṣāḥ.	*mūtra-purīṣa-vega-dhāraṇācca śarīre śaithilyaṃ vyādhi-nidānam eva. tena kṣudrādibhiḥ sva-pīḍātiśayāt. mātaryapi ca mṛtāyāṃ dīvyatyeva. kṛta-kṛtyeṣu ca na suhṛdbhir api kṛṣyate. taptāyasa-piṇḍavat para-dravyāṇi pariharato na pratyayate ca. kṣudhite durgate 'nnā-*	*mūtra-purīṣa-dhāraṇa-bubhukṣādibhiśca vyādhi-lābha iti dyūta-doṣāḥ (44—5). ... mātari ca mṛtāyāṃ dīvyatyeva kitavaḥ. kṛcchre ca pratipṛṣṭaḥ kupyati (48—9).*

[21] *kaup.* has evidently dropped out from Bhār.
[22] *prahāṇaṃ* of Bhār. seems better. [23] For *ghneṣu.*
[24] Bhār. probably read *āmiṣam.* [25] For *apratibhukta?*

	dyupapattyupekṣā viṣayatā sarva-guṇa-saṃpannasyāpi tṛṇa-vad avajñāyeta. iti dyūta-doṣāḥ.	
strī-vyasane tvapatyotpattiḥ pratikarma-bhojana-bhūyiṣṭham anusavanaṃ dharmārtha-parigrahaḥ. śaktā ca strī rāja-hite niyoktum apavāhayituṃ vā.	*strī-vyasane tvapatyot-pattiḥ pratikarma-bhojana-bhūyiṣṭhānubhavanaṃ*[27] *dharmārtha-parigrahaḥ. śakyā ca strī rāja-hite niyoktum apavāhayituṃ vā.*	*strī-vyasane tu snāna-pratikarma-bhojana-bhūmiṣu bhavatyeva dharmārtha-paripraśnaḥ.*[26] *śakyā ca strī rāja-hite niyoktum, upāṃśu-daṇḍena vyādhinā vā vyāvartayituṃ avastrāvayituṃ vā iti (50—1)*
strī-mṛga-vyasanayoḥ strī-vyasanaṃ garīyaḥ. adarśanaṃ kāryāṇāṃ,[28] *strī-vyasanāsaṅgeṣu*[29] *rāja-kāryeṣu nirvedaḥ. kālātipātanaṃ, dharma-lopaḥ, pāna-doṣānubandhaḥ, arthaghneṣu ca nṛttādiṣu prasaṅga iti.*	*strī-mṛga-vyasanayoḥ strī-vyasanaṃ garīyaḥ. adarśanaṃ kāryāṇāṃ, strī-vyasana-saṅgena rāja-kāryeṣu ca nirvedaḥ, kālātipātanaṃ, dharma-lopaḥ, pāna-doṣānubandhaḥ, arthaghneṣu cānṛtādiṣu prasaṅga iti.*	*adarśanaṃ kārya-nirvedaḥ kālātipātanād anartho dharma-lopaśca tantra-daurbalyaṃ pānānubandhaśceti (54).*
mṛgayāyāṃ tu vyāyāma[30]*-pitta-śleṣma-vadhaḥ*[31] *svedādi-nāśaḥ. cale sthire ca kāye lakṣa-paricayaḥ. praharaṇa-vaiśāradyopajananena āsana-paricayaśceti.*	*mṛgayāyāṃ tu vyāyāmaḥ pitta-śleṣma-bandhaḥ, medādi-nāśaḥ, cale sthire vā kāye lakṣya-paricayaḥ, praharaṇe vaiśāradyopajananaṃ grāmyajana-parijayaśceti.*	*mṛgayāyāṃ tu vyāyāmaḥ śleṣma-pitta-medaḥ-sveda-nāśaś cale sthite ca kāye lakṣa-paricayaḥ . . . (46).*

[26] Possible, but less attractive than Bhār.'s *parigrahaḥ. snāna* looks like an insertion into K. due to a misunderstanding of *pratikarma.*

[27] Note the misreading due to the unusual word *anusavanam,* and the ready confusion of the syllables *sa* and *bha/ma* in some scripts.

[28] The text of K. is doubtful here.

[29] *āsaṅgeṣu* is better, but the cause of our Medh.'s decline into *saṅgena* is uncertain.

[30] For *vyāyāmaḥ.*

[31] For *medaḥ?*

II

Bhāruci on M. VII, 52.

krodha-jasya tu trikasya daṇḍa-pātana-vāk-pāruṣyayor daṇḍa-pātanaṃ garīyaḥ. daṇḍa-pātane hi śarīra-vināśād aśakyaṃ pratisandhānaṃ, vāk-pāruṣye tvamarṣa-jaḥ krodhāgniḥ śakyate dāna-mānāmbhobhiḥ śamayituṃ. vāk-pāruṣyārtha-dūṣaṇayor vāk-pāruṣyaṃ garīyaḥ. tejasvino hi paruṣa-vacanaṃ citta-saṃkṣobhe bheṣajānāsādyate. tathā ca pravādaṃ: —

sthiraṃ svādhyam[32] *itaṃ gāḍhaṃ bhitvā*[33] *strī*[34]*-saṃpraveśitaṃ*
niśalyam[35] *aṅgān kṛntanti na vāco hṛdayād adhi*[36]
saṃrohati śarair viddhaṃ varaṃ[37] *paraśunā hataṃ*
vācā duruktaṃ bibhatsaṃ[38] *na rohati parikṣataṃ.*[41]

bhāgyāyattatvād arthasya ca tejasvino 'rtha-dūṣaṇaṃ na gaṇayanti.

Medhātithi on the same.

krodha-jasyāpi ca daṇḍa-pāta-doṣānubandhaḥ arthaghneṣvevānṛtādiṣu saṅgaḥ. daṇḍa-pāta-vākpāruṣyayor daṇḍa-pātanaṃ garīyaḥ. daṇḍa-pātane hi śarīra-vināśād aśakyaṃ pratisaṃdhānaṃ. vākpāruṣye tvamarṣa-jaḥ krodhāgniḥ śakyate dāna-mānāmbhobhiḥ śamayituṃ. vākpāruṣyārtha-dūṣaṇayor vākpārusyaṃ garīyaḥ. tejasvino hi pāruṣya-vacana-citta-saṅkṣobhe bhayaṃ nāsādayanti. tathā ca pravādaḥ: —

sthiraṃ sādhvasitaṃ kāṇḍaṃ bhitvā vā 'sthi-praveśitaṃ
viśalyam aṅgaṃ kurvanti na vāco hṛdayād api
rohate sāyakair[39] *viddhaṃ vanaṃ paraśunā hataṃ*
vācā duruktaṃ bībhatsen[40] *na saṃrohati vāk-kṣataṃ.*

bhāgyāyattatvād arthasyeti na tejasvino 'rtha-dūṣaṇaṃ gaṇayanti

[32] For *sādhim* (or *svādhim*), 'painful'? [33] For *bhittvā*. [34] For *'sthi*.

[35] For *niḥśalyam* ('readily', 'harmlessly').

[36] For *api*. Surgeons can remove deep and painful foreign bodies from the bone, but no surgery can remove the word from the heart. An unidentified *sūkti*. But Kauṭ. himself has a somewhat similar idea in a quotation at 8. 3, 25—6. Bhār. perhaps decided to improve upon it.

[37] For *vanaṃ*. [38] For *bībhatsaṃ*.

[39] *rohate sāyakair* is curiously the reading of MBh in the Roy and R.A.S. editions, also in KRESSLER's TjD, i.e. STERNBACH's CNT IV at śl. 216.

[40] MANDLIK read *bībhatsaṃ*, which is the reading adopted in the Poona MBh, V (Udyogap.), 34. 75.

[41] Neither the Poona MBh (see pp. 147, 693) nor L. STERNBACH, *Mahābhārata verses in Cāṇakya's Compendia*, J.A.O.S., lxxxiii, 1, 1963, 30ff., at p. 47, no. 46, notes this variant. Neither the MBh nor the Pañcatantra has Bhār.'s reading. Medh. has the MBh. reading, which STERNBACH follows, ubi cit. The verse, Dr. STERNBACH kindly tells me (a letter of 9 Ap. 1964), is found also at SR. 385. 322 (for the abbreviations see his article). I am obliged to Dr STERNBACH for identifying this śloka for me. Besides the MBh. and the CNT IV the verse appears also at Sāra-samuccaya, 128 (see L. STERNBACH, *Sanskrit Subhaṣita-saṃgraha-s in Old-Javanese and Tibetan*, Annals B.O.R. Inst., xliii, 1963, 115 ff., at p.140, where further references are given).

III

Bhār. on M.VII, 54.	Medh. on the same.	Kauṭ. I, 10.[42]
purohitaḥ svalpe kārye rājñā vyājenākṣiptaḥ amṛṣyamāṇaḥ sa-śapatham ekaikam amātyam upajapet. adhārmiko 'yaṃ rājā. sādhu dhārmikam ekaṃ kulīnam avaruddham eka-pragraham asāmantam āṭavikaṃ vā pratipādayāmaḥ. anyebhyaśca mantribhya etad rocate, bhavatas tu katham iti. pratyākhyāte[44] *dharmopadhā-śuddhaḥ.*	*purohitaḥ svakārye rājñā vyājenādhikṣiptaḥ bahunā 'rtha-saṃpradānenāpta-puruṣair ekaikam amātyam upajapet rāja-vināśāya. 'etacca sarva-mantribhyo rocate, atha kathaṃ bhavate' iti pratyākhyāne dharmopadhā-śuddhaḥ.*	*purohitam ayājya-yājanādhyāpane niyuktam amṛṣyamāṇaṃ rājāvakṣipet. sa sattribhiḥ śapatha-pūrvam ekaikam amātyam upajāpayet adhārmiko 'yaṃ rājā. sādhu dhārmikam anyam asya tat-kulīnam aparuddhaṃ*[43] *kulyam eka-pragrahaṃ sāmantam*[45] *āṭavikam aupapādikaṃ vā pratipādayāmaḥ. sarveṣām etad rocate, kathaṃ vā tava iti pratyākhyāne śuciḥ iti dharmopadhā (2—4).*
senāpatir asatpratigraheṇāvakṣipto rājñā sarva-pratyakṣaṃ bahunārtha-saṃpradānenāpta-puruṣair ekaikam amātyam upajaped rāja-vināśāya. etacca sarva-mantribhyo rocate, 'tha kathaṃ bhavata iti. pratyākhyāte 'rthopadhā-śuddhaḥ.	*senāpatiḥ kenacid apadeśena pūrvavad adhikṣiptaḥ bahunā ca saṃpradānenāpta-puruṣair ekaikam amātyam upajapet rāja-vināśāya. 'etacca sarva-mantribhyo rocate, atha kathaṃ bhavate' iti pratyākhyāne*[46] *arthopadhā-śuddhaḥ.*	*senāpatir asatpragraheṇāvakṣiptaḥ sattribhir ekaikam amātyam upajāpayet lobhanīyenārthena rāja-vināśāya. sarveṣām etad rocate, kathaṃ vā tava iti. pratyākhyāne śuciḥ. ityarthopadhā (5—6).*
parivrājikāntaḥ-pure labdha-viśvāsā ekaikam	*parivrājikā antaḥ-pure labdha-viśvāsā ekaikam*	*parivrājikā labdha-viśvāsāntaḥ-pure kṛta-*

[42] This marvellous piece of panditry is preserved in the Kāmandakīya at VI. 9—12, but in a truncated and cryptic form. In Soma-deva's Nītivākyāmṛta, however, at X. 14 (text, Bombay, 1923, at p. 111) we have explicitly *dharmārthakāmabhayeṣu vyājena para-citta-parīkṣanam upadhā.*

[43] GM read *avaruddhaṃ*, as Bhār. A preferable reading?

[44] Bhār. may originally have read *-āne ubique.*

[45] Bhār.'s *asāmanta* may be a scribal error.

[46] Jhā's text (II, p. 18) has here a large dittographical error.

amātyam upajaped rāja-mahiṣī bhavantaṃ kāmayate tat-kṛta-samāgamopāy (lacuna)	*amātyam upajapet sā rāja-mahiṣī bhavantaṃ kāmayate kṛta-samāgamopāyeti pratyākhyāne kāmopadhā-śuddhaḥ.*	*-satkārā mahā-mātram ekaikam upajapet rāja-mahiṣī tvāṃ kāmayate kṛta-samāgamopāyā, mahān arthaśca te bhaviṣyati iti. pratyākhyāne śuciḥ.*[47] *iti kāmopadhā (7—8).*
(lacuna) *āpta-puruṣaḥ kaścid amātyeṣu mantraṃ avaśrāvayed idaṃ*[48] *pravādam upaśrutya bhavatāṃ nigraho rājñāvadhṛta iti. teṣām eva cānyatamaḥ kṛta-saṃvitkaḥ pratyekaṃ tān rājāmātyeṣūtsāhayet. tatra ye pratyācakṣate te bhayopadhā-śuddhāḥ.*	*rāja-prayuktā eva kecit puruṣāḥ pravādam āviṣkuryuḥ, kṛta-samayair amātyai rājā hanyata iti. upalabdha-pravādaḥ purohitasyāptaḥ kaścid amātyeṣu mantraṃ śrāvayet, imaṃ pravādam upaśrutya bhavatāṃ nigraho rājñā kriyata iti. teṣām eva cānyatamaḥ pūrvam eva kṛta-saṃvitkaḥ pratyekaṃ rājāmātyeṣūtsāhayet. tatra ye pratyācakṣate te bhayopadhā-śuddhāḥ.*	*prahavaṇa-nimittam eko 'mātyaḥ sarvān amātyān āvāhayet. tenodvegena rājā tān avarundhyāt. kāpaṭikaścātra pūrvāvaruddhas teṣām artha-mānāvakṣipta, ekaikam amātyam upajapet, asat-pravṛtto 'yaṃ rājā, sādhu enaṃ hatvānyaṃ pratipādayāmaḥ, sarveṣām etad rocate, kathaṃ vā tava iti. pratyākhyāne śuciḥ. iti bhayopadhā (9—12).*

IV

Almost the whole of Bhār.'s commentary on M. VII, 147 is taken with slight adjustment from Kauṭ. (I, 15). This again is repeated with hardly an alteration in Medh. (on M. VII, 146), in a portion of text omitted in error by G. JHĀ, but present in MANDLIK's edn. (on 147) and represented in JHĀ's trans. at iii, 368. It is significant that neither dharmaśāstra scholar has anything of his own to add from any other source. Manu stresses secrecy, but says nothing of 'five parts'.

Bhār.	Medh.	Kauṭ.
pañcāṅgaṃ mantrayeta. tad yathā karmārambhopāyaḥ puruṣa-drav-	*mantra-pañcāṅgaṃ darśayiṣyate. imānyaṅgāni karmaṇām ārambho-*	*... mantrayeta. karmaṇām ārambhopāyaḥ puruṣa-dravya-sampad*

[47] *mahān ... śuciḥ* seems to be an addition, as it exemplifies a variety of *upadhā* which involves both *artha* and *kāma*.

[48] Bhār. apparently uses *pravāda* in the n. gender.

yasampad deśa-kāla-vibhāgaḥ vinipāta-pratīkāraḥ kārya-siddhir iti. tān ekaikaśaḥ pṛcchet samastāṃśca. hetubhiḥ sarveṣāṃ mati-pravivekaṃ vidyād. avāptārthaḥ kālaṃ nātipātayen na ca dīrgha-mantraḥ syāt. na ca teṣāṃ pratyakṣa-mantraṃ mantrayet yeṣām apakuryāt. gupta-mantraś ca syāt.

pāyaḥ puruṣa-dravya-saṃpat deśa-kāla-vibhāgaḥ vinipāta-pratīkāraḥ kārya-siddhir iti. athavā prārthanā-kālaṃ nātipātayet tatra dīrgho mantraḥ syāt. na teṣāṃ brūyāt, gupta-mantraśca syāt.

deśa-kāla-vibhāgo vinipāta-pratīkāraḥ kārya-siddhir iti pañcāṅgo mantraḥ (41—2). tān ekaikaśaḥ pṛcchet samastāṃśca. hetubhiścaiṣāṃ mati-pravivekān vidyāt. avāptārthaḥ kālaṃ nātikrāmayet. na dīrgha-kālaṃ mantrayeta, na tesāṃ[49] *pakṣīyair*[50] *yeṣāṃ apakuryāt. (43—6). tasmād rakṣen mantraṃ (12).*

V

Similarly the greater part of the commentary on VII, 153 is derived from Kauṭ. I, 20, with its characteristic appeal to 'historical' precedent. Once again, the material comes exclusively from the arthaśāstra.

Bhār. on M. VII, 153.

kakṣyāntareṣvantarvaṃśika-sainyādhiṣṭhito 'ntaḥ-puraṃ praviśet. tatra sthavira-strī-pariśuddhāṃ devīṃ paśyen nāpariśuddhāṃ devyā gṛha-nilīno[51a] *hi bhrātā Candrasenaṃ*[52] *jaghāna, mātuḥ śayanāntargataṃ*[53] *ca putra*[54]*-*

Medh. on the same.

kakṣāntareṣvantarvaṃśika-sainyādhiṣṭhito 'ntaḥ-puraṃ praviśet. tatra sthavira-strī-mati-śuddhāṃ devīṃ pariśyen nāpariśuddhāṃ devīṃ. gṛha-līno hi bhrātā Bhadraseno mātuḥ śayanāntargataḥ rājānaṃ jaghāna. kupuru-

Kauṭ. I, 20.[51]

kakṣyāntareṣvantarvaṃśika-sainyaṃ tiṣṭhet. antargṛha-gataḥ sthavira-strī-pariśuddhāṃ devīṃ paśyet. devī-gṛhe līno hi bhrātā Bhadrasenaṃ jaghāna, mātuḥ śayyāntargataśca putraḥ Kārūṣaṃ. lājān madhuneti vi-

[49] *na ca teṣāṃ* is read in M2.

[50] From KĀṄGLE's apparatus it is clear that the reading of this word was much disputed. Bhār.'s effort was apparently to elucidate a corruption?

[51] The curious list of assassinations is different in Soma-deva, Nītivākyām. XXIV. 35ff. (text, pp. 231—2), where the commentator refers us to the Bṛhatkathā. KĀṄGLE, trans., p. 56, refers to the Harṣacarita. Kāmandaka (6th cent.), VII. 51ff. nearly follows K. in giving Bhadrasena, Kārūṣa, Kāśirāja, Sauvīra, Vairanta (sic), Jārūṣa, and Vidūratha. Varāha-mihira (? 6th cent.) gives only Vidūratha and Kāśirāja in that order (Bṛhatsamhitā, lxxviii, 1, p. 393—4 of 1865 edn.).

[51a] So D. [52] For Bhadrasena. [53] for *-gataś*. [54] For *putraḥ*.

-Kāruśaṃ[55] *viṣa-digdhena nūpureṇa Vairantaṃ*[57] *jaghāna. mekhalā-maṇinā Sauvīraṃ veṇyāṃ nigūḍhena śastreṇa Vidūrathaṃ.*[58] *tasmād etānyāpadaḥ-sthānāni yatnataḥ parīkṣeta.*	*ṣa*[56]*-śaṅkha-viṣa-digdhena nūpureṇāvantyaṃ devī jaghāna mekhalayā. Sauvīraṃ veṇyāṃ gūḍhena śastreṇa Vidūrathaṃ. tasmād etāni visrambha-sthānāni yatnataḥ parīkṣeta.*	*ṣeṇa paryasya devī Kāśirājaṃ, viṣa-digdhena nūpureṇa Vairantyaṃ, mekhalā-maṇinā Sauvīraṃ, Jālūtham ādarśena, veṇyāṃ gūḍhaṃ śastraṃ kṛtvā devī Vidūrathaṃ jaghāna. tasmād etānyāspadāni pariharet.*
muṇḍa-jaṭila-kuhaka-pratisaṃsargaṃ bāhyābhiśca dāsībhir antaḥ-pura-dāsīnāṃ pratiṣedhayet.	*muṇḍa-jaṭila-kuhaka-pratisaṃsargaṃ bāhya-dāsībhir antaḥ-pura-dāsīnāṃ pratiṣedhayet.*	*muṇḍa-jaṭila-kuhaka-pratisaṃsargaṃ bāhyābhiśca dāsībhiḥ pratiṣedhayet. (13—18).*

VI

The same phenomenon is apparent at M. VII, 154. The śloka itself refers to another *pañca-varga* ('five-fold group') in a cryptic manner, and so calls for the artha-śāstra gloss, which is a compilation.

Bhār. on M. VII, 154.	Medh. on the same.	Kauṭ. I, 11; 12.
kāpaṭikodāsthita-gṛha-patita[59]*-vaidehaka-tāpasa-vyañcanāḥ. paramarma-jñaḥ pragalbhaś chātraḥ kāpaṭikaḥ. tad-artha-mānābhyām upasaṃgṛhya mantrī brūyād rājānaṃ māṃ ca pramāṇī-kṛtya yatra yad akuśalaṃ paśy (asi tat tadānīm evāśrāvy) aṃ tvayeti. pravrajyāyāḥ*[59c] *pratyavasita udāsthitaḥ, sa ca prajñāśauca-yuktaḥ. sarvān-*	*kāpaṭikodāsthita-gṛha-pati-vaidehika-tāpasa-vyañjanāḥ. parama-dharma-jñāḥ pragalbhacchātrāḥ*[59a] *kāpaṭikāḥ. tān artha-mānābhyām upasaṃgṛhya mantrī brūyāt rājānaṃ māṃ ca pramāṇaṃ kṛtvā yatra yad akuśalaṃ tat tadānīm evāśrāvyaṃ tvayeti. pravrajyāyāḥ pratyavasita udāsthitaḥ. sa ca prajñāśauca-yuktaḥ sarvānna-pradāna-sa-*	... *kāpaṭikodāsthita-gṛhapatika-vaidehaka-tāpasa-vyañjanān* ... *paramarma-jñaḥ pragalbhaś chātraḥ kāpaṭikaḥ. tam artha-mānābhyāṃ protsāhya*[59b] *mantrī brūyāt rājānaṃ māṃ ca pramāṇaṃ kṛtvā yasya yad akuśalaṃ paśyasi tat tadānīm eva pratyādiśa iti. pravrajyā-pratyavasitaḥ prajñāśauca-yukta udāsthit-*

[55] For *Kārūṣaṃ* (GM have *Kārūśaṃ*). Has Bhār. omitted *lājān ... rājaṃ?* But note the omission of *Jālūtha* below.

[56] The plainest example of Medh.'s inability to read Bhār.

[57] So Kāmand. [58] So GM. Vidūr. in purāṇa and MBh.

[59] For *patika.* [59a] So read by K. in mss. G1, M3, but in the singular.

[59b] GM read *utsāhya.* [59c] The reading of D.

na-pradāna-samarthāyājā prabhūta-hiraṇyāntevāsinaḥ karma kārayet. kṛṣi-ka(rma-phalācca sarva-pravrajitānāṃ grāsācchādanā)vasathān pratividadhyāt. teṣāṃ ye vṛtti-kāmās te[60] *upajapet, evam etenaiva vṛttena rājārthaś caritavyo bhakta-vetana-kāle copasthātavyam iti. sarva-pravra(jitāśca svaṃ svaṃ va)rgaṃ upajapeyuḥ.*	*marthāyām bhūmau prabhūta-hiraṇyāyāṃ dāsa-karma kārayet. kṛṣi-karma-phalaṃ tacca sarva-pravrajitānāṃ grāsācchādanāvasathān prati vidadhyāt. teṣāṃ ye vṛttikāmās tān upajaped evaṃ etenaiva vṛttena rājārthaś caritavyaḥ. bhakta-vetena-kāle copasthātavyam iti. sarva-pravrajitāḥ svaṃ svaṃ karmopajapeyuḥ.*	*aḥ. sa vārttā-karma-pradiṣṭāyāṃ bhūmau prabhūta-hiraṇyāntevāsī karma kārayet. karma-phalācca sarva-pravrajitānāṃ grāsācchādanāvasathān pratividadhyāt. vṛttikāmāṃścopajapet, etenaiva veṣeṇa rājārthaś caritavyo bhakta-vetana-kāle copasthātavyam iti. sarva-pravrajitāśca svaṃ svaṃ vargam evam*[61] *upajapeyuḥ (1—8).*
karṣako vṛtti-kṣīṇaḥ prajñāśauca-yukto gṛha-pati-vyañjanaḥ. sa kṛṣi-karma kuryāt yathoktāyāṃ bhūmāv iti.	*karṣako vṛtti-kṣīṇaḥ prajñāśauca-yukto gṛha-pati-vyañjanaḥ. sa kṛṣi-karma kuryād yathoktāyāṃ bhūmāv iti.*	*karṣako vṛtti-kṣīṇaḥ prajñāśauca-yukto gṛha-patika-vyañjanaḥ. sa kṛṣi-karma-pradiṣṭāyāṃ bhūmau — iti samānaṃ pūrveṇa.*
vāṇijiko vṛtti-kṣīṇaḥ prajñāśauca-yukto vaidehaka-vyañjanaḥ. sa vaṇik-karma kuryāt [vaṇik] pradiṣṭāyāṃ bhūmāv iti samānaṃ pūrveṇa.	*vāṇijiko vṛtti-kṣīnaḥ prajñāśauca-yukto vaidehika-vyañjanaḥ. sa vaṇik-karma kuryāt pradiṣṭāyāṃ bhūmāv iti samānaṃ.*	*vāṇijiko vṛtti-kṣīṇaḥ prajñāśauca-yukto vaidehaka-vyañjanaḥ. sa vaṇik-karma-pradiṣṭāyāṃ bhūmau — iti samānaṃ pūrveṇa.*
muṇḍo jaṭilo vā vṛtti-kāmas tāpasa-vyañjano nagarābhyāśe prabhūta-jaṭila-muṇḍāntevāsī śākaṃ yavasa-muṣṭiṃ vā māsa-dvimāsāntaritaḥ prakāśam aśnīyāt. dharma-vyañjana-gūḍhaṃ ca yatheṣṭam āhāraṃ. tāpasa-vyañjanān-	*muṇḍo jaṭilo vā vṛtti-kāmaḥ tāpasa-vyañjanaḥ. sa nagarābhyāśe prabhūta-jaṭila-muṇḍāntevāsī śākaṃ yava-muṣṭiṃ vā māsāntaritaṃ prakāśam aśnīyād dharma-vyājena gūḍham yatheṣṭam āhāraṃ. tāpasa-vyañjanāntevā-*	*muṇḍo jaṭilo vā vṛtti-kāmas tāpasa-vyañjanaḥ. sa nagarābhyāśe prabhūta-muṇḍa*[62]*-jaṭilāntevāsī śākaṃ yava*[63]*-muṣṭiṃ vā māsa-dvimāsāntaraṃ prakāśam aśnīyāt, gūḍham iṣṭam āhāraṃ. vaidehakāntevāsinaś cai-*

[60] For *tān*. [61] GM omit the *evaṃ*.
[62] *muṇḍa* is omitted in D. [63] *yavasa* (Bhār.) is read by GM.

tevāsinaś cainaṃ siddha-yogair arcayeyuḥ, śiṣyāś cāsyopadiśeyuḥ. lābhaṃ nidānaṃ[64] *cora-bhayaṃ duṣṭa-vadha-bandhanaṃ videśa-pravṛttim, idam adya śvo vā bhaviṣyatīdaṃ vā rājā kariṣyatīti. tad asya gūḍhāḥ sattriṇas tat-prayuktāḥ sampādayeyuḥ.*	*sinaś cainaṃ prasiddha-yogair artha-lābham agre śiṣyāścādiśeyuḥ. dāhaṃ caura-bhayaṃ duṣṭa-vadhaṃ ca videśa-pravṛttam idam adya śvo vā bhaviṣyatīdaṃ vā rājā kariṣyatīti tasya gūḍha-mantriṇas tat-prayuktāḥ saṃpādayeyuḥ.*	*naṃ samiddha-yogair arcayeyuḥ. śiṣyāś cāsyāvedayeyuḥ asau siddhaḥ sāmedhikaḥ iti. samēdhāśāstibhiś cābhigatānām aṅga-vidyayā śiṣya-saṃjñābhiśca karmāṇy abhijane 'vasitānyādiśet — alpa-lābham agni-dāhaṃ cora-bhayaṃ dūṣya-vadhaṃ tuṣṭi-dānaṃ videśa-pravṛtti-jñānam, idam adya śvo vā bhaviṣyati, idaṃ vā rājā kariṣyati iti. tad asya gūḍhāḥ sattriṇaśca saṃpādayeyuḥ. (9—18).*
ye cāsya rājño 'vaśyaṃ bhartavyās te lakṣaṇa-vidyām aṅga-vidyāṃ jambhaka-vidyāṃ māyāgatam āśrama-dharmaṃ nimitta-jñānaṃ cādhīyamānāḥ sattriṇaḥ syuḥ. tatrājaitāḥ pañca-saṃsthā etair mantribhiḥ saha sva-viṣaye para-viṣaye cāvasthāpayet. mantri-purohita-senāpati-yuvarāja-dauvārikāntarvaṃśikādiṣu śraddheya-deśa-veṣa-śilpa-bhāṣāvido janapadopadeśena sattriṇaḥ sañcārayet.	*ye cāsya rājño vaṃśa-lakṣaṇa-vidyāṃ saṅga-vidyāṃ jambhaka-vidyāṃ māyāgatam āśrama-dharmaṃ nimitta-jñānaṃ cādhīyānā mantriṇas tatra rāja etat-pañca-saṃsthāya tair mantribhiḥ sva-viṣaye 'vasthāpayet. mantri-purohita-senāpati-yuvarāja-dauvārikāntarveśikādiṣu sad-vyapadeśa-veṣa-śilpa-bhāṣā-vido janapadāpadeśena mantriṇaḥ saṃdhārayet.*	*ye cāpyasaṃbandhino 'vaśya-bhartavyās te lakṣaṇam aṅga-vidyāṃ jambhaka-vidyāṃ māyāgatam āśrama-dharmaṃ nimittam antara-cakram ityadhīyānāḥ sattriṇaḥ, saṃsarga-vidyāṃ vā (12, 1) ... tān rājā sva-viṣaye mantri-purohita-senāpati-yuvarāja-dauvārikāntarvaṃśika-praśāstṛ ... āṭavikeṣu śraddheya-deśa-veṣa-śilpa-bhāṣābhijanāpadeśān bhaktitaḥ sāmarthyayogāccāpasarpayet (6).*
tathā kubja-vāmana-kirāta-mūka-jaḍa-badhirāndha[65]*-chad-*	*tathā kubja-vāmana-kirāta-mūka-jaḍa-badhirāndha-naṭa-*	*... kubja-vāmana-kirāta-mūka-badhira-jaḍāndacchadmāno*

[64] For *agni-dāham?*

[65] This agrees with the reading of D, minus *-jaḍa*.

mano naṭa-nartaka-gāyanādayaśca striyaścābhyantara-cāraṃ vidyuḥ	*-narttaka-gāyanādayaḥ striyaścābhyantara-cāriṇyoṭavyāṃ*	*naṭa-nartaka-gāyana-vādaka-vāgjīvana-kuśīlavāḥ striyaścābhyantaraṃ cāraṃ vidyuḥ (9).*
vane vanacarāḥ[66] *kāryāḥ śramiṇāṭavikādayaḥ, para-pravṛtti-jñānārthāḥ śīghrāścāra-paramparāḥ.*	*vanecarāḥ kāryāḥ, grāme grāmīṇakādayaḥ, puruṣa-vyāpārārthāḥ sva-vyāpāra-paramparāḥ.*	*vane vanacarāḥ kāryāḥ śramaṇāṭavikādayaḥ, para-pravṛtti jñānārthāḥ śīghrāścāra-paramparāḥ. (23).*
parasya caite boddhavyās tādṛśair eva tādṛśāḥ, cāra-sañcāriṇaḥ saṃsthā gūḍhāścāgūḍha-saṃjñitāḥ.[67]	*parasparaṃ caite boddhavyās tādṛśair eva tādṛśāḥ, vāri-saṃcāriṇasthā gūḍhāśca gūḍha-saṃjñitāḥ.*	*parasya caite boddhavyās tādṛśair eva tādṛśāḥ, cāra-saṃcāriṇaḥ saṃsthā gūḍhāścāguḍha-saṃjñitāḥ. (24).*

[66] For *vanecarāḥ*, as D ? See next note.

[67] These verses appear with a commentary in Nandana's Mānava-vyākhyāna (see MANDLIK, p. 827), on which see the end of this note, between 154 and 155. The readings, but not the source (curiously), are indicated in JHĀ, *Notes*, Pt. 1, p. 254, as of 153 A and 153B (*sic*). But reports by JHĀ are always open to suspicion of inaccuracy. *Vanecarāḥ* is read; for *grāme grāmāṇakādayaḥ* (as our Medh.) we have the variant exactly as in Bhār.; *para-pravṛtti-jñānārthaṃ* is read, also *śīghrācāra* (or *śīghrāścāra*) likewise correctly *parasya caite*; but *śaṭhāśca* as well as *gūḍhāśca* (not *-āścā-*) appears. Whence did 154A and 154B arise ? Did Nandana obtain them from Kauṭ. ? Nothing known about that mysterious commentator suggests this. We do not know whether he found them between 153 and 154 or between 154 and 155. It is easy to write ślokas from a commentary into the text, since very often commentators' quotations in śloka form are written similarly with the ślokas of the work upon which he is commenting. Exactly this mistake was made by GHĀRPURE himself as indicated by JHĀ, *Notes*, Pt. 1, p. 261. The * possibility that Nandana's copy of Medh. was free from our Medh.'s errors must be dismissed, since whatever Nandana's age he is certainly post-jīrṇoddhāra. That he had direct access to a copy of Bhār. seems unlikely; but he may well have had access to a copy of the Manu-smṛti into which verses cited by Bhār. have crept in the manner stated. KĀṆE can tell us nothing about Nandana except that he is 'late' (op. cit., 157). BÜHLER has a lot to say (op. cit., pp. cxxxiii-cxxxv). In his view Nandana must be a *southern* writer, and his reasons are convincing. Moreover there are mysterious readings and interpolations which agree with southern mss. of Manu. In philosophical pieces he follows a commentator on Manu not otherwise known (could it be Bhār. at second hand ?). Nandana was the son (or younger brother) of one Lakṣmaṇa and a friend of one Vīra-malla. Vīra-malla suggests a descendant of one of the peninsular royal families, for example, Pallava, Gaṅga, or Cālukya. It has an antique flavour and suggests a period earlier than a 'very modern date'. One might guess the 17th century at the latest.

Conclusion

It is perhaps superfluous to dwell on the historical importance of discovering the manner in which the Manu-smṛti has been explained through the centuries. The availability of materials to the great commentators is as much a matter of importance as the emergence of new ideas, and new needs for reinterpretation of the text. Why did Viśvarūpa cite Kauṭilya's predecessors but not, so far as we know, Kauṭ. himself? From the facts which emerge from this present study it would be quite improper to suggest that Viśvarūpa was earlier than Bhāruci, on that ground alone. The chances that a complete copy of Kauṭ. was available to Viśvarūpa might seem far greater than that one should be available to Medh.; but one cannot be sure. Nor can we assume that Viśvarūpa did not prefer the older material, which may still have circulated with agreeable commentaries; nor can we assume that Bhār., who was content to quote from a metrical nīti-śāstra of Uśanas (Śukra), did not actually reject the predecessors of Kauṭ. whom Viśvarūpa cites. The vast complexity of these problems is demonstrated by the discovery outlined in * this paper.

ADDITIONAL ANNOTATIONS

p. [120], n. 2. Kāty. 20.

p. [121], l. 28. Bṛh. and Uśanas are cited by Medh. at M.VIII.284. Kāty. 20 is cited only in Medh. on M.VII.1, where Medh. says that Manu uses only that non-Vedic material (obviously including *arthaś*.) which was not opposed to *dharmaś*.

p. [123], l. 12-13. Jha, *Notes Pt. III*, 1929, xxxiv says that the references to the *Adhyakṣap.* at VII.61 could not be verified!

p. [127], n. 20. For Ṛju see also Medh. at M.VIII.172 (trans., but text has *kaścid*). For Medh. ref. to Bhār. see Derrett, *Bhāruci's Commentary on the Manusmṛti* (Wiesbaden, 1975), I, 10.

p. [137], l. 15 of n. 67. Also *Notes. Pt. II*, 543.

p. [138], l. 17. In order better to evaluate Bhāruci's quotations of Kauṭ. it is necessary (i) to remind ourselves that Kauṭ. was available to referees (above), and (ii) that Nārāyaṇa in his *Vyavahāra-śiromaṇi* (for particulars see Derrett, *Bhāruci's Comm.* (1975), I, 308-9) quoted Kauṭ. in the same 'loose' or paraphrastic style; but it is still a quotation.

"*QUID POSSIT ANTIQUITAS NOSTRIS LEGIBUS ABROGARE*"

THE ROLE OF THE JURIST IN ANCIENT INDIAN LAW

Justinian's 'constitutio' *Deo auctore* prohibits scholars and jurists from searching the existing literature and records : *et nemo ex comparatione veteris voluminis quasi vitiosam scripturam arguere audeat.* Justinian's own laws, though based mainly on the works of the jurists of the classical and post-classical period, though purporting to be Roman law and nothing but Roman law, were intended to be a fresh start. The possibility that his advisers were *wrong* in their law was not to be contemplated. There is much of this attitude to be found in Europe ever since. Legislation, validly passed, cannot be wrong. The professor can only interpret it, and the judge apply it.

In honour of a scholar who has worked on the operation of the characteristically European conception of law and legislation in a non-European environment, it may be appropriate to compare the Indian jurists' methods of digesting and transmitting law, which throw much light upon the choices which the Romans, at various stages in their history, made--and were not, it seems, necessarily obliged to make.

First, some preliminary remarks, The Indian legal system, now conveniently, briefly, and most perceptively described in relation to its ancient sources by M. Robert Lingat(¹), did not provide for general legislation by the king. The king was often a source of law, in the sense that his edict (Skt.*śāsana*) would determine many disputed matters; but his edicts were of a regulative effect, tending either to purely individual and private matters, or to sanction the decisions of social groups (such as castes), or to disallow customs which, in his view, were no longer entitled to survive the disapproval which the *dharma-śāstra,* the "science of righteousness", the "book-law", generally expressed for customs contrary to its own outlook and tenor. The *dharma-śāstra* could not be modified by any ruler, or indeed any assembly, but only by scholars with appropriate qualifications acting in the course of their functions (which we must describe below). Whatever law the ruler enforced in his courts, a law which might be influenced by political and expediential considerations, the *dharma-śāstra* (which provided the norms and the ideals) went on regardless. No king could abrogate *śāstra*, or render its provisions obsolete.

Next we should note that the sources of the *dharma-śāstra* were, at all times material to our study, *written.* It is quite likely that roughly about the 6th century B.C. that statement could not have been made with certainty. The passage of oral learning, oral maxims, into written legal texts was not yet complete. The ancestors of our oldest texts may not have been in a form resembling their present, and the difference may have to be attributed to the moulding effect of oral sources upon the nascent written literature. Most of such reflections are, and must remain, conjecture. Yet several centuries before our era the principal *sūtras* were already in existence(²) and the forerunners of our principal *smṛitis* were almost certainly current. It remains a mystery in which parts of India, a vast sub-continent, which *smritis*

(¹) *Les Sources du Droit dans le Système traditionnel de l'Inde* (Paris/La Haye, Mouton, 1967)

(²) S.C. Banerjee, *Dharma Sutras* (Calcutta, 1962).

arose or were composed. The tendency to avoid these questions admirably fits the tendency of the jurists with whom we are concerned : they did not care from which area or from what period their sources came.

The continuous *smritis,* more numerous in the past than they are now, and the fragments of *smriti*-like textual law, were the raw material of the jurists who welded the whole into a single, coherent legal system. The work of the jurists seems to have been consigned to writing at a very early stage. Bhāruchi, the earliest commentator on Manu(3) and one of the early commentators--perhaps a member of the earliest generation of juridical scholars now available to us--may be assigned tentatively to A.D.600-700, perhaps nearer the later than the earlier part of that century. Yet it is quite evident that numerous jurists known to him had been working on the Manu-*smriti,* but their own works have not survived. His own survives in only one manuscript (which is incomplete) and its apograph. From the generation of Bhāruchi until the scholars who worked for the Maharajas of Tanjore (Madras State) in the nineteenth century, the work of reducing *smritis* into a practical and coherent shape went on without interruption, and in every quarter of India. The language of the texts was Sanskrit, a strange, crisp, terse *lingua franca* of the scholars which made no concessions to beginners.

The judicial advisers, whose task it was to report to the ruler or his appointed judge what was the ruling of the *śāstra* on any point at issue, had been trained in the *śāstra* by first studying the Veda, later the science of interpretation and logic, and finally the *smritis* and their interpretation at the hands of leading jurists. Since *smritis* differed considerably from each other in many places, and since even the same continuous *smriti* might contain contradictions, the task of reconciling the divergent *smritis* was the foremost task of the jurists. When this was done there was no question of going back to the literal meaning of any particular *smriti.*

The status of smriti vis-à-vis the commentator.

It must be remenbered that the question with which we are concerned is a practical matter. In spite of the so-called "codification" of Hindu law which took place in India in 1955-6, considerable areas of law (especially that relating to the property of the joint family) remain unaffected by statute, except such piecemeal statutes as the Hindu Gains of Learning Act, 1930(4). In those areas the Sanskrit texts are still the sources of law and not a few cases from the last five years can be cited to exemplify the judges' reliance upon the original authorities (including, naturally, their judicial interpretations and amplifications). There is even one instance (from Kerala) in which the Sanskrit authority (Vijñāneśvara's *Mitākṣarā*), a work of the twelfth century, is exclusively relied upon, and judicial authorities which glossed it in the nineteenth century in the state of Madras are deliberately rejected.

Very early in the British period it was realised(5) that the British courts must not follow the *smriti,* though the *smriti* is the primarary source in a historical sense. The commentators comment upon the *smriti* and it would be reasonable to suppose that it, and it alone, should be relied upon. Philological and rational inquisition into the supposed meaning of the *smriti*-writer might have been allowed : but it was not. Following the traditional English view that no foreign law is to be applied unless it has been "received" into the area in question, their Lordships of the Privy Council laid it down that the courts were to apply not the *smriti* as such, but the meaning put upon it by the commentator or commentators whose works were primarily consulted by the native experts (the *śāstrīs* or doctors of law) in the district in question.

---

(3) Derrett at Z.D.M.G. 115, pt. 1 (1965), 134 ff ; J.A.O.S. 84, no. 4 (1964), pp. 392 ff ; *Adyar Library Bulletin* 30, (1966), pp. 1-22. The commentary is due to be published by the writer from Brussels (Editions de l'Institut de Sociogie).

(4) Derrett, *Introduction to Modern Hindu Law* (Oxford University Press, 1963), App. III.

(5) *Collector of Madura* (1868) 12 Moore's Indian App. 397, 436. See Derrett, *Religion, Law and the State in India* (London, Faber & Faber, 1968), 299-303.

The French in Pondicherry and elsewhere([6]) attained a nearly similar result by not allowing any written text as such to be a direct source of law, but by referring the question to a committee of experts who were at liberty to consult *smṛiti,* commentary, and custom, and to report accordingly--an extremely sensible and workable method.

The attitude of the British coincided more closely with what the native jurists themselves required. To them, the *smṛiti,* without its authorised commentary, was a snare and a delusion. The art of arranging and correlating *smṛitis* was so detailed and required such care, that to take out from its context any particular *smṛiti* or even a group of *smṛitis,* would have the effect of distorting the *śāstra,* which latter meant only what the *śāstrīs* said it meant. Moreover, numerous *smritis* had been declared obsolete under the *kali-varjya* doctrine([7]). In the eighth or ninth century A.D. certain jurists, fearful, apparently, that strict śāstric rules would be assumed or enforced in an excess of zeal for "orthodox" Hinduism, declared that certain practices (amounting to, eventually, thirty or so in number) were obsolete, and to be avoided in the present, "*kali*", age of the universe. This was accepted by jurists all over India with some alacrity, and it was founded on an undoubted *smṛiti* rule that, irrespective of what the *dharma-śāstra* might prescribe, any rule which met the determined opposition of any section of the public was to be ignored, and was not to be enforced : it was *asvargya,* it did not lead to Heaven, though it was consistent with *dharma,* the "righteousness" of the book-law([7a]).

The native jurists were thus quite able to decide what was, or what was not obsolete. Jimutavahana, for example, a writer of the Bengal school of about 1100 A.D., admits that when brothers share their deceased father's property after his death the *smṛiti* texts require an elder brother to be given one or other of several alternative types of "preferential share" as against his younger brothers. But, he says([8]), in his day either elder brothers did not behave as elder brothers should, or younger brothers were defective in respect of veneration for their elder brothers : so that in actual practice this requirement was not observed. A judge therefore who recommended in Bengal that those preferential shares should be deducted would be putting the clock back, and would be censured by the scholarly public, who never allowed mere textual law to overrule general public practice--provided, that is to say, the latter was not derived from demonstrably dishonest, low, or otherwise disreputable usages or motives.

Thus to allow the British Indian courts to administer only the approved ancient commentators' version of *smriti* law was to follow faithfully in the steps of the native jurists themselves.

Native professors, like Vijñāneśvara and Jīmūtavāhana, or still more the controversial author of the *Dattaka-mīmāmsā,* Nanda-pandita, would admit that the *smṛiti* is their "source" : but only in the sense in which they take it. It means only what they recognise it to mean. Why ? Obviously because they want their and their friends' lives to be ruled by it ! This is why they would say without hesitation, if they knew Latin (as a *few* in the first three centuries of our era may have done), *quid possit antiquitas nostris sententiis abrogare ?*

The orientalists' viewpoint.

When Europeans first became acquainted with *dharma-śāstra* they not unnaturally likened it to canon law. But the degree of difference between *śāstrīs* on apparently simple questions horrified them. They failed to realise that India was vast in extent and also in varieties of populations. They failed to see that the existence of one single science of righteousness, as the only book-law, incapable of modification by general statute, must be not only very flexible in its application, but also capable of expressing itself in different "schools", and even sub-schools. The elaborate work of Jagannātha Tarkapañcānana at the end of the

([6]) For the considerable bibliography of French works on Hindu law see the work cited in the previous note, p. 283.

([7]) See Lingat, *op. cit.*, also P.V. Kane, *History of Dharmaśāstra* (Poona, 1930-62) at vol.III, ch. 34.

([7a]) Derrett, *Religion, Law and the State in India* (cited above). 90.

([8]) In Colebrooke's translation, II, ii, 24.

eighteenth century, translated by H.T. Colebrooke in what has ever since (unfairly) been called "Colebrooke's *Digest*", exemplifies the divergent methods of interpretation of carefully selected *smṛitis*, and the failure to chose between or even to categorize the divergencies was found frustrating by British judges, who simply wanted a certain rule to enforce.

When the orientalists of the next two epochs approached the *dharma-śāstra* they too were horrified, but for another reason. They were obsessed by the need to determine, to publish, and to translate, the *original smṛiti* texts, and to their disgust they discovered that the variant readings presented by the commentators were so full of imponderable factors as to make it exceedingly difficult to determine whether Manu, for example, ever had a single, definite text for a particular verse. Verses circulated with, sometimes, widely variant readings ; and it could be argued that from the juridical standpoint both or all of these were right ! Further, it was evident that the commentators "tortured" their texts. They sometimes made them mean the opposite of what they literally said ! How could one have confidence in such people ? And so, oblivious of the practical needs of an age-less but still vital system of law and righteousness, the orientalists tended to record the interpretations of commentators in a patronising and depreciatory manner, more in sorrow than in anger.

But there is a point which orientalists have overlooked, and which is admirably brought out by M. Lingat[9]. Numerous kings asked their ministers to make, or to have made, digests of law. Some (but not all) of the more famous digests, and also the *Parāśara-mādhavīya*, a commentary on a *smṛiti*, owed their compilation and celebrity as much to the initiative of kings as to the scholarship of the *śāstrīs* employed on them. It was plainly intended in many cases that the interpretations offered, and the texts selected, should alone be referred to by judicial advisers throughout the king's territories, and perhaps further. It was a matter of prestige that the kingdom should be ruled in accordance with *dharma*, and this was one method of achieving it. Therefore the work of the scholar, his interpretations of the *smṛitis*, was taken seriously by properly constituted civil authority.

It is true that the resulting masterpieces, notably the *Sarasvatī-vilāsa*, the *Prithvīchandrodaya*, or the *Vīra-mitrodaya*, to name a few only, did not, in fact, put an end to scholarly debate, or even prevent earlier treatises, such as the *Mitāksharā*, from being consulted. On the contrary, some earlier works remain, as M. Lingat has noticed, of more prestige than the heavy and cumbersome efforts of the *paṇdits* of the royal courts. The fact is that commentators as a whole exclude from consideration the literal words of the ancient *smṛitis* (as distinct from the gloss upon them), but do not exclude consideration of each other, or close the door to future decisions between opposing opinions as to the cumulative effect of those *smṛitis*. New material, from *smṛitis* or *purāṇas* of doubtful authority, may be admitted to help out, to develop or adjust the law which is being described by the jurist. But the *smṛiti* can never be resurrected to confound the commentator, by giving it a "historical" or philological rebirth.

It is time now to turn to the work of the jurist and to see a few examples illustrating how he did it.

The function of the commentator.

The first task of the commentator is to establish his text. Early commentators frequently have special readings (e.g. those of Bhāruchi and Nandana on Manu VIII.15) which do not later obtain general currency. He must also determine the order of verses, which may be in dispute, because a different order may raise widely differing implications (e.g. Manu VIII. 33/34). The settled order which he adopts can itself be valuable for purposes of interpretation. The commentator must account for the order and explain why the topics appear as they do. Bhāruchi utilizes the order at Manu VIII.24-25 and 106-7. The most famous deduction from the order of treatment is that of Vijñāneśvara in the *Mitāksharā*. When tackling the thorny problem of the widow's right to inherit he notes, *inter alia*, that the

(9) Op. cit., p. 255.

verse which states the widow's claim (Yājñavalkya II.135) occurs between verses dealing with partition and others dealing with reunion between separated co-heirs : thus it is the widow of the separated and unreunited man who obtains his estate.

Each *smriti* text must be identified for what it is. Many are mere summarising-verses (Bhār. on Manu VIII.76 and *passim*). Some give reasons why a rule should be observed, and are not rules in themselves (Bhār. on Manu XI.96). Some *smritis* make statements which are later contradicted in the same work : these are *pūrva-paksas,* i.e. *prima facie* positions intended to be controverted (Bhār. on Manu IX.124).

It is important to detect whether a text is an injunction or an *arthavāda,* a mere declamation needed to support an injunction at another verse. Manu (IX.121), speaking of the expectation of a (secondary) son, says, "According to *dharma* the 'secondary' does not acquire the right of the 'principal'. The father is principal in begetting him, therefore he should divide him according to *dharma*". This extremely obscure *smriti* is explained by Bhāruchi in this way : a conflict with previous law will be avoided if we take this not as an injunction (which would, be reason of its contradiction of another, allow an option) but as a declamation belonging to the previous verse, which establishes the son's right.

In other cases the choice may be between taking the *smriti* as a reason or as a declamation : there is much to be said for taking the ancient statement as a mere declamation. Manu XI.93 : "Liquor indeed is the 'dirt of grains' and sin also is called dirt, therefore a Brahmin. . . should not drink liquor". Bhāruchi comments that this is a declamation, for otherwise too many things would be prohibited, and a chain of reasons would be called up (why are grains objected to ? etc.). Manu X.84 : "Some think agriculture is good : but that profession is blamed by all. The iron-tipped wood damages the earth and creatures living in the earth". Bhāruchi : This commends other professions open to the Vaiśya (the commercial caste), and is a declamation tending to prohibit actual (personal) ploughing. Manu X.61 : "The kingdom, where the people are born of a violation (of the order of castes), defilers of caste, perishes speedily, together with the inhabitants". Bhāruchi : A depreciatory text, to encourage the king to ward off that state of affairs, and aiming to commend the opposite.

It is often necessary to determine whether a *smriti* is a *niyama* (a 'faculty'), or an injunction of an original character. Manu IX.118 : "Their brothers should give to the unmarried girls separately out of their own individual shares a *fourth* part of each one's share. They would be 'fallen' if they declined to give". Bhāruchi : This is a 'faculty'. They may give if they wish. Only what will suffice for the marriages *need* be given--otherwise the brothers might find they have no property left over.

It is not always possible to adhere to the general rule that *smritis* do not repeat themselves. Cases where rules are repeated cannot always be avoided ; though, as we see from Bhāruchi's comment on Manu VIII.63, repetition (which weakens the force of the *smriti*) is admitted only in the last resort.

Once it is clear that the *smriti* is an injunction, the next question is what force is to be given to the words. Each *smriti* in the book must harmonize with the rest, incongruities must be eliminated, coherence with the propositions of *smritis* attributed to other authors must, if possible, be achieved, the text must be supplemented and corrected where necessary to provide a viable sense, and meaning must be obtained from the words (even the particles) so as to make the text meaningful for the current era. The result of this is that some texts are emasculated, while others are expanded and developed with the aid of reason, or analogy (as at Bharuchi's commentary on Manu IX.151). There are totally unintelligible *smritis* (as Manu IX.21), and with them the poor commentator must do the best he can.

At all times he must seek to be brief (cf. Bhār. on Manu XI.97) and not to give details which are of no relevance in his locality. If he is not brief his work will perish for want of copyists. And a rational and practical approach is called for at all times, even though his *smritis* belong to the world of ideals and norms, rather than mere statements of what actually happens in any particular place or amongst any particular caste. Bhāruchi, on Manu XI.130 and elsewhere makes the shrewd comment, "Who will buy for 10 *paṇas* what is available for 1 *paṇa* ?", meaning to say that if we were to interpret the various penances prescribed for sins in the *śāstra* as alternatives to each other the harder penances would never be employed and would cease to have any validity. Consequently the texts must be construed as requiring an accumulation, not an option !

Let us see, in about thirty examples, how the process actually went on.

Avoiding incongruities is a heavy task for the commentator. Manu XI.157 says "If a twice-born person who has not returned from his preceptor's house eats the food of the monthly rite (*śrāddha* for dead ancestors) he should fast for three days. . . ." Bhāruchi : To avoid incongruity with III.234, this does not apply to a student who is *invited* (as a daughter's son, etc.). Manu IX.140 : "The son of the 'appointed daughter' shall offer the *piṇḍa* (in the *śrāddha* ceremony) first to his mother, the second to his father, and the third to the father's father". Bhāruchi : This is to be taken as a mere repetition of a previous rule (132) under which the father and the maternal grandfather are to be given *piṇḍas*. Manu IX.113 : "The eldest and the youngest (brothers) shall receive their bonuses as stated--those other than the eldest and youngest shall have the property remaining over". On this Bhāruchi comments that discrepancies between this verse and the previous are to be resolved with reference to the *merits* of the middlemost brothers. Manu IX.10 reads "No one is able to guard women forcibly : they can however be guarded if these methods are employed : –", on which Bhāruchi comments that no contradiction can be contemplated between the two halves of the verse, so this means that the following methods are *commended.* Legal acumen is frequently called for. Manu VIII.270 provides that a Śūdra (a member of the fourth caste) abusing a twice-born (of a caste superior to his own) should have his tongue cut. Bhāruchi says that if the Śūdra abuses a *Brahmin* (267) he is put to death : therefore this verse relates to a Śūdra abusing a Kṣatriya or a Vaiśya (who are also twice-born, though inferior to a Brahmin).

At XI.173 Manu says "One who emits semen in non-human females, in a male, in a menstruating woman, in places other than the female organ. . .should perform the *santapana kricchra* (a severe penance)". Bhāruchi says that "non-human" means mares, etc. There is another penance for bestiality with a *cow.* As this has not been stated here it must be explained from another *smṛiti* (Gautama XXIII.13).

Necessary interpretation gives life to the text. Manu XI.97 : "When the Veda which has entered his body (during studentship) is once deluged with an intoxicant his Brahminhood leaves him and he becomes a Śūdra". Bhāruchi : "Intoxicant" does not refer to the *kind* of drink but to its intoxicating quality. Manu at IX.136 says, "The son whom she (the daughter) bears to a man of the same caste whether she be 'appointed' or not is the cause of his mother's father's having a grandson and should give the *piṇḍa* and take the property" ; on which Bhāruchi comments that this gives alternative rules : where the daughter is 'appointed' the son is entitled facultatively, but in other cases he has an option whether to take or not. Plainly the status of the daughter's son as an heir was highly disputed in Bhāruchi's time and place.

Meaning sometimes has to be squeezed, as it were, out of the words. Manu XI.163 : "For the taking of men and women, a field or a house, or water, wells or tanks, the expiation is traditionally a *chāndrayaṇa* (penance lasting a month)". But why is "water" mentioned as well as "wells" ? Bhāruchi : "Water" is for one's own enjoyment ; "wells" for that of others also--or some other solution to this doubt may be adopted ! Manu X.86 says "He must avoid all flavours, prepared food and sesamum (i.e. he must not sell them), stones, salt, cattle and human beings". Bhāruchi comments that since Brāhmins cannot be totally prohibited from handling salt, salt here cannot be one of the flavours ; it cannot be rock salt, for that is a "stone" ; therefore it is any *other* salt.

Words are often to be taken as illustrative of a much larger group or class. Manu XI.193 : "Whatever property Brahmins acquire by a blamed act, they are purified by abandoning it, by repeating texts and by austerities". Bhāruchi : "Brahmins" means all the twice-born. The penance referred to is the particular prescription laid down in the individual connection, not some other penance. Manu IX.198 : "The property that may have been given to a woman by her father the maiden who is a Brahmin by caste may take (after her death), or it shall belong to her issue". This obscure verse is interpretated by Bhāruchi in this way : (i) *all* the woman's property is involved ; (ii) "Brahmin" means "of the next higher caste", whichever that might be. Manu IX.178 lays down certain consequences "if a Brahmin, through lust, begets a son on a Śūdra woman. . .", but Bhāruchi says that "Brahmin" must be taken to include Kṣatriya and Vaiśya also (see above). Manu IX.54 : "If seed, carried away by rain or wind, grows up in a man's field, that must be known to belong to the owner of the field--the sower takes no profit from it". Bhāruchi adds that "rain or wind" is illustrative, so that sowing by theft or force produces the same result. Manu IX.188 provides, "In the absence of all these (heirs) the Brahmins are entitled to the estate. . ." Now Manu himself does not provide for widows or even other female dependants to inherit a man's estate. Bhāruchi says, in an important passage, that "all these" implies that only in the absence even of the deceased's womenfolk will the right pass to the Brahmins. Thus Manu is reconciled both with other *smriti*-writers, such as Yājñavalkya and Bṛihaspati, but also (evidently) with * local custom.

The particles *cha* and *api* ("and" and "even") can be given much greater force than the *smriti* literally would require. Medhātithi, commenting on Manu IX.2 ("*and* if they become attached to sensual objects"--a point obscured in Jha's translation), says that the word "and" shows that the duty of protecting women falls both upon their menfolk and the women themselves. Bhāruchi places such inclusive significance upon the word *cha* at Manu VIII.58,190 and X.3 ; and upon the word *api* at IX.236. The most celebrated example is that of the *Mitāksharā's* construction of the words "the wedded wife, the daughters *also*" in Yājñavalkya (cited above). The word "also" must have some meaning and therefore we infer that the daughter's son is an heir after the daughter though Yājñavalkya himself does not mention him at this place.

The literal meaning may sometimes be deserted. Manu XII.9 says "Through faults of *karma* (action having an occult effect) born of the body a human being becomes an immovable object, through those of speech a bird or a beast, through those of the mind, he becomes a person of the lowest class". Bhāruchi comments that this does not demonstrate the connection between cause and effect, which would conflict with the *śāstra* and with reason--but it shows the relative seriousness of *adharma* (sin). At IX.3 Manu says, quoting an ancient maxim, "The father guards her (a woman) while she is unmarried, her husband guards her while she is young, her son when she is old--a woman does not deserve independence". Bhāruchi : this is an injunction meaning only that all woman must always have the protection of their relatives.

Unexpected manipulations of the text occur, not unfrequently. Manu XI.180 : "*In a year* he 'falls' who associates with a fallen (outcasted) man by sacrificing for him or teaching him, or by matrimonial alliance, but not by riding, eating or sitting with him". Bhāruchi : by riding, eating and sitting with him one 'falls' not "in a year", but rather immediately. Alternatively another meaning may be derived, bearing in mind another *smriti*. An important piece of law is, according to Bhāruchi, secreted in Manu XI.5, which says "If a man who has already married acquires other wives after begging, he obtains delight as his only fruit and the progeny belong to the giver of the property". This means to convey a prohibition of a man's acquiring a second wife while his first is fit for *dharma* and offspring.

Manu X.112 tells us something arcane about means of acquisition in times of distress- - the moral implications are not to be forgotten : "The Brahmin unable to maintain himself may glean ears of corn and pick up grains from any place. Gleaning is better than acceptance (a qualified kind of begging)..." Bhāruchi says that the acceptance spoken of is acceptance from the "non-good" (i.e. unworthy persons, from whom a Brahmin should never accept gifts). Even gleaning is objectionable because one may glean the property of the "non-good". By contrast, there are instances where the fundamental propositions of the *śāstra*, against which a *smriti* is quite properly to be read, enrich the interpretation markedly. Manu IX.76 : "If the man went abroad for a duty of *dharma* he is to be awaited for eight years ; if for learning and fame, then six years, but if for his own fancy, three years". Bhāruchi adds that the basic rules on chastity, and on the "appointment" *(niyoga)* of widows to raise up seed to their deceased husbands, show that this verse does *not* sanction the unchasity of deserted women. The provisions of the *śāstra* on the subject are paramount.

Ingenuity can produce interesting results. Manu VIII.373 deals with the punishment for reiterated fornication. "If the convicted man is accused again a year after he shall pay a double fine..." Bhāruchi manipulates this in a curious fashion. If he (the offender) is taken with a woman *within the year* (from his previous conviction) the fine shall be 12 times as much in the first month of that year, 11 times in the second and so on until at the expiring of the year the fine is only double !

Enrichment is frequent, but, for the same ultimate purposes, emasculation is frequently called for. Manu X.123 : "The Śūdra's service of the Brahmin is praised as a special duty : whatever else he does is without fruit for him". Bhāruchi comments, this is a deprecation of *rituals* by the Śūdra, and thus commends his serving Brahmins. Naturally (we add) Bhār. understands the text as not deprecating, still less prohibiting, activities between those two poles. At X.109 Manu says "Amongst acceptance (see above), sacrificing, and teaching the acceptance is the lowest and is blamed for a Brahmin after death". Bharuchi holds that this deprecation of acceptance simply means a commendation of other means of livelihood. Manu IX.98 says "Not even a Śūdra should take a bride-price when giving his daughter ; for he who takes a bride-price makes a disguised sale of his daughter". Bhāruchi interprets this as follows : – this means that accepting a bride-price is blameworthy--but the Śūdra is not prohibited. Obviously in Bhāruchi's area Śūdras used to take bride-prices, as many of them still do. At Manu VIII.78 we are given a rule apparently about the admissibility of evidence : "What they state naturally should be accepted as relevant to the case, whatever they state apart from this, though it be for the sake of *dharma*, is useless". Bhāruchi says that the *nature* (i.e. demeanour) of the witness should be scrutinized by using inference to discover, e.g., why he is nervous--a comment tending to the question of credibility, not admissibility (as often in the ancient world).

One of the more celebrated examples of emasculation is that by which some jurists, notably Vijñāneśvara in his *Mitāksharā* (on Yājñ.II.24 : see Lingat, *op.cit.*, p. 182), dealt with the *smritis* which appeared to give a title in property to one who had held it unchallenged for a definite period of time (a kind of *longi temporis praescriptio*). These texts were so interpreted that they only gave to the possessor a right to undisturbed enjoyment of the fruits, on the footing that the true owner must have lost his right to reclaim them through his own laches or neglect.

It is always a delight to see the jurist tackling his apparently absolute and monolithic text with the beneficial aid of logic or reasoning.

Manu X.96 says "If any man of low caste...lives by the function of superiors, the king should deprive him of his property..." Bhāruchi says that though the context would indicate that the offender should be of the Kṣatriya caste, the object of the rule is the same, and therefore Vaiśya and Śūdra offenders should be treated as included in it. Manu IX.291 : "He who sells what is not seed, as well as he who pulls up seed and also one who breaks a covenant, shall have the 'slaying' which is disfiguring". Bhāruchi's comment : to inflict this mutilation there must be an accumulation of offences and aggravating circumstances, otherwise so heavy a deterrent would be unreasonable. Manu IX.287 (a very obscure *smṛiti*) says "He who acquires an unequal thing with equal things even by value, that man should have the first fine or even the middlemost". It seems that in very ancient times people used to barter goods for goods of the same volume or weight, irrespective of the market value, and this text was intended to prohibit the use of such a type of barter even when the value of the commodities *was* equal. But Bhāruchi has no time for such old-fashioned nonsense and says, "this refers to fraudulent sales : the size of the fine in any case must depend on the nature of the goods, and not be governed by so general a rule". Manu IX.286 similarly provides "For spoiling articles which are unspoiled, for breaking or wrongly boring gems, the punishment is the first 'violence'". Bhāruchi points out that gems are of various values, and the first 'violence' is a mere illustration, a hint. At IX.249 Manu says "The king's *adharma* is seen to be great if he strikes one who should not be struck as if he releases one who should be struck ; but *dharma* belongs to the one who chastises". Bhāruchi admits that this is literally true in the realm of penances. Kings must see that penances are performed. But in the realm of the royal policies (cf. 232) 'striking' is not obligatory and any effective form of coercion is satisfactory.

Likewise Manu IX.224 says "He who does gambling or betting. . .the king should strike. . .", but Bhāruchi alleges that 'strike' means only 'beat' (not 'kill'), for there is no breach of *dharma* involved in mere gambling.

At Manu IX.219 it is provided, in relation to the mechanical arrangements for partition of joint-family property, "A cloth, a conveyance, an ornament, prepared food, water, women, a maintenance-grant-way : these they say are not to be divided". Bhāruchi says *immo*, they may divide even these if they wish ; it is improper to forbid a gift in any case where the owner is willing to make it.

Reasoning can develop rules which the text gives only in, as it were, embryo form. Manu VIII.268 says, "For abusing a Kṣatriya the Brahmin should be fined 50, in the case of a Vaiśya 25, of a Śūdra 12". It is obvious that the fine is related to the *laesio honoris*, and consequently the *smṛiti* affords a model upon which other rules can be founded. Bhāruchi appeals to reason, and says that if a Kṣatriya abuses a Vaiśya the Kṣatriya should be fined double the amount prescribed for a Brahmin. When a Vaiśya abuses a Śūdra he should pay three times the penalty to be imposed on a Brahmin. Other methods of working this out would be possible, on the basis that a senior man's fault needs a greater deterrent, but that remains pure conjecture so far as we are concerned.

No doubt there are instances where the jurist cannot make up his mind. He knows that the judicial adviser will have his own preferences, and an absolute determination is requried only by those who have no training, and no judgement, of their own (like foreign administrators !). Sometimes Bhāruchi says, after stating an opinion which he cannot refute, "that deserves to be considered fully on its merits". At Manu IX.147 we read, "If an 'enjoined' woman (who has undergone *niyoga* : see above) bears a son either to her younger brother-in-law or to some other person, that son they declare. . . incapable of taking the estate. . ." Bhāruchi says, this is a deprecation of begetting otherwise than according to the injunctions (relative to *niyoga*), as a commendation of those children who are born under the injunction. Or there may be both an entitlement and a deprivation : so that the judge would determine solely on the claimant's merits. Such a solution, so well suited to the facts of ancient Indian litigation, is surprisingly seldom offered.

Conclusion

As is well known to modern Indian lawyers, the ancient and mediaeval commentators introduced into their texts elements favourable to contemporary customs. This is why they were selected by the British as the true textual sources of the law, rather than the fundamental *smṛiti*-texts themselves upon which the commentaries were based. Occasions where the commentaries have been neglected for the *smṛitis* can be found, but they are rare, and deservedly so.

Lest it might be thought that the technique of the jurists was in some way an innovation, it must be pointed out that the *smṛiti*-writers were themselves doing exactly the same.

It is very little realized as yet, but many *smṛitis* are reconstructions and tendentious manipulations of maxims and other more ancient sources of law. Two examples will suffice. The *smṛiti*-author Bṛihaspati in one place gives and explains the four sources of law, to which the judge must apply his mind. *Dharma*, the practice of the courts, custom, and the royal order are to be consulted, and each later in this series overrules or derogates from the earlier in the series. But Bṛihaspati, and indeed other *smṛiti*-writers, are dissatisfied with the implications of this (though they were perfectly practical) and attempted to expound the proposition as if the sources were not sources, but means of proof in actual litigation([10]).

A second example from the same source (or apparently the same source) will illustrate further what went on. There was (and still is) a custom to refer to ownership of land not by some abstract term--abstract terms being a sign rather of a sophisticated than a primitive stage in legal development--but by a collection of eight items implying different rights of enjoyment over the soil. Brihaspati takes these terms and gives his own explanation for them, an explanation tendentious in character and differing from the literal meaning([11]).

Perhaps it could be said that each generation of jurists relies upon the previous generations, and yet (though secretly) aims to supersede them. Modernity, whilst retaining a hold upon the indisputable sources of tradition, is the ideal of the commentator.

When Pratāparudra, in the preface to the *Sarasvatīvilāsa* (early 16 th century), stated that he aimed to make previous digests, which were troublesome to compare and reconcile, * absolutely superfluous([12]), he did not try (for he knew it impossible) to forbid the use of earlier works--and time has shown that his praiseworthy and idealistic optimism was unjustified. For his modernity was intellectual and fictitious, and the public retained its affection for the older sources.

---

(10) Derrett, *Religion, Law and the State in India* (cited above), 148 f, 155 f.

(11) L. Renou, Indo-Iranian J., 6 no. 2 (1962), p. 95.

(12) Mysore edn., 1927, pp. 11-12, 14-15. P.V. Kane, op. cit., vol. I, p. 411.

ADDITIONAL ANNOTATIONS

p. [146], para. 1. An interesting parallel is Mask. on Gaut. VII.25 (resort to arms by a brahmin): prāṇa-saṃśaye brāhmaṇo 'pi śastram ādadīta. *Comm.*: *prāṇa*-grahaṇena putra-dāra-hiraṇyāder api grahaṇam, "prāṇā hy ete bahiścarāḥ" iti darśanāt. When life is in danger is a condition wide enough to include danger to one's son, wife, or gold, *etc.*

p. [149], l. 22. For the commentators' and digest-compilers' motives in their own words now see also Derrett, *Dharmaśāstra and Juridical Literature* (1973), nn. 331, 337, and pp. 55-6.

A JURIST AND HIS SOURCES: MEDHĀTITHI'S USE OF BHĀRUCI

Medhātithi is the most amusing, and almost certainly the most interesting of the Hindu jurists of the pre-British period. Though Dr. Ganganatha Jha's translation is not a faithful representation of the text (from which it constantly differs) the world may obtain an excellent impression of Medhātithi's commentary on the *Manu-smṛti* without actually utilizing the Sanskrit text itself. He is the earliest Hindu jurist (he lived and wrote in Northern India about A.D. 825-900) whose methods are open to close inspection, and whose objects and achievement can be ascertained without much doubt. He was under the impression that the *Manu-smṛti* was a practical source of information about the *dharma-śāstra*, and his sparing use of citation of other Smṛti-s shows that he regarded Manu as a code in himself.[1] Grammar and Mīmāṃsā are used from time to time to clarify a text which less seriously-minded commentators might have left without those aids. Medhātithi (hereafter referred to as Medh.) refers to variant readings and very frequently

[1] A general treatment of Medhātithi by the present writer is due to appear in the *Festschrift* for Otto Spies. Another general appreciation is at Ganganatha Jha, *Manu Smṛti*, Notes, pt. 3, Calcutta, 1929, pp. ix-xl (introduction). *

to conflicting opinions about the meaning of the *smṛti*, which had evidently lost its original certainty of meaning (if in all respects it had one) in very many *śloka-s*. Most writers are content to give their own opinion, and every later commentator on the *smṛti* does this, with very occasional citation of opinions which differ. This rare citation of variant opinions is motivated by a desire not to neglect a prestige-holding opinion or one put to use in practice in the area under contemplation, whilst sparing the student the labour of making himself conversant with a confusing array of opinions. One factor which must surely have hastened Medh.'s own obsolescence is his constant setting forth of two, three or even four different views about Manu. Where did he get these views from? His own teachers and the learning popular in the area in which he worked must have been the obvious sources. But the way in which he used Bhāruci (hereafter referred to as Bhār.) can very plausibly be used as an indication of his general methods.

Bhāruci's *Manu-śāstra-vivaraṇa* has already been referred to by the present writer.[1] An opportunity was needed to show in detail Medh.'s depend nce upon him. In the seventh book, the *rāja-dharma* portion, Medh. copied, as best he could, quantities of Bhār.'s commentary. But that atmosphere was somewhat specialized: the material was after all *Arthaśāstra*, and Medh. did not have a copy of all

[1] *JAOS*, 84 (1965), 392-5.

Kauṭilya's work.[1] What of other books and other areas of law? Illustrations are in this article taken from the eighth and later books. They are a selection, arranged in a very rough general order. They will be found to illustrate the following phenomena: Medh. copies Bhār. word for word; Medh. paraphrases Bhār. with an apparently correct appreciation of his point and intention; Medh. takes Bhār.'s words and attempts to improve upon them stylistically; Medh. takes Bhār's words and attempts to improve upon them from the point of view of the idea; Medh. fails to grasp Bhār.'s idea and misrepresents it unconsciously; Medh. cannot read Bhār., and does the best with his text that he can; Medh. follows Bhār. in intent but not in words; Medh. gives Bhār.'s opinion faithfully, but accords it no importance, treating it as inferior to his chosen view; Medh. treats Bhār.'s opinion as unsuitable to be taken seriously. We cannot reprint typical instances where Medh. completely ignores Bhār.'s point, either because his manuscript is defective or because he thought it unworthy of discussion, nor the places where Bhār. himself, though writing a much slimmer and less luxurious work, seems plainly to have served in some degree as an inspiration for Medh. Bhār. too liked to record variant readings and the views of others.

[1] *ZDMG*, 115 (1965), 134-52.

Sometimes Bhār.'s variant reading is actually picked up by Medh., who very often follows Bhār.'s own readings of the *smṛti* itself.

What can we conclude from this survey? First that the welter of opinions, readings and interpretations of the *Manu-smṛti* provided jurists with a challenge, and the *smṛti* was still sufficiently important to deserve the luxury treatment they gave it. Bhār. was already an old and rare author by the time Medh. wrote. His opinions were entitled to the respect Medh. gave them, but he was not the leading pre-Medh. authority for the area which Medh. had under contemplation. Naturally Deccani or Drāviḍa traditions about Manu would carry prestige in Northern India where traditions of Hindu scholarship had suffered due to invasions and racial admixtures. We cannot tell whether a copy of Bhār. coming to the North inspired Medh. to write, or whether, intending to write a definitive commentary, he or his patron sent out requisitions for Manu commentaries from all quarters. But by comparing the two texts we are able to see how Medh. worked and what were the factors which inspired him. The first point that emerges fits with the fact that Medh. seems never to have obtained a great vogue in the South. Of course Vijñāneśvara refers to him, but not in any detail, and it may be a second-hand reference. Medh. was evidently biassed in favour of traditions of interpretation current in his own area or likely to obtain ready currency in his own area which would only be possible if there was a predisposition to that effect. Next, Medh. felt the need of the cognate sciences to determine the meaning of Manu and this is hardly foreshadowed in Bhār. The latter expresses authoritatively as a teacher whose exposition stands on its own feet. He was aware of other views than his own, but he seldom felt it necessary or desirable to refute them. Perhaps they were not worthy of refutation, or perhaps neither etiquette would allow this, nor would the current toleration of mutually independent or even personal lines of interpretation make it seem desirable. Medh.'s contribution, then, in contrast to an eminent predecessor, was to pull all available threads together, to cut the knots where they could not be untied, and to leave evidence of the competition through which his solutions had emerged triumphant. But in the course of his work Medh. was hampered by a text of this particular predecessor which was in places not clear, and unintelligible even to such an expert. Medh.'s work ultimately serves as a warning not so much to those who would write without fully appreciating their predecessors' achievements, as to those who fear that inadequacy of documentation and material must be fatal to an intellectual enterprise. Medh. remains for all his difficulties a monumental and, as I have already said, a unique specimen of Indian juridical writing.

The parallel passages follow: in the passages which * are compared the text of Bhāruci appears (as the earlier) on the left, and that of Medhātithi on the right.

XI. 256. B.

'deva-kṛtasyainasa' ity evam-ādayo 'ṣṭau mantrāḥ śākala-homīyāḥ. etair *ghṛtam abdaṃ hutvā sugurv apy apahanty enaḥ.* sarvamahāpātakāny apīty arthaḥ. *japtvā vā 'imā* rudrāya tavase kapardine kṣayadvīrāya' ity etan-mantraṃ saṃvatsaram eva. etāṃ siddhim avāpnuyāt antareṇāpi śākala-homaṃ. tad idaṃ vaikalpikaṃ japa-karma pūrveṇa śākala-mantra-homena prāyaścittam. anye tu *japtvā vā mana ity ṛcam.* sā tu śiṣṭebhya āgamayitavyā 'mano nv āhuvāmahe' ity eṣā.

M. (XI. 255)

'deva-kṛtasyainaso 'vayajanamasi' (*Vāj. S.* VIII. 13) ity evam-ādayo 'ṣṭau mantrāḥ śākala-homīyāḥ. tair *ghṛtam abdaṃ hutvā gurv apy apahanty enaḥ* sarva-mahāpātakāny apīty arthaḥ. japitvā 'namo rudrāya tavase kapardine' ity evaṃ mantraṃ saṃvatsaram evam etāṃ siddhim āpnuyāt, antareṇāpi śākala-homam. tad idaṃ vaikalpikaṃ japa-karma pūrveṇa śākala-mantra-homena prāyaścittam. anyena vā japitvā vā mana ity ṛcam. sā tu śiṣṭebhyaḥ sugamayitavyā.

XII. 5. B.

tathā ca vyāsaḥ: 'anabhidhyā parasveṣu sarva-sattveṣu sauhṛdam | karmaṇāṃ phalam astīti trividhaṃ karma saṃsmared' iti.

M.

tathā ca bhagavān vyāsaḥ: 'anabhidhyā parasveṣu sarva-sattveṣu sauhṛdam | dharmiṇāṃ phalam astīti trividhaṃ manasā smaret.'

IX. 155. B.

tathā ca gautamaḥ śūdra-prakaraṇa āha: ' aparigṛhītāsv api śuśrūṣuś cel labheta tad vṛtti-mūla-<m a>ntevāsi-vidhinā.'

M.

yathā gautamaḥ śūdrā-putra-prakaraṇa evāha: ' aparigṛhītāsv api śuśrūṣuś cel labheta vṛtti-mūlam antevāsi-vidhinā ' (XXVIII. 36).

X. 126. B.

evaṃ ca vyāsaḥ: ' na ceha śūdraḥ patatīti niścayo na ceha saṃskāram ihārhatīti ca । śruti-prayuktaṃ na ca dharmam aśnute na cāsya dharma-pratiṣedhanaṃ smṛtau ' iti.

M. (X. 127)

tathā ca bhagavān vyāsaḥ: ' na ceha śūdraḥ patatīti niścayo na cāpi saṃskāram ihārhatīti । smṛti-prayuktaṃ tu na dharmam aśnute na cāsya dharme pratiṣedhanaṃ smṛtam ' iti.

XII. 106. B.

tathā cetihāsaḥ: ' kaccin na lokāyatikān brāhma-
* ṇāṃs trāsate vase(?) । anarthakuśalā hy ete mūrkhāḥ paṇḍitamāninaḥ ' iti. kevalāgamo vā. tathā ca vyāsa-śloko bhīmasena-vacanānuvādī. ' śrotriyasyeva te rāja-nandakasyālpa-medhasaḥ । anuvāka-hatā buddhir naiṣā sūkṣmārtha-darśinī ' iti.

M.

tathā ca mahābhārate bhagavatā kṛṣṇa-dvaipāyanena darśitam: ' śrotriyasyaiva te rājan mandakasyālpa-buddhayaḥ । anuvāka-hatā buddhir naiṣā sūkṣmārtha-darśinī ' . . . tathedam aparam(uta) 'kaścin na lokāyatikān brāh-
maṇān smārta(?) sevate । *
anartha-kuśalā hy ete mūrkhāḥ paṇḍitamāninaḥ ' iti.

IX. 257. B.

tatra ye kraye vikraye m ā n a-t u l ā di-viśeṣaṇaṃ muṣṇanti dravyāṇām āgama-sthāna-nirgamān nāvekṣate[1] te *prakāśā vañcakāḥ*. *pracchannās* tu rātri-carās taskarā ity arthaḥ. na ca kevalam eta eva, kiṃ tarhi ime cānye yān ita ūrdhvaṃ vakṣyāmaḥ.

M.

tatra ye kreyārthaṃ māna-tulā-viśeṣeṇa muṣṇantī dravyāṇām āgama-sthāna-nirgamanāpekṣārthaṃ kurvanti te *prakāśa-vañcakā* vāṇijakāḥ. *prachannās* tu ye rātrer anuharanti te. *stenā āṭavikā* vijane pradeśe vasanti. apare tu prasahya hāriṇo na kevalam eta eva, kiṃ tarhīme cānye yān ūrdhvaṃ vakṣyāmaḥ.

VIII. 51. B.

karaṇaṃ ca yat saṃdigdhe vastuni nirṇaya-sādhanaṃ, tat punas tri-prakāram. evaṃ cośanā paṭhati: ' yatra na syāt kṛtaṃ patraṃ karaṇaṃ ca na vidyate | na copalambhaḥ pūrvoktas tatra daivī kriyā bhavet.'

M.

kāraṇaṃ pramāṇaṃ trividham. tad anyair iha saṃbhavatīti parigaṇitam. tathā cāhuḥ: ' yatra na syāt kṛtaṃ patraṃ sākṣi caiva na vidyate | na copalambhaḥ pūrvokto daivī tatra kriyā bhavet ' iti.

IX. 239. B.

evaṃ ca sati vyādhyādi-yoge 'py eṣu dayā na kartavyā. jyaiṣṭhyādi-guṇa-

M.

vyādhyādi-yoge 'py eṣu dayā na kartavyā. jyaiṣṭhyādi-guṇa-yoge 'pi ca

[1] MS.: nirgamānanavekṣya.

yoge ca naite namaskāryāḥ, pratyutthānābhivādanādibhiḥ.[1] eṣa eva cātra vacana-sāmarthyād dharmo vijñeyaḥ.

naite namaskāryāḥ pratyutthānādibhiḥ. eṣa eva vacana-sāmarthyād dharmo vijñeyaḥ.

X. 39. B.

evaṃ ca saty ayaṃ caṇḍālād api pāpataro vijñeyaḥ. tad etad ānantyāt saṃkarasya pradarśana-mātraṃ vijñeyam.

M.

ataś cāṇḍālād api kutsitataro vijñeyaḥ. tad etad ānantyāt saṃkarāṇāṃ pradarśana-mātraṃ kṛtam.

XI. 85. B.

yathā loke ' paṇa-labhyaṃ hi na prājñaḥ krīṇāti daśabhiḥ paṇair ' iti evam ihāpi syāt.

M. (XI. 39)

' paṇa-labhyaṃ hi kaḥ prājñaḥ krīṇāti daśabhiḥ paṇaiḥ.'

VIII. 219. B.

dharmārtha-yukteṣu prayojaneṣu rāja-kāryāvirodhiṣu go-pracārodaka-rakṣaṇa - devatāyatana - pratisaṃskaraṇādiṣu grāmādīnāṃ yā saṃvid utpadyate, tatra vyabhicāriṇaṃ tasmād deśād rājā nirvāsayet.

M.

grāmādīnāṃ yat kāryaṃ —yathā pāra-grāmikair grāmo no 'pahata-prāyaḥ asmākīne go-pracāre gāś cārayanti udakaṃ ca bhittvā nayanti. tad yadi vo mataṃ tad adya etad eṣāṃ kartuṃ na dadmaḥ. evaṃ naḥ pratibadhnatāṃ yadi

[1] MS.: pratyutthānādivādibhiḥ.

B.	M.
	taiḥ saha daṇḍādaṇḍir bhavati rāja-kule vā vyavahāras tatra sarve vayam eka-kāryāḥ. no ced upekṣāmahe. tatra ye saṃvidate—bāḍham—kim iti prāktanī grāma-sthitis tair vyatikramyate ity evaṃ protsāhya visaṃvaded balāt tair eva saha saṃgaccheta sveṣu vā nābhyantaraḥ syāt—sa rājñā svarāṣṭrān nirvāsayitavyo niṣkāsayitayaḥ. sva-viṣaye 'sya vastuṃ na deyam.

VIII. 376. B. M.

B.	M.
kṣatriyasya daṇḍādhikyaprayojanam uktam. viduṣo 'tikrame daṇḍa-bhūyastvam iti.	kṣatriyasyādhiko daṇḍo rakṣādhikṛto rakṣati tat punaḥ sa evāparādhyati.

IX. 93. B. M.

B.	M.
smṛtyantareṣv ayaṃ śloko, na tv atra samāmnāyate.	kecid āhuḥ amānavo 'yaṃ ślokaḥ.

XI. 24. B. M. (XI. 23)

B.	M.
evaṃ ca bhikṣaṇād ayācitaḥ śreyān iti vijñāyate. tathā coktam: ' ayācitopapannānāṃ dravyāṇāṃ yaḥ	bhikṣaṇam atra niṣidhyate. ayācitopapannaṃ tu na duṣyati. tathā coktam: ' ayācitopapannānāṃ dra-

pratigrahaḥ | sa viśiṣṭaḥ śiloñchābhyāṃ taṃ vidyād apratigraham ' iti.

vyāṇāṃ yaḥ pratigrahaḥ | viśiṣṭa-loka-śāstrābhyāṃ taṃ vidyād apratigraham ' iti.

VIII. 193. B.

p a v i t r ā sanenāśādānena s v a-k a l a t r a-saṃ-<bhoga->nyāsenāgāmi-kālopakārapradarśanenety evam-ādibhir *upadhābhiḥ* para-dravyāpahārī. . .

M.

iha tu vitrāsanaṃ rājata upakāra-darśanaṃ kanyānurāga-kathanam ity evam-ādyā gṛhyante. caurās tvāṃ muṣṇanti yady ahaṃ tvāṃ na rakṣāmi. rājā tavātyantaṃ kupito mayā tu bahu samāhitaṃ. rājatas te nagarādhikāraṃ dāpayāmi mukhyaṃ vopakāraṃ karomi. puṣpamitra-duhitā tvayyatyantam anurāgiṇī maddhasta idam upāyanaṃ preṣitavatī ityevam-ādy anṛtam uktvātmīyam upāyanam āsajya bahu pratinayanti. tat-samakṣaṃ ca rājani tat samaṃ vā kāryāntaram upāṃśu nivedya kathayanti. tvadīyaṃ kāryam upakrāntam ity evam-ādyābhir *upadhābhiḥ para-dravyaṃ* ca bhuñjate.

IX. 75. B.	M.
agarhita-śilpa-jīvanam. . . jālikādi-karaṇam. etena vidhavāyā ajāta-putrāyā vṛttyupāyo vyākhyātaḥ. garhitaṃ ca vastra-nirṇejanādi.	kartana-jālikā-karaṇādinā. garhitāni vastūni vijanādīni. eṣa eva vidhavādīnāṃ nija-śrama-janyo vṛttyupāyaḥ.

IX. 323. B.	M.
prāyaṇaṃ ca rājñaḥ prathama-kalpaḥ. atas tad-abhāva itare kalpā yathā syuḥ sva-kāma-prayāṇāvirodhaś cāsya vyākhyātaḥ.	ātma-tyāge saṃgrāmaṃ kuryāt. yadi kathaṃcid antyāvasthāyāṃ raṇaṃ nopalabheta tadāgnyudakādinā śarīraṃ jahyāt. phalātiśaya-saṃpattis tu raṇe samāsañjanaṁ āropaṇam.

IX. 274. B.	M.
ā l a s y e nānabhidhāvanto *nirvāsyāḥ*, ye tu coropakṣepān nānudhāvanti te coravadhena vadhyāḥ.	śaktau satyām ālasyādinā te *nirvāsyāḥ*. ye tu cauraiḥ kṛta-saṃketās teṣāṃ pūrvatra vadha ukto ' ghātayed ' iti.

X. 90. B.	M.
acira-sthitān ity argha-pratīkṣaṇa-pratiṣedhaḥ.	*acirasthitāḥ*. arthādikaṃ lābham anapekṣya. svalpaṃ mūlyam adya, kālāntare cāgāmini bahu-mūl-

	yaṃ labheyety evaṃ na pratīkṣitavyam.
XI. 73. B.	M. (XI. 72)
viduṣāṃ prāyaścittīyo 'yam ity evaṃ jānatāṃ, iṣvastra-jñānāṃ vā, catuṣ-pādaṃ dhanur-vedam adhīyānānām.	*viduṣām* ity eva jānate prāyaścittopadeśo 'yam iti. athavā dhanur-veda-jñānām.
VIII. 415. B.	M.
yas tu vidyamāna-vibhavaḥ śūdraḥ sva-śaktyā jīvati nāsau paramārthato dāso veditavyaḥ.	tataś cānicchato na dāsyam asti. ato yadi śūdro vidyamāna-dhanaḥ svātantryeṇa jīved brāhmaṇādyanapāśrito na jātu duṣyet.
IX. 113. B.	M.
bahu-putrasya jyeṣṭha-kaniṣṭhayor guṇavator yathoktam uddhṛtya nirguṇānāṃ bahūnām api madhyamānāṃ guṇavato madhyamasya yaś catvāriṃśad-bhāga ukto 'nantara-śloke sa bahubhir api ca madhyamair vibhajanīyaḥ. sama-guṇānāṃ tu madhyamānāṃ sarveṣām ekaikasya pūrvavac catvā-	tribhyo 'dhika-putrasya jyeṣṭha-kaniṣṭhayor guṇavator yathoktam uddhṛtya bahūnām api madhyamānāṃ guṇavato madhyamasya yaś catvāriṃśattamo bhāga ukto 'nantara-śloke bahubhir api madhyamaiḥ sa vibhajanīyaḥ. sama-guṇānāṃ tu madhyamānāṃ sarveṣām ekaikasya pūrva-vacanāc catvāriṃ-

riṃśad-bhāga uddhāryaḥ.

śattamo bhāga ukta uddhāryaḥ.

IX. 119. B.

ajāvikaṃ tu vibhāga-kāle yadi viṣama-saṃkhyayā vibhaktum aśakyaṃ taj *jeṣṭhasyaiva* syāt. na tad anyasya dravyāṃśa-pātena samatāṃ nayet, vikrīya vā tan-mūlyaṃ khaṇḍayet.

M.

eka-śapham aśvāśvatara-gardabhādayaḥ vibhāga-kāle sama-saṃkhyayā yad vibhaktum *ajāvikaṃ* na śakyate *jyeṣṭhasyaiva* syān na tad anya-dravyāṃśa-pātena samatāṃ nayed vikrītaṃ vā tatas tan-mūlyaṃ dāpayet.

VIII. 49. B.

ācaritena vābhojana-gṛha-dvāropaveśanādinā loka-samācaritena; *balena vā* sva-gṛha-bandhanādinā mā bhūd asyārtha-kṣayo rāja-samāveśanena.

M.

acaritam abhojana-gṛha-dvāropaveśanādi. *balaṃ* rājādhikaraṇopasthānaṃ. tatra rājā sāmnāprayacchantaṃ nigṛhya ca prapīḍya dāpayatīti.

VIII. 103. B.

prāḍvivākas tac chūdrānuyoga-vacanam anyathā go-rakṣakādiṣu brāhmaṇesu vadan *dharmato 'rtheṣu* vyavahāreṣu, ye sākṣiṇaḥ teṣu jānann api yathā-varṇam anuyogaṃ nādharmeṇa

M.

anyais tu pūrva-vidhi-śeṣatayāyaṃ śloko vyākhyātaḥ. tad etad go-rakṣakādiṣv anuyoga-vākyeṣu brāhmaṇeṣu bhavitavyam. anyathā brāhmaṇeṣu satyaṃ brūhīti yathā brāh-

yujyate. yena *daivīm* śāstravatīṃ *vācaṃ vadanti tāṃ* smṛtvā manv-ādayaḥ 'viprān śūdravad ācared' iti.

maṇā ete kathaṃ śūdravad anuyojyā iti tad vidvān api na duṣyatīti yato manv-ādaya evaṃvidhāṃ *vācaṃ vadanti* yathaite śūdravad ācaraṇīyā iti.

IX. 237. B.

lalāṭe 'ṅkana-pratiṣedhavidhau lalāṭa-grahaṇāt.

M.

lalāṭāṅkanam. pratiṣedhavidhau 'nāṅkyā rājñā lalāṭe syuḥ' (IX. 240) iti tac-chravaṇāt.

IX. 162. B.

etena darśanenāniyuktāsutādaya itaratrānaṃśārhatvād bījino 'ṃśaṃ labhante.

M.

aniyuktā-sutādayo 'satsu sapiṇḍeṣu janayitū rikthaharā bhavantīti.

IX. 230. B.

vikarma-sthānām etad aparādhānurūpataḥ śiphādibhis tāḍanaṃ. na pātakinām api cāpalatā vijñeyā.

M.

mahāpātakināṃ sāmyāt tac-chiphādibhis tāḍanam.

IX. 285. B.

dhvajo rājñāṃ devatāyataneṣu vā. *yaṣṭir* nāgāyatane, bali-yaṣṭir vā grāmeṣu.

M.

dhvajaḥ cihnaṃ rājāmātyādīnām. devāyataneṣu ca *yaṣṭiḥ*.

IX. 299. B.

pīḍanāni: jagatām aśani-
pāta-durbhikṣādīni; sva-
kṛtāni *vyasanāni* trayāṇi
deha-daivātma-gatāni kṣa-
ya-hetūni.

M.

pīḍanāni naraka-durbhikṣa-
pātādīni. tathāvarṣādi-var-
ṣ a-p a r janya-mūṣika-śala-
bhāśani-prabhṛtayaḥ. *vyasanāni* kāma-krodha-samu-
tthāni sva-putra-saṃprāp-
ta - daiva - vighaṭanayopan-
yāsena vā.

X. 32. B.

vāgurā-vṛttitvam āraṇya-
paśu-hiṃsanākhyaṃ yuk-
tam āryāṇāṃ deva-pitrar-
tham auṣadhārthaṃ ca.
p r ā ṇ a-yātrā-mātrārthaṃ
vā putra-dārātyayaṃ prā-
ptasya.

M.

vāgurā araṇya-paśu-hiṃsa-
nam. tac cāryāṇāṃ daiva-
pitryārthaṃ kṣudhārthaṃ
ca, na tu vyādhavat paśūn
hatvā māṃsa-vikrayeṇa
jīvanam. rāja-niyogād
bahu-prāṇivadho jīvikār-
thaḥ.

X. 47. B.

h a ṃ s a-patha-vāri-pathā-
khyāḥ.

M.

s t h a l a-patha-vāri-pathā-
diḥ prasiddhaḥ.

XII. 92. B.

na hi nityānāṃ karmaṇāṃ
parityāgo 'sty ātmecchayā.
śāstratas tu parityāgaḥ
pākṣikaḥ puruṣa-medhā-
diṣv anutyāgena.

M.

karmāṇi parihāyety asyālaṃ-
banaṃ praśasta-devatāya-
tana - pradakṣiṇa - mantra-
guru-gamanādīni muktvā-
py ātma-jñānam abhyas-

yet. na hi nityānāṃ karmaṇāṃ svecchayā parityāgo 'sti puruṣa-dharmādiṣu vihite nāsti tyāgena vinā.

IX. 162. B.

yadi jātāpatyo 'tharvaṇa-pakṣa-kriyayā punaḥ sarvaṃ kṛtvā putrān utpādayet, tayoś ca bīji-kṣetriṇor dhanaṃ strīgataṃ syāt, tayor eṣa vibhāgaḥ.

M.

klībasya prāgupātte kṣetraje ' yas talpa-jaḥ pramītasya vyādhitasya vā ' iti, paścād auṣadhe kathaṃcit klībatva-nivṛttau saṃbhavati, tadīyam evāsau rikthaṃ labheteti.

IX. 290. B.

śruti-smṛti-bāhyeṣv *abhicāreṣu* khādira-sūcī-nikhanana-pada-pāṃsu-grahaṇādiṣv idam ucyate. atrābhicārārhasyāyaṃ daṇḍo na vidyate. tathāyaṃ prāyaścittaṃ vakṣyaty anabhicaraṇīyasyābhicāre ' abhicāram ahīnaṃ ca tribhiḥ kṛcchrair vyapohati ' (XI. 197) iti. *mūla-karmaṇi cānāptaiḥ* kriyamāṇe. na mātṛ-bhaginyādibhiḥ, adhikārāt tāsām. *kṛtyāsu* ca vetāḷādyāsu bhū-<ta-> tantra-

M.

vaidikāḥ śyenādayaḥ laukikāḥ pāda-pāṃsu-grahaṇa-sūcī-bhedanādayaḥ. *mūla-karma* vaśīkaraṇādi. *āptāḥ* pautra-bhāryādayas tato 'nye '*nāptāḥ*. *kṛtyā* abhicāra-prakārā eva mantrādi-śaktayaḥ, uccāṭanaṃ suhṛd-bandhu-kuläddhi vicittīkaraṇādi-hetavo bhūta-vidyāḥ prasiddhāḥ.

2

vihitāsv asaṃbandha-kṛtāsv eva.

IX. 292. B.

taṃ nikaṣa-parivartana-tulā-saṃcaraṇādiṣu anyāyeṣu pravṛttam.

M.

parivartana-tulāntaratāpacchedādibhiḥ apaharanti gṛhṇate.

X. 38. B.

mūla-vyasanaṃ māraṇa-vṛttir ity arthaḥ. vadhya-māraṇaṃ rājādeśād, anātha-śava-nirharaṇaṃ tad-vastrādi-grahaṇaṃ preta-piṇḍa-bhojanam ity evam-ādi-vṛttiḥ *pulkasyāṃ caṇḍālena* jāyate.

M.

vyasanaṃ duḥkhaṃ tasya *mūlaṃ* māraṇaṃ tad-vṛttir vadhya-māraṇaṃ rājādeśād anātha-śava-vahanaṃ tad-vastrādi-grahaṇaṃ preta-piṇḍa-bhojanam ity evam-ādi-vṛttiḥ *pulkasyāṃ cāṇḍālena* jāyate.

VIII. 399. B.

yad yatra pracuraṃ yatra ca durlabhaṃ tat tasya *rājñaḥ prakhyātaṃ* bhavati. tathodīcyeṣvājāneyā aśvāḥ, kuṅkumaṃ kāśmīreṣu, prācyeṣv agaru-karpūrādi tad anyatra na nirhāryam. anirhṛtaṃ hi durlabhatvād itaretaraṃ rājñāṃ kārya-pratibandhād upāyanaṃ bhavati.

M.

rājñaḥ saṃbandhitayā prakhyātāni yāni *bhāṇḍāni* rājopayogitayā: yathā hastinaḥ, kāśmīreṣu kuṅkumam, prācyeṣu paṭṭorṇādīni, pratīcyeṣv aśvāḥ, dākṣiṇātyeṣu maṇimuktādīni. yad yasya rājño viṣaye sulabham anyatra durlabhaṃ tatra tasya prakhyāpanam bhavati. tena hi rājāna itaretaraṃ saṃdadhate.

IX. 101. B.

na tu puruṣasya strīvad anyopagama-pratiṣedhaḥ. 'tasmād ekasya bahvyo jāyā bhavanti naikasyā bahavaḥ saha patayaḥ' iti śrutiḥ. striyās tu puruṣāntara-saṃkalpenāpi vyabhicāra ity uktaṃ ca.

M.

yac cāhuḥ: 'aparityāgo 'trāvyabhicāraḥ, itarathā strīvat puruṣasyāneka-bhāryā-pariṇayanaṃ na syāt' —tad ayuktam. asti puruṣe vacanaṃ 'kāmatas tu pravṛttānām', tathā 'vandhyāṣṭame 'dhivettavyā' iti. na tu striyāḥ. tathā ca liṅgāntaraṃ syāt 'ekasya bahvyo jāyā bhavanti naikasyā bahavaḥ saha patayaḥ' (*AB*, III. 3) iti.

IX. 249. B.

adṛṣṭārtheṣu tāvad evam. dṛṣṭārtheṣu tu rājya-tantra-vidhy-artha upadeśe yad vadha-śravaṇaṃ yathā dviṭ-sevinaś ca hanyād (232) ity uktaṃ tatra dṛṣṭa-prayojanārthatvād upadeśasya na niyato vadhaḥ. evaṃ ca saty upāyāntareṇāpi bandhanādinā <*vi*> *niyacchato* na doṣaḥ.

M.

dṛṣṭārtheṣu rājya-tantra-siddhy-artham upadeśeṣu pravacanaṃ, yathādṛptaṃ yodhāṃś ca hanyād ity uktam. tatra dṛṣṭa-prayojanatvād upadeśasya na niyato vadhaḥ. evaṃ ca saty upāyāntareṇāpi bandhanādinā *viniyacchato* na doṣaḥ.

VIII. 198. B.	M.
anyas tv āha: *apasaraḥ* krayād anyo dhanāgamaḥ.	athavā. . .*apasaraḥ* krayād anyaḥ pratigrahādir āgamaḥ.

VIII. 315. B.	M.
ekārtha-viṣayo vikalpo musalādīnāṃ brāhmaṇa-varjam. anye tu varṇa-krameṇaiṣāṃ musalādīnām upadeśaṃ manyante.	varṇānām anukrameṇa musalādīnām upadeśaṃ manyante, tad ayuktam.

XI. 117. B.	M. (XI. 116)
etad eva go-ghāta-prāyaścittaṃ sarvopapātakeṣv atidiśyate. tad-vikalpena cāndrāyaṇam eva. evaṃ ca sati go-hatyāyāś cāndrāyaṇaṃ na syāt, tad-vaikalpika-sāmarthyāt, yathānyeṣūpapātakeṣu. ata eva pṛthaṅ nirdeśaḥ.	*etad eva* iti go-ghātaka-prāyaścittaṃ sarveṣūpapātakeṣv atidiśati. vaikalpikaṃ cāndrāyaṇam api. upapātakitve viśeṣopadeśān na go-ghnasya cāndrāyaṇam icchanti. teṣām upapātakitva-vacane go-ghnasya prayojanaṃ mṛgyam.

XI. 178. B.	M. (XI. 177)
apare tv akrodhāṃ śūdrāṃ *vṛṣalīm* āhuḥ. pāṭhāntaraṃ ca kurvanti: 'tribhir māsair' iti. tat punar	vṛṣalī-śabdo nindayā prayukto na jāti-śabde. . . yat tu 'tribhir māsaiḥ sevitvā vṛṣalīṃ' śūdrām

na nyāyyam anadhikṛtatvāt tasyā ity apare.

evācakṣate, tad apy ayuktam. śūdrā-vivāhasyāvihitatvāt, svairiṇyāś ca laghu-prāyaścittasyopadeśād anyasyāś copapātakatvād gurutaram idam ayuktam.

VIII. 348. B.

dvijātīnāṃ ca varṇānāṃ viplave varṇa-saṃkarādau vyavasthā-bhaṅge. *kāla-kārite* rāja-vyasanena kenacit kadācic ca dharmoparodhād atra śastra-grahaṇam adoṣam. yato 'sya na tatra sāhasika-daṇḍo yujyate. kiṃ ca *ātmanaś ca paritrāṇe* paritaḥ sarvatas trāṇe sa-kuṭumba-draviṇasyātmanaḥ. *dakṣiṇānāṃ ca* apahāra-paritrāṇa iti vartate. dakṣiṇā-grahaṇaṃ sarva-yājñiya-dravyopalakṣaṇārtham.

M.

varṇānāṃ viplavo 'vyavasthānaṃ varṇa-saṃkarādi. *kāla-kārite* rāja-maraṇādau. tatra sva-dhana-kuṭumba-rakṣārthaṃ śastraṃ grāhyam. anye tu parārtham apy asminn avasare. tathā ca gautamaḥ: 'durbala-hiṃsāyāṃ ca vimocane śaktaś ced' iti. uktaṃ yajña-vināśa-saṃkaranivṛttyarthaṃ śastra-grahaṇam. nimittāntaram āha *ātmanaś ca paritrāṇe*. pariḥ sarvatobhāve śarīra-bhāryā-dhana-putra-rakṣārthaṃ *ghnan dharmeṇa na duṣyati. dakṣiṇānāṃ ca saṃgaro* 'varodhaḥ yadi yajñārthaṃ kalpitā dakṣiṇāḥ kaiścid apahriyeraṃs tadā tan-nimittaṃ yoddhavyam. anye tv evam abhisaṃbadhnanti —dakṣiṇānāṃ hetoḥ saṃgare—yadyuparodhaḥ pravṛtto dharme 'pravṛtte ' dakṣiṇā-saṃgara ' iti.

VIII. 78. B.

[*svabhāvena* iti sabhāyāṃ] grāmiṇām anyeṣāṃ cāprāgalbhyād apratibhāna-kampādayo jāyante. teṣāṃ vyāvahārikaṃ bruvatāṃ sva-bhāva upalakṣayitavyo 'numānataḥ puruṣa-śīlato vā, kim eṣām amī mithyā-vacana-kṛtāḥ kampādayaḥ, utāprāgalbhyād anucita-mahājana-samavāyād vā. yena hy anumānāgamyaṃ kiṃcin nāsti evaṃ dhṛṣṭa-prāgalbhyānām api svabhāvo 'vadhāraṇīyaḥ

M.

anye vyācakṣate: yad aprāgalbhyādibhiḥ skhalita-padam udāharanti na tāvatā tad anādeyaṃ, kiṃtu svabhāva eṣām upalakṣitavyo 'numānena, kim amī aprāgalbhyāt skhalanti, utāsatyābhidhāyitayeti. tat tu prāg uktaṃ na cākṣarārtha ity upekṣyam.

ADDITIONAL ANNOTATIONS

p. [151], n. 1. See next chapter.

p. [155], l. 28. It will be found that the text of Bhār. as given here and in all comparisons with Medh. fails to correspond with the text as printed in my edn. (1975). The reason is that the comparisons were made with the manuscript (now at S.O.A.S.).

p. [157], ll. 18, 25. The original was *tāta sevase*.

THE CONCEPT OF LAW ACCORDING TO MEDHĀTITHI, A PRE-ISLAMIC INDIAN JURIST

This essay, an attempt to encourage the comparative study of Islamic and Hindu legal ideas, is dedicated to Otto Spies, in recognition of his services to India, to Islamic studies, and to comparative law.

First, to define the scope and intent of this essay. Medhātithi was pre-Islamic in that at the time he wrote (between 800 and 900 A.D.) Islamic legal notions cannot have been widely known to any scholars in India, with the possible exception of the sea-ports of Sindh, Kathiawar, Kutch, Gujarat, and perhaps Malabar. We have no knowledge of any such contact intellectual or personal, and although Al-Biruni was, not long afterwards, to obtain a very thorough knowledge of Hindus and Hinduism, we have no reason to suppose that Hindu scholars made any sympathetic investigation of Islam even at that period. Medhātithi wrote before Muslim adventurers obtained any foothold in Northern India (where he seems to have lived), and his jurisprudence is Hindu pure and simple (in so far as anything Hindu could be called simple).

Next, what is meant by « concept of Law » ? All readers of this essay will not be agreed as to what is meant by « law ». It is a phenomenon about which agreement is indefinitely postponed. For this very reason an investigation of the concepts of various great jurists is worthwhile. The danger here is that, since the Skt. word for law, *naya*, may not occur in Medhātithi at all, and since the words which certainly occur do not correspond to any commonly accepted word for « law » in modern languages, the search may be misdirected or futile. It is necessary, therefore, to frame a definition of « law » for our present purposes, and then to search in our source for information relative to it. Such an investigation has not, so far as this writer knows, been done. The most usual attempt is to fasten upon the concept *dharma* (« righteousness »), a virtually untranslatable term characteristic of Hinduism as *fiqh* is of Islam, and to describe it and its sources and manifestations. Most investigations are made into the *dharma-śāstra*, or science of righteousness, taking illustrations from every period and from authors dwelling in any part or parts of the sub-continent. The great hindrance to an objective, as opposed to a *śāstric*, investigation was that very little was known of the actual practices of Indians contemporary with the jurists. A little progress has been made in this respect [1], and Medhātithi has himself been very helpful : perhaps more so than any other jurist of ancient times [1a].

For the purposes of this investigation we may define « law » as follows :

Law is that body of rules (namely positive and negative injunctions, commands and prohibitions) which can be enforced by judicial action. A rule which will not be observed, directly or indirectly, in a court or before a tribunal is not law. What ought (in some people's opinion) to be law, is not law. Pious hopes or fears are not law. Ethical injunctions are not law. That which is left to choice is not law.

Did law exist in ninth-century India? Certainly. Did the jurists write about it? Certainly. How and why they wrote about it must be understood unless we are to fail to appreciate what they were doing when they went into detail about any legal problem. We shall try to answer that question in reference to Medhātithi in this essay.

Why Medhātithi? He was probably the greatest jurist of his science : a substantial distinction [2]. Of the hundreds of jurists whose works are available to us none has laboured in quite the same manner as Medhātithi, and many of his qualities are unparalleled. This can be said with confidence although the text we possess is not his original in all respects [3]. His chief claims to attention are these : first, he is very old : there are few writers older, and they are all short and laconic. Next he devotes his work (the

[1] See DERRETT, « Law and the social order in India before the Muhammadan conquests », *J.E.S.H.O.* VII (1964), pp. 73-120.

[1a] Vivid illustrations occur : on VIII.180 (p. 231), law of evidence; VIII.193 (p. 241), frauds; VIII.219 (pp. 266-267), by-laws.

[2] On Medhātithi see P.V. KĀNE, *History of Dharmaśāstra* I (Poona, 1930), pp. 268-275, also G. Jha, *Manu-smṛti. Notes. Part III, Comparative* (Calcutta, 1929), pp. xxxviii-xl (original and liberal). He is cited in the *Mitākṣarā* of Vijñāneśvara and occasionally even in litigation : e.g., *Ambu Bai* v. *Soni* Indian Law Reports. [1941] Madras 13, at p. 25.

[3] On the so-called *jīrṇoddhāra*, or « restoration », which took place before any archetype of our surviving copies was produced, see the comment of Jhā discussed and, to a certain extent, evaluated in DERRETT, « A newly-discovered contact between Arthaśāstra and Dharmaśāstra : the role of Bhāruci », *Z.D.M.G.* CXV (1965), pp. 134-152.

Manu-bhāṣya, his earlier *Smṛti-viveka* [4] having been lost) to a minute exposition of the *Manu-smṛti*, the most famous of Indian law-books, with the intention of making his commentary a textbook in the *śāstra* and making it possible for people of his own day to use Manu with confidence as a foundation for śāstric teaching. Finally, in the course of his exposition he continually brings in views opposed to his own, and disposes of them by reasoning, rather than by the citation of conflicting texts from other *smṛti-s*, which is, all too often, the method adopted by his successors in the science. His reasonings are often subtle, but they are as often practical and have an eye to actual usage. It is from Medhātithi we obtain glimpses of what people actually said and did : and more than once a sense of humour is to be detected [5], which is usually buried (if at all present) in lesser writers.

Another reason why Medhātithi repays close study is that in his day the development of *purāṇic* contamination of the *dharmaśāstra* was barely beyond its commencement. *Purāṇa-s*, which purported to be encyclopaedic accounts of history and learned tradition, were usurping the task of the *smṛti-s* in stating what was righteousness and what was duty. The contamination of the textual sources of *dharma* was going on apace. The belief that the ancient sources were to be referred to as authorities and that new sources could not be manufactured was now so deeply rooted (as Hinduism advanced and embraced more and more sub-Hindu communities), that forgery and spurious « traditions » found an open door. The effort to take over from the decaying remnants of Buddhism and the distinctive ways of the Jains coincided with an internal explosion in the Hindu *śāstra-s*, of which the proliferation of spurious *smṛti-s* and *purāṇa-s* was a symptom [6]. Medhātithi stands at the point where the desire to uphold the « genuine » *śāstra* against its intellectual rivals is paramount, but the need to rely upon all and every more or less antique text had not penetrated into jurists' technique. A

[4] A verse work, as appears from the citation in the *Manu-bhāṣya* at II.6, pp. 63, 65-66 in Jhā's Sanskrit text.

[5] What the present writer regards as comical passages occur at II.6 (p. 206); III.26 (p. 50), III.33 (p. 58); III.281 (p. 291); IV.138 (p. 418); IV.228 (p. 477, a delicious example of a confidence trick); V.83 (p. 98); VII.75 (p. 250); VIII.104 (p. 128); VIII.163 (p. 208-209); IX.14 (p. 11); IX.260 (p. 203).

[6] Observations on this subject in Derrett, « The Purāṇas in Vyavahāra portions of mediaeval smṛiti works », *Purāṇa* V (1963), pp. 11-30. Kāne in his *H.D.*, vol. V, part 2, devotes a chapter to *purāṇa* material in *dharmaśāstra*. What appear to be *purāṇic* citations occur in Medh. at III.124 (falsely numbered 134 in the trans., p. 159); VII.29 (p. 291); and perhaps at II.202 (falsely numbered 212 in the trans., p. 234).

certain intolerance, which was one of the main-springs behind the *purāṇic* movement, is therefore visible in the jurist's writings themselves, an intolerance which begins to disappear with the more flexible and supple ratiocinations of mediaeval writers.

Medhātithi has a great attraction for us in that his commentary on Manu has been translated. The translation, made by *Mahāmahopādhyāya* Dr. Gaṅgānātha Jhā [7], was more or less commissioned by Sir Ashutosh Mookerjee, the celebrated judge and patron of learning. The translation lacks accuracy in many places. Dr. Jhā was not a *dharmaśāstrī*, but a *mīmāṃsaka*, and though this skill was extremely useful in unravelling many of Medhātithi's reasonings, it was not appropriate for all the demands which the text made upon its translator. But, for all that, the newcomer to the *śāstra* will find Medhātithi, in the guise of Jhā's English translation, readable and, on the whole, intelligible. In what follows references are made to the volumes and pages of Jhā's translation and to the books and verses of Manu with the *Manu-bhāṣya* of Medhātithi as published by Jhā himself some years afterwards [8].

I. The Factual Situation

What we know of the practice of law in Medhātithi's time is either to be found out from passing references in Medhātithi himself or from inscriptions or from references in literary works. Material from later centuries will not necessarily be irrelevant. Some well-known usages of Hindus today correspond exactly with what Medhātithi himself says.

[7] Published in five volumes by the University of Calcutta from 1920 to 1926. The five volumes appeared in nine parts and the reader of this article will need to know that the pagination is continuous for both parts of vol. I, both parts of vol. II, both parts of vol. III, both parts of vol. IV, and through vol. V, which appeared in one volume. Vol. I of the trans. covers Manu, books I-II; vol. II covers books III-IV; vol. III covers books V-VII, vol. IV covers book VIII (the one with which this article is most concerned), while vol. V contains the remainder of the work.

[8] Asiatic Society of Bengal, *Bibl. Ind. ser.*, 256, vol. I (Calcutta, 1932), vols. II and III (index and prelims.) (Calcutta, 1939). The occasional discrepancies between the numbering of the verses in the text and the trans. must be watched. In the interval between 1926 and 1932 Dr. JHĀ changed his mind regarding several readings, but the fact is not noted anywhere.

Law operated in three contexts. (*i*) Between the subject and the king, the king's prerogatives and powers had *de facto* the force of law [9], and this was recognised in the *dharmaśāstra,* though the latter sought to restrain the king from acts of tyranny. Between the subjects themselves there were two main fields in which law operated. The first is more familiar to us. One subject wronged another. The latter could commence proceedings in front of the appropriate judicial authority, and a decision would be arrived at. It does not follow that the decision would agree with another given in a similar case in the same place previously, and it does not follow that the *śāstra* would invariably be consulted, or if it was consulted that it would be consulted to any particular depth. (*ii*) The second field was that of unilateral breach of a sanction. Again there could be two types of sanction : the sanction might be of a « civil » character in that the village or district had enacted what amounts to a by-law or regulation [10], restraining inhabitants from certain acts or requiring inhabitants to cooperate in an enterprise, either subject to a penalty, or with the penalty for breach unexpressed — or (*iii*) the sanction might refer to some purely ritual or superstitious act, what should be done, or what should not be done, particularly in a social context. For example, if a villager cohabited with a widow, and if it was against local or caste custom to cohabit with widows, the appropriate local or caste tribunal might take cognizance of this and sentence him to a penance, or, if he failed to conform, to excommunication [11].

The basic sanctions depended upon custom, and therefore upon agreement. The immobile force of social convention was the ultimate real authority, and even the king's edicts had to be understood within this framework. There were authorised or conventional scopes within which kings could issue edicts [12], that is to say, with expectation of their being obeyed. But since custom was always being questioned by those who claimed equality in social terms, and since breaches of custom were the subject of debates, some urging that a breach should be punished with rigour, and some urging that it might be justified — a fundamental, scientific basis for all rules

[9] Illustrations : one must not stare at the king's wife : Medh. on Manu VIII.125; king may prohibit certain commercial transactions, subject to a death penalty : *ibid.*, IV.226 (text p. 406, trans. (correct ?), p. 478).

[10] Derrett, *J.E.S.H.O.* VII (1964), p. 89. See also Medh. on Manu VIII.41.

[11] On the effects of this see the article cited in the previous note.

[12] Derrett, « Bhāruci on the royal regulative power in India », *J.A.O.S.* LXXXIV (1964), pp. 392-395. Examples of royal proclamations are given at Medh. on IX.232. Cf. Yājñ. II.186.

of every kind, whether legal or moral, was in demand, and this demand it was the *dharmaśāstra's* task to satisfy. A commentator upon any prime *śāstric* work would therefore be dealing with rules which were by no means legal, as well as rules which were legal in the sense we have defined. A rule, the breach of which could lead to out-casting, with its consequence of submission or in default exile, or rebellion, was indubitably a legal rule, though the court which would administer it would not be presided over by a judge, but by some elders, local or caste notables, people of natural leadership, whose common sentence would be obeyed.

In prescribing law, therefore, Medhātithi is joining that task with much wider responsibility. It was the theory of his author, Manu, that all duties, of whatever character, ethical, moral, and legal, had an existence independent of the individuals concerned (subject to the theory of the ages of the universe) [13], and that all duties could be traced back to creation. The actual fact that duties are learnt from elders was taken to its logical conclusion, that duties had a single common origin in an effort of instruction immeasurably far back in time. In explaining this theory in terms intelligible to his contemporaries Medhātithi proceeds to show that the content of *dharma* is as varied as we have seen, and recognizes the distinctions between the classes of injunction. To him the transcendental and the practical are equally real. Those who do not accept the transcendental must accept the practical, or they will suffer in this world. Though it is the task of the *dharmaśāstra* to teach both, since the problems of avoiding re-birth were seen to be as real as those of avoiding imprisonment, the teacher is aware of the greater urgency of the latter to most people, and, what is often overlooked, the reality of a caste's or a village's superstitions when these express themselves in terms of punishment or excommunication.

We are now in a position to approach Medhātithi's conception of law in India as he saw it.

[13] On the whole question of ages (Skt. *yuga-s*) a forthcoming publication of Ludo ROCHER is awaited. Time, in Hindu eyes, brings decay, and the amount of *dharma* which can be performed decreases, thus *smṛti-s* become obsolete. The doctrine is worked out fully in the *puranic* period under the title *kalivarjyāni* (acts to be avoided, though *dharmic*, in the Kali, i.e. the present, age), a subject treated by KĀNE at *H.D.* III (1946), pp. 885-968 and by Batuknāth Bhaṭṭāchārya in a thesis entitled *The « Kalivarjyas » or Prohibitions in the « Kali » Age* (University of Calcutta, 1943). See also R. LINGAT, « Dharma et temps », *J.A.* 1961, pp. 487-495.

II. Law in Litigation

A study of Hindu law causes the mind to become inured to inconsistencies and contradictions, and encourages it to be quick to see distinctions and to split hairs. But in the early mediaeval period the anomalies were sustained in a less artificial and fictional manner, and the distinctions were plausible enough to have been sustained through centuries of oral and eventually documentary scholarship. In what follows numerous propositions will emerge which seem to tread uncomfortably upon each other's heels. A careful survey will show that Medh., like most of his contemporaries, was adept at reconciling divergent opinions and trends, and at minimising the logical faults of the system which the public, after all, needed.

We have seen that litigation, in the sense of appeal to law in conflicts occurring in society, took place not only in the royal courts (including courts held or sanctioned by grant from the sovereign) but also before tribunals of a customary character. The subject matter of litigation could be breach of civil law, of criminal law, or of social etiquette. The *dharmaśāstra* itself made no such distinctions, but it did carefully avoid giving prescriptions which would limit the judges' freedom in dealing with etiquette questions. The *dharmaśāstra* did not therefore give a complete code which covered all types of litigation. Manu did not do so, and therefore Medh. himself does not purport to do so, but many of his remarks, especially those *obiter*, reveal his understanding of the range of litigation.

We may deal first with civil litigation. The ruler is bound to supply means for resolution of the subjects' mutual disputes because one of his tasks is « relief from oppression », just as the basis for his administration of what we should call criminal law is his duty to relieve the subjects from the pains they would suffer in the other world or worlds for their offences [14]. Subjects fall into sin in their maltreatment of each other and in their offences against the king (e.g. non-payment of taxes) and if the king does not protect the subjects from sin he himself incurs sin [15], and it is understood that this consideration authorises him to take the initiative in the restricted class of criminal cases where he can start proceedings *suo motu*. Since hearing cases provides him with an income, the restraint referred to is a real one.

[14] On VIII.1 (p. 2).
[15] On VIII.304 (p. 338).

In the actual hearing of cases three questions arise : does the law require the judge to act as umpire or inquisitor, does the judge proceed according to a fixed and unchangeable procedure, and does the law applied to the facts as found out derive from the *śāstra*, from custom, from equity, or from some mixture of sources ? Does the law itself lay down answers to these questions ? Medh. is unusually frank and open on this subject, upon which the public must have been sensitive; since if the *śāstra* is an optional guide or an incomplete guide the question remains whether it is a guide at all, and, if it is not, one cohesive factor in the common Hindu civilization disappears. In Medh.'s view the judge must act as inquisitor, and once he is seized of the case he must pursue it to its end, no matter what the witnesses say or fail to say or how the parties behave [16]. It is perfectly true that compromise of an action at law may be the best solution [17], but the agreement of the parties cannot authorise the judge to depart from the established methods of arriving at a decision [18]. In arriving at a decision on facts the judge must not be hampered by considerations of jurisprudence, however learned. A *smṛti* (such as Manu himself) may tend to fossilize the categories of facts, and this tendency must be resisted. The true state of facts of a given case must never be ignored because of any incompatibility with a *smṛti* text [19].

Litigants may often be disappointed with the result. Appeal to law is appeal to *dharma*, in the wide sense of that word. The function of the judge, which is never entirely immune from taint of sin (for no judgment can be perfect), must be approached as if it were the performance of a religious obligation. And yet the results are often far from what strict truth would require. Medh. frankly acknowledges this and claims that Manu did so too. The better cause may be lost through the factor of litigation [20], and yet it is a requirement of the sacred law that the decision be implemented. True, a review of a decision is possible in many cases : that which conflicts with law may be annulled, and, says Medh., fines may be doubled (there were fines payable even in civil cases) [21].

The law to be applied to the facts as discovered by the court could achieve injustice unless it were plastic and supple, and yet undue suppleness would

16 On VIII.14 (p. 26).
17 On VIII.1 (p. 3).
18 On VIII.3 (p. 10 top).
19 On VIII.3 (p. 15).
20 On VIII.148 (p. 182).
21 On IX.233 (p. 188).

lead to instability and the collapse of the judicial system. The solution appears in the following manner : the first task was to determine whether the *smṛti* rules were barred by custom. Customs must be examined minutely, lest they be novel [22], or incongruous with the *śāstra*. Before incongruity is surmised the custom (if otherwise unimpeachable) must be compared with the *smṛti* which is alleged to be incongruous with it. If the *smṛti* is faultless it will take precedence. But *smṛti-s* can be faulted on a number of grounds. First a great many *smṛtis* in *vyavahāra* (litigation) contexts are based either (*i*) upon custom, or (*ii*) upon the author's preference in each case [23]. In either case the proved custom will take precedence. A *laukika* (popular) rule will normally provide the rule for decision so long as *some śāstric* support for it can be found [24]. But one must take care, since many *smṛti-s* which purport to make up the *śāstra* are themselves only reflexions of customary provisions (*vyavasthā-s*), and therefore of no independent authority [25]. Thus it may come about that practical rules having no literal counterpart anywhere in *smṛti* may have to be applied. When however resort is felt inevitably to be to the *smṛti*, it does not follow that *smṛti* rules will supply the answer unaided by other sources of decision. Where *smṛtis* are markedly in variance, none of them is authoritative without more [26]. When a *smṛti* appears in a context which is not perfectly appropriate to it, this affords a ground for ignoring it [26a]. And it is for these reasons that *smṛti* itself particularly lays down a scope for judicial discretion [27]. Naturally, when the litigants are non-aryans, and not bound by the *śāstra* in any event, their customs cannot be disapproved as repugnant to the *śāstra* [28].

The judicial procedure itself is governed by *smṛti* rules. But the rules all subserve a practical (« seen ») purpose (see IV below) and are therefore subject to rational limitation and adjustment to meet the needs of the case [29]. A certain number of these *smṛti-s* may be ignored entirely, for the following reason. *Smṛti*, as we shall see, derives its authority from factors external

[22] On VIII.8 (p. 21).

[23] On VIII.3 (p. 10).

[24] On VIII.3 (p. 11).

[25] On VIII.3 (pp. 12, 14, 17).

[26] On IX.180 (p. 159).

[26a] IX.94 (on ages for marriage) does not occur in the marriage chapter and therefore does not bear on the ritual; therefore persons of other ages may validly marry : on IX.94 (p. 78).

[27] On IX.213 (p. 177).

[28] On VIII.41 (p. 55).

[29] On VIII.72 (p. 96).

to itself, such as the Veda or the behaviour of persons learned in the Veda. If there is no practical support for a *smṛti* rule, one is justified in supposing that it is a rule derived from the Veda, and therefore possessing spiritual compulsive power, which one neglects only at one's spiritual risk. But if the context is purely practical, and has nothing to do with action (*kārya*) in the sacrificial sense, as is plainly the case with questions that arise in the course of litigation, the *smṛti* is deprived of all support, and is not to be followed [30]. Moreover, there is another reason why rules found in the *smṛti-s* should not hamper judicial procedure. The judicial function itself exists for the *rājya-sthiti*, namely the security of the state or kingdom, and it is for this reason that *artha-śāstra* (economical and political) considerations as well as the *dharma-śāstra* should be taken into account in that context [31]. If the requirements of order and good government demand that *smṛti* provisions should be modified in practice, modification is authorised [32].

Subjects should not engage in litigation unless other means of resolving their difficulties have failed [33]. When the king's criminal jurisdiction is invoked (which to this day is thought the most effective method of bringing pressure to bear on the opposite party) other considerations apply. The king is not authorised to compromise [34], or to sanction compromises by the aggrieved parties. Criminal penalties are better than Hell [35]. *Daṇḍa*, the symbol of *dharma* and generic name for penalties of all kinds, is a quality of government having an almost religious mystique [36]. Punishment produces invisible effects as well as its essential function of deterrence [37]. *Dharma* requires rigour in administration of the criminal law, for the criminal's own benefit, apart from any other consideration. Yet, the punishment to be inflicted must be chosen by reference to other factors besides the *smṛti* text. Mere application of the written text will produce unjust punishments [38].

It follows from our survey both of criminal and civil law that knowledge of the *śāstra* is by no means the chief requirement. Indeed, before the king's court litigants need not expect to be judged according to strict *smṛti* rules.

[30] On VIII.56 (pp. 75-76).
[31] On VII.1 (p. 273). Now see D. Schlingloff at W.Z.K.S.O. IX (1965), pp. 1-38.
[32] On VIII.24 (p. 35).
[33] On VIII.49 (p. 68).
[34] On VIII.56 (p. 77).
[35] On VII.2 (p. 275).
[36] On VII.14 (p. 281).
[37] On VIII.318 (pp. 350-351).
[38] On VIII.127 (p. 154).

The court does not absolutely require perfect *smṛti*-knowledge [39]. Procedure and evidence can be mastered by an intelligent person who does not have (and perhaps by reason of caste might not be entitled to have) recourse to the *śāstra* as laid down in the *smṛti-s* [40]. This is an admission of an extraordinary character, introducing an element of reality into the jurisprudential scene which is all too rare in our *dharmaśāstra* literature. [40a]

III. Law as a Social Reality

An even more surprising revelation is the acknowledgement by so eminent a scholar that, not only (as we have seen) may a properly conducted trial lead to unjust results, but also it may happen that in pursuance of his legal rights a litigant may properly incur censure. The *śāstra*, in his view, already contemplates the dichotomy well-known to the West, that what is lawful, in the sense that it may be successfully pursued in litigation, may be immoral, so that the successful litigant may become liable to spiritual or social penalties or both [41]. This recognition of the split in the sacred law between the possible and the desirable is a sign of maturity which, one feels certain, the *smṛti-s* themselves cannot have anticipated. There is indeed a survival, even in Medh. himself, of a more ancient outlook. Outside the field of *vyavahāra* and in the field of pure social and spiritual sanction doubts may occur (as they constantly occur amongst orthodox Jews) as to cleanness, purification, and the like. The *śāstra* allows even one Brahman specialist to pronounce finally upon such questions [42]. How is he to determine? One should follow the decisions of cultured men (i.e. Brahmans living by customs inherited from a pure ancestry known to have preserved Vedic learning), for one may have faith that there can be no two opinions in matters of (such) *dharma* [43]. Here we meet the apparently naïve, but yet normal concept amongst *śāstrī-s* that in a quandary (especially a quandary induced by divergent *smṛti-s*) a final reconciliation is possible, in which all scholars can eventually be brought to agree.

39 On VIII.20 (p. 30).

40 *Ibid.*

40a It is, however, consistent with Kauṭilya's rule that the king's edicts must be founded on practical considerations, righteously, whereupon the edict will exclude the *smṛti* text *pro tanto* (III.1, 44-5).

41 On IX.209 (p. 173).

42 On II.6 (p. 204).

43 On XII.108 (pp. 640-641).

The scene with which Medh. was familiar was one of infinite variety, yet the whole society, with all its castes and even tribes who claimed to have been Hinduized, sheltered under one jurisprudential umbrella. For centuries Brahmans, cultivating their ancestral usages, had served as models for other, less pure castes to follow. But one must accept the fact that the process of modelling was not far advanced, and where it was advanced at all was unevenly so. The *śāstra* itself seemed to acknowledge the incompatibility of what went on in the world with what was, apparently, subsumed by the *smṛti* rules. The *smṛti-s* set an impossible standard. Sleeping in the daytime was a sin and so was cow-killing. The public regarded the latter with abhorrence, but took no strong line with reference to the former. Yet, says Medh., repeated performance of either act would bring about degradation from caste, for the *smṛti* intends this [44]. But, whatever the standard, no one was justified in pretending that it was met, and thus turning one's back on the facts of life. Marriage, the chief institution of the law, must be admitted and recognised, even though people married for motives, such as the receipt of large dowries, which the *smṛti* altogether ignored and would certainly have deplored [45].

In practice the public were constantly agitated by failures to conform to patterns of behaviour. If it came to a dispute and the law was appealed to, what had law to say? The basic conception accorded remarkably well with social habits. What made an act sinful, and therefore fit for an accusation tending towards penance or excommunication in default of performance of penance, was not the nature of the act when analysed by a rational man, but the fact that the act was prohibited. Killing is sinful, not because of the killing, but because of the prohibition [46]. The reader will comment that this explains why, to judge from traditional Indian practice, robbery of a castefellow is reprehensible, while robbery of a non-castefellow is either non-reprehensible or even laudible. The actual terms of the *śāstra* give no countenance to any such proposition, for acts savouring of sinful attitudes of mind are there seen as sinful from the point of view of the owner of the mind, not so much by reference to the victim — but the presence of rules discriminating in favour of classes of wrongdoers who have wronged

[44] On XI.181 (p. 490).

[45] On IX.88 (p. 75).

[46] On II.6 (p. 188). Of course reasons why one should not kill are available : on V. 40 (pp. 49-50).

members of lower castes goes far to show that such notions could, somehow, seek support even from the sacred text.

Outside the sphere of litigation the operation of the law is visible. A disobedient servant may lawfully be deprived of his wages, but he is also sinful, and must therefore clear himself by some penance [47]. The system did not regard an offender as cleared merely because he had paid compensation; some penance (perhaps payable to the caste itself) was also required. A criminal penalty however, as we have seen, had the effect of being also a penance.

A great sanction, which Medh. elaborates in numerous places, is the force of public opinion. By « public », of course, is meant not the whole body of citizens or villagers but the caste which, for the time being, can effectively discipline its members. The subject of occupations is something of a test. The *śāstra* condemns those who deviate from the occupations laid down in the *smṛti-s*. A medieval commentator is likely to ask himself how much reality may be attributed to these rules, which, if they were to be taken seriously, would give a perpetual income to the authorized recipients of penance-money. Medh. emphasises that no occupation should be taken up, even though distinctly sanctioned by the *śāstra*, if the result would be blamed by the world [48]. It is obvious that this can work both ways and that the authorised and indeed proper occupations could not be returned to if the community objected. Family usage may prevent a person from taking up an occupation, whether or not the *śāstra* also prohibits it [49]. For it is a *loka-vyavahāra* which one observes; one must avoid unpopularity [50]. For a *smṛti* tells us that what is *loka-vidviṣṭa* (hated by the world) is *asvargya*; it does not lead to heaven, which means no more nor less than this, that, whether one is permitted to do it by the *śāstra* or not, social (and possibly spiritual) penalties will follow from availing oneself of the facility [51]. What appears to be a *smṛti* of unascertained authority is cited for the rule that it is wrong to incur popular disapprobation [52]. That this opens the door to social pressures not contemplated in so many words by the *śāstra* is obvious.

[47] On II.28 (p. 255).

[48] On IV.3 (p. 302); IV. 176 (pp. 440-441); IV.209.

[49] On IV.15 (p. 317).

[50] On IV.18 (p. 320).

[51] On IV.176 end. On V.48 (p. 57); V.103; VIII.127.

[52] On V.88 (p. 106). An offering should be made to the spirit of a dead reprobate *loka-garhā-bhayāt*.

Yet the author does not allow the *smṛti* to convert offenders into outcastes with undue expedition. Manu V.19 does not mean that a man becomes an outcaste by virtue of his offence (says Medh.), but outcasting follows only when he refuses to perform penance for the offence; unless one prefers to say that what is intended is that the offender shall perform the penance which one who had been outcasted would have to perform in order to obtain reinstatement.

The *dharma* encirclement of Indian (Hindu) society is not to be forsaken, however. Those who are outside the pale of *dharma* are not capable of entering society and claiming a purity which on other grounds some Hindus could claim by virtue of their function. Non-Hindus could by no means escape from the law's ban on social intercourse [53]. The dwellers on the very fringe of Hindu society, the scavengers, Chaṇḍālas, had not yet reached the stage when their very shadow conferred impurity [54], but Medh. evidently does not allow their habits, standards, or feelings any say in deciding what the law requires. So far as the pure castes are concerned, their customs regarding purity are themselves authoritative as *samācāra* (usage) and must be observed, whether or not positive support for the customs could be found in any *smṛti* [55].

On this basis one would suppose that popular religious usages — whether or not these were recognised or recorded in *smṛti* or Veda — would come within the concept of law. On the contrary, though the law in litigation might recognise that such rituals were in use, sacrifices which did not conform to *śāstric* precepts were to be condemned, for the *śāstric* material on the duties towards the gods and the unseen world could not be argued away or displaced by evidence of custom as such [56].

IV. Practical v. Transcendental

This brings us to the difficult and involved subject of the distinctions between injunctions to be found in the *smṛti* literature. Any commentator has to determine whether a text which in fact conflicts with practical usage is valid and binding upon a court or a customary tribunal, or can be distin-

[53] On V.128 (p. 156).
[54] On V.131 (falsely 132) (p. 159).
[55] On V.110 (p. 138).
[56] On V.37-38 (pp. 47-49).

guished as applicable only in a sphere uncontemplated by the suit in question. To clarify the position : in civil litigation it might be argued that a *smṛti* must be applied, as for example, to the effect that the transaction in question, having been recorded in a fashion which does not comply exactly with the requirements of *smṛti*, is void and of no effect. Money might have passed, and the suit might be for the performance of the promise stipulated for. Since it would be manifestly unjust to deny relief to someone who was following usage merely to comply with a formality prescribed by the text, the court would seek to avoid the textual law, if not on an equitable principle, then at least because the text did not mean exactly what it said. Likewise in marriage, where the texts recommend the selection of a girl who is not a close relation and who *has* brothers, there might be a dispute over a marriage where the girl was a near relation and had *no* brothers. The court might in fact hold that the violation of the first rule would render the marriage void, whereas the violation of the second alone would not have had that effect. There are two categories of injunctions which have to be considered, though the categories overlap. The first is the category of « seen-ness », i.e. does the purpose which the text subserves relate to the seen world of perceptible causes, or does it refer to the unseen world in which effects arise out of causes in ways not knowable otherwise than through the *śāstra*? The second category is that of « sacrificiality ». If the rule is directed to the fulfilment of a sacrifice (however indirectly) it is different in kind from one which is directed to the conduct of an individual (e.g. a sacrificer or other « actor »). The first classification of rules is into injunctions which are *dṛṣṭārtha* (directed to a « seen » object) and *adṛṣṭārtha* (directed to an « unseen » object). We could say loosely that the first are « practical », the second « unpractical ». The second classification is between *kratvartha* injunctions (those directed to the sacrifice) and *puruṣārtha* injunctions. A breach of a *dṛṣṭa* rule involves no more than practical inconvenience. A breach of an *adṛṣṭa* rule involves usually nothing more than spiritual hazard [56a]. A breach of a *kratvartha* rule means that the *kratu*, the « act »,

[56a] That is why the rules of chivalrous warfare are *adṛṣṭārtha* : on VII.90 (p. 340). Likewise non-compliance with an *adṛṣṭa* rule somehow detected at IX.219 (impartible effects in a *prima facie* partible estate) would not produce sin (or so the text seems to say at IX.219, trans. p. 181). But the proposition that breach of an *adṛṣṭa* rule would not involve sin seems insecure. If the rule is a *yama*, breach involves outcasting; if it is a *niyama* breach simply means loss of spiritual advantage : see Medh. on Manu IV.204 (p. 458). To define a rule as a *niyama* would therefore be to the advantage of an intending offender. A thorough survey of all these classifications is still awaited.

comes to nothing — it is therefore an important rule; whereas a breach of a *puruṣārtha* rule affects the individual and will lay him open to the consequences, which, as the case may be, may amount to penance or fine or both if the circumstances permit. We may proceed to see how Medh. manipulates these distinctions.

It must be understood at the outset that a *smṛti* rule which is not to be discarded for any of the reasons set out in previous sections of this paper must be given *some* force. If it is not *dṛṣṭārtha* it must be *adṛṣṭārtha*. The lawyers hold to the maxim that no *smṛti* must be given an *adṛṣṭārtha* sense (which is in practice emasculating) if it is somehow capable of being given a *dṛṣṭārtha* sense. In the *vyavahāra* sections of *smṛti-s* one naturally starts out with the presumption that the rules are *dṛṣṭārtha* [56b]. Customary rules and by-laws are all *dṛṣṭārtha*, though they may have *adṛṣṭa* overtones. But exceptions will throw light on the way the presumption works in practice. At Manu VIII.33 it is said in the *smṛti* that thieves of lost property must be killed with the aid of an elephant. Medh. says that the specification of the elephant is *adṛṣṭārtha* [57]. In other words the judge may order any other form of execution, while any penance he performs for failing to obey the *śāstra* will cover the spiritual fault of failing to use an elephant. Law works, as it were, upon wheels oiled by the judge's willingness to incur spiritual guilt (the present author's figure of speech). At Manu VIII.223 the text says that after ten days from an agreement constituting a sale of an object the purchaser who is dissatisfied shall not return the object. It might be argued that it is sinful to return the object *even with the seller's consent*, which would certainly be the case if the text had an *adṛṣṭa* force. But in fact [58] its force is merely *dṛṣṭa*, and the meaning is that the seller shall not be *compelled* to receive the article back again and refund the price. Further at VIII.179 the text tells us that « The wise man shall entrust a deposit to one who is born of good family, is endowed with character, cognisant of the law, and truthful, has a large following, and is wealthy and honourable ». What happens when the depositor chooses one who is not truthful, has no large following or is not wealthy? Does it mean that the deposit is void, or that he incurs sin by so entrusting his property? What force does the *smṛti* have? We should not be alarmed, says Medh., for the text is *advice*

[56b] On VIII.72 (p. 96).

[57] On VIII.34 (p. 47). However, in the light of the text to n. 62 below, it is to be suspected that the reading should have been *dṛṣṭārtha*. *

[58] On VIII.223 (p. 271).

as it were to a friend [59], and is not an injunction at all, still less is it an injunction even of an *adṛṣṭārtha* character, as would be injunctions on how to perform a sacrifice. The advice is of good practical value, and he explains with an illustration how good it is. Other instances where no transcendental purpose (*adṛṣṭārtha*) is seen could be multiplied in the field of litigation, but a final instance would serve. Manu prescribes precise relationships between the punishments to be awarded to culprits of various castes. Medh. says that these prescriptions have no *adṛṣṭa* force (though the concept of punishment itself is, of course, mixed) [60], with the consequence that the court is not in any sense bound by them literally.

Kingly duties appertain to *dṛṣṭārtha* [61]. If the king performs them he gains a transcendental reward. But his function is purely practical. Therefore instructions given in *smṛti* regarding penalties are *dṛṣṭārtha*, and lesser penalties may be awarded if they are effective for the king's purpose [62]. But this does not prevent the *smṛti-kāra*, such as Manu, adding an essentially *adṛṣṭa* force, for the purpose of emphasizing its obligatory character : but that will not render breach of the rule a spiritual offence as a matter of course, since the words are not to be taken in their literal sense : i.e. whereas at IX.327 Manu says that Prajāpati (Lord of Creatures) having created cattle, made them over to the Vaiśya caste (to tend) and an impression is thereby created that if others than Vaiśyas (i.e. Śūdras) tend cattle they will be afflicted with supernatural penalties, in fact all that the *smṛti* means is that the Vaiśya, if in fact he does tend cattle, must tend them in a particularly solicitous fashion [63]. Still less could it be urged that Śūdras tending cattle are to be punished or that Vaiśyas are to be punished if they do not tend cattle.

So many examples have been given of the denial of an *adṛṣṭa* character. A transcendental purpose may however be seen in injunctions relating to etiquette, caste-behaviour. The *brahmachārī*, or religious student, having fetched fuelsticks is told, by Manu at II, 186, to place them in the air. If placing them in the air would have the effect of drying them no *adṛṣṭa* purpose is to be inferred; but if in many cases the removal from dense forest and placing in the open would have the opposite effect the only motive

[59] On VIII.179 (p. 230).
[60] On VIII.337-338 (p. 367).
[61] See on IX.249 (p. 196).
[62] *Ibid.* The doctrine was held by Bhāruci before our author.
[63] On VIII.327 (p. 235).

could be *adṛṣṭa*, and so some scholars opined [64]. It would be possible to take action against a student who did not place his sticks in the air, but of course not in the king's court, only in a tribunal vested with jurisdiction in such matters. A nice contrast between the practical and the transcendental is to be seen at Manu IV.133-4 [65]. One should not pay attention to someone else's *woman*, and this prohibition is *dṛṣṭa*; one should not pay attention to another man's *wife* : this is both *dṛṣṭa* and *adṛṣṭa*.

The importance of an *adṛṣṭa* command must not be underrated. That which is commanded for an *adṛṣṭa* purpose may still be exacted in the appropriate forum if it is easily stirred into action. People may be excommunicated, evidently, for failure to perform superstitious acts which the *śāstra* does not oblige them to do by any threat of civil or criminal penalty. That arises when the acts are intended for practical welfare [66]. One is entitled to infer an *adṛṣṭa* command even in *smṛti-s* which are concerned with purely practical matters if, without the scriptural injunction, the person concerned would in any event tend in the same direction. An elder brother would wish to take a larger share than his younger brothers (IX.153), the result is not that the *smṛti* therefore has no injunctive force (see below) but that the *smṛti* contains an *adṛṣṭa* force. Breach of the rule without the authorization of custom will therefore lead to penance, and the social sanction is thus ensured. Needless to say this method of interpretation would be considered controversial by *śāstrī-s* generally today.

The conflict between the practical and the transcendental is like that which we have already noted between the legal and the moral. In the world of contractual relations there are many contracts which are prohibited or not recognized as legal by the *śāstra*. From the point of view of *dharma* they cannot be enforced and those that enter into them may be liable to spiritual sanctions. Excessive interest, sale of wife and children, gift of all property : these are the illustrations Medh. adopts [67]. The transactions, though defective from an *adṛṣṭa* standpoint, may well have a practical effect.

Our final illustration may be taken from the law relating to suicide, which is rather special in that punishment for violation is hardly practical. The *śāstra* as expounded by Medh. does not flinch from dealing with the

[64] On II.186 (p. 479).

[65] On IV.133-134 (pp. 414-415). See also on IV.171-172 (p. 435).

[66] On IV.145-6 (pp. 422-423). Customary rituals which operate as precautions against calamity, though irrational, may not be om.it-ted out of indifference to calamity.

[67] On VIII.164 (p. 214).

subject because the objections to suicide operated in a transcendental sense, so that the many suicides with which ancient India was familiar could lead, unless properly authorised by the *śāstric* system [68], only to Hell [69], for there would be no opportunity for penance.

The distinction between *kratvartha* and *puruṣārtha* is less common. At Manu VII.93 a set of *niyamas* or rules are laid down concerning enemies who should not be slain : « Nor one in distress, nor one severely wounded, nor one who is frightened, etc. ». These interesting humanitarian provisions, in everyone's interest, one would have thought, become the object of controversy. What ill befalls one who breaks this commandment, and kills a terrified and unarmed enemy? Presumably his military courts will not be in a position to punish him, even if they were disposed to do this, which is unlikely. If the *niyamas* were *kratvartha* (as might be urged by those interpreting the whole section in terms of the king's spiritual gains through honourable conquest, or war in defence of his people) failure to observe them would merely hinder the king's attainment of Heaven, which need not be a pressing consideration either for the king himself or his soldiers! Therefore the jurist determines that the text sets out a prohibition which is addressed to the hearer in his own interest, not mere advice, but a *śāstric* prohibition, of the *puruṣārtha* category, like the prohibition of eating flesh of an animal killed by a poisoned arrow [70].

V. Sources of Law

Enough has been said to show that the sources to which the judges must apply their minds are far more extensive than the *smṛti* texts themselves. Even in interpreting and applying those they must use skills of a character ancillary to the *śāstra*. But what does Medh. recognize as sources of injunctions which provide the starting-point in all disputes? This subject is involved and complex, and there is a superabundance of information. Any student of Hindu law knows that the Vedic texts take precedence, in a dispute, over any *smṛti* text on precisely the same subject-matter; but that there is an obligation to obtain harmony if possible between *smṛti-s* where they are discrepant. In *vyavahāra* topics the effort is not made so

68 On V.88 (p. 106); cf. p. 109; VI.32 (pp. 212, 215-216).

69 On V.27 (p. 40), 43 (p. 55). *Sati* is forbidden (V.155).

70 On VII.93 (p. 343). But cf. n. 56a above.

conscientiously or so confidently as in the non-*vyavahāra* contexts, in which, after all, the application of social or spiritual penalties took place in an atmosphere in which reliance upon *śāstric* learning might be more widely tolerated or encouraged. On *adṛṣṭa* questions the ultimate determination of the Brahmans might well be acquiesced in, whereas in questions of property such sources as the *smṛti-s* were open to objections. It is likewise well known that when the act enjoined by the *smṛti* was one which would be done even without an injunction the *smṛti* had no coercive or injunctive force, it was merely reiterative, illustrative, or mere exhortation [71]. But assuming that the act or abstention would not be instinctive or automatic, what fundamental standards determined the rule of law?

One of the curiosities of Medh. is that he frankly admits that there are many sources of law which are not on the one hand instinctive, conscientious, or automatic, nor on the other hand Vedic or derivable from the *smṛtis* or from custom which can be said to be based on lost Vedic or *smṛti* material. Apart from legislation to which we have given a glance already and which will be mentioned in brief below, there are in practice many avenues through which injunctions may come, to which the individual is positively bound to give attention or to live at his peril. The mass of the *śāstra* repeats, like an incantation, that no conduct but that of pure Brahmans learned in the Veda can ever be a standard for anybody, but this was evidently not merely a counsel of perfection, but also a dangerous generalisation. For example, the student is to take lessons from the Sūdra servant of his teacher on matters entrusted to the former [72]. A stranger visiting a village he does not know, must find out what are the rules and regulations operating in that area, and cannot decline to receive warnings even from untouchables [73].

The attitude towards the *smṛti* is cynical, and in places comical [73a]. No doubt Manu had access to materials not available to us and gave us the benefit of the relevant information from the Veda [74], but he was no more

[71] On V.27 (p. 35); cf. VIII.105 (p. 132); VIII.410 (p. 428).

[72] On II.223 (p. 518).

[73] On II.238 (pp. 529-530) *paro dharma* means local regulations, and *dharma* can mean nothing more than *vyavasthā*.

[73a] In one place Medh. says that the verse does not belong to Manu at all, according to « some ». In fact Bhāruci supports him. IX.93 (p. 77).

[74] On II.6 (p. 190).

than a man, he condensed his material misleadingly [75], used unnecessary words to fill up his metre [76], and borrowed heavily from practical life, not to say from common sense, which in *vyavahāra* weakens the force of his injunctions [77]. The attitude to custom attempting to derogate from the *smṛti* is even more cynical. Widespread customs, like that of marrying the maternal uncle's daughter, spring from accidental origins [78]. Deviant practices spring from greed or ignorance [79]. Injunctions are valid if they come from the practice of « good » people [80], but never if they emanate from the traditions of non-Hindu peoples or beliefs [81]. A statement on *dharma* must always be authenticated by reference to texts or to a custom which can be approved in such a manner. An actual usage, so long as it is not objectionable, can be used to clarify what the law is [82]. As for the relationship between custom and the *smṛti*, the *smṛti* may lie dormant, as it were, until the custom itself dies away, in which case the *smṛti* becomes, in that region, for the first time obligatory [83]! One of the uses of *smṛti* is to show us what, upon that footing, can be done, since what the *smṛti* prohibits is obviously in use somewhere [84]! *Smṛtis* can be very terse : they obviously incorporate by reference local usages, some of which might have no similarity with the provision in the text [85]!

VI. Political Power and the Law

In all this variety the one factor which has not appeared is political power. Judicial discretion, equity, scope for interpretation of texts, competition between sources of law, all these are evidenced ; but there is no question

[75] On IV.25 (p. 328); V.13 (p. 19). He sums up material in other *smṛti-s* : on III.206 (falsely numbered 216 in the trans., p. 239).

[76] *Passim.* He often comments on the curious phraseology of his author and denies him the right to devise a style of his own.

[77] Because of the rule noticed at places cited at n. 71 above.

[78] On II.18 (p. 233).

[79] On II.6 (p. 175).

[80] On II.6 (p. 205).

[81] On II.6 (pp. 173-174).

[82] On V. 88 (pp. 108-109).

[83] On VIII.151 (p. 188).

[84] On VIII.153 (p. 194).

[85] On VIII.222 (p. 270).

of the king himself being a source of law in competition with the *śāstra*, nor could political advantage as such vary the sacred law or its method of interpretation. Yet, though the king's subordination to the law is repeatedly asserted, there were loopholes through which the administration of justice, and the nature of what we have called law, could be modified in practice, and Medh. was content that he saw justification for this modification even in *śāstric* theory.

The word *dharma*, as we have seen, can comprehend very diverse factors, *śāstric* and non-*śāstric*. Provided they were not contravening an undoubted *śāstric* rule local bodies, corporations, could enact by-laws or regulations which would be enforced with all the rigour of a *śāstric* rule to which no exception could be taken [86]. The king was under a *śāstric* obligation to recognise and put into effect the resolutions of guilds, associations, sects. And for these classes of people an opportunity therefore existed to conspire against the remainder of the public, and from the great wealth that merchants were able to accumulate in ancient times (obviously with the royal sanction) it is evident that they were in the main successful. Medh. insists that while Manu speaks only of a judicial setting aside of gifts, mortgages and sales the king may in fact render void fraudulent devices by cultivators, traders and artisans [87] which aim to subvert the public interest.

VII. Conclusion

The demands we make upon law are these : it must be certain, ascertainable, intelligible, and suited to the needs of the people. We do not require that it look after our spiritual needs as well as our secular needs, nor that it take care of our social responsibilities as well as our financial. No doubt there was a time when government in Europe in theory at least attempted all those tasks, as the Hindus seem to have attempted during the whole of their known history. What does Medh.'s conception of law reveal as *his* demands upon the law? To him it is clear that practicality was the first consideration, suppleness and ready adjustability to circumstances. These requirements were flatly contrary to the professed character of the Hindu jurisprudence, which, for all its very occasional references to equity and

[86] On VIII.46 (p. 62). See article cited at n. 12 above.
[87] On VIII.165 (p. 216). Read with Medh. on VIII.41 (p. 56).

common sense, in fact tries to codify duty in all possible spheres with all possible precision. Manu is an exception to the extent that he is vague and comprehensive in some of his more sweeping condensations and generalisations. The spirit of the *śāstra* is very far from the flexible and contingent standard which Medh. presents as Hindu law. If so many qualifications are to be applied before one can know what rule would be administered in a particular court — and we must bear in mind that an individual might have several tribunals before which he might be summoned to answer for his conduct — the law as a body of rules is no entity which can qualify for the adulation and worship normally attributed to it.

The answer seems to be this, that the intellectual exercise was intended to achieve two results. First the supremacy and inter-regional character of the *śāstra* was to be upheld. The public believed in some supernatural forces, they only differed on what these were and what their effects might be. The *śāstra* purported to cater for all points of view which could be claimed as « Hindu ». Secondly no kingdom could claim to be a Hindu kingdom unless the *śāstra* played some role in its administration of justice, and provided it played *some* role there was really no concern on anyone's part how substantial that role was or how pervasive the influence of the *śāstra* might be. This did no harm to the individual subject because, though the law was not certain and was barely ascertainable by the learned, let alone by the man in the street, he belonged to a unit, a family, clan, tribe, caste, or village, which would defend him independently of the merits of his case, and without whose support he was powerless how meritorious so ever he might be. Action would be rare at all times, in a country which has never ranked activity as such high, and mature deliberation and delay would precede any act. The approval of the authorities would be sought for almost any transaction of real importance, and the insistence on witnesses and documentary evidence is only a symptom of this subconscious desire to implicate as many people as possible in whatever was done.

The absence of a need for continuous development of the law (as opposed to the *śāstra*), for recorded precedents, for recorded reasons for judgments; the absence of need for juridical as opposed to *ad hoc* predictions as to what effects an act would have; the absence of concern about prejudice (despite the *śāstra's* fulminations on the subject), bribery, corruption of other kinds; the absence of a concern for true justice as opposed to what would suit the majority of the influential persons involved; all these absences account for the confused and illogical, though in the circumstances eminently practical, jurisprudence which emerges from a study of Medhātithi's commentary on the *Manu-smṛti.*

ADDITIONAL ANNOTATION

p. [189], n. 57. I now feel sure that *dṛṣṭārtha* is correct, and the text's inference wrong.

THE RELATIVE ANTIQUITY OF THE MITĀKSHARĀ AND THE DĀYABHĀGA. *

The present is a time when the theories of *Jīmūtavāhana* and *Vijñāneśvara* are being subjected to close scrutiny. It has been proposed to abolish the *Mitāksharā* joint family, and those who resist the abolition are anxious to know what superiority the *Mitāksharā* conception of the family's property rights has over that of the *Dāyabhāgā*, which until 1951 the reformers wanted to extend from Bengal over all India. Naturally we cannot appreciate either of the remarkable treatises unless we know which was prior to the other.

MM. Dr. P. V. Kane, on page 327 of Vol. I of his *History of Dharmaśāstra*, sums up his discussion of the problem whether *Jīmūtavāhana* was criticizing the *Mitāksharā* or not in the *Dāyabhāga* by saying, "All that one can advance is that it is quite within the bounds of possibility that *Jīmūtavāhana* criticizes the *Mitāk-shārā*". The purpose of this article is to show, by an analysis not attempted before, that there are no sound grounds for believing that the author of the *Dāyabhāga* ever saw the text of the *Mitāksharā*. There is evidence consistent with *Vijñāneśvara's* having seen the text of the *Dāyabhāga*, but it is not conclusive. The solution is a matter of real importance because, although we are already aware of the existence of at least two different schools of thought on the subject of inheritance even before the time of these protagonists, it is so commonly said that *Jīmūtavāhana* wrote in order to refute the arguments of the *Mitāksharā*, that students, and legislators, may justifiably judge the worth of the *Dāyabhāga* with reference to its quality as such a refutation. This would be, it is submitted, a great injustice to *Jīmūtavāhana*.

First of all, neither writer makes direct reference to the other. But certain very late commentators, such as *Mitra Miśra*, imply that *Jīmūtavāhana* was refuting the *Mitāksharā*. This is neither here nor there, for, as Kane says[1], those writers had no idea of chronology ; they were concerned with jurisprudential problems horizontally, as it were, and not vertically.

There can be no doubt but that *Jīmūtavāhana* and *Vijñāneśvara* were contemporaries. Internal evidence in the former's *Kālaviveka* shows that the years 1091 and 1092 A.D. were almost certainly within his lifetime.[2] The *Mitāksharā* was unquestionably published between 1121 and 1125 A.D., for the details in the colophon point to the period of the greatest prosperity of the emperor *Vikramāditya VI Cālukya*. The chances, then of *Vijñāneśvara* having read *Jīmūtavāhana's* work seem on the face of the matter greater than *vice versa*. But there is a means of settling the question by a brief comparison of the point of view of the two writers on identical topics. This process is apt to be a trifle tedious, but it gives the answer to the problem.

---

1. History of Dharmaśāstra, Vol. I, pp. 242,   2. Kane, History of Dharmaśāstra, Vol. I.
327.   pp. 325-6.

First let us take the 33 topics on which a distinct difference of opinion can be detected between the authors. Of these, 10 instances, which we will mention first, clearly show the priority of *Jīmūtavāhana* or alternatively his ignorance of the *Mitāksharā* text; six instances suggest strongly that if *Vijñānesvara* is not correcting *Jīmūta vāhana* he is refuting a person with similar views; the remaining 17 instances are inconclusive and equally consistent with either author's priority. There is not one instance which suggests the priority of the *Mitākshará* unmistakably.

(1) *Dāvabhāga.* I : 6 : Is "*dāyabhāga*" the splitting of a divided thing into parts, or a matter of a part not being united to the *dāya*? The first suggestion is wrong because there would be a disappearance of the *dāya* itself; the second also because we find people saying even when property is undivided, "This is not my separate property, it is my brother's!" (The text and meaning are both open to dispute here.) *Mitāksharā* I 3 7, 17 : "*Dāyabhāga*" is the arrangement of multiple ownerships, which have as their subject-matter a conglomerate mass of possessions, into individual lots in respect of these possessions. Ownership exists before partition.

Dāyabhāga. I 7, 8 : "*Dāyabhāga*" is not the apportioning in respect of particular objects of a right of property produced by an identity of relationship over all the possessions, because (1) relationship so long as there is another relation with competing claims will not produce proprietary right over the whole, (2) it is needlessly complicated to imagine proprietary rights in the whole of the father's goods being born and being destroyed, and (3) it would be useless, through the absence of the power to use at will, *i.e.*, no proprietary right could have existed before partition. Thus "*dāyabhāga*" is the manifesting by lot or some other method of a proprietary right which never extended beyond a part of the possessions and had previously been unascertained because no ocaasion had arisen for its ascertainment. *Mitāksharā* I (i) 17-23 : Five arguments listed against property existing before partition : (1) Father to whom a son is born would not be able to lay the sacred fire; (2) there would be no necessity to prohibit division of property given out of affection by a fatner to a joint son; (3) the text concerning gifts of affection to a wife would not be pertinent, for the husband would not be competent to give; (4) the text, "Father is master of gems, pearls and corals", shows that the sons have no birth-right in moveables. whatever right they have in immoveables; and (5) in the case of an only son the estate passes without partition (the demise of the owner being the sole cause of property). All these arguments are met.

Dāyabhāga. I 11 : *Nārada's* text is authority for the statement that sons have no proprietary right in the father's property before partition. Partition alone is not a cause of property, for one can partition the goods of a stranger. *Mitāksharā* and *Aparārka* and all later peninsular writers unanimously hold that the rights of the sons, etc., are by birth and that this fact is a matter of practical observation. If one looks closely at the expressions, it is clear that as regards sons, etc., there is no fundamental difference : *Jimūtavāhana* is anxious to ensure the father's independence. The point about partition alone not being a cause of property is aimed not at the *Mitāksharā* school but at some other. *Mitāksharā* I i 23 : partition relates to effects belonging to several owners (as of course you can partition the effects of business partners); partition does not apply to goods vacant or unowned by the persons making the partition.

It emerges from all this that *Jīmūtavāhana* was attacking the school which the *Mitāksharā* represents in an earlier and less developed form. His phrases, as in *Dāyabhāga* I i 6, 7 above, which he thinks portray that school's view are cruder and less exact than those we find in the *Mitākshara*. No one who would have read the latter could have used the more awkward expressions. It was not a *divided* thing which was split into parts, nor was it *identity* of relationship which produced the proprietary right. The *Mitākshara* gathers and deals with more objections than the *Dāyabhāga* itself produced. It adds the point, though with tongue in cheek, that if the birth-right were to be denied a stranger could with impunity run off with the deceased's goods before the heirs partitioned them. It is worth adding that *Jīmūtavāhana* did not enter into the discussion on the origin of *property*, whether or not exclusively ascertainable from the *śāstra*. His acumen could here have been applied with excellent effect: at the least he could have demonstrated again his famous "moral obligation is not legal obligation" theory.

(2) *Dāyabhāga* I 13, 14 : It is said that birth, the act of a son, is an act of acquisition, and that birth alone makes a son proprietor in his father's estate; this is a mistake, for *Manu* says that the brothers have no power while the parents live. *Dāyabhāga* I 16 : "Have no power" does not mean "have no independence" for here we are not told that they have any proprietary interest. *Mitākshara* I i 27-30 lays out the details of the son's birth-right in the following way: (*a*) sons have the right to inherit on the father's death (*Jīmūtavāhana* does not deny this); (*b*) sons are co-owners with their father in the grandfather's property; (*c*) sons cannot prevent the father's disposing of his ancestral moveables for special necessity or his self-acquired moveables for any purpose; (*d*) the father must obtain the son's permission to alienate the immoveable estate, however acquired, under any circumstances unless (i) there is an emergency and (ii) the co-owners are minors or incapable of giving consent. *Mitākshara*, *Aparārka*, *Varadarāja* and later southern authors insist that *Manu's* text *does* mean that sons lack independence in dealing, but not ownership. It is clear that had *Jīmūtavāhana* read this description of the powers which the birth-right gave he would have been in a position to make a powerful criticism of the theory underlying them. The *Mitākshara* view is based upon a compromise between the traditions of northern and southern schools and, like most compromises, offers a wide scope to critics. A conclusive passage is *Dāyabhāga* I 19, where *Jīmūtavāhana* calmly says that if sons had ownership in their father's property partition could be enforced by will of the sons and against the will of the father: in the south by this time such partitions not only occurred (in respect of ancestral property) but the *Mitākshara* had deliberately sanctioned them. *Jīmūtavāhana* clearly did not know this, for we know him to be a man interested in practical experience, and not a mere theorist.

(3) *Dāyabhāga* I 38, 39 : There are two times for partition: when the father's right of property ceases and by his choice. It is wrong to see *three* periods. *Mitākshara* I ii 7 gives *five* periods, four during the lifetime of the father and one after his death. It is unnecessary to go into the details, which are easily available, but the third time, *i.e.*, when the father is indifferent to wealth and not sexually active, serves as an answer to *Jīmūtavāhana's* objection to a period on the ground that there could not according to that view be a partition of the father's property if he became a hermit. This again proves that *Jīmūtavāhana* was aiming at an earlier and less considered account of the times of partition.

(4) *Dāyabhāga.* II 9 and III 22, 23 : *Yajñāvalkya's* text, " the ownership of the father and son is the same in land acquired by the grandfather, etc.," is according to *Udyota* an explanation that when *A*, having two sons *B* and *C*, is predeceased by *B*, who himself leaves a son *D*, and then *A* himself dies, *C* does not take the whole estate, but shares it with *D*. *Mitākshara* I v 3-9 explains that the text was required to meet the argument that as, according to the previous text (" among claimants by different fathers the allotment of shares shall be by regard to fathers ") the sons of each brother get the share of their respective father between them, when the father is separate or has no brothers one of two things happens : either the maxim applies only when the father is dead, and therefore the sons cannot demand a share of the father's father's property in the father's lifetime, or, if a partition does take place, it must be at the pleasure of the father. Here it is clear that the *Mitākshara* copes with arguments, similar to those brought forward by *Jīmūtavāhana*, and leaves nothing to be said in the way of bringing out the meaning of *Yājñavalkya* II 121. Had *Jīmūtavāhana* seen this interpretation he would have been bound by the conventions of his science to meet it in some way. No writer of consequence could ever pass an important argument of an opponent by, on pain of being ridiculed as ignorant by contemporary *śāstris*.

(5) *Dāyabhāga* II 11 : If sons had birth-rights in the property of the grandfather during the life of the father, then all the sons by all the fathers would at a general partition take equal shares with their fathers in the whole. This argument is fully answered by *Mitākshara* I v 2, which *Jīmūtavāhana* cannot possibly have seen, as it demolishes his position.

(6) *Dāyabhāga* II 22 : *Yājñavalkya* says, " the father is master of the gems, pearls and corals and of all ; but neither father nor grandfather is so of the whole immoveable estate." Moveables inherited from the grandfather, or otherwise acquired, are owned exclusively by the father. *Mitākshara* I i 21 : the text refers to immoveables descended from the father's father ; the text " By favour of the father clothes and ornaments are used, but immoveable property may not be consumed even with the father's indulgence " is to the same effect. It is to be noticed that *Jīmūtavāhana* does not quote the latter text—it is contrary to his position—but had he read the *Mitākshara* he would have been obliged at least to circumvent it. We are the losers, because his method of interpreting the text would have been interesting.

(7) *Dāvabhāga* II 49 : If a father and son were to share equally the grandfather's wealth, the fact that the father must have a double share leads to the conclusion that if *A* and his son *B* and his brother *C* were dividing the property of his father *X*, *C* would be left with a fifth share. This situation could not have been suggested seriously by anyone who had read the *Mitākshara* which in I v 2, 7 and I iii 3-4 makes such a conclusion impossible according to the " birth-right" school.

(8) *Dāyabhagā* III ii 36, 39, 40, 42 : The rule that daughters who are unmarried are entitled to 1/4th of a son's share on a partition between their brothers is to be interpreted elastically so that the sons will not be impoverished *Mitākshara* I vii 5-14 is an answer to the difficulty and a refutation of the solution which *Jīmūtavāhana* offered. The 1/4th is obligatory, but will not impoverish the sons because it is a 1/4th, not of the share which the son might have taken had there been no daughters, but of what the daughter would have obtained had she been a son,

(9) *Dāyabhāga* VI ii 38-9 : A single heir recovering by his own labour land formerly lost may retain only 1/4th in addition to his share on a partition. *Mitākshārā* I iv 2 and I v 11 show that *Vijñānesvara* believed that the consent of the other joint members was a vital factor in deciding whether the acquirer in such a case retained the 1/4th or not : the *Mitākshārā* proviso is a protection against fraud which *Jīmūtavāhana* would have incorporated, though perhaps in a modified form (*e.g.*, " with consent of father ") had he known it.

(10) *Dāyabhāga* XI iii 1 and iv 3 : Father comes before Mother in the order of heirs. Though the mother surpasses the father in the respect which is due to her this does not prefer her in this connection. *Mitākshārā* II iii 1-5 gives more than one reason why the mother should be preferred. Grammatical, sentimental and physiological considerations are urged, to which *Jīmūtavāhana* would have been bound to give an answer had he been informed of them.

This completes the list of those instances which clearly point the way of the present writer's opinion : it remains to mention those which tend to show that *Vijñānesvara* was correcting either *Jimūtavāhana* or some writer of his school.

(I) *Dāyabhāga* II 7 : The death of both parents is one period of partition of an estate inherited from a grandfather, and the other is the choice of the father when the mother is past child-bearing. *Mitākshārā* I v 8 is a direct contradiction of the second half of this proposition while the first half is answered by the whole of I vi.

(II) *Dāyabhāga* II 20, 35, 37 : Father can take a double share even of ancestral property. *Mitākshārā* I v 7 : The text enabling a father to keep two shares applies only to self-acquisitions.

(III) *Dāyabhāga* II 21 : The verses of *Manu* and *Vishnu* which say that a father recovering paternal wealth need not share it with his sons seems to suggest that a partition by the will of the son could occur in respect of ancestral property ; but the true meaning is that a father, setting about a partition, need not distribute the grandfather's wealth which he has retrieved. The *Mitākshārā* was not obliged to introduce this verse, but we find in I v 11 that the text obliges the father to divide with his sons the property acquired by his own father, however unwilling he may be, if they demand it of him. The meaning is better explained : the property is not that *lost* by the grandfather, but that lost by another ancestor and not recovered by the grandfather, for the latter is already accounted for by a different rule.

(IV) *Dāyabhāga* IV ii shows a different conception of *strīdhan* from that which we find in *Mitākshārā* II xi 12-25. Where, in *Dāyabhāga* IV ii 13-20, *Jimūtavāhana* says that "issue" in *Yājñavalkya* means the issue of the mother (*i.e.*, sons) instead of that of the daughters, *Mitākshārā* in II xi 17 makes it plain that the " issue " is that of the daughters.

(V) *Dāyabhāga* XI vi 18 : The text of *Manu* (" to the nearest *sapinda* the inheritance belongs ") does not indicate nearness according to birth. *Mitākshārā* II iv 5 quotes the text in order to show that those of half-blood are more remote through difference of mothers. Uterine half-blood, incidentally, were not contemplated by either author with reference to inheritance.

(VI) *Jimūtavāhana* agreed with *Vijñānēsvara's* predecessor, *Viśvarūpa*, that a coparcener who concealed joint property was not guilty of theft. *Mitākshārā* I ix 9 : It is criminal to withhold common property, and sinful. The kidney bean illustration, which *Jimūtavāhana* says had been used in a puerile manner by *Bāla* (=*Bālaka*), is carefully repeated in such a way as to show its proper application to this problem.

This survey would not be complete without a glance at the other notable divergences between the writers. These, as stated above, do not provide any conclusive evidence.

(i) The definitions of *dāya* are totally different. The full significance of the difference has been brought out admirably by Mr. I. S. Pawate in his "*Dāyabhāga*", published at Dharwar, 1945. *Dāyabhāga* I 4 : *Dāya* comes from the root *Dā*. It is the constituting of another's property after annulling the previous right of a person who has died, etc., but there is no abdication of the deceased, etc., in respect of the property. *Mitāksharā* I i 2 : *Dāya* is wealth which becomes the property of another solely by reason of his relationship to the owner.

(ii) *Dāyabhāga* I 42: *Sankha-Likhita* says that a partition does *not* take place if the father does not desire it, and the reading "if he be incapable of business, partition of wealth takes place" is corrupt. The *Mitāksharā* quotes *Sankha-Likhita*, but not to this effect. *Vijñānesvara* quotes a text from that source which supports his case, but which *Jimūtavāhana* had not noticed in his account. The topic of dividing the goods of the maternal grandfather (*Dāyabhāga* I 45) is nowhere noticed by the *Mitāksharā* at all. The general rules cover it adequately, and it is an emanation of *Jimūtavāhana's* eccentric interpretation of the texts allowing sons to step into control when the father is incapable.

(iii) *Dāyabhāga* II 5 and III 1 : Division of the father's estate ought to be made after the death of the mother. This is based simply on *Manu's* "*ūrddhvam pituśca mātuśca*". *Mitāksharā* I vi is based upon the assumption that a partition can take place in the lifetime of the mother : posthumous sons are accounted for.

(iv) *Dravyam*, of course, means "goods" or "money." *Dāyabhāga*, II, in a curiously significant manner explains it as "slaves" in *Yājñavalkya's* text. *Mitāksharā* I v, 4 goes out of its way to explain that *dravyam* means gold, silver etc.

(v) *Dāyabhāga* II 59 : *Ekaputra* in the text of *Sankha-Likhita* means "son of one father." *Mitāksharā* does not answer this eccentricity.

(vi) *Dāyabhāga* II 71 : Father takes two shares of the property acquired by his son. *Mitakshara* I iv, 12 : "It is well known that what is acquired by one belongs to him only and to no other person." Incautious, but one would think that if *Jimutavahana* had read the *Mitāksharā* he would have had to confute the texts which support the statement.

(vii) *Dāyabhāga* III ii 32 : Only son-less wives of the father should have a share in a partition at the father's option. *Mitāksharā* I ii 9-10 and vii 1: All wives then take a share.

(viii) *Dāyabhāga* IV i 23 : Where a husband has given his wife immoveables she may not alienate them even after his death (*Nārada*). *Mitāksharā* maintains silence on this topic, implying no restriction.

(ix) *Dāyabhāga* IV i 11 : The limitation of 2,000 *paṇas* on the widow's inheritance is to be rejected. *Mitāksharā* does not mention it, but refutes a similar view of limiting the widow's estate attributed to *Śrīkara*. The 2,000 paṇas limit is found in *Kauṭilīya*, *Vyavahāra-nirṇaya* and *Smṛti-candrikā*, and is quoted in a verse of *Vyāsa* by the southerner *Haradatta* on *Gautama* 28, 19.

(x) *Dāyabhāga* V deals with outcastes. No reference there to their daughters. *Mitāksharā* makes a point of protecting the daughters, in II x 12-3. *Aparārka* is even more explicit.

(xi) *Dāyabhāga* VI i 17-20 : Gains of learning even without the use of joint funds must be shared with those coparceners who are equally or more learned. *Mitākshara* I iv 13, 15 partially answers this and denies it by implication.

(xii) A severe poser is set by the distinction between *Dāyabhagā* (XI i 1-26) and *Mitākshara* views on the estate to be taken by a vidow. *Mitākshara* says that the widow of a separated unreunited member takes his entire property. The *Dāyabhāga* makes no such restriction. In all probability the text of the *Mitākshara* does not give us the views of the author fully. Epigraphy and the evidence of Jaina law for instance show us that the old texts which did allow the widow to inherit when issueless contemplated her taking her husband's interest in the joint family property.

(xiii) *Dāyabhāga* XI ii 30 : If an unmarried daughter-heiress dies, the inheritance goes not to her heir but to the married daughter and then to a daughter's son. The *Mitākshara* saw women having less obstructed ownership than men, and hence makes no such provision.

(xiv) *Dāyabhāga* XI v 13-37 and *Mitākshara* II ix 1-12 deal with the difficult passage of *Yājñavalkya* on inheritance from reunited persons. The latter is much more thorough, answering a question which *Jīmūtavāhana* does not touch, *i.e.*, the result when reunited full brothers compete with unreunited half brothers by the same mother, and when reunited half-brothers compete with unreunited half-brothers.

(xv) The whole of the *Dāyabhāga* section on inheritance reeks of the religious benefit theory explained in a most comprehensive manner. *Mitākshara* denies that *sapiṇḍaship* is a matter of religious benefit but in such an odd manner that one may doubt whether he is correcting *Jīmūtavāhana* or a predecessor of *Jīmūtavāhana* of whom we have now lost sight. We read, on *Yājñavalkya* I 51, that *sapiṇḍaship* must not be understood as a handing on of the *piṇḍa* which has to be offered in the *śrāddha*, for if that were the case there would be no *sapiṇḍaship* with one's mother's issue or one's brothers' sons (one must read here "*bhrātṛvya-pitṛvya*"), paternal uncles and so on. This is the strongest piece of evidence for *Vijñānesvara's* never having read the *Dāyabhāga*, though it neither strengthens nor weakens the case regarding *Jīmūtavāhana's* having read the *Mitākshara*. Of course *Jīmūtavāhana's* explanation of the significance of *sapiṇḍaship* in inheritance is very much wider than this. *Vijñāneśvara's* point is that one's uterine brothers, one's brothers' sons and one's paternal uncles cannot be called *sapiṇḍas*, if one understands the word in the sense of "those who have identity of *piṇḍa*, i.e., those who offer the same type and quality of *piṇḍa*". At that rate brothers alone would be *sapiṇḍas*. Since that is not the case, the true meaning of *sapinda* must be "connected by particles of the same body." But it must be repeated that the *Mitākshara* nowhere distinctly denies that the right to perform *śrāddhas* has a significance in determining priority of heirs.

(xvi) Sarvadhikari, in his analysis of the arguments of the two authors has shown that *Jīmūtavāhana* desired agnate and cognate *bandhus* to take in a different manner from that envisaged by the *Mitākshara*. Cognate *bandhus* were intended to take immediately after agnate *bandhus* in the same class, whereas in the *Mitākshara* all agnates precede cognates. It must be remarked that the whole analysis depends upon a number of conjectures, and the subject is still in an unclear state. At any rate no evidence exists that the one author was correcting or amplifying the views of the other. Had a clear statement been found the present doubts would not exist, and Allahabad and Madras would be at one on heritable *bandhus*.

A final point needs to be mentioned : *Jīmūtavāhana* often pours scorn upon an opponent. There is no ground for thinking that this is *Vijñāneśvara*. *Jīmūtavāhana's* chief opponent (*Dāyabhāgha* II 64) is " he who continually explains *Manu*, *Gautama*, *Dakṣa* and others in a vague sense " and thus " demonstrates his own unsettledness." This is *Bālaka*, who is probably the same as *Bāla*, mentioned in *Dāyabhāga* XI i 51 and ii 27. Kane, op. cit. pp. 283-4, tells us that he was an easterner, not long prior to *Jīmūtavāhana* himself.

Kane op. cit. on p. 327 quotes some occasions when *Jīmūtavāhana* in his *Vyavahāramātṛkā* seems to refer to the text of the Mitakshara. There is no clear reference, and the one which Kane has thought apt for quotation is a commonplace, a stock illustration of types of absurdities in plaints.

From internal evidence, after reviewing all the important places where conflict exists between the authors, it seems undeniable that the old belief that *Jīmūtavāhana* wrote his *Dāyabhāga* to refute the *Mitāksharā* is unfounded. There is so much against it, and nothing for it. *Jīmūtavāhana* did not lack opponents even in 1100 : both schools of thought were very old already. *Jīmūtavāhana's* own contribution, a new evaluation of the notion of *sapiṇḍaship*, is totally independent of contact with the *Mitāksharā*.

A piece of external evidence completes the picture. The date of *Aparārka* is well known. Ample data fix the compilation at about 1125. (*See* Kane, History of Dharma Śāstra, Vol. I, p. 334). It can be suggested with reason that a legal author who did not know *Aparārka's* commentary could not have known the *Mitāksharā* either. Now in the commentary on *Yājñavalkya* II 121, *Aparārka*, or his editorial committee, used an argument which would have been of great service to *Jīmūtavāhana* had the latter wanted to refute the *Mitāksharā*. It was used to refute those who said that a son could not have rights by birth because this would prevent the father of a new-born son from performing *agnihotra* and other obligatory rights which must be performed with one's own property. It is said, " even if his property is common to himself and his son, nevertheless he is able to perform the *agnihotra* and so on, either by the (implied) consent of his son or by the earning of additional property, the son's share having been put to one side ; *and it is not the case that the genesis of the (father's) ownership comes about by a partition since that would deprive the father of ownership prior to the partition.* For " partition " is the arranging . . . . ."

One of the logical weaknesses of the southern conception of family-joint-ownership as expressed in the *Mitāksharā* is the implication behind the twin definitions of *dāya* and *vibhāga*. All the *dāyādas* have proprietary rights in one another's property by reason of their relationship ; when there are many ownerships in respect of the aggregate a partition arranges who will be *apratibandha* owner of which part of the whole. It follows that until a partition takes place among *dāyādas* of the same class and bearing the same relationship within that class, no one should be able to say who is independent owner of a particular part. But we find that the southern writers are content to talk of partitioning the "father's" or "grandfather's" property as if there were a superior proprietary right existing prior to the partition in the father or grandfather. How is this? Surely if all sons, for example, have rights by birth over the property of their father, the second son would be born at a time when the father would have no separate property in which he could acquire rights, quite apart from the consideration that the father's brothers and father would have ***sapratibandha*** rights over it already. In fact if partition is the only means of deciding who is the owner, broadly speaking, of which part of the family property, before a partition a father would have no ownership at all; and yet we see that practice and the ***smṛti*** texts give the father exceedingly wide powers.

Had ***Jīmūtavāhana*** perceived this particular mode of attack upon the *Mitāksharā* position he could hardly have failed to employ it. The peculiar skill which is required of a legal author working in a field of this nature demands the utilisation of all possible arguments. It is possible that ***Aparārka*** did not realise that his commentary was supplying an argument against himself. The shrewd Bengali would not have rejected a gift of this nature. Hence we conclude that ***Jīmūtavāhana*** did not know ***Aparārka's*** publication, and this tends to support the general conclusion that he did not know the ***Mitākshar*ā** either.

ADDITIONAL ANNOTATIONS

Tit. S. now L. Rocher, 'Schools of Hindu law', *India Maior* (*Jan Gonda Fel. Vol.*) (Leiden, 1972), 167-76. And the same, '*Janmasvatvavāda* and *uparamasvatvavāda*: the first chapters on inheritance in the Mitākṣarā and the Dāyabhāga', *O.H.* XIX/1 (1971), 3-13.

p. [203], l. 43. See below, p. [217].

SHOWING A BIG BULL: A PIECE OF HYPOCRISY IN THE MITĀKṢARĀ?

There is no doubt but that Vijñāneśvara's *Mitākṣarā,* or to give it its correct name, *Ṛju-Mitākṣarā,* stands at the pinnacle of indigenous Indian law-books. Its prestige remains even in the current version of Hindu law which governs the management and enjoyment of joint-family property. Through the centuries since its composition (c. 1125) it has enjoyed respect throughout India, mainly because in its explanation of the meaning of the stanzas of the *Yājñavalkya-smṛti* it has managed to state, in a small compass, all that matters of the Dharmaśāstra. It is interesting to find any inadequacies in it, and now we shall consider the translation of an intriguing short passage,[1] in which the author seems to have fallen into hypocrisy—a very rare quality in Hindu legal literature. Fantasy, a formal regard for propositions which no longer held the attention of the public (if ever they held any substantial section of it), and perhaps even a refusal to recognise the challenge of custom and the need to expand the *śāstra* to accommodate long-tried practical institutions: these accusations could conceivably be made against the jurists. But this present writer has not seen a straightforward piece of hypocrisy before; and that is why he is interested in this item.

Yājñavalkya says at I. 109:

> *mahokṣaṃ vā mahājaṃ vā śrotriyāyopakalpayet*
> *satkriyānvāsanaṃ svādu bhojanaṃ sūnṛtaṃ vacaḥ.*
>
> "Let him make available to a Śrotriya a large ox or a large goat, *
> kindly treatment, precedence, sweet food, and courteous speech."

Now it is obvious that Yājñavalkya intends these items to be given to a

1. The passage is mentioned by P. V. KANE, *History of Dharmaśāstra*, V (Poona, * 1962), p. 1270, n. 2071, from the point of view of the concept of *loka-vidviṣṭa.* In the same work, vol. III (Poona, 1946), p. 946, KANE, speaking of *madhuparka* (which he had mentioned at II, 776 and in connection with *Kali-varjya* at III, 928), makes the following comment on Viśvanātha who, in the *Māṃsatattva-viveka* "takes up the cudgels on behalf of flesh-eating by brāhmanas in sacrifices, *śrāddha*, *madhuparka*, in danger to life and when ordered by a *brāhmaṇa* and charges those who totally forbid flesh-eating with being the followers of the doctrine of Bauddhas...", the relevance of which last remark will presently appear.

Śrotriya, namely a Brāhmaṇa of especial devotion to the Vedic lore,[1] and not to every Brāhmaṇa guest. In the previous verse he has been speaking of feeding friends, relatives and kinsmen. In the following verse he speaks of giving *argha,* ceremonial welcome, to the *snātaka,* preceptor, the king, the friend (? and) the son-in-law, as well as the priest at the time of a sacrifice. The large ox or the large goat are reserved for the Śrotriya. As we shall see, this was not always so. But let us pass to Vijñāneśvara's commentary on the passage.

mahāntam ukṣāṇaṃ dhaureyaṃ mahājaṃ vā śrotriyāyokta-lakṣaṇā-yopakalpayet bhavad-artham ayam asmābhiḥ parikalpita iti tat prītyarthaṃ na tu dānāya vyāpādanāya vā. yathā sarvam etad bhavadīyam iti. prati-śrotri-yam ukṣāsaṃbhavāt, "*asvargyaṃ loka-vidviṣṭaṃ dharmyam apy ācaren na tu*" *iti niṣedhāc ca.*[2] "He should make available to a Śrotriya who has the above-mentioned qualities a great ox, that is to say a draught-ox, or a large goat, with the words "we have chosen (or 'got ready') this one for your sake", in order to give the guest pleasure but not as a gift to him nor in order that it should be slaughtered. Just as when one says, 'all this is yours'. The reason is twofold: there are not enough oxen for every Śrotriya to be given one, and there is a prohibition expressed in the words "But he should not practise what is repugnant to Heaven and detested by the public, though it may be consistent with *dharma.*"

What on earth is the point of "making available" the animal if the Śrotriya guest is neither to have the option to take it or eat it? Let us see how other commentators have taken the verse of Yājñavalkya. Viśvarūpa (I, 108) says *upakalpana-vacanāt tad-anujñāpekṣo mahokṣādi-vadhaḥ.* This is a text which Vijñāneśvara had in front of him, and on which he was improving. It is a correct statement of the Vedic *dharma* on the subject: "The word *upakalpayet* indicates that slaughter of the great ox, etc., takes place only if he permits it." In other words it is up to the guest to decide whether or not to ask for the animal to be slaughtered. Originally it is evident that an ox or a cow used to be offered to special guests who arrived for ceremonial reception. The king, a Śrotriya, and especially a Brāhmaṇa son-in-law, were entitled to elaborate ceremonial reception, at which many offerings, including sweet speech, were made to them, and then the host

1. Yājñavalkya's reference to a Śrotriya is in itself a restriction. *Madhuparka* was to be offered to important guests, of whom the *snātaka,* learned Brāhmaṇa, the king, and the son-in-law were the chief. See KANE, *Hist. of Dharmaś.* II (Poona, 1941), pp. 542–6. The qualification for being a Śrotriya is knowledge of the Veda.

* 2. The text, *Yājñ.* I. 156, may be compared with *Manu.* IV. 176, *Viṣṇu-purāṇa* III 11, 7 and *Bṛhannāradīya-purāṇa* I, 24, 12, all of which are cited by KANE at n. 2071 at his vol. V, p. 1270.

announces the animal, " The Cow." The guest has the option to say " Do it (i. e. slaughter it)", or to take pity on the animal and order it to eat grass (i. e. as nominal owner he relinquishes the animal back to his host, saving its life).[1] Originally the slaughtering of the animal was supposed to be a service to the guest in that it atoned for his sins.[2] This also was part of the hospitality, and the somewhat tough meat which would then be served up to the guest as his meal would be another aspect of hospitality. Thus to say, as Viśvarūpa does, that the animal is not slaughtered unless the guest requires it, is correct. Why should Vijñāneśvara differ from this ? If the guest had conscientious scruples—as some guests obviously had in very early times, not less than a thousand years before—it was up to him to pursue them and to save the animal's life, naturally to the relief of his hosts upon whom, in a sense, he was already imposing by visiting them in this ceremonious manner.

Let us see what post-*Mitākṣarā* commentators have to say on the same verse. Śūlapāṇi takes a point of view somewhat similar to that of Vijñāneśvara, though he does not express it so elegantly. **upakalpayet** *vyāpādayet mārayet. Vasiṣṭhaḥ (IV. 8): " api Brāhmaṇāya rājanyāya vā mahokṣaṃ mahājaṃ vā pacet. evam asyātithyaṃ kurvanti ". etad go-vadhenātithyaṃ na Kalau. yathā Brahma-purāṇam :—" dīrgha-kālaṃ brahmacaryaṃ dhāraṇaṃ kamaṇḍaloḥ, gotrān mātṛsapiṇḍād vā vivāho go-vadhas tathā. narāśvamedhau palyaṃ ca Kalau varjyā dvijātibhiḥ. "*

Now there is no doubt but that the Kalivarjya theory would prohibit the slaughter of cows.[3] This however does not affect the duty to offer a large goat. And Śūlapāṇi leaves us with the impression that the text of Yājñavalkya enjoins upon the host to slaughter a large goat (" cow " including " ox ") in order to feed his guest. Indeed slaughtering would be to no

1. The texts are briefly discussed by KANE at *Hist. of Dharmaś.* II, pp. 544-5. Batuknath BHATTACHARYA, *The ' Kalivarjyas ' or Prohibitions in the ' Kali ' Age* (Calcutta, 1943), pp. 28 ff., deals with the basic texts. These are *Śāṅkh. Gṛ. S.* II. 15.1 (should any one of the six persons to whom Arghya reception is due visit, let him make ready a cow, a goat, or what he thinks most like). *Hiraṇ. Gṛ. S.* I. 4. 13. 13. *Āśvalāyana Gṛ. S.* I 24. 30–32. *Śat. Br.* III. iv. 1.2 (S. B. E. 26, p. 85) = 3. 3. 2. 2. *
(Kashi Skt. Ser. ed. 1937) (the last is the *śruti* cited by Aparārka (see below). *Pār. Gṛ. S.* I. 3. 26–31. *Āp. Gṛ. S.* I. 3. 9, cf. *Āp. Dh. S.* II. 4. 8, 7. Doubts about cow- or ox-eating are expressed at *Śat. Br.* III. i. 2. 21 (S. B. E. 26, p. 11). Vasiṣṭha is quoting the *Śat. Br.* III. iv. 1. 2. *

2. *Hir. Gṛ. S.* : " Drive away my sin and the sin of N. " *Pār. Gṛ. S.* : " I kill my sin and N.'s sin. " " My sin and N.'s sin have been killed. "

3. BHATTACHARYA, *ubi cit.* KANE, III, pp. 945 f. At p. 929 he cites a quotation by Aparārka (p. 233) of the *Mārkaṇḍeya* which must, however, be read along with our passage in the same author (see below). The cow is not to be killed, but that does not exclude the *goat* from *madhuparka : mādhuparkika–paśur atra gaur eva.*

purpose if the guest were not to be fed with its meat. Thus, apart from the Kalivarjya theory, which emerged some time between the days of Viśvarūpa and, it would seem, those of Vijñāneśvara himself, the law would allow or require the host to slaughter the animal. Śūlapāṇi does not refer to the guest's option. By the way, we may notice that the 13th-century jurist Devaṇṇa-bhaṭṭa ignores the verse of Yājñavalkya when discussing the duties * of hosts to guests in his *Āhnika-kāṇḍa*.

The *Vīramitrodaya*, which belongs to the seventeenth century, commenting on the verse itself, is clear that *upakalpayet* means " one should cook ", and he cites in support a *śruti* which coincides with Vasiṣṭha as quoted by Śūlapāṇi. Thus the northern Indian agrees with the Bengali. A somewhat similar position is taken by Aparārka (twelfth century), who belonged to the Konkan area. He says *mahāntam ukṣāṇaṃ balīvardam, tad-alābhe ajam, śrotriyāya madhuparkārhāya gṛham āgatāya upakalpayet pacet saṃskuryād iti yāvat*. Preferably an ox, or if that is not available, a goat, is to be slaughtered and prepared for the guest's entertainment. *Śruti* is cited, in a more extended form than in the *Vīramitrodaya*: for the *śrotriya* or the king a large ox or a large goat must be cooked. He also cites a long text from the *Bahvṛca-brāhmaṇa* which refers to hosts entertaining with an ox. He continues: " Someone has said that ' he should make available to a Śrotriya ' means only offer it to him verbally, but should not injure the animal: but this is repugnant to the Veda. Nor does the prohibition, ' he should not injure all creatures', stand in the way of injury to animals who are ancillary to the *madhuparka* offering any more than in the case of the animal sacrificed to Agni and Soma. "[1] He proceeds to quote Manu 5.41 which permits injury to animals in sacrificial contexts and in the *madhuparka* (which is our context). He then quotes the words of Śaunaka in a lost *gṛhya-sūtra* which recapitulate the Vedic position, in which the guest has the option to ask the animal to be slaughtered (in view of his own atonement) or to have it released (i.e. save its life). In fact the *madhuparka* starts, says Aparārka, with the making available of the great ox. And so, he implies at this point, the *Mitākṣarā's* actual solution is unacceptable.

1. At pp. 154–5 of the Poona edition of Aparārka's commentary on the *Yājñavalkya-smṛti*. The same passage appears at p. 79 of S. S. SETLUR, *The Mitākṣarā with Viśvarūpa*,...I (Madras, 1912). It should be read along with that at p. 233 cited by KANE (above). It will be observed that Aparārka is actually commenting upon I. 156 (the *asvargyaṃ loka-vidviṣṭam* half-verse), and what he prescribes is *not* the abolition of animal-slaughter in *madhuparka* but an option, a permitted alternative (*anukalpa*) in the case of the cow (or ox). Thus the goat in his view is to be slaughtered if the guest wants it and (of course) if the host is unable to produce an ox. But it is open to the host, out of deference to public feeling as expressed in the *Mārkaṇḍeya-purāṇa*, to substitute a golden vessel instead of the cow (or ox).

There is no reason for supposing that Aparārka actually knew the *Mitākṣarā* on this point, but he certainly knew its solution to the problem. The real objection to slaughtering the ox or goat was really that the public were not disposed to allow animal slaughter for hospitality, even if they were disposed to allow it for sacrificial purposes properly so called. The development of a doctrine of total *ahiṃsā* was, we know, slow in coming. The objections to slaughtering a cow may have led, but the antipathy to animal-slaughter was much broader-based.[1]

Today there is no trace of a guest's being offered an ox or a goat, and the present writer has never heard of the guest being given the option of asking for it to be slaughtered or to be " released. " The most recent commentary on Yājñavalkya is probably that by Bālam-bhaṭṭa on the *Mitākṣarā,* a commentary to be dated at the very end of the eighteenth century. We find that the *Mitākṣarā* solution is fully accepted. The text of Vasiṣṭha is first cited, and then the Kalivarjya point is raised. A Śrotriya is explained as either a Brāhmaṇa or a king. And the form of " making available " appears in the formula which the *Mitākṣarā* has provided. The words are said only to please the guest (one wonders how?), because that is the natural intention of the formula (it could have no other object). He continues: " *But not as a gift*. . . . The order of dealing with the topic has aroused some expectation, and therefore he says this in order to remove the possibility that the action should totally lapse *(asya adṛṣṭa-caratva-nirāsāya āha). Just as when*. . . Now he begins his explanation. *There are not enough oxen*. . . . he means there is not one ox to each Śrotriya. Secondly he cites this: *He should not practise*. . . . Because injury has been prohibited in general terms that option has become improper and the ceremony tends to be neglected if this is the footing. But merely because Vasiṣṭha's rule is barred in the Kali age we should not suspect that the injuries enjoined by the Veda are all on a par ; so that there is no public opposition to them (all): that is the point." Since on this footing the guest will get small pleasure from the ritual, the other acts of service are prescribed by the author in order to make the hospitality genuine.

The position seems to have been this. In very ancient times the arrival of guests having a very special claim to hospitality such as the king, or a son-in-law at the time of marriage, or a learned Brāhmaṇa, was an excuse

1. KANE II, 777–782. See W. Norman BROWN, " The sanctity of the cow in Hinduism, " *Economic Weekly*, Feb. 1964, pp. 245–255, an outstanding treatment (mentioning our *madhuparka* at p. 246, col. 1), the main ideas of which are utilised in his *Man in the Universe : Some Continuities in Indian Thought* (University of California Press, Berkeley and Los Angeles, 1966). The *Mitākṣarā* did contemplate the eating of meat at *śrāddhas* offered by *kṣatriyas* and *vaiśyas* (I. 200–1 : KANE V, 1269, n. 2070).

for conspicuous consumption. An esoteric reason for the acts of hospitality had to be alleged and the symbolic value of animal-slaughter at that time was found out. Later, respect for cows still able to provide milk or otherwise contribute to sacrifices led to doubts as to whether such cows ought to be slaughtered even for so great a purpose as hospitality, and bulls came within this doubt also. It was left to the conscience of the guest whether or not the animal should be slaughtered. At first, no doubt, the largest valuable animal was used. Later, due to the poverty of hosts, or the frequency of guests, or the dislike of cow-slaughter, or a combination of any of these, a goat was substituted. And it is at this stage that we have the *śruti* about the "large ox or large goat" and the text of Vasiṣṭha which virtually copies it. Now as a *ritual*, which hospitality was and to some extent still is, the Vedic and śāstric requirements would take precedence over individual convenience and preference, and general moral notions would tend to flow around it as around an island. The right to give such hospitality and the right to take it when offered would long survive the public's doubt whether animal slaughter should take place at all. And the public would have greater doubts on this subject in the Central and Southern regions of India, where meat-eating could safely vanish from the habits of the non-manual working classes.[1] At this point we may look to the Buddhist law on the subject, which seems to fit into Northern Indian attitudes at a time when the laws of hospitality survived in full vigour and the virtue of abstaining from taking life was already widespread, so that two portions of ethics, the one backed by the literate culture and the other backed by popular religion or superstition were in direct confrontation.

The story of Sīha, which is well known, shows how the Buddha was looked to as an authority (a virtual legislator) in such a controversy.[2] Where the host has slaughtered cattle for a feast the Buddhist monk may well eat the meat, without conscientious scruples, but he may not eat meat which has been slaughtered for him. Sīha killed a large ox to provide meat for the Buddha and his monks and the food was accepted. The rule that was formulated was that no monk should eat flesh where he has reason to believe that the animal had been specially killed for him. In order to emulate the Buddhists the Hindus would have to deny the possibility that the guest should say "Do it (slaughter it)", and therefore they would have to

1. J. R. GHARPURE, *Yājñavalkya Smṛti* (*The Collection of Hindu Law Texts*, vol. 2, pt. 1, Bombay 1936), p. 303 n. 3 (misprinted 2) speaks of "two types of civilization having special usages in the country for which the two authors (Vijñāneśvara and Mitra Miśra) speak – a specimen of how different Schools arose."

2. *Vinaya Piṭaka* I, 233 f (ed. OLDENBERG); *Mahāvagga* VI, 31, 13–14 (S. B. E. 17, pp. 116–117); *Aṅguttara Nikāya*, iv. 179 f. See also S. CHATTOPADHYAYA, *Evolution of Theistic Sects*, p. 69 for the *Pāśupata Sūtra* on eating meat one has not killed.

deny the guest the opportunity of exercising his ancient option. The only way in which this could be done would be to interpret Yājñavalkya and Vasiṣṭha in a different sense. If one accepted the Kali–varjya doctrine (and this by the twelfth century was becoming common), it followed that *dharma* allowed a large ox or a large goat to be *offered* to a guest (provided he was suitably qualified), but the dharmic position, according to which the guest might order the animal to be slaughtered and eat its meat, would be counteracted by the popular antipathy to animal–slaughter. Two paths might be followed. Either the jurist might take the view that *madhuparka* is Vedic, rare, ceremonial, sacrificial, and therefore out of the reach of the popular sentiment—which is the view adopted by Aparārka, Śūlapāṇi, and Mitra Miśra (in the *Vīramitrodaya*) : or he could contend that the entertaining of guests was specifically within the popular objection (the *Nāradīya–mahāpurāṇa* and other Kali–varjya sources specifically denied the right to offer an animal to a guest in the *madhuparka*),[1] but that the objection did not eliminate the ritual as such. The word *upakalpayet* does not mean slaughter, nor " give ", but " make available " (i. e. so that the option might be exercised) and this could be read with the adjacent material so as to mean merely that the animal should be shown as a formality. Once upon a time (he seems to say) our ancestors used to offer a fine animal to especial guests to complete the hospitality, and the guests could, if they wished, have it slaughtered for their food. Nowadays this does not take place, but the animal is shown in order to indicate that the requisite trouble has been taken. If the ox were not shown the inference would be that the host was too poor. Similarly once upon a time hosts were so selfless that they offered their entire household to their guests in affection and *atithi–pūjā*. Nowadays people neither make such offers nor have the impudence to accept them : but the formula " All this is yours " is still employed. It is less hypocrisy than the survival of a courteous usage into a more practical age.

Without accepting the Buddhist position, which would allow the guest to eat meat which had been slaughtered irrespective of his coming, the *śāstrīs* eventually decided to keep the formalities of hospitality whilst depriving the host of his former right to give the guest a meat-meal. It might be

1. KANE, III, p. 928, n. 1798. BHATTACHARYA cites, besides several passages negativing *go-vadha* in general terms, Śrīdhara (12th century) (p. 4 : *madhuparke paśor vadhaḥ*) ; Devaṇṇa–bhaṭṭa (p. 6 : *varātithi-pitṛbhyaś ca paśūpahanana–kriyā*) ; and the *Bṛhannāradīya purāṇa* (p. 9). The *Vīramitrodaya* refers to the same notion in the *Paribhāṣā–prakāśa* (BHATTACHARYA, p. 200). It is extremely interesting that Vidyākara Vājapeyi in his *Nityācārapaddhati* (ibid., p. 202) says that the killing of a cow for the guest–offering, etc., are forbidden in the Kali age in order to prevent excessive addiction, and so the individual has an option whether to do them or not. Being cited by Raghunandana this author is prior to 1500 (so KANE).

argued that at this rate popular prejudice had got the better of Vedic prescription. No, says Bālam-bhaṭṭa, almost certainly rightly; by restricting the force of *upakalpayet* and making the showing of the great ox, etc., a mere formality, an offer which cannot be accepted, one is admitting the force of the Kali-varjya rule, or rather of the popular exaggeration of the Vedic (limited) rule against injury to living beings, without at the same time prejudicing the right of sacrificers to sacrifice animals in Vedic sacrifices where these are still observed. Popular repugnance is to be taken into account in a sphere where it may properly operate.[1] This is one way of reconciling the conflicting forces. It is interesting to see that at the time of Bālam-bhaṭṭa it was still desirable to view popular repugnance as by no means capable of delimiting the validity of Vedic sacrificial prescriptions. Had the *madhuparka* been totally obsolete by that time it is unlikely that this caveat would have been superadded.

We may return to our initial question. Was this a piece of hypocrisy? Aparārka believed that the offering of the bull or goat was required by the *śāstra* and that a merely formal offering was repugnant to the Veda and so not good law. His near-contemporary Vijñāneśvara believed that a purely formal offering was necessary, the host implying almost in so many words that the animal is not a gift to the guest. This would give no real pleasure to the guest, and was an empty sham. Indeed a bull could be hired out to hosts (if they did not have draught-cattle of their own) for completing this part of the ceremony. The jurists' certainty that this is a draught-ox makes it even clearer that the guest could not possibly think of asking for it to be slaughtered, with the attendant inconvenience and cost to the agriculturalist host—and it is conceivable that these vegetarian Brāhmaṇas may have known that the flesh of a recently-slaughtered draught-ox would hardly be capable of being eaten.

The answer must be not that Vijñāneśvara, whose point of view won, connived at a piece of blatant hypocrisy, emasculating his author's text, but rather that the ancient ceremony was intended to be preserved in its dignified form, notwithstanding that the original intention could not, in respectable society, be followed out to its logical conclusion. The first argument, namely that there would not be enough oxen for every Śrotriya who came, is not so weak as it seems since, although a goat can be substituted, the text of Yājñavalkya implies that one must always be in a position to offer a large ox or a large goat—to offer only a goat must have been detrimental to the host's prestige, which could never have been the object of the verse. Consequently

1. It is presumed here that GHARPURE's text of *Bālambhaṭṭī* (*Collections of Hindu Law Texts*, No. 5, Bombay, 1914), p. 359, is accurate.

rather than risk that the ceremony should collapse because the sacrificial overtones ran headlong into popular prejudice, and so the text might fail to have any kind of relevance, a compromise was adopted as *dharma* which was almost certainly known in some places as a fact (because guests would never dream of asking for the animal to be slaughtered). And thus Vijñāneśvara supports his text and gives it a vitality which it might otherwise not have been guaranteed.

The instance is thus not of hypocrisy but of concern for the validity of a text: rather it should operate in an emasculated form, consistently with the growing literature expressing popular superstitious repugnance, than that one should adopt an austere Vedic stance, and insist upon the Veda and nothing but the Veda, with all the evil consequences which that would have.

Modern Indian law follows, in some States, popular prejudice against animal sacrifices, and the *loka-virodha* has indeed won. But it is noticeable that this has not yet happened in Northern India or Bengal : and so the pattern of the ancient *śāstra* is (probably unawares) faithfully preserved.[1]

1. The anti-cow-slaughter legislation of e. g. Uttar Pradesh and Bihar is of course not directed specifically against sacrifices ; and it does not affect the slaughter of goats. An indirect result is that Hindus may not sacrifice cows – but no Hindu in Northern India has contended in recent centuries that his religion required the slaughter of cows.

ADDITIONAL ANNOTATIONS

p. [207], l. 21. *upakḷp* is associated with *kḷp*, a root which can have the sense of dividing, apportioning, assigning a sacrificial victim (as is relevant here): O.H. de A. Wijesekera, 'A socio-semantic analysis of the Sanskrit *kalp-*', *A.B.O.R.I.*, 1968, 161 ff., at 164. For the definition of Śrotriya see Āpast. dh. sū. II.3.6,4-5.

p. [207], n. 1, l. 1. Also II, 750.

p. [208], n. 2. S. R. Lingat, *Classical Law of India* (1973), 190-3.

p. [209], n. 1, l. 6. Kane, *H.D.*, II, 750.
l. 10. Vas. is trans. at Jha, *Manu, Notes*, III, 367.

p. [210], l. 7. He says however that the ox is bound to be offered, since failure to offer it, though common, is not a *śiṣṭācāra* (see Lingat, *C.L.I.* for this concept) but the absence of *śiṣṭācāra*—in other words the *offering* is obligatory (Mysore edn., *Vy.k.*, ii, 1916, 621, ref. by Kane, H.D., II, 629. Devaṇṇa-bhaṭṭa finds fault with Viśvarūpa's saying that the ox or goat is not practised because *śiṣṭācāra* is against it, but this citation cannot be traced in Viśvar.).

p. [211], n. 1. L. Alsdorf, *Beiträge zur Geschichte von Vegetarismus und Rinderverehrung in Indien* (Wiesbaden, 1962); J. C. Heesterman, *Ind.-Ir.J.* 9 (1966), 148.

A STRANGE RULE OF SMṚTI, AND A SUGGESTED SOLUTION

Since the period between May, 1955, and December, 1956, when the Hindus of India lost their system of " personal law ", and the latter was replaced by a new system comprised in the so-called " Hindu Code ", the Sanskrit books which contain the accumulated learning of the *dharmaśāstra*, or so much of the ancient Indian " science of religious-and-civil law " as survives the ravages of time and the neglect of private owners of manuscripts, have ceased to be the fundamental source of Hindu law, and it is only in marginal contexts that for practical purposes reference to them will ever again be made in that country. Yet the relegation of their ancient learning to practical uselessness may be expected to have a beneficial effect on the study of the *dharmaśāstra* itself, and that literature, which has been widely neglected in all continents, may once again receive the volume of attention which it could command about eighty years ago. About that time it was still very doubtful what the *śāstra* had to say on topics of practical importance, and Bühler and Jolly, for example, could be sure that their researches, despite their predilection for the ancient and the " original ", would be of use in the Courts in addition to providing material for academic exercises. By the end of the first decade of this century it was evident that at least as far as British India was concerned the law was about to develop along lines which were to a certain extent incompatible with the *śāstra*, and the relation of academic study to practical advocacy became intolerably delicate. Cases might occur in which elaborate *śāstric* learning was required and would gain its reward; but these were a small minority amongst the mass of decisions which were more or less cheerfully given in an atmosphere of indifference towards the *śāstra* which an English statute had made the fundamental source of law for Hindus in matters of their most intimate concern. Simultaneously public rewards for an expert knowledge of the *śāstra* had been diminishing, and Indian Universities on the whole neglected to provide courses on and examinations in *dharmaśāstra*, or *smṛti*, as it is often called. Even in the cases of the honourable exceptions, the careers open to those who had mastered what was admittedly a difficult subject were so few or so narrow that a flow of able students was not to be expected. The revolution of 1955–6 may now be expected to modify the situation in the West, and in course of time this alteration in academic prestige cannot but affect trends of interest in the country where the subject took its birth.

It is the purpose of this article to draw attention by means of an example to the sort of problem which is repeatedly posed by the *smṛti*-texts which form the basic working-material of the *śāstra*; and to suggest to those who may be intrigued by the way in which it arises not merely that there exists a need to search for an intelligible solution, but also that there is a likelihood that such a search, if suitably directed, may meet with success. The *śāstra* contains many oddities which may only be understood after elaborate literary studies in other fields of Indology, or through the often more rewarding process of sociological "field-work" in Indian villages [1]; but this example is illustrative of the substantial class of problems which may perhaps be solved by looking into the books of the *śāstra* themselves.

One of the most striking (and perhaps for some years to come the most troublesome) of the innovations introduced by the Hindu Succession Act, 1956, was the abolition of the so-called Hindu women's limited estate, and the substitution in all except special cases of an absolute estate for women.[2] This was part of the programme to place women, so far as was deemed necessary or practicable, upon an equal legal footing with men. When this has been rendered a living reality amongst the mass of the Hindu population (an event which cannot be anticipated within a lifetime) the end will have been reached of a process of development from a situation in which women were denied any right to *own*, as distinct from enjoying, objects of whatever character.[3] That they became the beneficiaries of generosity long before the arguments against their

[1] The student of the *śāstra* is able to take advantage of the modern trend of social anthropology in India away from the exclusive study of tribes and towards a broader survey of the population.

[2] Section 14 of Act XXX of 1956. The "women's estate" was a topic of law of such magnitude that it occupied sixty pages in the current edition of Mayne on Hindu Law and Usage.

[3] The *locus classicus* on the subject is Jaimini, *Mīmāṃsā-sūtra*, vi, 1, 10–14. The text with Śabara's commentary is conveniently printed in Lakshmaṇ Śāstrī Joshī, *Dharma-kośa, Vyavahāra-kāṇḍa*, Wai, 1938, 1424. Reference to this most useful modern digest will be made below as *Dh.k.*

being owners were consciously formulated goes without saying. But in course of time the usefulness of permitting women to own in their own right impressed itself upon Sanskrit jurists, and it was admitted that certain classes of presents, defined according to their sources and the times when they might be given, should belong to the donee [1] in such a way that their abstraction by her husband or sons would be a conversion, subject always to the former's right to take them in an emergency.[2] In other words the strict theory of patriarchal Āryan law broke down in the face of the demands of practical utility, and no doubt under the influence of pre-Āryan customs, some of which we know allowed substantial proprietorial rights to women.

For at least a millennium and a half it was a matter of acute controversy whether women might inherit property, as opposed to their being donees of gifts *inter vivos*. No one ever doubted, of course, that they were entitled, so long as they did not remarry, to be maintained adequately either out of the joint family property belonging to the deceased husband and his agnates or, alternatively, by his heir, if any. This was not always satisfactory, but the consequences of permitting a widow to disrupt the joint stock and to carry away her share possibly into the bosom of another, and even a competitor family, were more than the average Hindu could bear to contemplate. Yet authors of the greatest respectability, perhaps influenced by Dravidian usages, declared that the widow and the daughter were heirs to a sonless man.[3] Though the daughter's position was relatively unchallenged the majority of the *smṛtis*, including Manu, could find no place for the widow as heiress. It became a work of art to reconcile the conflicting texts, which were of equal authority. Some thought that the widow should be understood tacitly to decline in favour of the agnates [4]; some that only a widow of special, and in some areas rare, qualifications might inherit: thus she must be free from potential as well as actual blemishes of character (!) [5]; she must be about to bear a son, or be willing to submit to *niyoga*, that is to say to bear a son to her

[1] Manu, ix, 194; *Dh.k.*, 1431*b*.

[2] Yājñavalkya, ii, 147; Devala, *Dh.k.*, 1461.

[3] Yājñavalkya, ii, 136; Viṣṇu, xvii, 4; *Dh.k.*, 1470*a*; Vyāsa, *Dh.k.*, 1524*a*.

[4] Aparārka's commentary on Yājñ., ii, 135–6.

[5] Ibid. This is not quite so foolish as it appears. Public examinations of childless widows were held in southern India according to the testimony of Medhātithi, *Manu-bhāṣya*, ed. Gangānāth Jhā, ii, 73; trans. *idem*, iv, pt. 1, 10.

deceased husband at the command of the family elders by some near agnate of the deceased [1]—though since *niyoga* was nominally obsolete in the current epoch the qualification was such as to remove the problem totally—and finally it was suggested that she must have been married in an "approved" form.[2] Alternatively others permitted her to inherit provided that she accompanied her husband's corpse upon the funeral pyre! [3] Others more rationally restricted her right to movable property,[4] or to cases where the estate was very small and her right to maintenance in jeopardy.[5] Finally, the celebrated *Mitākṣarā* reconciled the texts by allowing her to inherit when her husband was "separate", that is to say, she might take his share in the joint estate if it had already been ascertained that no more harm could be done thereby to the agnates.[6] The Hindu Succession Act, by contrast, aims to equate the inheritance-rights of males and females, and the latter are entitled to claim their shares unless, in a few cases, they have remarried prior to the opening of the succession. The widow's vested rights in the joint family estate were first created in 1937.[7] Until that date the rights of a female to inherit had been the subject of a prolonged and obstinate struggle; she obtained the right to inherit from the Sanskrit jurists long after she had obtained the right to own property, but the latter had been accorded to her the more readily for the known obstacles to her attaining the former.

[1] Viśvarūpa (on Yājñ., ii, 139, p. 241) does not allow a non-pregnant widow to inherit, but if a daughter is born she may hold the property in trust for the daughter. That *niyoga* alone qualified the non-pregnant widow was the view of King Bhoja, *alias* Dhāreśvara, whose opinion is immortalized in the *Mitākṣarā* (Colebrooke's trans., II, i, 8).

[2] An artifice of Devaṇṇa-bhaṭṭa in the *Smṛti-candrikā* (pp. 290–1). As an Āndhra or Tamilian he knew perfectly well that most marriages in his part of India were celebrated in the Āsura, an unapproved form.

[3] The view of a certain Udayakara commenting upon Manu, and referred to in the *Vivāda-ratnākara* (p. 590) and the *Vivāda-cintāmaṇi* (p. 237; *Dh.k.*, 1514*b*). The reference in the latter text is obscured by the translation of Gangānāth Jhā, Baroda, 1942, at p. 267, whereas the old translation of P. C. Tagore (Madras, 1865, p. 290) faithfully preserves it. Steele reports a custom in the Deccan tending to confirm such a practice, and there is an inscription in Mysore, one amongst many *satī*-stones in the north-west of the State, relating that despite the repeated deprecations of her relations the lady commemorated burnt herself on her husband's pyre, *having first distributed all the property* (evidently her husband's estate).

[4] *Sarasvatī-vilāsa*, sections 512–5 (Foulkes' edn.).

[5] This was the view of Śrīkara and others, refuted in the *Mitākṣarā*, II, i, 31.

[6] II, i, 39.

[7] The Hindu Women's Rights to Property Act, 1937, repealed by Act XXX of 1956.

While the process was in motion Kauṭilya, who is generally believed to have written during the fourth century B.C., wrote [1] :—

vṛttir ābandhyaṃ vā strī-dhanam | para-dvisāhasrā sthāpyā vṛttiḥ | ābandhyāniyamaḥ | |

" 'Females' property' consists either of their maintenance or their ornaments. Maintenance should be fixed at not more than 2,000. Ornaments are not subject to restriction."

Kātyāyana, author of a *smṛti* greatly respected for its detailed practical provisions, living perhaps two centuries later than Kauṭilya, says [2] :— *

pitṛ-mātṛ-pati-bhrātṛ-jñātibhiḥ strī-dhanaṃ striyai |
yathā-śaktyā dvi-sāhasrād dātavyaṃ sthāvarād ṛte | |

" 'Females' property' should be given to a woman by her father, mother, husband, brothers and kindred according to their ability, within 2,000 ; this is over and above landed property."

The proviso contained in the last words was differently interpreted by old writers hostile to the widow's claim to succession in particular and to the ownership of landed property by females in general. The words *sthāvarād ṛte* to them could mean nothing but " to the total exclusion of immovables ". But since " 2,000 " can only refer to coins the other translation is more logical.

Vyāsa, whose age is not more certain than Kātyāyana's, but who is not probably older than the first century B.C., says [3] :—

dvi-sāhasra-paro dāyaḥ striyai deyo mṛtasya tu |
yac=ca bhartrā dhanaṃ dattaṃ sā yathā-kāmam āpnuyāt | |

" But the inheritance of a dead man to be given to a woman is limited to 2,000 ; and whatever property was given to her by her husband she may retain at her pleasure."

[1] Trivandrum edition, ii, p. 14 ; *Dh.k.*, 1430*a*. MM. Gaṇapati Śāstrī understood the word *para-dvisāhasrā* as *kārṣāpaṇa-sahasra-dvaya-paramāvadhiḥ*, that is to say, " having as its upper limit 2,000 *kārṣāpaṇas*." As we shall see the insertion of the coin chosen is wrong, although the *Smṛti-candrikā* and *Nṛsiṃha-prasāda* provide precedents (*Dh.k.*, 1454*b*), but the interpretation of the compound is correct. Dr. Shāmashāstry in his trans., Mysore, 1929, p. 172, wrongly says, " above two thousand." Since the king is advised as to what amount ought to be given to women the limit must be a maximum and not a minimum, as the reference to ornaments shows. *

[2] Kane's edn., 902 ; *Dh.k.*, 1454*b*. The *Smṛti-candrikā* reads *dvi-sāhasram*, implying that the full 2,000 ought to be given, and not more.

[3] As Colebrooke notes on Jīmūtavāhana, *Dāyabhāga*, trans., IV, i, 10, this text is variously read. See below *re* Lakṣmīdhara's reading, and the citations given in *Dh.k.*, 1460*a*. *dvi-śāhasra-paro* could mean, " more than 2,000," and doubtless was adopted by many jurists with that object in mind.

The *Mahābhārata*, in a passage which may be no earlier than Vyāsa the law-giver, says [1] :—

* *dvi-sahasra-paro dāyaḥ striyai deyo dhanasya vai* |
bhartrā tac=ca dhanaṃ dattaṃ yathārhaṃ bhoktum arhati | |

" Out of the property an inheritance extending to 2,000 should be given to a woman, and whatever property was given by the husband she is entitled to enjoy according to propriety."

No one will question the eminence of Lakṣmīdhara as a jurist. He flourished in northern India about A.D. 1050. In his Digest the text of Vyāsa appears in a form very closely resembling that printed above, but reading *dvi-sahasrapaṇo dāyaḥ*, thus making it plain (it would otherwise have remained ambiguous) that the inheritance is not to exceed 2,000 *paṇas*.[2] *Paṇas* of copper, silver, and even gold are heard of, but the *smṛtis* are almost certainly referring to a copper *paṇa*.

But what is the purport of these 2,000 *paṇas* ? Figures are rare enough, as also fractions, in the science of jurisprudence as developed in India, and wherever they occur we have reason to suppose that they were chosen deliberately. But what motives could have induced the jurists to be so precise in this isolated and extremely important instance ? The *smṛti*-texts set out above appear in very respectable commentaries and digests, being treated seriously, besides the works cited above, in the *Vyavahāra-nirṇaya*,[3] the *Smṛti-candrikā*,[4] the *Parāśara-mādhavīya*,[5] the *Vivāda-ratnākara*,[6] the *Vivāda-candra*,[7] the *Sarasvatī-vilāsa*,[8] the *Madana-ratna-pradīpa*,[9] and the *Vyavahāra-mayūkha*.[10] While Vijñāneśvara does not think fit to cite any of them in his *Mitākṣarā*, his contemporaries Jīmūtavāhana [11] and

[1] The connection of this text with Vyāsa's is evident, but as yet unexplained. As Colebrooke notes, *ubi cit.*, many manuscripts read *tri-*, that is to say, " 3,000."
* The *Dh.k.*, 1429*b*, prints the text so (xiii, 47, 23), but when the *BORI* Critical Edition of the *Anuśāsana-parva* appears we may confidently expect to find the reading *dvi-* well represented.

[2] *Kṛtya-kalpataru, Vyavahāra-kāṇḍa*, Baroda, 1953, 684.

[3] At p. 450.

[4] At p. 281.

[5] At III, 548–9.

[6] At p. 510.

[7] At p. 82 ; *Dh.k.*, 1521*a*.

[8] At p. 377 ; section 523.

[9] At p. 376.

[10] At p. 154 of Kane's edn.

[11] *Dāyabhāga*, text (Calcutta, 1930), 117, trans., IV, i, 10.

Aparārka [1] cite Vyāsa ; so does the *Vivāda-tāṇḍava*,[2] a work only a little less important than the *Mayūkha*, which was written by the author's nephew. Amongst the galaxy of southern works it is not surprising to find the late *Vyavahārārtha-samuccaya* [3] also citing Vyāsa. The *Nṛsimha-prasāda* [4] and its much more distinguished successors the *Vīramitrodaya* [5] and the eighteenth-century *Bālambhaṭṭīya* [6] are alike in citing Kātyāyana. And to close this impressive list the very eminent Jagannātha Tarkapañcānana [7] gives us a discussion of the meaning of Vyāsa, himself approving the interpretation of the ancient digest, the *Prakāśa*, now lost. Some of these authors [8] take the view that the limit of 2,000 applies only to gifts made in any one year ! Plainly a fall in the value of money would make 2,000 copper *paṇas* insufficient for the lifetime's needs of a young widow who remained faithful to her deceased husband, and the position would be little better in the case of a female member of a rich family even if the *paṇa* were a silver *paṇa*. Writers hostile to the widow's alleged right of succession went the other way, and took the word *dvi-sāhasra* to mean "2 in every 1,000". We shall not be surprised to find these conflicting "interpretations" being employed, but what astonishes us is that not one of the authors, from the *smṛti*-writers onwards, condescends to tell us why 2,000 is the figure chosen.

In the face of this unbroken silence even an ingenious solution cannot be accepted as conclusive ; and until a new and more enlightening text is published we can proceed only upon hypothesis. But fortunately a hint is to be found, and the source of the intriguing figure can be surmised. The *Smṛti-candrikā* quotes a text of Nārada [9] to the effect that a virtuous widow is entitled to be allowed for her maintenance, out of the property in which her husband had an

[1] On Yājñ, ii, 143 ; *Dh.k.*, 1460. *

[2] At pp. 439–40.

[3] A digest made in the time of Rāja Śarabhojī of Tanjore (*circa* A.D. 1820).

[4] At p. 237 of the P. W. Saras. Bhav. Series edn. of 1934.

[5] At p. 544.

[6] At p. 731 of the Chowkāmbā Sanskrit Series edn. of 1914.

[7] *A Digest of Hindu Law . . . translated by H. T. Colebrooke* . . ., London, 1801, iii, 583 ; Madras, 1865, ii, 600–1 = V, ix, text 482.

[8] For example Mādhava, Madanasiṃha, and Nīlakaṇṭha. *

[9] At p. 293. For the text see *Dh.k.*, 1402*a*, where the variant reading, "34," is shown. Devaṇṇa-bhaṭṭa says that *paṇa* means *kārṣāpaṇa* ; that may have satisfied his contemporaries, but to us it is merely misleading.

interest, twenty-four *āḍhakas*[1] of grain plus forty *paṇas* per annum. It is well known that the needs of any person connected directly or even indirectly with agriculture could be met by an allowance in grain, which served not only to feed the recipient but also as a means of exchange for services upon a wide scale. But certain services or commodities cannot be paid for even to-day otherwise than in coin, and thus a small allowance of cash is essential, where the family concerned normally comes by such a thing. The *smṛti*-writer Viṣṇu, quoted in the *Sarasvatī-vilāsa*,[2] goes further, and throws some light on our difficulty. He says: "Year by year 40 *paṇas* and 24 *āḍhakas*; or else 100 *kārṣāpaṇas* as long as she lives; or one-half of this." Viṣṇu seems to be improving upon Nārada. His 100 *kārṣāpaṇas* as an alternative are plainly a commutation for the yearly allowance in grain and coin, and it appears that it is intended to serve as an entire quittance for the family paying it. A widow entitled to be maintained but unwilling to remain in her father-in-law's or her brother-in-law's house might claim her future maintenance as a lump sum. Her grain allowance could not practicably be anticipated, and her food might come either from her own father's family, or from the landed property, if any, of which Kātyāyana speaks. But the cash might be obtained in a lump sum. A yearly allowance of 40 *paṇas* was thought to be practicable as a maximum. How this figure was arrived at remains a mystery.

[1] L. D. Barnett, *Antiquities of India*, 1913, 208, gives several equations showing the weight of an *āḍhaka*, but certainty has yet to be achieved, due to the variety of standards. S. K. Maity, *The economic life of Northern India in the Gupta Period*, Calcutta, 1957, at p. 39 deals carefully with the *āḍhaka* and finds it equivalent to about 16 seers (of rice). Manu (vii, 126 recommends or prescribes just twice this allowance of grain to a working man.

[2] Section 527; *Dh.k.*, 1428*a*. One must record, in all fairness, that the *Sarasvatī-vilāsa* cites Viṣṇu and indeed other *smṛti*-writers quite frequently in cases where no other writer cites them and for opinions which do not always harmonize readily with the views of the same authorities in their recognized and frequently-cited texts. This has led to a suspicion that the compiler manufactured texts and attributed them to known authors of *smṛtis*. Puzzling as the problem is, it is unlikely that this is the solution, since (i) such frauds were relatively easily detected and detection meant the literary death of the work, which was already dangerously long for its hopes of survival; (ii) the names of *smṛti*-writers whose works did *not* then survive in entirety would have been chosen; and (iii) the forger would not have fabricated texts containing rules the meaning of which was ambiguous and required explanation and, as happens in several instances, the comparison of the views of other commentators thereon. It seems that better, if less simple, explanations must be found. See "*Kuttā*: A class of land-tenures in South India," *BSOAS.*, xxi, 1958, 61, and seqq. at 69.

If there were 16 *paṇas* to the *kārṣāpaṇa*, 100 *kārṣāpaṇas* is a sum based upon an actuarial assessment of a widow's probable life: forty years. But Nārada tells us [1] that in the east a *kārṣāpaṇa* was worth 20 *paṇas*. 2,000 *paṇas* is more generous in an age when girls might be widowed at 12, and assumes (i) that the widow can always claim as if she were likely to live for fifty years; and (ii) that if she anticipates living longer it is up to her to invest her capital profitably, while if she lives a shorter period the loss falls on the family which has encouraged or forced her to leave their roof. Naturally a "half", that is to say, proportionately less, will be allowable where the standard of living is lower. Grants in lieu of maintenance have always been regular, and it is not the practice to question a widow as to her method of disposing of hers. The Courts have always considered themselves capable of assessing the rate at which a female should be maintained, and there is nothing in the least incongruous in fixing a figure at which these pious and social duties should be met. Whether the above references solve our present problem or not, it is clear that similar work to that done in the past will continue to be done, if in a more complex manner, when the Hindu Adoptions and Maintenance Act, 1956, is put into operation, and the manner in which dependants are to be maintained out of intestate and even testate estates comes to be worked out in practice.

[1] Barnett, op. cit., 207: so *Nārada-smṛti*, xxi, 57, as published by Jolly. However, as *Dh.k.* shows, 532*a*, the majority of the sources read *ṣoḍaśaiva*, "16." Viṣṇu's own description of a *kārṣāpaṇa* is not particularly helpful, but he understood it to be a copper coin: iv, 13: *Dh.k.*, 526. The reading "20", if it is genuine, is evidently very much older than the proportion 16 : 1 which appears to be almost universal in later text-books. But the equation 20 *māṣas* = 1 *paṇa* which is found in Nārada and other *smṛtis* (*Dh.k.*, 532–3) would seem to throw additional doubt upon this otherwise helpful reading; particularly since, to make confusion worse confounded, Kātyāyana says that a *kārṣāpaṇa* contains 20 *māṣas* (*Dh.k.*, 533—note variant readings). However, if we are to assume, as Kātyāyana's words very strongly suggest, that he understands *māṣa* here not as a subdivision of the *paṇa*, but a variant of it (he says the *kākiṇī* is a fourth part of a *māṣa* and of a *paṇa*), his text is even more helpful to us than Nārada's, and he appears to be supported by a text of Uśanas cited by Haradatta on Gautama (see Kane's edn. of Kātyāyana, 493, p. 213, and note thereon). Maity, op. cit., 171, accepts the equation of 20 *māṣa/paṇa* = 1 *kārṣāpaṇa*, and on p. 172 comments, "It . . . seems that the Smṛiti writers are not thinking in terms of coinage, but rather of goldsmith's weights." He is relating the texts to Gupta coins.

ADDITIONAL ANNOTATIONS

p. [221], l. 8. These texts are discussed at *Muthukaruppa* v. *Shellathammal* (1914) 39 Mad. 298, 303 (they are directory, not mandatory). The judgment in the case is of interest as to the purpose and status of texts (see extract at H. S. Gour, *Hindu Code*[4], Nag., 1938, 49 n.).

p. [221], n. 1, l. 7. The text is Kauṭ. III.2.14-15 (R. P. Kangle's crit. edn., 99). Kangle translates, 'maintenance is an endowment of a maximum of two thousand (*paṇas*); as to ornaments, there is no limit'. S. *The Kauṭilīya Arthaśāstra Part II* (Bombay, 1963), 228. He says, ibid., n., that *sthāpyā* is a noun, another name for *vṛtti*; improbable at first sight, this is supported by the usage at III.2.19, 3.12 (which he cites). My trans. must thus be amended. It comes to the same thing : a 'fund' has to be fixed.

p. [222], l. 3 and n. 1. It is very extraordinary that the MBh, crit. edn., 1966, p. 285, gives not a single instance of a Ms. reading *dvi-*. The author of the MBh. thus deliberately *revised* the *smṛti* rule. The 'unidentified' comm. (see p. 1075) clearly takes the limit as directory: and it should be allotted to her *over and above* the needs of religion and the maintenance of the household.

p. [223], n. 1. Haradatta cited our Vyāsa twice.

p. [223], n. 8. Add Aparārka (Jolly, *T.L.L. 1883*, 251).

p. [224], n. 2. See below p. [280].

SURETYSHIP IN INDIA :
THE CLASSICAL LAW AND ITS AFTERMATH

I. The Background of the Study

Suretyship is one of the neat, precise, concrete topics of *dharmaśāstra* which enables us to compare the juridical achievement, as well as the legal history, of Indian law with its coevals of Judaism and Rome. The system under discussion is the classical system, which pervaded scholarly juridical discussions throughout India from the centuries immediately preceding the commencement of our era until the enactment of the Anglo-Indian codes in British India, or the introduction of the Civil Law by the Portuguese, Dutch, and French rulers in their territories. The institution of suretyship, superseded as to land revenue matters already in the early 19th century, became obsolete as to the majority of commercial and juridical matters with the enactment of the Indian Contract Act in 1872 (see Act IX of 1872, ch. VIII). But in practice the English notions of suretyship, not without some apprehension of civil-law notions [1], were already extruding the native Hindu rules and also the Islamic rules in use between Muslims as early as the beginning of the century in the Company's courts in the

---

[1] See ch. 34 of George Bowyer's *Commentary on the Modern Civil Law* (London, 1848) written for, and used in, India.

mufassil (i.e. the country apart from the Presidency Towns). In the Supreme Courts, which were royal courts functioning under the King's charter [2], the native laws of contract were specifically reserved [3], and the Hindu law of suretyship would certainly be enforced until the enactment of the statute referred to above [4]; but those Courts had jurisdiction in a limited class of cases, chiefly those arising between inhabitants of those Presidency Towns (Calcutta, Madras, Bombay). A curious remnant of the Hindu law of suretyship, not recognised for what it is, does indeed survive in the topic called the Pious Obligation, of which a sufficient account will be given below. There is every prospect that this will survive for some time to come, since the codification of the law relating to the Hindu joint family in India is as yet only a project.

Sources of information on this system are in practice (with the exception of the document given in paraphrase in the Appendix below) nearly limited to the *dharmaśāstra* texts and a few modern discussions of them. Mahamahopadhyaya Dr. P.V. Kane devotes pp. 435-8 of vol. III of the *History of Dharmaśāstra* (Poona, 1946) to the subject of suretyship, and the topic recurs in two other places to which we refer in due course. N.C. Sen-Gupta in his *Evolution of Ancient Indian Law* (London/Calcutta, 1953) mentions the subject very briefly (at p. 238). There is a long and competent chapter on suretyship in Dr. Ludwik Sternbach's *Juridical Studies in Ancient Indian Law*, Pt. I (1965), ch. 5. G. Mazzarella's studies began in 1903 and culminated in the massive *Etnologia Analitica*

---

2 See *Garabandho* v. *Parlakimedi* (1943) L.R. 70 I.A. 129.

3 The Act of Settlement, sometimes called « Burke's Act », 1781, 21 Geo. III, c. 70, s. 17; Government of India Act, 1915, 5 & 6 Geo. V, c. 61, s. 112. *Jacob* v. *Jacob* 1944 2 Cal. 201. Sir George Rankin, *Background to Indian Law* (Cambridge, 1946), 8, 9 ff.

4 Sir Thomas Strange, *Hindu Law ... in the King's Courts*, I (London, 1830), ch. 12. T.L. Strange, *Manual of Hindu Law*[2] (Madras, 1863), ch. 14. Derrett (op. cit. n. 5* inf.), 264.

dello Antico Diritto Indiano, which (though neglected) merits attention for its comparative ethnological value [4*]. But the major ancient authorities on the subject are cited by Sternbach, to whose views many references will be found below. The original *smṛitis*, that is to say the verse, or verse and prose maxims or oracles setting out the fundamental rules, are collected for the most part in Gaṅgānātha Jhā's *Hindu Law in its Sources*, I (Allahabad, 1930), pp. 177-189. He gives references to the places where the *smṛitis* are to be found when, as is frequently the case, they are located only in digests and commentaries, and some notes of the deviations from and explanations of the *smṛitis* in those medieval works. As a short introduction to suretyship, free from comparative 'contamination', Jhā is very useful. In a somewhat similar manner Jhā's translation of the *Vivāda-cintāmaṇi* of Vācaspati-miśra contains a section relating to suretyship, pp. 22-25, in which material is brought from other sources to throw light on the text. The digest entitled *Dharma-kośa*, published by Lakshman-śāstrī Joshī, contains the *smṛitis* and extracts from commentaries at length, at pp. 661-667 (*Vyavahāra-kāṇḍa*, vol. I, pt. 2, publ. Wai, 1938) — this is a most authoritative compilation, enabling the reader of Sanskrit to see at a glance the contributions of the respective jurists. The somewhat dépassé section in Priyanath Sen's *General Principles of Hindu Jurisprudence* (Calcutta, 1918 — the work was compiled in 1909), pp. 320-4, still contains in simple terms the gist of the subject.

Suretyship (in Skt. *prātibhāvyam*) is an institution which is as old as Hindu law. It is mentioned in the ancient *smṛitis*, amongst whom we may count Gautama and Hārīta, appears in full in the later *smṛitis* amongst whom must (for this purpose) be placed Manu, Yājñavalkya, Nārada, Bṛihaspati, Kātyāyana, and is dealt

[4*] See « Il prestito nell'India antica », Rev. it. di Sociologia 7 (1903), 47 pp. *E.A.A.D.I.* (Catania), esp. V (1927) 67-68; VIII (1932) 111; XI (1935) 148; XIV (1937) 361.

with also in *smṛitis* whose authenticity is uncertain and are in any case very late, such as Vyāsa. It is referred to in Kauṭilya's (or Kauṭalya's) *Arthaśāstra*, where there appear some puzzling phrases, and there cannot be any doubt but that *prātibhāvyam* was known much as it appears in our texts from circa 500 B.C. It has been mentioned already up to how recent a period the institution has maintained life and validity. The word *pratibhū*, 'surety', is evidently an ancient word (resembling *punarbhū*, the remarried woman) and probably refers to the surety's being in some non-juridical and popular sense a deputy or substitute for the original debtor. The word occurs in contexts other than the securing of a debt [5]. He has another ancient name, *lagnaka*, which seems to refer to the surety's 'following closely after' the original debtor, as if 'backing him up', supporting and clinging fast to him. These vague semantic indications may have a legal historical value. And another testimony to age is the presence in this context of words having a strictly applied meaning, a small technical vocabulary.

Before we commence to review the topics undertaken for comparative study special, individual mention must be made of the material upon the subject of suretyship in Jagannātha Tarkapañcānana's *Vivāda-bhaṅgārṇava*, which has been (on the whole) adequately translated by H.T. Colebrooke in his *Digest of Hindu Law on Contracts and Successions*... (citations below are from the Madras, two-volume, 1864-5, edition). Sureties are treated in ch. IV of Book I (pp. 159 and ff.), and the treatment is ample and sufficient. A lawyer of the 1850 period would certainly have been content to refer to this chapter, and to treat it as absolutely authoritative for the administration of Hindu law on the subject to Hindu litigants. There is no doubt that it would have been considered superflu-

[5] *Lekhapaddhati* (see Appendix below), p. 10 : 'guarantor', i.e. mediator of a royal grant. The three there provided for were to see to the carrying out of the conditions of the grant. The glossary to the *Dh.K.*, *Vyavahārakāṇḍa* (s.v.) does not give this or any other meaning. For other meanings of *avastha* see n. 19 below.

ous to refer to the original *smṛitis* upon which Jagannātha founded his work and which he cites and explains. However, we have discovered that Jagannātha was questioned and almost certainly advised to some extent by a common lawyer (perhaps by Sir William Jones himself or some attorney-at-law practising in Calcutta), and the work reflects a certain influence of European approaches if not also European legal ideas. There is no reason for excluding the possibility that in this chapter as in others Jagannātha was tempted to arrange his material in a manner not characteristic of his predecessors. Thus his very commencing with the question, who may be accepted as a surety, reflects a non-traditional arrangement. The *Śukranīti*, a work of the first half of the 19th century, is much cited by Sternbach, but its usefulness is even more questionable than Jagannātha's [5*]. After this word of warning we may safely proceed to our topics.

II. History of the Institution

We have seen that suretyship is of great age. The *smṛitis* contain phrases the exact meaning of which is open to debate, and consequently the commentators take advantage of this to amplify or contract the law at their discretion (a usual phenomenon); but it is to be noticed that no fundamental changes of importance in the law relating to suretyship are to be observed throughout the two millennia of its observed history. The present writer (unlike Sternbach or Mazzarella) cannot detect signs of evolution. Hence the creative work must have been done long before the Christian era.

The definition of suretyship given by Vijñāneśvara (c. 1125) in his commentary on the *Yājñavalkya-smṛiti* is this :
prātibhāvyaṃ nāma viśvāsārthaṃ puruṣāntareṇa saha samayaḥ. This can be translated, « The word 'suretyship' means the contract or agreement with a third party which has as its object (or 'for

[5*] Derrett, *Religion, Law and the State in India* (London, 1968), 169 n., 247-248.

the purpose of') confidence (in the second party)». Sternbach is not satisfied with this [6], and says, «This definition is not detailed enough. From the point of view of ancient Indian law, the contract of suretyship should be defined in the following manner : a contract of suretyship is a contract whereby a man binds himself to be personally answerable for the obligation of another, as an accessory debtor [7], in addition to the person principally liable ». One would not quarrel with Sternbach's definition, based as it is on a scrupulous investigation of the *smṛitis*. But one could observe, first that jurists like Vijñāneśvara were highly trained minds, and versed in logic, whence it follows that the definition is deliberate. Now it follows that the classical definition insists upon aspects which Sternbach would not necessarily see as uppermost : firstly, *prātibhāvyam* is the actual contract itself, and not an abstract notion. There is a suretyship when an agreement to answer, if necessary, for another man's obligation is still valid and binding. Secondly, Sternbach's intrusion of the word 'personally' could give rise to misunderstandings. If anything is clear it is that the surety's obligation does not necessarily die with him (as Sternbach fully explains in his article), and, moreover, the obligation attaches to the surety's property — indeed, without the liability of the surety's property (the surety, as we shall see, should be an independent, rich man) the institution of suretyship is a mockery. Next, the classical definition insists that the institution exists for the purpose of

[6] *Op. cit*, 23.

[7] Sternbach at p. 163 denies that the surety is an accessory debtor, saying that he is liable only if the principal debtor does not repay the debt. The document in our Appendix would make the sureties liable along with, or rather indistinguishably from, the principal debtor. The general law would seem to have been that the liability of a surety was conditional upon the principal's default. It will be observed from Kauṭilya's *Arthaśāstra* III, 11, 14 (Kangle, p. 113; R. Shamasastry's trans., p. 198) that co-obligors, i.e. co-debtors, and sureties are carefully distinguished. But the text goes on to read (ibid., 15) : *na prātibhāvyam anyat*, 'suretyship operates in this way only (i.e. in the absence of the debtor, his heirs, or a co-obligor)'. His further comment (ibid., 16) that a minor's suretyship is inchoate (*asāra*) is plain.

inducing *confidence* : and there can, therefore, be a suretyship in the eyes of the Hindu jurists though no definite or even envisaged obligation is in question at the time of the agreement. As we shall see, the Hindu jurist was interested in the confidence aspect rather more than in the debt aspect : though this is not to suggest that there was any defect in the agreement — evidently there was no suretyship without an explicit undertaking to indemnify the third party in case the confidence should turn out to be unjustified. And this would apply with equal force and with equal validity whether the confidence turned out to be unjustified by chance, misfortune, or fraud : what is in view may as well be speculation as normal business undertakings. The institution of suretyship existed to enable risks to be taken, and not only risks in respect of the second party's honesty and integrity [7*].

Furthermore, Sternbach, keeping close to his authorities, overlooks what they have indeed overlooked. To the Hindu jurists — unlike the Société Jean Bodin — there was not suretyship unless there was an agreement. In other words all suretyships arose out of agreement, or imputed agreement (since the word *samayaḥ* can, and certainly must here, include the village-compacts [8] with regard to payment of revenue and the like which were binding upon each generation in turn, as with our Acts of legislative assemblies, so that a son or other successor, or a newly settled immigrant, would be bound by a subsisting village-compact). Yet, as a matter of fact, suretyship by law existed, in which no element of contract or agreement arose : this was not recognised as suretyship because the liability of the male issue of a man, not separated from him, to pay his debts whether or not he left separate assets was a survival from a period when 'separate assets' had not yet achieved legal recognition, and the sons' liability was viewed as an aspect of their joint ownership with their father, and attributed to a religious obligation — which we shall investigate more closely.

[7*] Juridical analysis of *Havālā* is needed (see n. 13 inf.).

[8] Manu VIII, 219.

Ignoring, then, these suretyships by virtue of law, the *dharmaśās-tra* knows six main types of suretyship, six heads, under which all known agreements could be classified. Some *smṛitis* would contend that there are only three types [9], some more, and Sternbach would find seven types, and suggests that there are two additional instances not properly classified (about which it is possible to differ from him in interpreting the technical terms) [10]. The six heads are these :

a) (i) Suretyship for the appearance of the second party to answer charges against him, or to submit to penalty or attachment of his person, or otherwise [11].

(ii) Suretyship for the honesty of the second party, i.e. that confidence may be placed in a state of facts, e.g., his ability, reliability, and so forth [12].

---

[9] Yājñ. II, 53 (*Dh.K.* 665b, Jha, *HLS*, 177); Nārada I, 118 (*Dh.K.* 669a); Viṣṇu VI, 41 (*Dh.K.* 662a); Medhātithi on Manu VIII, 158.

[10] Op. cit., 171. *gṛhīta-bandhopasthāna* could mean « rendering up a pledge which had been taken », and would therefore be a variety of head (iv). A surety for the due payment of produce from a mortgaged field is surely another example of the same head. The surety *lekhye 'kṛte* could be a surety required where no document is executed, since without one or the other interest (according to Hārīta quoted in the Smṛti-candrikā, *Dh.K.* 608b) cannot be obtained.

[11] *darśana*, *pradarśana* (appearance, perception). Yāj. II, 53; Viṣṇu VI, 41; Nārada I, 118; Bṛh. (R. Aiyangar's ed.) X, 73; Kātyāyana (Kane's ed.), 530; Hārīta, ubi cit. Guild-courts insisted on sureties : Medhātithi on Manu VIII, 2 (Jha, IV, p. 7) (see n. 16 inf.).

[12] Sternbach, op. cit., 160. *Pratyaya* (confidence), *viśvāsa* (trust, id.). Citations as in last note. It is a desire that the principal debtor (the second party) shall be given credit. Sternbach shows, relying upon Nārada, that the surety for honesty was not liable if the debtor failed to pay through inability or ill-luck. The two types of suretyship must be distinguished. A surety for honesty does not guarantee a debt as such. Sternbach finds fault with Jagannātha for attempting (pp. 165-6) to show that a surety for honesty is liable only where his representation turns out to be false. But Jagannātha seems to be correct : a surety for confidence makes representations after all, upon the faith of which the lender lends or entrusts, etc. Hence the representation must be strictly construed. Jagannātha (to Sternbach's surprise) insists that if the surety warrants a man honest and in fact he had always been so, but he is afterwards dishonest, the surety is not liable, unless he promises that the proposed borrower shall not be dishonest for the future. For he warrants only the

(iii) Suretyship for the payment by the second party of a sum of money that will be lawfully due from him [13].

(iv) Suretyship for the restoration by the second party of objects which he will be or is due to render up, whether these be (a) his own effects, which are pledged, such as moveable property with which the second party might abscond [14], or (b) effects, such as a jewel, deposited or loaned, to the second party by the third party [15].

b) (v) Suretyship for the second party's performing all obligations that will arise out of his instituting, or defending, litigation [16], and suretyship for the second party's taking the oath or performing the ordeal which the course of litigation might impose upon him [17]. It has been sugges

---

state of affairs as these are capable of being ascertained. The exceptional understanding of the nature of a representation betrays the assistance of English law. It appears that a form of guarantee of honesty or fitness was in ancient times practised in the context of joint undertakings by villagers and others. They were authorised to insist on individuals' taking ordeals, supplying documentary proof or *madhyasthas*, literally 'umpires', 'stake-holders', before commiting themselves (Bṛhaspati, XVII, 7, ed. R. Aiy., p. 150; *Dh.K.* 873b).

13 References as in n. 11 above. It is to be understood that formulae as such had no significance at Hindu law, but the formulae frequently given by the commentators and even in one *smṛiti* in this context are reliable as showing to what the surety was agreeing. Here the formula would (according to the Mitākṣarā on Yājñ. II, 53) be « if this man does not pay then I shall certainly pay ». The implication from this is that the agreement between surety and third party precedes the agreement of loan. Yet the document in our Appendix does not confirm that this was the principle. For the modern *Havālā* see VAIDYA at 71 Bom. L.R., *J.*, 7-10 (1969).

14 Reading *ṛiṇi-dravyārpaṇa* (delivery, e.g. return, of chattels of the debtor). Bṛh. X, 73. Possibly known to Kāty. as well (Sternbach, 164-5).

15 The interpretation of Bṛh. (above) by Vācaspati-miśra, who reads, with Śūlapāṇi, *ṛiṇe dravyārpaṇe* (for debt, for delivery of the chattel). See Sternbach at para. 17, Jagannātha, p. 165. Sternbach's text here (p. 165, para. 16) should be corrected by reference to the translation of the *Vivāda-cintāmaṇi* at p. 22.

16 Yājñ. II, 10; Kāty. 530 (*Dh.K.* 673a — *vādeṣu*, in disputes). Jagannātha, 168-9. Kane, *H.D.* III, 289 n. 395, 291-2. Sternbach, 166. Kauṭilya, III, 1, 17 (Kangle, p. 97) : *avastha* is equivalent to *pratibhū* (Shamasastry's trans., 169, is defective).

17 *divya* (ordeal); *śapatha* (curse). Kāty. 530. Jagannātha, p. 169 (creditor only). Sternbach, 168.

ted [18] that to this category must belong suretyship for 'the peace', i.e. a turbulent individual may be offered an alternative between finding a surety for his good behaviour, or imprisonment, and this is an aspect of litigation [19].

c) (vi) Another, alternative view is that the classical suretyship for 'the peace' relates properly to the sphere of international law, where a hostage guarantees the performance of his obligations by a king towards another; and in principle the same institution would apply to agreements guaranteeing the good behaviour of princes, ministers, governors, and so forth [20].

These six categories of suretyship were evidently essential to the running of commercial and political life. Litigation certainly could not have developed without suretyship (including the notion of bail) to guarantee the honesty and fitness of the parties to prosecute their claims before the judge [21]. Throughout the scheme the notion is that an individual, totally independent of the second

---

[18] Kane, op. cit., p. 434 touches on this very lightly. P.N. Sen, however, op. cit., p. 321, is more sure.

[19] *abhaya* (security, safety). Hārīta, ubi cit. Yājñ. II, 209 (*Dh.K.* 1781b). In Kauṭilya III, 18, 11 (Kangle, p. 125) *avastha* appears (cf. n. 16 above). Monier-Williams' Dictionary does not show the meaning 'surety', but it is evidenced in that sense not only at III, 1, 17 (above) but also at II, 8, 29 (see Kangle's glossary). He shows *avasthā* as « guarantee » and *avasthāpanā* as « giving a surety ». Shamasastry (trans. p. 219) translated *avastha* « security » which is not impossible, and T. Gaṇapati Śāstrī (II, p. 105) glossed the word *pratibhū*. Sternbach's interpretation (p. 170) that surety is needed after the wrongdoer is sentenced to a fine seems unnecessary. At Kauṭ. II, 8, 29 *avastha* seems to mean less « surety » (as Kangle would have it) than « one who assures, certifies » concerning an event (he may have been obliged to supply a deposit in evidence of his good faith).

[20] There is a thorough discussion at Kauṭilya VII, 17. The word *pratibhū* here signifies « hostage » in the sense of deputy for the contracting party. Not in every case would suretyship, properly so called, arise.

[21] The judicial system was peculiar in that the defeated party often had to pay a fine as well as the disputed sum (Kane, op. cit., 294), and often to lose his wager as well (ibid., 263). The successful litigant paid a court-fee. The surety could therefore play an integral role.

party and the third party, and of ample financial means, supports as accessory the undertakings of the second party. The only other suretyships known, namely that of villagers for each other in respect of payment of revenue, and of the male issue to pay the debts of their ancestor, escaped notice as distinct types of suretyship, the first because it was, after all, only a variant of (iii) above, the second because it lacked the common ingredient of all 'true' types of suretyship.

It is not surprising that the ancient authors were content, for the most part, to summarise all suretyships under *three* or at the most four heads [22], namely appearance, honesty, and payment (and delivery), and taking the latter in a rather wide sense it is practical so to understand the scheme; and so it is understood to this day in the Anglo-Hindu law relating to the sons' liability to pay their father's suretyship debts (see below) [23].

III. Fundamental characteristics of suretyship

The surety could undertake either a general responsibility, such as in the case of suretyship (ii), which might involve him in great expense if the second party robbed his employer (for example), or a specific responsibility, as in the case of suretyship (iii), as where, for example, the second party undertook to pay a principal debt with interest to a stipulated or customary amount. The obligation of the surety was secondary to and accessory to the obligation of the second party (the debtor). This feature is preserved in the document in the Appendix, where some departures from the common Hindu law are visible. One surety could guarantee any

[22] See n. 9 above. Yājñ. (3); Bṛh. (4); Hārīta and Vyāsa (both of doubtful age and authenticity; 5). Jha, *HLS*, 177-8.

[23] *Tukarambhat* v. *Gangaram* (1898) 23 Bom. 454; *Choudhuri Govinda* v. *Hayagriba* (1930) 10 Pat. 94; *K. Lakshminarayana* v. *K. Hanumantha Rao* (1935) 58 Mad. 375. These references are to the « Indian Law Reports » series.

number of obligations or debts, and one obligation or debt could be guaranteed by any number of sureties, the latter acting as partners, or independently as co-sureties, liable jointly and severally for default of the second party. The creditor, or third party, had freedom to demand pledges and sureties, or either of these, and the terms of the original agreement between the second party and the third party might depend fundamentally upon the presence or absence of these.

Up to this point we have not discussed the relation between husband and wife and between partners. It might be asked whether the development of credit was not assisted by the availability of sureties drawn from such close associates. The answer is negative. Though the property of the wife was not available for the payment of the husband's private debts, nor vice versa (subject to an exception which cannot be discussed at length here) [24], the ancient theory of the indivisibility of husband and wife prevented spouses acting as sureties for each other. Similarly, though coparceners (co-heirs of ancestral undivided property) could rely on family debts' being paid by the managing member for the time being, whoever had contracted the debts, this was not a case of suretyship, because no debts were binding unless they were for family purposes, and the family funds could be pledged (normally by the manager only) exclusively upon that footing. Partners likewise could bind each other by proper acts within the scope of the partnership, but they, like the coparceners, could not be sureties for each other. A surety must, after all, not be joint in estate with his principal [25]. Thus co-owners or partners could very well act as sureties for other people, and indeed a partnership would make a very suitable surety, since the risks would be widely spread though only one

[24] The husband's right to appropriate his wife's *strīdhan* to pay his own debts in an emergency (Yājñ. II, 147, Kāty. 914) : Kane, op cit., 785-7. The husband's creditors had no right to attach or sell the wife's property. P.W. REGE, *The Law of Strīdhana...*, Ph.D. Thesis, London, unpubl., 1960, pp. 303-5.

[25] See the rules of Hindu law set out below at text to notes 44-6 inf.

partner might appear as surety in the agreement; but the payment of family debts or partnership debts by any co-owner or partner is not an instance of suretyship.

The fact that a surety in category (iii) would be liable *together with his sons* (*only*), so that if he died the third party could call upon his sons to make good the guarantee, strongly reinforced the value of this suretyship. Under certain conditions even sureties in categories (i), (ii), and (iv) could offer the same security; but these conditions will need to be studied in detail before the significance of this can be grasped. How suretyship could be inherited, and why it could be inherited only by the first generation of male issue, is something of a puzzle which no comparative jurist has yet solved.

IV. Suretyship and Pledge or Mortgage

We have seen that the creditor, or third party, might choose which security to use; and even in litigation the parties might (one supposes) use the pledge method rather than suretyship. It would be in the discretion of the court whether to accept one, the other, or both. On the whole the ancient society must have favoured suretyship, since it combined prestige and property, and was not tied to a particular place. If chattels were pledged the borrower often had to maintain them in the possession of *ādhipālas*, who were, as stakeholders, in a sense guarantors of the pledge, and thus an additional risk for the lender. The settled and developed society no doubt preferred the mortgage of land to any other security. But there might be occasions where mortgage might have involved difficulties or expenses for the creditor, and rights of exacting the obligation from a suitable surety might have been ample and satisfactory by comparison. It is not easy to generalise from our existing information. The document reproduced in our Appendix shows that pledges and sureties were frequently taken, yet it would seem to show that, as between pledges and sureties, the lender was under an obligation to call upon the sureties first (§ 5) and only upon their failure to pay might he sell the pledges [25*].

V. The Juridical technique of Suretyship

a) *Creation of the security*

We have seen that *prātibhāvyam* was created by an agreement, and was voluntary. The customary mutual suretyship of villagers in respect of land-revenue is very little known and it is not practical to give details here, the subject requiring close research amongst the limited and scattered sources. Here, at any rate, there must have been an implied agreement even if in fact no actual agreement could be discovered, and to this extent this class of suretyship was exceptional. The agreement normally required two parties, the surety and the third party. The second party was not a party to this agreement, though of course he benefited from it. In the Appendix we find no trace of the surety's agreement to the terms exacted by the lender from the borrower, and the proper inference is that another agreement was required between surety and lender — which the book does not exemplify [26]. The surety was bound in any case by his promise, and not by the borrower's. As is normal in classical Hindu law, no consideration was required in order to make the promise of suretyship binding upon the surety himself. Nevertheless it was plainly a common thing for sureties to undertake the responsibility of suretyship only upon an understanding, that is to say, a contract, between themselves and their second parties. In order that A should agree to guarantee C's loan to B, it was

---

[25*] Mazzarella thought suretyship applied where pledge was impossible : Riv. it. di Soc. 7 (1903), p. 29 of offprint.

[26] Jagannātha (p. 169) confirms the statement here, and suggests that sureties (in his day) usually wrote their agreements *in the margin* of the agreement of loan executed by the borrower : this should be borne in mind when noting the structure of §§ 12, 13 of the document.

common for A to exact from B a promise, not of reimbursement should A be obliged to repay the loan to C — for this is an aspect of the relationship between A and B which was implied by the law itself and required (as we shall see) no stipulation — but a promise of payment for his services, for his taking the risk. Thus in ancient India we already had an institution of suretyship for reward : some called it a 'black' (reprehensible) means of earning [26*]. This was [27] similar to our indemnity-insurance policies, in which, for a reward, insurers undertake to guarantee loans or to indemnify against risks. Furthermore, the surety might undertake to guarantee the loan only after B had consigned to him, or hypothecated to him, a valuable piece of property [28] which C himself refused to accept as security, or was unable to accept as security. In other words, the right of reimbursement, implied by law, had itself to be secured, at the surety's option. We have reason to believe that by depositing wealth to secure a person's suretyship was one of the well-known ways of losing one's capital [29].

In the cases where the surety has given his undertaking to the

---

26* Nārada explained by Medh. on Manu IV, 226 (Jha, II p. 477).

27 So I understand Manu VIII, 161-2 (see n. 71 below). Sternbach, 194. Hindu jurists (e.g. Jagannātha, pp. 175-6) were keen to show that the consideration must not have been given to the surety as a gift; i.e. a deposit (probably *not* a pledge) would serve. But reward is certainly not excluded, and a survey of the texts, which are reticent, suggests that proposed sureties used to take pledges, on the understanding that if the debtor paid the debt, so that his surety was not called upon, the pledge would be returned upon payment by the debtor of the surety's expenses. In earlier times these would doubtless have been little, but when suretyship became a business and risk was involved in guaranteeing loans by relatively unknown people it is quite likely that a fee was charged in all cases, for which the existing *smṛiti* law would make provision without the invention of new provisions.

28 Kāty. 534; Mitākṣarā on Yājñ. II, 54; Jagannātha, p. 174. Sternbach, 193.

29 The family deposit or charge wealth to secure the honesty of a member. The deposit is not returned or the charge released during all the years he is employed, the occasion for the transfer is forgotten and the surety and his successors become owners : such is to be inferred from Medhātithi on Manu VII, 83 (Jha's trans., *ubi cit.*, p. 331 is not precise).

third party after receiving (a) a payment, or (b) a pledge, or the equivalent, the contract of suretyship was strengthened by the fact that the son of the surety would make good his undertaking after his disappearance or death [30]. These are the exceptions to the rule that only sureties in category (iii) are represented by their sons [31]. It follows as a matter of course that third parties greatly preferred sureties who acted for reward (a natural result of professional skill and mercantile enterprise) or accepted a security of their own. It is possible, therefore, that although on the surface mortages of immoveable property might be a better security than a surety, insistence on the second party's providing a surety of

[30] See last note. The general rule, given in Gautama XII, 41 was that sons were *not* liable for suretyship debts. This was later construed to mean debts for suretyship for appearance and honesty. Haradatta (Poona ed., p. 97, *śloka* 38) cites Manu, Yājñavalkya and Viṣṇu to this effect. Kauṭilya III, 16, 9, (Kangle, 122) exempts sons, etc., from payment of suretyship debts. See next note. Another reading of K.'s text would exempt from payment of *fines* incurred through suretyship — which fits the *smṛiti* law more closely. Kauṭ. III, 11, 18 is translated differently by Shamasastry, J.J. Meyer and Sternbach (p. 189, n. 60). Son and grandson *are* liable for debts (i.e. suretyship debts, *vide* context) provided these are unlimited as to country and time (cf. our Appendix, para. 3) (ibid. 17); if one makes the small alteration of reading — *pratibhāvyaṃ saṃkhyāta* — the sense is exact : — they are liable for limited suretyship (in point of country and time) provided it be suretyship for a livelihood (i.e. « honesty »), a marriage (or betrothal) or landed property (to be mortgaged or sold, etc.). Kangle (trans. 263) would exclude liability for *debt*, but not financial liability.

[31] Who pay capital, *not* interest (with the possible exception of sons of co-sureties — a very confused topic). Sternbach, § 39. S., p. 186, sees an historical progression in the texts, the earliest (Gautama, Vasiṣṭha and Kauṭilya — though the latter be an *arthaśāstra* writer) absolving the son from all liability, the middle (Manu, Yājñ., Viṣṇu, Bṛhaspati, Kāty.) holding him liable for sureties for payment or delivery of assets, the latest (Vyāsa) holding him liable for all suretyship debts. Since the meanings of the texts are not beyond doubt and the priority in age is far from established this interesting theory (see Sternbach's *Jur. St. in Ancient Indian Law*, I, pp. 508-529) cannot as yet be regarded as more than plausible. The late Rangaswami Aiyangar disagreed with those who sought to see progression in the greater detail in *smṛiti* texts, or their deviations from each other. S. believes, for example, that some jurists « thoughtlessly copied » their predecessors, which is a large assumption.

the type who acted only after receiving a pledge or hypothecation might give the third party the best of both worlds. There is evidence that in such cases the lender might charge a higher rate of interest lawfully than could be allowed in conscience if he had taken the pledge himself [32]. *Volunteer* sureties could even be fraudulent [32*].

The special case of the male issue who must pay their father's debts other than suretyship debts (subject to reservations to be discussed below) has been noticed already. Their agreement was not necessary for their obligation to arise. It was supposed that the religious duty to secure the deceased ancestor from the pains of hell was inherent in sonship [33]. Originally the son was liable whether he were separate from his father at the time of the latter's death or not, but only if he were above the age of majority. Originally the son was liable for all the debt, with interest; the grandson without interest; and the great-grandson likewise only if some property of the great-grandfather (however small) actually reached his hands [34]. The unlimited liability of sons remained in Bombay Presidency until the last century, when it was abolished by statute [35]. Elsewhere it was felt, under British administration, that sons' obligations should be confined to the properties they received from their ancestor; that the obligation did not arise for the first time on the ancestor's death [36]; and that there was no

[32] Jagannātha, p. 174.

[32*] Medhātithi on Manu VIII, 165 (Jha, IV p. 216).

[33] Kane, *op. cit.*, 442-443. Derrett at Z.SAV.St. (rom. ab.) 86 (1969).

[34] Mitākṣarā on Yājñ. II, 51, Smṛiti-candrikā (Mysore edn., III, pt. 2, pp. 397-400); Mitra-miśra, *Vīramitrodaya*, Vyavahāra-prakāśa, p. 264; Viṣṇu VI, 27-8; Bṛh. X, 114; Kāty. 556 — all cited and discussed carefully by Kane, op. cit., 443-5.

[35] Kane, op. cit., 445. Hindu Heirs' Relief Act, Bombay Act 7 of 1866, a reaction to *Narasimhrav* v. *Antaji* 2 Bom. H.C.R. 61.

[36] See the fifth proposition in *Brij Narain* v. *Mangla Prasad* (1924) 51 I.A. 129; Kane, op. cit., 450. This has hardly any śāstric justification : Nārada IV, 14; Viṣṇu VI, 27; Kāty. 548-50 only contemplate payment by the sons when the creditor's hopes of realising the debt from the living father have been dim, as, for example, 20 years after the father's disappearance, or when the father has become blind or an outcaste. Mysore State until 1954 did not recognise the Pious Obligation while the father was alive : *Hutcha Thimmegowda* v. *Dyavamma* A.I.R. 1954 Mys. 93FB.

difference between the position of the son, the son's son, and the son's son's son [37]. So far as joint-family property was concerned the debt enabled the father during his lifetime, or the court acting in his stead, to alienate the undivided interests of the male issue to pay his debts [38], provided that the debts were antecedent to the alienation (and so already binding upon the male issue) [39]. Debts contracted by the ancestor which were not 'recognised' for this purpose by the Hindu law could not be exacted from the sons, etc., and for such purposes the interests of those male issue could not be alienated [40]. The modern formula is that the male issue are not under a Pious Obligation to pay the tainted, i.e. illegal or immoral debts of their ancestor [41]; nor are they obliged to pay untainted debts which are not antecedent, nor which were incurred posterior to the separation from the ancestor of the male issue sought to be made liable [42].

b) *Extent of the security*

The male issue referred to above had, and have, a liability which extends as far as the property available, that is to say the entire undivided interest in joint-family property may be taken to satisfy any untainted, antecedent, pre-partition, private debt of

---

37 *Masit Ullah* v. *Damodar Prasad* (1926) 53 I.A. 204, *Lachman Das* v. *Khunna Lal* (1896) 19 All. 26 — the grandson is liable for interest as well as principal (it was a mortgage of joint-family property). See also *Ladu* v. *Gobardhan* (1925) 4 Pat. 478.

38 See *Brij Narain* cited at n. 36 above.

39 Kane contends that antecedency was not known to the *śāstra* (op. cit., 450). It is suggested by the present writer that Kane failed to grasp the nature of « antecedency ». See DERRETT, *Introduction to Modern Hindu Law* (Oxford University Press, Bombay, 1963), paras. 447-9. Antecedency was accepted into Mysore State in *Hutcha* (cited at n. 36 above). *Faqir* v. *Sardarni* A.I.R. 1967 S.C. 727.

40 KANE, *op. cit.*, pp. 446-447. 'Interests' = 'undivided rights (droits)'.

41 DERRETT, *op. cit.*, paras. 507-11.

42 *Pannalal* v. *Naraini* A.I.R. 1952 S.C. 170. A partition to evade payment of binding debts incurred personally by the father, etc., is « fraudulent » and ineffective to that extent — the separated shares are proportionately liable.

the father. But the more normal categories of suretyship anticipate three types of personal obligation : (a) the unlimited, as in suretyship of category (ii); (b) the strictly limited as in categories (i), (iii), (iv) and vi); and (c), in category (v), the peculiar unlimited type of obligation which admits however of reasonable conjecture. The fines imposed and the sums to be awarded can be calculated with reasonable exactness, and the risks can be judged with fair accuracy. The surety is not liable beyond the liability of the second party.

c) *Qualifications for being surety*

We have seen that individuals on their own behalf or as representatives of a partnership might become sureties. The Hindu law of the classical period provided a long and interesting list of persons who should not be accepted as sureties by the third party. As usual with the *dharmaśāstra* the list does not distinguish between the persons who are *incompetent* to be sureties in the case under consideration, and those whom it would be *inadvisable to accept* as sureties. We can make the distinction for ourselves.

Incompetent to act as sureties are :

(i) husband for his wife, and vice versa [43];
(ii) one co-heir for another co-heir, unseparated [44];
(iii) father and a son unseparated from him [45];

though the presupposition is that the debt contracted by the second party is in respect of the property joint between himself and the proposed surety. If the second party be dealing with property

[43] Sternbach, 178-9. The early stage, when the property of spouses was joint (was there such a stage ?), explains the rule, he suggests. Authorities for the jointness of property between husband and wife are discussed at Z.V.R., 64 (1962), pp. 62-64. Yājñ. II, 54, Jha, *HLS*, 180.

[44] *Smṛitis* cited in the last note.

[45] Ibid.

which is not joint between himself and the surety the incompetence of the latter does not arise [46].

Unsuitable to be tendered as sureties are :

(i) a person who is not well-known [47];
(ii) one who is of bad character, or is already liable to pay a fine [48];
(iii) one who is a close prisoner, or is not at liberty to pursue his rights against the second party [49];
(iv) one upon whom the third party is himself dependent, as also a servant of such a one [50];
(v) one who is an enemy of the third party, or an intimate friend of the second party; or his pupil [51];
(vi) one who has abandoned the world [52];
(vii) the king, or a minister of the king [53];
(viii) one unable, or reputed to be unable [54], to pay the sum which is in issue, or who could not pay a fine of an equal amount [55].

There may be debate as to the reasons for these ancient rules, but their general good sense is evident. Two additional rules are of great interest :

(ix) one should not be accepted as surety who has a father living [56];

---

[46] Jagannātha, 161-3.

[47] Kāty. 116 (*Dh.K.* 682, Jha, 179).

[48] Ibid., 114. In the view of L. Renou (Ét. Véd. Pan. xi, 1963, 94-95) the three verses of Kāty. were inspired by a prose passage attributed to Bṛihaspati (R. Aiy., X. 79) of which R. gives a French trans.

[49] Ibid.

[50] Ibid.

[51] Ibid., 114, 115 (reading *mitraṃ* instead of *ṛikta* as Kane reads).

[52] Ibid., 115. Some understand the word (Sternbach, 176) as ‹banished›.

[53] Variant readings of Kāty. 115b are discussed by Jagannātha, 160. He says it is superfluous for the king or his minister to be a surety, for the king is by nature a universal surety, and royal servants can overawe courts and litigants and should not be accepted on that ground also.

[54] Jagannātha, 160.

[55] Kāty., 116.

[56] Ibid. Jagannātha, 161.

(x) nor should one choose him who acts 'according to his sweet will' [57].

This reinforces the basic supposition, that the surety ought to be an independent man (which a man whose father is living is in theory incapable of being), and that a reputation for responsible conduct is essential. Though the surety must be independent and thus capable of doing his duty without anyone else's consent, he must not be so independent as to have no regard for God or men, so as, for example, to disregard his obligations to the third party, or overawe the court, or otherwise bring the legal system into contempt.

The question arises, what would be the effect if the third party, or the court, accepted as a surety an insolvent, particularly a man who was in fact insolvent, but not yet so to his own knowledge. It seems that the rule *factum valet* is applicable — one should not appoint or accept such a person as a surety, but if he has been accepted his obligation exists. And the same remark seems applicable to the other nine instances of persons who are unsuitable sureties. No question arises, but that the loan of C to B is unaffected by any defect in B's surety, A [58].

Primitive legal systems must have considered the question whether a surety himself might require to be guaranteed by a sub-surety or 'counter-surety'. A story to some such effect is found in Jewish *midrashim*. But in the Hindu legal sources no idea of sub-suretyship is found. The relationship involved in suretyship appears to be exclusively triangular, and no doubt it is for this reason that in our Appendix we find sureties and pledges coupled together. But in pre-British times counter-sureties are in fact

[57] Kāty., 116. Jagannātha, 160, suggests that this means an idiot or prodigal. Kane would interpret the word *icchā-pravartaka* (the meaning of which is far from self-evident) as one who had incited the debtor (Sternbach, 176). In reconstructing the probable meanings of these *ad hoc* technical expressions one must bear in mind that the immediate context by no means supplies a conclusive indication. The words are arranged to suit metre rather than sense.

[58] So STRANGE, I, 300, quoted by the editor at Jagannātha, p. 159, f.n.

found. We are unable to draw any inference from the names being Persian in origin [59].

d) *The relationship between the surety and the creditor*

The third party can take up and enforce the obligations of the surety only when the debtor, the second party, has failed in his obligations : the document in the Appendix bears this out [60].

When the suretyship is in category (i) the surety is allowed an interval according to the terrain and circumstances in which to produce the second party [61]; if he ultimately fails he is liable to the fine or penalty which would have fallen upon the second party had he appeared and been condemned [62].

When the suretyship is in categories (iii)-(vi) the surety is obliged to pay the value in dispute [63]. He is entitled to claim time in which to find the principal debtor, if necessary [64]. In order to protect the second party from undue pressure by the surety after the latter has made payment two provisions are laid down : (i) the surety must not make payment to the third party until the latter, after failing to obtain payment or satisfaction from the second party, has recourse to the surety. It is not in order for the surety

---

[59] *Jhyntee Ram Misser* v. *Raja Mhypal Sing* (1819) 2 Macn 's S.D.A. 316 : an *arzāmini* (see H.H. Wilson, *Glossary*, s.v.).

[60] See § 5 there : the sureties are liable after (a) default of the debtor, (b) sale of the pledges, leaving an amount outstanding. See the formula at n. 13 above. In *Ochubanund Gosaen* v. *Hurindernaraen Bhoop* (1808) 1 Macn.'s S.D.A. 234 the court seem to have believed that the creditor must give notice to the borrower before claiming against the surety.

[61] Kāty. 532. See Nīlakaṇṭha-bhaṭṭa, *Vyavahāra-mayūkha* (trans. J.R. Gharpure, p. 148). That author is valuable on this topic in comparison with the majority of commentators, but he is not in all points in agreement with the majority.

[62] Kāty. 531. There is an excuse if the principal is missing due to act of God or the king.

[63] Vīramitrodaya, p. 324, Jha, 182-3, texts of Pitāmaha (a dubious authority, perhaps very late). Kāty. 533, 535, 536, Jagannātha, 170-3.

[64] Bṛh. XI, 42 (*Dh.K.* 672a, Jha, 182); Kāty. 532. Jagannātha 171.

to make payment spontaneously [65]. However, once the third party has applied to the surety, it is the latter's duty to make payment without necessitating the third party's applying distraint, or otherwise harassing him. For in the latter case (ii), should he have to suffer distraint at the hands of the third party [66], he will have a right of special recourse against the debtor, the second party.

The question may well arise whether the surety, when applied to for payment by the third party, has the right to dispute the debt alleged to be owing. The curious terms of the document in our Appendix strongly suggest that ordinarily he has [67]. Naturally, where the suretyship was for the payment of what should be due or what should turn out to be payable by the second party it would be fraudulent if the surety were not entitled to raise any objection or call for any account which the principal debtor could have insisted upon. Therefore we have evidence of a right in favour of the surety similar to subrogation [68]. It is for this reason that when the institution of pleading (in litigation) by *vakils* (attorneys) arose in the last part of the 18th century the Hindu jurists visualised the *vakils* as not merely agents but even sureties for their clients, the latter having not merely authorised them to conduct litigation on their behalf, but actually investing them with their own rights *vis-à-vis* the third party, so that a decree against the surety would be in effect a decree against them, and the *vakils* would be entitled to full reimbursement from their principals [69]. This theory, of considerable juridical interest, is evidenced, but it did not survive,

---

65 Bṛh. X, 83 (*Dh.K.* 672, Jha, 189).

66 See n. 82 below.

67 See §§ 6, 7. The conjecture is supported by Pitāmaha cited in the Smṛiticandrikā at p. 356 of the vol. cited : if the surety, on behalf of the debtor, disputes with the creditor and having done so meets with obstacles (*sopasarga*, a rare expression), he is to be fined a double amount... (cf. Jha's, *HLS*, p. 184).

68 It is curious that the texts do not give details of this right — they tend to concentrate on limiting rights of demand and rights of complaint, assuming that disputes are inevitable.

69 Jagannātha, 169, 172 (« the representative of the party who pleads his suit »).

since *vakils* operated as agents, and it is in that guise alone that legal representation exists in India, Pakistan and Burma at present.

When the suretyship is in category (ii) different considerations arise. The third party could require the surety to pay the value of any loss caused to him by the fault or default of the second party, both where the latter was dishonest or where he was incompetent [70]. Here there could often be no question of subrogation. In many cases the second party might not be under any legal obligation whatever. But the debt would arise simply out of the contract between the surety and the third party, and the surety would have a right in his own person to dispute the amount alleged to be due from him by the third party.

If the surety is missing when the third party's claim arises his sons and heirs are liable in all cases where the suretyship was undertaken for reward [71] (a rule no longer observed in the Anglo-Hindu law) [72], and the sons are liable in all cases where the suretyship was for payment. It is of interest that while the sons and grandsons of both lender and borrower figure in the agreement given in our Appendix (§ 4) the sons of the sureties do not—plainly the legal liability was sufficient. When a pledge or other security was taken by the surety himself, at *dharmaśāstra* the sons and heirs would be liable [73], but this rule also has been abandoned in Anglo-Hindu

[70] Bṛh. X, 78; Nārada I, 119 (Jha, *HLS*, 180-1). Jagannātha, 164-6. Sternbach, 159-61

[71] Kāty. 534 discussed in *Dwarka Das* (cited below). See Medhātithi on Manu VIII, 161 (Jha's trans., IV, pt. 1, 205) which, like the *Vyavahāra-mayūkha*, leaves it open to be supposed that consideration was received for suretyship. Such was understood to be the case by the very learned judge Chandavarkar, J., in *Narayan* v. *Venkatacharya* (1904) 28 Bom. 408. This may have been the field in which the doubtful text of Hārīta discussed by Sternbach at p. 193 functioned.

[72] *Sarwan* v. *Kunji Lal* A.I.R. 1951 M.B. 49, differing from dicta in *Dwarka Das* (below) at pp. 679-80, which rely upon the law as set out in the *Vyavahāra-mayūkha* V, 3, 1 (in Kane's edn. it is at p. 177; see also ibid., p. 330; Gharpure's trans., p. 149).

[73] STERNBACH, 194. Manu VIII, 162. Kāty. 534. *Dwarka Das* v. *Kishan Das* (1933) 55 All. 675.

law [74]. In the cases of suretyship for payment or delivery the sons alone are liable [75], for the rule of the Pious Obligation has most curiously not been extended to the grandsons and greatgrandsons for this class of debt. The texts expressly confine the obligation to the surety's sons [76]. The rights of the third party against these representatives would be the same if the surety had disappeared or died [77].

If there are many sureties the law depends on the agreement. If these are co-sureties, jointly and severally liable to guarantee the obligation of the second party, the creditor, the third party, may demand the entire amount from any at his choice. That surety, after payment, failing to obtain reimbursement from the second party, has no right of contribution from the other co-sureties. If however the sureties have jointly undertaken to guarantee only portions of the amount, as would happen in the case of a revenue-farmer, who might require numerous sureties in fractions, the third party is entitled to take up the obligations according to these fractions, and the sureties' rights against the second party would likewise be related to those same fractions [78]. We notice from the document in our Appendix that the borrower undertakes that the lender many recover the entire debt from any surety and that none of his sureties (the document does not contemplate less than two) may direct the lender to have recourse to others.

---

[74] See *Sarwan* (cited above). The *son* is liable to pay, out of the pledge, a suretyship debt incurred by way of suretyship *for payment* : *Dwarka Das* (above). See N.R. Raghavachariar, *Hindu Law*, 4th ed., Madras, 1960, p. 309. It is of great interest that Jagannātha, at p. 174, would convert a surety for payment of a debt contracted from a money-lender into a surety for appearance.

[75] Provided the father himself *was* personally liable : see cases cited at Derrett, *Intro. Mod. Hindu Law*, para. 506.

[76] Kāty. 561. Vyāsa in the *Smṛiti-candrikā*, p. 352 (Jha, *HLS*, 185).

[77] Sternbach, 195.

[78] See n. 85 below.

e) *The relationship between the surety and the debtor*

After the surety has paid or otherwise satisfied the third party he has a right of recourse against the second party. The Hindu law was formerly very strict here. The subject of interest on loans is complicated and it would be out of place to repeat here observations set out at length in another connection [79]. Let it suffice that after an interval of six weeks the amount paid by the surety begins to carry interest [80], and apparently (if the texts are to be interpreted literally and not as more recent Hindu jurists would wish) at a peculiar rate. After the interval, during which the absconding or defaulting second party could be apprised of the position, the capital of the debt is doubled : and even at the expiry of the seventh week the surety is entitled to realise at one time twice the amount of the debt [81]. Was this some kind of compensation?

This penal rule applies only when the third party has had to enforce payment from the surety by public process [82]. In other words, where the surety holds out in case somehow he can arrange for the second party to meet his obligations by another method, and has failed, the second party must pay dearly for his dishonesty or incompetence. The institution, which is most peculiar, is evidently intended not so much to encourage people to become sureties as to discourage borrowers from too readily utilising the facility of having a surety. The text of Hārīta penalising those who exact from a surety the extent of double or triple [83] is probably intended to prevent creditors from taking this rule as an advantage for themselves.

---

[79] For the right of recourse see Kāty. 540. Jagannātha, 181-2. For the rates of interest see Derrett in *ZVR*, 65, 2, 1963, at p. 181.

[80] Sternbach, 185. Kane, op. cit., 438.

[81] Bṛh. X, 82 (*Dh.K.* 672a, Jha, 188); So Kāty. 539. Jagannātha, 180. Sternbach, 184-5. Mazzarella divines fault of co-sureties : *E.A.A.D.I.* III, p. 89.

[82] Yājn. II, 56 (Dh.K. 670, Jha, 188). Utathya (whoever was he?) in *Smṛiticandrikā*, p. 358 (Jha, ibid.). The double amount applies only to the case where the surety applies in vain to the principal debtor.

[83] At *Vīramitrodaya*, p. 310 (Jha, *HLS*, 183).

We have already discussed the surety's right of stepping into the second party's shoes if necessary to dispute the amount claimed from him by the third party, claiming set-off, and the like.

Prior to payment the surety has no right secured to him by law, but it is evident that he is entitled to follow his second party if necessary, or to apply pressure to him, short of distraint (for he is not himself yet a creditor) in order to persuade him to answer to, or otherwise meet, his liabilities. Manu says (VII, 17) that Punishment (*Daṇḍa*) is the 'surety' of the four Stages or Orders of society, i.e. it keeps them to their duties as real sureties do not allow debtors to deviate or go astray [84].

f) *The relationship between co-sureties*

So far as this is known we have covered the topic in sec. d) above. The *dharmaśāstra* does not in so many words proceed further to explain the rights of sureties, except against the second party. This is evidently because of the custom for sureties who had no sentimental or political motive in acting as sureties to take pledges, hypothecations or mortgages of property belonging to the second party, thereby securing themselves against loss. Where one of a number of co-sureties is forced to pay the amount, he has, strangely, no right of contribution against the others [85]. Co-suretyship was,

---

[84] Medhātithi on Manu, *ubi cit.*, (Jha's trans. III, pt. 2, 1924, p. 283) : *yathā pratibhūs-calitum na dadāti.*

[85] Yājñ. II, 55; Nārada I, 20; Viṣṇu VI, 42; Jagan; 176-8. *Viv. cint.*, tr. 24; Kane, III, 437-8; Sternbach, 195ff. S. however sees this in some commentators! But the evidence does not proceed further than that if there are several joint sureties (each securing the entire debt) and the creditor does not express any preference as to whom he requires to pay the debt (e.g. if he serves a notice to pay on all of them) the sureties are liable for the debt in equal shares upon the presumption (maxim) that in default of evidence of intention the result is equality : *samaṃ syād aśrutatvāt* (an extraordinarily interesting maxim discussed by Kane, *H.D.*, V, pt. 2, pp. 1330, 1350). This view appears in the *Vīramitrodaya* and the *Smṛiticandrikā*. It is however by no means the only method of interpreting the *smṛitis*. The *Vivādārṇava-setu* (late 18th century), Halhed's trans., 1777 edn., p. 13, shows that this view was

after all, a voluntary relationship. The law did not become controversial [86]. Bṛihaspati (X.111-2) exempts the *son* of a *deceased* co-surety from all but his father's share, but the point is not debated.

g) *The extinguishing of suretyship*

Upon payment by the second party, or other compliance with his obligations, e.g. appearance on the day of his trial, etc., the obligation of the second party has ceased, but there is no automatic extinction of the obligation of the surety. True, it is not necessary that the third party should explicitly release the surety, but the obligation of the surety ceases to be enforcible — though the result in point of fact is the same. For this reason, it seems, the lender would agree that conditions which released the one would release the other — for such would be in the inference from §§ 7, 8 of the document in our Appendix. When the second party has paid there is no cause of action between the third party and the surety, since the obligation that was the subject of the guarantee has been extinguished.

---

established at that period; but several mediaeval texts take the view that liability by shares is the exception, and that when sureties independently undertake to guarantee the loan the creditor may exact the debt from any at his choice. This would seem to be the view of the *Vyavahāra-mayūkha* for example.

Where a surety for appearance supports the guarantee given by a surety for payment, the sureties are ranged in order, and are not co-sureties.

[86] Traces of an ancient debate upon the meaning of *ekacchāyāsthiteṣveṣu dhanikasya yathāruci* (Yājñ. II, 55b, in the *Bālakrīḍā*, II, 57b) appear in Viśvarūpa's commentary (Trivandrum edn., p. 221, *Dh.K.* 667), where the author denies the suggestion that the co-guarantors indicated by the words with which the line commences (words that the pronoun shows relate to the sureties in the previous line) were really co-enjoyers, or users, of the amount taken on loan. That such a misunderstanding could have occurred is to be attributed to a desire to confine the creditor's right to demand payment « at his option » to cases where the loan is taken by partners or other co-obligors; in other words the possibility, later taken for granted, of co-sureties for the whole amount being at the mercy of the creditor without benefit of contribution must have been uncongenial. But this supposition remains to be substantiated by positive evidence. Renou (ubi cit.), 98 deals with Bṛihaspati.

If the second party defaults, the suretyship is extinguished by the surety's payment. It can be extinguished, of course, like any other debt, by the release of the third party. There being neither a law of insolvency, nor a law of limitation of actions for debt, no other method of extinction is available except the death of the surety, *except* in the cases when the sons or heirs are bound to meet the obligation (see above), in which case the suretyship comes to an end when these pay the amount or die without having paid it. The death of the third party, or acts by him, will not terminate the obligation, unless the acts amount to a release, if validly given.

VI. Conclusions

One notices the relative simplicity of the Hindu law relating to suretyship, except for the portion at present surviving in the Anglo-Hindu law, where certain complications (in particular relating to the nature of the debt and the question of taint) survive. The age and the consistency of the institution speak for its efficiency.

Granted that this must be so, the question remains why was it superseded by the Indian Contract Act? Naturally the determination to supplant both Hindu and Islamic laws of contract was at the bottom of the programme put into effect in 1872. But the new rules relating to suretyship bore a close resemblance to their Hindu predecessors, except for the provision about the double payment for the defaulting second party, the original debtor. For this there is no counterpart in any Anglo-Saxon system of law. Examples of coincidence between the systems are not few. For example, the consideration for the contract of suretyship, the guarantee, passes from the third party to the second party and not to the surety himself; again, if the nature or extent of the obligation owed by the second party is varied by the third party that will terminate the liability of the surety, for he has promised only to enable the third party to have confidence in the second party with respect to the matter in existence at the time of that promise. The Indian Contract Act is a little more strict in that it provides, in s. 135, that the surety is discharged if the third party (the creditor) gives time to the second party (the principal debtor) or promises not to sue him in court. At Hindu law a mere prolonging of the time available or variation in the method of seeking a remedy would not necessarily discharge the surety. Both systems agree in the rule that the discharge of one co-surety does not discharge other co-sureties. But the Act diverges from the ancient law in providing that the surety is discharged in any case if the third party does any act inconsistent with the surety's rights, or omits to do any act which the surety has required him to do. It seems to the present writer (the sources are not decisive) that the agreement of suretyship would not be terminated by such conduct under the old system, but that when the third party sought to enforce his rights the surety would be enabled to contend that a condition had been broken, for which he would be entitled to ask for a set-off, or that the third party was guilty of fraud, in which case the court would adjust the equities between the parties. The insistence of the agreement in the Appendix upon the surety's not raising objections to the lender's proceedings (§§ 6, 7, 11) speaks for itself.

A major difference between the old law and the Act is to the advantage of sureties, and supplies a reason for the superiority of the new law over the old, the European over the native. Under the old law the third party must first exercise his rights against the second party, including, it seems, the sale of pledges; only when the second party's obligations remained outstanding was it possible for the third party to apply for performance of his obligation by the surety. The evidence of § 5 of the agreement below, which requires the reverse, can be relied on for this. Under the Act, s. 141, which follows the English law, the surety, having paid the debtor's debt, is entitled to the benefit of all securities which the creditor has against the principal debtor, whether the surety knew of the existence of such securities or not. Furthermore the loss or release of such securities by the creditor would discharge the surety to the extent of the value of the security lost or discharged. This aspect of subrogation does not seem to have been required or understood in the original Hindu law.

Though it is true that at the ancient law the relation between surety and third party is contractual, whereas at the modern Indian law it is fiduciary, the difference (though not negligible in practice) cannot be regarded as decisive of our question, since all cases in contract were fit, in the pre-British Indian courts, for being treated with a regard for equity, for equity and law went side by side. Thus where a surety was deceived by his third party he could plead this defect either in order to have his contract set aside, or to have his obligations modified *pro tanto*. There is a remarkable improvement in the law by an introduction of an English rule in the Indian Act, s. 146 read with s. 43. It provides not only the right of a creditor to proceed against one or more co-sureties, but also their obligation of contribution as between them. The Indian Act does not indeed mention suretyship by shares, but the illustrations sufficiently cover such a case (Ill. (b) to s. 146). One may conclude that the Indian Contract Act offered what was required by the public, and that the penalty of the double payment by the defaulting original debtor was not of such importance in practice that the public deemed it requisite to retain it. The Act, in any case, did not purport to regulate the arrangements which might subsist between a proposed debtor and a proposed surety, and a bond might well be conditioned for the former to pay a penalty to the latter — a penalty which an Anglo-Indian court might refuse to recognize in practice but which the natives might, at least for some decades, treat as binding in conscience between themselves.

APPENDIX

A close paraphrase of the *Covenant of Debt supported by Pledge and Collateral Security* provided in the (originally) 13th-century book of forms and precedents called *Lekhapaddhati* (ed. C.D. Dalal and G.K. Shrigondekar, Gaekwad Or. Ser. 19, Baroda, 1925), at pp. 19-21.

1. Particulars of date, place, reigning sovereign, title of document : 'document of *drammas* borrowed upon the security of pledged valuables'.
2. Statement that 2404 *drammas* of a particular quality have been borrowed from *A* by *B*, upon pledge by *B* of 8 buffaloes, 16 oxen, 50 cows, and 2 (?) stud-bulls. The rate of interest is 2 per cent per mensem.
3. These *drammas* must be rendered up at a particular festival without dispute and without remonstrance by the borrower, before (?) the eighth hour, in a lump sum even if the lender is abroad. If the lender is not in the village, then the *drammas* must be rendered up by the borrower, to the like amount, within the threshold of a brother of the lender who is joint in estate with him, or of a son of his.
4. Should one or other of the giver or taker die by act of Fate, or be missing, or should either suffer some misfortune by decree of Fate, or evil chance happen to him, then the *drammas* must be given, upon the authority of the document, even by sons or grandsons.
5. If the borrower does not deliver to the lender on the stated day in a lump sum the *drammas* together with interest thereon, or if he does not render up the total *drammas* in a lump sum, then the *drammas* which remain in arrears and unpaid according to the terms of the document, after taking into account the number of *drammas* that may have been rendered up, may be obtained by the lender by selling (after due notice to the borrower and sureties) the chattels written above and placed in pledge, in the same manner as vegetables are sold in (open) market. Should the *drammas*, together with interest and costs as indicated in the document not be realised from the pledged articles, then the *drammas*, together with interest, must be paid to the lender by the sureties, after they have obtained them at interest from some other lender or sold some article from their own house.
6. No plea or defence is to be raised in the court between the borrower and his sureties and the lender. But if a dispute arises the entire costs are to be borne by the party defeated in the action.
7. Should any of the items included in the pledged chattels be damaged by Fate or ill-chance, should there be a loss through fire, theft, or flood, then the borrower and the sureties become free from liability after paying to the lender, according to the authority of the document, the entire *drammas* together with costs and interest. In such a case no dispute or controversy or scandal is to be raised against the lender in reference to the loss of the pledges.
8. In the event that, at any time, the lender has need of the *drammas* to be delivered into his hands by reason of some necessity that has arisen in his own house, the lender may take the *drammas* together with interest, setting upon the borrower and his sureties and quartering soldiers upon them (as a form of distraint). In such a case whatever costs arise in respect of the soldiers employed shall be borne in their entirety by the borrower and his sureties.
9. The two sureties are fully responsible to the lender, precisely as if they were themselves borrowers, for (i) compliance with the conditions written above; (ii)

securing the payment of the *drammas* together with interest and costs in accordance with the terms of the written document; and (iii) supplying the pledged chattels with their maintenance, according to the custom of all other borrowers.

10. Where there are many sureties they make payments jointly, i.e. payment by one is on behalf of all, and payment for all releases any one of them. Between the principal and his sureties no distinction is to be recognised. The entire payment of the *drammas* according to the written document, with interest and costs, must be complied with, exactly like the borrower, by a single surety, without replying to the lender that there are other sureties.

11. It will be presumed that the borrower himself has been approached by his sureties. Payment of the *drammas* with costs and interest according to the authority of the document must be made to the lender by the keepers of the pledges and sureties, abandoning all complaint and pursuing entirely the custom of sureties.

12. The keepers of the pledges are four persons of ... village, ... relationship, ... names.

13. Signatures of (i) pledge-keepers; (ii) borrower; (iii) five witnesses.

14. Particulars of the scribe, who writes at the request of both parties. Document to be valid in spite of clerical errors.

Appended Note

Long after this article was completed the following work came to hand : HERAMBA CHATTERJEE SASTRI, *The Law of Debt in Ancient India* (Calcutta Sanskrit College Research Series, No. 75) (Calcutta, 1971). It is the most recent work in *dharmaśāstra* and gives a thorough picture of the topic *ṛiṇādāna*. Suretyship is dealt with in Chapter IV, pages 135-203.

AN EXAMPLE OF TAX-EVASION IN MEDIEVAL INDIA *

The medieval Indian king was Lord of the soil, and in that capacity claimed and enforced his right to taxes, many of which, whatever their nomenclature, amounted to what is nowadays called ' land-revenue '. The total of the demand, so far as may be ascertained from the surviving data, was liable to vary with the varying needs of central and local governments, but it would appear that in at least one extensive Hindu kingdom an effort was made to stabilize the principal demand under the name *siddhāya*, which at least in a substantial number of cases amounted to a ' permanent settlement '.[1] Whether the king

[1] On this see Derrett, *The Hoysaḷas*, Oxford (to be published), 195 ff., and for a general description of taxation policy in South India see Mahalingam, *South Indian polity*, Madras, 1955, index sub tit. *Taxation, Taxes.*

was in fact able to restrain himself for long from adding under special pressure to the total thus fixed is another matter, and it is certain that conquering kings would have no difficulty in disregarding their predecessor's *siddhāya* should they feel that the land, perhaps in other hands, could produce a better revenue. We have certain details of the assessments made on estates in the hands of *agrahāra* Brahmans in the Hoysaḷa empire, and these provide valuable indications.[1] It is evident from them and from collateral material that the assessment on *brahmadeya* land might be much lower than that on the same land when it was in private hands. But it is equally certain that no land could entirely escape taxation unless the king especially granted, or confirmed, immunity and made it *sarva-mānya.* Land owned by temples was generally free of taxation, and, provided the subsisting burden of taxation were accepted by the previous owner, or a corporation, or by some other private person for a consideration, there was seldom much difficulty in obtaining the king's permission to alienate land virtually free of tax to a god or to a religious community.

The practical situation was therefore this, that the king did not make a profit out of land granted by himself, or his ancestors, or his subjects with his permission, to a god. Where land was granted to Brahmans in an *agrahāra*, or to a community of *Vīra-śaivas* or even to the *guru* of a particular sect, the king might agree to a lower rate of assessment than was normal in the district in question, and his readiness to agree to this might be the greater for another party's undertaking to bear a proportion or the whole of taxation otherwise lost to the State. Attempts to dedicate land to a god without the king's permission and in the hope that some indirect or illicit benefit might be derived from a subsequent claim of freedom from taxation were almost certainly
* frowned upon, though evidence of this is not readily forthcoming in India. In Ceylon, however, precisely the same situation existed,[2] and there is not the least doubt but that fraudulent dedications did take place when the government officials were insufficiently vigilant, and when the British assumed responsibility for the administration of the Kandyan Provinces in 1815 they soon found it advisable to make close inquiries as to the genuineness of these allegedly tax-free endowments.

An instance of the ingenuity of a certain wealthy official and landholder, by name Gōpāla-daṇṇāyaka, merits attention not merely because the arrangements which he made were intended to evade taxation, and because the details of his attractive scheme were published for all the world to admire on the face of a stone *śāsana*, but also because the scheme had evidently been submitted for the king's approval (though this is not explicitly stated in the record) and was a complete success. The particulars are given in the inscription

* [1] *India. Archaeological Survey, Epigraphia Carnatica*, v, Hasan 84 (1223); ix, Bangalore 6 (1253); v, Belur 74 (1261); vi, Kadur 49 (1291).

[2] See F. W. Hayley, *A treatise on the laws and customs of the Sinhalese including the portions still surviving under the name Kandyan Law*, Colombo, 1923, sub tit. *rājakāriya.*

dated 1261 published in *Epigraphia Carnatica*, XII, no. 2 of *tāluk* Chiknayakanhalli. Before describing them it might be helpful to look at the establishment of two temples endowed about twelve years previously in another part of the empire: in both cases the schemes were carried out by authority of government.

The Brahmans of Uṅgurager̲e were permitted [1] by Bommana-daṇṇāyaka, * obviously the General Officer in command of the district (he bore the titles *mahā-pradhāna, hiriya sandhi-vigrahi*), to transfer from the State their dues in respect of *siddhāya* to an account on behalf of the upkeep of two temples and their worship. Bommana himself had 'set up' (i.e. dedicated) images of various gods in 1246 and 1249 respectively in an *agrahāra* of his own foundation called Vijaya-Sōmanātha-pura, and it was quite natural that he should approve an arrangement of this kind—it being understood that Bommana himself would make good the loss to the treasury. The Brahmans were in fact guaranteeing the upkeep of and worship at temples in which the founder himself had an interest. What is instructive to us, though, is the scale on which provision was made. The *siddhāya* would have amounted to 95 *gadyāṇas*, and we are given an account of how each *paṇa* [2] of this sum was to be spent. It is unfortunate that many of the terms are as yet unintelligible, but the general picture is clear. The account tells its own tale:—

5 *pūjāris* (to perform worship) .	*ga.* 25	*pa.* –
2 attendants	4	–
4 cooks	10	–
Persons to draw ornamental patterns	2	5
Clerk	11	–
2 *bhaṭṭa-gutta* (?)	5	6
8 *davasiga* (?)	17	–
2 garland-makers	5	–
2 *angharika* (?)	8	–
2 grove-gardeners	4	–
2 potters	2	2
Washermen	–	7
Total	*ga.* 95	*pa.* –

Thus full-time as well as part-time staff are accounted for, and some might think that the provision was bordering upon the lavish.[3] The provision for the Clerk looks suspiciously like a sinecure for a poor relation of the founder, but we cannot be sure. When we turn to the scheme set up by Gōpāla we find the comparison illuminating.

[1] The record is *Epigr. Carn.*, V, Channarayapatna 238, at Nuggihalli. The text is printed in Kannaḍa script at p. 671 of part II of the volume.

[2] The monetary system was 1 *gadyāṇa* (gold) = 10 *paṇas* (gold); 1 *paṇa* = 4 *hāgas*; 1 *hāga* = 2 *bēḷes*.

[3] A Brahman teacher of literature at an endowed institution during this period could expect an annual salary of 6 *gadyāṇas*.

At a village called Seṭṭikere in the year 1261 the minister Gōpāla-daṇṇāyaka created an *agrahāra* under the name Bharita-prakāśa-pura out of lands in that village and its hamlets given to him for that purpose by the Hoysaḷa king Nārasiṃha III. The tax due to the treasury is specified as 41 *gadyāṇas*, 4 *paṇas*, 1 *hāga*, and 1 *bēḷe*. This was a very moderate revenue-assessment, as is evident from the proportion it bore to the income available from the whole land in question, and there is every reason to believe that the tax was specially assessed when the original gift was made to the minister for the charitable purpose which the king had in view. Gōpāla proceeded to divide up the land into 47 shares. Each share would bear its proportionate part of the land-revenue. Thirty-six of them were bestowed upon Brahmans of various *gotras*. Out of the remaining 11 one was set aside apparently to enable the founder to meet some of his own expenses and to exonerate him from charges on account of local cesses. The remaining 10 he conveyed to the god Yōganātha which he had set up in the *agrahāra*, under the Brahmans' corporate administration, they agreeing to pay the proportion of the *siddhāya* to the government, to pay for a yearly feast in the founder's name in honour of a certain Bharita-prakāśa Yōgēśvara, to provide for the upkeep of the temple and its adjacent buildings, the garden and the gardeners, and last but not least the god's ornaments, and finally 8 shares were specifically appropriated to the provision of a total of 151 *gadyāṇas* for the following purposes intimately connected with the temple :—

Offerings and *nambis* (officiants)	*ga.* 6
Decorators (or ? dancing girls)	6
Attendants	4
Cooks	4
Water-carriers	2
2 drummers, 1 garland-maker, and 1 sweeper . .	22
Bhariteya-daṇṇāyaka as Manager and Treasurer of the endowment	40
Siṅgeya-daṇṇāyaka as Clerk and Inspector . .	40
Bāyakka, daughter of Gōpāla, as Superintendent of gardens, lands, and granary	20
Preparer of meals, rice, cooked food, and pigments .	2
Oilmonger, potter, and washerman . . .	2
Vaiṣṇavas	3
Total	*ga.* 151

It does not appear that the worship at this temple was more elaborate, nor that the actual provision for its upkeep was necessarily more lavish than that which prevailed in regard to the two temples whose estimates we have reviewed from the record of 1250 above. But what is very clear is that while the persons who, whether whole-time or part-time, performed the real work were given what must have been no more than a reasonable reward, certain other individuals are given an absurdly extravagant emolument. We wonder who Bhariteya and Siṅgeya were. We cannot be certain about the latter, for the name was fairly common, while nothing is known of any officer with the former name. But there cannot be very much doubt. Bāyakka, the founder's daughter, is given an excellent income (for what, incidentally, might prove a more onerous task than those undertaken by the male beneficiaries), and these two men must have been close relations of the founder. They can hardly have been his sons: it is much more likely that they were his sons-in-law. Had Gōpāla kept the land under his own control he would have had to pay a much larger assessment to *siddhāya*. On the basis that the village was to be turned into an *agrahāra*, a charitable endowment if ever there was one, the land-revenue was fixed at a very reasonable figure. The astute founder then proceeded to provide for an income (in the nature of a *nibandha*, and thus hereditary) for his own nominees, who, of course, took the benefit tax-free. We cannot be sure that this method of tax-evasion was widely practised. Perhaps it was not. This is the only example extant with reference to that part of India and that century. But the idea was a good one, and it deserved wider employment.

ADDITIONAL ANNOTATIONS

Tit. It should be explained that the instance is not one of tax-*avoidance* only, but an arrangement whereby burdens were shifted correspondingly to other taxpayers by a subterfuge : an element of evasion is therefore present.

p. [261], l. 27. S. Nārada XVII.46 (Jolly).

p. [261], n. 1. Examples of division of lands for the god, drummers, musicians, the manager, prostitutes, their manager/the steward (always well remunerated), and dancing master are to be seen at E.I. XIII, pp. 168-70 ; similarly, cf., S.I.I. XI/i, 103, pp. 99-102 ; 86 ; K.I. II, 34 of 1940-1 ; 16 of 1940-1, pp. 62ff. ; K.I. I, 17 of 1939-40, p. 20.

p. [262], l. 6. Attention should be drawn to the Munirabad Stone Ins. of A.D. 1088 (Hyd. Arch. Ser. no. 5, 1922) (= A.R.I.E. st. ins. no. 483 of 1959-60). The lands dedicated included 113 *kamma-s* of garden land, 750 *kamma-s* of irrigated land, and 60 other *kamma-s*. The *pūjāri* was allotted *ga.* 6, two attendants *ga.* 6, and a *bhaṭṭa* to recite the *purāṇa-s ga.* 4 (all annually). The cash scale seems higher than that at Uṅguragere̱, and, seemingly, Seṭṭikere̱ (it is unlikely that the value of money had appreciated in the meanwhile).

PROHIBITION AND NULLITY: INDIAN STRUGGLES WITH A JURISPRUDENTIAL LACUNA

EVERY legal system requires a mass of prohibitions, and it may be a source of confusion to some of the lay public (who tend to think of law rather in terms of 'must nots' than 'musts') that it has this feature in common with a concurrent system of ethics. The confusion will be worsened if a great many prohibitions appear, perhaps in slightly different guises, in both. The human mind is quick, however, to discover 'what you can get away with', and in practice the distinction in modern times between a legal and a moral or ethical prohibition is well understood. There is indeed scope for holding *quod fieri non debuit, factum valet.*[1] There remains a difficulty, nevertheless, when in a purely legal context we attempt to discover the effects of a prohibited act, and the distinction between a void and a voidable transaction is of immense importance and is consequently eagerly detected.[2] Provisions, again, in legislative enactments may appear to inhibit the acquisition of a particular status, and yet the law that results from their practical application may stop short of denying that acquisition, whatever penalties may incidentally be exigible from the individual who has attempted to acquire the status illegally.[3]

But whatever the remaining problems in our own and contemporary systems, the fundamental difficulty was much more acute in countries and periods when law was emerging from a pre-legal era, that is to say when 'must nots' and 'musts' were becoming the concern of the community as judge rather than of the same community as priest, when superstitious and sentimental sanctions were not strong enough to give injunctions almost automatic efficacy amongst adults, and the opinions and feelings of the community had deliberately to be put into operation by devising and regulating penal sanctions. At this critical stage in human development—a stage perhaps of immense duration in certain societies—prohibitions are investigated, rationalized, and classified, and subtle distinctions may be drawn between the prohibited act

1 See for example M. Hale, *Historia Placitorum Coronae*, London, 1736, I, 194; also refs. in *Byrne's Dictionary of English Law*, 1923, 730.

2 See (1953) 55 Bombay L.R. (Journal) 105–11. In our Bankruptcy Act, 1883 (see now 4 and 5 Geo. 5, c. 59) a voluntary settlement stated to be 'void' may bind a *bona fide* purchaser for value. See also the Infants Relief Act, 1874 (on which see a valuable article in 73 L.Q.R. 194 and following): *Stocks* v. *Wilson*, [1913] 2 K.B. 235; *Valentini* v. *Canali*, (1889) 24 Q.B.D. 166; and the valuable summary in 4 *Stroud's judicial dictionary*, third edition, 1953, 3227–32.

3 In *Catterall* v. *Sweetman*, (1845) 163 E.R. 1047, it was said, 'The Court will not hold a nullity to be created by mere prohibitory words unless such nullity is expressly declared in the Act', and we see from the references in the previous footnote that even in such cases nullity may not be an inevitable result. Examples of the rule in *Catterall's case* may be found in the earlier *R.* v. *Birmingham* (*Inhabitants*), (1828) 108 E.R. 95, and in the very recent Indian case of *Ganeshprasad* v. *Damayanti*, I.L.R. [1946] Nagpur 1 SB.

which is valid in law and the prohibited act which not only draws vengeance upon the perpetrator but is otherwise legally ineffective. Although it would be a mistake to suggest that traces of these efforts are not to be found in many societies [1]—for indeed to this day the Canon law perpetuates rules bearing unmistakable traces of the stage we are discussing [2]—there is much interesting material in Sanskrit which seems to have been neither closely nor sympathetically investigated. It is the purpose of this article to summarize the manner in which the Indian jurists of the period stretching from the sixteenth century to the commencement of the British period attempted to meet the requirements of the fully-developed legal era for which they were catering.

Discussions of this sort show the *dharmaśāstris* at their best, and it is high time that a specimen of such work, the fruit of profound thought and wide learning, was made available to a non-Sanskritist public. It may be suggested that it is a great many years since Colebrooke published his translation of Jagannātha's *Vivāda-bhaṅgārṇava*,[3] in which a very lengthy investigation of this problem is to be found ; and it may be added that if *Mahāmahopādhyāya* Dr. P. V. Kane has not given much attention to the matter in his *History of dharmaśāstra* it has at least been treated in outline by the late Dr. Priyanath Sen in his *General principles of Hindu jurisprudence.*[4] The present writer does not believe that this excuses him from entering into the subject once more, since Jagannātha's work, meandering and leisurely as it is, still requires an introduction, and is coloured by a characteristic 'Bengali' bias ; while Priyanath Sen was satisfied to lay out the bones of the matter, to adopt Jagannātha's analysis, and somewhat complacently to accommodate the result with what he considered were fundamental and universal principles of jurisprudence.[5] He seems unaware that he was observing a remarkable example of rational creation, and indeed his main object was to show (as was far from unnecessary in his day) that the Hindu law could stand comparison with foreign systems.[6]

Our story commences with the *smṛti* texts, few of which need be dated

[1] The Islamic law is still in difficulties over the distinction between 'forbidden' and 'void' marriages : J. N. D. Anderson, 'Invalid and void marriages in Hanafi law', *BSOAS*, XIII, 2, 1950, 357–66 ; N. U. A. Siddiqui, *Studies in Muslim law, I, Batil and Fasid marriages*, Dacca, 1955.

[2] *Corpus Juris Canonici*, can. 1035, 1036, 1042, 1138–41.

[3] *A digest of Hindu law on contracts and successions : with a commentary by Jagannátha Tercapanchánana translated from the original Sanscrit by H. T. Colebrooke, Esq.*, . . . , London, 1801. The references below (see pp. 208, 213, 214, 215) are to the two-volume edition, Madras, 1864–5.

[4] *TLL* for 1909, Calcutta, 1918, 83–94.

[5] See p. 86 : '. . . having regard to the general principles of transfer of ownership, I think it will be going too far to say that although the owner makes a gift of his own property, no title will pass, simply because the Sastras have condemned such a gift as improper'.

[6] See p. 90 : 'I do not know how it may strike you, but it seems to me that these rules and the distinctions on which they are based exhibit a deep logical insight, a marked development of juristic ideas, and a high moral standard of which we, as the distant descendants of those who laid them down, may justly be proud'. The reader may compare the material upon which this remark is based with that contained in and referred to in this article.

later than the second century of our era and all of which were treated as binding authorities by the medieval jurists. Amongst the mass of negative injunctions we may at once discard those which are not capable of leading to the conflict in which we are interested. Examples are the injunctions against saying 'hum' to one's teacher, against touching an untouchable, against eating the leavings of another's meal, and against passing water in a river. Injunctions against marrying a woman of the same *gotra* [1] and against marrying before one's elder brother or elder sister as the case may be [2] are indeed of the kind in which we are interested, for the question arises whether marriages contrary to the injunctions are valid, voidable, or void.[3] But it is more convenient to pass on to a list of injunctions of a purely financial implication, and we may revert to the preceding question in our conclusion.

Various *smṛtis* prohibit:

(1) acquisition of assets otherwise than according to a set of rules (devised caste-wise by Gautama and others for normal and emergent circumstances) [4];

(2) acquisition from a person who has taken something either (i) not given to him or (ii) not lawfully capable of acquisition by him: in other words from a thief [5];

(3) acquisition by acceptance by a Brahman from a *caṇḍāla* (outcaste) [6];

(4) acquisition by acceptance upon the banks of a river [7];

(5) acquisition by acceptance of a ewe, etc. [8];

(6) alienation of land by sale [9];

(7) alienation to *B* of what has been promised to *A* [10];

(8) alienation by gift of all one's assets [11];

(9) alienation of common assets [12];

[1] For example, Manu, III, 5.

[2] ibid., III, 170; XI, 61; and *Mitākṣarā* on Yājñavalkya, III, 265.

[3] See below, p. 214, n. 8.

[4] Gautama, X, 38–41, 48 = *Dharmakośa* (*Vyavahāra-kāṇḍa*, Wai, 1938), 1124–6; cf. Manu, XI, 70 (in Medhātithi = 69), also XI, 194 (Medh. = 193), 254. Also Kane, op. cit., III, 548, and *Madanaratna-pradīpa*, Bikaner, 1948, 323 and seqq.

[5] Manu, VIII, 340 = *Dh.k.*, 1397 (Medhātithi is particularly valuable on this).

[6] Manu, X, 109; XI, 176 (see also Medhātithi); *Mitākṣarā* on Yājñ., III, 290; *Svatva-rahasya*, ch. V.

[7] A *purāṇa* qu. *Dānakriyā-kaumudī*, Bibl. Ind., Calcutta, 1903, 85. See Kane, op. cit., II, 885–6, for reference to the *Dāna-candrikā*.

[8] *Brahma-purāṇa*, qu. Hemādri, *Caturvarga-cintāmaṇi*, *Dāna-kāṇḍa*, Bibl. Ind., Calcutta, 1873, 57; cf. Manu, IV, 188; *Mitākṣarā* on Yājñ., III, 290. *

[9] Anon., *apud Mitākṣarā* on Yājñ., II, 113 (ed. Nirnayasagara, Bombay, 1909, p. 200) = *Dh.k.*, 1589b.

[10] Yājñ., II, 175 = *Dh.k.*, 796b; Nārada, V, 5 = *Dh.k.*, 798b; Bṛhaspati (ed. Rangaswami Aiyangar, Baroda, 1941), XIV, 2 = *Dh.k.*, 802a.

[11] Yājñ., II, 175; Nārada, V, 4 = *Dh.k.*, 798b; Dakṣa, qu. Lakṣmīdhara, *Kṛtya-kalpataru*, *Dāna-kāṇḍa*, 17 = *Dh.k.*, 807a.

[12] Yājñ., II, 179 (*Bālakrīḍā* only); Nārada, V, 4; Dakṣa, *ubi cit.*; Bṛhaspati, XIV, 2 = *Dh.k.*, 802a.

(10) alienation of son or wife [1];

(11) alienation of ancestral assets without the consent of male issue, except under exceptional provisions of law [2]; and

(12) alienation of assets in respect of which one is bailee or mortgagee.[3]

This list is not exhaustive, but its five prohibitions of acquisition and seven prohibitions of alienation serve our purpose adequately.

In some cases the *smṛtis* specifically provide that anyone who transgresses the prohibition shall perform a penance, or incurs sin (which comes to the same thing).[4] The implication to the unreligious whose situation is such that outcasting need not be feared for practical purposes is that he may act as he chooses: failure to perform the penance would in the cases of other people involve serious social and perhaps legal consequences,[5] but he can 'take a chance' with his spiritual welfare, for his status in the next or other worlds or lives may not interest him. The ancient pre-legal sanction is thus useless, and the prohibition a mere *brutum fulmen*. In other cases the *smṛti-kāra*, evidently alive to the difficulty, prescribes a punishment for transgression of the rule.[6] The one who contemplates wrongdoing is now taking a heavier risk, and the prohibition, so armed, is as near to being effective in one sense as many prohibitions can ever be. But will he take his chance, undergo his punishment, pay his fine (or whatever it may be that is inflicted upon him), and then feel satisfied at having achieved his object, even at such a price? This might not seem unattractive to a rich and powerful wrongdoer. The prohibition is thus only half-armed after all, and we need to know whether the act completed by the wrongdoer will be legally valid notwithstanding the penalties prescribed—for if the actual invalidity of the act is not stated in so many words the implication might well seem to be that it is penalized, but none the less operative. Here it is very rare for the *smṛti* to be explicit.[7] Indeed it is only where the obnoxious present is still legally the property of the outcaste, or the common assets still remain within the ownership of the whole body of co-owners, or if the Court may grant a decree in such terms, that the prohibition has really done its work. Common sense tells us that unless a prohibition is well-armed it might as well be omitted; and although it is perfectly true that procedural

[1] Yājñ., II, 175; Nārada, *ubi cit.*; Bṛhaspati, *ubi cit.*; Kātyāyana (ed. Kane, Bombay, 1933), 638–9, p. 79 = *Dh.k.*, 804a, 805a. Authority for *gift* of a son is found in the celebrated text of Vasiṣṭha on the subject. On the husband's Property in his wife see *BSOAS*, XVIII, 3, 1956, 492, n. 4. The subject cannot be disposed of briefly.

[2] Bṛhaspati, XIV, 5 and 6 = *Dh.k.*, 803a, b.

[3] Nārada, V, 4 = *Dh.k.*, 798b; Dakṣa, *ubi cit.*

[4] Viṣṇu, qu. *Sarasvatī-vilāsa* (Mysore, 1927), 278 = *Dh.k.*, 794b; Nārada, V, 6 = *Dh.k.*, 799a; Dakṣa, *ubi cit.*; anon., qu. Bhavasvāmi, *Nāradīya-manu-saṃhitā-ṭīkā*, V, 5 = *Dh.k.*, 807b; Hārīta, qu. var. *Dh.k.*, 808a; and cf. *Mitākṣarā* on Yājñ., III, 290.

[5] Since *pātitya* ('fall from caste') involved loss of property: see *BSOAS*, XVIII, 3, 1956, 487, n. 4.

[6] Viṣṇu, V, 174 = *Dh.k.*, 794b; Nārada, V, 11 = *Dh.k.*, 801b; Manu, qu. var. digests *Dh.k.*, 796a; and *Matsya-purāṇa*, qu. *Kṛtya-kalpataru*, *Vyavahāra-kāṇḍa*, 377 = *Dh.k.*, 808.

[7] The dubious text of Śaṅkha, qu. *Sar. vil.*, 251, clearly tells us that the donor may recover the improperly given object.

limitations control the persons who may question an act and the time within which they may do so, in order that innocent third parties may be protected, and it is necessary to stipulate carefully in what circumstances an act may be treated as void *ab initio* and thus capable of being ignored without resort to litigation,[1] it remains evident that ambiguity in the terms of a particular prohibition is capable of being more radically fatal to its efficacy. Now Sanskrit, with its habitual employment of the optative mood, which may lead to translations of a single term as varied as 'he shall not', 'he should not', 'he may not', and 'he must not', directly encouraged ambiguity of such a kind.[2] Moreover the perhaps fortuitous omission of details of penance and punishment for breach, not to speak of rules regarding nullity, if any, lent ample opportunity to commentators and digest-compilers to make the distinctions which they knew from practical experience were vitally necessary.

It is interesting that the discussions did not start in real earnest until the twelfth century (if so early).[3] Up to that time, and indeed in important instances until long afterwards,[4] jurists were inclined to assume that if an alienation was forbidden it was voidable, i.e. capable of being set aside at the suit of an interested party.[5] This was often very inconvenient, and therefore even from

[1] The following modern cases are enlightening: *A.* v. *B.* (1952) 54 Bombay L.R. 725 (with which compare *K. Malla Reddy* v. *K. Subbama*, A.I.R. 1956 Andhra 237 = [1956] Andhra W.R. 590); *Tattya Mohyaji* v. *Rabha* (1952) 55 Bombay L.R. 40 = I.L.R. [1953] Bombay 570 (with which compare *Palani Goundan* v. *Vanjiakkal*, A.I.R. 1956 Madras 476 = [1956] 1 Madras L.J. 498); and *Shah Hiralal* v. *Shah Fulchand*, A.I.R. 1956 Saurashtra 89. See also p. 203, nn. 2, 3 above.

[2] This fact was carefully considered by their Lordships of the Privy Council in the very important case of *Sri Balusu Gurulingaswami* v. *Sri Balusu Ramalakshmamma*, (1899) L.R. 26 I.A. 113= I.L.R. 22 Madras 398.

[3] The *Sar. vil.* credits Lakṣmīdhara with distinct views in this controversy. It is curious that nothing clear on the point is to be found either in the *Vyavahāra-* or the *Dāna-kāṇḍa*. The *Smṛti-candrikā* (c. 1250) is the earliest work to give definite evidence of thought on this topic. The author says (ed. Gharpure, Bombay, 1918, II, 190) that both parties must be punished, *and the given object must be restored to the donor as the gift is ineffective and Property has not passed.* He does *not* distinguish between *adeya* and *adatta* (and deserves credit therefor). He is quoted extensively in the *Sar. vil.* at p. 281, and Mitra-miśra explicitly follows him (apparently in preference to Śaṅkara): *Vīramitrodaya, Vyavahāra-prakāśa*, Benaras, 1932, 307. It is true that Aparārka (*c.* 1130) says (on Yājñ., II, 175, at p. 779) that *adeyaṃ* is *apahāryaṃ*, and Varadarāja (*c.* 1200), *Vyavahāra-nirṇaya*, Adyar, 1942, 287, says that *adattaṃ* means *asthiraṃ nivartanīyaṃ*, and thus clearly intend that such gifts are voidable, but their discussions are brief to the point of insignificance.

[4] See previous note. For the *Smṛti-sāra* see below, p. 214, n. 1. Nīlakaṇṭha, Śaṅkara's son, merely says that the donor sins and the transaction is invalid: he is evidently content to follow his father (*Vyavahāra-mayūkha*, ed. Kane, Bombay, 1926, 203 = ed. Mandlik, II, 123). Kamalākara, Śaṅkara's nephew, might have been expected to be helpful but his *Vivāda-tāṇḍava* (Baroda, 1901, at pp. 604–5) avoids the point and refers us to the *Dāna-Kamalākara*, which does not appear to be extant now. Neither the *Nṛsimha-prasāda* nor, surprisingly enough, the *Madanaratna-pradīpa* are of any help to us. Nor does Śūlapāṇi offer any remarks (comm. on Yājñ., II, 175, ed. Gharpure, Bombay, 1939, at p. 61), but because he was a Bengali there may be some significance in that; see p. 215, n. 2, below.

[5] In the present writer's view absolutely void alienations cannot have been known in ancient and medieval India except perhaps in cases of alienation by non-owners or owners limited by *pāratantrya* ('dependence'), and not in all of those. But the matter is obscure.

the late *smṛti* period conditions began to be fastened upon the words of the rule in question so as to make the prohibition consort more happily with common sense and usage. These authorities then forbade one to give away all one's assets when one had a family to maintain, or so long as its maintenance had not been secured already [1]; similarly to alienate common assets without the consent of co-owners or in the last resort except to the extent of one's own undivided interest therein [2]; or to alienate one's son or wife unless in the former case a specific textual authority could be called in aid or unless in either case the alienated relation gave his or her consent [3]; or to alienate, finally, ancestral property without the consent of male issue unless the latter were already divided in interest from the alienor.[4] But this type of tinkering only touches the surface of the problem, leaving us in the dark about the exact effect of a transgression of the now limited prohibition, while it in any case leaves many prohibitions untouched. The problem was complicated by the fact that usage varied from district to district, and what was an acceptable transgression in one part was shocking in another.

Our authors were eventually obliged to turn their attention to the real problem: were transactions in defiance of prohibitions voidable or, on the contrary, valid? Three schools of thought emerged. According to one the transaction is valid, but the transgressor sins and is perhaps liable to punishment, depending upon the case. According to the second the transaction is voidable and the transgressor does not sin. The third opinion holds that the transaction is voidable and the transgressor does sin and is liable to punishment in an appropriate case. The handiest summary of the arguments leading to the first opinion is to be found in Jagannātha. His text is unfortunately not in print,[5] but Colebrooke's translation is extremely reliable.[6] The second opinion is not found independently, but is represented in the text of the best source for the arguments supporting the third view, namely Śaṅkara-bhaṭṭa's [*Dharma-*]*dvaita-nirṇaya* (*c.* 1580–1600). This work contains, as one of its miscellaneous collection of *quæstiones*, a most acute investigation of the topic *dattāpradānikam*. Commencing with a rehearsal of the basic text on *adeyatva* ('ungivability'), and accepting as correct the statement of Vijñāneśvara (*c.* 1125) that *adeyatva* is based partly upon the absence of Property in the alienor in respect of the object and partly upon the force of the prohibition,[7] Śaṅkara goes on to select for special consideration the most crucial as well as the most difficult instance, that of the gift of an object promised to another, a gift *prima facie* in the power of the donor because of his remaining, as Vijñāneśvara

[1] Kātyāyana, *ubi cit.*, also texts cited in the *Kṛtya-kalpataru, Dānakāṇḍa*, 16; Jagannātha (Colebrooke), I, 410.

[2] *Madanaratna-pradīpa*, 207; Jagannātha, I, 403 and seqq.

[3] Kātāyana, *ubi cit.*; *Kṛtya-kalpataru*, ibid., 18; Jagannātha, I, 408–9.

[4] Aparārka on Yājñ., II, 175.

[5] Colebrooke's original copy is MS I.O. 1770 = Egg. 1534, in which see Part III, ff. 2a–10a.

[6] The entire passage is contained in I, 399–422.

[7] *Mitākṣarā*, 244–5.

pointed out, owner despite the promise. An extract from his treatise is given below with enough annotation to make it intelligible to the non-specialist. The original may be found on pp. 123–4 of Principal J. R. Gharpure's edition, Bombay, 1943.[1] A very handy summary, unfortunately marred by some needless errors, may be seen in the *Dvaita-nirṇaya-siddhānta-saṅgraha* of Śaṅkara's grandson Bhānu-bhaṭṭa,[2] who is to be congratulated at any rate upon having concentrated on our extract, which is undoubtedly the best part of the passage. The extract from Śaṅkara now follows.

In this context we may consider whether, when a gift is made contrary to the prohibition,[3] 'That which has been promised to *A* shall not be given to *B*',[4] the donor sins, merely, while the Property of the donee is effected [5]; or on the contrary Property is not effected, neither does the donor sin.[6] Now the fact is that he does indeed sin, while Property is *not* effected.[7]

1. It is suggested that Property must be effected, since gift cannot be completed without the production of the Property of another.[8] Moreover gift on the one hand and acceptance on the other are two entirely distinct operations; consequently just as, in the case of one who makes an acceptance in contravention of the prohibition against accepting a ewe and so on,[9] the gift materializes,[10] since *gift* as

[1] This edition groans under an exceptional load of misprints. But other defects trouble the reader besides. On p. 123 for *tad-viṣaya-nirvarttanānupapatteḥ* it is probably better to read, with MS I.O. Bühler 174 = Egg. & Keith 5627, *nivartt-*. Similarly for *yaccādṛṣṭārtha* read *-arthaṃ*; for *phalatā-mānaṃ* read *-mātraṃ*. On p. 124 the MS correctly has (on f. 162a—Keith's foliation in the Catalogue is wrong) the essential *na* in *atas tad api na bodhyate*. For the barbarous *nanu saṃbhāvanā-mātreṇaitat siddhyatīti dṛṣṭe saṃbhavaty=adṛṣṭa-kalpanā nāvakāśa-nyāya upāsyaḥ* read *na tu* and (?) *kalpanayā'vakāśa-*, for which in the first case the manuscript gives support, while in the second it has *kalpanāvakāśa*. Could *kalpane 'navakāśa* be correct? In the next paragraph the manuscript suffers from a haplography, which appears even to have affected Gharpure's sources or some of them, for instead of *-pratigraheṇaiveha niṣiddhenāpi tena svatvam utpattyavirodha* we should surely read *dānena svatvotpatty=avirodha*.

[2] P. W. Sar. Bhav. Texts, No. 75, Benaras, 1937, 120–1. It is quite extraordinary that the editor prints without comment *kṛte dāne dātā* na *pratyavaiti . . . prathamaḥ pakṣaḥ*| *dvitīyas =tu svatvam eva notpadyate dātā tu* na *pratyavaiti*| The first *na* is to be omitted, while the second is correct, as a glance at the *Dvaita-nirṇaya* itself would have confirmed. MS I.O. 1395b = Egg. 1575 (f. 43b) omits the first *dātā*, leaving us an opportunity of guessing how the corruption came about.

[3] A paraphrase of part of Yājñ., II, 175.

[4] If the author proves his point in this connexion it will apply *a fortiori* to other *adeyas* in the *vyavahāra* section of the *dharmaśāstra*.

[5] This is the characteristic Bengali view, for which see p. 215, n. 2, below.

[6] See § 2 below.

[7] At first sight a paradox, this is proved in § 3 below.

[8] For gift is conventionally defined as (i) *sva-svatva-dhvaṃsaka-para-svatvāpādaka-tyāga* or (ii) *svatva-tyāga-pūrvakaḥ para-svatvotpatty=anto vyāpāro*: both definitions implying that as Property is at the commencement so Property must be at the end of it.

[9] See p. 205, n. 8, above.

[10] This is not considered open to question in view of the conclusion in *Mitākṣarā* I, i, 16, on acquisitions contrary to the *śāstra*; in view of *Gautama-dh.sū.-pariśiṣṭha*, II (Adyar, 1948), X, 15–16, on the duty to give away what one ought not to have accepted from *mlecchas*, etc.; in view of the texts on usury: Manu, IV, 225, and X, 73; and the most explicit passage in Śrī-Kṛṣṇa's comm. on Śūlapāṇi's *Śrāddha-viveka* (Calcutta, 1939), 38–9. One may recall the argument of the *Mitākṣarā* (text, p. 213: Colebrooke, I, xi, 10) that the prohibition of the adoption of a son except in a time of distress binds the giver only and not the taker (!), an argument repeatedly followed. Manu, VIII, 153, supplies an example from *smṛti* of a *bilateral* prohibition.

such is not prohibited, so though it is gift that is prohibited in our context and we are confronted with a donor notwithstanding the prohibition, the effecting of Property is in no way inconsistent with the prohibition since the perfecting of the transaction is the act of the donee [1] and his acceptance is not prohibited.

Furthermore, admitting that, comparably with the effect of a prohibited acceptance of a ewe, etc., there is in our context no inconsistency in the effecting of Property by means of a gift which happens to be prohibited; yet the donor sins, merely. This must be so, for it would be nonsensical for the subject-matter of a prohibited proceeding to be under restraint, without the act in question itself giving rise to sin.[2] But this brings us to the following distinction. In our context mere gift is indifferently prohibited. But both sorts of gifts are comprehended, that which is secular and directed to a ' seen ' object [3] such as a gift to a friend and so on, as well as that which is directed to an ' unseen ' object, being to a technically indicated recipient, whether the gift be regular, purposive, or purely voluntary,[4] such as a gift by a *dīkṣita*.[5] So far as concerns the gift of a non-technically enjoined character [6] all the prohibition tells us is that transgression gives rise to sin. But where a technically enjoined gift [7] is in issue there must be a basis for restraint, since the reverse would involve a contradiction,[8] and consequently restraint is implied in information that there is no basis for proceeding.[9] Inevitably the only information to be obtained in such a case is that there is no possibility of achieving the desired object which was to be expected from that act and that act alone. And this is a permanent state of affairs, for we can never escape from the position that the absence of a basis for restraint would be an absurdity. Indeed should any persons, despite their evidence of the unattainability of the desired object (which is laid down in the texts and was to be expected accordingly) none the less decide to proceed to their own satisfactions under the impression that somehow or other that very desired object may be achieved, it is impossible to restrain them.[10]

[1] Jīmūtavāhana took the view (Colebrooke, *Dāyabhāga*, I, 22–4) that acceptance was not required to constitute the donee owner, but his opponents were numerous and include Dr. Kane. See *BSOAS*, XVIII, 3, 1956, 492–3.

[2] For the doubt as to the text here see p. 209, n. 1, above. It is a general principle that any transgression of an injunction must be expiated by penance: Manu, XI, 44; Yājñ., III, 219 and 220, and *Mitākṣarā* thereon. The word for ' sin ' here is not *pratyavāya* as previously but *aniṣṭa*, literally ' undesirable ' or ' harmful '. We follow Colebrooke in taking ' sin ' as its most helpful translation in this context. See *Mīmāṃsā-nyāya-prakāśa*, New Haven, 1929, § 320, where *anartha* is used instead with similar connotations.

[3] Bharadvāja, qu. *Sar. vil.*, 288 = *Dh.k.*, 807b. The distinction between ' seen ' and ' unseen ', i.e. secular (or rational) and spiritual, objects is explained in *Mīmaṃsā-nyāya-prakāśa*, p. 277, and in Pārthasārathi-miśra, *Śāstra-dīpikā* (trans. Venkataramiah, Baroda, 1940), index, sub tit. *adṛṣṭa*; and is illustrated by Kṛṣṇa Yajvan, *Mīmāṃsā-paribhāṣā* (Belur Math, 1948), 21.

[4] Reading *nityan=naimittikaṅ=kāmyañ=ca*. See Āpastamba, I, 5, 12–13; Kane, op. cit., II, 848, and p. 211, n. 3, below.

* [5] A person ritually prepared to perform a *soma* sacrifice. See Kane, op. cit., II, 1137–40, 1151, 1188–90. The subject is discussed by Anantarāma in his *Vivāda-candrikā* (MS I.O. 1278b = Egg. 1530) at ff. 16b and seqq.

[6] *avaidha*: not laid down by the Veda, the ultimate source of all injunction as such.

[7] *vaidha*: laid down by the Veda.

[8] Because the injunction to give is countered by a prohibition against giving a particular object.

[9] Restraint, or determent, must be there, but where is it to be found? In the power of the prohibition to tell us that there is no ground for following the positive injunction in the circumstances.

[10] The donors have an option of proceeding if they are not persuaded by the prohibition. So, the *pūrva-pakṣin* argues, the secular result can come about notwithstanding the prohibition.

If the prohibition does *not* tell us of the sin incurred in transgressing it, then it follows from that assumption that it does not even convey what has already been shown above.[1] One might perhaps object that it is false reasoning to deduce a comprehension of the absence of possibility of achieving the desired object which is expected, a comprehension which is produced first, from the comprehension that sin will be achieved, a comprehension which is produced afterwards.[2] But this is not true, since it would be absurd to posit an absence of a basis for restraint comparably with a regular rite.[3] In fact whereas one individual may proceed because of the possibility of achieving the desired object which he expects, another may desist from fear of achieving sin as the fruit of his prohibited act. In such circumstances as these an absence of a basis for restraint, upon the lines of a regular rite, is totally precluded.[4] It is therefore established that in cases of enjoined gifts [5] what is revealed by the prohibition is as much the absence of the possibility of achieving the expected desired object as the fact that what *is* achieved is sin. Accordingly the donor who gives to *B* what he has promised to *A* sins, merely, while by virtue of the donee's acceptance the Property of the latter is effected. So much for the first point of view.

[1] For a difficulty with the text see p. 209, n. 1, above. It might be claimed that the prohibition does not in fact inform us of the ' harmful ' or ' sinful ' result of a transgression of itself, but that we have to infer this *aliunde*. On the power of a prohibition, and the meaning of a negative in an injunction (a highly controversial subject), see *Śāstra-dīpikā*, 29–35, also Kishori Lal Sarkar, *The Mimansa rules of interpretation as applied to Hindu law*, *TLL* for 1905, Calcutta, 1909, 313 and seqq.

[2] The *pūrva-pakṣin* says, ' We may assume, if you will, that the text tells us nothing about sin : if that be so it tells us nothing of the unfruitfulness of the act either (for the two must be connected). But since we know that sin is produced it must follow that unfruitfulness is also present '. The imaginary objector points out that unfruitfulness is known from the plain sense of the words, and cannot be made to depend from the presence of sin, which is ascertained only by reference to another authority, referred to on p. 210, n. 2, above. A kind of inversion is thus the result of assuming that ' no basis for proceeding ' implies ' no fruit from the completed act ' and then making this depend upon the sinfulness of the act.

[3] *nityavan=nivarttanāviṣayatvānupapatteḥ*. A *nitya-karman* (which will include a *nitya-dāna*) is a fixed rite, required to be performed on stated occasions all through life, and hence may not be omitted even by one who can only perform it imperfectly, and who therefore has *prima facie* grounds (i) for expecting that the normal fruit in the way of spiritual reward will not be forthcoming and accordingly (ii) for being deterred or restrained from proceeding with it. See *Mīmāṃsā-nyāya-prakāśa*, § 237 ; Sarkar, op. cit., 51, 403. Consequently where a *nitya-karman* is concerned there is a *nivarttanāviṣayatva*, whereas with *naimittika-* or *kāmya-karmans* the absence of a necessary ingredient will provide a *nivarttana-viṣayatva*. Our author points out here and in § 3 that this very contrast, however it might otherwise attract him, cannot be extended so as to assist in a case where (*a*) there is an injunction to give and (*b*) there is a prohibition against giving objects promised to a third party. In the latter case a *nivarttana-viṣayatva* is permanently present, there is a basis for restraint, and the donor sins, on the one hand, and fails to produce the desired spiritual result on the other. Consequently the assumption of unfruitfulness (*pratipanneṣṭa-sādhanatvābhāva-kalpanā*) is logically sound and not a deduction from a comprehension posterior to itself.

[4] The theory that the doctrine relative to *nitya-karmans* should be extended to make these prohibited gifts fruitful would be an embarrassment, since, the public being (it is argued) at liberty to choose between the alternatives before them, the position is quite distinct from the *nitya* situation, in which the fruit is certain and the act must always be done. And since that doctrine is excluded it follows that, although the spiritual fruit is always missing, the secular result is unaffected thereby. Thus a *nitya-dāna* of this sort, being both compulsory and prohibited at the same time, has no spiritual result but may have a secular result. All this springs from the initial assumption that in a *vaidha-dāna* the prohibition, like the injunction, has nothing to do with secular results.

[5] See p. 210, n. 7, above, and the previous note.

2. According to the second viewpoint Property is *not* effected, while the donor does not sin. What happens is (it is argued) as follows : The ' effecting of Property ' is not an integral component of the sense of the root ' to give ', so that the completion of gift causes the ' effecting of Property ' in the donee ; but the *accomplishing* of Property in him is a constituent of the composite entity, gift, being an operation functioning in a manner conducive to the ' effecting of Property ', identical with the process commencing with ' designation of the donee ' and comparable with the act of relinquishing the object given.[1] By contrast the ' effecting of Property ' is the fruit of this operation, being a distinct entity, like Heaven and the rest.[2] Consistently with this we may conjecture as follows : where a gift is made in contravention of the prohibition Property is not effected.[3]

But, merely on the ground that this is established by conjecture only, we must not employ the Maxim of Scope,[4] by positing an ' unseen ' purpose in the rule where a ' seen ' purpose is perfectly possible.[5] And as a general rule positive and negative injunctions which are found in a *śāstra* appertaining to practical affairs [6] are to be understood as having only a ' seen ' object ; and accordingly we are not to posit any sin here.[7] As for the suggestion that, just as with a gift despite the prohibition of acceptance of a ewe, etc.,[8] so here, should an acceptance come about notwithstanding the prohibition of gift, Property is effected ; and therefore just as there is no obstacle to the effecting of Property even by a forbidden acceptance of a ewe, etc., so there is none to its being effected by a forbidden gift : that argument has been refuted already in the words commencing, ' And as a general rule . . .'.[9] In fact just as in our very context the rule, ' What has been promised must be given ',[10] is a rule concerning gift which is not directed to an ' unseen ' object, but is directed merely to the effecting of Property,[11] so this prohibition of gift is purely for the purpose of the non-effecting of Property : for the *śāstra* containing it is a practical *śāstra*. So much for this view.

[1] A clever argument. Both the *Svatva-vicāra* and the *Svatva-rahasya* are agreed that gift (*dāna*) causes Property. But *dāna* = designation of the donee + intention to relinquish in his favour + divesting of ownership by relinquishment [+ acceptance (see p. 210, n. 1, above) by the donee] : the fruit of all these is the effecting of Property. The accomplishing of the donee's Property (*svatva-sampādanaṃ*) is said to be a part of *dāna*, and corresponds to the first ingredient above.

[2] On the nature of Heaven, the result of sacrifices, see Jaimini, *Pūrva-mīmāṃsā-sūtras*, IV, 3, 15, also VI.

[3] Because the completion of *dāna* fails to produce Property because of the obstructive power of the prohibition. This gets round the verbal argument in § 1, para. 1.

[4] On the difficulty in the text see p. 209, n. 1, above. It appears as if a maxim of interpretation known as *avakāśa-nyāya* (or ? *anavakāśa-nyāya*) was being availed of. None of that name is known to the present writer. But the general sense is plain. Bhānu-bhaṭṭa says simply *dṛṣṭe saṃbhavaty=adṛṣṭa-kalpanāyā anyāyyatvāt*, which meets the case exactly.

[5] *Mīmāṃsā-nyāya-prakāśa*, § 187 (see p. 277). Use of this rule is common in *dharmaśāstra* works : e.g. Medhātithi on Manu, VIII, 1, 2, 9, 179, Aparārka on Yājñ., I, 29 (p. 57), and Vācaspati-miśra, *Vyavahāra-cintāmaṇi* (Ghent, 1956), §§ 772²–773⁵.

[6] *vyavahāra-śāstra* : what a century and a half ago would be called ' an institute of civil law '.

[7] Here *pratyavāya*, not *aniṣṭa* (see p. 210, n. 2, above).

[8] See p. 209, n. 10, above.

[9] Because the rule regarding acceptance of a ewe, etc., is part of a non-*vyavahāra* set of injunctions, partaking partly of *ācāra* (what gifts are meritorious ?) and partly of *prāyaścitta* (what penance will purify one who has accepted such a gift ?), and we know already that the natural secular effect is not touched by these rules (see p. 209, n. 10, above).

[10] The first words (inverted in the text) of Yājñ., II, 176.

[11] Being the complementary half of the rule we are discussing, this rule indicates that the *śāstra* intends merely that the promisee should have the object.

3. We come to our conclusion. In the case of the rule, ' What has been promised must be given ', just as in any case where a punishment is prescribed,[1] the quality of belonging to a practical *śāstra* is to be found, and accordingly the element of direction towards a ' seen ' object is certainly present; nevertheless, by reason of the assumption of sin in the one who fails to give,[2] the element of direction towards an ' unseen ' object exists too. Thus, in the rule prohibiting the making of a gift of what one has promised to another, a restraint[3] along the lines of a regular rite would be an absurdity. Indeed just as one individual may proceed to his own satisfaction in regard to an act of thieving,[4] which may serve to feed him and so on, although it cannot produce his own Property[5]; so another may proceed to his own satisfaction in the gift of a promised object, which cannot produce the Property of the other party.[6] Where an individual is proceeding to his own satisfaction in taking such an object, just as in a case of theft, an absence of basis for restraint upon the lines of a regular rite is precluded, in order that he may be placed under guard or otherwise prevented.[7] Consequently the donor's sin is posited.

The great merit of Śaṅkara's treatment of this important question lies not in the novelty of his conclusion, for it coincides with that of another outstanding *dharmaśāstra* author, the editor-compiler of ' Pratāpa-rudra's ' *Sarasvatī-vilāsa* (*c.* 1500–25),[8] but principally in its concentration upon the true criterion for solving the problem. It was not satisfactory to fasten upon linguistic clues in the *smṛtis* themselves, nor to draw assistance from the presence or absence of explicit penance- or punishment-prescriptions in association with the individual prohibitions. No assistance could be sought, as the author of the *Smṛti-sāra* thought[9] and even Vācaspati-miśra[10] was inclined to

[1] For breach of these rules, or for breach of any others. [2] See p. 210, n. 2, and p. 212, n. 10, above.

[3] *Scilicet* ' absence of restraint '; the text is almost certainly faulty.

[4] Theft is sinful, deserving of punishment, and incapable of giving rise to the thief's Property, and so it is comparable with our situation in respect of the first two characteristics, and thus (?) by the Maxim of the Staff and Loaf (Sarkar, 362) one may assume that the last characteristic is also attributable to our act.

[5] See *BSOAS*, XVIII, 3, 1956, 480–1. [6] This is our author's contention.

[7] See p. 211, n. 3, above. The reason is that, whereas with a *nitya-karman* there is no basis for restraining the officiant, within a gift of this character there is a definite basis not merely for restraining the officiant (who may refuse to be restrained) but also for restraining the projected acceptor, who, our author believes, is indirectly harming the former promisee, and has in any case no right to the object.

[8] His discussion is at pp. 277 and seqq. When assessing the value of this work one should not ignore the fact that it relies curiously often on *smṛtis* which are not traced elsewhere. However, the lengthy and learned disquisition contains the following interesting features: the ultimate conclusion agrees with that of Śaṅkara; no Property is produced by such a gift because *para-svatvāpatti-paryantā svatva-nivṛttir=nāsti*, ' there is no cessation of *P* enduring up to the commencement of the *P* of the donee '; and he deals with the view of those who hold that all the prohibitions against gift rest upon a rational basis and the opposed view of Lakṣmīdhara and others that the prohibitions derive their force from the texts alone (i.e. have an ' unseen ' force). He approves the latter view. At the end of the passage occurs a unique discussion of whether the customary tenancy which he refers to as *kuttā* (cf. Tel. *gutta*; Mar. and Kan. *guttā*; Tam. *kuttakai, kuttaka-kāraṉ*) is or is not an instance of pledge.

[9] Qu. in the *Vivāda-cintāmaṇi* (Calcutta, 1837, 36; trans. G. Jha, Baroda, 1942, 58) and in Jagannātha (I, 414 = MS I.O. 1770, Pt. III, f. 16b, which seems to be a paraphrase; I, 423 = f. 26a). He believed that though the donor sinned, Property had always the property of causing a valid gift, and thus an owner could always give.

[10] See previous note. As one would expect, Vācaspati's passage is as penetrating as it is brief.

believe, from the definition of Property itself.[1] It was only partially satisfactory to divide the prohibitions against alienation into two categories, those in respect of owned, and those in respect of unowned assets, and to characterize alienations of the former as valid and those of the latter as void[2]: for this provided no answer to problems of prohibitions of other sorts. Nor could the rule-of-thumb suggested by Jagannātha[3] and gratefully adopted by Priyanath Sen,[4] namely of treating *adeya* ('ungivable') grants as valid and *adatta* ('ungiven') grants as void,[5] be of any further assistance, if it could indeed help us so far. In fact the only satisfactory criterion is whether the prohibition (to adopt the *śāstrī's* language) occurs in a *vyavahāra-śāstra* or not. The more modern of the *dharma-śāstras* contain a large, and in some cases a strikingly preponderant volume of *vyavahāra* material, that is to say, of material directed to the assistance of the King in solving disputes. The remainder of the work is usually given to *ācāra* ('conduct') or *prāyaścitta* ('penance'), and a quantity of treatises are concerned almost exclusively with these. Rules found in such sections were intended to be applied in a pre-legal environment, and continued until recently to be applied if at all as extra-legal rules. An offender might be boycotted in the last resort, but practical affairs, in the civil law, were not affected by his transgressions: no means of nullifying the practical consequences of his prohibited act had been devised. The prohibitions in the *vyavahāra* ('civil law') section came into another category: they were devised in an atmosphere which assumed the King's ability to 'put things right'. Non-*vyavahāra* rules in a *vyavahāra* setting, and vice versa, could be detected by applying the test, 'Has the rule (merely) an "unseen" object?'

Consequently prohibitions (1) to (5) in our list, together with prohibition (6), though it is not quite comparable,[6] coming as they do in non-*vyavahāra* contexts, are prohibitions which do not invalidate transactions in breach thereof.[7] The same criterion applies equally to the prohibitions we have cited regarding marriage: the faults of the parties do not invalidate the marriage.[8] But

See pp. 36–7 (trans. 58–60). Transgression leads to absence of fruit + sin + secular efficacy of gift, where donor is owner. Contrast the nullity of gifts by dependent persons: the same author's *Vyavahāra-cintāmaṇi*, § 772². But, discrepant though it is, we must not fail to observe the passage in the latter work (§ 755²) in which gifts of all property by a person having a son living are treated as a legal impossibility (there is a precedent in Medhātithi on Manu, VIII, 164, and the *Kṛtya-kalpataru*, *Vyavahāra-kāṇḍa*, 271).

[1] The author of the *Smṛti-sāra* (probably Harinātha, but we cannot be sure as our only manuscript, MS I.O. 301 = Egg. 1489, is mutilated: cf. Kane, op. cit., I, 372–4) calls *P kḷpta-kāraṇa*. But see *BSOAS*, XVIII, 3, 1956, 481–5.

[2] Vācaspati-miśra: investigated by Jagannātha at I, 400, 402, 406, etc.

[3] I, 405, 411–12. *Smṛti*-authority was not wanting: see Nārada, V, 2 = *Dh.k.*, 798a.

[4] At pp. 83, 85–6.

[5] Nor can we accept Jagannātha's own idea, that prohibited gifts will be free from defect if given for pious purposes: I, 400, 410, 422.

[6] Being an alienation with an obvious 'seen' motive—but the *Mitākṣarā* steadily ignores this fact.

[7] See p. 212, n. 9, above.

[8] The subject cannot be treated fully here. See first two cases cited in p. 207, n. 1, above, also (1952) 54 Bombay L.R. (Journal) 115–19; also Devaṇa-bhaṭṭa, *Smṛti-candrikā*, 83 (where texts indicating nullity and/or divorce are said to apply to 'previous ages'). A *sagotra* marriage

prohibitions (7) to (12) are alike in appearing in a *vyavahāra* context—even though some *smṛtis* prescribe penances for breaches [1]—and they are therefore alike in rendering transactions in breach thereof liable to be declared void. This conclusion will not suit a follower of Priyanath Sen ; it is not consistent with the traditional Bengali solution of such problems [2] ; it implies that a bare promisee has an interest, however inchoate, in the promised asset [3] (which is difficult to admit, but far from impossible) ; and it obliges us to scrutinize every prohibition more carefully in case any further exceptions can be fastened upon it. But it has the merit of avoiding irritating and artificial distinctions between transactions which the *smṛtis* treat together ; and, moreover, the *smṛtis* being after all historical documents as well as law-books, it pays to history the tribute that is her due.

(legal since 1949) was valid according to the *śāstra* but the husband had to live with the wife *tamquam sorori* : see Kane, op. cit., II, 497. It is perfectly true that the *Mitākṣarā* says (on Yājñ., I, 53a, p. 15) *sapiṇḍāsamānagotrāsamānapravarāsu bhāryātvam eva notpadyate* ; the status of wifehood is denied to those women who are forbidden by reason of sameness of *gotra*, etc., but the author's meaning is that they are unfit for intercourse or for the wifely duties in general, not that they need not be maintained or that they are free for marriage with any other person, since the marriage though seriously defective was not altogether a ullity. See references cited by Sir Hari Singh Gour, *The Hindu Code*, fourth edition, Nagpur, 1938, 136, and E. J. Trevelyan, *Hindu family law*, London, 1908, 40. During the British period such a marriage was void unless permitted by custom : see *Madhavrao* v. *Raghavendrarao*, (1946) 48 Bom. L.R. 196=I.L.R. [1946] Bombay 375.

[1] See p. 206, n. 4, above.

[2] Jīmūtavāhana's famous text (Colebrooke, *Dāyabhāga*, II, 30) : ' a fact cannot be altered by a hundred texts '. Followed by Jagannātha, I, 411–12. See Colebrooke in 2 Strange 432–3, also Sir Francis Macnaghten, *Considerations on the Hindoo law . . .*, Serampore, 1824, 33, 248, 274, 292, 301, and H. H. Wilson, *Works*, V, 273. It is at this stage that we may advert to the difficulties of the Privy Council in this connexion. They were strongly influenced by the Bengali view (probably because Bengali legal texts were well represented amongst those that first reached the public in translation) in *Raja Rao Balwant Singh* v. *Rani Kishori*, (1898) L.R. 25 I.A. 54, and in *Sri Balusu Gurulingaswamy* v. *Sri Balusu Ramalakshmamma*, (1899) L.R. 26 I.A. 113, which the reader will find of great interest after studying this article. See also *Muniammal* v. *P. M. Ranganatha Nayagar*, A.I.R. 1955 Madras 571, *Anilabala Debi* v. *Somendu*, A.I.R. 1955 N.U.C. (Cal.) 811, and A.I.R. 1953 Journal 52–3, 57–62.

[3] Otherwise he could not sue to have the gift set aside. The reader, in attempting to appreciate Śaṅkara's (and ' Pratāpa-rudra's ') point of view—however opposed it may be to what is conventionally accepted—must recollect that at Hindu law prior to the early decades of the nineteenth century (as at French law to-day) no consideration was required to support a contract. Moreover, the Bengali view had its own difficulties, as Jagannātha half admits (I, 422) : what is the predicament of the promisee ?

ADDITIONAL ANNOTATIONS

p. [268], n. 8. Acceptance of a horse may be sinful: see *Śab. bhā.* III.iv.10 (*sū.* 28).

p. [272], n. 3. A connected rule was read by some into Manu IV.209 (see Medh. thereon).

p. [273], n. 5. The rule that a *dīkṣita* must make no offerings is stated at Medh. on M.III.120. The anthropological reason for this is explained in the classic study by J.C. Heesterman, 'Brahmin, ritual and renouncer', *W.Z.K.S.O.* 8 (1964), 1ff., esp. at 2,24. The *dīkṣita*, about to be reborn, is 'charged with the evil of death'. The *mīmāṃsā* discussion of gifts by a *dīkṣita* occurs at Jaimini, X.8,12 and Śab. thereon (Jha's trans., III, 2042). A maxim is *dikṣito na dadāti na juhoti na pacati* ('the initiated person does not make gifts, or offer libations, or cook'). This is a *paryudāsa* (exception) to a rule such as *ahar ahar dadyāt*, 'one should make gifts every day'. The prohibition is not confined to the sacrificial situation itself.

KUTTĀ: A CLASS OF LAND-TENURES IN SOUTH INDIA

ONE of the most important problems faced by the administration in the early days of British rule in India was how to ascertain and distinguish the different types of land-tenure prevalent there. It was obvious that a great variety of rights existed by custom in respect of land, and when the government proposed to collect revenue it was essential to know from which party or parties it could be expected and in what manner and proportions it should be levied. The task was completed by elaborate local inquiries,[1] but very little help was anticipated or received from legal textbooks in Sanskrit, which might have been expected to provide information upon so obviously fundamental a subject. But here and there details which throw light upon medieval practices are to be found in the books, and these seem to connect tolerably well with the results of the inquiries made during the nineteenth century. An instance of this seems worthy of quoting, not merely for its comparative rarity and for the juristic skill exhibited by the author, but chiefly because of the intrinsic interest of one of the tenures in question, which has a high curiosity-value and is probably of a species confined to India.

The most interesting of a set of passages is found in the *Vyavahāra-kāṇḍa* (' Civil law section ') of the gigantic digest called *Sarasvatī-vilāsa* (*c.* A.D. 1500–25) attributed to the Emperor Pratāpa Rudra Gajapati.[2] *Arthaśāstra-viśārada Vidyālaṅkāra* Dr. R. Shama Sastry printed this section in the Mysore Sanskrit Series in 1927, and the first extract is to be found on pp. 281–3. But since he did not abstain from printing some gibberish as well as some more or less obvious mistakes it is necessary to print a clearer version of the passage before proceeding to a translation.[3]

Towards the end of the subsection entitled *Dattāpradānikam*, or ' Non-delivery of Gift ', when he is considering the meaning of the prohibition of gift of *sāmānyādi-dravya*,[4] ' assets in which more than one person has an interest, and the like ', he turns to the general proposition that an owner of an inferior interest might donate the asset in question with the assent of the owner of the

[1] An example of the fruits of such work may be seen in C. P. Brown, *Three treatises on Mirāsi right*, Madras, 1852.

[2] P. V. Kane, *History of dharmaśāstra*, I, Poona, 1930, 410–14; on the true authorship of the work see further P. K. Gode, *Studies in Indian literary history*, I, Bombay, 1953, 423 and seqq.

[3] A rapid comparison will reveal the orthographically minor corrections; but it is necessary to place on record that the learned editor prints without comment at p. 282, l. 15, the following (corresponding to a part of the third sentence of the second paragraph of the extract given next): *nivṛttau pravṛttāyāṃ gururabhyuddheyaḥ pravayāḥ pratyuddheya ityādyupanītadharmāṇām* . . .

[4] A prohibition laid down by Bṛhaspati, quoted ibid., 277.

superior interest. This apparently unobjectionable theory is countered by an opposite argument to the effect that the owner of the inferior interest could not convey more than the same inferior interest (if so much, of his own volition) and that the assent of the owner of the superior interest could not clothe him with a power which only the latter possessed in his own right.[1] Assuming that this last theory was sound our author was reminded of a practical difficulty. There existed in his own part of India (Āndhra-Orissa) a peculiar tenure called *kuttā*.[2] The tenant of the *kuttā* might, and perhaps often did, run the risk of forfeiting his tenure for breach of its conditions and/or—and here was an immediate problem—for transfer of the land to a third party. Similarly the owner might wish to transfer his own title, but would this be valid ? How was this tenure to be coped with ? First of all one must decide into what category of relationship it should be placed. Our author proceeds as follows :

loke kuttākhyo vyavahāraḥ. mūla-svāminas sakāśād gṛha-kṣetrādikaṅ gṛhītvā, tad-upacayāpacayau kauttikasya mayaiva soḍhavyāv iti pāribhāṣikas samasti. aparañ ca kuttākhyo mūla-svāmina aurdhva-daihikādikaṃ tat-kṛtam ṛṇañ ca tadīya-gṛha-kṣetrādinā nivartya saṃśodhya cāvaśiṣṭam asti cet grahītavyam, nāsti cen māstv iti pāribhāṣikaḥ.

sa ca kuttākhya upacaya-padābhilapyas: tasyopacayākhya-pāribhāṣikatven-aupādhika-svatva-saṅkramopādhitayā, etat-prakaraṇe ṛṇādānākhye vivāda-pade gopyādy-adhikāre 'ntarbhāva evāstv iti cet, maivam. ṛṇādānākhyaṃ vivāda-padaṃ śodhya-mocya-koṭi-dvayāvalambanena pravṛttam; śodhyam abandhakam

[1] This is the view attributed to Lakṣmīdhara and others by the *Sarasvatī-vilāsa*, ibid., 281.

[2] The word is plainly Dravidian. Tamil has *kuttakai* ' lease ', ' rent ' ; Mr. J. R. Marr kindly ound an instance in classical Tamil where a grove was leased as a shrine. Compare the Telugu *gutta* in the same senses ; in Kannaḍa *guttā* is given by Kittel (correcting Wilson's *gutta* : *A glossary of revenue and judicial terms . . . by H. H. Wilson . . .*, London, 1855, 191) in the sense of *guttige* ' farm ', ' monopoly ', while *guttige* was used in medieval times to mean ' assessment ' upon a land-holder, and is given by Kittel as meaning, in addition to the above, ' rental on land '. For the initial voiced plosive see Burrow, Dravidian studies I, *BSOAS*, IX, 3, 1938, 711 and seqq. Compare the Kannaḍa form *gutte* and the Marāṭhī *guttā* and *gutā* (Wilson, ubi cit.) : s this Kannaḍa form a back-formation from Marāṭhī ? Malayālam has *kuttaka* and *kuttata* according to Wilson, op. cit., 305. Gundert gives meanings suggesting ' monopoly '. The conviction that the word is Dravidian is by no means diminished by the possibility of the Nēpālī *guṭhi* (Turner, Nēpālī dictionary, 143) being ultimately derived from the same source (see p. 68, n. 1 below). The *Hindī Śabdasāgar*, I, 1916, gives as a dialectical word *guttā*, which appears identical with the Marāṭhī word in the senses of ' a leasing of land ' and ' rent ' ; while Platts (*Dictionary of Urdū, classical Hindī and English*, 1884) adds the meanings ' monopoly ', ' contract ', and ' farm '. He suggests a derivation from the Skt. root *grath*. So far the sense of ' lease ' or ' rent ' heavily predominates, with a distinct revenue context, which might, of course, be a secondary development. More interesting and more relevant perhaps may be the material in Oḍiyā. G. C. Praharaj (*Pūrṇnachandra Orḍiā Bhāshākosha*, II, 1932) gives *kuta* : ' appraisement of the produce of a field, tree, or tank ' ; *kuta* (or *gutā*) *debā/nebā* : ' to give/take a lease of a land or tree under a system of appraisement '. It might seem probable that whereas the element of contract or lease now or until recently predominated, in Āndhra-Orissa of the sixteenth century the word *kuttā* evoked primarily the notion of offering and assuming a future responsibility after appraising the probable income from the land demised.

ṛṇam; mocyaṃ sa-bandhakaṃ gopyādi-prakṛtikam; evan dvi-prakāram ṛṇādānākhyaṃ vivāda-padam. loke upacayāpara-paryāya-kuttā-rūpasya śodhya-mocya-rūpa-prakāra-dvayāsambhavāt. kiñ ca ṛṇādāne uttamarṇa-gata upacayaḥ, kuttātmake tv adhamarṇa-gata iti na tatrāntarbhāva aupacayikasyeti.

apara āhuḥ:—gopyādāv antarbhāvo vācya iti. Devadatta-kṛtarṇāpākaraṇe jāte prakṛta-vivāde mocanīya-viṣayatā 'sti. kintu yāvaj-jīvānuṣṭeya-pitṛ-kriyā-karaṇasyādhi-rūpeṇa svī-kārāt tan-mukhena na vimocyatvam. upanayana-saṃskārasyādhyāpana-kriyāṅgatvena tan-nivṛttyā nivṛttau pravṛttānāṅ gurur abhyuttheyaḥ pravayasaḥ pratyuttheya ityādy upanīta-dharmāṇāṃ yāvaj-jīvānu-vṛttes tan-mukhenopanayanasyāpi yāvaj-jīvānuvṛtti-vat, maivam, prakṛtasya vyavahārasyāhita-dravya-viṣayatvābhāvāt. pratyuta pākṣikāpacaya-bhāra-sahitatvād ādhau tadabhāvāt, kuttākhyasyaupacayikasya ṛṇādāne 'ntarbhāvayitum aśakyatvāt.

dattāpradānike 'ntarbhāvo nyāyyaḥ. dattāpradānikañ caturvidhan dānam avalambyāvatiṣṭhate: dattam adattan deyam adeyañ ceti dānamārgaś caturvidha ity uktaṃ prāk. dattan dvividham: sopādhikan nirupādhikañ ceti. kuttātmakan dānaṃ sopādhikam iti kṛtvā sopādhika-datta-rūpatvenaupacayikasya tatraivāntar-bhāva iti rahasyam. Devadattasyarṇāpākaraṇan tad-uddeśa-prasakta-deva-pitṛ-kriyā-karaṇaṃ vā viṣayī-kṛtya pravṛttam aupacayika-viṣayan dattāpradānike 'ntarbhavati.

This may be translated as follows:

In practice we have a transaction known as *kuttā*. A man takes a house or lands and so on from their original owner and both the profit and the loss therefrom accrue to the tenant-in-*kuttā*, i.e. must be borne by himself, and there is a special contractual term to this effect. Moreover—the technical definition of this right proceeds—the tenant, with the aid of the house, lands, and so on, carries out the funeral and subsequent religious rites appertaining to the original owner of the property and pays off the debts which he has incurred, and if any balance remains over he may appropriate it, while if there be none it cannot be helped. *

It may be suggested that this *kuttā* ought really to appear in that section among the topics of litigation dealt with in this chapter which treats of Non-payment of Debt, where we deal with the rights of mortgagees in possession for custody and other varieties of mortgagees,[1] on the ground that the word *

[1] Mortgage (*ādhi*) could be of two principal sorts, *gopya* 'to be kept' and *bhogya* 'to be enjoyed'. In the case of the former the land was lost to the owner if he did not repay the amount borrowed with interest at the stipulated time, if any, and the mortgagee had no right over the income from the land unless this were specially stipulated. See also below, p. 76, n. 1. In the case of the latter no interest had to be paid, since the creditor took the profits of the land in lieu of interest. See Kane, op. cit., III, Poona, 1946, 427 and seqq. Kane does not deal with this *kuttā*. Assuming for argument's sake that the transfer of land in the *kuttā* is in the nature of a pledge, and thus only an alienation of a subordinate interest in the soil, one may inquire how it might conceivably enter within the definition either of *gopya* or *bhogya*. The incidents of the tenure as we are told them point rather to the latter type than to the former,

' profit ' is employed in describing it, and therefore it possesses the character of a transfer of Property which is qualified by the technical term relative to profit.[1] But this is not so. The section on Non-payment of Debt proceeds upon the basis that there are two alternatives : debts to be paid and debts to be released. A debt which is ' to be paid ' is an unsecured debt, while a debt ' to be released ' is a secured debt of the nature of a possessory mortgage for custody and so on [2] ; consequently the section called Non-payment of Debt has a double aspect. But in practice neither aspect of either sort, secured or unsecured, is present in the form of the *kuttā*, which consists in the risk of making a profit, or its reverse. Moreover, in Non-payment of Debt the profit accrues to the creditor,[3] while in the *kuttā* it accrues to the debtor. Consequently the party entitled to the profit cannot be treated in that section. This is my view.

Others hold the view that the *kuttā* is comprehended within a mortgage in possession for custody or some other type of mortgage. In a normal lawsuit, when debts incurred by *X* are paid off, the question of releasing securities which he granted may well arise : but when land has been *taken* by way of security for the performance of ancestral worship to be continued as long as the taker's life lasts, there can for that very reason be no question of releasing the security.[4] One might indeed object that this is quite comparable with the fact that in a sense even the rite of the thread-ceremony persists throughout life simply by reason of the life-long continuance of the duties proper to one who has been invested with the sacred thread, such as standing up to greet the teacher and standing up to show respect for elders,[5] duties which persist in and from the

but the true *bhogyādhi* was connected with an advance in cash to the owner, and could be terminated upon his tendering the same amount at or after an appropriate interval : neither feature is present here. But since the transfer was connected with the transferee's promise, and the transferor impliedly promised not to resume the property so long as the transferee did not repudiate his obligations, the element of pledge might well be thought to be present.

[1] The reason given for suggesting that the *kuttā* is a kind of pledge or mortgage is that the tenant's tenure consists in his right to take a profit. One might object that in *gift* also the donee is expected to ' make a profit '. But what our author means is that the tenant has undertaken to *pay out*, and is induced to do so by the chance of ' making a profit ', just as a moneylender will accept a mortgage when there is a high probability of his earning thereby.

[2] This has already been discussed in the *Sar. vil.* at pp. 221 and seqq.

[3] The party who advances money : if the mortgage he takes is a *bhogyādhi* it follows that all the profits are his in any event ; but even if it be a *gopyādhi* any increase in value of the mortgaged land accrues to the creditor-mortgagee should the owner fail to repay the loan with interest. In the *kuttā* the party who is here called the debtor is the tenant, who has undertaken to make payments after the original owner's death.

[4] The tenant takes the land as a security (if at all) for his reimbursement, having in view a more or less heavy expenditure on the owner's death. Who can release this security ? After all, the duties which he engages to perform do not terminate during his own lifetime—and the question whether his heirs have to continue the religious rites indefinitely is left open. If we inquire whether the heirs of the original owner (if they can be traced) can settle with the tenant and redeem the land, we must be met with the answer that the original contract is broken thereby, and in fact the practical difficulty of making such a settlement is nearly insuperable.

* [5] See for example Lakṣmīdhara, *Kṛtya-kalpataru*, *Brahmacāri-kāṇḍa*, Baroda, 1948, 188, 192.

moment when the thread-ceremony ceases and which actually persist by reason of the cessation of the thread-ceremony, by virtue of the fact that that sacrament forms a portion of the rite which consists in the duty of teaching the Veda to the initiate.[1] But this would be a mistake, since in the institution in question there is no suggestion of assets being mortgaged. On the contrary, since the tenure carries with it the liability of a contingent loss—a feature which is absent in either kind of mortgage—it is impossible to include within the purview of Non-payment of Debt the party entitled to the profit in the case of a *kuttā*.

Inclusion within the scope of Non-delivery of Gift is, however, consistent with logic. Non-payment of Debt is founded upon a basis of the four-fold Gift. We have already seen that, 'The way of Gift is four-fold: "given", "ungiven", "givable", and "ungivable" '.[2] 'Given' is itself two-fold: conditional and unconditional. If we assume the *kuttā* to be a conditional gift the mystery is solved[3]: the party entitled to the profit is included in this section by virtue of the gift made to him having been conditional. When the party entitled to the profit is involved in any issue in which we are concerned with the payment of *X's* debts or the due performance of divine or ancestral rites in conformity with *X's* instructions the section to consult is Non-delivery of Gift.

From this passage we gather that it was a practice in our author's region and period for persons who were, no doubt, in poor health or destitute of capital, and who had no sons or grandsons (legitimate or adoptive) or sons-in-law upon whom they could depend to work their land, to maintain them, and to see to the payment of their debts, the repose of their souls and the maintenance

[1] The objector's argument (which is acceptable so far as it goes) is ingenious. He says in effect, 'I agree that the security is incapable of release, but what of that? The situation of your tenant, whose duties arise potentially from the moment of the transfer and, when they materialize, go on for the rest of his life, is not unlike that of a Brahman boy who has received the sacred thread. The latter acquires at a definite point of time a set of duties which gradually unfold, and which he could neither come to know nor be burdened with until then. He can never be released from these duties, some of which are irksome or irrational, since they depend from the status which he voluntarily acquired at his initiation. But his duties are none the less of the nature of obligations, and the relation between the *guru* and his *upanīta* is (at any rate in theory) one of reciprocal and permanent indebtedness: the *guru* must teach the Veda to the pupil and even when he has finished this task his relationship lasts for the rest of their lives and even beyond those limits. So with the tenant-in-*kuttā*'. It is argued that the tenant's relation to the owner is none the less that of debtor and creditor for the impossibility of the 'security's' being released.

[2] The quotation is really a syncope of Nārada, VII, 2: *Dharma-kośa, Vyavahāra-kāṇḍa*, Wai, 1938, 798a; qu. *Sar. vil.*, 277, as from Manu.

[3] *iti rahasyam*: one should resist the temptation to translate: 'So says the *Rahasya*', for no work of that name likely to have a bearing on the subject is known to have been available at this period. The Hindu law of gifts did not hesitate (as did the Islamic law) to contemplate gifts subject to a condition, and the gift of an absolute estate subject to a defeasance clause was perfectly valid: there is a splendid example in *Corpus Inscriptionum Indicarum*, III, ed. J. F. Fleet, London, 1888, 235, and see also *Pulamuthu Pillai* v. *Azhaku Pillai*, (1930) 46 Travancore L.R. 227.

of the necessary regular oblations to gods and ancestors,[1] to give a part or the whole of their lands to strangers (who should not be without the necessary qualifications in point of caste) subject to an undertaking by the latter to ' see all square with them ' at and after their death.[2] Of course such a transaction must be a speculation on the part of the donee. It is true that he is the owner of the land in all but name, but its profits cannot always be anticipated correctly. He cannot be sure in advance how deeply indebted the original owner will be at his death, even if he can make a fairly accurate estimate of the annual cost of the religious ceremonies which will encumber him. If he decides that working the land himself is not the best course to follow, and wishes to lease it to a third party, is this consistent with his tenure ? Our author says almost in so many words that it is not : for although he is owner by the conditional gift, the original owner, the donor, retains so much of his ownership as will serve to prevent alienations in fraud of the stipulations and to recover (vicariously, in the person of the donor's heir) the whole property for default in performing the conditions. There are thus two owners, the property is *sāmānya*, and the tenant-in-*kuttā* (Skt. *kauttika*) cannot alienate validly even with the original owner's assent : the act must be that of the original owner himself. As for the latter, so long as the transaction is a *gift*, he cannot transfer his interest (albeit encumbered) to a third party.

The conditional gift operates at once, and the donee can draw profits from the land donated without being obliged to wait for the donor to die and for the conditions to become binding upon him. Since these encumbrances seem remote, not being in vigour at the time of the transfer, and since the size of the pecuniary burden is doubtful and, while hypothetical, fluctuating (to however little an extent), grounds certainly exist for wondering why anyone should have supposed that such a transaction was a mortgage. It is at once evident that if it *were* a mortgage a right of transfer might remain with the owner.

Now South India and Ceylon are familiar with a phenomenon (which may be peculiar to that part of the world) according to which the sale outright of ancestral property is so obnoxious to its owners, however impoverished they may be, that they will go to any lengths to avoid it.[3] When they cannot

[1] That such duties still weigh heavily upon the minds of those who anticipate dying without close relatives to follow them is proved by the facts in *Lekshmi Pillai Karthiyayani Pillai* v. *Narayani Pillai Easwari Pillai*, A.I.R. 1955 NUC (Travancore-Cochin) 3482, a case which is of peculiar value in our present context. The tenant-in-*kuttā* was plainly *not* adopted, or the whole transaction would have been pointless, but that there was some kind of customary adoption (i.e. not legal in the *śāstric* sense) in such cases cannot be ruled out. Reference may also be made to *Gopinath Shetty* v. *Santhamma*, [1956] 2 M.L.J. 38.

[2] For an instance of a deed of gift partly in consideration of past services and partly to secure payment of debts and maintenance of the donor in the Kandyan Provinces in 1872 see *Kandy D.C. No. 70480* in J. M. Perera, *A collection of select decisions of the Supreme Court on points of Kandyan law* . . . , II, Colombo, 1892, 91–2.

[3] Perhaps the best example is the mortgage known as *Peruverthom* described in C. Ramachandra Aiyar, *A manual of Malabar law* . . . , Madras, 1883, at pp. 38, 136 ; but compare the perpetual lease (see ch. VIII of the same work) and the mortgage known as *Jemmpanayom* (see ibid., 38, 138).

work it they lease it, and since the concept of the lease seems to have just missed occurring to the Northern Indian jurists of ancient times, probably on account of the historical priority of the concept of, and the astounding proliferation of the variety of, mortgages, what we should call a lease used to be given (subject to what is said below) by way of mortgage or under the guise of a kind of mortgage.[1] The status of mortgagor neither was, nor is, considered contemptible or deserving of pity, and when the owner exacted a premium from his tenant as a condition precedent to the latter's occupation of the land, he was content to think of this as a debt secured by mortgage. Mortgages properly so called were in any case almost invariably possessory. What we should call a deposit to secure regular payment of rent, or 'rent *
in advance', Indian jurists called a debt incurred by the owner on the security of his land, and the relationship of owner and tenant was described as that of debtor and creditor. It was natural, therefore, for the Indian lawyer of the pre-British periods to think of every tenant as a mortgagee in possession, who might retain part or the whole of the profits from his tenure in lieu of interest on the premium (or mortgage amount, according to the viewpoint), and in most cases in practice, should the tenant have stipulated (for example) to pay over half the crop to the owner year by year for a twelve-year term, the lawyer would view the tenant as a mortgagee bound to make regular additional advances to the mortgagor upon the security of the land and its yearly produce.

In the case of this *kuttā*, however, the condition subject to which the land was held was a condition which only in certain instances would be financially advantageous to the tenant. In those instances indeed he might be called *aupacayika*, 'the party entitled to the profit', and in this capacity he was indistinguishable from a mortgagee in possession whose advance upon mortgage had not been paid promptly but had been promised at and after the death of the mortgagor. Our author quite properly notices that he will be a debtor, if choice must be made from the alternatives, and certainly not a creditor. Of course the fact that the amount borrowed (assuming the donor to be a borrower) was unascertainable until the death of the borrower made no difference to the validity of the comparison. But the risk of loss did make a difference. The tenant-in-*kuttā* stood a substantial chance of not 'breaking even', especially if he had to maintain his own family out of the income from the lands. And where in fact he lost in carrying out his obligations (and he could be forced

[1] Material on this subject may be sought in C. Ramachandra Aiyar, op. cit., in chh. VI and VII, where *kānam*, and *oṟṟi* (otherwise *otti*), the two basic types of mortgage are investigated, followed by a discussion of *kuzhi-kānam*, *kuṭṭi-kānam*, and *verumpattom* leases. G. D. Patel, *The Indian land problem and legislation*, Bombay, 1954, deals with the subject briefly at pp. 313 and 345 and seqq. See also A. C. Mayer, *Land and society in Malabar*, Oxford, 1952, ch. 4. On the *otti* in Ceylon see H. W. Tambiah, *The laws and customs of the Tamils of Jaffna*, Colombo, 1950, ch. XX, and the same author's *The laws and customs of the Tamils of Ceylon*, Colombo, 1954, 48 and seqq., 71. On the position at Kandyan law see F. W. Hayley, *A treatise on the* *
laws and customs of the Sinhalese . . ., Colombo, 1923, 503 and seqq. For a modern investigation of the legal implications of the various types of mortgage in Malabar see *N. K. Rajaraja Varman Thirumalpad* v. *K. K. Krishnan Nair*, [1956] 2 M.L.J. 46. *Distinguish* 'mortgage by lease'.

to carry them out on pain of forfeiting the estate) his similarity with a mortgagee broke down. He was in fact making one or more gifts in return for another; the land could not be a security in the ordinary sense of the word (for in taking a qualitatively unlimited interest in it at the time of the transfer he had exhausted its capacity to satisfy him); and there was no means by which the heirs of the donor could pay off the encumbrance and thus reacquire, or 'redeem', the property. His interest was in effect what we should call an absolute estate subject to a condition subsequent, an estate defeasible upon failure to perform the services stipulated for by the demisor.

The present writer would be most grateful if any reader who knows of instances of such a tenure, whether it be from ancient, medieval, or modern India or in any other part of the world, would kindly bring them to his attention.[1]

If we had only the foregoing passage to rely upon we might be inclined to suppose that *kuttā* meant only a special kind of relationship between demisor and demisee, according to which the former made over the corpus of the property and the latter agreed to pay the debts and perform the religious rites required by the demisor. We should then be at a loss to account for the fact that the word *kuttā* appears, in various forms,[2] in modern Indian regional languages of the Peninsula without any suggestion that the transaction referred to has either a religious object or the satisfaction of the demisor's creditors as a normal component term. On the contrary we are obliged to explain how it is that the word, in whichever form it appears, is used to mean a lease, and apparently that kind of lease which obliges the tenant to pay in advance the rent for the season or period stipulated, or to pay at stipulated intervals an amount previously agreed upon as the value of his tenure, while retaining all the direct income of the lands (or other exclusive right demised to him) for himself, without obligation to account to the demisor, though perhaps liable for (legal) waste. It is quite extraordinary that in Sanskrit legal literature no word for 'lease' has so far been identified, and no word has been discovered in the printed *smṛtis* which could possibly cover the type of transaction alluded to in the regional languages referred to above. One was ready to accept (as stated previously) that the Northern Indians, Āryans or sub-Āryans, had not inherited the concept of lease and that when it was required the previously emerging concept of mortgage was made to serve all the purposes that were required. But it remained to be marvelled at that even in South India, where very substantial sections of the population have for centuries drawn their living from inferior tenures of the soil, no trace of a discussion of their legal position

[1] Professor J. Brough has kindly drawn to the author's attention the institution known in Nēpālī as *guṭhi* and in Nēwārī as *guthi* which, to his knowledge amongst the Nēwārs at any rate, enables land to be 'tied-up' (perhaps as some sort of *fideicommissum*) for generations amongst the settlor's descendants in order that its income might be exclusively devoted to defraying the cost of *śrāddhas* and other religious ceremonies in which the settlor would have a vicarious interest. That this institution has some ulterior similarity with the *kuttā* cannot be denied.

[2] See above, p. 62, n. 2.

could be found in the *śāstric* texts. In fact the *kuttā* supplies the key, and the *Sarasvatī-vilāsa* supplies the general background as well as the peculiar details set out above.

The passages are to be found at pp. 161–6 of the edition of 1927 [1] and their unique interest, legal and lexicographical, demands their republication along with the curious passage we have just examined.[2] They demonstrate that *kuttā*, for all its absence from the Sanskrit dictionaries, was in the sixteenth century the word for 'lease', and they outline the juristic basis of lease as then understood. They go further, and point out that the word *kuttā* was believed by the ancient commentator Bhāruci to have been used by the *smṛti*-writers Gautama and Viṣṇu, and was expounded by him. Bhāruci is believed to have been a South Indian writer, and his work (except for a commentary on Manu) has been lost for many years. It is fairly certain that his work on Manu [3] does not include the matter which the *Sarasvatī-vilāsa* copies out for us, and we are once again given cause to reflect upon the undoubted fact that the author of that work quotes more frequently than any other *dharma-nibandha* compiler from *smṛtis* which are not quoted elsewhere. The crucial texts cannot be traced. This casts some suspicion upon the genuineness not merely of the references to Bhāruci, but upon the whole discussion, since if the texts of Gautama and Viṣṇu which are relied upon are indeed spurious the technical *śāstric* quality of the passage is negligible, and it will not suffice to pass the blame on to Bhāruci. On the other hand the practical importance of such a discussion in a work specially commissioned by one of the great emperors of the eastern half of the Peninsula, a work intended for use, and doubtless gaining wide notoriety in its own day, cannot be underestimated, and it is for this reason that the present writer feels encouraged to offer an explanation (however far-fetched it may seem) for the curious fact that the discussion hangs upon texts which cannot be traced.

There is good reason to believe that Gautama's text was received in a fuller form than is now extant [4]; the same may well have been the case with Viṣṇu. *

[1] These passages, buried in parts of the digest where few would expect to find them, were pointed out to the present writer by his pupil, Mr. P. W. Rege.

[2] The passages were reprinted in the *Dharmākośa*, ubi cit., 107–9 under the unlikely heading of *darśanopakrama*. This reprint, which falls far below the standard of caution and supervision commonly used in that publication when selecting published and unpublished *śāstric* material for inclusion, bears all the mistakes, large and small, of the Mysore edition and actually adds, through mistaken zeal, a couple more of its own. The present writer hopes that the text which he prints below avoids the difficulties raised by these defective copies, but he cannot certify that the original text of the *Sarasvatī-vilāsa* has been definitively restored.

[3] A mutilated copy of a *Manu-śāstra-vivaraṇa* by Ṛjuvimala (*alias* Bhāruci) was identified by the late Dr. T. R. Chintamani and has been acquired for eventual publication by the present writer.

[4] Vijñāneśvara quotes Gautama as saying that Property is taken by birth; no one, not even in the seventeenth century in Bengal, could trace the original, and it is always cited as 'Gautama, in Vijñāneśvara'. The *Sar. vil.* refers to Gautama on p. 277 to the effect that improper gifts fail to create Property: the *sūtra* he quotes cannot be found either in Maskari or in Haradatta. Yet both of these were Southern authors, and Maskari is very old, being quoted in Viśvarūpa. *Per contra* for Gautama's text *utpattyaiva* cf. Medh. on M, IX, 156. *

Bhāruci, whether in his researches on Manu or in an independent work on Viṣṇu, would have had material available to him which was in many senses more antiquated than was available to the commentators and digest-writers of the twelfth century and after. His texts of Gautama and Viṣṇu may well have been pruned before transmission to later centuries,[1] and it was always a permissible practice to eliminate *sūtras* which could not be explained in a sense agreeable to current authorities—a practice which was much more common before the *smṛtis* acquired almost superstitious authority. Bhāruci was at least eight centuries and possibly almost a millennium older than the compiler of the *Sarasvatī-vilāsa* ; his work was very lengthy and detailed, and such works were doomed to comparatively rapid extinction. A copy was available (? at second hand) to Vijñāneśvara (*c.* A.D. 1125), but not to Varadarāja (*c.* A.D. 1200) nor to Devaṇṇa-bhaṭṭa, the author of the *Smṛti-candrikā* (*c.* A.D. 1250). In fact the *Sarasvatī-vilāsa* is the only work which makes constant, and obviously first-hand, reference to that ancient and valuable authority. A reason why these texts of Gautama and Viṣṇu, though present in Bhāruci, should have dropped out of their original collections may not be far to seek. It has long been suspected that Gautama was a *smṛti*-writer patronized chiefly in the South. The reference to the *kuttā* may have been inserted into his text, as doubtless other insertions were made, during the period when his text was far from settled and he was being acclimatized to the South. Northerners, who could for long claim an exclusive right to determine the genuineness of *smṛti*-texts, could not understand what this *kuttā* was, and ejected the supposititious *sūtra*. The same may well have happened to Viṣṇu, but there an additional inducement to reject the texts was present. As we shall see, the tenant in a 'without-profits' *kuttā* was allowed the benefit of an implied term in his contract that one-quarter of the profit over and above the rent due or paid in advance belonged to the tenant. This provision may well have been satisfactory in the ninth century A.D., when perhaps the pressure of population upon the land was much less heavy than it afterwards became, but would have been inappropriate in an age when the landlord could afford to insist that all losses should be borne by the tenant, and would exact a rack-rent, while the best that the tenant could do to protect himself was to stipulate not for a fixed rent, but for a share in the income, whatever it might turn out to be. In a tenants' market, at a period when, as we shall see Bhāruci saying, the motive behind the institution of *kuttā* was to enable the owner to obtain some income from land which he could not farm himself, it was natural that the owner, desiring to secure good farming, should say, 'Take the balance, if any, for yourself'. He might well feel inclined to approach the matter from another angle, to demand all the profits beyond a fixed amount, but to fix that amount high, and to stipulate for a generously low rent. Viṣṇu's implied term served to encourage good farming in a tenants' market, and protected owners who were in no position to stipulate for a high rent. But in

[1] This is the view which Kane accepts : op. cit., I, 70, n. 118 ; 266.

a landlords' market the tenant was not able to beat down the rent stipulated for, and the possibility that he would be left with a balance after meeting his own expenses would be remote. If then the law demanded that three-quarters of the net income also should be handed to the landlord, the economic rent would become almost impossible to fix, since it would be a pure speculation what the tenant's quarter might amount to. Hence the offending parts of the *smṛti*, if not capable of being interpreted into innocuity, suggested their own deletion.

At pp. 161–2 the *Sarasvatī-vilāsa* was discussing the effect of an *āsedha*, a word which is often translated ' arrest ', but which also means ' attachment ' (pending trial of an action), and had been commenting upon the question as to the proper reading of a text of Nārada on the function of this process, when reference to the *kuttā* in quite general terms is found :

ato Bhāruci-vyākhyānam eva samyak, Viṣṇu-vacanānurodhitvāt. nanv evam ayuktam, Viṣṇu-vacanānurodhābhāvāt; tathā ca Viṣṇuḥ ' āseddhuḥ phalam evāsedhya ' iti — maivam. bhavatā Vaiṣṇava-vacana-tātparyāparijñānāt. tat-tātparyan tu likhitāsedhāt phalāsedhanaṃ balavat. sarveṣāṃ phalārtham eva pravṛtteḥ. phalāsedha-karaṇe tat-pūrva-kṛtā likhitādyāsedhā aprayojakā eveti tat-prābalya-jñāpanārthatvāt tad-vacanasya iti. tathā ca Gautama-sūtraṃ ' phalāsedhaḥ kauttika-vat ' iti. tasyārtho vivṛto nibandha-kāreṇa — atra dvitīyārthe vatiḥ; kauttikaḥ *kuttā-jīvikaḥ, yathā āsedha-viṣayaḥ. evaṃ sarvatra phalam evāsedha-viṣaya iti. yathā kauttikaḥ kuttā-kāreṇa gṛhīta-pāribhāṣikārthātiriktopacita-dravya-svīkāra-daśāyām āsedhyaḥ. evaṃ sarveṣu vyavahāreṣu phala-svīkāra-daśāyām āsedhaḥ kartavya iti. phala-svīkāra-daśāyāṃ phalam evāsedhyam, na sva-rūpam iti tātparyam. kauttika-grahaṇan tu kuttā-viṣaye itara-vyavahāra-vat pūrva-kālāsedhā na santi, kintu kuttāyāṃ phalam evāsedha-viṣaya iti tāvan-mātra-viśeṣa-jñāpanārtham ity avagantavyam.*

This may be translated as follows :

Hence the explanation of Bhāruci is correct, since it is conformable to the text of Viṣṇu. If you reply that this solution is unsatisfactory, since it does not actually conform to Viṣṇu's text, and because what Viṣṇu says is, ' The income alone belongs to the attaching party after his attachment ', I must disagree : for you have not really grasped the meaning of Viṣṇu's text. Its meaning is, on the contrary, that an attachment of the income takes precedence over an attachment by written notice.[1] Naturally, since all such proceedings are instituted with the object of obtaining access to the profits. In other words the

[1] On the different sorts of attachment the *Sar. vil.* has spoken on p. 160. Kane, op. cit., III, 290–2, gives an account of the institution with references. Neither the *Sar. vil.* itself nor its most substantial Southern predecessor, the *Smṛti-candrikā* (ed. Gharpure, Bombay, 1918, II, 29–31), speaks of *likhitāsedha*, literally ' written attachment '. It is not impossible that the word means ' attachment of the kinds detailed in Nārada, I, 48 ', but the likelihood that it means attachment by a written notice not to depart out of the village, not to dispose of the property, and so on seems on the whole greater. Vācaspati-miśra, *Vyavahāra-cintāmaṇi*, ed. and trans. L. Rocher, Ghent, 1956, is most disappointing on this subject.

purpose of that text is to inform us that where there has been an attachment of the income prior attachments by written notice or by other methods are quite useless, on account of the greater efficacy of the former method. And Gautama's *sūtra*, ' Attachment of income occurs as in the case of a *kauttika* ',[1] is on the same point. The author of the Digest [2] has explained its meaning as follows : ' Here the ending *vat* (" as ") is to be understood in the accusative sense.[3] *Kauttika* means a tenant-in-*kuttā*,[4] that is to say one who may be the object of an attachment. Thus in all cases it is the income which is the object of attachment. For example a tenant-in-*kuttā* may be subjected to attachment by way of interception of assets accruing over and above the amount stipulated for in the terms he accepted with his tenure. Similarly in every sort of litigation attachment is to be made by way of interception of the income '. The expression ' by way of interception of the income ' implies that income alone is to be attached and not the actual corpus itself. But the expression *kauttika* is to be understood as brought in to convey this distinction alone, namely that in the case of a *kuttā* there can be no prior attachments, as would be possible in other types of litigation, but in respect of a *kuttā* nothing can be the object of attachment but the income.

Although this passage does not tell us more about the meaning of the *kuttā* than we know already (from the passage dealing with the question whether *kuttā* is a mortgage or a gift), it was perfectly rational to explain that where a tenant does not own the corpus, and becomes the defendant in an action, whether brought by his landlord or a stranger, the latter cannot obtain an attachment of anything beyond such portion of the income as is left over when the landlord's rights are satisfied. In our *kuttā* for payment of debts and performance of religious rites, the part of the income available for attachment will be that over and above the cost of those two quasi-charges upon the property. Much more light on the central concept of *kuttā* is available from a passage on pp. 163–6, where the compiler digresses into a discussion on a *kuttā*-deed as a document of title, and its evidential value :

Kuttā-lekha-bala-vicāraḥ. nanu likhitādīnāṃ prāmāṇyam āgama-nirūpaṇa-dvārā. āgamābhāve tat-prāmāṇyaṃ praśithila-mūlatayā dṛdhan na bhavati.

[1] Not traced in Maskari's or Hardatta's versions of Gautama.

[2] Who this is is uncertain. It may well be Bhāruci (though not in his work on Manu), or possibly Halāyudha ?

[3] Otherwise the expression might mean nothing more than that a *kauttika* could attach.

[4] One must resist the temptation to translate *kuttā-pradātā* (= *uttama*, we are told) ' landlord ', and *kauttika* ' tenant '. Whereas the latter would not be strikingly inaccurate, as the rights of a *kauttika* are undoubtedly those of a tenancy of a sort or sorts, the owner or demisor may be of wider kinds than are indicated by the English word ' landlord '. On the whole, while the general discussion may employ the English words in a non-technical sense, it seems better in the translation of our source to remain as close to the apparent sense as possible. The ' author of the Digest ' glossed *kauttika* as *kuttā-jīvikaḥ* and Bhāruci (see below) as *kuttōpajīvī* ; these are synonymous, meaning ' one who derives his living from a *kuttā* '.

āgamās tu keṣāñcin mate 'sapta. tathā ca smṛtiḥ 'sapta vittāgamā dharmyā' iti. Gautamādīnāṃ mate tu riktha-kraya-saṃvibhāga-parigrahādhigama-pratigraha-nirveśādayo 'ṣṭa-vittāgamā iti. Bhāradvāja-mate tu parivṛtter api vittāgama-rūpatayā nigaditatvāt tayā sārdhan nava-vittāgamāḥ. eteṣāṃ madhye kuttākāra-kārita-paribhāṣitārthasyāparigaṇanād āgama-prakāra-nirūpaṇāśaktau kuttā-lekh-asya tad-ārūḍha-sākṣiṇāñ ca daurbalyaṃ prāptam. 'anāgaman tu yo bhuṅkte bahūny abda-śatāny api, cora-daṇḍena taṃ pāpan daṇḍayet pṛthivī-patiḥ' iti smṛteḥ, āgama-śūnyāyā bhukteḥ pramāṇa-koṭi-niveśābhāvaḥ pratīyate. yat tu bhogāgamayoḥ sāmyaṃ Bṛhaspati-vacanāt pratīyate: tat tu kevala-bhukter daurbalya-jñāpana-paratayā na viruddham. tathā ca Bṛhaspatiḥ: 'bhuktyā kevalayā naiva bhūmi-siddhim avāpnuyāt, āgamenāpi śuddhena dvābhyāṃ siddhim avāpnuyāt'. tathā ca Vyāsaḥ 'sāgamo dīrgha-kālaś ca niscchidro 'nyaravojjhitaḥ, pratyarthi-sannidhānaś ca pañcāṅgo bhoga iṣyate' iti. atra 'pañcāṅgo bhoga iṣyata' iti vadann ekāṅga-vaikalye 'py aprāmāṇyaṃ bhogasyeti darśayatīty uktaṃ prāk. ataś cāgama-nirūpaṇe tad-abhāva-pratīteḥ mūla-śuddhy-abhāvāt tad-gamaka-pramāṇa-dārḍhyābhāva iti.

atrocyate. kvacit paribhāṣā api vittāgama eva, yathā 'ādhiḥ praṇaśyed dviguṇe dhane yadi na mokṣyate' ity atra dhana-dvaiguṇya-nibandhana-paribhāṣā vittāgama-madhye 'parigaṇitā 'pi sopādhikaṃ svatvam avagamayatīti Vijñāneś-varaḥ. Candrikā-kāras tu dhana-dvaiguṇya-paribhāṣā parivṛtti-rūpeṇa tila-vrīhi-vinimayavat svatvāpādakety āha. Vijñāneśvara-matāvalambanena paribhāṣāyā vācika-dānāntargatatayā svatvāpādakatvam asti. aupādhika-sthale 'py upādhi-nivṛttau svatvasya dṛḍhatvāt. tathā hi kṣetrādes tasmād etāvad dhanam asmabhyan dīyatām avaśiṣṭaṅ gṛhyatām; yad vā etāvad dravyaṅ gṛhītvā tad-ṛṇaṃ saṃśodhya-tām avaśiṣṭaṅ gṛhyatām iti paribhāṣāyām avaśiṣṭa-dravye svatva-nivṛttiḥ para-svatvāpatti-paryantā bhavaty eveti dṛśyate. athavā Bhāruci-matāvalambanena kuttākāra-kārita-paribhāṣāvaṣṭambhita-mānasika-dānāntatayā svatvāpādakatvaṃ paribhāṣāyās samasti.

nanu saṅkalpa-mātrāt svatvan notpadyate, kin tu saṅkalpāt svatvam apaiti. svatvotpattis tv arjanād eveti dhanārjana-naya-siddhatvāt tad-vyākopo mānasika-dānāntatayā paribhāṣāyās svatva-hetutvoktāv iti cet, maivam. yadi dhanārjana-nayas svatvāpāya-hetu-mānasika-kriyaiveti syāt tadā 'yan doṣaḥ prāduṣyāt, na ca tathā svatvāpāya-hetuḥ kvacit saṅkalpaḥ kvacin mahāpātakādir ity uktam. ataś ca tasyāpy adhikaraṇasya laukika-vyavahārānurodhitayā svatvasyāpi laukikatvāc ca yathā loke dṛṣṭan tathā svīkartavyam. kuttādi-vyavahāre mānasikī kriyaiva svatva-hetur iti sammataṃ laukikānām. tathā ca dṛśyate. bahuśo bahavaḥ Kāyasthāḥ kṣetrādikan deśa-grāmādikaṃ vā kuttā-kāreṇa gṛhṇantaḥ pākṣikā-pacaya-bhāra-sahiṣṇavo dṛśyante. tatra grāmādi-kṣetrādi-deśādy-upacita-pāribhā-ṣika-dravye teṣāṃ vyavahāriṇāṃ svāmyaṃ vidyata eva. sa cāgamas sādhīyān eva. nanu kuttā-kāreṇa gṛhīta-dravye upacayo vidyate cet tam upacayaṅ kuttā-pradātāra uttama-padābhilapyās svīkurvanti paridṛśyante ca, maivam. yadi kauttikas tv apacaya-bhāra-sahiṣṇur na bhavet tadā 'py uttamasyāpy upacayā-pāya-sahiṣṇutvan na syāt. kauttikatva-prasiddhir yā 'varuddha-bhoga-pradānān-yathā-karaṇa-mūlā. ata evoktaṃ Viṣṇunā 'kauttiko 'pacaya-bhāra-sahiṣṇur uttamas tūpacayāpāya-sahiṣṇur' iti. atra Bhāruciḥ: kuttopajīvī kauttikaḥ; *kuttā-pradāt*ottamaḥ; kuttā-*nāma gṛha-kṣetrārāma-grāma-deśādi-padārtha-samṛddha-phala-prāpty-artham yasmai-kasmaicid vyavahāriṇe tad-gṛhādi-padārtha-jāta-sandānam iti.* sandānan *nāma samyag-dānan na bhavati aupādhika-dāna-rūpatvāt kuttāyāḥ, api tu sandānaṃ bandhanam, uttamasyāpy upacayānaṅgī-kāreṇa kauttika eva bandhana-rūpatvāt. sandānaṅ kuttety upacaryate.* sandānan *nāma tyāga-mātram iti kecit. atrāyaṃ viśeṣaḥ: yady anayoḥ kauttikottamayor vādyate samayaḥ 'upacayaś cen mayottamena soḍhavyaḥ apacayaś cet tvayā kauttikena soḍhavya' iti, tadā saṃvid-anusaraṇe upacaye vidyamāne 'pi Viṣṇu-vacanānusāreṇa pāda-mātropacaya eva svāmyaṅ kauttikasya. tathā ca Viṣṇuḥ 'pāda-mātropacaye kauttikasya svāmyam' iti. atra Bhāruciḥ: so 'yam upacayaḥ kuttātaḥ; pāda-mātrañ cet tasminn evopacaye uttama-manasā imam upacayaṅ kauttiko gṛhṇīta, anyadā āya-nāśayos svāmy-adhīnatvam, na tu kauttikasya; pādādhikya eva svāmyāt tasyeti smarati. tadā tasmin pāda-mātropacita-dravye uttamasya svatva-nivṛttiḥ parasvatvāpatti-paryantā bhavatīti tātparyam iti. ayam āśayaḥ: mānasikam api dānan tyāgatmakaṃ svatvāpādakam iti Vaiṣṇavaṃ matam iti. uttama-manasā 'yaṃ kauttika imam upacayaṅ gṛhṇātv iti vadatā Bhārucinā yāvaty upacite dravye uttamasya mānasika-tyāgaḥ tāvaty api svatvaṃ Vaiṣṇavaṃ pādam iti matam. tato nyūnena na bhavitavyam iti. atra kecid āhuḥ: anenaiva nyāyena kuttāyāḥ apacaye vidyamāne 'pi pāda-mātram uttamena soḍhavyam. tato nyūnan dūrata eva, tatrādhikam aicchikam iti Viṣṇu-vacanasya tātparyārtha iti.*

This may be translated as follows:

A discussion of the value of a deed of *kuttā*. You may well point out that the evidential value of deeds and other documents is derived from their capacity to declare title.[1] In the absence of title the evidential character of such material is open to challenge, for its very foundation is of the weakest. Now according to many authorities titles are no more than seven in all. A *smṛti* tells us,[2] 'Seven acquisitions of wealth are consistent with *dharma*'. On the other hand, Gautama and others believe that there are eight 'acquisitions of wealth' namely inheritance, purchase, partition, garnering, finding, acceptance, wages, and so on. Yet Bhāradvāja believes[3] that since even exchange has been pronounced to be a type of 'acquisition of wealth' we must include it, and

[1] Documents were valued as evidence in disputes concerning debts or title to land or grants of income. Naturally if the transfer was itself of an impossible or illegal character the evidence was worthless.

[2] Manu, x, 115. Gautama's text next referred to is x, 39–42, and the phrase 'so on' stands for 'conquest'. Both texts are accompanied by exhaustive and varied commentaries in the *Dharma-kośa*, ubi cit., 1122 and seqq.

[3] His text is not cited independently in the *Dharma-kośa*, in Lakṣmīdhara's *Gṛhastha-kāṇḍa* (where one might well expect to find it), in the *Vyavahāra-nirṇaya*, the *Smṛti-candrikā*, or the *Vīramitrodaya*; but the *Sar. vil.* refers to a view of his on exchange on p. 314 (also 319). It is clear from the many quotations in the *Vyavahāra-nirṇaya* that Bharadvāja or Bhāradvāja was known as the author of a verse work on *vyavahāra*, which may well have been composed comparatively late.

so we have nine 'acquisitions of wealth'. The subject-matter of the terms stipulated by way of a *kuttā* is not enumerated amongst these nine, whence it appears that a deed of *kuttā* cannot possibly declare a kind of title, and we are faced with the fact that neither it nor any oral evidence depending from it can be of the least validity! Moreover, a *smṛti* says,[1] 'The King should punish with the punishment appropriate to a thief one who enjoys an object without title, even if he is able to point to possession for many centuries'; and thus we know that possession devoid of title is not included among the alternative permissible types of evidence of title. As for the text of Bṛhaspati which gives us to understand that possession and title amount to the same thing, it does not contradict the point raised, since its intention is to inform us of the invalidity of bare possession. Bṛhaspati says in fact,[2] 'One may never attain certainty of tenure of land by possession unaided; one may attain certainty by *both*, if his title is clear'. And to the same effect Vyāsa says,[3] 'Possession prevails if it be five-fold: accompanied by title, of long duration, uninterrupted, free from the adverse claim of others, and in the presence of the opposite party'. And it has already been shown that, by the use of the expression, 'possession prevails if it be five-fold', he explains that if possession be short in respect of even one of those qualifications it has no evidential value. Consequently, when it is proposed to declare a title, and the fundamental contention is open to question by reason of our knowing that such a title is non-existent, there can be no validity in evidence tending to prove such a contention. Such might be my objector's argument.

But my answer is as follows. There are occasions where a contractual term [4] amounts to an 'acquisition of wealth', as for example in the

[1] Nārada, I, 87, discussed in the *Vyavahāra-cintāmaṇi* at § 462.

[2] *Bṛhaspati-smṛti*, ed. Rangaswami Aiyangar, Baroda, 1941, VII, 30. The learned editor prefers *bhuktiḥ* to *bhūmi*, and *sidhyati nānyathā* instead of *siddhim avāpnuyāt* in the second half of the *śloka*, following the reading in the *Smṛti-candrikā*, ubi cit., 70. There is no material difference in the sense rendered.

[3] The text is quoted in this form as Vyāsa's in the *Vyavahāra-cintāmaṇi* at § 452, and is there referred to Vyāsa, ed. Jolly, 1881, I, 84. But the Mysore edition of the *Sar. vil.* prints *vicchedoparavojjhitaḥ*, and there may have been some confusion with a text attributed to Pitāmaha in the *Smṛti-candrikā*, ubi cit., 70, which reads *cāvicchinnāparavojjhitā* (the line commencing *sāgamā*) and concludes the *śloka* with *bhuktiḥ pañcavidhā smṛtā*. However our text is attributed to Vyāsa and/or Kātyāyana and even Nārada in the form printed here: see *Dharma-kośa, Vyavahāra-kāṇḍa*, 406b, 416b, and cf. 420b, 419a.

[4] *paribhāṣā*. This has been translated here sometimes 'contractual term' and sometimes 'legal term'. In the first passage the word *pāribhāṣika* is used, as an adjective governing *vyavahāra*. In this passage again we find *pāribhāṣika-dravya*. Monier-Williams does not give this meaning of *paribhāṣā*, though the meanings given for *pāribhāṣika* may be said almost to cover what is required. In Nīlakaṇṭha-bhaṭṭa's *Vyavahāra-mayūkha* we have the now famous distinction between *pāribhāṣika-* and *apāribhāṣika-strīdhana*. *paribhāṣā* in this sort of context means a term by reason of which a particular legal right can be predicated, particularly (though by no means necessarily) if it is created by agreement; *pāribhāṣika* means 'having such a term as its characteristic', or 'in accordance with such a term'. In Nīlakaṇṭha's case the meaning is that the first class of *strīdhana* is that strictly marked out by the text of Kātyāyana. The word for 'contract' is not *paribhāṣā* but *samaya*, 'the meeting of two minds', as Anglo-American jurists would say, or *saṃpratipatti, or saṃvid.* *

text,[1] ' A mortgage may perish if it be not redeemed with the double amount', where, although the legal term charging the land with double the mortgage-amount is not enumerated among the 'acquisitions of wealth', Vijñāneśvara tells us [2] that we are to infer a conditional Property. On the other hand, the author of the Candrikā has said [3] that the legal term of the doubled amount is a means of creating Property because it is a variety of exchange, like an exchange of sesamum for rice. If we rely upon Vijñāneśvara's view, the legal term is a means of creating Property because it is an example of an oral gift. For in a case of a conditional transfer Property is validly effected upon the performance of the condition. So in examples like, 'You must give me out of this field (etc.) such-and-such an amount, and the balance you may keep for yourself', or, 'You may take such-and-such goods and pay this debt, and the balance you may keep for yourself', it is evident that there is a cessation of Property persisting up to the production of another's Property.[4] Alternatively, relying upon Bhāruci's opinion, the contractual term does indeed possess the capacity to create Property since it ends with a mental gift dependent upon the term stipulated for by way of the *kuttā*.

You may object that by intention alone Property is not produced, whereas by intention Property ceases.[5] The principle of acquisition of assets is established in the terms, 'Only by means of acquisition does Property come about',[6]

[1] Yājñavalkya, II, 58. This is well commented upon by Vijñāneśvara. It is clear even from the *smṛti* that it is only a *gopyādhi* (see above, p. 63, n. 1) that can be foreclosed in this manner. In the case of a usufructuary pledge, on the other hand, the rule is (Yājñ., II, 64) that after the income in the mortgagee's hands has reached double the amount of the loan, the mortgagee's right to possession ends, and the pledge with it.

[2] *Mitākṣarā* comm. on Yājñ., II, 58; ed. Nirṇaya-sāgara Press, 1909, 159. J. R. Gharpure (*Yājñavalkya Smṛti with the commentaries of (1) The Mitākṣharā by Vijñaneśvara Bhikṣhu . . . , Chapters I–VII. . . . An English translation with notes . . . Second edition*, Bombay, 1938, 821–2) translates as follows: '(To this) the answer is: Even the act of pledging itself is considered as a circumstance, although coupled with a contingent condition, creating the creditor's ownership. The acceptance of a pledge also is well known in the world as a circumstance, also coupled with a contingency, creating the creditor's ownership. So when the amount becomes doubled, and also when the appointed time has arrived, the right of paying the amount becomes entirely extinct, and therefore under the present text there occurs an entire cessation of the debtor's right of ownership, and the ownership of the creditor becomes absolute'.

[3] Devaṇṇa-bhaṭṭa, *Smṛti-candrikā*, ubi cit., 141. The sale of sesamum was prohibited by the religious law to certain persons (see texts in Kane, op. cit., II, 127) but the restriction was overcome by allowing exchanges: cf. Āpastamba referred to by Kane, ibid., 129. Consequently the agreement according to which land is taken instead of a sum of money due but not capable of being paid is an exchange and therefore a lawful means of acquisition, although not mentioned by Gautama.

[4] This is the definition of transfer of title according to the compiler of the *Sar. vil.* See ibid., 277.

* [5] On this general problem see *BSOAS*, XVIII, 3, 1956, 475 and seqq. On *saṅkalpa* as a cause of the cessation of Property see *Svatva-rahasya* (to be published), IV, § 10.

[6] This is an inverted statement of Prabhākara's gibe: *pralapitam idaṅ kenāpi 'arjanaṃ svatvan nāpādayati' iti vipratiṣiddham.* It is rubbish to say that acquisition does not produce Property. But there was more in the suggestion than Prabhākara was prepared to admit, and all his juristic followers have missed the point. But that is a subject for treatment elsewhere.
* The reference is *Bṛhati* on Jaimini, IV, i, 2. See *J. Econ. and Soc. Hist. of the Orient*, I, 1957, 66–97.

and accordingly this rule would be contradicted if we were to declare the legal term we have been discussing a cause of Property on the ground of its culminating in a mental gift. But this is not true. It has been pointed out that if the method of acquiring assets were merely the mental act causing the cessation of Property that difficulty would be greatly weakened, and it would not be the case that a cause of the cessation of Property might be seen at one time in an intention to dedicate, for example, and at another in the commission of a grave sin and the like.[1] And so, since even this chapter of the law observes conformity with the world of practical affairs,[2] and since even Property has a purely practical character,[3] what is observed in practice must be accepted by the jurists. That in a transaction such as the *kuttā* the very mental act alone is a cause of Property is agreed amongst all students of practical affairs. And this is what is actually observed. Very frequently a great number of Kāyasthas [4] accept fields and so on, or a District, a village and so on, by way of

[1] The sentence at first reading is obscure. In fact it is a rather brilliant suggestion, considering the state of the subject at that time. It was conventionally accepted that Property was destructible, and Property was producible ; but an instance of the one would not by any means necessarily lead to an instance of the other. This was not unreasonable since one might destroy one's Property by, for example, forgetting about a buried object, by determining to abandon it, or by dedicating it for the public use ; and in each case no Property was caused by one's act or omission. The objector has pointed out that a mental gift is no transfer of Property (as contrasted with a ceremonial gift in the presence of the donee and with pouring of water, etc.) since mere *saṅkalpa*, ' intention ', does not *create* Property. But, says our author, what about (i) dedications to an idol, where the idol's Property is traced to the *saṅkalpa* of the dedicator, and (ii) grave sins, which cause ' fall ', and thus the loss of all Property, so that the heirs inherit as if on death ? Is there any substantial point in saying that the *saṅkalpa* is not a *cause* of the idol's Property, and that the sin is not a *cause* of the heir's succession ? Assume that, as we observe, they are in fact causes, they create and do not merely destroy, and we are a long way to removing your difficulty, which is of a purely technical origin. We must, as he says next, have regard to what actually happens.

[2] It is a maxim of the *śāstra*, stressed most frequently in the sixteenth and seventeenth centuries, that the *vyavahāra* portions (to which all these discussions belong) are ultimately based upon practical requirements and actual usage, notwithstanding the fact that *smṛti*-texts are the authoritative hooks upon which the rules are hung.

[3] A doctrine accepted from the Mīmāṃsakas, who had a vested interest in such a view. Dhāreśvara, i.e. Bhoja, objected to this, and he had some following, but the majority of the jurists are content to accept a conclusion which gave less trouble to the public. The matter has been investigated elsewhere (see p. 76, n. 6, above). A good reference is K. L. Sarkar, *The Mimansa rules of interpretation as applied to Hindu law*, *TLL* for 1905, Calcutta, 1909, 390 and seqq. Madana-siṃha (attrib.), *Madanaratnapradīpa*, *Vyavahāra-vivekoddyota*, ed. Kane, Bikaner, 1948, has an excellent passage on the subject at pp. 323 and seqq.

[4] The mention of this caste, well-known in Bengal, Eastern India generally, Uttar Pradesh, and even in Maharashtra, is significant. The author did not want to use the actual caste name * of the people who most frequently participated in this transaction as *kauttikas*, because that would have the effect of limiting the application of what he was saying, but it is extremely likely that he had a caste such as the Reddis in mind. Although in many places castes lower than Kāyasthas (who are held to be Śūdras by some decisions of modern courts and *dvijas* by others) must have been frequent tenants of ordinary farming leases, it is quite probable that government revenue-leases were monopolized by a particular class. Valuable material about Kāyasthas is collected in Kane, op. cit., II, 75–7, and it is evident that their identity commenced with an occupational aptitude, namely in administration of a more or less subordinate character. Vijñāneśvara, on Yājñ., I, 336, where Kāyasthas are classed with *cāṭas* (p. 81 inf.) and thieves,

kuttā, and are observed to bear the risk of a contingent loss. In such cases no one doubts but that there is Ownership on the part of these businessmen in any profit accruing to them from the village, field, District, or whatever it may be, so far as is covered by the legal term in question. And this title is beyond dispute. You might reply that if in the property taken by virtue of the *kuttā* a profit results, the demisors-in-*kuttā*, who are known by the name *uttama*,[1] appropriate the profit to themselves and are commonly observed to do so. But you are wrong. If the *kauttika* were not willing to undertake the risk of a loss, the *uttama* would certainly not undertake the risk of a diminution of the profit.[2] If anything is established about the status of a *kauttika* it is that it is founded upon an exact compliance with the mode of transfer of a strictly limited possessory right. It is for this reason that Viṣṇu says,[3] 'The *kauttika* is liable to suffer the loss, while the *uttama* is liable to suffer a diminution of the profit'. Here Bhāruci explains, 'One who lives on a *kuttā* is a *kauttika*; the demisor-in-*kuttā* is the *uttama*; the word *kuttā* refers to the *sandāna* to any second party of the items consisting of the demisor's house, field, garden, village, District, and so on for the purpose of realizing the whole income therefrom'. The word *sandāna* does not equal *samyag dāna* ('a full and entire gift'), since the *kuttā* has the quality of a conditional gift, but means 'binding'.[4] For the *kuttā* has the character of a 'binding', at any rate from the point of view of the *kauttika*, in that the *uttama* does not acquire the profit.[5] 'Binding'

accounts for the sage's singling them out for especial supervision by the King on the ground that they are normally highly in his favour and possess extraordinary cunning. They were not mere accountants in Aparārka's eyes (*c.* A.D. 1100), for when he comments on the same *śloka* (there = I, 334) he says *kāyasthāḥ karādhikṛtāḥ*, i.e. those that supervised the actual collection of the revenue. Śūlapāṇi in his *Dīpakalikā* (on I, 336), written between 1420 and 1465, is more cautious, since many Kāyasthas in Bengal were not employed in government service. He says
* *rāja-sambandhāt prabhaviṣṇavaḥ*, i.e. only those in a position to oppress the public because of their official status at Court. More to our present purpose, however, is the fact that in Āndhra during the thirteenth century at any rate Kāyasthas were in a position to carry on an independent territorial rule, for in A.D. 1239 the powerful Āndhra emperor Gaṇapati Kākatīya of Wāraṅgal had to subdue by force Kāyasthas ruling in the region corresponding to the modern Cuddapah and Kurnool Districts. See K. A. Nilakanta Sastri, *A history of South India*, Oxford, 1955, 210, 211. Whether the preferential right to clerical appointments to Government was still evident in the sixteenth century may be open to doubt. The mention of the word *deśa* 'District' makes it quite clear that these people might be revenue-farmers as well as private tenants.

1 The choice of this word, unknown to the compilers of lexicons, is strongly reminiscent of *uttamarṇa* 'a creditor'.

2 Cases where the *uttama* takes profits over and above the premium are, he says, to be attributed to a special agreement to that effect. There is a certain reciprocity in the relationship. The *kauttika* can be forced to pay his rent, whether the income reaches that amount or not; similarly the *uttama* must take a chance whether there is any profit. If the *kauttika* stipulates that he shall not be liable for loss, i.e. agrees to pay over as rent a proportion of the net income, there can be no question but that the *uttama* will oblige him to pay over that proportion, however large the income may turn out to be.

3 The text is not found in Jolly's edition.

4 The root *dā* is found (very rarely) in the sense 'to bind'.

5 See Monier-Williams for the usual senses of *sandāna*. In the normal *kuttā*, says our author, the corpus of the property is 'bound' to the *kauttika*, so that he may take all the income to the exclusion of the *uttama*, subject to his performance of his part of the bargain.

is used metaphorically for the *kuttā* itself. There are some, however, who take *sandāna* here to mean no more than 'relinquishment'.

But the following distinction should be observed: if the agreement between the two parties, namely the *kauttika* and the *uttama*, is this: 'If there be any profit it is to be taken by me, the *uttama*; but if there be a loss it must be borne by you, the *kauttika*'; then should there be a profit after the terms of the contract have been performed, the *kauttika* actually has Ownership in not more than one-quarter of the profit, in accordance with a text of Viṣṇu. Viṣṇu says, in fact,[1] 'The *kauttika* has Ownership in the profit only to the extent of one-quarter'. Bhāruci comments: 'The purport of the *smṛti* is this: the profit referred to here is that realized from the *kuttā*; if this amounts to no more than a quarter [2] the *kauttika*, by virtue of the *uttama's* intention, may take this "profit" in that profit; but as to other circumstances [3] both profit and loss would accrue to the Owner, and not to the *kauttika*; for as to the excess above the quarter the Owner has the ownership. The meaning is that in such cases there is a cessation of the Property of the *uttama* persisting up to the creation of the Property of another in respect of the goods which represent the profit of not more than a quarter'. What this amounts to is that according to Viṣṇu's opinion even a mental gift has the character of a relinquishment and may produce Property. When Bhāruci says that according to the *uttama's* intention this *kauttika* may take this profit, his opinion appears to be that Viṣṇu's 'quarter' is the Property arising in so much of the goods representing a profit as the mental relinquishment by the *uttama* covers. Consequently we are to understand that it cannot arise in less than a quarter.[4]

[1] This text is likewise not traced in the printed edition.

[2] The sense is not perfectly clear, since the whole extract has been affected by misunderstanding in the course of the transmission of the text. What should have been read *uttama-* has twice been written *uttamo*, and the true subject of the verb *smarati* has been missed, apparently by both editors. It would seem that Bhāruci's notion of Viṣṇu's meaning is that the profit is the total income; out of this the rent is deducted and there is another 'profit' remaining over. If this amounts to a quarter of the whole, but not more, the *kauttika* may, in this special kind of *kuttā*, keep it. The law allows the *uttama* mentally to relinquish a quarter, even when he says that he relinquishes none of the profits over and above the rent.

[3] i.e. when the *kauttika* makes no profit at all, or his profit amounts to less than a quarter of the total income, or it amounts to more than a quarter.

[4] At first sight this is an odd rule. We commence with the position that the *uttama* claims, and the *kauttika* admits that the *uttama* is entitled to, all the profits which accrue from the tenure over and above the rent or premium. Then we are told that according to Viṣṇu a *kauttika* is entitled to a profit of 'only' a quarter. We might suppose that the text of Viṣṇu refers to quite a different situation, where the *kauttika* pays a heavy fee for the right to work the land, and might *prima facie* claim all the profits, whereupon a customary rule comes to the aid of the *uttama* and secures to him three-quarters of the profits. It may well have been the case at some stage in the history of land-tenure in South India that tenants paid three-quarters of the gross produce to the owners and kept only a quarter for themselves, but we may doubt whether this situation prevailed far or for long. Is it not more likely that this text (if genuine) applies to a situation where a quarter of the net profit is secured to a tenant, whatever the value or extent of his premium, in order to secure good farming? The *Sar. vil.* understands Bhāruci to say that the quarter is estimated on the total profit from the *kuttā*, and that probably means the total gross income. Whichever method of calculation is correct the principle is clear that the tenant is

Some object that according to this reasoning if the *kuttā* produces a loss, a burden not exceeding a quarter of it ought to be borne by the *uttama*.[1] Consequently the full meaning of the text of Viṣṇu, they say, is that while a falling-short is totally excluded an excess is optional.[2]

From these fragments, introduced into the work in different places and with totally different motives, we are able to piece together the basic concept of the *kuttā*. The owner most commonly offers to a stranger the right to work a piece of land (or some other source of income) and to keep all the income for himself, and the stranger agrees to pay the owner a premium, which he has carefully calculated by appraising the probable productivity of the source in advance, as a consideration for the exclusive right in question. The period might be as long as a season, or indefinite subject to an implied right to novate the agreement should conditions alter markedly. When the premium demanded is very high, or if its payment is deferred and its amount is not capable of exact computation, the possibility of the tenant's suffering a loss is worthy of consideration. If the premium is low, as might have been frequently the case in early times, a large net profit to the tenant might be regarded as inequitable

protected. We are told that the situation in which this protection is available to him is that in which the *uttama* demands all the profit, leaving the possibility of loss exclusively with the *kauttika*. Now we see why an exact quarter is under consideration and neither more nor less: the calculation of the rent would be impossible if neither party knew what proportion of the profit if any would belong to the tenant. The availability of a quarter would encourage him to work the land well, while any excess would be for the benefit of the owner. A loss would be borne, according to some only (see below), exclusively by the tenant, but any profits up to but not reaching a quarter would be claimable by the owner. To illustrate the rule two balances are given below. In both cases the *kauttika* estimated 'on the safe side'.

Tenant's Balance			*Revenue-farmer's Balance*		
Gross income:	Rs.	5,000	Gross Revenue:	Rs.	1,50,000
Expenses, including living expenses:	,,	3,500	Expenses of collection, including sub-contractor's expenses:	,,	5,500
Net income:	Rs.	1,500	Net Revenue:	Rs.	1,44,500
Rent:	,,	1,100	Contract:	,,	1,40,000
'Profit':	Rs.	400	'Profit':	Rs.	4,500
To owner:	,,	300	To Government:	,,	3,375
Real profit:	Rs.	100	Real profit:	Rs.	1,125

[1] This suggestion stems from a desire to protect the tenant still further. If Viṣṇu secures to the tenant a quarter in the event of a profit, in the same type of contract the tenant ought to be indemnified to the extent of a quarter (and neither more nor less) if the *kuttā* brings him in a loss, in order that the speculation may be reciprocal; and thus the calculation of the rent may be more favourable to both parties, and it may be easier to let land, the exact productivity of which may for special reasons be difficult to appraise in advance.

[2] Given that this reciprocity is justified by Viṣṇu's text, they believe that the owner can insist on the tenant's bearing three-quarters of the loss, and the tenant can insist on the owner's bearing three-quarters of the risk of an absence of profit; both, however, may be more generous if they like—the opposite course is not open to either.

and *extra contractum*. Thus the owner was legally entitled to claim, in the first situation that he was exempt from liability to repay any part of the premium or to suffer a reduction in the amount of the unpaid premium if any; and in the second situation that three-quarters of the net profit (or according to Bhāruci the gross profit) was due to him over and above the premium. In this way the owner was amply protected. The tenant's rights in the *kuttā* were confined to the profits. If the agreement said nothing about profits, they were all his; if the agreement said that the owner was to have all the profits, the latter could demand no more than three-quarters of them (however calculated). But if the year was bad, or the sub-tenants (if any) obdurate, or for some other reason the tenant was unable to recoup his initial outlay by way of premium or rent, a suggestion was made that the owner, besides bearing the risk that he will not make a profit over and above the premium, should undertake a liability to bear a quarter of the loss. To this view the *Sarasvatī-vilāsa* lends what is plainly somewhat qualified support, commenting that whereas the tenant can be sure of keeping a quarter but not less than a quarter, of any profit he makes, he may be able to call upon the owner to assist him to the extent of a quarter in the event of a loss, and the owner has an option to assist him still further, as Viṣṇu's text might suggest, just as he has an option to allow him to retain more than a quarter of the net profits, if any.

The first passage dealt with a peculiar type of demise for payment of debts and religious duties; the last very plainly deals primarily with government revenue-farming contracts. Yet it is clear that the same features of absence of Ownership in the tenants, the restriction of their rights to the income pending the non-performance of the conditions, and the speculative character of the undertaking, are present both in these and in the intermediate specimens which approach a modern farming-lease (where, however, legal relief against loss is not available to the tenant).

It seems that a case could be made out for a greater juristic maturity in the sixteenth century amongst the South Indians, than amongst their Northern colleagues, who not only do not know of the *kuttā* but also fail to tell us what are the essentials of any sort of lease, though they must have been familiar with many of them. *

ADDENDUM

Yājñavalkya's attitude to Kāyasthas (above, p. 77, n. 4) is indicated by the company in which he places them. J.Ph.Vogel, *BSOAS*, xx, 1957, 566–7, has shown that *cāṭa* meant 'head of a *parganā*', i.e. a middle-grade provincial civil servant. But Aparārka says it means 'an informer'; Vijñāneśvara equates it with a confidence-trickster; Śūlapāṇi thinks the word should be *cāra*, glossed 'one who gets the better of others'. The word became synonymous with a swindler who takes full advantage of a colour of authority, but between Vogel's sources (and see S. K. Maity, *Economic life of northern India . . .*, Calcutta, 1957, 64) and the fifteenth century *cāṭa* ceased merely to mean a grade of official, and the text of Yājñ. had to be glossed or modified accordingly.

ADDITIONAL ANNOTATIONS

p. [281], n. 2. *gutta* is a revenue demand at A.R.S.I.E. 1943/4 & 1944/5 (1955), App. E. GEI 1941-2, no. 18 (Telugu) (A.D. 1665). Earlier material on *guttige* is not scarce. K.I.II (1951), no. 9, pp. 27, 28 (A.D. 1075): *guttage* = rent. E.C.xi Dg 11: dēva-guttike tekoṇḍu biṭa bhūmi, 'land donated had been rented from the deity (?)'. More important for our purpose is B.K.Ins.II (1964), no. 99, p. 127: ī dēvara toṃtada araṇi-guttiga Bīcaṇa... B. undertook to supply garlands and flowers every day. He was the banyan-wood-fire-stick-contractor/lessee/monopolist in respect of the deity's garden.

p. [282], l. 22. An actual example of this kind of transaction appears at *Kalandi Parida* v. *Sadhu* A.I.R. 1967 Or. 74: the widow and another demised the husband's inheritance, 'the donee shall maintain us till we live. After our death, he shall according to the prevalent custom and usage perform our funeral and obsequies and sraddh ceremonies and would also take care of the daughter of the donee who is the sister-in-law of the second donor'.

p. [282], l. 32. *Kuttā* is studied within the wider context of Debt by Heramba Chatterjee (*sic*), Śāstrī, in *The Law of Debt in Ancient India* (Calcutta, 1971), 228-30, relying on this present article.

p. [283], n. 5. The author is really referring to the controversy raised and settled by Jaimini VI.2,21-2 on which see the *Śab. bhā.*, trans. G. Jha, II, 1031.

p. [286], l. 11. For the vocabulary of 'rent' see below, n. to p. [300].

p. [286], n. 1. Hayley is not entirely superseded by H.W. Tambiah, *Sinhala Law* (Colombo, 1968), ch. 31.

p. [288], l. 30. Viṣṇu (spurious?) cited on suicide by Vijñāneśvara on Yājñ. III.227.

p. [288], n. 4. There is an untraced citation of Bṛh. at *S.V.* 135, but it appears again in the *Vya.nir.* 132 (only). Vijñāneśvara also cites Gaut. on a man's need perpetually to attend to *dharma, artha, and kāma* (on Yājñ. II.135-6, Nirṇ. sāg. edn., p. 219, Colebrooke's divisions II, i, 22) but it cannot be located in the printed Gautama. An untraced citation of Viṣṇu is known to Govindarāja (pre 11th cent.) and cited in Jīmūtvāhana's Dāyabhāga XI,ii,23. See S.C. Banerji, *Dharma Sūtras*, 31.

p. [294], n. 4. Illustrations of the range of *paribhāṣā* may be of value. The concept *pāribhāṣikatva* (technicality) is discussed at length at *S.V.*, 244. Primarily we find it in *dharmaśāstra* with the sense of 'technical definition': pāribhāṣika-kṣetra-dāna means 'a gift of land subject to a precise limitation' (*Vya.may.* at Dh.k.1123). Mādhava in Par. Mādh. I, ii (B.S.S. edn., vol. 48), p. 81 says that if we take *kanyā* to mean a girl up to 10 that is a *pāribhāṣika* (technical) not a *loka-prasiddha* (popular) definition. Similar Medh. on M.XI.61/62 (usury). Viśvarūpa on Yājñ.I.53 (p. 63). *Vivāda-candra*, p. 76. Kṣīrasvāmin on Amara, 213 (1941 edn., p. 323): *dravya* can be used in a technical sense (meaning [moveable] property/wealth) or in the ordinary sense of 'a thing'. na kiṃcit paribhāṣyate, 'no condition is laid down' or 'superadded', said of a gift: Medh. on M.III.35 (Jha's trans., p. 64).

p. [295], n. 5. I.e. below p. [333].

p. [295], n. 6. I.e. Derrett, *Rel. Law and the State in India* (1968), 124, 137, 143-4.

p. [296], n. 4. He cites a text of Vasiṣṭha about them—or those of them who live by bribes on p. 34. There he also follows the comm. of Vijñāneśvara on Yājñ.I.336.

p. [297], l. 7 of n. Literally 'in power', sc. over villages: cf. *Śab. bhā.* on Jaimini VIII.1,34. Kāyasthas are scribes in M.A.R. 1928, 73, p. 74 (A.D. 1058).

p. [300], l. 33. One hired premises, hence rent, properly *stoma*, is a species of hire, and thus *bhṛti* or *bhāṭaka* are found. stomaṃ vāsamūlyam ('rent'): Lakṣmīdhara, *K.K.T.*, *Vya.Kā.* 411; Nārada at Dh.k.851b. The title of the chapter of the *K.K.T.* is *grahādi-bhāṭaka-vidhi* (sic) (see Aiyangar's n. at p. 411). Kane, *H.D.*, III 428, n. 704 notices that Haradatta explains *ye cādhim* in *Āp.dh.sū.* I.vi.18,19-22 as 'rent of a house' (svagṛhe parānvāsayitvā tebhyo bhṛti-grahaṇam ādhir yaḥ stoma iti prasiddhaḥ: Bühler's edn, p. 134). Kane comments 'that sense is very rare', but it would not have puzzled him had he realised the ambivalent history of lease by way of mortgage.

THE *DISCUSSION OF MARRIAGE* BY GADĀDHARA *

A PRELIMINARY INVESTIGATION

THE subject of marriage has a permanent fascination, but its definition has never been established to general satisfaction. In modern languages ' marriage ' or its counterpart can mean either the ceremony by which the married status of the spouses commences, or that married status itself. The question whether a couple have actually married often arises in law, and both the capacity to marry and the formalities requisite for achieving married status are carefully delimited. In India, where marriage has always had an overwhelming importance socially, careful definition in this sector would naturally be expected. Yet some curiosities emerge which have defied satisfactory treatment by courts of law right up to our own day, when the Indian Hindu Marriage Act persists in quite remarkable vagueness concerning the capacity to marry. The dark spots have always been child-marriage and the marriage of lunatics or idiots or impotent persons. Notwithstanding the gradual education of opinion, pockets of resistance remain where the marriage of a very young girl to a man she not only does not know, much less love, but would actually be unfitted to marry according to the sentiments of civilized countries, will take place according to the plans of her parents or guardians, and this will persist even though they now realize that when she comes of age she may well try to have the marriage annulled or even obtain a divorce. Aged and sick men, idiots, lunatics, impotent men, or even small boys, are, in these pockets of antiquated social convention, able to obtain wives if they or their guardians have the means to negotiate for them.

Not so very long ago there was the problem of Kulinism in Bengal. A man, poor in most cases, virtually made a living out of his caste and sometimes accumulated a dozen or more wives, whom he might not see more than once in his lifetime—a curiosity about which Ram Mohan Roy waxed eloquent. What sort of marriages were these? How would one define them? Not long ago it was frequently asserted that so long as the girl had undergone the ceremony, the *saṃskāra* of marriage, the 'sacrament', as it is often called, was obtained by her and that nothing in this world or the next could undo it. We can see that this is an obvious rationalizing of the social need for permanent dynastic and financial links: and the modern Hindu resistance to the institution of divorce seems to stem from similar sources. One wonders whether the old jurists were right in thinking of marriage in terms of a *saṃskāra*, and what was the effect of their pointing to the elements of the ceremony, the invitation of the bridegroom, the *kanyā-dāna* (or proffer of the virgin), the *pāṇi-grahaṇa* (in which the bridegroom grasps her by the hand), and the *saptapadī* (to which even our

Hindu Marriage Act refers, in which the pair walk seven steps before the sacred fire, the seventh step being completion of the ceremony so far as its capacity to marry the couple is concerned). What relation had these elements, or any of them, to the *saṃskāra*? What if the bridegroom was incapable of taking her (or anybody) by the hand? Could an agent do this for him? If he was incapable of knowing what marriage was, let alone whether he was being married, could this want of capacity be made good by his guardians', or his guardians' agents' participation in the ceremony? To investigate all such questions one must know what marriage is. Moreover, there were the problems of perennial Indian interest. Śūdra-s, the majority caste, were believed by some not to be entitled to the full marriage rites of ' higher ' castes. Were their marriages different in kind from the marriages of others?

In all investigations linguistics play some part, usually a restricting and frustrating part. Marriage, *udvāha* or *vivāha*, correctly gives the idea in Sanskrit of a ' taking away '. Not a mere taking, for this can happen at a *pāṇi-grahaṇa* or the customary equivalent, but the actual removal to the bridegroom's house or village. Even where in practice the bride is not at once removed there may be a symbolic, or as the lawyers would say, a ' constructive ' removal, to be followed by an actual removal some time afterwards. But this can hardly be insisted upon. The *saṃskāra* of marriage occurs, surely, even in those relatively rare cases where the husband does not remove the wife, but comes at the time of marriage or earlier and lives permanently with his parents-in-law. The process of ' taking ' can therefore hardly be the key to ' marriage ', and that marriage is called *vivāha* can well be misleading.

To isolate the actual cause of a thing, and to show how that cause is related to its effect, and so by what process causation occurs, one turns from the lawyers, who in this respect are pupils rather than teachers, to the logicians. In the course of the 17th and 18th centuries the school of New Logic, stemming principally from Nava-dvīpa in Bengal, got down to the task of analysing certain problems of the lawyers, and for this purpose assumed that the rules laid down in the *dharma-śāstra* were valid for argumentation in logical terms. An *ad hoc* marriage between law and logic followed, and numerous small treatises emerged, of which we have unfortunately only a depleted collection. (Note for example Gopāla Nyāyapañcānana's *Vicāranirṇaya*, known to us from R. Mitra's *Notices* 6 (1882), p. 210 (No. 2147); 7 (1883), p. 83 (No. 2310), and belonging to the beginning of the 18th century.)

The language of logic, and particularly that of the New Logic is repellent. Extremely condensed, treating abstractions as concrete realities, dealing with the abstraction in preference to the realities to which it refers, avoiding a phrase with four words where a phrase with three could serve, pruning the vocabulary to the barest minimum so that the same words and phrases recur interminably, repeating the same syntactical form over and over again, bracketing objections and counter-arguments within the principal demonstration without obvious distinction between the limbs of the argument, not to speak of the hair-splitting and paradoxes that one would expect from such a quarter—the treatises are opaque and puzzling even to one who knows the subject-matter thoroughly. This must have been the case even in the centuries when the best brains India had were channelled into logical studies, and when education in a higher sense meant nothing if it did not include a qualification in logic. When Europeans came to Bengal they found their best qualified native assistants, in all fields where intellectual ability was called for, amongst the former pupils of the schools of Nava-dvīpa. Small wonder that Indian logic has played an important part in education in India to this day. But the transmission of the texts has always been an acute problem.

The teachers and their immediate pupils used to copy out the compositions themselves, but as the prestige of the science carried their productions into unlearned hands, the inevitable happened. Scribes misread what they could not understand, or copied parrot-fashion. The present writer has copied quantities of *navya-nyāya* without a clue as to the meaning of most of it—just as was the case with the scribes of two centuries ago—and he knows how those howlers were made. The repetitions of jargon made for haplographies. The loss of paragraphs or sentences at once ruins a text, in which the experts in concise expression place a pageful of meaning in a short sentence. Every reader tried to make sense of his copy and altered, by making grammatical changes and insertions, in an attempt to reconstruct the sense according to his ability. Within half a century copies would diverge so widely from each other that only an expert could reconstruct the author's original. Modern editors do exactly this: they must in places alter their manuscript's reading to obtain any sense, and it is at times a matter of good luck whether they hit the mark. One can scarcely hope to obtain a good text from one manuscript, and the availability of many leads, at any rate in the first stage, to frustrations.

These editorial handicaps are partly the effect, and partly the cause, of the failure to carry on the tradition of Indian logic in all the richness of the varied textual sources. The famous, especially fundamental, works exist in many copies and many editions; the rest languish or perish. The work which we attempt to reproduce here survives, as far as is known, in only *two* copies. This is fantastic when we consider that the author was the marvellously prolific and deservedly famous Gadādhara, whose life spanned the entire seventeenth century, and whose major works have proved that whatever he might contribute on a legal subject would be of the greatest intellectual significance. When the great experts in law in Mithila and Bengal were for the most part trained also in logic, it is extraordinary that this little treatise should not have obtained a mention, not even within the writings of such a scholar as William Macnaghten, who lived about 130 years ago. As usual with works of this class, the title is uncertain. It seems to have been *Vivāhavāda.*

The sources of this edition are A, the edition by Dr. Herambanatha Chattopadhyaya Sastri (in *Saṃskṛta Sāhitya Pariṣat*—the monthly organ of the Sanskrit Literature Society—vol. 44, nos. 9-10, Jan.-Feb. 1962, pp. 179-82) of the manuscript in the Calcutta Sanskrit College Library (catalogue number 8/154, title *Vivāhavādārthaḥ*),[1] an edition which made no use of any other copy, and B, a manuscript belonging to Patna University Library kindly sent to the present writer by Professor R. S. Sharma, Head of the Dept. of History, Patna University. Whereas the Calcutta manuscript has plainly been tampered with in order to make some agreeable sense in places, it shows signs (barring two omissions) of being complete; B, the Patna manuscript, on the other hand, has lost long passages, perhaps because of their being fanciful, or because of their difficulty or unimportance from the copyist's point of view. Apart from these losses a substantial portion has disappeared through haplography. B was evidently taken from a Bengali original, as some of the errors look like an attempt to copy the unfamiliar Bengali compound consonants. These misreadings are not noted below, but other significant

[1] The manuscript figured in Hṛṣīkeśa Śāstrī and S. C. Gui's *Descriptive Catalogue*, III (Calcutta, 1900), pp. 311-2 (No. 558). Its latest description is in *Our Heritage*, vol. 4.1, 1956, pp. 136-7 (No. 3).

variations from the text are shown. It was unfortunately quite impossible to obtain a microfilm of the Calcutta manuscript which is the basis for A. The microfilm would have revealed what were the editor's changes. But since we are entitled to believe that he has departed from his original only where it was absolutely necessary we proceed upon the basis that A represents the manuscript. That manuscript has lost portions which appear in B, so that we are able to make good the loss in our present edition. Some use has also been made of C, a manuscript which once belonged to Pandit Damodar Jha, Ṭhārhī, Andhraṭhārhī P.O., Darbhanga. C was a complete and good manuscript, but of it we have only tiny fragments reported in K. P. Jayaswal and A. P. Sastri, *A Descriptive Catalogue of Manuscripts in Mithila*, I (Patna, 1927), p. 382, No. 338. The original came from Nava-dvīpa. It is a great pity that this manuscript has not been recovered and preserved. The other Mithila manuscript of the same work, reported in the same catalogue as No. 339, appears not to have been so good, but its loss is also much to be regretted.

The edition of the text and the settling of the translation are tasks that go hand in hand. The better the logician the greater the liberties he will be prepared to take with the text. For the logician's jargon one may consult D. H. H. Ingalls, *Materials for the Study of Navya-Nyāya Logic* (Cambridge, Mass., 1951), but Dr. E. R. Sreekrishna Sarma's edition and translation of *Maṇikaṇa* (Adyar Library Series No. 88,

1960) is a very useful guide for the beginner. The text and translation offered here are provisional. The purpose of this publication is to elicit comments and reactions from logicians. The change of an ending, the insertion of a particle, and a slight twist to the English rendering, can make all the difference between success and failure.

Given that text and translation are provisional, a residuum remains which enables us to know the author's ideas about marriage. Marriage (*vivāha*) is in his view not a *saṃskāra* at all, though it is the essential step without which the *saṃskāra* cannot come about. This *saṃskāra* is called by the logicians the ' final ' *saṃskāra*, in contradistinction from the *dharma-śāstra* which recognizes further *saṃskāra-s* after marriage.[1] The logicians' view is that the transcendental function of *saṃskāra-s* to remove sins is completed only by *vivāha-saṃskāra*, and that since it completes this process it is the final *saṃskāra*. What then constitutes the marriage? Is it the gift of the girl, or her acceptance by the man, or the knowledge that she is his wife? The view that the knowledge that she is his wife constitutes marriage has its adherents,[2] but this is hardly acceptable since

[1] Kane, *History of Dharmaśāstra*, vol. II (Poona, 1941), pp. 194-7. Note Manu, II. 16 and *Yājñ.*, I. 10.

[2] There is an interesting little essay on *vivāha* (under that heading) in Bhīmācārya Jhalakīkar's *Nyāyakośa* (rev. and ed. by Vasudev Shastri Abhyankar, Poona, 1928, p. 778). The alternative to the author's preference (which is *saptapadī-samāpanam*) is given in the following words: yena jñānena mameyaṃ bhāryā,

children and idiots can be married. Other people's knowledge that a couple are married is no substitute for this. Marriage must therefore be either the giving or the taking, the latter of course being, in such marginal cases, by an agent or representative. It can hardly be the giving, since gift is a matter of offer and acceptance; it therefore is the taking. Is the taking a matter of *pāṇigrahaṇa* or the mental condition (in *mīmāṃsā* terms also a *saṃskāra* itself) of knowing that the girl is one's wife, a condition created by the *svīkāra*, or acceptance, of the girl? It appears to be the latter. Thus the *vivāha* consists essentially in an acceptance, which produces the mental impression that this girl is the man's wife, and wifeness arises from her having undergone the *saṃskāra*, which *saṃskāra* itself could not occur but for the marriage. This circularity is a problem, but it can be avoided, as the author attempts to show, because wifeness is a condition distinct from that of being subjected to the *saṃskāra* associated with marriage. In fact (VII. 2) wifeness, which qualifies the woman, is an aspect of the *saṃskāra* itself, which has

mamāyaṃ patiḥ (note that both spouses are to have the knowledge) iti vyavahāro bhavati, tādṛśaṃ jñānam iti vivāha-śabdārthaḥ. tādṛśaṃ jñānaṃ tu saṃskārādinotpadyate (knowledge comes from the saṃskāra and not vice versa). tac ca saṃbandhaviśeṣeṇobhaya-niṣṭham (the knowledge is located in both by a difference in the relations). atredaṃ vicāryam: bhāryātvasaṃpādakaṃ jñānam ity atra bhāryātvasyopalakṣaṇatayā niveśaḥ. tena nānyonyāśrayaḥ iti (we can treat this as a conclusion because wifeness is only upalakṣaṇa, i.e. secondary implication and therefore there is no 'mutual resort' to invalidate the definition).

been shown to be a product of marriage. 'Wife' differs from 'woman' as 'milch cow' differs from 'cow': in each case the former terms are 'conventional' denotations. The capacity of being sucked by a calf turns a cow into a milch cow, and the capacity to be 'taken' by the bridegroom turns a woman into a wife. The significance of the appeal to usage, to linguistics, and to analogy will not be lost on the legal reader, who accepts such criteria without difficulty.

One obtains the impression that this little treatise is somewhat far from the end of discussion of the subject (which is unobjectionable), but it has at any rate performed the service of carefully distinguishing the ceremony from the *saṃskāra*, and both of these from the status achieved thereby by the married pair. To put his general conclusion in popular terms, he sees marriage as a preliminary to the *saṃskāra*, which from our point of view is a defect, in that those who do not accept the validity of the *saṃskāra* theory are precluded from marriage: though this may incidentally serve the *śāstrī's* purpose in that Muslim, Christian, and modern Indian 'special' marriages and the like, which are capable of divorce, will not have the associations traditionally coupled with the *saṃskāra*. But granted that marriage be merely a preliminary to a theory, the essence of the marriage is the activity of the bridegroom and the mental impression which it can create. The implications of this are somewhat paradoxical, but may well have had a social value at the time when the work was composed.

Text

I. 1. atha carama-saṃskārānukūla-vyāpāro vivāhaḥ. [1]tatra[1] caramatavaṃ svāvacchedaka-śarīrāvacchinna-svādhikaraṇa-vṛtti-saṃskāra-prāgabhāvāsamāna-kālīnatvam. tena na nāma-karaṇādāv [2]atiprasaṅgaḥ.[2] [3]atrānyadīya[3] -saṃskāram ādāyāsaṃbhava-vāraṇāya [4]svādhikaraṇa[4]-vṛttyantam. [5]avacchinnānta[5]-niveśācca [6]janmāntarīṇa[6]-saṃskāram ādāya nāsaṃbhavaḥ.

2. [7]nanu yatra kṛta-carama-saṃskāra eko mṛtaḥ taccharīre ca mṛta-saṃcāriṇī-vidyādinā satsaṃskāro 'tra praviṣṭo[8] mṛta-dvitīya-puruṣīya-saṃskāram ādāya pūrva-puruṣīya-vivāhe 'vyāptiḥ. ubhaya-puruṣīya-saṃskārasyaiva eka-śarīrāvacchinnatayā pūrva-puruṣīya-carama-saṃskārasya dvitīya-puruṣīya-carama-saṃskāra-prāgabhāva-samāna-kālīnatvād. ataḥ svādhikaraṇeti.

3. ' evam enaḥ śamaṃ yāti bīja-garbha-samud-

[1-1] B: atra.
[2-2] So AB, C: ativyāptiḥ.
[3-3] B: atra cānyadīya.
[4-4] B: omits.
[5-5] A: athāvacchinnānta.
[6-6] B: janmāntarīya.
[7] Para I. 2 is omitted in A.
[8] B: praviṣṭa.

Translation

I. 1. Next, marriage is the operation conducive to the final *saṃskāra*. ' Final ' here means not coincidental in time with the prior non-existence of a *saṃskāra* occurring in the locus of the self which [locus] is limited by the body which [in turn] limits the self. Thus there is no fear of the definition including the *nāma-karaṇa* and the *saṃskāra-s* that follow it. In the definition the words ' occurring in the locus of the self ' are needed to avoid the total non-applicability which would arise if one took the *saṃskāra* of someone else. And by the insertion of the phrase ' limited by . . .' one obviates the total non-applicability which would arise if one took the *saṃskāra* of another life.

2. One might object that our definition is defective where, if one man, having undergone the final *saṃskāra*, dies and another individual, who is also dead, and has already undergone the *saṃskāra*, enters his body by means of migratory learning and the like, taking the *saṃskāra* of the second dead man one would exclude the marriage of the first man; for, as the *saṃskāra* of both men is limited by a single body, the final *saṃskāra* of the first man is coincidental in time with the prior non-existence of the final *saṃskāra* of the second man. It is for this very purpose that the phrase ' in the locus of the self ' appears.

3. One is in no danger of the solecism of including the *saṃskāra* of *nāma-karaṇa* and *anna-prāśana* and the

bhavam ' ityādi-vacana-pratipādya-pāpa-viśeṣa-dhvaṃsātmaka-saṃskāra-niveśād eva [1]nāmānnaprāśanādi-[1] -saṃskāram ādāya nāsaṃbhavaḥ.

4. atha yasya nāma-karaṇādyanyatamam eka--mātram eva jātaṃ[2] tasya tad-anyatame 'tivyāptir iti cen na, sāmānādhikaraṇye[3] sva-bhedasyāpi niveśāt.

5. [4] nanu yatra nāma-karaṇādyanyatamaṃ dvitīya-saṃskāra-mātraṃ jātaṃ tatra dvitīya-saṃskāre 'tivyāptir iti cen na, svāvacchedaka-śarīrāvacchinna-svādhikaraṇa-vṛtti-bīja-garbha-samudbhava-pāpa-dhvaṃsa-samāna-kālīnatvasya vivakṣaṇīyatvāt.

6. na caivaṃ 'vivāha-mātra-saṃskāraṃ kuryāc chūdro 'pi sarvadā ' ityādi-vacanāt [5]saṃskārāntarāprasiddhyā[5] tadīya-vivāhe 'vyāptir[6] iti vācyam, tat-[7] -tad-vacanenaiva teṣāṃ saṃskāre mantrasyaiva niṣedhān na tu[8] [9]saṃskārāntarasyābhāvaḥ,[9] 'śūdro 'py evaṃ-

[1-1] A: snānācamanādi.

[2] A. -anyatamādika-. B: -anyatamād ekam eva. jātam omitted in A. B: jñātaṃ.

[3] B: -karaṇya-, omitting sva.

[4] Para I. 5 is omitted in A.

[5-5] A: saṃskārāntarāprasaṅgāt.

[6] B: 'tivyāptir.

[7] First tat omitted in B. A: tat-tad-vacanais.

[8] B: ca.

[9-9] A: saṃskārasya.

rest when one inserts '*saṃskāra*', the nature of which is to destroy specific sins, which are referred to in the text [of *Yājñ.*, I. 13]: 'Thus the taint ceases which arose from seed and womb. . .'

4. Now it might be argued that our definition must be over-pervasive, as it would include any one of the *saṃskāra-s* like *nāma-karaṇa* performed for *any* person who had undergone only that one. This however is not so, because we have introduced non-identity with the self, in the phrase 'having a common substratum'.[1]

5. Nor would it be right to object that there is another over-pervasion, as our definition would include a second *saṃskāra* where, amongst the *saṃskāra-s*, namely the *nāma-karaṇa*, etc. no more than the *second saṃskāra* had been undergone; because of what we were to explain about the coincidence in time with destruction of sins 'arising from seed and womb', a destruction 'occurring in the locus of the self which [locus] is limited by the body which [in turn] limits the self'.

6. Nor would it be correct to object that our definition is under-pervasive, in that it excludes the marriage of a Śūdra, since it is not established that he has other *saṃskāra-s* available to him, for there are texts like:[2] 'Even a Śūdra must always undergo one

[1] *Sāmānādhikaraṇya* being equivalent to *-adhikaraṇa-vṛtti* in § 1.

[2] Herambanatha points to a similar text from the *Brahma-purāṇa* cited by Devaṇabhaṭṭa in the *Smṛticandrikā*, I, p. 24. Of

vidhaḥ prokto vinā mantreṇa saṃskṛtaḥ' ityādi--vacanāt [1]saṃskārāntarasyāpi bodhanāt.[1]

II. 1. na ca tathāpi pāṇigrahaṇa-saṃskāram ādāyāsaṃbhava iti vācyaṃ, pāṇigrahaṇasya saṃskārāntaratvābhāvāt. pāṇigrahaṇa-mantrā vivāha -karmāṅgabhūtāḥ.

2. pāṇigrahaṇena na [2]bhāryātvaṃ, kiṃtu saṃ-skāreṇa,[2] 'saptame pade' ityādi [3]-Manu-vacanena [3] vivāhanirvāhasyaiva[4] bodhanāt.

III. dvitīyādi[5] -vivāhasya[6] nārī[7] -saṃskāra--janakatve 'pi vara-niṣṭha-saṃskārājanakatayā sva-samānādhikaraṇa-saṃskāra-prāgabhāvāsamāna-kālīna-tayā na dvitīyādi-vivāha-kartuḥ[8] prathama-vivāhe

[1-1] Omitted in A. B: bādhanāt.

[2-2] A: kṛtsnaṃ bhāryātvaṃ kiṃtu. B: jāyātvaṃ kiṃtu kṛta--saṃskāreṇa jāyātvam.

[3-3] A: Manu-vacanair. B: muni-vacanena.

[4] A: vivāhasyaiva.

[5] B: dvitīya.

[6] A: vivāhe ca.

[7] nārī omitted in B.

[8] B: -vivāhakatva.

saṃskāra alone, namely marriage'; for by those various texts what is prohibited is only the use of *mantra-s* at the marriages of Śūdra-s, not the absence of *saṃskāra-s* other than marriage. For, by reason of a text like 'A Śūdra is declared to be such, undergoing *saṃskāra* without a *mantra*,' we know that he may have other *saṃskāra-s*.[1]

II. 1. Nor should one object that it would be impossible to include within our definition the *saṃskāra* of *pāṇigrahaṇa* (taking the hand), since it is not a characteristic of *pāṇigrahaṇa* to be a different *saṃskāra* from marriage. The *mantra-s* of the *pāṇigrahaṇa* are accessary to the rite of marriage.

2. The status of wife is not created by *pāṇigrahaṇa*, but by the completion of the *saṃskāra*, for by the text of Manu (VIII. 227) 'at the seventh step', we are informed of the manner of performing a marriage.

III. In a second or subsequent marriage would there be an under-pervasion? Would our definition include the first marriage of a man who later makes a second or any subsequent marriage? In such a case

this there is a somewhat different reading in the passage from Raghunandana to be cited below. The whole question of a Śūdra's right to more *saṃskāra-s* than marriage is discussed by Kane in the *History of Dharmaśāstra*, II, pp. 198-9.

[1] Herambanatha cites this rule with a quotation from the *Varāha-purāṇa* to be found in the *Śūdrakṛtyatattva*. On the problem see Kane, op. cit., II, pp. 158-9.

'vyāptiḥ,[1] pāpa-viśeṣa-dhvaṃsātmakasya prathama--vivāhenaiva nirvāhāt. ata [2]eva tatra[2] jātyā [3]saṃskāram api na,[3] [4]sa ca vyāpāra-mātro[4] vivāhaḥ.[5]

IV. 1. atha[6] kanyādānam eva[7] vivāha-kartṛtvam. 'vivahati' ityādau cākhyātena tādṛśa-saṃbandhenaivāśrayatvaṃ bodhyate. ato na dātur vivāha-kartṛtvāpattiḥ, na vā tatra 'vivahati' ityādi-prayogaḥ. tasya kanyā-dāna-rūpataiva, 'brāhmo vivāha āhūya dīyate śaktyalaṃkṛtā' iti śaktyalaṃkṛtā kanyā yasmin[8] dīyate sa brāhmābhidhāno vivāha iti yathāśrutārthaḥ. evaṃ ca

'ācchādya cārcayitvā ca
śruti-śīla-vate svayam
āhūya dānaṃ kanyāyā
brāhmo dharmaḥ prakīrtitaḥ'

[1] B: 'prāptiḥ.
[2-2] eva tatra omitted in A.
[3-3] A: saṃskāram āpannaḥ. B: lakṣaṇam api na.
[4-4] A: sa-vyāpāro 'tra.
[5] vivāhaḥ omitted in B.
[6] atha omitted in B.
[7] After eva B inserts utthatā-saṃbandhena tadvatvam eva (? a misplaced gloss).
[8] A: yasmai. The whole sentence is badly corrupted in B.

though the *saṃskāra* of the woman is produced by the marriage it cannot produce a *saṃskāra* located in the husband. Accordingly there is, in the first marriage, a non-coincidence with a prior non-existence of a *saṃskāra* having a common locus with the self; and there is no under-pervasion to be feared, for the accomplishment of that which has as its nature the destruction of specific sins took place only through the first marriage. For this very reason marriage is not by generic character a *saṃskāra* itself, and it is merely an operation [conducive to one].

IV. 1. Next as for the *kanyādāna* (receiving the * maiden) it is [said to be] 'being the effector of marri- * age', and it is only through such relation that the receptacleness is denoted by means of the verbal suffix in expressions like *vivahati*, 'he marries' (lit. 'bears away'). Whence it is not the case that the effector of marriage is the giver, nor is the use of 'he marries' * found in that case. 'The Brāhma marriage is where, after summoning the bridegroom, a girl is given, adorned as well as her father is able' (*Yājñ.*, I. 58) literally means that that marriage is called Brāhma in which a maiden, adorned to the best of his ability, is given away. Similarly, in texts like 'the gift of a * daughter, after decking her, and honouring her, to a man learned in the Veda and of good conduct, whom the father himself invites, is called the Brāhma rite'

ityādy api yathāśrutaṃ saṃgacchate. brāhmādyaṣṭa-vidha-saṃjñā tasyaiva Manu-vacanaiḥ pratipāditā ca.

2. tena saṃbandhena tādṛśa-dānasyaiva saṃskāra-janakatayā 'mameyaṃ bhāryā' ityādi-svīkārādy-asamarthasyāpi bālakāder[1] vivāhe nāvyāptiḥ. anyathā teṣāṃ [2]vivāhānupapattyā[2] āśauca-vyavasthāyāṃ Smārtādīnāṃ[3] bahutara-likhanāsaṃgatiḥ syāt.

* 3. karmatā-saṃbandhena tadvattvam eva vivāha-karmatvam[4], ata eva 'kanyā-putra-vivāheṣu' ityādi saṃgacchate.

[1] A: bālāder. B: vaṇikāder (!) for bālakāder.
[2-2] B: tadasaṃbhave vivāhābhāvāt patyā.
[3] B: Mārtaṇḍādīnāṃ.
[4] A: kartṛtvaṃ.

(Manu, III. 27) the literal meaning is consistent. And by texts of Manu the names of the eight forms of marriage, i.e. Brāhma, etc. are explained for the *kanyādāna* only (Manu, III. 29).

2. As the *saṃskāra* is produced only by such a gift with the aid of that relation, there is no under-pervasion in the marriages of children and others who are incapable of acceptance and the like which imply a consciousness, 'this is my wife'. Otherwise, if their marriages were indeed impossible, there would be an incongruity with several passages of Raghu-nandana and others dealing with the problem of [death-] pollution.[1]

3. The state of being the 'object' of [the verb] *vivah* is to be known as merely possessing the character of being an 'object' (being effected) through the relation of objectness. For this reason we are in harmony with texts like 'On the occasion of the marriages of his daughter or of his son', etc.[2]

[1] In his *Śuddhitattva* (with the comments of Kāśirāma Vācaspati, ed. with Bengali translation by Hṛṣīkeśa Śāstrī, Calcutta, 1908, pp. 162-6) Raghunandana proves ingeniously that a marri-age may take place (though undesirable) prior to the sixteenth year. A 'law-abiding' Śūdra is assimilated to a Vaiśya. For him marriage takes the place of *upanayana*; for the age within which a Vaiśya's *upanayana* may take place he refers to *Yājñ.*, I. 14. A marriage at twelve is therefore not out of the question.

[2] The point of this citation from *Viṣṇu-purāṇa*, III. 13. 5, is this: Worship of the Nāndīmukha ancestors should diligently be performed by the householder whether the marriage is of his son or daughter. There may be a *vivāha* affecting either sex as object.

V. na caitasya sva[1]-ghaṭitatvād ananugamaḥ, tādṛśa-sāmānādhikaraṇya-kālika[2]-viśeṣaṇatobhaya-saṃbandhena tādṛśa[3]-prāgabhāvavadanyatvasya niveśanīyatvāt, sva-vṛtti-dhvaṃsa-pratiyogi-kāla-vṛttitva-tādṛśa-sāmānādhikaraṇyobhaya-saṃbandhena saṃskāravadanyatvasya vivakṣaṇāt. ata eva prāgabhāvānaṅgīkāre 'pi na kṣatiḥ. tādṛśānyatvāvacchedaka-saṃskāratāvacchedakāvacchinnatvasya vivakṣaṇān na kāpy anupapattir iti saṃkṣepaḥ.[4]

VI. 1. yat tu bhāryātva-saṃpādaka-grahaṇaṃ vivāhaḥ, tac ca grahaṇaṃ 'mameyaṃ bhāryā' ityākārakaṃ jñānaṃ. tasya ca samavāya-viṣayatayor bhedād vara-kanyayor vivāha-kartṛtva-karmatve. 'ācchādya' ityādis tu tādṛśa-grahaṇa-nimittībhūtaṃ kanyāyā yat tādṛśaṃ dānaṃ sa eva brāhmābhidhāno vivāha

[1] B: svatva.
[2] B: sakālika.
[3] tādṛśa is omitted in A.
[4] Here B ends abruptly.

V. And it is not the case that this [definition] is indeterminate, because of its containing the term 'self'. For otherness [or distinctiveness] from that having such prior non-existence, must figure in the definition from the double relation of (i) coexistence in one and the same substratum and (ii) the fact that simultaneity qualifies both of them, since otherness from that having the *saṃskāra* is signified by the double relation of (i) occurrence in time with the counterpart to the destruction and (ii) coexistence in one and the same substratum. Thus it is that even if one fails to accept the theory of prior non-existence, the proposition holds. There is no logical fault, because what is signified is limitedness by a limitor which limits *saṃskāra*-ness that is itself the limitor of that very otherness. This is to put the point concisely.

VI. 1. Then marriage is [said to be] 'a taking which effectuates wifeness,' and that 'taking' is knowledge in the shape of the notion 'this is my wife'. That taking possesses the characters both of cause and of effect of marriage of groom and bride respectively through the distinction between its inherence and its subject-matter.[1] A text such as 'The gift of a

[1] The groom takes, and the taking causes the marriage for him; the bride is taken, from this point of view (which is rejected) her being taken is the effect of the marriage. The words are apparently from Raghunandana's *Udvāhatattva* (edition with the *ṭīkā* of Kāśirāma and a Skt. comm. called *Tattvabodhinī* and Bengali trans. by Kṛṣṇa-caraṇa Tarkālaṅkāra, 2nd ed., Calcutta 1923, p. 3).

ity arthaḥ. na ca tad-grahaṇasya [1]sva-viṣayakatayā[1] madīyatvāder[2] api sattvād ativyāptiḥ, madīya-bhāryātva-prakāratā-nirūpita-viśeṣyatāyā eva karma-ghaṭakatvāt. ata eva mukuṭa-maṇyaṃśukādāv api nātiprasaṅgaḥ.

2. athodāsīnasya tādṛśa-jñānasya vara-niṣṭha-saṃskāra [3]-janakatvam iti cen na,[3] tādṛśa-tyāgoddeśyatva-viśiṣṭa-tādṛśa-jñānasyaiva karmatā-saṃsargeṇa bhāryātva-saṃpādakatvāt.

VII. 1. atha bhāryātvaṃ vivāha-janya-saṃskāravannārītvam. tathā ca tasya vivāha-ghaṭitatvena vivāhasyāpi tad-ghaṭitatayā anyonyāśraya iti cet, atra Smārtāḥ ' bhāryātvasya svarūpa-sadviśeṣaṇatvena netaretarāśraya-doṣa ' iti. tasya ca svarūpa-sadviśeṣaṇatve [4]upalakṣaṇa-vidhayā[4] vyāvartakatvena saṃpādaka-svīkāra eva vivāhaḥ. atra bhāryātva-nirūpita[5]-saṃ-

[1-1] A: sa-viṣayakatayā.
[2] A: madīyatvādāv.
[3-3] A: janakatvena.
[4-4] B: upalakṣaṇa-viṣaya.
[5] A: nirūpaka.

daughter. . .' (Manu, III. 27) means that the marriage called Brāhma is that kind of gift of a daughter which is the cause (or occasion) of such a taking. Nor is * there an over-pervasion, on account of the presence of mineness and the like as a subject-matter of that knowledge, because what constitutes the subject-matter is nothing but the qualificandness correlated by a chief-qualifierness consisting of 'my-wife'-ness. For this very reason we do not have to face the absurdity of including also the jewels, tiara or fine muslin [which are also 'taken' on the occasion].

2. Now if it be asked whether such knowledge on the part of a *third* party may produce a *saṃskāra* located in the bridegroom, the answer is no, because * the capacity to effectuate wifeness is possessed only by such knowledge qualified by [the knower's] being * the destination of such a relinquishment, and this happens by the relation of being the 'object'. *

VII. 1. Now wifeness is womanness accompanied by the *saṃskāra* which is born of marriage. And so if one objects that there is a circularity, in that, when it is constituted by marriage, marriage itself possesses the characteristic of constituting it, the answer is that given by Raghunandana: 'There is no fault of mutual resort because wifeness is a qualifier existing by nature.' And because of its being the qualifier existing by nature, marriage is actually nothing other than an effectuating *acceptance*, because of its capacity for excluding through the

pādakataiva svīkāre viśeṣaṇam.[1] bhāryātvaṃ prakṛta [2]-jñānāviṣayam api[2] saṃpādakatā-vyāvartakam.

2. yathā dhenu-pada-śakyatāvacchedakaṃ [na][3] dhānavad-gotvaṃ dhāna-karma-sāmānyatva-go-vṛttyā dhāna-karma-viśeṣa-sthāpakaṃ gotva-samānādhikaraṇa-dhāna-karmatvasyaiva śakyatāvacchedakatvāt, tathehāpi tādṛśa-janyatā-nirūpita-sāmānādhikaraṇyenaiva janakatvena sampādakatvaṃ vedyam ity arthaḥ. [4] yad vā svarūpa-sattā [4] vivāha-janyatārūpa-viśeṣa-rahitena vivāha-janyatāvacchedakībhūta-saṃskāra-niṣṭha-vilakṣaṇa-dharmeṇa viśeṣaṇatvena, svīkāre[5] vyāvartakatvenety arthaḥ.[6]

[1] After viśeṣaṇam A seems to add na tu viśiṣṭatvena.
[2-2] A: jñānāviṣayo 'pi.
[3] I would excise this na.
[4-4] A: svarūpatā. From here I follow C.
[5] A: saṃskārāntara.
[6] A: vyāvartakatety arthaḥ.

implication. There the capacity to effectuate, correlated by wifeness, is a qualifier present in the acceptance. Wifeness, though not the subject-matter of the * knowledge under consideration, is an excluder of that capacity to effectuate.

2. For example: that which limits the significance of the word *dhenu* (milch cow), 'cowness accompanied by the capacity of being sucked [by the calf]' particularizes the object of sucking by means of the occurrence in a cow having the general effect of being sucked [by the calf], because the significance [of *dhenu*] has as its limitor only being the effect of being sucked, which effect has a common substratum (or locus) with cowness.[1] * In exactly the same way, in our problem, the capacity [of taking] to effect [wifeness] is to be known as the capacity to produce [it] merely by means of a common substratumness correlated by such a producedness. Or, its [wifeness'] natural existence is due to its being a qualifier [of woman], which has the distinguishing property of being located in a *saṃskāra*, which has become the limitor of producedness by marriage, a property devoid of special aspects of producedness by marriage, that is to say because of the exclusive character possessed by the acceptance of her [by the bridegroom].

[1] For *dhenu* as an illustration of a *rūḍha* ('conventional') denotative power (*śakti*), see *Maṇikaṇa* (cited above), pp. 81-3.

VIII. brāhmādyaṣṭaka-tyāgānantara-tādṛśa-grahaṇam eva vivāha[1] iti [2] cen na,[2] tādṛśa-jñānāsamartha-bālakāder vivāhe 'vyāpteḥ.[3]

iti śrī-Gadādhara-bhaṭṭācāryasya Nava-dvīpa-nivāsinaḥ [4] vivāha-vādaḥ samāptaḥ.[4]

[1] vivāha is omitted in A.

[2-2] A: cet.

[3] A: 'vyāptiḥ.

[4-4] Omitted in A, which is apparently labelled *Vivāhavādārthaḥ*. B is entitled *Vivāhavādarahasyam*, so was Jayaswal and Sastri's No. 339 from Darbhanga. C is entitled only *Vivāhavādaḥ*. Only A gives the author's name.

VIII. [Consequently] if it is suggested that marriage is merely this taking immediately following a relinquishment, in the eight forms of marriage, namely Brāhma, etc., I deny it, for it would not cover the marriage of a child, etc., who is incapable of such knowledge.

So ends the *Discussion of Marriage* by Śrī Gadādhara Bhaṭṭācārya, resident in Nadiya.

ADDITIONAL ANNOTATIONS

Tit. The *Vivāhavādārtha* of Gadādhara (here) is virtually commented upon (and heavily plagiarised) by Śrī-Kṛṣṇa-caraṇa, author of the *Udvāha-pariśiṣṭa* printed at pp. 134ff. of Heramba Nath Chatterji, Sastri's, edn. of Raghunandana's *Udvāhatattvam* (Calcutta, Sanskrit College, 1963). S. the same, *Forms of Marriage in Ancient India* I (Calcutta, 1972), 23-4 and nn.

p. [308], l. 21. Reacting to this comment Pt. Aithal found nos. 7878, 7879[2] in *Des. Cat.* of Skt. Mss., R. As. Soc. Beng., and Heramba Nath Chatterji lists seven further Mss. actually at the Sanskrit College, Calcutta itself!

p. [311], n. 1. The funeral is called a *saṃskāra* by Kāty. also. at Dh.k.1524a.

p. [321], l. 12. Cf. Medh. on M.III.27 and Jha's *Notes* thereon.

p. [321], l. 13. Delete [said to be].

p. [321], l. 15. Delete '-al suffix'.

p. [321], l. 18. giver, as contrasted with the gift...

p. [321], l. 24. In fact it is the *saṃskāra* which is produced by the gift.

p. [322], l. 8. *karmatā* is the state of being the sufferer or recipient of the action.

p. [327], l. 3. Read : Nor is it the case that, on account of that taking having as its subject-matter some one who is one's own, there is an overpervasion, on account of the presence of mineness and the like (at other times), because what constitutes the object is nothing but...

p. [327], l. 13. ... third party (e.g. a guardian)... *saṃskāra* (i.e. by gift which produces it).

p. [327], l. 16. Taking = knowledge.

p. [327], l. 18. I.e. the girl is the object of a gift to the bridegroom.

p. [329], l. 3. Knowledge (taking) creates wifeness. Therefore wifeness is *not* the thing known. But if it existed already the knowledge which creates it could not arise.

p. [329], l. 13. I.e. just as sucking (being sucked) turns a cow into *dhenu*, so *being taken* turns a woman into a wife.

AN INDIAN CONTRIBUTION TO THE STUDY OF PROPERTY

(i) Introduction

FUNDAMENTAL concepts are often the more difficult to define because of their ubiquitous employment, and though the majority of people are content to do without a definition the lack of one stands as a perpetual challenge to human intelligence. Property is just such a concept, standing upon the frontiers of linguistics, law, and logic without deriving final shape from any of them. Since no legal transaction or dealing could take place without it, and since innumerable events familiar to daily life depend upon it for their effectiveness, it seems strange that it is so little understood. Many legal systems (which of necessity employ the concept at every turn) contrive to dispense with a definition altogether [1]; and the most acceptable definition of modern times makes a virtual sum of the incidents of Property,[2] just as if one were to define a blackboard as ' blackness + largeness + suitability-to-be-written-on-for-the-information-of-students '. Indeed, new problems perpetually arise (e.g. has the Coal Board the right to mine coal more than three miles from the shore of the United Kingdom ?) and if we knew what Property was we might be saved the embarrassment of producing a new rule from a heap of irreconcilable previous decisions upon related problems, whose individual relevance to the problem in hand will always be a matter of controversy. The situation outside the Anglo-American legal field may be no better for the existence of Codes, and for a

[1] Roman law and English law have persistently avoided the necessity. See Austin, *Lectures*, chh. 47, 48. Study of the incidents led Jolowicz to write : ' ownership, in the developed (Roman) law, may be defined as the unrestricted right of control over a physical thing, and whosoever has this right can claim the thing he owns wherever it is and no matter who possesses it '. This sounds very like *ius utendi fruendi abutendi* (denied by Buckland, *Text-book*, 187). But as soon as we say *ius* or *right* we fall foul of Hägerström and his school, who defy us to explain what these words mean. English law frankly denies that Property has any technical meaning : per Lord Porter in *Nokes* v. *Doncaster Collieries*, [1940] A.C. 1014 ; Paton, *Jurisprudence*, ch. 18. See also Vinding Kruse, *Right of Property* (trans. Federspiel), Oxford, 1939. It is curious that Rashdall, ' The philosophical theory of Property ', in *Property, its duties and rights*, London, 1913, seemed to be unaware that a philosopher requires Property to be defined before its justification may be attempted.

[2] Salmond, *Jurisprudence*, sec. 86 : ownership is the relation between a person and any right that is vested in him. This may be compared with the view of Noyes, p. 484, n. 2 below. According to the Romans a man might be *dominus* without possession and without any other right than to make a mancipation. At another extreme, Property has a residual aspect—' a very necessary vacuum for the law to abhor ' (Terry, *Some leading principles of Anglo-American law*, Philadelphia, 1884, 298). While ' relationships ' and ' rights ' beg more questions than they answer, a definition of *dominium* as the ' classificatory genitive ' (ibid. 296) seems to come nearer the heart of the matter : it tells us exactly what we might attempt to define. The French Civil Code (Art. 544) is the best authoritative example of the ' cumulative ' type of ' definition ' : *La propriété est le droit de jouir et disposer des choses de la manière la plus absolue, pourvu qu'on n'en fasse pas un usage prohibé par les lois ou par les règlements.*

neat exposition of the manner in which such problems are approached in the former system one cannot do better than consult a recent frank confession in the House of Lords.[1]

Courts and Codes perpetually take refuge in devices and fictions in order to evade a fundamental issue, with results which are often so incongruous that they could not be justified were the nature of the essential institution readily ascertainable. For example, if it be asked whether, when *A* sends a gift by post to *B* and it is lost in transit, the loss accrues to *A* or to *B*, it is held that it accrues to *A*,[2] on the ground that the Post Office is the agent of the sender, and its employees are thus accountable to *A* (though he might have thought that he had ceased to be interested in the object) and not to *B* ; whereas if the question is whether a contract was performed or an offer accepted on the day of posting or the day of receipt, or whether the sender or the addressee must bear the risk of deterioration in transit, the rôle of the Post Office is conveniently reversed, and it becomes the agent of the addressee, in order that Property may pass on posting [3] or that knowledge of the contents of the letter which he does not see until later or which he may never see at all may be imputed to the addressee at the moment in question. Examples of such anomalies might be multiplied. Refuge is taken for some purposes in distinctions between the various subdivisions of Property (for 'title' is divisible) and between Property and Possession. Nevertheless we know from our mercantile law that Property can 'pass' without delivery actual or constructive and it is perfectly possible that one's Property in an object may amount to no more than a liability to bear the risk if it is not duly delivered.[4] Despite the shifts, the recourse to analogy upon grounds of convenience, and perhaps even because of the multiplicity of instances from which a composite empirical picture of Property would have to be built up, a sound definition of Property remains as remote as ever.

The best studies of Property as a concept (as distinct from the questions whether private property existed in ancient civilizations, whether certain persons ought to own particular kinds of objects, or what are the conditions subject to which owned objects may be used and transferred to other owners or users) have been written by Indians. The literature is mostly in manuscript, and the excellence of the discussions is unknown not only to comparative lawyers and students of jurisprudence in the West but even to the majority

[1] In *Chapman* v. *Chapman*, [1954] 2 W.L.R. 723, 750, per Lord Asquith of Bishopstone : 'Nor, speaking more generally, does English jurisprudence start from a broad principle and decide cases in accordance with its logical implications. It starts with a *clean slate*, scored over, in course of time, with *ad hoc* decisions. General rules are arrived at inductively, from the collation and comparison of these decisions : they do not *pre-exist* them '. (First and last italics are mine.)

[2] *Whitfield* v. *Lord le Despencer*, (1778) 98 E.R. 1344, 1350.

[3] *Household Fire and Carriage Accident Insurance Co.* v. *Grant*, (1879) 4 Ex. D. 216 ; *Henthorn* v. *Fraser*, [1892] 2 Ch. 27 ; *Badische Anilin und Soda Fabrik* v. *Basle Chemical Works*, [1898] A.C. 200.

[4] The Sale of Goods Act, 1893, secc. 18, 20, 32. See in particular Rule 5 of sec. 18.

of Indian scholars as well.[1] This is due partly to the specialist appeal of the works themselves, copies of which have become extremely rare, and partly to the disrepute into which the study of *Nyāya* (Logic) has fallen since University courses of study began to be organized under the influence of a Westernized Indian political and social hierarchy. For whereas the *application* of the concept to individual problems was always the task of the jurists, some of whose works are still in vogue for the purpose of the administration of the Anglo-Hindu law, the *definition* of Property was the special concern of the logicians, who were extremely well-informed upon the sources of law, and who commenced a very thorough investigation of this subject from about the middle of the sixteenth century. The literature of *Navya-nyāya*, or the New School of logic, has been characterized as the most difficult literature the mind of man has produced, and once the great prestige which it gave its adepts ceased to attract students it is not surprising that it began to face extinction. A recent publication in America [2] has given the study a much-needed stimulus, and perhaps its future is now not to be despaired of. The present article does not, however, attempt to recreate the entire story of the study of Property at the hands of the *Navya-naiyāyikas*—indeed, without certain of the principal texts [3] it is doubtful whether it can ever be written—but perhaps lawyers other than Indologists may be interested in a work which was written while the central problems were hotly debated among the learned, which is brief, of wide range, and a notable

[1] Priyanāth Sen, *The general principles of Hindu jurisprudence*, TLL for 1909, Calcutta, 1918, referred in his second Lecture to the logical basis of the concepts of *svatva* and *svāmitva* but did not consider that his audience were likely to comprehend the subtleties of the arguments, and he rapidly passed on to a discussion of the more widely-known problems concerning acquisition and disposition and the nature of the authority behind the rules applicable to each. No one has taken up the earlier point, and Dr. P. V. Kane, *History of Dharmaśāstra*, III, Poona, 1946, makes an even briefer reference (at p. 547) giving as his authority the extremely condensed remarks of Kamalākara-bhaṭṭa in his *Vivāda-tāṇḍava* (which will be found in the edition with Gujarāti commentary printed Baroda, 1901, at p. 279). No reference to the fundamental controversies is to be found in the Wai *Dharmakośa* (Vyavahāra-kāṇḍa, 1941). Yet Indian jurists have been put on enquiry not merely by the reference in the *Vivāda-tāṇḍava*; the most explicit reference in Mitra Miśra's *Vīramitrodaya, Vyavahāra-prakāśa*, Benaras, 1932, at p. 422 to the 'category' theory and to the (then) availability of further information in the *Ākara* and 'the *Līlāvatī* and subsequent works' (a valuable reference which Golāp Candra Sarkar Śāstri unfortunately distorts in his translation (Calcutta, 1879) at p. 24); and the brilliant if superficial summary of the controversies given by Jagannātha Tarkapañcānana in his *Vivāda-bhaṅgārṇava* (MS I.O. 1768 = Egg. 1532, ff. 3b–10a = 'Colebrooke's Digest', two-volume edition, Madras, 1865, II, 186–93); but also by the very useful, though eclectic and summary, account sub. nom. *Svatva* in the *Nyāyakośa* (Bhīmācārya Jhalakīkar, revised Vāsudev-śāstri Abhyaṅkar, Poona, 1928) at p. 1049.

[2] D. H. H. Ingalls, *Materials for the study of Navya-nyāya logic*, Harvard University Press, 1951.

[3] Amongst the missing works the most to be lamented is the *Ākara*, referred to by Mitra Miśra (n. 1 above), by Kamalākara in the *Nirṇaya-sindhu*, by Jayarāma in his *Nyāya-siddhānta-mālā*, II, 128, 139, and by Gokulanātha in his *Padavākya-ratnākara* (twice) and in his (*Nyāya-*) *Siddhānta-tattva-viveka* (MS I.O. 1436b) at f. 116b. A less important loss generally, but much to be regretted in our immediate context, is the *Rāddhānta-saraṇi* of Jayarāma, referred to in his *Svatva-vādārtha* at p. 2 (this pagination refers to the MS (*nāgari*) in my possession which is a copy of MS Adyar Shelf No. 30.C.9, Serial No. 73879, a palm-leaf manuscript in Telugu script, supplied to me by the Librarian, Adyar Library and Research Centre, at very short notice, for which co-operation I wish to express sincere acknowledgments).

specimen of Indian legal literature. In the last regard it is somewhat peculiar, since the style is midway between that of the legal digest or commentary of the period and that of the typical logician of the New School: few of the characteristic terms employed by the latter appear, and hardly any of its excruciating subtlety.

The Sanskrit original [1] will, it is hoped, be published together with the *Svatva-rahasya*, the remains of Jayarāma's *Svatva-vādārtha*, and portions of * Gokulanātha's *Nyāya-siddhānta-tattva-viveka*, for all four authors were concerned with the same problem and are best studied in close proximity. The title of the work of which an English translation is printed here is as much of a mystery as its authorship. It is probably *Svatva-vicāra*,[2] 'A discussion of Property'. Its author was probably a Bengali,[3] but he may well have been a Maithila: if this is so Gokulanātha [4] may have regarded him as a remote predecessor. His date depends upon many factors, but at this stage the first quarter of the seventeenth century seems most likely. Aufrecht tells us [5] that a copy of a *Svatva-vicāra* by one Anantarāma had been found in private hands. Anantarāma is identified by Professor V. Raghavan [6] with the author of the *Vivāda-candrikā*,[7] which was certainly not written before 1773.[8] But apart from the discrepancies in viewpoint between these two works,[9] it is clear

[1] I gratefully acknowledge the encouragement and suggestions which I received while studying this text from Śrī Krishṇa Gopāla Goswāmi Śāstri, M.A., P.R.S., and from Dr. Ludo J. Rocher.

[2] Neither in MS I.O. 861 nor in MS A.S.B. I.B. 26 has the text a proper *incipit* or a colophon. But the copyist's endorsements on MS I.O. 861 make it clear that he believed that our work had this title.

[3] Since Bengalis of Nava-dvīpa virtually monopolized this particular branch of learning during the period to which I tentatively attribute this work. Yet no doubt Maithilas came to them as students, and because a work contains views which are not consistent with the characteristic 'Maithila' doctrines upon controversial legal questions it by no means follows that the author was not a Maithila by birth and associations.

[4] The great Maithila exponent of *navya-nyāya*. The opinion expressed by the editors respectively of his *Padavākya-ratnākara* (Kāñcī, 1904) and *Amṛtodaya* (*Kāvyamālā*, Bombay, 1896) that he belonged to the middle of the sixteenth century cannot be accepted. He certainly belongs, at the earliest, to the end of the seventeenth and the beginning of the eighteenth century.

[5] *Catalogus catalogorum*, I, 749.

[6] *New Catalogus catalogorum*, Madras, 1949, 138.

[7] MS I.O. 1278b = Egg. 1530.

[8] Since it refers to the *Vivādārṇava* on f. 19b. In the absence of a clue to the existence of a work of that title we are justified in assuming that the work referred to is that famous co-operative work compiled by Bāleśvara (or ? Bāṇeśvara), Kṛpārāma, Gopāla-Kṛṣṇa, Gaurīkānta, and other Pandits at the request of Warren Hastings and subsequently translated into Persian and thence into English and published by N. B. Halhed under the title *A code of Gentoo laws or, Ordinations of the Pundits*, London, 1776, and in later editions. The manuscripts of this Digest are divided between those which entitle it *Vivādārṇava-setu* (a very intelligible title) and *Vivādārṇava-bhañjana* (or *-bhaṅga*). MS I.O. 3145a = Egg. 1506 is an example of the former and MS B.O.R.I. No. 364 of 1875–6 is an example of the latter. P. V. Kane, *History of Dharmaśāstra*, I, Poona, 1930, 622, lists the two works separately, but their identity was proved by extracts very kindly supplied to me by Dr. P. K. Gode in a letter dated 22 November 1955.

[9] Anantarāma believed, for example, that Property in a father's estate was obtained by birth (f. 10b); that a *patita* could use the assets he owned before his *pātaka* for the purpose of performing penance; and that Jīmūtavāhana was wrong in holding that partition merely *manifests* Property (f. 11a).

that Anantarāma knew of the views of Śrī Kṛṣṇa Tarkālaṅkāra (*c.* 1750),[1] who carefully contradicts an opinion which is expressed in our work.[2] Since it was a general practice for writers always to refute a contrary doctrine which was generally known in their own day, a failure on the part of a specialist even to refer to an opposed opinion cited from an eminent scholar is strong evidence either that the two persons were contemporaries or that the former was anterior to the latter. Gokulanātha himself wrote a *Svatva-vāda*,[3] but his views as expressed at length elsewhere make it clear that he is of a different opinion as to the nature of Property from that of our author. Jayarāma (? Nyāya-pañcānana (*c.* 1650)) is certainly not the author of this work, for his own shows that he began when the debates had reached a much later stage. Gadādhara may well have written a *Svatva-vāda*, and it is open to doubt at present whether the brilliant but anonymous *Svatva-rahasya* is not his rather than Mathurānātha's.[4] The latter work undoubtedly presupposes such a treatise as ours, and thus the order in which the works appeared can be established even though we may remain in doubt as to their authorships. The *Svatva-vicāra* may be dated provisionally about 1600–10.

The text is based upon two manuscripts : *A*, which is MS I.O. 861 (Egg. 1538), is probably half a century older than *B*, which is MS I.B. 26 in the library of the Asiatic Society of Bengal ; both were copied within the period *c.* 1780–1830 from a manuscript which included, in that order, the *Svatva-vicāra* and the *Svatva-rahasya*. It is unfortunate that they are closely related, probably as cousins, but the text derivable from them is fairly satisfactory and the few orthographical corrections of importance which were necessary are mentioned in footnotes. Two remarkable omissions and one erroneous addition, however—substantial faults in the transmission—deserve fuller mention. The omission in VI of *kvacit pātityasya*, which the sense absolutely requires, can be attributed to haplography. In the same section the manuscripts read *kvacit pitṛ-maraṇasya*, which is nonsense in the context : perhaps a somewhat over-zealous and under-skilled student slipped in the word *pitṛ* under the impression that it would

[1] The famous jurist is quoted repeatedly (e.g. on ff. 8b, 19a).

[2] In his commentary on Śūlapāṇi's *Śrāddha-viveka*, Calcutta, 1939, 124, Śrī Kṛṣṇa points out that in the text *dampatyor madhyagaṃ dhanam* (for which see below) the word *dhanam* refers to the husband's and not the wife's estate, 'for the husband is not the owner of her *saudāyika* assets'. See the text below, IV (5).

[3] Aufrecht, op. cit., I, 749.

[4] The view characteristic of the author of the *Rahasya*, namely that *svatva* and *svāmitva* are one and the same category, is referred to by Gokulanātha in his *Siddhānta-tattva-viveka* at f. 115b as the view of 'Jyāya'. The ascription of the *Rahasya* is a matter of extreme difficulty. *
It was written after Jayarāma and, of course, before Gokulanātha. Titles tend, somewhat vaguely, to have the character of trademarks. The termination *-rahasya* is used widely by Mathurānātha and apparently less often by Rāmabhadra Sārvabhauma (who cannot be the author since his views expressed in the *Padārtha-tattva-vivecana-prakāśa*, Benaras, 1916, are much less mature), by Harirāma Tarkavāgīśa (a comparatively obscure author), and by Gadādhara. There is little doubt but that the *Rahasya* was studied by both Vācaspati Bhaṭṭācārya, the grandfather of Jagannātha Tarkapañcānana, and by Śrī Kṛṣṇa ; it was most unfortunate that Prīyanāth Sen died before he could pursue the interest which a rapid study of the manuscript at Calcutta obviously aroused in his mind.

improve the sense. A more serious fault may be observed in III, and since a false impression of the law would be created by ignoring it, a full description of it will be necessary. The text as the manuscripts would have it implies that Jīmūtavāhana (*c.* 1090–1110) and other authorities of the Bengal school (which must include the celebrated Raghunandana (*c.* 1510–60)) were of the opinion that a thief could give a good title in his stolen property to a third party, although he himself would be liable to (spiritual) penalties. Jīmūtavāhana in his *Dāyabhāga* [1] and the *Vyavahāra-mātṛkā* [2] does indeed glance at topics which relate to this problem, but nowhere does he suggest such an absurd proposition. Raghunandana is similarly guiltless, and in the summaries of doctrines on the subject found in the *Vīramitrodaya* (*c.* 1630) [3] and the *Vivāda-bhaṅgārṇava* (*c.* 1795) [4] we have no hint of such a suggestion from any authority whatever.[5] On the other hand it is indeed a frequently-made proposition, by implication in the *Dāyabhāga* and by other old authorities such as the *Mitākṣarā* (*c.* 1125), that where *X* acquires assets by a method which is reprobated in the *dharma-śāstra*, and subsequently alienates them, whether voluntarily or involuntarily, to *Y*, the fault attaching to *X*'s acquisition affects *X* alone, and not the property, so that in fact *X*'s failure to perform the appropriate penance will not affect the title of *Y*.[6] Similarly, where the *śāstra* forbids certain persons to alienate their assets under certain conditions,[7] it is commonly held that they may nevertheless alienate them validly, but the texts have an *adṛṣṭa* (' unseen ') force and the alienors must perform a penance.[8] In our present passage it is clear that some words have dropped out. Assuming an haplography we must read as follows :—

> tatra cauryyāpahṛta-dravyasya caureṇa dāne vikraye vā kṛte ⟨ādātrādinā ca dāne vikraye vā kṛte⟩ uttarādhikāriṇaḥ svatvaṃ siddhyaty = eva, kintu karttā pratyavaitīti Dāyabhāga-kāra-prabhṛtayaḥ.

[1] II, 27–30 (Colebrooke's translation and also Bharatcandra Śiromaṇi's edition, 1863).

[2] ed. A. Mookerjee, *Memoirs of the As. Soc. of Bengal*, III, 5, 1912, 277 ff., at pp. 341–52.

[3] Secc. 42–8 in Golāp Candra's edition.

[4] Book II, chh. ii and iv.

[5] This is not to deny that no one ever argued that injunctions such as *parasvaṃ nādadīta iti* made the thief liable to *sin*, while texts such as the famous lists of *āgamas* in Gautama and Manu sanctioned *purchase* as a means of acquisition without specifying from whom one should not make a purchase. But such arguments had little chance of success.

[6] *Mitākṣarā* (Colebrooke's translation), I, i, 7–16.

[7] A father, a coparcener, and a wife are especially inhibited. For instances we may take the texts of Vyāsa *sthāvaraṃ dvipadañ = caiva* (*Dh. kośa*, 1587a), of Nārada or Yājñavalkya *maṇimuktāpravālānāṃ* (*Dh. kośa*, 1219b), and of Nārada *bhartrā prītena yad dattaṃ* (*Dh. kośa*, 1448b). It is most important to remember, however, that where the owner's proprietary right is defective as in the case of a Mitākṣarā coparcener there can be no case for the texts' being taken in an *adṛṣṭa* sense, and the alienation will be invalid : even in the Bengal school many authorities believed that Jīmūtavāhana was wrong when he allowed an undivided coparcener unrestricted alienation of his undivided share.

[8] See nn. 6 and 7 above, and v(1) and VIII below. Jīmūtavāhana's point of view, however, has been widely misunderstood. He did not believe that a father might effectively alienate all the family property in all circumstances whatever. It is quite clear from what he says in his *Vyavahāra-mātṛkā* at p. 285 that a son could contest the alienation unless, as explained in the *Dāyabhāga*, the maintenance of the persons entitled to be maintained under the text of Manu would be jeopardized by failure to alienate.

This reconstruction is supported by (i) the fact that a thief is not merely liable to *pratyavaya* (' sin ') ; (ii) the donee is not really *uttarādhikāri* (' successor in title '), for in order for there to be an *uttarādhikāri* there must be a *pūrvv-ādhikāri* (' predecessor '), which the thief *re ipsa* cannot be, whereas his receiver can be ; and (iii) the thief is not a *karttā*, because his act (giving the goods to the receiver) is not condemned and made the subject of a spiritual penalty, whereas the receiver from a thief is a *karttā* of a *karma* which is *śāstra-niṣiddha*, namely accepting from a thief an object not given to the latter.

Before we pass to the text itself, however, we must put ourselves, rapidly, as nearly as possible in the intellectual position of its author. He does not recapitulate for us the whole history of the study of Property up to his time, for his readers did not require it : but our appreciation of his extraordinarily compressed treatise will be the greater for a summary understanding of developments which took place before, and also those which followed after its publication. Both the lawyers and the logicians had been content for a very long period to define *Svatva* (Property) as *yatheṣṭa-viniyoga-yojyatva*, or a notion not far removed from it.[1] ' The capacity of a thing to be employed at pleasure ' seemed a satisfactory description of the fact which distinguishes my thing from John's thing. Early writers had found, as they thought, the secret of Property in the right of use at pleasure. This demanded modification, since evidently the law does not permit absolute freedom of use and even, according to a powerful school among the jurists,[2] enjoins that owned assets should be employed in specified ways.[3] Hence an amended definition appeared by the beginning of the fifteenth century, namely *yatheṣṭa-viniyoga-yogyatva*, ' the fact that a thing may be applied to use at pleasure ' or, more intelligibly, *yatheṣṭa-viniyogārhatva*, ' the fact that a thing is morally and legally fit for employment at pleasure '.[4] But this was not a very substantial advance, it hides a fatal circularity, and when the famous logician Raghunātha Śiromaṇi (*c.* 1520–50) made his drastic revision of the ontological ' categories ' (*padārthas*)

[1] The expression is frequently used in the *Dāyabhāga* and accepted by Śrīnātha Ācārya-cūḍāmaṇi, Rāmabhadra Nyāyālaṅkara (an opponent of the ' category ' theory), and of course most authorities before Raghunātha Śiromaṇi's views gained the ascendancy. His influence affected even those who refused to accept the ' category ' theory : e.g. Vācaspati Bhaṭṭācārya (*flor. c.* 1695)—see Jagannātha (ref. on p. 477, n. 1 above). A link between this concept and *Svatva* was never abandoned however : see n. 4 below. See also Devaṇṇa-bhaṭṭa, *Smṛti-candrikā*, Bombay, 1918, II, 283, for a pre-Raghunātha example of the connexion between *yatheṣṭa-viniyoga-yogyatva* and *Svatva*.

[2] Represented by Dhāreśvara and the author of the *Smṛti-saṅgraha*. The question is treated by both Jīmūtavāhana and Vijñāneśvara (under the heading : the widow's right of succession).

[3] Such as maintenance of the family, sacrifices to the gods and offerings to deceased ancestors, etc.

[4] Prīyanāth Sen, 43–8. An excellent discussion is found in the *Madanaratna-pradīpa*, Bikaner, 1948, at pp. 324–5, from which Mitra Miśra seems to have borrowed largely in the *Vīramitrodaya* (sec. 43) ; but the latter bows to the influence of Raghunātha, and relates *yatheṣṭa-viniyogārhatva* to *Svatva* as ' capacity to produce sprouts ' is related to ' seed-ness '. It is interesting that Jagannātha's concept of the relationship is more simple and more antiquated (MS I.O. 1768 f. 6a), and this may perhaps be attributed to the influence of Annaṃ-bhaṭṭa (see p. 487, n. 1 below).

and declared that *Svatva* was an additional 'category',[1] further developments were inevitable. Followers of Raghunātha were content with the definition of *Svatva* as a special category, caused by listed causes, extinguished by listed causes of extinction (derived from the *dharma-śāstra*), inhering in the owner and in the thing and giving rise to that special conjunction between them which explains the most frequent and most subtle use of the Genitive Case. Some recognized as its *lakṣaṇa*, or characteristic, *yatheṣṭa-viniyogārhatva*, but of course they denied that the two concepts were identical.[2] Opponents of the 'category' theory searched for destructive arguments: some said that it was not a 'category' but *vyavahāra-viṣayatva*,[3] 'the fact that a thing may be the subject-matter of a legal transaction': since Property is detected chiefly, and can be adjudged only, in legal contexts, and forms the means by which transactions can be validated, this suggestion has very attractive features. Others again said that *Svatva* was a *śaktī-viśeṣa*, 'a particular potentiality'. Raghunātha had already defined *śakti* in general as a 'category'; and this definition, though it attempted merely to classify Property, brought its upholders into excessive difficulties at once, and we have hardly any trace of their viewpoint.[4] Next we come to the view expressed, and carefully substantiated, in our text, namely that Property is really a *saṃskāra*, 'a fixed impression',[5] founded upon knowledge that 'this is mine', a knowledge itself referable to the law for its validity. Very broadly speaking the difference between the 'category' and the 'impression' viewpoints, which are elaborately discussed here, in the *Svatva-rahasya*, and in the works of Gokulanātha and Jayarāma, may be said to be a difference between an *objective* and a *subjective* definition. The 'category' school held that Property had an objective reality of its own independently of a particular individual's consciousness, and for this type of definition ample legal support was forthcoming. The 'impression' party believed that Property was a special figment or condition of the brain, and that without consciousness of Ownership (based upon legally verifiable data) Property did not exist at all. They denied that any conjunction between

[1] On the meaning of *padārtha* see p. 486, n. 2. Raghunātha's opinion is given at length in the *Nyāya-līlāvati-prakāśa-dīdhiti* (often referred to as 'the Dīdhiti') of which MSS I.O. 62 and 1213b (each commencing at f. 10b) are both poor copies; and in brief in the *Padārtha-tattva-nirūpaṇa*, Benaras, 1916, at p. 62. With the printed text MS I.O. 2662c may usefully be compared, though a portion is omitted by haplography. The argument as given in the *PTN* may be summarized as follows: 'Fitness-to-be-used-at-pleasure' cannot = Property since all kinds of uses are comprehended, and if we attempt to restrain use in accordance with texts such as 'let him not take the *svam* of another' we find that the restrictions themselves depend upon the concept of *sva-tva*. The only way out of this circular difficulty is to posit *Svatva* a distinct ontological category.

[2] *Vīramitrodaya*, sec. 43; Anantarāma, *Vivāda-candrikā*, ff. 19a, b; Acyuta, *Dāyabhāga-siddhānta-kumuda-candrikā* (Bharatcandra's edition), p. 22.

[3] *Vivāda-tāṇḍava*, 279; cf. Raghudeva, Rāmabhadra Sārvabhauma, and Vēṇīdatta (following the first) on *Svatva* not being *yatheṣṭa-viniyogopāya-viṣayatva* (commentaries on Raghunātha). Jayarāma, *Svatva-vādārtha*, p. 2, denies that it is *dānādi-janakatva*.

[4] *Vivāda-tāṇḍava*, 279.

* [5] Colebrooke, *Digest*, II, 186 n., translates it 'faculty'.

'me' and 'my thing' existed, and their theory had to resort to devices to explain the Property of babies and lunatics—at least it must have done so, for we have hardly any trace of the actual arguments amongst the literature at present recovered.[1] The inherent weakness of the 'impression' theory led to a further development. The conjunction between the Owner and the thing, which the 'category' school subsume [2] but do not explain satisfactorily, and which the 'impression' school deny, struck yet another school of thought as the solution to the problem. The constant factors in the discussion were Time (the period during which Property exists), acquisition (which involves an acquirer), and loss or cesser (by which Property ends). It seemed that by an accurate linking of these factors a perfect definition could be achieved. The result was the following [3]:—

'Property is the conjunction of "Time posterior to acquisition" with the "occurrence" of "Time coincidental with acquisition", (conjunction) particularized by the persisting absence of alienation or by the absence at any relevant moment of alienation of any portion of the acquisition'.

'Time' is an eternal entity,[4] and 'Time' after an event is eternal; its relationship or conjunction, so long as no alienation has taken place, with the 'occurrence' of 'Time related to the acquisition' (we may dispense with the acquirer himself), constitutes the entity known as Property, which is thus not a 'category' but a special kind of conjunction. This brilliant notion inspired an attack from Jayarāma, who re-established upon a securer footing the already formidable 'category' theory. The latter also vanquished the theory that Property was the 'extinction' of acquisition particularized by the 'prior non-existence' of alienation.[5] By this time the *saṃskāra* or 'impression'

[1] Jayarāma in the *Svatva-vādārtha*, p. 6, says that *Svāmitva* (ownership) must reside in the 'self', otherwise the youth would not own a toy which he played with as a child—the self being the only continuous link between the child and the youth.

[2] Rāmabhadra Sārvabhauma alone, I believe, commits himself to the identification of the conjunction with Property: '*caitrasyedaṃ dhanam*' *iti pratīti-viṣayo dhana-vṛtti-caitra-vṛtti-sambandhaḥ* (comm. on Raghunātha, 117). I do not feel happy about the second *vṛtti*, which may be a mistaken reading. Yet the sense is plain.

[3] *krayādyanyatamotpatti-kāla-vṛttinā yāvad-vikrayādyabhāvena kvacit tad-vikrayābhāvena vā viśiṣṭaḥ tat-tat-krayādyanyatamottara-kāla-saṃbandhaḥ*: Jayarāma, *Svatva-vādārtha*, p. 1; cf. the view cited by Viśvanātha Siddhāntapañcānana in his *Padārtha-tattvāloka* (MS I.O. 1698c at f. 166a): *caitrīya-krayādi-kālīna-tad-dravyīya-vikrayādi-pratiyogika-yāvad-abhāva-vaiśiṣṭyaṃ tad-dravye caitrasya svatvam iti prācīna-mata-niṣkarṣa iti.*

[4] See Ingalls, op. cit., 78–9.

[5] Commentators on Raghunātha, *PTN*, and *Padārtha-maṇḍana*, Benaras, 1930, 32. It will be observed that the *nyāya* theory of causation recognizes that every activity (*karma*) is completed in the fourth moment (*kṣaṇa*) of the process (*kriyā*), and when the activity is 'extinguished', namely in the fifth moment, the product of the activity is in existence. Consequently Property cannot exist until the whole process of the *kriyā* known as purchase is exhausted, but once that moment has been reached a cause of the extinction of Property has to be produced (e.g. sale) before Property itself ceases: the interval, popularly speaking, between the events can be equated with Property itself. For the basic notion of *kriyā* reference may be made to Kuppuswāmi Śāstri, *A primer of Indian logic*, Madras, 1932, III, 20, and ibid., 48, for an explanation of the concept of 'prior non-existence', one of the three sub-divisions of non-existence according to *nyāya*. It is the idea of conceived specific futurity, in relation to a non-existent thing.

theory had long been left behind. An investigation of the merits of these theories and in particular those of the 'category' theory is a distinct undertaking and must be postponed.

It will have been observed that these discussions are not concerned with differences between various sorts of *tenures* or *interests*, of which there was undoubtedly some profusion in ancient and medieval India.[1] Proprietor, tenant, bailee, mortgagee—all appear to be thought of as, within their respective boundaries, *svāmis*.[2] Even the question of the rights of unincorporated associations, which is directly relevant to the last section of this work, is not investigated here. In fact none of these related works deal with either the capacity to own, except very incidentally, or the incidents of ownership, apart from the very general claim to 'employ at pleasure'. No emphasis need be placed on this, for discussions of this sort, which are appendages to the conclusions upon the fundamental question of the nature of Property, are to be found in the legal textbooks, where they belong. Indian jurists took it for granted that the incidents of particular manifestations of Ownership might differ, while the *svatva* of the King, the *svatva* of the landowner, the *svatva* of the tenant-farmer, and, in an extreme case, even the *svatva* of the mortgagee in possession (as against a trespasser) were all comprehensible under the single term of Property. This is not only logically defensible but historically explicable, since, as we have seen, the discussions started from a long-traditional definition of *Svatva* as the fact of the existence of a right of enjoyment at pleasure, a feature which is common, in varying measures, to all those manifestations. Another line altogether was taken by Western jurists, seemingly following the old Roman distinctions between *dominium, ususfructus, servitus, hypotheca, possessio*, and so on.[3] Whether in the modern representative systems of the Civil Law world,

[1] It is quite certain that, while the word *svāmi* (owner) is often used to distinguish the bailor, for example, from the bailee, the word is correctly used to describe one whose powers of disposal over the assets are severely limited. *Bhogopayogi-svatva*, or Property admitting of a right to enjoy the produce without rights over the corpus, is a familiar concept (cf. in Islamic law *manfa'a*: on which see K. Tyabji, *Limited interests in Muhammadan law*, London, 1949, 3 ff.). Kings in particular frequently made gifts of land specifically denying the grantees the rights of gift, sale, or mortgage, and our surviving inscriptions provide many examples of grants where, to convey the nearest title to an absolute estate which a subject could hold, the grantor made over the land in *aṣṭa-bhoga-tejas-svāmya* with rights to timber, minerals, treasure, etc., etc. Explicit passages are found in Śrī Kṛṣṇa and in Jagannātha, who relies upon the former, where *Svatva* is shown by illustrations to be qualitatively sub-divisible. See Priyanāth Sen, 49–53 (where his views about the King's ultimate ownership, though popular amongst contemporary scholars, are probably unsound).

[2] See previous note. C. Reinold Noyes, *The institution of Property*, New York/Toronto, 1936, 363, expresses a conclusion as to the nature of ownership which corresponds very closely with the assumption made by Hindu jurists—but it is violently in conflict with current Anglo-American formal jurisprudence.

[3] All these 'bundles of rights' differed actually or potentially, and it never occurred to the Romans to treat Property as the fundamental concept of which each was a manifestation. Consequently, when Property came to be thought of as equivalent to *dominium* (or even the so-called bonitary ownership), any rights which did not include that of alienation for value seemed to be distinct from Property. A further confusion was introduced by the relatively modern distinction between *iura in rem* and *iura in personam*, but the crowning absurdity was the notion (possible in England until 1925) that there was no such thing as Property in land, only estates.

or in the Anglo-American systems, Property tends to be sharply distinguished from all ' derivative ' titles or interests, and may even be detected in a person, for example a trustee, whose legal title gives him no beneficial interest whatever.[1]

We may now approach our text. The style, which is derived from the style of public debate, is difficult to follow, and is likely to give rise to misunderstandings when read instead of being listened to (as it demands). Europeans anxious to arrive at an author's conclusions have more than once complained of the manner of argumentation adopted, and even the deliberately facile diction of Jagannātha could not satisfy critics who found his material too deep to plumb quickly. Whether the style or the manner is the more irritating, we must read all such writers patiently and not jump to conclusions. Like algebra without symbols, such works must be read as a set of statements within concentric and contrasting brackets. In order, however, to obviate any doubt as to what our present author *says* I give a summary of his conclusions.

I. Property is not an objective entity *sui generis*. It is a ' settled impression ', dependent upon consciousness of acquisition, or rather of having acquired (v (2)), which in turn implies understanding of the permitted methods of acquisition. (The question of the rights, *adhikāra*, to which Property itself gives rise is not treated and is only incidentally referred to in III (3).)

II. The ' causes ' of Property can be enumerated (by reference to the *dharmaśāstra*). The five headings are self-explanatory (with the aid of existing treatises) except (ii) which is discussed in v and (iii) which is discussed in IV. ' Cause ' (iv) is mentioned incidentally in VII.

III. Would *acquisition* as a comprehensive ' cause ' obviate the need for distinguishing between those five headings ? Are they not examples of one and the same thing ? No, for if this were so theft would be a cause of Property. As this possibility is taken seriously by some authorities it is refuted.

IV. Death as a ' cause ' of Property is open to controversy, not only in logic—much depends upon the definition of ' death '—but also in the light of joint family law. It is indeed a cause, hence before partition the heirs are joint owners of the whole and alienations of undivided fractions without the consent of the co-owners are impossible. Hence, also, the father excludes the son in succession to the grandfather—though his tenure may be subject to certain restrictions upon alienation (this is not discussed). The author's views are found in IV (1) and (4). In (5) he explains that husbands have Property in

[1] The entire purpose of the devise upon a use, which the court of the Lord Chancellor perfected until it became the nucleus of our law of trusts, was to show to the world a legal owner who had no rights over the estate (unless he were simultaneously a *cestui que trust*) but only duties, such as to protect the estate and pay over or invest its income for the benefit of someone whom it might be inconvenient or impossible to nominate as legal devisee. The invention of the trust enables the Anglo-American system to evade many of the difficulties which beset lawyers who adopt definitions devoid of logic. This is aptly illustrated in the judgment in *New, Prance & Garrard's Trustee* v. *Hunting*, [1897] 2 Q.B. 19 and other cases cited in Lewin, *The Law of Trusts, 15th edition*, London, 1950, 51, n. (*y*).

their wives, and that wives do not have Property in their husband's estate during the latter's lifetime, but only in their separate assets (*strīdhana*) subject to special provisions of law.

V. Acceptance does not cause Property. Gift alone causes it. In other words acceptance is not a necessary constituent of 'gift'. The title vests upon the donation, provided a donee exists and is in the mind of the donor, but acceptance only manifests the title in the donee to his own consciousness and to that of those who do not know of the donation.

VI. The *dhvaṃsakas*, causes of extinction of Property, can be enumerated. They resolve themselves, though seven in number, into a group of five corresponding to the five 'causes'. The first group has already been discussed; (iv) is discussed in VII along with (vii), while (v) is discussed in a fragmentary manner in VIII and (vi), sale, is thought self-explanatory (with the aid of technical treatises).

VII. Change in the nature of an owned article is not an example of 'destruction of the subject-matter of Property'. One's milk turns to curds (or one's tadpole turns into a frog): just because there is no cause of ownership of the curds (or of the frog), as such, except lapse of time, we must not suppose that the destruction of the milk (or the tadpole), as such, destroys Property in the substance in question, and a technical objection to this solution is refuted.

VIII. Dedication to the public's use is not an example of gift. Property is extinguished in the dedicator, but a right of enjoyment, which is inferentially distinguishable from Property, is created in favour of all persons whatsoever, including the dedicator. The use of the word 'gift' is in an applied sense in this as in many other instances. Property is incapable of inhering in an indefinitely large class.

(ii) Translation *

'A discussion of Property' (*Svatva-vicāra*)

An obeisance to the Auspicious Gaṇeśa!

I. Now Property is to be defined. Many [1] contend that Property is a particular category [2] because one may cognize, 'this asset belongs to *X* and

[1] Raghunātha Śiromaṇi and all subsequent *navya-naiyāyikas*, with so few exceptions that these latter are quite properly called *svatantrāḥ*. See p. 482, n. 1 above.

[2] *Padārtha*: see Kuppuswāmi Śāstri, op. cit., III, 5 ff.; Ingalls, op. cit., 37. The great development of the 'category' theory at the hands of the author of the *Svatva-rahasya* (ch. 1) was the successful identification of Property with Ownership as a single category. Cognition of 'mine-ness' and 'non-mine-ness' was recognized as an essential feature of Property even as early as Medhātithi, and probably very much earlier, but the 'category' school carefully refrain from making such a cognition more important than evidence of the universal existence of the entity Property, without reference to its occurrences.

not to *Y*'; but more recent writers [1] take the view that it is a settled impression deriving from the particular knowledge that 'this is mine'.

II. The causes of Property [2] are (i) purchase, (ii) acceptance, (iii) the predecessor's death, his embracing the order of ascetics,[3] or his 'fall',[4] and (iv) finding an abandoned object.[5]

III. It is even suggested [6] that theft must actually be a cause of Property in an object in which the Property of another inheres.[7] The maxim of Grass,

[1] It is a slightly confusing habit of authors in this series to refer to a widely rejected view as that of 'former authorities' and their own as the 'modern' view. Since to students of *nyāya* at large the word *navyāḥ* would seem to refer to the *navya-naiyāyika* school this warning is necessary. Our author means Rāmabhadra Nyāyālaṅkāra, in all probability, but equally well-known in (?) subsequent adherence to this doctrine was Vācaspati Bhaṭṭācārya. A bitter opponent of the 'category' theory was the famous Annaṃ-bhaṭṭa: see his *Tarka-dīpikā* (Benaras, 1864, at f. 53a; Calcutta, 1897, at p. 102). The commentary on this by Nīlakaṇṭha is useful, also Y. V. Athalye's edition in translation (Bombay, 1897); and in order to establish the text reference should be made to the Grantha edition also.

[2] Even though not a category, Property still requires a cause: its scope of inherence is another matter, which is discussed in the other works of the series.

[3] Leaving one's own *āśrama* and becoming an ascetic (*saṃnyāsi*) by the appropriate renunciation of the world involved the cessation of ownership. Succession to one's estate took place as if one had died: *Dāyabhāga*, I, 4, 39. Thereafter one retained the capacity to earn and to own, within the limitations of the new status (*Mitākṣarā*, II, viii, 7–9), and on one's death a special order of succession applied (Kane, op. cit., III, 764–5).

[4] *Pātaka*, or 'sin', involved a special status called *pātitya*, one effect of which was to cancel ownership. One was supposed to earn new assets, for the purpose of support and performing penance, by begging, if necessary. The strict doctrine, upheld by our author and the author of the *Svatva-rahasya*, was adulterated by later writers, following Mitra Miśra and others, who asserted that the loss of ownership (and the consequent succession of the heirs) was conditional upon a 'fixed disinclination to perform penance'. This enabled the sinner to pay for his penance out of his previously owned assets, a clear fraud upon the *śāstra*, but logically useful as well as profitable to the persons likely to benefit from the 'penances'. On *pātaka* and *prāyaścitta* see Kane, op. cit., IV, chh. I–V.

[5] This cleverly avoids the controversy as to the basis for acquisition by virtue of lapse of time (see VII below). According to Jīmūtavāhana, whom our author clearly follows, a possessor cannot become owner until the owner has made *upekṣā* (abandonment); alternatively, lost property becomes fit for appropriation by the finder, similarly to common unowned articles such as grass and twigs or river-water, only when the owner has ceased to concern himself about his loss and ceased to take active steps to find the object. *Nidhi* (buried treasure), of course, besides the characteristic of being hidden, is fit for appropriation by the finder, subject to the rights of the King, immediately after the cessation of the ownership of the person who hid it, e.g. by his death.

[6] Traces of this suggestion in Raghunātha's *Dīdhiti* at f. 11a; Abhirāma Vidyālaṅkāra, * *Kaumudī* on Goyīcandra's *Saṃkṣipta-sāra-ṭīkā* on Kramadīśvara (MS I.O. 1404 = Egg. 832) at f. 10a; Bhavānanda Siddāntavāgīśa in his *Kāraka-cakra*, Calcutta, 1912, at p. 93; Viśvanātha Siddhāntapañcānana at f. 165b; and Jayarāma, *Svatva-vādārtha*, at p. 2. Reference may be made to Jagannātha on *asvāmi-vikraya*. The matter arises by two paths: prohibition of theft may not be distinguishable from (*a*) prohibition, as in Manu and Gautama, etc., of acquisition (*anāpadi*, i.e. in normal circumstances) by Brahmans by means of acceptance from bad people, trade, conquest, etc., and (*b*) prohibition of acceptance on the bank of the Ganges, and it was established that breach of such rules did not affect the validity of the title acquired; secondly, *svī-kāra* (= acceptance or acquisition) seemed to refer to a subjective standard of appropriation which would allow a thief to think, 'I have got it, so I own it'. But see pp. 480–1 above.

[7] Our author accepts the doctrine of the 'category' school, that Property inheres in the asset, just as Ownership inheres in the owner; it is common ground that Property cannot be caused in an asset in which Property already exists, any more than blueness can be produced in a blue object.

Tinder, and Jewel [1] is said to settle causality [2] here, for otherwise one could not escape the anomaly that one might be able to omit purchase,[3] even, and leave Property to be produced by acceptance and the causes that follow it in the list. Each one of these events, then, immediately causes Property. In this connexion we have the view of the author of the *Dāyabhāga* and others [4] that, if a thief makes a gift or sale of the stolen object and the recipient alienates it by gift or sale, Property is effectuated in the alienee, while the recipient-alienor has merely committed an offence.[5] Many writers are in dispute upon this, for since Property is never produced in that which is already the material object of Property,[6] how can the Property of a second person be produced in something which is already the object of some individual's Property ? Alternatively, how does it come about that if the original owner retakes the stolen object without the thief's consent the original owner does not commit an offence ? [7] And mere theft does *not* extinguish the original owner's Property, for there is no authority [8] for such a proposition, and the second difficulty is inescapable.

IV. (1) From the moment of the father's death, etc.,[9] Property is produced in all his sons [10] in respect of all the objects in which his Property inhered. Many [11] say that only after the extinction of *that* Property upon a partition

[1] MS *A* : *tṛṇāraṇi-nyāyena* ; better *tṛṇāraṇimaṇi-nyāyena*. One effect may be produced by a variety of independent causes : fire (which is unique) may be produced by a heap of grass (spontaneously), by touchwood (or tinder) upon which the stick is twirled (by friction), and by a jewel (acting as a burning glass). However disparate the causes, the effect is identical : upon what basis, then, is theft excluded ?

* [2] See Jagannātha (Colebrooke, *Digest*, II, 187).

[3] The first of the listed ' causes ' : if one method of *svīkāra*, theft, can be omitted, why not another ?

[4] See above, p. 480, and Jayarāma, *Svatva-vādārtha*, p. 2, where similar reference is made.

[5] With the words inserted as indicated at p. 480 above.

[6] See p. 487, n. 7 above. Upon this doctrine rests the theory of *obstruction* (*pratibandhakatva*) of which our author, Jayarāma, and the author of the *Svatva-rahasya* make constant use. See also Jagannātha, ubi cit., 188, 190–5.

* [7] This is an original point, for which no authority has yet appeared ; it probably stems from current practice. In III, V (1), and VIII, ' offence ' = sin.

[8] The *dharmaśāstri* and the *naiyāyika* are agreed that all propositions of law must proceed either from a text (*śruti* or *smṛti*), from the received practice (*sadācāra*) of men versed in the sacred law, or from logic, in which term for this purpose common-sense and equity are included. An authority (especially a text) may justify a rule for which logic unaided could supply no equivalent ; yet even a thousand texts cannot nullify an established logical precept.

[9] The author deliberately avoids saying, as Jīmūtavāhana did, that death *causes* the heir's Property—a proposition which long troubled logicians. The ' etc. ' refers to *pātitya* and *saṃnyāsa-grahaṇa* (see above, p. 487, nn. 3 and 4).

[10] The author ignores, perhaps *per incuriam* (?), disqualifications, for which see Kane, op. cit., III, 610 ff.

[11] This is a famous controversy. The practical point is simple. Joint families were, and to some extent still are, the normal media of enjoyment of ancestral and even acquired property. Many co-heirs were simultaneously owners of a large estate comprising various assets. At a partition it would be feasible to distinguish which heir was owner exclusively of which portion, but until then difficulties constantly arose as to the rights of heirs to alienate their undivided share, as to their rights over acquisitions made with the use of a particular asset, as to the effect of the birth of posthumous heirs, and so on. Raghunandana took the view that the heirs became owners of their shares at partition, but that until then their ownership extended over the whole

between them by casting lots, etc., is Property produced in each son in respect of individual items of the estate; but others [1] maintain that the casting of lots merely manifests the individual Properties and does not produce them. Thus, as a matter of fact, it is only in respect of that object in which the son's Property arises after partition that his Property is produced from the time of the father's death, etc., and it is not the case that Property is produced in all the sons in respect of all the estate. And of course the consent of all of them is not required to a gift of any particular item.[2] But in my view it is correct to * require the consent of all, because there is indeed Property in all of them in respect of the whole estate.[3] One may compare the consent of neighbours and disinterested parties taken in a sale of land [4]: this is relevant because the latter is required by texts, and because where a matter follows logically textual authority is absent and if a logical principle leads to a particular conclusion a text to the same effect would be redundant.[5]

(2) (There is a view [6] that) the death of the father produces Property in the son only in respect of assets personally acquired by the father, but that even during the father's lifetime Property is produced in his son in respect of the assets of the grandfather, because of the text:

'In that estate the ownership of father and son must be similar.' [7]

Therefore, it is provided, a son may oblige his father to give him a share in the assets of the grandfather.[8] Moreover, if the son's Property were *not* produced

estate: the consent of all co-heirs was therefore required to validate an alienation except in cases of emergency, which were covered by relevant texts. Jīmūtavāhana had taken the contrary view, that ownership began and remained fractional, and that a co-heir had the right to alienate his proportionate share without consent. Subsequent authors side either with the master, or with Raghunandana. All are agreed, however, that partition in no case creates a Property in the assets *for the first time*: Raghunandana's school say that the pre-existing Property is replaced at partition by a number of Properties in respect of the same assets.

[1] Jīmūtavāhana, *Dāyabhāga*, I, 6–9. The author of the *Svatva-rahasya* elaborately supports this view (ch. IV). Anantarāma in the *Vivāda-candrikā* refutes it.

[2] This is the point of the objector's argument. In an emergency, however, consent could be dispensed with according to both schools. It will be remembered that this dispute is *within* the Bengal school itself. The Maithilas, it must be taken for granted, never admitted fractional ownership.

[3] In other words our author sees no reason for positing an extinction of the original Property that was produced by the death and its replacement by a different Property, or rather set of Properties at partition, with retrospective logical effect. This is the better view, it would seem, since all the co-heirs might become disqualified except one, who of course would remain unable to make a partition.

[4] The text the author has in mind is *sva-grāma-jñāti-sāmanta-dāyādānumatena ca | hiraṇy-odaka-dānena ṣaḍbhir gacchati medinī* || (*Dh. kośa*, 901). He impliedly controverts the view of Vijñāneśvara (*Mitākṣarā*, I, i, 31), who holds that a transfer may be valid notwithstanding the breach of the rule, which is recommendatory. See also Misaru Miśra, *Vivāda-candra*, Calcutta, 1931, 151.

[5] See p. 488, n. 8 above. This argument is somewhat precarious. Nevertheless the form of the argument is orthodox. Because even strangers are required in a text to give their consent it follows, he says, that co-heirs' consent is obligatory.

[6] This is the assumed opponent's view, which is one midway between the Bengal and the Maithila doctrines.

[7] Yājñavalkya, II, 121b: the bed-rock of the Maithila (*Mitākṣarā*) doctrine.

[8] The *Mitākṣarā* asserts this (I, v, 5) and the *Dāyabhāga* denies it (II, 7–8).

in respect of that estate during the father's lifetime the son's consent would not be required to a gift or sale of any of it.[1] And it is not correct to ask, since one's Property obstructs another's,[2] how someone else's Property can be produced in respect of an object in which the father has Property. For when a predecessor's gift or sale is specially established as a cause of Property in his successor in title [3] there is no occasion to posit here the relationship of obstructer and obstructed. Moreover, if the relationship of obstructer and obstructed were sanctioned by authority in this connexion the wife's Property in assets in respect of which her husband has Property would never be produced. Nor would it be correct to deny authority for the production of a wife's Property in assets belonging to him, because the Vedic text [4]

'wealth is common between spouses'

establishes the wife's Property therein. The word 'common' means *impartible* in the sense of 'unfitted for partition'.[5] And so if the wife's Property were not produced in such assets what need would there have been for a declaration that that estate was 'impartible'?

(3) Moreover it is, of course, incorrect to argue that the doctrine that the *death of the father* causes Property in the son in respect of assets in which the father's Property inhered has been impaired. Since an object sold by a father passes into the ownership of a successor in title, there can be a production of a son's Property through acceptance, purchase, and the rest, and therefore we

[1] This assumes that the opponent relies upon the Maithila interpretation of the *śloka* of Yājñavalkya quoted above.

[2] See p. 488, n. 6 above.

[3] The opponent says that since we know that when *X* gives or sells his assets his Property is obstructed by that of his donee or vendee, it follows that when the grandfather's assets pass by descent to a father and that father's son simultaneously we have an entirely different kind of transfer in which the father and son do not stand towards each other as transferor and transferee.

[4] The text, *dampatyor madhyagaṃ dhanam*, is probably not Vedic. I have not traced it earlier than Śūlapāṇi, who refers to it in his *Śrāddhaviveka* at p. 124. It is likely that it originated as a description of a *communio bonorum* between spouses, which survives in Burma, among the Tamils of Jaffna (where the institution is probably *not* mainly due to Dutch influence), and (at any rate with reference to rights arising on a divorce) among the Kandyans, but seems to have no example in modern India. The text had been virtually emasculated even by the time of the author of the *Svatva-rahasya*, whose explanation (that it authorizes the wife to spend her husband's property in entertaining guests, etc.) is followed by Jagannātha who uses the text repeatedly. Śrīnātha Ācārya-cūḍāmaṇi and other commentators on the *Dāyabhāga* were quite familiar with the text, as was Balabhadra Tarkavāgīśa (see his *Dāyabhāga-siddhānta*, MS I.O. 1386c = Egg. 1529, f. 2a), and its authenticity can hardly be doubted. The nearest parallel in published *smṛti* literature is Āpastamba, II, 14, 16–20, on which see Haradatta's *Ujjvalā*, Poona, 1932, 178; see also Aparārka on Yājñavalkya, II, 52: a wife cannot stand surety for her husband because of their community of property. The concept is referred to in the following cases: *Jamna* v. *Machul Sahu*, (1879) I.L.R. 2 All. 315; *Indu Bhusan* v. *Mrityunjoy Pal*, I.L.R. [1946] Cal. 128; *Kamalabala Bose* v. *Jiban Krishna Bose*, A.I.R. 1946 Cal. 461; *Muthalammal* v. *Veeraraghavan Nayudu*, [1952] 2 M.L.J. 344.

[5] The rule that there can be no partition between husband and wife is axiomatic in the Hindu system.

may avoid the anomaly [1] : therefore to apprehend the death of the *grandfather* *
as the real cause would be extremely cumbersome. For it is fully established that when the father dies during the grandfather's lifetime and Property is produced in his son, that grandson's Property in the estates of *both* father *and* grandfather will in the circumstances be due to the relationship of cause and effect.[2] Moreover, by positing a relationship of cause and effect in the manner mentioned previously [3] we are in danger of an anomaly. This is the argument.

(4) Not so, for the Property of one person obstructs the Property of another. Nor should we say that there is no need of admitting the relationship of obstructer and obstructed when we posit the relation of cause and effect in the father's death, etc., in the order stated : since the father's ' fall ' and his embracing the order of ascetics are specified causes that would be extremely cumbersome.[4] So, to put it shortly, the cause (of the son's succession) operates through the non-existence of any thing characterized by his father's Property.[5]

(5) Further, it is incorrect to ask how, in that case, Property is produced in the wife in the assets in which her husband has Property, since the wife's Property in the husband's estate is not produced at all.[6] Otherwise we should have the unsatisfactory position that the son's Property would not be produced during the lifetime of the mother,[7] since the Property of one person obstructs

[1] The anomaly put up by an imaginary objector to the imaginary opponent is that if a son takes his father's property by reason of the death of the father this automatically excludes his taking property *together* with his father. But, the opponent says, there is nothing to prevent a son taking his father's property by gift or sale (the latter proposition being possible at *Dāyabhāga* law in the case of all sons), hence there is no rule that a son takes his father's assets only by succession, to which an anomaly might be feared.

[2] The cause is the death of the ancestor in each case. For the manuscripts' *hetusadbhāva* (twice) read *hetu-hetumad-bhāva.*

[3] If a son cannot succeed to his grandfather except through his father (which is the general proposition laid down in *Dāyabhāga* (III, i, 19)) one is at once in difficulty in explaining the rule that the son of a predeceased son takes by representation (ibid., II, 9).

[4] Everyone agrees that death, *pātitya*, and *saṃnyāsa* are upon the same footing, and that in each case the Property arising in the successor excludes, or ' obstructs ', the Property of the predecessor. If he is dead no question of his Property arises (for the Hindu law unlike the Imperial Roman law and the Islamic law is not prepared to pretend that a dead man's estate can own itself or that he remains alive for the purposes of owning his shroud and paying his debts) ; if he is a *patita* he cannot regain his pre-*pātaka* estate by any means other than buying it back with subsequently-acquired assets ; and if he has become a *saṃnyāsi* he is supposed to be dead to worldly concerns. Upon the maxim of the staff and loaf (*daṇḍā pūpa-nyāyena*) the position explicable with regard to the last two causes of the extinction of Property applies equally to the first, so that if the father succeeds to the grandfather's estate he will exclude his own sons and (for this is what our author is aiming at) when the father dies *after* the grandfather it is the father's and not the grandfather's death that makes the sons owners of the ancestral estate.

[5] This brilliant definition cannot be understood unless it is appreciated that in *nyāya* there are no ' abstract ' concepts, and ' non-existence ' is just as real and potent as ' existence '. Jayarāma, *Svatva-vādārtha*, p. 5, gives a comparable but less attractive definition.

[6] This paradox is necessitated by what follows.

[7] The order of succession, which is established by homologation of texts, places son before widow : hence if the widow be co-owner with her husband we have to discover a means of extinguishing her Property on her husband's death in order that the son may exclude her.

the Property of another. Nor is the death of the owner the cause of the extinction of the wife's Property,[1] since there is no authority for this and since such a position would be cumbersome.[2] If one were to ask, what then is the point of the text, 'wealth is common between spouses', I admit the difficulty; yet all are agreed that females have Property in *strīdhana* ('females' estates'),[3] while in that estate even the husband's Property inheres, because the husband has Property in the females themselves.[4] And the point of the text is that such an estate has an *impartible* character. We need not prolong this discussion.

V. (1) It is the settled opinion of some [5] that acceptance produces Property: an unattractive doctrine. If it were true it would follow that, if one were to make a gift in favour of a recipient at Benaras,[6] the latter's failure to accept it would result in the non-production of Property in him in respect of that object, and it would be *res nullius*. Thus if it were stolen no offence would be committed. There has been, in that situation, an extinction on the part of the predecessor of Property which admits of relinquishment by him, but (it is

[1] An estate *pur autre vie* does not seem to have occurred to Hindu jurists. Yet it has been created by Anglo-Hindu jurisprudence.

[2] The defect of 'cumbersomeness' is technical: see Ingalls, op. cit., 47. In this case the fault alleged is that more hypotheses are posited than are required to produce the desired conclusion.

[3] On this institution see Kane, op. cit., ch. XXX.

[4] This is a perverse view, which one had thought had been exploded by Jaimini, whose treatment of the question is found in the *Mīmāṃsā-sūtras*, VI, i, 10–16 (*Dh. kośa*, 1424–5); cf. *Nirukta*, III, 4. Moreover Bhavadeva, in the *Vyavahāra-tilaka*, quoted in *Vyavahāra-cintāmaṇi*, 122, 307, had been definitely against it. But there is evidence that sales of wives, though deprecated, were considered possible: Jīmūtavāhana, *Vyavahāra-mātṛkā*, 285; frequent instances of sales are recorded in south Indian inscriptions. One should not fail to notice the remark of the author of the *Viṣṇupurāṇa* that the reflecting man ought not to consider even his wife his own property. Sales and gifts of children were probably more common. In communities where bride-prices were usual this attitude is not difficult to understand, and from Kandyan as well as South Indian practice it is evident that transfer of relations to pay debts was legal and not disapproved.

[5] *Svī-kāra* would naturally be expected to be the cause of Property, rather than *dāna*, yet *dāna* is mentioned in many texts and *pratigraha* (acceptance) in others as the cause of Property. *Nyāya* will not permit that a thing can have *two* causes. Modern devices work fairly well, but only with the aid of ancillary devices such as special rules of guardianship, trusts, and rules enabling infants to take the benefit but not the liability of certain contracts. A rule such as that in the Indian Transfer of Property Act, 1882, sec. 122, requiring both gift and acceptance for transfer of the interest is logically absurd and permits problems such as the following: if *A* offers a block of shares to *B* and the latter accepts them a year later, to whom does the accruing dividend belong? The Companies Act provides a pragmatic answer, but many analogous cases are not so happily answered. The Anglo-American system demands acceptance before a gift is completed, and if the donee is incapable of accepting and has no generally authorized agent or guardian to make acceptance on his behalf the donor may constitute himself a trustee for the donee's benefit. The Hindu jurists preferred if possible to solve the problem fundamentally: the ultimate conclusion seems to have been that *dāna* extinguished the title of the donor, but the donee's assent was presumed to the donor's maintaining control over the object until acceptance; acceptance then manifested the donee's Property, being the cause of *yatheṣṭa-viniyoga-yogyatva*, which is still distinguished from Property. Though this approaches a modern Western standpoint it is not entirely satisfactory. The 'acceptance' school included Abhirāma Vidyālaṅkāra, the author of the *Svatva-rahasya* (ch. V), Vācaspati Bhaṭṭācārya, and Jagannātha.

[6] Any place distant from the point of view of the imaginary donor.

argued) a Property remains in him sufficient for protection and superintendence,[1] a Property of a somewhat less than general character; otherwise if that object were stolen by someone other than the donee in whose favour the predecessor has relinquished it, the predecessor would have no legal remedy against that other person. This argument has an element of truth, but positing a Property of such a character may be said to be cumbersome [2] and accordingly it is maintainable that what is posited by the donee's acceptance is the *manifesting* of Property, not its production.[3] Nor should one deny that a gift made without the formula, '"I give": "Yes, give!"', is legally perfect, since *
even such a gift is authorized by the Vedic text [4]:

> 'having designated the recipient mentally let him cast water upon the ground'. *

(2) At this stage some say that it cannot be the function of acceptance to *manifest* Property unless Property is a distinct category.[5] Only if we were to admit that acceptance causes the *production* of Property could Property be a settled impression deriving from the knowledge that 'this is mine', and our object is achieved merely through the relationship between knowledge and impression, being cause and effect. But knowledge of previous acquisition does not lead to a settled impression, since the essence of Property lies in a settled impression deriving from knowledge that 'this is mine'—knowledge that one has currently made an acquisition. Therefore if, since the cause of a settled impression which is not consistent with this can only be a knowledge

[1] It is alleged in support of the 'acceptance' theory that the donor can divest himself of some of his Property (for who could prevent him if he is the owner ?) but not all of it. In support of the 'acceptance' theory our author ought to point out that if an outcaste makes a gift to a Brahman at a remote place and property passes by *gift*, the unfortunate Brahman could not avoid *pātitya*, for the law subjects him to penalties if he accepts from an outcaste.

[2] See p. 492, n. 2 above. See Mitra Miśra, *Vīramitrodaya*, *Vyavahāra-prakāśa*, 427–8.

[3] This is the majority view. Jīmūtavāhana energetically maintained (*Dāyabhāga*, I, 22–4) that gift alone conveyed the assets to the donee. By the time of Gokulanātha it was maintainable that gift put an end to the donor's Property without necessarily creating the donee's Property, which would have been a paradox a century earlier, when the accepted definition of *dāna* was that *tyāga* in favour of a sentient being which extinguished the Property of the donor and produced the Property of the donee. For a more elaborate definition see Jagannātha, ubi cit., I, 454. It will be observed that gifts to unborn persons and gifts of future assets were alike impossible, and that gifts to gods, ancestors, and animals were only 'gifts' in a figurative sense. See *Siddhānta-tattva-viveka*, f. 117a.

[4] Once again the text is almost certainly not Vedic and has not been traced. It is the third *
of four lines which are seldom quoted together. They appear in Jayarāma's *Kāraka-vāda*, Bombay, 1914, *sub tit.* *Vādārtha-saṃgraha*, 24 ff., at pp. 31–2: *tīrthe saṅkalpitaṃ dravyaṃ yadyanyatra pradīyate* | *dātā tīrtha-phalaṃ bhuṅkte pratigrāhī na doṣa-bhāk* || manasā pātram uddiśya bhūmau toyaṃ vinikṣipet | *vidyate sāgarasyāṃto dānasyāṃto na vidyate* || (for the text of the first line compare MS I.O. 3317 = Keith 5861 at f. 10a). Although this text (except for the last line, which looks like a *locus communis*) does not appear in Lakṣmīdhara's *Dāna-kalpataru* it must be genuine since Jīmūtavāhana and most of his successors rely upon it. Closely similar is the text of *Bṛhat-parāśara* printed by Jīvānanda Vidyāsāgara, Calcutta, 1876, II, 239: *pātraṃ manasi sañcintya guṇavantam abhīpsitaṃ* | *apsu brāhmaṇa-haste vā bhūmāvapi jalaṃ kṣipet* ||

[5] The 'category' school open the attack. If acceptance manifests Property the inference seems to be that Property is there to be manifested, independent of the consciousness of the acceptor.

which is itself inconsistent,[1] one were to contend that there is no solution without the relation of cause and effect,[2] I reply that, even so, to posit Property's being a distinct category as you do is extremely cumbersome. Moreover, in my view, the fact that relinquishment extinguishes Property is an instance of the fact that, assuming two incompatible entities, knowledge of one of them extinguishes a settled impression deriving from knowledge of the other. Our purpose is served merely by that relationship of extinguisher and extinguished. In your view Property is a distinct entity, and you accordingly posit that the extinction of Property can be brought about by relinquishment quite inde-
* pendently:[3] an exceedingly cumbersome position. Moreover, following our view that knowledge that ' this is mine ' *manifests* Property, your position is in conflict with the Mīmāṃsā.[4]

(3) It is upon this very basis that the gods acquire rights in a sacrifice.[5] Here ' sacrifice ' means only relinquishment of an oblation in favour of a deity whose name is muttered mentally.[6] My contention must be correct for immediately after the occurrence of knowledge that ' this offering belongs to the gods, not to me ' there arises an impossibility of knowledge that ' this is mine '. No such possibility exists. In that situation there is no question of Property being produced by knowledge that ' this is mine '.[7] If acceptance (in the form of such knowledge) merely manifests Property the gods cannot lack their right, surely? Quite so. Their rights are settled by textual authority.[8] According to your opinion a relinquishment of an oblation in favour of a single god would make it impossible for another god to have a right therein[9]

[1] Admittedly the knowledge, which our author claims is the root of Property, must take its colour from the circumstances which are known.

[2] Nevertheless the opponent may say that, assuming as we do Property to be a category, we can reach our desirable conclusion (that acceptance merely manifests Property), and only by positing that very assumption. Gift creates Property which from that moment exists in favour of the donee, and the donee's mental impressions are not related to his Property as cause and effect: hence Property is a category.

[3] For after all one relinquishes assets, not Property! Our author attacks the ' category ' school at a weak spot: if knowledge of title has nothing to do with Property, as they suggest, how do they account for an individual's extinguishing his Property by voluntary transfers? In fact the list of *svatva-dhvaṃsakas* relied upon by the ' category ' school is a fabrication, being the correlative of the list of causes of acquisition given in the texts of Manu and Gautama—texts which of course tell us nothing about the *nature* of Property.

[4] For the immediately following reason.

* [5] The gods have no knowledge, and cannot *own*, except in a figurative sense. Gifts to gods produce unseen fruit merely because Vedic texts tell us so: indeed, the very description of the gods themselves may depend upon this fact. Jaimini, op. cit., IX, iii, 35–40, demonstrates the *adhikāra* which gods have, even jointly, in sacrifices.

[6] This definition is not quite orthodox. The reading of the manuscripts is not quite clear and I adopt *dhī-japta-devatoddeśyaka-havis-tyāga.*

[7] An exclusively human attribute.

[8] See p. 489, n. 5 above.

[9] If Property is produced by acceptance. Whereas oblations to groups of gods are usual and in a sacrifice to gods named in the plural any one of that class would be entitled to participate, and would not exclude others. Moreover, if the indicated god failed to accept, others would benefit and the fruit of the sacrifice would not be lost.

from which it follows that a god's general right in sacrifices is put in question.[1]

(4) Moreover the doctrine that (acceptance in the form of) knowledge that ' this is mine ' *produces* Property lays one open to the question how an *ātma-śrāddha* [2] (' commemorative oblation to oneself ') can be effected, on account of the impossibility of the simultaneous knowledge that ' this is mine ; this is not mine ' : yet even the *ātma-śrāddha* exists upon the authority of the Vedic text [3] :

' to the descendants of Manu and likewise to himself '.

And we cannot say that all that takes place is a relinquishment on his part in respect of the offered objects,[4] since Śūlapāṇi has declared emphatically that *śrāddha* partakes of the characters of both gift and sacrifice.[5] It is for this reason that some scholars say that if mere relinquishment amounted to *śrāddha*, *śrāddha* would be a universal phenomenon.[6]

VI. Now the extinction of Property is caused by (i) death ; (ii) embracing the order of ascetics ; (iii) ' fall ' ; (iv) destruction of the object in which

[1] The true position is known from Jaimini. See Kane, op. cit., II, ch. XX, for examples of offerings to groups of gods.

[2] *Śrāddha* covers all ceremonies in which offerings of food and water are made to deceased persons. The spiritual welfare of both deceased and living depended upon these oblations being performed. As Kane says, op. cit., IV, 545, people ' went crazy with the idea of śrāddhas and invented (a) new mode to satisfy that craze '. If there seemed no prospect of a *śrāddha* being faithfully performed a man might perform his own while he was still alive ! The ritual is prescribed in the *Baudhāyana-gṛhya-śeṣa-sūtra*, the *Liṅgapurāṇa*, and (according to the *Jīvacchrāddha-prayoga* of Nārāyaṇa-bhaṭṭa (MS A.S.B., G. 2325 = I.O. Micr. Reel 366)) in the *Brahmapurāṇa*. The subject was dealt with by Lakṣmīdhara, Hemādri, and Mitra Miśra (see references given by Kane, op. cit., IV, 542) and in a treatise in the Bombay University Library attributed to Śaunaka. A pilgrim's *śrāddha* to himself at Gayā must also be considered (Kane, op. cit., IV, 670). The *kartā* relinquishes a rice-ball with the words, ' a *piṇḍa* to me of such-and-such a *gotra* (lineage) for my benefit in the other world : *svadhā namaḥ* '. Hence the comment in the text.

[3] Once again, this is not a Vedic text. In fact, as we see from Śūlapāṇi (*Śrāddha-viveka*, 31), it is a fragmentary quotation from the *Narasiṃhapurāṇa*, reading as follows : *divya-pitṛbhyo devebhyaḥ sva-pitṛbhyaś = ca yatnataḥ | dattvā śrāddham ṛṣibhyaś = ca* manujebhyas = tathātmane || It is the last word which provides authority for the strange phenomenon. *

[4] In an attempt to ignore the *ātma-śrāddha* and to adhere to the doctrine that knowledge that ' this is mine ' *produces* Property, the objector suggests that the *kartā* relinquishes the *piṇḍa* (and so extinguishes his Property) without the corresponding production of Property in anyone, while the *piṇḍa* itself is eaten by birds, etc.

[5] Our author rather disingenuously utilizes the famous definition of Śūlapāṇi (op. cit., 66) to crack the opponent's very reasonable objection with a hammer which seems too heavy for the purpose. Since every *śrāddha* is defined as partaking of the character of *gift*, it follows that Property must be produced as well as extinguished by the act in question, and this production must be due to the oblation, i.e. the alienation only. This is unsatisfactory, since Śūlapāṇi undoubtedly meant that *dāna* was involved in the gifts to Brahmans, whereas the deceased ancestors, etc., benefited by *yāga* (sacrifice), not *dāna*. The *kartā* is neither an invited Brahman (for these are provided for in the ritual) nor a deceased ancestor. Moreover a *śrāddha* has been held to be possible without the presence of any Brahmans, so that the definition of Śūlapāṇi suffers from *avyāpti*. But see Mitra Miśra, op. cit., *Śrāddha-prakāśa*, Benares, 1935, 8.

[6] I do not feel entirely happy with this rendering. The text appears to be : *kevala-tyāgasya śrāddhatve śrāddhaṃ jagatām eva syād iti vadanti.*

Property inhered; (v) relinquishment; (vi) sale; and (vii) lapse of a specific period.

VII. Where milk in which one's own Property has inhered has turned into curd, how is Property produced in that curd when the milk has been destroyed in which the former Property inhered? Since the atoms of which milk is composed actually constitute the curds, and as there was Property in those very atoms, Property is produced in the molecules through the Property in the atoms, and through the Property in the molecules Property is produced in the corresponding visible particles and in this way we can see the production of Property in respect of the whole by means of Properties in its components.[1] This explanation has some truth in it, but it would lead us to the unsatisfactory position that Property would be produced in that person in respect of pots and other objects which are constituted of just such atoms.[2] For it is not possible to claim that at the critical moment there is no Property in respect of such atoms, since at that moment there is nothing to extinguish that Property. Nor should we say that on occasions such Property (in the curds) may be produced in him in conjunction with the *supernatural*,[3] since in that case if Property could come about under all conditions merely in particular conjunction with the supernatural the result would be that acceptance and the other technical causes would cease to produce Property.[4] In reply it is argued that an extinction of the Property in those atoms happens in conjunction with a lapse of time,[5] and for this reason it is quite impossible for Property to be produced in respect of pots, and so on. It is indeed true that a lapse of time is heard of as a factor extinguishing Property. For when land is taken by force in the presence of the owner and 20 years have elapsed without his disputing it, his Property is extinguished,[6] and this is a case where a lapse of time extinguishes Property. But, one might reasonably comment, there the

[1] Reading *krameṇāvayavi-svatvotpattir iti* for *-avayava-*. On primary, binary, and triad atom-forms see Keith, *Indian logic and atomism*, Oxford, 1921, 213. Viśvanātha Siddhāntapañcānana, at f. 166a, denies that Property in the curds comes about by a conjunction with (lapse of) time. Jayarāma, *Svatva-vādārtha*, p. 5, obviously follows our author, but supplies a solution to the difficulty of the pots, etc. (see next note): Property in the curds may be attributable to the same cause as Property in the crops grown on one's land. For the commencement of the problem see Gautama, *Nyāya-sūtras*, III, ii, 13–17, and Vātsyāyana thereon (Poona, 1939), at pp. 202–3.

[2] It is a basic theory of *nyāya* that atoms are eternal and indistinguishable, so that once one posits that Property inheres not in the thing but in its atoms one is in danger of depriving Property of a defined locus.

[3] The last resort of the harassed logician!

[4] A cause is either a cause or it is not; if it is, then it is an invariable concomitant, and the intervention of other factors is permanently excluded.

[5] The relationships between 'Time' and the milk and between 'Time' and the curds are plainly different, and it is suggested that the difference between them may be the reason why the owner of the milk is owner of the curds.

[6] The text the author has in mind is obviously *pratyakṣa-paribhogāt tu svāmino dvi-daśāḥ samāḥ | ādhyādīnyapi jīryante strī-narendra-dhanād ṛte ||* (Nārada: *Dh. kośa*, 405a), but that of Vyāsa (*varṣāṇi viṃśati bhuktā*: *Dh. kośa*, 422a) and of Yājñavalkya (II, 24; *Dh. kośa*, 389a) are relevant. See now Vācaspati Miśra, *Vyavahāra-cintāmaṇi*, ed. L. Rocher, Ghent, 1956, 112–16, 291–8 (trans.). For our manuscripts' reading *dvādaśa* we must read *dvi-daśa*.

extinction of his Property is due simply to a distinctive enjoyment,[1] not to a lapse of time, for if the latter were the case Property might be extinguished even without enjoyment. Yet a lapse of time *does* extinguish Property in the instance of buried treasure[2]; there we cannot assume that the former owner's Property still persists, since if that were so Property could never be produced in the finder's favour in respect of that object after however long an interval.[3]

VIII. 'Finally,[4] if we apply the principle that the Property of one person obstructs the Property of another, when a tank is relinquished and there is a production of public Property through the relinquishment in favour of all, an absurd conclusion results that a person born subsequently to the date of the gift, not being in existence at the moment when the tank was relinquished,[5] has no Property in respect of its water. And we must not say that in that situation a mere relinquishment in favour of all has taken place but that by that act Property is not produced in the public,[6] since relinquishment in favour of someone cannot fail to produce that person's Property.' Only thus could one believe that when a gift of an object has been made in favour of a person at Benaras and, according to *your* view, no Property has been produced because of his failure to accept it, no offence is committed by anyone who appropriates the object.[7] Quite so. In that context no knowledge that 'this is not mine but that man's' has either extinguished the donor's Property or produced the donee's Property.[8] In our instance, however, while there *is* knowledge that 'this is not mine', there was no intention to this effect: 'let it belong to the public!' Of course it is reasonable to ask how then can

[1] Enjoyment qualified by (i) absence of legitimate title and (ii) cessation of ownership in the former owner. The subject is highly controversial. Kane, op. cit., III, ch. XII. The topic is a great feature of Jīmūtavāhana's *Vyavahāra-mātṛkā* as of Vācaspati Miśra's *Vyavahāra-cintāmaṇi*. Like many judges in England and Ireland before the Act of Will. IV the Hindu jurists could not understand how title could be acquired by wrongdoing. *

[2] Kane, op. cit., III, 175–6. *Nidhi* is defined in the *Svatva-rahasya* (IV, 36), in brief, as the capacity to be common Property prior to its extinction by the extinction of Property on the part of all except the finder.

[3] The element of time serves eventually to extinguish the owner's Property, but it must be borne in mind that as long as the owner lives the object is *nidhi* only after he has ceased to concern himself about it. *

[4] From 'Finally' to 'Property', nine lines below, we have the words of the imaginary opponent. He is shown attempting to demolish the theory of *pratibandhakatva*, upon which our author strongly relies.

[5] This is a cardinal rule of the Hindu law of gifts, that no one other than a person in being at the time of the gift can benefit. It follows that where a 'gift' is made to a deity who is not yet installed, or whose image is fashioned anew every year for a short festival and then thrown in a river, we are dealing with a transfer which is distinct from gift properly so called. For difficulties caused by Hindu doctrines in modern times see *Gadadhur Mullick* v. *Off. Trustee of Bengal*, (1940) L.R. 67 I.A. 129.

[6] Our author is hitting at the words *in favour of all*. According to him there is no *uddeśa*.

[7] The argument introduced in order to be refuted is set out in V (1) above.

[8] Our author believes that knowledge in the terms, 'this is not mine', serves to extinguish Property; knowledge in the terms, 'this is mine', gives rise to the *saṃskāra*, or impression, which he says *is* Property. When a man relinquishes a tank he has no idea of a successor-in-title.

a gift of a tank be made in favour of the public.[1] The intention is to this effect: 'let it be for the enjoyment of the public!', not an intention to this effect: 'let the Property of the public inhere in it!' That is the difference. Hence it is that he himself takes water from a reservoir which he had relinquished in favour of the public.[2] A man who appropriates gold which he has relinquished in favour of a Brahman commits an offence[3]; the purport was this: his intention was: 'let this belong to a Brahman! It is not mine'; but in our instance the intention is 'it is for the enjoyment of the public'—a substantial distinction. Moreover, a gift dedicating Property to the public is an impossibility, since it would conflict with the *pariṣad-adhikaraṇa* text,[4]

'what is given to a group is ungiven',

which means to say that receipt of an object dedicated to an indefinitely large class is impossible.[5] If one enquire, then, about the formula, 'I give to Brahmans',[6] my reply is that it should not be employed, but rather, 'I give to a Brahman'. The matter has been concisely stated.

[1] Compare with the above text the passages in Jayarāma's commentary on the *vṛsotsarga* portion of the *Pāraskara-gṛhya-sūtra*, Benaras, 1925, at p. 621 and Śrī Kṛṣṇa on the same subject in his commentary on the *Śrāddha-viveka* at pp. 39 ff. The latter concludes that the bull released ceremonially at that time remains in the ownership of the releaser; nevertheless the institution is an excellent example of relinquishment (*tyāga*) failing to effect Property in another or others because of the absence of *uddeśa*. See Kane, op. cit., II, 893. One wonders in what respects public rights of enjoyment differ from public 'Property'. Our author seems to deny that the latter exists.

[2] In other words our author believes that the dedicator's *saṅkalpa* does not affect his own Property, nor conveys any Property to others, but amounts to an irrevocable general licence. As indicated in the previous note there are unresolved difficulties latent here. Jagannātha did not resolve them when he remarked (cf. Bhavadeva, quoted in *Vyavahāra-cintāmaṇi*, 122, 307) that when one dedicates water to 'all creatures' the aquatic inhabitants do not acquire Property in their element: MS I.O. 1768, f. 8b = Colebrooke, *Digest*, II, 191. Another interpretation of his text denies that worms, etc., up to elephants acquire Property therein, but admits inferentially that humans may. If this is correct it still leaves his view unstated, as to whether *occupatio* as well as being a beneficiary of the dedication is required to create this Property.

[3] Kane, op. cit., IV, 22–3. One might relevantly quote the well-worn and parallel text *svadattāṃ paradattāṃ vā yo haret vai vasundharām,* | etc. The ending usual in inscriptions differs from that printed in the so-called *Vṛddha-gautama-saṃhitā* by Jīvānanda Vidyāsāgara, II, 541; but both threaten dire punishments after this life.

[4] The text has not been traced. There is probably an indirect reference to Jaimini, *Mīmāṃsā-sūtras*, X, iii, 50–2.

[5] The meaning is merely that Property cannot be produced in a group, unless the membership be certain, in which case title vests by shares. All dedications to the public use must be by way of renunciation of personal ownership in favour of the enjoyment of the class of beneficiaries. It may be asked why, since this view posits the absence of an owner, the assets, being literally *asvāmika*, cannot be appropriated by the first occupant. Presumably this is, like *deva-grāma* and *hasti-grāma*, an instance where the absence of Property is not significant, since the King was under an obligation to protect the dedication.

[6] Not 'I give to any persons who can claim to be Brahmans', but 'I give to you, who are all Brahmans'. This formula would be used at various rituals, at *tīrthas*, and particularly at *śrāddhas*. The donor was interested in the caste of the recipient since that factor ensured spiritual merit as the reward for his generosity. Alternatively, 'I give to Brahmans (resident at Kāśi)'. The object would be similar.

ADDITIONAL ANNOTATIONS

p. [336], l. 8. Heramba Nath Chatterji draws attention (*Forms of Marriage in Ancient India*, I, 23 n.) to Gadādhara's *Svatva-janakatā-vāda-vīci* in the *Vādavāridhi*, Chowkhamba Skt. Ser., no. 469.

p. [337], n. 4. S. ch. 21 below.

p. [340], n. 5. As is common in *nyāya*. I prefer to reserve the word 'faculty' for *niyama* in *dharmaśāstra* contexts.

p. [342], n. 1. On this whole subject see my study of Property in Vol. 2, and more shortly my *Concept of Property in Ancient Indian Theory and Practice* (Groningen, 1968).

p. [344]. Subheading. For the Text see ch. 20 inf.

p. [344], n. 2. S. above, p. [336], n. 8.

p. [345], n. 6. See p. [358]. Mitra-miśra, *Vīramitrodaya*, Vya. prak., 423-4 (ed. and trans. G.C. Sarkar, Sastri, Calcutta, 1879, I, § 46, trans., 26). The argument seems to have been: there is no need to deny the *śāstraika-* theory because of the inconvenience of *asatpratigraha*; for the latter does produce Property, and it is only where punishment is provided that Property is not produced. To this M -m. replies, even *asatpra-* leads to no Property if you accept the *śāstraika-* theory, for there can be no distinction. Medh. on M.V.110 treats seriously the possibility that theft could lead to Property.

p. [346], n. 2. S. Raghunātha, *P.T.N.*, LXIII.4-LXVI.1, explaining it fully.

p. [346], n. 7. See p. [358].

p. [347], l. 8. See p. [358-359].

p. [349], l. 1. See p. [359].

p. [351], l. 9. Mitra-miśra says (p. 427 = G.C. Sarkar, Sastri, I, § 50, trans. 33-4) the correct term is not *dāsye* or *sampradade* but *utsrakṣye* (var. lect. *utsṛje*) (see last sent. of this art.).

p. [351], ll. 11-12. The reason for casting or pouring of water is simple: Āpastamba. dh. sū. II.4.9,8: sarvāṇy udaka-pūrvāṇi dānāni, 'all (religious) gifts must be preceded by (pouring of) water'.

p. [351], n. 4. Jīmūtavāhana quotes this text in the form *manasā pātram uddiśya ityādi-śāstre* at Dāyabhāga § 13, p. 22 of the Calcutta, 1930, edn., but Colebrooke could not understand it (*Two Treatises*, Dāyabh. I.22); it is repeated by Mitra-miśra, *Vīra-mi.*, 426 (= G.C. Sarkar, ed., 14; trans., 32 = I, 49, where the passage is filled out in translation).

p. [352], l. 10. See p. [359].

p. [352], n. 5. On this subject see G.-D. Sontheimer, 'Religious endowments in India: the juristic personality of Hindu deities', *Z.V.R.* 67 (1964), 45-100; M.VIII.242 with the comm. of Bhār., also XI.26 with Bhār. The question arose in *Jogendra* v. *Commr. of I.-T.* A.I.R. 1969 S.C. 1089, where it is learnedly discussed.

p. [353], n. 3. For texts on the 'self-śrāddha' see Hemādri, *Caturvarga-cintāmaṇi*, *Pariśeṣa-Khaṇḍa*, śrāddha.

p. [355], n. 1. The intriguing topic is best read in Lingat, *C.L.I.*, 160-5.

p. [355], n. 3. It is desirable to review the *smṛti-s* dealing with the rights of finder and owner in respect of *nidhi*: M.VIII.35-39; M.VIII.35-6, Viṣṇu III.63-4, and Nār. X.8 are reproduced at Lakṣmīdhara, K.K.T., *Vya. k.*, 791. A summary is given by Kane, *H.D.*, II, 146, and (with Kauṭilya's details) at III, 175. It is also significant that several *smṛti-s* deal with the competing rights of the king and true owner of property lost or abandoned, depending on the lapse of time: Kane, op. cit., III, 175-6.

THE ANONYMOUS SVATVA-VICĀRA : A LEGAL STUDY BY A SEVENTEENTH-CENTURY LOGICIAN

The work which is published for the first time below was translated by me with an introduction and notes at *B. S. O. A. S.* 18/3 (1956), pp. 475-498. In the interval I drew attention to another work in the short series of treatments of Property, the *Svatva-rahasya*, in the Centenary Volume of the *Annals of Oriental Research*, Madras, pp. 42-48. About half a dozen treatments of Property exist, most of them unpublished, as explained in those articles. There is also the Svatva-janakatā-vāda to be found in the *Vādavāridhi*, published in the Chowkhamba Sanskrit Series (pp. 34-5). In order to obtain a better idea of the date of these works it is desirable to place them together and compare the development of ideas; but before that can be done all must be published. Perhaps Dr. Herambanatha Chatterjee Śastrī, who has developed a reputation in this rather special field where dharmaśāstra and *navya-nyāya* overlap, may further this branch of study amongst his **students ?**

The date of this present work is evidently earlier than the flowering of the *navya-nyāya* techniques in the field, as exemplified in the *Svatva-rahasya*. A work called *Svatva-vicāra* is in the Calcutta Sanskrit College Library (8/128) and it is dated 1693. I was not able to consult that text. The present edition is based on I. O. L. Skt. MS. 861 (Egg. 1538) and Asiatic Soc. Bengal MS I. B. 26.

Now that readers have the Sanskrit text in their hands they will be able to form their own impression of my translation. Since I published that I have changed my mind about certain passages. At p. 487 n. 6 I would draw attention to Medhātithi on Manu IV. 226, VIII. 197 and XI. 11 (12). At p. 488 n. 7 I would refer to Yājñavalkya cited in the *Vivāda-ratnākara* and the *Vivāda-cintāmaṇi*, text 192 at p. 48 of Jha's translation of the *Vivāda-cintāmaṇī*. At p. 489, text to notes 2-5 I should experiment with an alternative rendering : 'It is indeed incorrect to ask why we require the consent of all...whereas the requirement of the consent of all presupposes that (according to our view) all have property in the whole, for this rule is based on a text, as is the case of the consent of neighbours to a sale of land. For when the matter is logical there is no text, and if the matter were logical, etc.' At pp. 490-1, the last sentence onwards on p. 490, I would experiment with an alternative rendering, 'If one said that it would be going much too far to posit as the cause the death of the *grandfather* merely on the ground that there must be an exception in the nature of an anomaly when the Property of a son takes place as a result of acceptance, purchase, etc., in view of his capacity to be a transferee of an item sold, etc., by his father, I entirely agree, for when, during the grandfather's lifetime, Property is produced in a son born after the father's death, it is universally established that that very relationship of cause and effect (produces) the property in all items created after the death of the said grandfather on the part of the said grandson. Moreover, there is fear of an anomaly by positing a relationship of cause and effect in the manner previously mentioned. No...' At p. 494, the last sentence of (2) : 'Moreover, your view that knowledge that 'this is mine' manifests property is in conflict with the Mīmāṁsā.' In VII perhaps 'an unseen factor' is better than 'the supernatural'.

These works, for all their technicality, have a special call on Sanskritists' attention. This is the field (along with Marriage) in which the logicians applied themselves to factually verifiable topics. Yet, if they ventured into law, they had to use texts. Many of these texts were of doubtful meaning, since contact with the societies in which they first appeared had long been lost. Jurists used their work, for Mitra Miśra and others show an awareness of this kind of investigation. There is no reason to doubt but that jurists encouraged these studies in order to produce generalised propositions which could serve to throw light upon new problems, for which the *smṛti* texts alone could not be relied upon. Colebrooke found Bengali jurists fully persuaded that this class of research was valid for the furtherance of legal research. It is the coincidence of a theoretical enquiry, divorced from practical needs, with the practical urgencies of the jurists which produced this rather difficult literature, and it deserves to be rescued. A comprehensive, serial, treatment along the lines I suggested in 1956-7, is a desideratum. It is sad that the British period ultimately, though indirectly, put an end to such discussions : but they have an educational value and should not be allowed to slide into oblivion.

SVATVA-VICĀRA

1. atha svatvaṁ nirūpyate. tatra "caitrasyedaṁ dhanaṁ na maitrasya" ityādi-pratyayāt svatvaṁ padārtha-viśeṣa iti bahavaḥ. "mamedam" iti jñāna-viśeṣa-janya-saṁskāra iti tu navyāḥ.

2. tatra svatvaṁ prati kvacit krayaṇasya, kvacit pratigrahasya, kvacit pūrvādhikāriṇaḥ maraṇa-sannyāsa-grahaṇa-pātityānāṁ, kvacit tyaktavastūpādānasya ca hetutvam.

3. para-svatvāspadī-bhūta-dravye cauryasyāpi hetutvam ityapi kaścit. "kāraṇatvaṁ tṛṇāraṇi-maṇi[1]-nyāyena; anyathā krayaṇaṁ vināpi pratigrahādinā svatvotpādād vyabhicārāpatteḥ. tathā ca svatvāvyavahitottara[2]-svatvaṁ prati teṣāṁ hetutvam. tatra cauryāpahṛta-dravyasya caureṇa dāne vikraye vā kṛte uttarādhikāriṇaḥ svatvaṁ siddhyatyeva, kintu kartā pratyavaitīti Dāyabhāga-kāraprabhṛtayaḥ." atra vivadante bahavaḥ. svatvavati svatvānutpatteḥ katham ekasya puṁsaḥ svatvavaty aparasvatvotpādaḥ? kathaṁ vāhṛta-dravyasya pūrva-svāmi-grahaṇe vinā caurānumatiṁ pūrvasvāmino na pratyavāyaḥ? na ca cauryam eva pūrva-svāmi-svatvanāśakaṁ, mānābhāvāt, dvitīya-doṣānuddhārāc ceti.

4 (i). atra ca pitṛ-maraṇāditaḥ tat-svatvāspadī-bhūta-yāvad-dravye sakala-putrāṇāṁ svatvaṁ jāyate. teṣāṁ vibhāgottara-tādṛśa-svatva-nāśānantaraṁ tat-tad-dravya eva tat-tat-putrasya guṭikā-pātādes tu svatva-janakatvam iti bahavaḥ. anye tu guṭikā-pātanaṁ tat-tat-svatva-vyañjakaṁ, na tūtpādakam. tathā ca pitṛ-maraṇādito vastu-gatyā vibhāgānantaraṁ yad dravye yasya svatvaṁ bhavati tatraiva tasya svatvaṁ jāyate, na tu sarvatra sarveṣām iti. na ca tarhi yat-kiñcid-dravyasya dānādau sarveṣām anumatiḥ katham apekṣitā, asman mate tu sarvatra sarveṣāṁ svatvam astīti sarvānumater apekṣeti vācyam, bhū-vikraye pārśva-vartyudāsīna-saṁmativat tasya vācanikatvāt; api ca nyāyaprāpte 'rthe vacanābhāvāt, tadarthasya nyāye tādṛśa-vacana-vaiphalyāc ca.

(ii). pitrupārjita-dhana eva putra-svatvaṁ prati pitṛ-maraṇasya hetutvam. pitāmaha-dhane tu pitari jīvatyapi putra-svatvotpādaḥ, "tatra syāt sadṛśaṁ svāmyam pituḥ putrasya cobhayoḥ" iti vacanāt. ata eva pitāmaha-dhane putrasya pitrā saha vibhāgo 'py uktaḥ. kiñca jīvati pitari tatra dhane putrasya svatvānutpāde tādṛśa-dhanasya dāna-vikraye putra-saṁmater apekṣā na syāt. na ca tat-puruṣīya-svatvaṁ prati tad-anya-puruṣīya-svatvasya pratibandha-

1. MS I.0.861 reads tṛṇāraṇi.
2. MSS : sva-svāvyav.

katve kathaṁ pituḥ svatvavaty aparasya svatvotpāda iti vācyam. pūrvādhikāriṇo dānavikrayasyottarādhikāri-svatvaṁ prati viśiṣya hetutve siddhe, kṛtam etādṛśa-pratibandhya-pratibandhaka-bhāva-kalpaneneti. api ca tādṛśapratibandhya-pratibandhaka-bhāvasya prāmāṇikatve svāmi-svatvavati dhane patnī-svatvotpādo na syāt. na ca tad-dhane patnī-svatvotpāda eva mānābhāva iti vācyam, "dampatyor madhyagaṁ dhanam" iti śrutes tad-dhane patnī-svatva-siddheḥ. *madhyagam* avibhājyam, vibhāgānarham iti yāvat. tathā ca tādṛśa-dhane patnyāḥ svatvānutpāde 'vibhājyatvasya pradarśanaṁ kim iti kṛtam ?

(iii) na ca tarhi pitṛ-svatvāspadībhūta-dhane putra-svatvaṁ prati pitṛ-maraṇasya hetutva-bhaṅgaḥ syād iti vācyam. pitṛ-dattavikrīta[1]padārthasyottarādhikāritvāt pratigraha-krayādi-janya-putra-svatvasyāpādād vyabhicārātmakoddhāraḥ syād iti pitāmaha-maraṇasya hetutvakalpanam eva mahāgauravam iti cet, satyam, pitāmahe jīvati pitṛ-maraṇottara-jāyamāna-putra-svatvotpāde tādṛśa-pautrasya tādṛśa-pitāmaha-maraṇottara-jāyamāna-tat-tad-dhana-svatvaṁ prati tādṛśa-hetu-hetumad[2]-bhāvasya sakalatvābhisiddhatvāt. kiñca pūrvokta-yuktyā hetu-hetumad[3]-bhāva-kalpanena vyabhicārāśaṅketi. tad asat, tat-puruṣīya-svatvaṁ prati tad-anya-puruṣīya-svatvatvena pratibandhakatvāt. na cokta-krameṇa pitṛ-maraṇāder hetu-hetumad-bhāve kṛtaṁ tādṛśa-pratibandhya-pratibandhaka-bhāvādareṇeti vācyam, pituḥ pātityasya tat-sannyāsa-grahaṇasya viśiṣṭa-hetutve mahāgauravam iti lāghavāt. tat svatvāvacchinnābhāvatvena hetutvam iti.

(iv). na ca tarhi svāmi-svatvavati dhane kathaṁ patnī-svatvotpāda iti vācyam, svāmi-dhane patnī-svatvānutpādāt. anyathā pitṛ-maraṇottaraṁ mātari jīvantyāṁ putra-svatvānutpāda-prasaṅgāt tat-puruṣīya-svatvaṁ prati tad-anya-puruṣīya-svatvatvena pratibandhakatvāt. na ca svāmi-maraṇasya patnī-svatva-nāśaṁ prati hetutvam, mānābhāvāt, tathā-kalpane 'tigauravāc ca. tarhi "dampatyor madhyagaṁ dhanam" ity atra kā gatir iti cet, satyam, strīdhane strī-svatva-sattve 'vivādāt, tatra ca svāmino 'pi svatvaṁ tiṣṭhati, strīṣu svāmi-svatva-sattvāt. tādṛśa-dhanasyaivāvibhājyatvam iti kṛtaṁ pallavitena.

5 (i). pratigrahasya svatvotpādakatvam iti mataṁ keṣāṁścit: tan na ramaṇīyam. tathā sati kāśi-sthaṁ puruṣam uddiśyātra kenacid dāne tādṛśa-dhane tasya svīkārābhāvena svatvānutpādād asvā-

1. MSS : pitṛ-vikrīta.
2. MSS : hetu-sad.
3. MSS : hetu-sad.

mikam eva tad-dhanaṁ syāt. tathā ca tad-dhanāpahāre pratyavāyo na syād iti. atha tatra pūrvādhikāriṇā tyāgārha-svatvasya nāśaḥ; rakṣaṇāvekṣaṇopasāmānya-svatvaṁ tu vartata eva. anyathā yam uddiśya tad-dhanaṁ pūrvādhikāriṇā tyajyate, tad-anyena tādṛśa-dhanasyāpahāra-karaṇe tad-anyasya pūrvādhikāriṇā na daṇḍaḥ syād, iti cet, satyam. etādṛśa-svatva-kalpane mahāgauravaṁ syād iti tasmāt para-svīkārasya svatva-vyañjakatvaṁ kalpyate na tūtpādakatvam iti. na ca "dadāni : dadasva" iti vinā yad dānaṁ kṛtam tad vaidhaṁ na bhavatīti vācyam, "manasā pātram uddiśya bhūmau toyaṁ viniḥkṣipet" iti śrutyā tad-dānasyāpi vaidhatvāt.

(ii) atra kecit svīkārasya svatva-vyañjakatvaṁ svatvasyātirikta-padārthatvaṁ vinā na sambhavati, tasya svatvotpādaka-hetutve "mamedam" iti jñāna-janya-saṁskāraḥ svatvam iti, jñāna-saṁskārayoḥ kārya-kāraṇa-bhāvād eva prakṛta-nirvāha iti. athāhārya-jñānasya na saṁskārakatvam, tadā āhārya-jñānam iti "mamedam" iti jñāna-janya-saṁskārasya svatvatvabhāvāt. tādṛśa-vijātīya-saṁskāraṁ prati vijātīya-jñānatvena hetutvam iti, hetu-hetumad-bhāvaṁ vinā na niṣkṛtir iti cet, tathā 'pi tvan-mate 'tirikta-padārtha-kalpanam eva mahāgauravam. kiñca tyāgasya svatvanāśakatvam asman mate virodhi-jñānasya virodhi-jñāna-janya-saṁskāranāśakatvam. tādṛśa-nāśya-nāśaka-bhāvād eva prakṛta-nirvāhaḥ. tvanmate svatvasyātiriktatvāt svatva-nāśaṁ prati tyāgasya svātantryeṇa janakatva-kalpanam eva mahāgauravam. api ca "mamedam" iti jñānasya svatva-vyañjakatve Mīmāṁsā-virodhiḥ[1]

(iii). tathā hi devānāṁ yāge 'dhikāro 'sti. tatra dhī-japta[2]-devatoddeśyaka-havis-tyāga eva yāgaḥ. tathā "devatānāṃ, na mamedam" iti jñānāvyavahitottara-kāle "mamedam" iti jñānāsambhavāt. na tathā sambhavaḥ. tatra "na mamedam" iti jñānasya svatva-janakatvaṁ sambhavati. svatvavyañjakatve teṣām anadhikāraḥ kim iti cet, satyam, vācanikatvāt. tasya tvan-mata eka-devatoddeśyaka-havis-tyāge 'nyasya devasyāsambhavāt, kathaṁ devasya yāga sāmānyādhikāraḥ ?

(iv). api ca yadi "mamedam" iti jñānasya janakatve "manujebhyas tathātmana" iti śrutes tatrātma-śrāddhasyāpi sattvāt tatra "mamedaṁ na mamedam" iti jñānasyaikadā 'sambhavāt katham ātma-śrāddha-siddhiḥ ? na ca tatrātmanas tatra dravye tyāga eva bhavatīti vācyam, tatra śrāddhasya dāna-yāgātmakatvam iti Śūlapāṇi-kaṇṭharaveṇoktatvād iti, kevalatyāgasya śrāddhatve śrāddhaṁ jagatām eva syād iti vadanti.

1. MSS : virodheḥ.
2. The readings of the MSS are obscure here.

6. atha svatva-nāśam prati kvacit maraṇasya,[1] kvacit sannyāsa-grahaṇasya, kvacit pātityasya,[2] kvacit tat-svatvāśraya-dravya-nāśasya, kvacit tyāgasya, kvacid vikrayaṇasya, kvacit kālaviśeṣasya hetutvam.

7. itthañca yatra sva-svatvāspadībhūta-dugdhaṁ dadhi jātaṁ tatra kathaṃ tādṛśa-dadhiṣu svatvotpādaḥ, pūrva-svatvāspadībhūta-dugdhasya nāśāt ? atha tatra dugdhārambhaka-paramāṇor eva dadhyārambhakatvāt tādṛśa-paramāṇu-svatva-vidyamānatvāt, tādṛśaparamāṇusvatvād dvyaṇuka-svatvotpādaḥ, dvyaṇuka-svatvāc ca tādṛśa-traśareṇu-svatvotpāda ity avayava-svatva-krameṇāvayavi[3]-svatvotpattir iti cet, satyam. tathā sati tādṛśa-paramāṇuto jāyamāna-ghaṭādiṣu tat-puruṣīya-svatvotpatti-prasaṅgaḥ. na hi tādṛśa-paramāṇau svatvaṁ tadānīṃ nāstīti sambhāvyeta, tadānīṁ tādṛśa-svatva-janakābhāvād[3a] iti. na ca tasyādṛṣṭa-sahakāreṇaiva kvacit tādṛsa-svatva-janakatvam iti vācyam, tathā sati sarvatrādṛṣṭaviśeṣa-sahakāreṇaiva svatva-sambhave pratigrahāder api svatvājanaka-tvāpatteḥ. atra vadanti kāla-viśeṣa-sahakāreṇa tādṛśa-paramāṇuṣu svatvasya nāśaḥ iti, ghaṭādiṣu na svatvotpatti-saṁbhāvanāpīti. nanu kāla-viśeṣasya svatva-nāśakatvaṁ kvacana dṛṣṭacaram iti cet, sat-yam, svāmisamakṣaṁ balād bhūmer āharaṇe dvidaśa[4]-vatsara-madhye svāmino 'vivādina etasya svatva-nāśa iti tatra kāla-viśeṣa-sya svatva-nāśakatvam iti; atha tatra vilakṣaṇa-bhogād eva tasya svatva-nāśaḥ, na tu kālaviśeṣāt, tathātve bhogaṁ vinā 'pi svatva viśeṣasya svatva-nāśakatvāt.[5] na ca tatra pūrva-svāminaḥ svatvaṁ tiṣṭhatyeveti vācyam, tathā saty uttara-kālaṁ tādṛśa-dravye aupā-dānika-svatvānutpādāpatteḥ.

8. atha tat-puruṣīya-svatvaṁ prati tad-anya-puruṣīya-svatvasya pratibandhakatve puṣkariṇī-tyāge sarvoddeśyaka-tyāgena sarveṣāṁ svatvotpāde, tādṛśa-puṣkariṇī-tyāga-kāle 'vidyamānasya tad-uttaraṁ jāyamānasya puṁsas tādṛśa-jale svatvānutpāda-prasaṅgaḥ. na ca tatra sarvoddeśyaka-tyāga-mātraṁ kriyate. nahi tena karmaṇā sarveṣāṁ svatvotpāda iti vācyam, taduddeśyaka-tyāgasyaiva tat-puruṣīya-svatva-janakatvāt. katham anyathā ? kāśi-stha-puruṣo-ddeśyaka-dravya-dāne kṛte tvan-mate tasya svīkārābhāvena svatvā-nutpādāt, tādṛśa-dravyasya kenacid apahāre, tasya pratyavāyo na syāt iti cet, satyam. tatra "na mamedaṁ kintu tasya puṁsaḥ" iti

1. MSS : pitṛ-maraṇasya.
2. kvacit pātityasya inserted by J.D M.D.
3. MSS : āvayava. 3a. MSS : nāśakābhāvad.
4. MSS : dvādaśa.
5. MSS : nāśakatvaṁ.

jñānaṁ na dātuḥ svatva-nāśaḥ saṁpradānasya svatvotpattir vā. atra tu "na mamedam" iti jñānam bhavati, na tu "sarveṣāṁ bhavatu" itīcchā bhavati. kathaṁ tarhi puṣkariṇī-dānasya sarvoddeśyakatvam iti cet, satyam. "sarveṣāṁ bhogāya bhavatu" itīcchā 'pīti veśeṣaḥ. ata eva sarvoddeśyaka-tyakta-jalāśayasya jalaṁ svayam api gṛhṇāti. brāhmaṇoddeśyaka-tyakta-suvarṇasya tasyāyam āśayaḥ : "brāmaṇasyedaṁ bhavatu, na mama" itīcchā bhavati; atra tu "sarveṣāṁ bhogāyetyeva" iti mahān viśeṣaḥ. api ca sarva-svatvoddeśyaka-dānam api na saṁbhavati, "pariṣad-dattam adattam" iti-pariṣad-adhikaraṇa-virodhāt, nānoddeśyakam eva dānaṁ na sambhavatīti tad-arthāt. atha tarhi "brāhmaṇebhyo dade" iti kathaṁ vākyam iti cen, na kartavyam eva tathā vākyaṁ, kintu "brāhmaṇāya dade" ity eva kartavyam iti saṁkṣepaḥ.

SVATVA RAHASYAM: A 17TH-CENTURY CONTRIBUTION TO LOGIC AND LAW

The famous *Navya-nyāya* school in Bengal eclipsed in brilliance and prestige all other Indian educational products; consisting of a succession of brilliant teachers, themselves the fruit of that orthodox system of *guru-śiṣya-paramparā* which enabled education to be the common enjoyment of successive generations of persons of like inclinations and often of close neighbourhood, they found in Logic the best medium of instruction to elicit the mental gifts of the cream of the intelligent youth of the country. The object of this paper is to give a brief description of a treatise which was produced while that school was in its prime. A typical product of the *navya-nyāya* technique, a specimen of the tools with which the masters cultivated learning, the *Svatva-rahasyam* ("The Secret of Property") is characteristically anonymous and challenges those who may be interested in it to attribute it to its author, or at least to its proper period. This is a task which can be attempted by one who is interested in the *subject matter* of the work, but his suggestions can only be tentative until a master of the *navya-nyāya* itself has confirmed or rejected the attribution upon purely stylistic grounds—a possibility open to one who has studied the voluminous literature (most of which is still in manuscript) on Logic in general, and to no other.

The *Svatva-rahasyam* has a peculiar fascination. Its topic is, the present writer believes, the only one which directly links Logic with practical everyday affairs, and one of the very few topics in which the hyper-realism of the Logicians will tolerate the condominium of a *śāstra* and a *smṛti* other than their own In dealing with Property the *naiyāyika* is obliged to admit the *pramāṇa* of the texts of the *dharma-śāstra*, and we have the entertaining picture of a confirmed observer of experience grappling with authorities which in the majority of cases are several stages removed from direct experience. And the subject of Property occupied the minds of the "new logicians" from the time of the celebrated Raghunātha Śiromaṇi (c. 1520-50) at the latest until Jagannātha Tarkapañcānana (c. 1790) at the earliest; and between those periods a number of highly interesting speculations were put forward in a number of works and tested in turn by reference to law and to practice. The series is not quite complete, since vital links have disappeared, but one, apparently, of the earlier works after Raghunātha was the *Svatva-vicāra* (tentatively dated c. 1600-10), which has been edited in translation in the B. S. O. A. S. for 1956 (Vol. xviii), and of the remaining works and fragments, Jayarāma's *Svatva-vādārtha*, parts of the works of Gokulanātha, and lastly the *Svatva-rahasyam* itself are shortly to be prepared for publication along with the *Svatva-vicāra*.

Apart from the views which the author expresses there is no internal evidence of any sort which would assist a close dating of this work.[1] We are forced therefore to rely upon the views expressed for our purpose, and this can, within certain limits, be a suitable method to employ. The practice of all members of this school was to mention, so far as was relevent and consistent with brevity, the views of predecessors : and this practice, essential for scholarly productions, was adhered to with exceptional rigidity where the previously-published views were to be refuted if the author's thesis was to be sustained. Any other course would have led to ridicule. If therefore we find that a view is not mentioned by an author which conflicts with his own, or which would have been of assistance to him, we are justified in supposing that the view was not known to him ; and the only exception arises in a case where the view in question was notoriously unpopular and did not at that time require to be mentioned, since refutations of it were too trite to repeat. By this method we can go a long way towards attributing the *Svatva-rahasyam* to its author, although as yet we are unable to go to the final stage in the process.

But first a few words on the work itself. It is found in very few manuscripts and all are in poor condition, unless we except the one described by M. M. Haraprasad Sastri in his *Notices of Sanskrit Manuscripts* (New series), ii, p. 226 (No. 259), which cannot be traced. Not one of our manscripts has a proper *incipit* with invocation ; the colophons are not very helpful, except the three Sanskrit verses which are printed by Haraprasad Sastri from his "find" and which, apart from a perhaps not altogether useless

1. He refers to the *Mitākṣarā*, to Śūlapāṇi, to Vācaspati Miśra, to Hariśarma (whose date is as yet quite uncertain), apparently to Bhaṭṭācārya-cuḍāmaṇi, who was Jīmutavāhana. The reference to * Cūḍāmaṇi is not perfectly clear as all the manuscripts are corrupt and the reading may possibly be Hariśarma-bhāṣyācārya cūḍamaṇi ; and Ācāryacūḍāmaṇi was of course Śrīnātha, the oldest commentator on the *Dāyabhāga*.

praise of Kṛṣṇa[2] give no plain information of which we can make use at this stage. The Madras manuscript (R. No. 3217) in Grantha characters is called *Svatvavāda*, which seems to be a librarian's label, since the text is a substantial fragment from the middle of our work and lacks both *incipit* and colophon. Ms. IO. 861 commences *atha svatva-vicāraḥ* and ends *iti svatva-rahasyam* ; Ms. A.S.B , I.B. 26, a close relation of the preceding, reads likewise ; Ms. A. S. B., G. 3913, which is perhaps a better manuscript, omits the *atha svatva-vicāraḥ* and ends *iti svatva-vicāra*-(followed by an erasure) ; Haraprasad Sastri's manuscript commenced without the *incipit*, as does the last-mentioned, but ends *iti svatva-vicāraḥ* G. 3913 is labelled *Svatva-vicāra-rahasyam*, although we cannot be sure upon what authority. Such a title, though not impossible, would require some explanation, and upon the whole I think that *svatva-rahasyam* is the most appropriate title that could be bestowed upon this work. The differences between the readings in the manuscripts are multitudinous, and some are very difficult to account for unless the author's dictation was differently reproduced by different pupils. But that is a subject for another disquisition.

The work may be divided into six chapters, each dealing copiously with an aspect of the problem ; all these aspects having been discussed, it would appear, very largely by previous writers. Some, we can see, were of great practical importance, and large sums of money might change hands should a Judge follow one rather than another solution in a given dispute. The contents of the chapters may be summarised as follows :

Chapter I : Admission that Property is a distinct 'category'[3], assertion that Ownership is another 'category' ; the sixth (i.e. genitive) case denotes either ; investigation of the denial that Ownership is a 'category' ; assertion that Property and Ownership are one and the same 'category'.

Chapter II : How is Property produced ? By abandonment, and by mere *pātitya*, for example. Investigation of the father's death as the 'cause' of his sons' Property. Life is not a cause of Property. The Property of one person obstructs the Property of another. The father, etc., are succeeded by their descendants because the extinguishing of their Properties permits a particularly qualified *birth* to 'cause' something characterized by the successor's Property.

2. Mathurānātha Tarkavāgīśa was a Vaiṣṇava, and praises Kṛṣṇa in some of his colophons.

3. For a brief introductory account of these and other doctrines
* mentioned here and below see the article in B. S. O. A. S. (1956) xviii referred to above.

Chapter III : Investigation of life being a general cause of Property. The text of Gautama, "wealth is taken by birth alone ",[4] refers to the birth of children to slaves and cattle, and not to Property being produced by the birth of sons, etc., in themselves. In fact the 'cause' generally of something characterized by the Property of a determinator is the absence of death, not life.

Chapter IV : Discussion of the question whether an estate descends to sons as a unitary or a fractional Property. After scrutinising the prevailing view that Property in an estate is unitary he asserts that it is fractional from its inception and that the casting of lot merely manifests a pre-existing Property in the sharer. The text, " wealth is common between spouses ", merely gives the wife authority to make certain uses of her husband's property. Sons have no right in their fathers' property during his lifetime. 'Buried treasure' is defined as " the capacity to be Property when every element of Property has been extinguished which was characterized by the existence of a Property over the whole other than that of the finder. "

Chapter V : The 'cause' of Property in a gratuitous transfer is not gift but acceptance. There can be a theft of an object which does not belong to anybody.

Chapter VI : Discussion of relinquishment. There are six sorts, viz. sacrifice, oblation, gift, sale, distribution, and renunciation. *
A relinquishment which is followed by Property is a gift. The definition of gift as " that transaction which gives rise to the extinction of Property and produces the special Property of another " is wrong. Appropriation is of four kinds, acceptance, finding, purchase, or exchange. In the *vṛṣotsarga* the Property of the releasor is extinguished. The release of a tank is both *homa* and a *dāna*. *Śrāddha* is not a conjunction of gift and sacrifice, but is merely oblation.

It does not require much searching to discover that a work which contains these opinions, expressed in the manner in which they are expressed, is later than a group of writers which have been dated in the period c. 1610—50. Our author is certainly later than Kamalākara,[5] and almost certainly later than Mitra

4. The backbone of the Mitākṣarā system of family law, now, after eight centuries and a quarter of ostensible authority, laid low by the Hindu Succession Act, 1956.

5. For his date see P. V. Kane, *History of Dharmaśāstra*, i, 437. He deals with the nature of Property in the *Vivāda-tāṇḍava*, ed. Baroda, 1901, 279, as follows: tatra svatvam padārthāntaram eveti Śiromaṇi-bhaṭṭācāryāḥ. svam iti vyavahāra-viṣayatvam śakti-viśeṣo vetyanye.

Miśra;[6] he is definitely later than Viśvanātha Nyāyapañcānana,[7] Rāmabhadra Sārvabhauma,[8] Jayarāma Nyāyapañcānana[9] and Raghudeva Nyāyālaṅkāra[10]. He is quite clearly earlier than Gokulanātha, who refers to him[11]—but this is of little assistance to us since we do not

6. For his date see Kane, op. cit., 446. He agrees that Property is a 'category' (Vīramitrodaya, *Vyavahāra-prakāśa*, 24) but does not investigate the means. He is prepared to admit that *śrāddha* is *yāga* and *dāna*(*śrāddha-prakāśa*, 8). He agrees that acceptance perfects gift (*Vya-Pra.* 33), but has a less exact idea of what right the donor retains if the acceptance is delayed (34-5). *Pātitya* as a cause of extinction of Property is that which is coupled with the non-performance of penance: a view which our author counters. Mitra Miśra adheres to the principle of unitary right and has an unsatisfactory concept of the function of a partition (42).

7. Who appears to have lived about 1640, though there is some doubt about it. His celebrated *Bhāṣā-pariccheda* does not so much as hint that *svatva* as an *atirikta-padārtha* deserves discussion—indeed he totally ignores it, and thus silently differs from Raghunātha Śiromaṇi. Viśvanātha Siddhāntapañcānana [if distinct] was prepared to attack the *saṃskāra* school, but is not elaborate on *padārthatva*.

8. His view was: "caitrasyedam dhanam" iti pratīti-viṣayo dhana-vṛtti-caitra-vṛtti-sambandhopītyarthaḥ, tat svatvam (*Padārtha tattva-vivecanaprakāśa*, Benaras, 1916, 117). I am much exercised in mind as to what is the connection, if any, between this Rāmabhadra and the Rāmabhadra (? Nyāyālaṅkāra) who wrote the *Dāyabhāga-vivṛtti*. See note 15 below.

9. He is generally dated about 1650. His *Svatva-vāda* laments that the work of Śaṅkara (? Śaṅkara Miśra) is now out-of-date, and this makes it impossible that the *Rahasyam* could have existed in Jayarāma's day apart from the fact that the many views which Jayarāma there investigates are more superficial and less original than those of the *Rahasyam*. He obviously knows the *Svatva-vicāra* and holds views which the *Rahasyam* condemns such as that which Mitra Miśra held about *pātitya* and the view that estates descending to multiple heirs are held in one property. In the *Kārakavāda* (in *Vādārthasamgraha*, Bombay 1914 at 24 and ff.) he expresses views condemned in the *Rahasyam* including an objectionable (but then regular) definition of *dāna* as sva-svatva-dhvaṃsāpara-svatva-proyojakaṃ.

10. The commentator on Raghunātha Śiromaṇi (reprinted from *The Pandit*, Benaras, 1916). He differs from Rāmabhadra Sārvabhauma somewhat; and on p. 64 appears a definition of property with reference to acquisition and alienation which Jayarāma sets out to deal with in his *svatva-vāda*, and which is not taken seriously in the *Rahasyam*.

11. Gokulanātha's attitude to the subject is much more advanced and might be compared with Śrī Kṛṣṇa Tarkālaṅkāra's. His reference to our author, by his characteristic theory of the oneness of Property and Ownership, appears in the *Siddhānta-tattva-viveka* (Ms. IO. 1436 b) at f. 115b.

know Gokulanātha's date for certain. That he is obviously earlier than Śrī Kṛṣṇa Tarkālaṅkāra[12] (c. 1750) would be useful to some extent if there were not better evidence at our disposal. In fact it seems quite evident that Vācaspati Bhaṭṭācārya, the paternal grandfather of Jagannātha Tarkapañcānana, had studied this subject very fully, had read this work and the *Svatva-vicāra*, and evolved a new synthesis of his own[13]. This viewpoint would certainly have been mentioned in the *Rahasyam* if it had been known to its author, but since it seems to presuppose reasoning such as is to be found in the *Rahasyam* it is very likely, if not certain, that Vācaspati Bhaṭṭācārya was a successor and not merely a contemporary of our author. The date of Vācaspati Bhaṭṭācārya is not difficult to fix. Jagannātha was a very old man when he compiled the *Vivāda-bhaṅgārṇava*,[14] and lived thereafter well over his century. It seems that he was born about 1690, and this must be his grandfather's *floruit*, or if not, then it fell not long before that date.

In the interval between c. 1650 and c. 1690 brilliant *navyanaiyāyikas* were not rare, but amongst those of front rank two stand out

12. Śrī Kṛṣṇa's views are discussed in Jagannātha's passage (see below) but scattered throughout his works are innumerable instances of difference from the *Rahasyam*. One obtains the impression that he felt a substantial difference in development between himself and that work, and a century in point of time might not be too much. In numerous cases he improves on our author, e. g. the effect of the *vṛṣotsarga*; the text "wealth is common to both spouses" refers to the husband's property and does not imply a common ownership; he develops the notion of Property-ness; and disposes of the awkward text of Gautama in a fashion somewhat more attractive than the *Rahasyam*.

13. Vācaspati's views are given very fully by Jagannātha in the *Vivāda-bhaṅgarṇava* (Ms. IO. 1768 = Colebrooke's *Digest*, 2 vol. edn. Madras, 1864-5, ii. 186-93). He follows our author in the view that acceptance, not gift, causes Property, and that there can be theft of a given-but-not-accepted object. But his most striking depature from the *Rahasyam* is found in his remarks on the nature of Property. Our author comments: kecit tu-svatvam eva padārthāntaram; tannirūpakatvam eva svāmitvam, na tu tadapi padārthāntaram; and then he goes on to prove his theory of the oneness of the two concepts. Vācaspati Bhaṭṭācarya, however, utilising the fact that the author of the *Rahasyam* did not spend any time on the *saṃskāra* theory (which is fully dealt with in the *Svatva-vicāra*), concocts the following: svatvam tāvat tat-tad-dravya-vṛtti-saṃskāra-viśeṣa [iti Mīmāṁsaka-matam]; naiyāyika-mate tu taddravya-nirūpita-svāmivṛttya*pūrvvam* eva svāmitvam, tacca nirūpakatā-sambandhena dravyavṛttir iti. This is evidently an advance on the plain and straightforward *Rahasyam*, but as to whether it is the last word *anyad etat*.

14. On this see Kane, op. cit., 465.

immediately: Mathurānātha and Gadādhara. Mathurānātha was related to Rāmabhadra Sārvabhauma as pupil's pupil, and, if the identification were correct, this might be significant, since undoubtedly the author of the *Rahasyam* was acqainted with a Rāmabhadra's views, which seem to be the immediate predecessors of his own.[15] Again Mathurānātha was related to Jayarāma Nyāyapañcānana as pedagogical nephew,[16] and Jayarāma's attitude to the subject, though not lacking in zeal, lacks the form and profundity of our author's. However, I am not prepared to be certain that Mathurānātha was the author of our work. Gokulanātha refers to him as *Jyāyān* and I am not aware that this was a title of Mathurānātha. Until better evidence of ascription appears, or evidence destructive of the suggestion is produced, I am prepared to hazard that the author of the *Svatva-rahasyam* was Gadādhara. A discussion of the merits of his approach to the problem in comparison with his predecessors and
* successors will, it is hoped, appear shortly in another place.

15. The identification of Rāmabhadra Sārvabhauma and Rāmabhadra Nyāyālaṅkāra might be suggested ; at any rate the date of the latter is not certain. In his commentary on the *Dāyabhāga* (Bharatcandra Śiromaṇi's edn., 15,) he says : vastuto dhana-niṣṭham na svatvam nāma padārthāntaram kintvātma-niṣṭham svāmyam, dhanam tan-nirūpaka-mātram, and later on, naiyāyika-naye svāmitva-nirūpakam eva svatvam. This is definitely a stage not far removed from that which the author of the *Rahasyam* reached, and some connection between them will probably be made out. On the whole, until evidence is produced, it seems more likely that the commentator on the *Dāyabhāga* was not the Sārvabhauma, and if the author of the *Rahasyam* were indeed Gadādhara the likelihood that this close predecessor was some distance from Jayarāma seems both high and satisfactory.

16. See D.H.H. Ingalls, *Materials for the study of Navya-nyāya Logic*, Harvard, 1951, 21-22.

ADDITIONAL ANNOTATIONS

p. [366], n. 1. Read '... who was Janakīnātha, the father of Rāmabhadra Sārvabhauma, and of course ...'.

p. [367], n. 3. I.e. p. [333].

p. [368], l. 23. Read '... sale, exchange and renunciation'.

p. [371]. At end, add :

When W. Ward was in Bengal (1799 onwards) both the *Svatva-vicāra* and the *Svatva-rahasya* were recommended to him as books on the Law of Inheritance (W. Ward, *View ... of the Hindus*, i, Serampore, 1818, 448). This proves not only how well established they were, but also that they could be referred to in highly practical contexts (which one might not guess from a perusal of their contents and an appreciation of their style!).

INDEX OF INDIAN CASES

INDEX OF NAMES AND TOPICS

Bṛhan-Nāradīya, 83, 85, 208n
Bṛhaspati, 120 n.2, 121, 139, 149, 234 n.12, 243 n.34, 246n, 249n, 250n, 252n, 254, 268n, 269n, 280n, 294
Bṛhatparāśara, 351n
brideprice, 147
British, the, in India, 1, 2, 3, 141; in Ceylon, 261
British period, 56, 64, 141, 280
brothers, 142, 144
Brown, W.N., 211
Brunner, H., 110
Buddha, the, 54
Buddhism, 7, 17, 55, 212
Bühler, G., 121
bull, big, 207ff.
Burrow, T., 110, 281n

Cāḷukyas, 9, 10, 38n
Caṇḍeśvara, 15
canon law, 142, 267
Carstairs, M., 34 n.1, 41 n.6, 45 & n, 46 n.3
caste-disputes, 86ff.
caste-system, 6, 18, 56, 58, 62, 73, 75, 85, 108, 113, 148
caste-tribunals, 68
castes, mixed, 89ff., 92, 97
cattle, 190
celibates, 111, 114
Ceylon, 261, 285 n.2, 286n, 301
charities, 8, 16, 261ff.
chastising, 148
chastity, 147
Chatterjee, Sastri, H., 259, 301, 309, 332, 357, 358
Chintamani, T.R., 120
Chōḷas, 9, 38n
climate, 18
coercion, 67
Colebrooke, H.T., 49, 110, 143, 221n, 230, 267
columns, 46
comedy, 176 n.5, 193
commendation, 144
commentators, 121, 141f., 143ff.
communication, 17, 24
compensation, 186, 252
compromise, 181, 183
condition, 294-5, 301
confiscation, 40
conqueror, 7, 10
conquest, 8, 10
consensus, unanimity, 73
consumption, conspicuous, 20, 115, 212
contract, Indian law of, 227-8, 255ff.
contradictions, 144, 182
Coomaraswamy, A.K., 33
coronation, 33, 41, 45
corruption, 24, 75
court fee, 236
courts, 72, 227-8, 234 n.11
cow, wishing-,34
creative work in law, 231
criminal law, 15, 24, 72, 180
criminal tribes, 62n
cryptic texts, 134
cultivators, 5
curse, 118
custom, 67, 68n.25, 86, 111, 140, 146, 178, 182, 187, 194

Dakṣa, 268nn
danger, 150
Dasgupta, R., 51n, 54n
Dasgupta, S., 34 n.1
daughter, 147, 201
daughter's son, 145
Dave, J.H., 85
Dāyabhāga, the, 198ff.
debts, 282
debts, father's, 233, 243-4, 254
debts, husband's, 238n
debts, the three, 117
Deccan, 9, 11, 13
declamation, 144
deeds, 240 n.26, 257-9
democracy, 53
deposit, 189
Derrett, J.D.M., 4 n.3, 49, 61n, 71n, 112, 113n, 149n, 150, 175nn, 176n, 178nn, 231n, 243n, 244n, 251n, 277 n.8, 301
desertion, 147
despotism, 59
deterrence, 183
Dev Raj, 46 n.5
devas, 33, 35, 41, 43, 45, 352
Devala, 98
Devaṇṇa-bhaṭṭa, 216, 220, 339n, *see also* Smṛticandrikā
Dhāreśvara, 339n, *see also* Bhoja-rāja
dharma, 23, 97, 113, 148, 174-5, 184, 191, 194
dharma and kings, 7, 39, 46, 58, 59, 80
dharmaśāstra, 39, 41, 45, 69, 71, 80, 82 & n, 86, 107, 108, 111, 114, 121, 140, 143, 179, 180, 183, 186, 196, 301

dharmaśāstra literature, 38, 87, 114ff., 132, 222, 267, 287-8
digests, 143
Dikshitar, V.R.R., 41nn, 43nn, 44nn, 117nn
discretion, 182
dishonesty, 24
disloyalty, 9-10, 19
dissidents, 67
disputes, 13, 86
dissension, 13
Doge, 34
Drower, E.S., 49
durbar, 10
Dutch, the, in India, 2

Earth, the, 33; and cow, 34; and gifts of, 40 n.3
East India Company, 40, 57, 67
eclectic readings, 124 n.12
edicts, 178, *see also* legislation
Eggermont, P.H.L., 7n
ekavākyatā, *see* harmony of texts
election, 66, 70, 74
elephant, 189
Ellis, F.W., 39 n.2
emperor, 9, 10, 15; personality of, 16, 20; ineptitude of, 24
empire, gives kingly caste its scope, 7-8; empire-building, 8; desire for, 15
empires, Hindu, 1ff.; definition of 'empire', 1-2; rise of, 4ff.; development of, 8ff.; decay of, 11; fall of, 15ff.; Muslim, 25ff.; British, 27ff
engraving, 107
equality, want of, 14
ethics, 212
evidence, 147
evolution, 231
excommunication, 178, 187, 269
experience, learning by, 7

fact and fiction, 52
factum valet, 266
'faculty', 144
fame, 44
family, imperial, 16, 19, 20, 23, 25
family, joint, 23; *see also* joint family
fatalism, 18
feudatories, 9, 24
feuds, internecine, 16, 18, 22, 24
fines, 15, 147, 148, 181, 189, 236nn
flexibility, 111
foreigners, 40
fornication, 147
Fortune, 38
fraudulent devices, 195
freedom, 50
French, the, in India, 2, 142
Frykenberg, R.E., 25n
funeral, 282

Gadādhara, 308, 337, 357, 371
gambling, 148
Ganapati Sastri, T., 121n, 123, 221n
Gautama, 88, 93, 105, 106, 107, 150, 242n, 268 & n, 288
Gharpure, J.R., 137n, 212n, 272n
Ghoshal, U.N., 42 n.3, 54n
gifts, 8, 16, 148, 268, 272n, 275 & n, 280-1, 284, 287, 301, 312, 350, 355
gleaning, 146
Gledhill, A., 61 n.13
goat, large, 207
Gode, P.K., 85, 280n, 336n
Gokulanātha, 335n, 336, 369
gold, 83, 85
Gonda, J., 33, 34 n.4, 35nn, 36nn, 41-2, 42 n.3, 43nn, 44nn, 45nn, 46 n.4, 49, 97n
Gopal, L., 49
Gopāla, 10n
Goudriaan, T., 98 n.2
Goswami Sastri, K., 34 n.1
Govindarāja, 122, 127n, 301
Govindasvāmī, 93
grants of land, and decay of empire, 11
gṛhyasūtras, various, 209nn
grievances, 68-9
Gros, F., 79
guest, 208, 211
Gune, V.T., 72n
Guptas, 8, 12, 17-18
gurus, 115, 118

Halāyudha, 34 n.3
Haṃsarāja, 33 n.1, 34 n.2
Haradatta, 242, 302
Hariśarmā, 366n
Hārīta, 234n, 236n, 252, 269n
harmony of texts, 84
Harṣa, 9, 16
havālā, 233n, 235n
Hazra, R.C., 116 n.29, 119
headmen, 58
heaven, 35, 275 n.2

Heesterman, J., 45 n.2, 48nn, 53, 216, 279
Hemādri, 357
hereditary principle, 13
historians, Indian, 2-3
historical scholarship in India, 7
horses, 91, 97
hostage, 10-11, 236
householder, 111, 114, 117
Hoysaḷa, 9, 10, 11n, 38n, 263
humanitarian rules, 192
Hūṇas, 12, 13, 18
Huntington, R.M., 49
husband and wife, 238, 245, 348
hypocrisy, 207

ideological factors and empire, 7
illustrative interpretation, 146
immunities, 41
impartiality, 52
impregnation, 43
incongruities, 145
Independence, Indian, 3
Indo-Greeks, 2, 16, 17
Indra, 34, 35, 36, 37, 39, 42 & n.6, 43, 44 & n.4; flagstaff of, 45
Indra, Prof. 8n
inheritance,. 143-4, 145, 146, 202, 204-5, 220, 346, 368
inscriptions, 36 & n, 47n, 56, 61, 87ff., 110, 113 n.12, 114, 115nn, 220n, 261-3, 265, 284n, 301
insecurity, 23, 25
instruction, religious, 114
insurance, 241
interest, 191, 244n
intoxicants, 145
intrigues, 17, 19, 20n, 23, 24
invasions, and empire-building, 13, 16; and collapse, 17, 18, 23

Jābāla, 118
Jagannātha-tarkapañcānana, 40 n.2, 142, 223, 230, 234n, 235n, 240n, 241n, 243n, 246n, 247n, 248n, 249n, 250n, 251n, 252n, 267, 271 & nn, 277n, 278n, 338, 370
Jaimini, 91, 96, 110, 218 n.3, 275n, 279, 295n, 301, 356n; *see also* Śabara
Jain, H.M., 113n
Jainas, 55
Jayarāma, 335n, 337, 341n, 349n, 356n
Jayaswal, K.P., 51, 71n
jealousies, 9, 14, 24
jewels, 34
Jha, D.N., 49
Jha, G., 9, 110, 122, 124, 131n, 132, 137n, 139, 151, 216, 220n, 229, 245n
Jīmūtavāhana, 142, 198ff., 222, 273, 278n, 301, 338, 347nn, 351nn, 355n, 357
joint family, 198ff., 219, 233, 244, 269
Jolly, J., 121 n.5a, 123
judges, 69, 142, 148, 184, 192; as inquisitors, 181; penances and punishments, 189
judicial advisers, 141, 148
jurisdiction, 14-15
jurists, work of, 143ff.
Justinian, 140

Kālāgnirudra, 116
Kalhaṇa, 34nn, 36n, 37nn, 40 n.4, 43nn
Kali Age, 116, 142, 179n, 209
Kālidāsa, 34nn, 35nn, 36nn, 37nn, 38nn, 42 n.3, 43nn, 44 n.5, 45
Kamalākara, 270n, 335n, 368
Kāmandakīya, 121, 131n
Kammāḷas, 86ff.
Kampili, 11n
Kane, P.V., 33 n.3, 35 n.3, 36 n.1, 39, 40 n.2, 41nn, 42nn, 44 n.5, 45 n.4, 46 n.3, 51n, 65n, 69n, 80n, 83n, 85, 88n, 91n, 92n, 98n, 110, 113n, 114n, 116n, 117nn, 120n, 122n, 123, 124, 125n, 127n, 176n, 198, 205, 207n, 208nn, 216, 228, 236n, 243nn, 244nn, 253n, 267, 280n, 282n, 296n, 311n, 319n, 335n, 336n, 356n, 357, 370
Kangle, R.P., 121n, 123, 133nn, 226
Kāraṇāgama, 102
Karkācārya, 92
karmas, of Brahmins, 92
Kāśyapa-jñāna-kāṇḍa, 98
Kathāsaritsāgara, 37 n.3
Kātyāyana, 40 n.2, 82n, 139, 221, 225n, 234n, 235nn, 241n, 243nn, 246n, 247n, 248n, 250n, 251n, 252n, 269n, 271n, 332
Kauṭilya, 36, 38, 42nn, 55, 88, 109, 120, 123, 124, 127ff., 139, 184n, 221, 226, 230, 232n, 235n, 236nn, 242nn
Kāyasthas, 296-7, 301
Kedar, T.J., 85
Keith, A.B., 61
Kern, F., 7n
kingly rule, 55
kings, and examples, 7; a potential con-

money-lending, 113-114
Mookerji, R.D., 6n, 17
mortgages, 282-3, 285, 302
Mukerji, J., 79
Murti, G. Srinivasa, 7n
Muslims, the, in India, 1, 9, 10, 11, 13, 17, 18, 20-21, 25-27, 52, 227

Nāgas, 34
Nanda-paṇḍita, 93, 118, 142
Nandana, 137n
Nārada, 41, 42 n.3, 82, 85, 90, 223, 234nn, 241n, 243n, 250n, 253n, 265, 268nn, 269nn, 277n, 284n, 294, 302, 338n, 354n, 357
Nārāyaṇa, 139
Narain, Dhirendra, 3
nationality, want of, 18
Nikam, N.A., 7n
Nilakanta Sastri, K.A., 7n, 18, 30, 36 n.6, 56n, 70n, 87n, 297n
Nīlakaṇṭha, commentator, 80
Nīlakaṇṭha-bhaṭṭa, jurist, 248n, 250nn, 253 n.85, 270n
Nirṇaya-sindhu, 116
Nītivākyāmṛta, 20
niyoga, 2, 19-20
nullity, 266ff.
Nyāyakośa, 311n

oaths, decisory, 85
obsolescence, 142
'obstruction', 348, 349-50, 367
occupations, 186
O'Flaherty, W.D., 49
officials, recruitment and pay of, 11, 19, 22
oligarchies, 5
oppression, 17
optimism, 6-7
ordinances, 70; *see also* legislation
orientalists, 142
outcasting, 187, 269
ownership, 40

pacifism, 10n, 17
Pādma-saṃhitā, 99, 102
Paiṭhīnasi, 98
Pālas, 9, 10n
Pāñcarātra texts, 97, 99, 104, 106, 110, 119
panchayat, 62n, 66 & n, 67, 68 n.25, 72
Pāṇḍyas, 9
Paramapuruṣa-saṃhitā, 104
Parāśara-mādhavīya, 116, 124n, 143, 301; *see also* Mādhavācārya
Parjanya, 42, 43
Parṇadatta, inscription of, 12
Parthians, 2
participation in government, 69
partition, 148, 199, 200-1, 202, 203, 244
partners, 238
Pāśupatas, 111ff., 119
patronage, 17
peace, 4 n.3
penances, 145, 146, 178, 186, 189, 338
personalities and empire, 20
phallic symbols, 47 & n
Philips, C.H., 3 n.2, 53 n.4
piety of Indians, 3
pious obligation, the, 233, 243-4
Pitāmaha, 248n, 249n
pledge, 239
police, 70-1
politicians, 72, 75
politics, 121
Portuguese in India, 2, 21
possession, acquisition by, 147, 294, 354-5
Prabhākara, 295 n.6
practicality, 144, 296
practice, public, 142
Prakash, B., 17n
Prapañca-tantra, 103
Prapañcottara-vidyā-sūtra, 103
Pratihāras, 9
pratiloma, 87, 94, 96, 97, 99, 107
precedent, 196
precision, 222
prestige, ingredients and importance of, 13-14, 15, 16, 23, 24, 115
prohibition, 185, 192, 194, 266ff.
promises, 275, 278n
proof, means of, 82
propaganda, 7n
property, 272-6, 295-6, 333ff., 357, 367-8
protection, 11, 22
Pṛthu, 33
Pṛthvīcandrodaya, 143
psychology of rulers, 22; of subjects, 25, 26
public opinion, 186
public policy, 68n
punishment, 183, 189, 190, 253
purāṇas, various, 34, 35 n.9, 43, 49, 106, 114n, 116, 117, 119, 176, 208n, 265, 323, 353n

purification, 184
purity, 187
purveyors, 40
Pylee, M.V., 61 n.14
pyramid of dependence, 13-14, 22, 23

quotations, 139

radicals, Tamil, 113
Raghavachariar, N.R., 113n, 251n
Raghavan, V., 120, 336
Raghunandana, 318n, 323, 325n, 327, 332, 338
Raghunātha Śiromaṇi, 339-40
rain, 35, 36, 42, 43
Rāma Rāya, 20
Ramachandra Dikshitar, V.R., 33 n.3
Rāmānuja, 41 n.5
Rangaswami Aiyangar, K.V., 33 n.2, 35 n.5, 36 n.1, 41 n.1, 43 n.11, 45, 65 n.21, 85, 120 n.2
Rankin, G.C., 228n
Rāṣṭrakūṭas, 7n, 9, 10n
Rathakāras, 87ff.
Rau, W., 35 n.5, 41 n.2, 44
readings, variant, 143, 151, 153-4
realism, 184
reasoning, 147-8; *see also* logic
rebellions, 18, 23, 58; *see also* revolts
reception of law, 141
reciprocal obligations, 14
reciprocity, 22
recitation, 97
reconciliation of divergent texts, 184
recovery of land, 202
referees, legal, 87, 89, 93, 94, 98, 106, 107 & n
reinstatement of kings, 9
relatives, *see* feuds
religion, and imperial policies, 6, 7, 25
religious benefit, 204
Renou, L., 149n, 246n, 254n
rent, 302
reopening of conflicts, 68
repetition, 144
representation, political, 61-2
repression, 84
republics, 54, 66
rescission of sale, 189
revenge, 13
revenue-payers, 19; -receivers, 24, 300
revolts, 17, 68
rice-growing areas, 12
risks, 233
rivals, 16, 19, 24
Ṛju-vimala, *see* Bhāruci
Rocher, L., 206n
Ruben, W., 79, 86

Śabara on Jaimini, 40 n.3, 43, 48 n.2, 85, 117 n.39, 279, 301
'sacred' king, 33
sacrifices, 35, 36, 117, 118 n.47, 188, 279
Sagara, 38
Śaivism, 112, 118; literature on, 112 n.6, 119
Śakas, 2, 13
sale of wife and child, 191, 269, 271; of land, 268, 347; prohibited, 295n
salt, 145
Sāḷuva Narasiṃha, 7n
Samant, S.V., 66n
Sanatkumāra-saṃhitā, 116, 119
sanctions, 178
Śaṅkara-bhaṭṭa, 271ff.
Śaṅkha, 91, 93, 96-7, 269n
Sāṅkhya, 34 n.1
Sanskrit texts, 87, 104, 107, 109, 117-18, 140
sannyāsī, 44, 73, 111ff.
Sarasvatī-vilāsa, 84, 143, 149, 222, 224, 270n, 276, 280
Sarasvatīya, 105
Sarkar, Jadunath, 30
Śāśvata, 37
Sātavāhanas, 8
Śaunaka, 210
Sāyaṇa, 35, 42 n.5, 44 n.4, 48
Schlerath, B., 49
scholarship, unnecessary in judges, 184
schools of law, 142, 212n
seal, 115
securities, 283, 287
security, public, 5
seed, 146
'seen' and 'unseen', 188, 273
self-consciousness, Indian, 40
self-government, local, 51, 58
self-sufficiency, 6
semen, 43
Sen, A.K., 69n, 71n
Sen, P., 229, 236n, 267, 335n, 339n
Sen-Gupta, N.C., 228
sexual imagery and religion, 34
Shama Sastry, R., 280
shares, 142

INDEX OF SANSKRIT WORDS

CORRIGENDA

Relatively few of my writings have been published and printed by native English-speakers. Thus I have been deprived of the normal services of publishers' readers, printers' readers, and compositors' cooperation, not to speak of editorial functions taken for granted in one's own land. Consequently some misprints remain which might confuse one not throughly acquainted wth the subject-matter or the language. The following corrections should be made by the reader.

p. 2, l. 26 Parthians; p. 6, l. 8 ac-; p. 6, l. 31 emphasised,; p. 7, n. 6 Phoenix; p. 9, l. 17 desperate; p. 19, l. 26 had; p. 20, l. 26 of; p. 21, l. 13 allegiance; p. 27 l. 16 were; p. 58, l. 27 every village; p. 63, l. 6 those villages; p. 88, l. 9 not the; p. 88, l. 17 that which; p. 91, l. 24 smṛtā; p. 95, l. 15 *upanayanaḥ.*; p. 95, l. 17 *amantrikā*; p. 97, l. 25 of the *pratilomas*; p. 103, l. 3; tasyānveṣayet; p. 120, l. 7 Bhāruci's; p. 120 n. 1a : delete.

LIBRARY OF DA'